CW00794397

THE GLAMORGANSHIRE AND ABERDARE CANALS

Surviving Glamorganshire Canal Company boat number plate, rescued by the author Ian Wright.

A 'swim in' on the Glamorganshire Canal at Rhydyfelin, circa 1930. A full caption for this view can be found on page 14. Glenys Williams photo

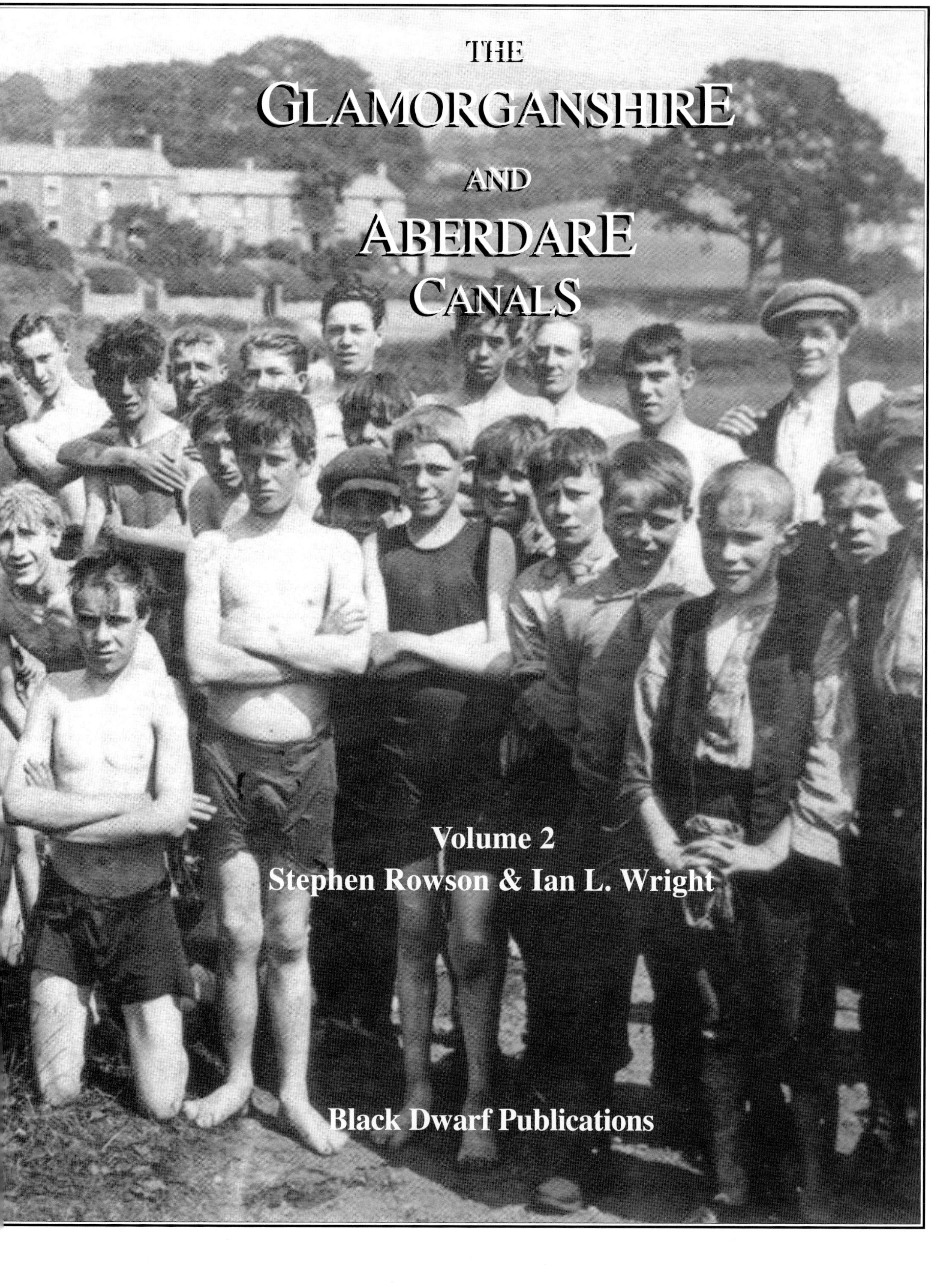

THE GLAMORGANSHIRE AND ABERDARE CANALS

Volume 2

Stephen Rowson & Ian L. Wright

Black Dwarf Publications

A unique image of the Cyfarthfa Iron Wharf at the peak of trade on the Glamorganshire Canal, in the 1850s. Three prospective customers, perhaps, are inspecting the vast stock of iron rails in William Crawshay's yard. On the right, three men unload iron from a canal boat, while several sea-going vessels lie at the wharf next to the warehouse and canal company offices, which survived into the 1980s. Petherick's watercolours are remarkably true representations. The buildings near the river, on the left horizon, are the goods shed and train shed of the South Wales Railway's Cardiff Station, Brunel's broad gauge railway having arrived at the town only a few years earlier. The station platforms were under cover; the eastern entrance is shown. The building behind the trees is the original Dowlais Company's steam mill where, in 1860, J. Chivers of Pontypridd then built his vinegar works. The tower of St John the Baptist Church in the town centre is prominent behind the ships' masts.

Courtesy National Museums and Galleries of Wales

THE GLAMORGANSHIRE AND ABERDARE CANALS

TWO WELSH WATERWAYS AND THEIR INDUSTRIES

Volume 2

Pontypridd to Cardiff

Stephen Rowson & Ian L. Wright

Black Dwarf Publications

The canal at Nantgarw, looking north, circa 1910. The bridge carried the main road from Caerphilly to Llantrisant across the canal and beyond are the kilns of Nantgarw Pottery. A tiny section of unwatered canal survives here today, including the bridge, whilst the pottery now houses a museum. John Ryan collection

Designed by Neil Parkhouse

British Library Cataloguing-in-Publication Data. A catalogue record for this book is available from the British Library

ISBN 1 903599 12 1

Black Dwarf Publications
120 Farmer's Close, Witney, Oxfordshire OX28 1NR
Unit 144B, Lydney Trading Estate, Harbour Road, Lydney, Gloucestershire GL15 4EJ
www.lightmoorpress.co.uk

Printed by Cromwell Press, Trowbridge

VOLUME 2
PONTYPRIDD TO CARDIFF

CONTENTS

GLAMORGANSHIRE CANAL BOAT OWNERS MARKINGS

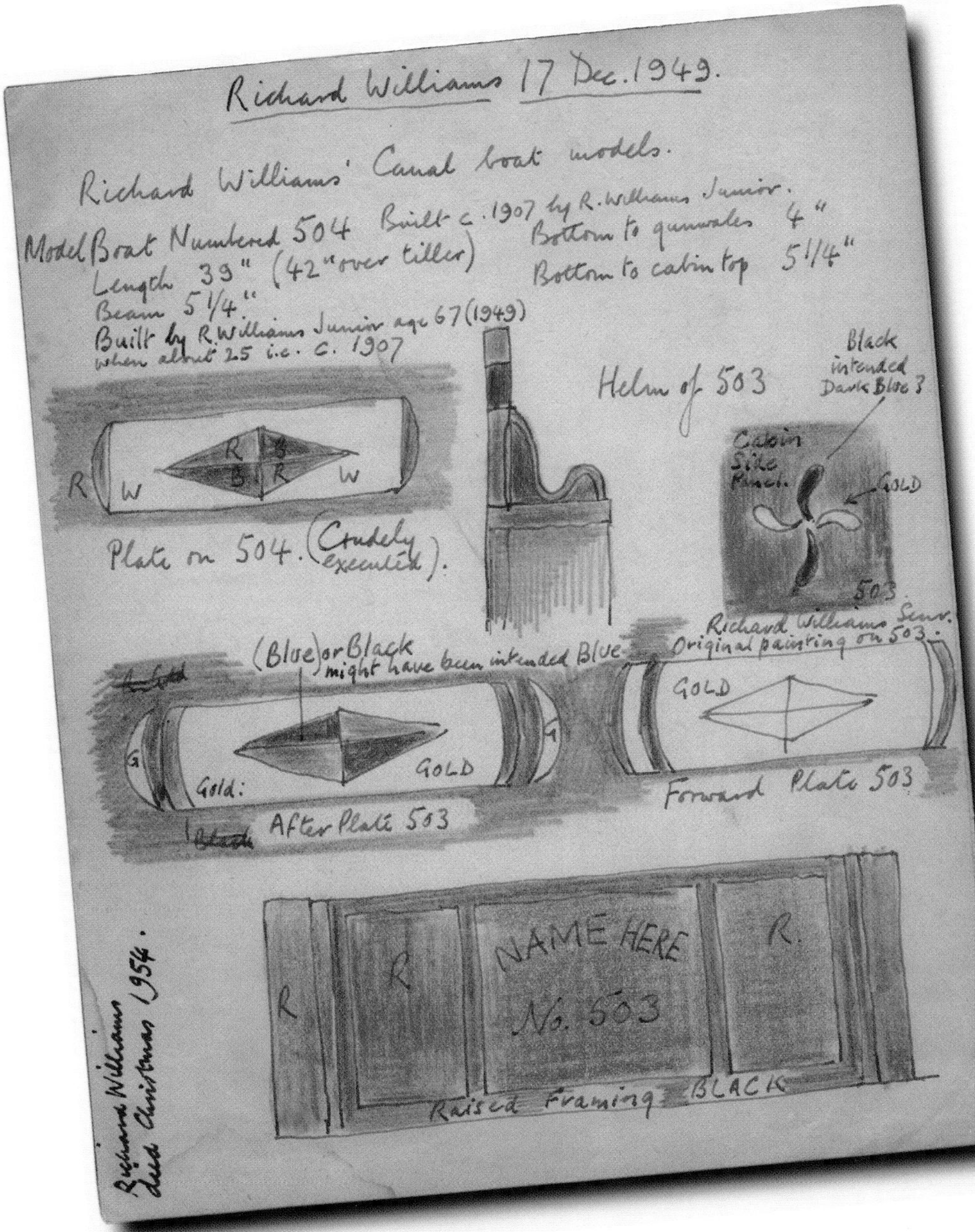

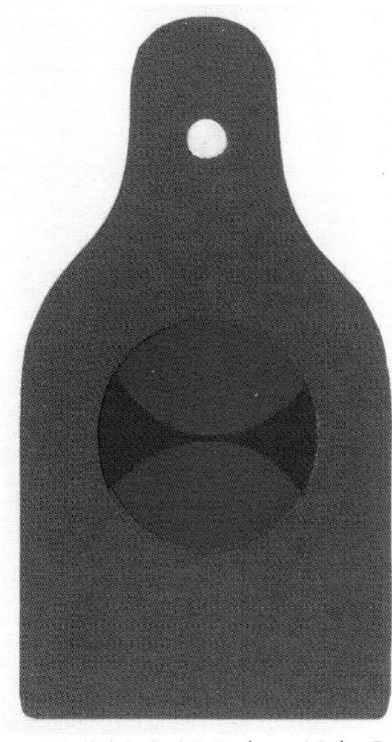

MEAT BOARD late 19th C. 12ins x 8ins. Recorded 1948 at Llandaff North. The decorated reverse side is depicted . This side would have been displayed in the boatman's cabin. The owner was Thomas Jones, a canal bye-trader and one-time owner of boat No 111 Lady Margaret. ILW

Ian Wright's original sketches made in 1949 of the colours and designs used on Richard Williams' Glamorganshire Canal boat models (see pages 91-2). Note the later addition, bottom left corner, recording Richard Williams' passing at Christmas 1954. ILW

SALT BOX, 1869, wood, 10ins x 9ins. Recorded at Dyffryn, Rhydyfelin 1949. The box was made by boatman Richard Williams snr. for hanging in a boat cabin in the days when meals were cooked on board. Until the late 1930s, salt was commonly retailed in the form of solid blocks, which were later cut down to smaller, more manageable lumps. It is thought unlikely that the two artifacts depicted here have survived. ILW

KEY – OWNERS MARKS (opposite page)

- A Leading cabin bulkhead of boat No 289 *Jubilee*, c1890. Owner: Thomas Taylor, Contractor, Pontypridd. Reconstructed from recollections of W. Gomer, Rhydyfelin.
- B L. Gueret Ltd.
- C The painted nameplate of *Bute*, a steam tug owned by the Glamorganshire Canal Co 1893-1914.
- D Examples of GCC cabin side number plates and register plates.
- E Star Patent Fuel co number plate, 1917. The company also marked boats with an incised star and number.
- F Bye trader's bow and stern design. Invariably a quartered diamond on a white plate with crescents either side. Colours red and blue.
- G Robinson, David & Co Ltd No 1 was a canal based timber importer's lighter.
- H Bye trader's fully panelled and lettered cabin side c1890. Reconstructed from recollections of W. Gomer, who recalled three owners running boats in the Pontypridd district. The two boatmen's models at Rhydyfelin authenticate the design.

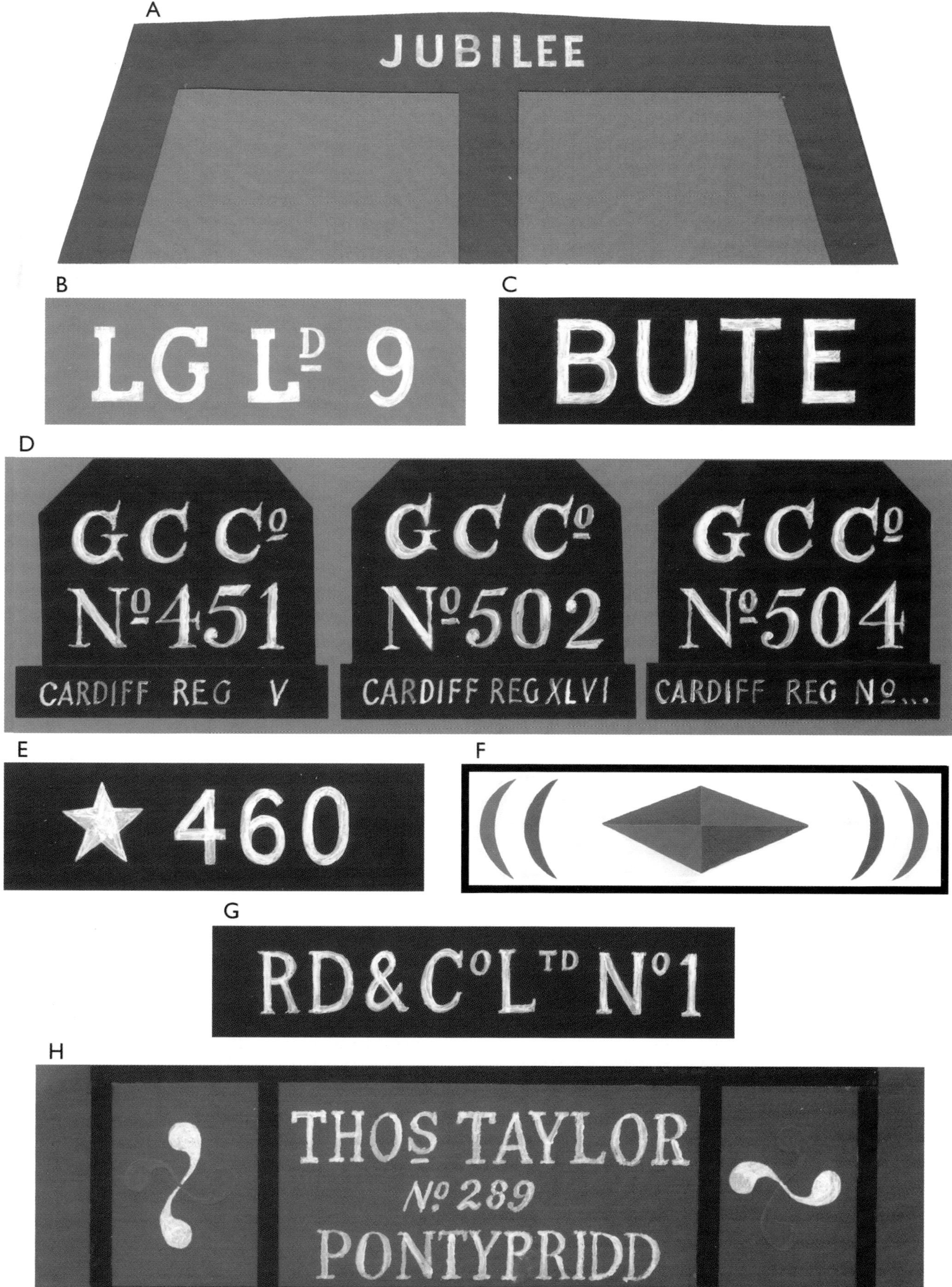
A
JUBILEE
B
LG L^D 9
C
BUTE
D
GCC^o
N° 451
CARDIFF REG V
GCC^o
N° 502
CARDIFF REG XLVI
GCC^o
N° 504
CARDIFF REG N^o...
E
460
F
G
RD&C^oL^TD N^o1
H
THOS TAYLOR
N° 289
PONTYPRIDD

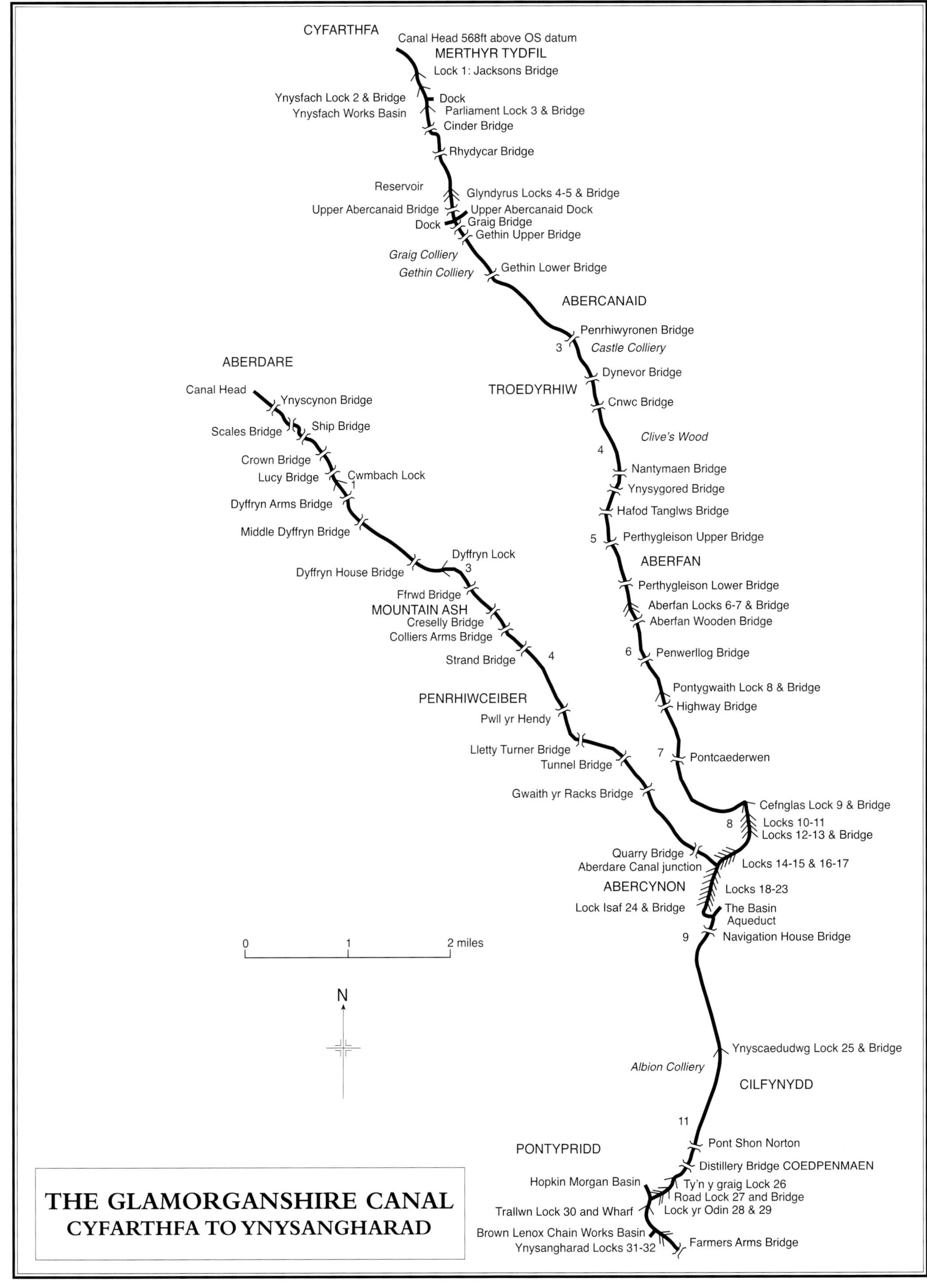
CYFARTHFA
Canal Head 568ft above OS datum
MERTHYR TYDFIL
Lock 1: Jacksons Bridge
Ynysfach Lock 2 & Bridge
Ynysfach Works Basin
Dock
Parliament Lock 3 & Bridge
Cinder Bridge
Rhydycar Bridge
Reservoir
Glyndyrus Locks 4-5 & Bridge
Upper Abercanaid Bridge
Upper Abercanaid Dock
Dock
Graig Bridge
Gethin Upper Bridge
Graig Colliery
Gethin Colliery
Gethin Lower Bridge
ABERCANAID
Penrhiwyronen Bridge
3
Castle Colliery
ABERDARE
Dynevor Bridge
Canal Head
Ynyscynon Bridge
TROEDYRHIW
Cnwc Bridge
Scales Bridge
Ship Bridge
Clive's Wood
4
Crown Bridge
Nantymaen Bridge
Lucy Bridge
Cwmbach Lock
1
Ynysygored Bridge
Dyffryn Arms Bridge
Hafod Tanglws Bridge
Middle Dyffryn Bridge
5
Perthygleison Upper Bridge
Dyffryn Lock
ABERFAN
3
Dyffryn House Bridge
Perthygleison Lower Bridge
Ffrwd Bridge
MOUNTAIN ASH
Aberfan Locks 6-7 & Bridge
Creselly Bridge
Aberfan Wooden Bridge
Colliers Arms Bridge
6
Penwerllog Bridge
Strand Bridge
4
Pontygwaith Lock 8 & Bridge
PENRHIWCEIBER
Highway Bridge
Pwll yr Hendy
Lletty Turner Bridge
7
Pontcaederwen
Tunnel Bridge
Gwaith yr Racks Bridge
Cefnglas Lock 9 & Bridge
8
Locks 10-11
Locks 12-13 & Bridge
Quarry Bridge
Aberdare Canal junction
Locks 14-15 & 16-17
ABERCYNON
Locks 18-23
Lock Isaf 24 & Bridge
The Basin
Aqueduct
9
Navigation House Bridge
0
1
2 miles
N
Ynyscaedudwg Lock 25 & Bridge
Albion Colliery
CILFYNYDD
11
Pont Shon Norton
PONTYPRIDD
Distillery Bridge COEDPENMAEN
Hopkin Morgan Basin
Ty'n y graig Lock 26
Road Lock 27 and Bridge
Trallwn Lock 30 and Wharf
Lock yr Odin 28 & 29
Brown Lenox Chain Works Basin
Farmers Arms Bridge
Ynysangharad Locks 31-32
THE GLAMORGANSHIRE CANAL
CYFARTHFA TO YNYSANGHARAD

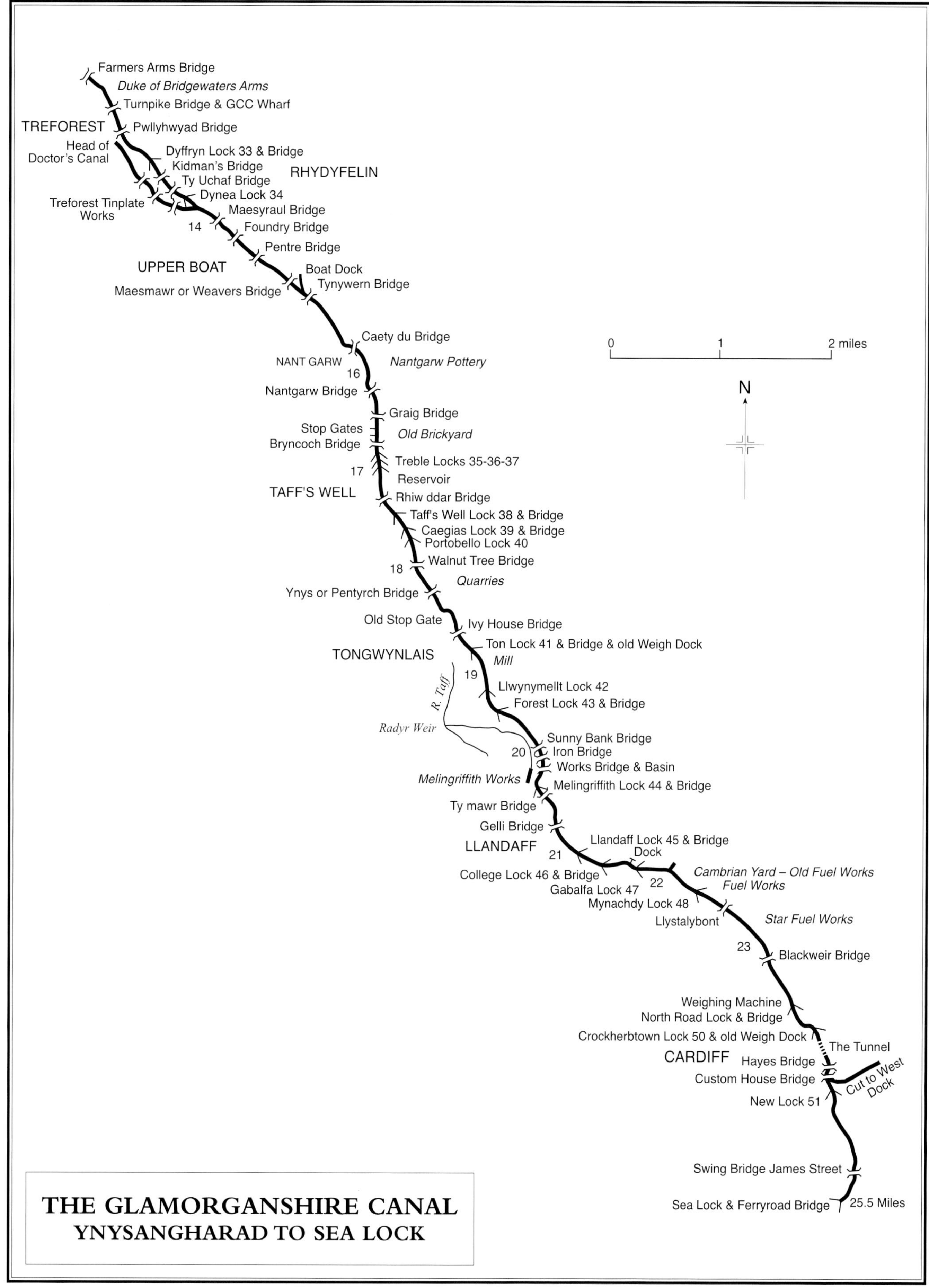
Farmers Arms Bridge
Duke of Bridgewaters Arms
Turnpike Bridge & GCC Wharf
TREFOREST
Pwllyhwyad Bridge
Head of Doctor's Canal
Dyffryn Lock 33 & Bridge
Kidman's Bridge
Ty Uchaf Bridge
RHYDYFELIN
Dynea Lock 34
Treforest Tinplate Works
Maesyraul Bridge
14
Foundry Bridge
Pentre Bridge
UPPER BOAT
Boat Dock
Tynywern Bridge
Maesmawr or Weavers Bridge
Caety du Bridge
NANT GARW
Nantgarw Pottery
16
Nantgarw Bridge
Graig Bridge
Stop Gates
Old Brickyard
Bryncoch Bridge
Treble Locks 35-36-37
17
Reservoir
TAFF'S WELL
Rhiw ddar Bridge
Taff's Well Lock 38 & Bridge
Caegias Lock 39 & Bridge
Portobello Lock 40
Walnut Tree Bridge
18
Quarries
Ynys or Pentyrch Bridge
Old Stop Gate
Ivy House Bridge
Ton Lock 41 & Bridge & old Weigh Dock
TONGWYNLAIS
Mill
19
R. Taff
Llwynymellt Lock 42
Forest Lock 43 & Bridge
Radyr Weir
Sunny Bank Bridge
20
Iron Bridge
Works Bridge & Basin
Melingriffith Works
Melingriffith Lock 44 & Bridge
Ty mawr Bridge
Gelli Bridge
LLANDAFF
21
Llandaff Lock 45 & Bridge
Dock
College Lock 46 & Bridge
22
Cambrian Yard – Old Fuel Works
Fuel Works
Gabalfa Lock 47
Mynachdy Lock 48
Llystalybont
Star Fuel Works
23
Blackweir Bridge
Weighing Machine
North Road Lock & Bridge
Crockherbtown Lock 50 & old Weigh Dock
The Tunnel
CARDIFF
Hayes Bridge
Custom House Bridge
Cut to West Dock
New Lock 51
Swing Bridge James Street
Sea Lock & Ferryroad Bridge
25.5 Miles
0
1
2 miles
N
THE GLAMORGANSHIRE CANAL
YNYSANGHARAD TO SEA LOCK

Thomas Hornor's 1819 panorama of the Vale of Taff was painted for the Duke of Sutherland, as a souvenir of his tour of South Wales. At that time, the Duke of Bridgewater's Arms was still 'the' place for travellers to stay, before they continued up the Rhondda or Cynon Valley on their way to the head of the Vale of Neath. Depicted here is the short-lived footbridge of 1816, which the canal company had given Mr Newman of the Duke's Arms permission to erect at his own expense. By 1830 it had disappeared but a little upstream there was a quarry bridge leading over the canal to a waste tipping place on the river. Evidence of that was swept away by the PC&N railway embankment. Hornor shows smoke rising from the Brown Lenox forge chimneys, dominated by the escarpment of Graig Evan Leyshon in the far distance. Private collection

Left: *Cardiff Harbour, circa 1850s, by J. Petherick. The original painting, incidentally, is around this size.*

Page right: *The Sea Lock pound in 1936 by Bill Harris.*

Full captions for both of these paintings are on page 14.

CAPTIONS TO PREVIOUS PAGE PICTURES

Top: *Cardiff harbour was a safe haven for shipping because it lay in the lee of Penarth Head. Over the years, there were countless proposals to build shipping facilities there, at Cogan Pill. John Petherick painted this scene from the Grange Moors in the 1850s, a decade before Penarth Dock was eventually built. The estuary of the River Ely lies to the right, whilst the River Taff flows in from the left. Hidden by the river bank is the Sea Lock of the Glamorganshire Canal but the Sea Lock buildings can be seen and the red ensign flies boldly. Perched atop Penarth Head is St Augustine's Church, which was to be rebuilt in the 1860s.* Courtesy National Museums & Galleries of Wales

Bottom: *This water colour of the Sea Lock pound, executed by Bill Harris in 1936, shows the Trinity House pilot (probably* Sylvia*) at her mooring opposite the Old Sea Lock Hotel and the New Sea Lock public house. The licence of the Old Sea Lock was transferred in 1892 to the Avondale Hotel, which was built on Clarence Road close to the GWR railway station.* Courtesy Heath family

CAPTION TO TITLE PAGE PICTURE

The canal as amenity. A poignant scene on the Glamorganshire Canal at Rhydyfelin, probably during the late 1920s or early 1930s – a time of industrial depression and unemployment in the South Wales valleys. The 'swim in' is likely to have been unofficial but the lock keeper at Lock Lewis would have told the organiser of this well-managed group that the canal would be free of an approaching horse and boat from Cardiff. This example of intensive exploitation of local resources raises Health and Safety issues that would worry the regulators of today but the sense of community evoked by this powerful photograph is truly remarkable. The location is Springfield Terrace, off Gellidawel Road, the stretch of canal a few hundred yards upstream from Dyffryn Lock, now lost under Ilan Avenue. Glenys Williams photo

ACKNOWLEDGEMENTS

The following, over the years have helped the authors in some way with information towards the writing of this book. To them we express our sincere thanks:

Colin Chapman, Brian Davies (Pontypridd), Chris Evans, John Evans (Blaenafon), Tom Evans (Aberdare), Bill Hamlin, Joseph Gross, Keith Harries, Bill John, Steven K. Jones, Tony Jukes, Andy King, John Mear, Harold Morgan, Tom Morgan, John R. Norris, John Owen (Caerphilly), John Owen (Dowlais), Don Powell, Terry Powell, Gordon Rattenbury, Peter Tann, Dave Thomas (Ponthir), Mike Thomas, Richard Watson, Doug Williams, Angus Watkins, Robin Williams and Matthew Williams.

Members of Oxford House Industrial Archaeology Society, and staff at the following institutions: Aberdare Library, Aberdare Museum, Cardiff Central Library, Cyfarthfa Castle Museum, Glamorgan Record Office, House of Lords Records Office, Institute of Civil Engineers, Ironbridge Gorge Museum Trust, Merthyr Tydfil Library, National Library of Wales, National Museum of Wales, Pontypridd Historical Heritage Centre, Public Record Office, Welsh Folk Museum, Welsh Industrial and Maritime Museum, Worcestershire Record Office, the National Maritime Museum and Bristol Industrial Museum. Finally, those who have generously allowed photographs from their collections to be reproduced are acknowledged with the accompanying captions.

Volume 1 Errata

p14	Spelling Ynyscaedudwg not Ynyscasdudwg
p15	Spelling Pwllyhwyad not Pwllywhyad
p33	Pamplin's second view, the painting of Canal Head Merthyr, has been reversed
p36	End note 47. Date should be 1795 not 1745
p38	Spelling Sir Benjamin Hammett not Hammel
p56	First sentence – Ynysfach cinders tramroad not Plymouth
p63 and Index	William and John Powell should read Walter and John Powell (Richard Hill's solicitors)
p64 & note 23, p81	James Brindley married Hugh Henshall's sister not daughter
p78	Lord Plymouth wasn't really in his infancy, he had not come of age but was 19 years old.
p91	The gravestone of Morgan Morgan and his wife has not been removed but is still *in situ* at Graig cemetery
p91-3	Spelling Locket not Lockett
p121	Spelling Tredwen not Tredwin
p204 caption	Spelling William Bladen not Willian
p216	Ynys House, whilst owned by the Melingriffith Company, was not the residence of T.W. Booker (who lived at Velindre)
p243 and Index	Ann Dadford was wife of Thomas junior, not senior
p266	Appendix G not Appendix E
p268	T.W. Booker's dates were 1830-87; those given are of Thomas William Booker-Blakemore
several	Inconsistent spelling of Nant Mabon or Mafon. Should be Mabon
several	Inconsistent spelling Hafod Tanglwys or Tanglws. Correct is Tanglwys
several	Inconsistent spelling Creselly or Cresselly
Dust Jacket	Photograph at Pontycafnau – date should be 30 May 1994 not 7 May 1995

INTRODUCTION TO VOLUME TWO

If our book had been written before the 1980s it would have been appropriate to contrast the dirty, noisy and bustling industrial environment of the Taff, Cynon and Rhondda valleys with the natural beauty which preceded the age of iron and coal. This is the geographic area served by the Glamorganshire and Aberdare canals. Within the past few decades, heavy industry has disappeared from the South Wales valleys and most visible evidence of its operation has been eradicated too – some would say, with indecent haste. The deliberate removal of some waste tips and redundant pit-head buildings can be traced quite naturally to safety concerns following the tragedy of the Aberfan disaster but the bland landscaping resulting from 'land reclamation' of iron works and colliery, and the rapid removal of final coal mining evidence of the 1980s, was a disservice to the communities whose historical existence was based on those industries. The pre-industrial landscape could not be restored. Valley residents can now enjoy a special standard of living close to a renewed, if sometimes artificial, rural environment.

Two hundred years ago, when Benjamin Heath Malkin wrote of his two Glamorgan excursions in 1803 and 1806, the three valleys were sparsely populated and had a raw natural grandeur which, above all his contemporaries, Malkin was able to describe best in juxtaposition to the insidious impact of encroaching industry.[1] Roads, canals and tramroads created to serve pockets of iron making and coal extraction were also conveniently making the three valleys accessible to the foreign traveller. Malkin was one of the first to describe Rhondda, a few years before its sale-coal was to be sent down the canal.

> '*The parish of Ystradyvodwg exhibits such scenes of untouched nature, as the imagination would find it difficult to surpass: and yet the existence of the place is scarcely known to the English traveller … Those who know the banks of the Taff, the two Ronthas, and the Cynon, the wilds of Aberdare and Ystradyvodwg, have seen such woods and groves as are rarely to be found.*'[2]

In over twenty pages of the book's second edition, we follow his wild trek up the Rhondda Fawr Valley and over the mountain to the Neath Valley. At only one spot does he note as an aside the existence of coal pits. He concludes the account with:

> '*… a necessary caution to my reader to inform him, that he must travel thirty miles from the Duke's Arms in the vale of Taff to Pont Neath Vechan, without expecting the most humble accommodation.*'[3]

The traveller would have done exceedingly well to cover the terrain between dawn and sunset in one day, even on horseback.

Earlier in his account, Malkin first enters the Taff Valley from Llantrisant and, after spending time describing William Edwards' bridge and the Berw Falls at Newbridge (Pontypridd), he heads southward past the canalside Duke of Bridgewater's Arms:

> '*The road from New Bridge to the Duke's Arms, a respectable inn, passes along the river side, with which a very curious canal keeps pace. The canal is esteemed a remarkable instance of art triumphing over the obstacles thrown in its way by nature. The course of the river continues dark, rocky, interrupted, and romantic. The hills that close in the narrow vale are lofty and precipitate, but clothed with an almost exhaustless magnificence of wood.*'[4]

Once through the Taff gap and past Castell Coch, Malkin describes Melingriffith Tinplate Works as '*perhaps the largest in the kingdom*':

> '*The numerous ranges of buildings for the habitations of the workmen give this part of the vale an air of bustle and business: while the canal, passing parallel with the Taff, and not being carried in a straight line, infringes less on nature and beauty, than almost any other artificial construction of its kind. The banks opposite the towing path are steep, though not lofty, and richly ornamented with hanging woods.*'[5]

It is clear in those early years, when the cut was fresh and new, that observers such as Malkin already felt it enhanced rather than detracted from the scenery. The industries it served were what created the scars and prompted most critical comment. Whenever he mentions the canal, Malkin

The lower end of the Sea Lock pound in about 1830. This was a very busy period for the canal and the artist may have restricted the number of boats and ships that he, or she, had to paint. On the left are the imposing glass cones from Guest's Works of 1824 and, beyond that, some sea-going vessels lie at the coal wharves, just before the Sea Lock entrance. On the right, a gaggle of geese graze on what remains of the Dumballs marshland next to the timber wharves, of which there is evidence in the floating timber and the timberman in his lighter in the foreground. An old cannon is in use as a mooring post (several were saved from this area and are now on display at Cardiff Castle). Behind the geese is the complex of buildings around the Sea Lock Hotel and the lockkeepers housing. In the right distance is the imposing Penarth Headland and St Augustine's Church.

Courtesy National Museums & Galleries of Wales

Although this engraving of the Taff Vale was executed half a century after Malkin's journeys, the view would have altered little except for the imposition of the Taff Vale Railway, crossing the River Taff on its original wooden viaduct – later replaced in stone when the railway was widened in the 1860s.
From *Mr and Mrs Hall's The Book of South Wales, the Wye and the Coast*, London 1861

is sympathetic to Thomas Dadford's engineering achievement. For example he describes the Abercynon flight:

> *'The wonders of art in this neighbourhood almost rival those of nature. There are just here eighteen locks on the canal in the space of one mile, eleven of which follow each other in such immediate succession, as to occupy only one quarter of that mile.'*

Another potential intrusion on the landscape, the Merthyr Tramroad, was even newer than the canal and had been in operation to the Basin for only one year when Malkin made his first trip. He is aware of the original intention of the shareholders to build the railway all the way to Cardiff:

> *'At the aqueduct, where the canal is carried over the river, an iron rail-road, for the present, ends; and from the wharf at this place the canal is the only conveyance for heavy goods to Cardiff. The length of it, as far as it has already been completed, is about ten miles; but it was designed to have extended from Merthyr Tydvil to Cardiff; and it is said that one horse would have been able to draw forty tons of iron the whole distance of twenty-six miles in one day. I understand, however, that it is not likely to be finished; and indeed it is much more necessary where it is now made, from the occasional want of water, than lower down, where the confluence of many streams affords a more certain supply to the canal.'*[6]

He is also well briefed on the un-executed Aberdare Canal and when describing the Cynon Valley he relates:

> *'A canal to join the other is carried the length of seven miles and an half, beside a rail-way eight miles and an half further; and a turnpike road through the vale is in agitation. It is yet doubtful whether these improvements will be carried to their proposed extent.'*[7]

Of Aberdare itself, Malkin remarks on the paradox of an industrial community springing up in the middle of nowhere:

> *'I found the village of Aberdare more populous and better arranged than I expected. This is to be attributed to its having become, in common with Merthyr Tydvil, a manufacturing place, though its establishments bear no comparable proportion with that metropolis of ironmasters. It produces a sudden and rather in-explicable sensation in the mind, to meet with the modern improvements of scientific ingenuity, and the activity of commercial enterprise, in a country which seems to have precluded all such possibilities, and appeared but just before like the very headquarters of solitude. I did not visit, and of course do not describe, either the works of Aberdare belonging to Mr. Scales, or Hirwaun Furnace, at the distance of four miles to the north, whose columns of smoke, rising from the station at the black and barren extremity of this Alpine vale, obscure and stifle those rural images, produced on the fancy by the sportive creations of nature. Such arrangements are everywhere similar; and as I was to see the most extensive and perfect hereafter [at Merthyr], I was glad to escape from the contusion of anvils, the blast of furnaces, and the whirl of wheels.'*[8]

The mountain road leading from Aberdare to Merthyr and passing Scales' Llwydcoed Works, was in constant use, presenting a scene *'widely different from the unfrequented wilds of Aberdare.'* From the road's summit Merthyr Tydfil came into view. By that time it was already the largest town throughout Wales by a long chalk, the previous largest being Swansea which now had only half the population of Merthyr:

> *'The first perception of singularity that it occasions in the mind, is the extreme disproportion between the population and the visible means of sustenance. A mountain valley, overspread, as far as the eye can reach, with the comparatively commodious habitations of masters, agents, engineers, and workmen, seems to have been peopled in the teeth of every obstacle, and to assert the triumph of fact over probability ... The mountains are bleak, barren, and devoid of wood:*

the bottom has its sprinkling of successful cultivation: but the inhabitants live on the contributions of distant parts, and enhance the prices far beyond their natural level, at the same time that they drain the surrounding country of its labours. It is seldom that so populous a district and so bare a soil are found to coalesce.'

The observant Malkin goes on to say that because of the demand for food, local farmers had been encouraged to improve their land '*so that all sorts of corn, in very good and plentiful crops, are now raised upon lands, where it was once taken for granted that no corn could possibly be produced.*'[9] Such crops, however, would only supplement in a small way the large quantity of foodstuffs imported into the district on the Glamorganshire Canal.

Malkin's description of the coal levels on the Garth above Pentyrch acts as our introduction to this second volume:

'*On the left of the road* [from Llantrisant] *about Pentyrch, are very extensive collieries among the hills, which likewise abound in iron ore, and are thought to be capable, by the application of industry and enterprise, of rivalling Merthyr Tydvil in quality and copiousness. The country, as in all such neighbourhoods, is wild and black; and one of the largest mountains in Glamorganshire overhanging these mines gives a magnificence to the sooty complexion of the scene.*'

The ironworks of the southern outcrop were not destined to rival Merthyr's but their modest output was indeed carried on the Glamorganshire Canal. More importantly, the main commodities to join and compete with the through traffic to Cardiff from the heads of the valleys were significant quantities of bituminous coal from the lower Rhondda, tinplate from Treforest and Melingriffith, and Patent Fuel from the northern outskirts of Cardiff.

Our present volume is concerned primarily with the southern portion of the Glamorganshire Canal, from Pontypridd to Cardiff. It must not be forgotten, however, that the proprietors of the Pentyrch Ironworks and the Melingriffith Tinplate Works stood shoulder to shoulder with those of the four Merthyr ironworks in promoting the building of a canal to Cardiff.

From the same source as the previous illustration comes this view of Garth Mountain, which Malkin described in some detail. The chimneys of Pentyrch Ironworks are visible at its foot, whilst the colliers village of Gwaelod y Garth rises spectacularly up the somewhat exaggerated steeply wooded slopes of the mountain, which stood sentinel at one side of the Taff gap.
From *Mr and Mrs Hall's The Book of South Wales, the Wye and the Coast*, London 1861

NOTES TO INTRODUCTION

1 Benjamin Malkin *The Scenery, Antiquities and Biography of South Wales*, London 1807.
2 Ibid pp83-4.
3 Ibid pp280-303.
4 Ibid p150.
5 Ibid pp152-3.
6 Ibid pp252-3.
7 Ibid p258.
8 Ibid pp256-7. This passage was quoted partially in Volume 1 of the present work but the word 'contusion' was incorrectly replaced with 'confusion'.
9 Ibid pp258-60.

Bill Bladen of Llandaff North leads his horse 'Dick' and their empty boat out of Ynysangharad Locks on a summer's day in the 1930s. The prominent white building is Underhill and to its right is the Chain Works chapel of 1873, facing the entrance road across the canal to the Brown Lenox chain and anchor works. The photograph was taken a few minutes after that reproduced on page 201 of Volume 1.
SR collection

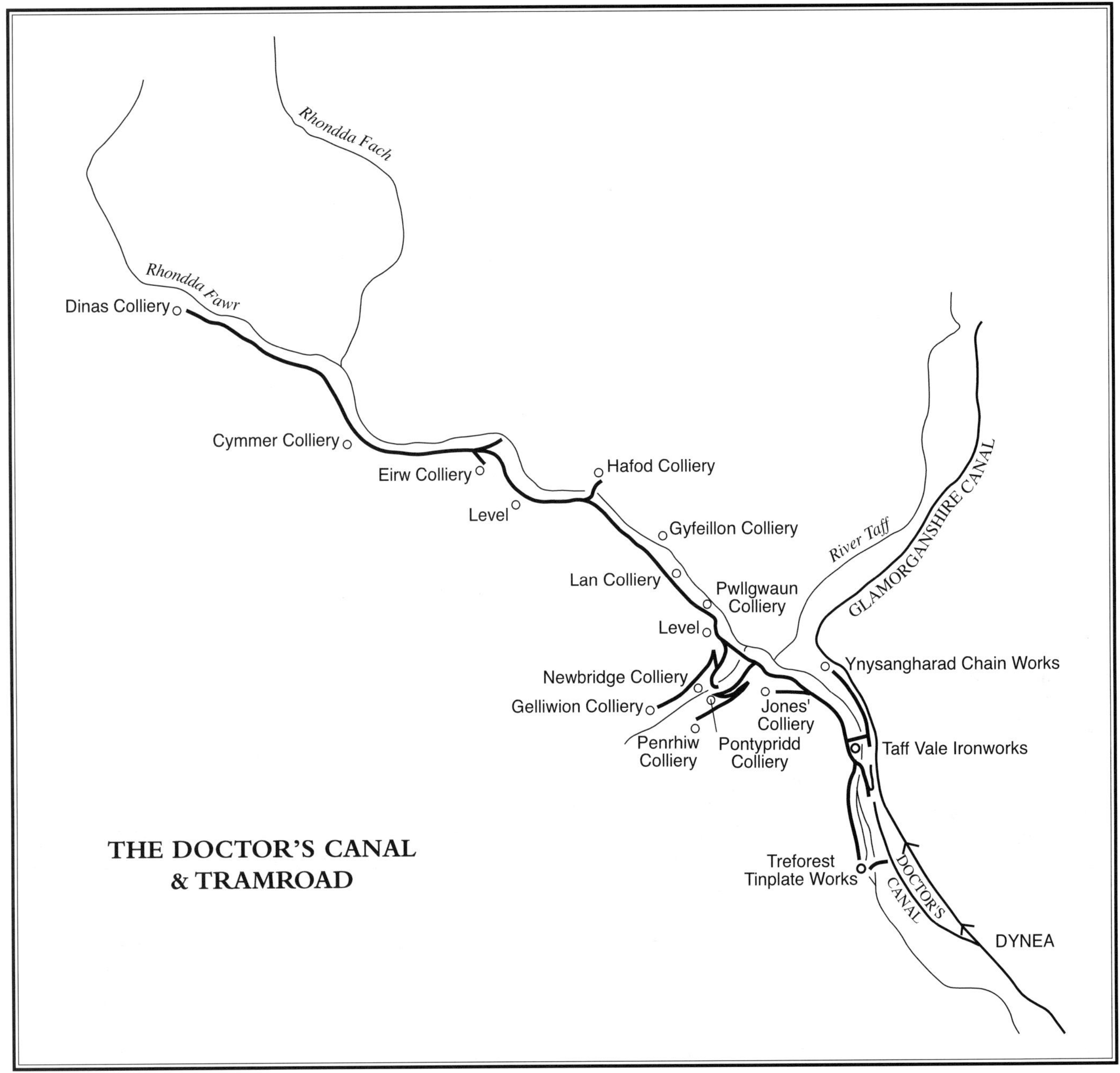

This map shows the Doctor's Tramroad and Canal, and the various connecting tramroads. Coffin's tramroad ran from Dinas Colliery to a junction with Griffith's tramroad at Hafod.

Chapter 1

COAL SOUTH OF PONTYPRIDD

This photograph of Pwllgwaun Colliery, looking south, was taken in the final years of operation of the Doctor's Tramroad. The tramroad can be seen snaking its way towards the pit beneath the Barry Railway embankment on which is travelling a passenger train bound for Barry. Pwllgwaun Pit was only 45 yards deep. The distant smoke is from Maritime Colliery. SR collection

Rhondda Coal: The Doctor's Canal and Tramroad

Richard Griffiths was born at Gellifendigaid in the parish of Llanwonno, near Pontypridd, in 1756. He qualified as a doctor of medicine and took up practice in Cardiff with his partner Dr Richard Reece. He became renowned for his hedonistic lifestyle, as he just about balanced a vocation in medicine with his love of gambling. However, it was his business interests which really left their mark.[1] E.D. Lewis doubts Charles' statement that it was Griffiths, in 1790, who opened the coal level at Gyfeillon, near Trehafod, in the Rhondda Valley.[2] Yet at that time he was certainly one of the promoters of the Glamorganshire Canal and would have foreseen the benefits the canal could bring to his property in Rhondda. He was at the first meeting of the shareholders in June 1790 when they were appointing the committee and where he acted as proxy for Wyndham Lewis. In that year, one thing which would have attracted the gleeful admiration of the canal company's autocratic chairman, Richard Crawshay of Cyfarthfa Ironworks, was Griffiths' successful defence of a lawsuit brought by Crawshay's bitter rival in trade at Merthyr, Samuel Homfray of Penydarren Ironworks. Homfray had accused Griffiths of cheating him at a game of cards. Two years later Griffiths was involved publicly in another incident and pleaded guilty to assault.[3]

The doctor visited the four Merthyr ironworks regularly in his role as coroner, from the 1780s until he retired from office in 1810. Fatal accidents were so frequent that Griffiths is on record several times for showing typical impatience in his job. In 1806, he wrote to Josiah Guest at Dowlais '*In future, upon any accidental death, unaccompanied by purposeful violence, you need not take the trouble of writing … it will save*

This extremely rare and magnificent postcard photograph shows a journey of drams, drawn by three horses, about to leave Pwllgwaun pithead on the Doctor's Tramroad. The postcard was sent in 1912 but it is known that the tramroad fell out of use around a year earlier. It may well be that the photograph celebrates the last journey of drams about to leave Pwllgwaun Colliery in 1911, by which time the plateway for surface transport was a rare survival in South Wales. The haulier is George Grove and the lady behind the dram on the right with the two children are quite possibly his family. There are 6 drams in the journey, each laden with around a ton and a half of coal, making for a combined weight, including the drams themselves, of upwards of 10 tons which the horses will be hauling from what appears to be a slight uphill start. Good detail of the design and construction of the drams is provided by the view of the one on the right. Brian Lewis collection

you trouble and the County some expense.'[4]

Richard Griffiths became a committee member of the GCC himself in 1793 and it was he who hosted the celebrations at Bradley's, in Cardiff, when the canal was opened to the town in 1794. From 1793 until 1809 and from 1815 until his death in 1826, he was a leading figure on the canal company's committee, occasionally acting as chairman at their meetings. However, Griffiths often neglected his medical commitments for these other activities. In 1797 his partner, Reece, brought an action against him for a breach of their articles of partnership and inattention to their patients. Amongst Reece's claims were that Griffiths had been absent for six weeks at a time in London attending canal business (he had been promoting their second Act of Parliament), had been at Newmarket on pleasure (at the racecourse no doubt) and had been '*at Cardiff in the Ball Room last Races and not immediately attending a Call.*' On the other hand, the trial heard that Griffiths was '*displeased with Mr Reece because he talked Politics to the patients.*' As the judge found in favour of Reece, he remarked of the partners that the case had been '*founded in Malice and brought forward in bitterness.*'[5] By 1803, he was either more responsible or had found a more tolerant colleague, for he was in partnership with another Cardiff surgeon, Thomas Vaughan, and their articles were renewed for another nine years from April 1808, despite Griffiths' growing preoccupation with the emerging sale-coal industry.

Whether or not Griffiths had begun his industrial adventures earlier, it is certain that 1808 saw him lease lands at Hafod Fawr in Cwm Rhondda, on very reasonable terms from his brother-in-law Evan Morgan, husband of Griffith's youngest sister, Catherine. For a 99-year term, he was to pay £40 per annum along with 400 horse loads of coal. He then set about sub-letting the coal level at Hafod on more commercial terms to Jeremiah Homfray, Samuel's brother, who began working the coal. In this way, through a succession of sub-leases to various parties including, in later years to John Calvert and the Great Western Colliery Company, Griffiths and his heirs were able to benefit substantially more from the mineral reserves at Hafod than did Morgan and his heirs during the 99 year period of the lease.[6]

Griffiths seems to have adopted a model used in later years by the Marquess of Bute – that of leasing mineral rights and providing his lessees the means of bringing their coal to market rather than running the collieries himself. He recognised that the success of his enterprise depended on adequate transport of his coal from Rhondda and he was no doubt encouraged in this respect by his tenant Jeremiah Homfray, who went on to make similar arrangements at Llanfabon with Sir William Smith.[7] In testing his plans, Griffiths had already approached the Glamorganshire Canal Company in 1807 for an allowance of £3,000 on tolls towards the making of '*a Dram Road to join the canal from a colliery near Newbridge.*' Perhaps he had in mind the allowance the Dowlais company had been given for building their railroad to the canal in 1791. In spite of or because of his place on the committee, the GCC replied that an unspecified clause in their Act prevented them from granting an exemption from tonnage payments. Yet the following year, the company did allow the doctor to carry building materials free of tonnage for making his intended canal and tramroad. The next spring, Homfray too was granted free tonnage of limestone for erecting buildings on the tramroad then being constructed.[8] It may have been a perceived conflict of interest that then caused Griffiths to leave the Glamorganshire Canal committee during this period, while he was developing his own transport infrastructure.

The Doctor's Tramroad was built under the four mile clause of the Glamorganshire Canal Act. This allowed any business situated within four miles of the canal and wishing to use the canal to transport its product, to build a branch canal or tramroad to the canal without having to apply to Parliament for permission to purchase the necessary land or wayleaves. The Doctor's Tramroad was of 3 foot gauge, making it compatible with the underground tram lines. It used tramplates of L-shaped section, following the fashion introduced by George Overton in 1802 for the Merthyr Tramroad, although the gauge of the Merthyr Tramroad was a much sturdier 4ft 2in. We have not been able to discover who Griffiths used as surveyor and contractor but that the engineering was sound is proven by the large quantity of coal it carried and the long period of its operation. The tramroad ran for 3¼ miles from Homfray's house in Cwm Rhondda (where Griffiths built an access bridge from the Hafod level across the river), then through Pwll Gwaun where it crossed the Gelliwion Brook by another bridge, through the southern part of Newbridge (Pontypridd) to Treforest.[9] At Treforest, it crossed the River Taff by a substantial stone bridge of three arches built in 1809 and known as Pont y Doctor. Its alternative name, Machine Bridge, derives from the practice of weighing the loaded coal trams there before they crossed the Taff on their way to the canal. At Machine Bridge and opposite the weighing machine, a tramroad turn-out supplied a large warehouse which lasted into the early years of the 20th century. The bridge is believed to be the oldest surviving railway viaduct in the world but in February 2003 the local council was considering its demolition.[10]

Not content with the tramroad, Griffiths also built his own canal. At Treforest, he built a lockless length of private waterway to link the terminus of the tramroad with the Glamorganshire Canal. In this way, he was able to provide the capacity for transshipment of increasing tonnages of coal from tram to canal boat without hindering the flow of boats on the main line of the Glamorganshire Canal. But Griffiths still needed to safeguard the water supply to his cut. The Doctor's Canal was nearing completion in August 1809 but, in spite of Griffiths' rights under the four mile clause, Richard Crawshay wrote to his friend making it quite clear where his own priorities lay:

> *'Hearing you are proceeding with your Canal & have begun to break into the Banks of the Glamorganshire Canal ... it is my duty to repeat in this letter that you cannot join the*

John Calvert's Newbridge Colliery of 1844, in the Gelliwion Valley. The railway lines in the foreground are on the line of the tramroad branch from Penrhiw Colliery, which also led past Pontypridd Colliery to a tipping wall on the TVR. The slightly higher level parallel line across the stream is the original tramroad branch to Gelliwion Level. Rhondda Fawr is in the distance. SR collection

Canal unless you bring water to supply yours, by any other mode than a Tram or some other Road – my whole Iron Trade and the Works of the Country are of too much Importance to suffer any Person for his Individual Emolument or Caprice to do Injury to this Canal & Iron Works. Any further step you take to injure them will send an Injunction to stop you of greater Authority than your Friend & Obt Hble Svt.' [11]

As we have shown, an arrangement was made and the canal was finally opened in 1813.[12]

E.D. Lewis records that the tramroad was opened on 29 September 1809,[13] enabling Griffiths to be first in sending Rhondda coal to outside markets. In the first few years, the doctor's coal must have been transshipped directly to the Glamorganshire Canal at Treforest, most probably at Pwllyhwyad Bridge where William Harrison's 1830 survey of the canal and later 19th century OS plans indicate tramroad connections up a short steep slope to the Glamorganshire Canal towpath quite near to the Doctor's Canal head. With the commissioning of his canal in 1813, Richard Griffiths' clients enjoyed the advantage of transshipping their coal from tramroad to boats at his own Treforest terminal free from disruption and interference to boats and horses passing on the main line. Settlement around the canal head was encouraged by these activities and, in the first decades of the 19th century, Treforest expanded to become a place of greater importance than Newbridge.

Homfray was not the only freighter encouraged by the building of Griffiths' tramroad. In 1809, Walter Coffin, a 24-year old Bridgend man started developing coal levels at Dinas, two miles further up the valley from Hafod, on farms which his father had purchased in 1801. Coffin and Griffiths had a shared vision. In December 1809 they entered into a written agreement for usage of the tramroad and canal. Coffin was to be charged 2d per ton per mile (coal and iron ore) reducing to 1½d once the tramroad had made £2,000 profit for Griffiths. Lime and limestone was to be charged at 1d per ton per mile and all other articles at 5d.[14] No waggon was to carry more than 25 cwt and tonnage was to be charged long weight. Coffin was given second choice after Homfray of where to lay his wharf at the canal head. Coffin and Griffiths would share the cost of a boat dock for their joint use (we assume this was a boat repairing dock rather than a loading dock, since the latter would seem to have been unnecessary on what was already in effect an elongated loading basin).[15] In another similar agreement of 25 March 1812, the Bassett sisters, Eleanor and Joan, of Penrhiw, Pwllgwaun and Eirw Isha, and Richard Hoare Jenkins of Eirw Ucha, agreed their tonnage rates and were allowed to select wharves on the Doctor's Canal within one boat's length of Homfray's and Coffin's landing places. They were to be allowed use of the boat dock that Griffiths and Coffin had made. A clause stipulated they were not to use any other tramroad in the Rhondda.[16]

It is unclear whether tenants of the Bassett sisters and

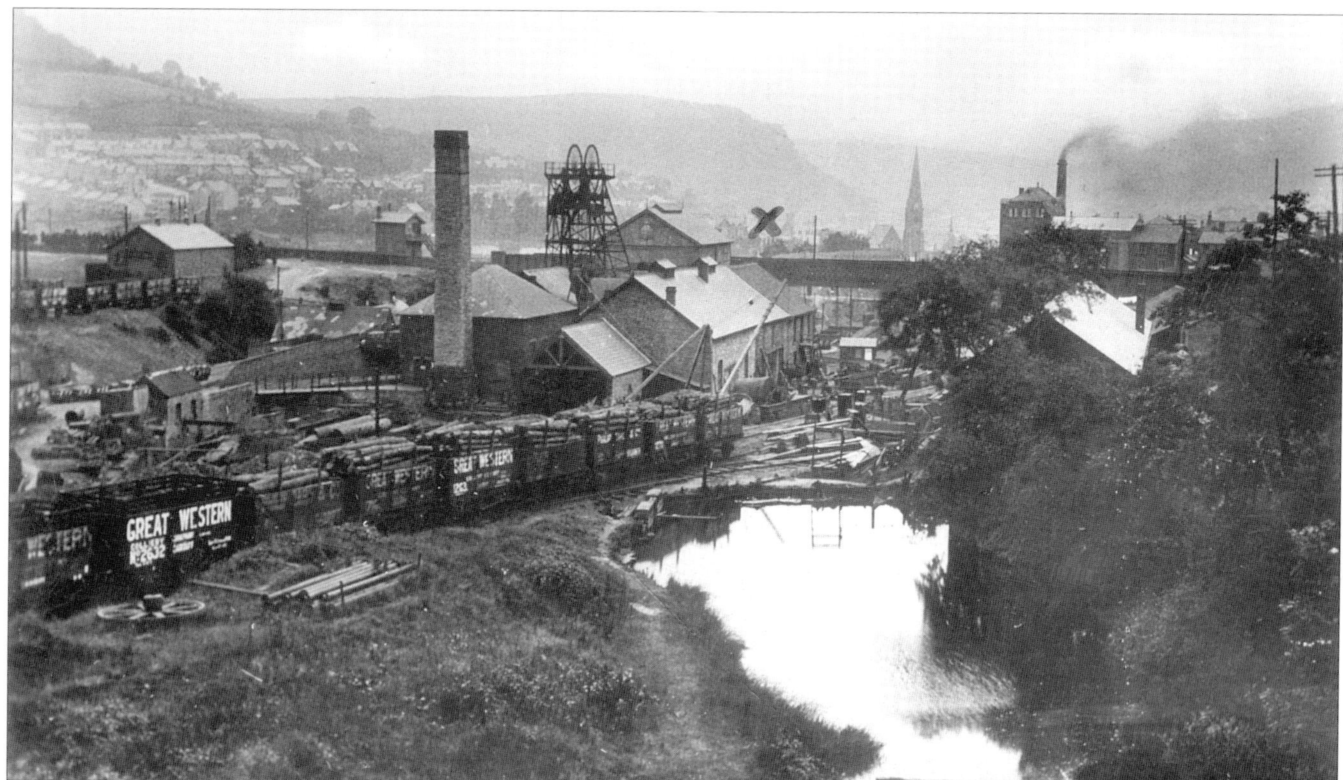

Maritime Colliery, looking towards Pontypridd and Craig yr Esg. This was formerly John Edmunds' Pontypridd Colliery of 1841. The high level Rhondda line of the Barry Railway crosses behind the colliery and beyond this is the Glen View Brewery. Penrhiw Colliery lay just behind and to the right of the photographer. The wagons in the foreground laden with pit props belong to the Great Western Colliery Company, who took over both Maritime and Penrhiw collieries around 1900. SR collection

Hoare Jenkins exercised their rights straight away to use the tramroad, or indeed whether they opened coal levels or pits on their land in these early years. Coffin's agreement certainly fulfilled the hint of riches to come. Walter Coffin proceeded to build his own extension of the tramroad along the right bank of the Rhondda Fawr, from Hafod to his several levels and later pits at Dinas. Although the route distance of the combined tramroad and canal was more than four miles, Coffin got away with building his portion of the tramroad under the four mile clause, because Dinas lay fewer than four miles as the crow flies from the Glamorganshire Canal at Newbridge. The building of both tramroads and the Doctor's Canal occasioned something of a flurry among the landowners on the line, so several meetings of the canal commissioners were convened by their clerk, Charles Brown, to value the land. At the meeting of 17 August 1810, held at the Duke of Bridgewater's Arms, an eager number of twenty four qualified landowners volunteered their services to act as commissioners and the selected fourteen valued the land belonging to Joanna Jones, comprising a strip 45 ft wide and 5,823 ft long from the bridge over Pwllgwaun Brook to the Taff River bridge (Machine Bridge) at £21 per annum rental or £630 outright purchase. Even the Marquess of Bute's rights to the waters of the River Taff had to be respected when Machine Bridge was constructed.[17] The landowners could not fight the compulsory seizure of the land by Griffiths under the Act but they could use the commissioners to get the best valuation. By the time these meetings took place, the tramroad and canal had already been built. On a rough plan of Jones' property, on paper with an 1812 watermark, the length of tramroad is given as 2,024 yards (6,072 feet) and a branch is shown to the west '*to Mr Jones Colliery*'.[18]

The Doctor's Canal, one mile in length, ran roughly parallel with the Glamorganshire Canal and the turnpike road, passing south-easterly through Rhydyfelin and Dyffryn on its way to the junction with the main canal at Dynea.[19] While the Glamorganshire Canal passed through two locks in this distance and dropped some 19½ feet, there were no locks necessary on the Doctor's Canal. At the Cardiff end of the Glamorganshire Canal, both Homfray and Coffin were granted 21 year leases each of coal yards with 190 feet wharfage on the Sea Lock pound – an indication of their intentions to promote a maritime trade.[20] Homfray's account with the GCC opened in October 1810 but his quarterly tonnage charges only once exceeded £100 (Jan 1813). On the other hand, Coffin's account opened in July 1811 and by 1812 was already averaging over £200 per quarter – as a coal shipper second only to Brockett Grover's, whose Maesmawr loading wharf at milepost 15 was one mile closer to Cardiff than Dynea.[21]

The year 1810 was a growth year for the coal trade on the Glamorganshire Canal, with the opening of both the Doctor's Tramroad from Rhondda and Sir William Smith's tramroad from Llanfabon. However, the Glamorgan coal owners were at a disadvantage when competing with the established coal trade out of Newport, whose shippers continued to benefit from the clause in the Monmouthshire

Canal Act that exempted them from excise duty. The Cardiff-based coal owners got together and petitioned Parliament for the clause to be revoked. Among those petitioning were Walter Coffin and Jeremiah Homfray (who now, as High Sheriff of Glamorgan, had been knighted towards the end of November 1809[22]). The accustomed Griffiths gave evidence to the House of Commons committee on behalf of the petitioners, speaking more as a land owner than a colliery proprietor but they were unsuccessful and it took several more attempts before the duties were repealed eventually in 1831.[23] This early defeat did not deter Coffin and the quantities of Dinas coal he shipped out of Cardiff to Ireland rose steadily. In spite of his claim to the Parliamentary committee not to be a coal shipper, Griffiths took a lease of a coal wharf on the Sea Lock pound at Cardiff in 1811 but the surviving GCC accounts to 1815 show that his own coal shipments were insignificant.[24] Homfray, on the other hand, was bankrupt in 1812 – a victim (some would say a contributory cause) of the spectacular crash of the Tappenden investments at Aberdare. The sale of Homfray's effects and estate on 20 November 1813 included 32 tram waggons of 3ft gauge, 30 tons of tramplates, three iron boats and two wooden boats for the Glamorganshire Canal.[25] This bankruptcy did not prevent Homfray from continuing to trade on the canal until 1814.[25]

Dr Griffiths died in 1826 aged 70, leaving all the property and leaseholds to the children of his eldest sister Jane, who was widow of Thomas Thomas of Llanbradach.[26] The two brothers, the Reverend George Thomas of Ystrad Mynach and Llandaff Court and his brother Thomas Thomas of Pencerig, Radnor, continued to work the tramroad and canal. 'The Rev George Thomas's Canal' was now the official name of the little waterway but such was the impact of Griffiths on popular memory that 'The Doctor's Canal' remained the preferred name for almost another century, to its end. As for the tramroad, it continued to be the only means of bringing coal down the valley until the Taff Vale Railway opened its Rhondda branch line, from Newbridge to Dinas, for mineral traffic in 1841. In 1830, Walter Coffin sent down 46,000 tons of coal on the tramroad and T. & G. Thomas themselves contributed 11,400 tons, all of which passed on to the Glamorganshire Canal at Dynea. In 1839, Coffin's tonnages had risen to 56,000 tons – a quarter of the 214,200 tons carried down the Glamorganshire Canal that year.[27] A glance at the tithe map for Llantrisant parish shows what a 'Klondike' Dinas had become in the otherwise peaceful Rhondda Fawr – with Walter Coffin the prominent lessee operating several collieries there.

Whilst Coffin was certainly the prime shipper of Rhondda coal on the Doctor's Tramroad and Canal until the opening of the TVR, he had to share the facilities with other sale collieries who were also shipping their coal out of Cardiff. In October 1829, the coal levels at Gelliwion were up for sale as being connected to the tramroad and canal. The sale included '*Boats, Trams etc to be taken at a valuation*'.[28] About that time, George Insole started shipping quantities of their coal from his yard on the Sea Lock pound

The Doctor's Tramroad approaching the Taff Vale Ironworks in Broadway, Treforest, a photograph taken in the late 1880s by Thomas Forrest & Sons. Courtesy Pontypridd Heritage Centre

These two rare late 19th century views of the centre of Pontypridd provide us with photographic evidence of the Doctor's Tramroad in operation. Much of Pontypridd and Treforest grew around this tramroad and here, on the left, a lone waggon loaded with coal stands on the plateway at the Tumble – a name suggestive of coal transshipment, possibly from Penrhiw Colliery, or simply of where the town coal yards originally were and where the coal was tumbled out of the tramroad waggons. Of interest is the platform on which the men in the foreground are sitting. Perhaps this too was where passengers embarked for their trip back to Rhondda from shopping in Pontypridd market. In the view below, the photographer has turned his bulky camera and tripod to the right, to look across the tramroad and down High Street.
Courtesy Pontypridd Heritage Centre

at Cardiff. Some of the boatmen taking Gelliwion coal from the Doctor's Canal to Cardiff were Moses Thomas, Henry Williams, Thomas Linnet, Richard Williams, William Prichard, Thomas Jacob and William Richards.[29] In 1837, Homfray's old Hafod Ucha Colliery was being worked by John Edmunds and the agreement to use the tramroad stipulated that his '*Tram Waggons* [could be] *drawn by Horses or other Cattle (but not by Steam Carriages)*'.[30] The rate the Thomases were charging under that agreement was 7d per long ton (2,400 lbs) for any distance along their tramroad and canal. The agreement in turn allowed the Thomases to use the colliery's tramroad to bring stone from the quarries at Hafod to their own tramroad, at a tonnage rate of ½d per mile per long ton. The maximum capacity of a tram waggon was set for Edmunds at 3,120 lbs. John Edmunds was son of Edward Edmunds of Penrhos, one of the pioneer traders on the Glamorganshire Canal and agent to the Penydarren Ironworks and the Melingriffith Tinplate Works. In 1839, when Coffin had shipped 51,100 tons of Rhondda coal on the Glamorganshire, John Edmunds had shipped 14,073 tons.[31] By 1845, Edmunds was also working

This 1949 view of the derelict canal at Ynysangharad provides evidence of where the 1826 tramroad extension from Pentrebach entered the works. It passed through a gap in the stone wall and carried on within the works, alongside the lower works basin.
ILW photo 16 Sept 1949, neg 901

The lower basin at Brown Lenox, with two cabin boats awaiting loading with chain outside the Testing Shop. The canal towpath crosses the exit to the basin. On the right is a section of the internal works tramway, laid on what must have been the line of the tramroad from Pentrebach.
Robin Williams collection

A circa 1907 view of the chain works and canal, looking south from Pontypridd Common towards Treforest, showing the wide towpath that had once taken the 1826 tramroad between Brown Lenox and Pentrebach. On the left, the former Cardiff - Merthyr turnpike passes the Pennant sandstone quarries at Pentrebach. At Ty ar y Graig (Rock House) on the first bend, was a tunnel under the road leading from the quarry to a stone wharf on the canal opposite Nightingale Bush (the row of cottages beneath the towpath). Just beyond Nightingale Bush are Rose Cottage and Grove House, before the canal is crossed by the Farmers Arms Bridge. The railway embankment surmounted by long coal trains is that of the Alexandra (Newport and South Wales) Docks & Railway Co. SR collection

Five very lucky children enjoy an unofficial trip on board a GCC working horse boat at Pontypridd in the 1930s. The boat is on its way back to Cardiff, after delivering a consignment of flour to the Hopkin Morgan Bakery at East Street.

Apart from its value as a social document, this picture is an unusually informative record of the on-board layout of the boat and clearly shows the moveable floor planks, running plank and supporting cross planks. The round 6-foot towing mast is being used in the inclined position, because the boat is empty and therefore high in the water. Only inclined like this would an empty boat's mast clear the canal's low bridge arches. The photograph was taken from the Farmer's Arms Bridge looking north-westwards towards the Brown Lenox chainworks. The stretch of canal from Ynysangharad to this point is now preserved in water as a nature reserve, under the ownership of the Wildlife Trust of South and West Wales.

The youngsters are, from left to right, Mary Morgan, Cyril Morgan, Margaret Starr, Jessie Thorne and Audrey Thorne. We are unable to identify the boatmen in charge but at this period the masters would have been William Thatcher, Thomas Frazer or William Bladen.
Courtesy Pontypridd Library, Cyril Morgan donation

Left: *The iron upright members on Farmers Arms Bridge were dated 1879. The tipping in the background is for the A470 road works – cause of the destruction of much of the canal's archaeology.* ILW photo 27 Oct 1971, neg 2281C

Right: *The derelict canal at Farmers Arms. The public house has since been demolished, to allow widening of the entrance to industrial units in the old Gibbons quarry.*
Courtesy Pontypridd Library

The original Gwern y Geryn Bridge at Llanbradach Arms in 1899, before it was rebuilt to carry Pontypridd electric tramways. The GCC warehouse, from which deliveries by horse drays were made to Treforest shopkeepers, is on the left. It was closed in 1941. The stone on the towpath is an indication that work on the bridge was just about to start. Thomas Forrest & sons photo, courtesy Pontypridd Heritage Centre

A southbound loaded cabin-less boat approaches the cameraman at Llanbradach Arms Bridge in the winter of 1905-6. In the background is the bridge at the A(N&SW)D&R Glyntaff station. The collection of white buildings is the former Duke of Bridgewater's Arms, which dated from the opening of the canal. Legend and the canal's table of distances record there was an arch under the turnpike road from the inn to the canal bank. The two breaks in the wall shown here opposite the school seem to lead to a small wharf or mooring point next to the road. SR collection

Glyntaff and Treforest, as seen by Henry Gastineau from above the stone quarries at Pentrebach. It was a few years yet before Treforest became built up as a result of the establishment of the tinplate works. All that can be seen on the west side of the river is the warehouse and group of buildings around the Thomas brothers' weighing machine at Machine Bridge. On the other hand, there are quite a number of dwellings on the canal side of the river around Glyntaff and Gwern y Geryn. From *South Wales Illustrated*, London 1830

From a similar viewpoint to the Gastineau engraving but executed thirty years later, this view of the Taff Valley also shows the Aberdare Iron Company's rolling mills at Treforest – the Taff Vale Ironworks. The three tall chimneys are at the re-heating furnaces and the others are at the forges themselves. Note the tramroad viaducts leading from the mills; the one to the left of the mills leads to the (hidden) river bridge and the canal. The three-arches are of Machine Bridge.
From *Mr and Mrs Hall's The Book of South Wales, the Wye and the Coast*, London 1861

Pontypridd Colliery, across the Pwllgwaun Brook from Gelliwion and sunk by him in 1841. His landlord, Richard Fowler Rickards, had built a connecting tramroad for him from the colliery and coke ovens to a junction with the main tramroad. An attempt to link up to a tipping wall on the Taff Vale Railway at that time came to nothing.[32] Also in 1844, John Calvert sank Newbridge Colliery on the Gelliwion line and was able to use that branch to get his coal to the Thomases' tramroad. Another user of the tramroad and canal was Richard Lewis from his level at Cymmer, whose coal was shipped from Cardiff for a short period in 1843 by Insole.[33]

As well as sale coal, the tramroad was also part of the infrastructure supplying other local industries. Foremost of these were the Aberdare Iron Company's rolling mills at Treforest (later to become the Taff Vale Ironworks), the Brown Lenox chain and anchor works at Ynysangharad, and Treforest Tinplate Works – which William Crawshay II had built for his son Francis to manage. The last were established in the early 1830s and William Crawshay opened the Gwaun yr Eirw Level near Hafod to supply it and their Hirwaun Ironworks with coking coal.[34] A long tramroad branch, again on Rickard's land, was built to connect the tinplate works with Thomas's tramroad. Iron for the works, brought down from Hirwaun on the Aberdare and Glamorganshire Canals, was delivered along another tramroad branch – either that through the Aberdare Iron Company's rolling mills from the wharf at Pentrebach or the one from the wharf at Pwllyhwyad Bridge. From the 1840s, finished tinplate left the works by yet another tramroad crossing the Taff by the Julia Bridge at Rhydyfelin and ran to the Doctor's Canal where there was a wharf with crane. The tramroad extension along the canal towpath from Ynis Geryn Bridge to Brown Lenox was authorised by the GCC in 1826 but tonnage charges were to be paid to the canal company as if the canal had been used.[35] By the time of the 1875 25 inch OS map, this extension had been curtailed at Pentrebach where the wharf and sidings for the Taff Vale Ironworks lay.

Despite its many customers, information on the operation of Griffiths' tramroad and canal seems practically non-existent. It is said that the weighing machine at Machine Bridge was used not only to ascertain the tonnages payable by the collieries to Griffiths or the Thomases but also to calculate the piece-rate wages of the coal hewers. This eventually caused a coal strike at Dinas, with the result that Coffin agreed to pay his colliers per the weight at pit head.[36] The best source of information on the tramroad

Fifty years later again, the same view of the village of Treforest, with its three river bridges, now includes Glyntaff Halt on the A(N&SW)D&R.. The nearest bridge, opposite the Duke of Bridgewater Arms, is that built in 1851 by the Aberdare Iron Company to receive iron carried via the Aberdare Canal to its rolling mills at Treforest. Its replacement included the original stone abutments and survives to this day. Iron would also have been carried this same way, from William and Francis Crawshay's Hirwaun Ironworks to the Treforest Tinplate Works. The next bridge is Machine Bridge which had carried the Doctor's Tramroad. The photograph is taken after Machine Bridge had been widened with reinforced concrete parapets in 1913. The building on the canal bank is the Llanbradach Arms, which dates from before 1841. Finally, downstream is the Castle road Bridge, which connected the Treforest market place with the terminus of the Doctor's Tramroad at the head of the Doctor's Canal. The rolling stock at Glyntaff Halt is of interest; it includes two of the three ex-Barnum & Bailey coaches which the railway company had purchased in 1909, when Buffalo Bill Cody and the circus returned to the USA. SR collection

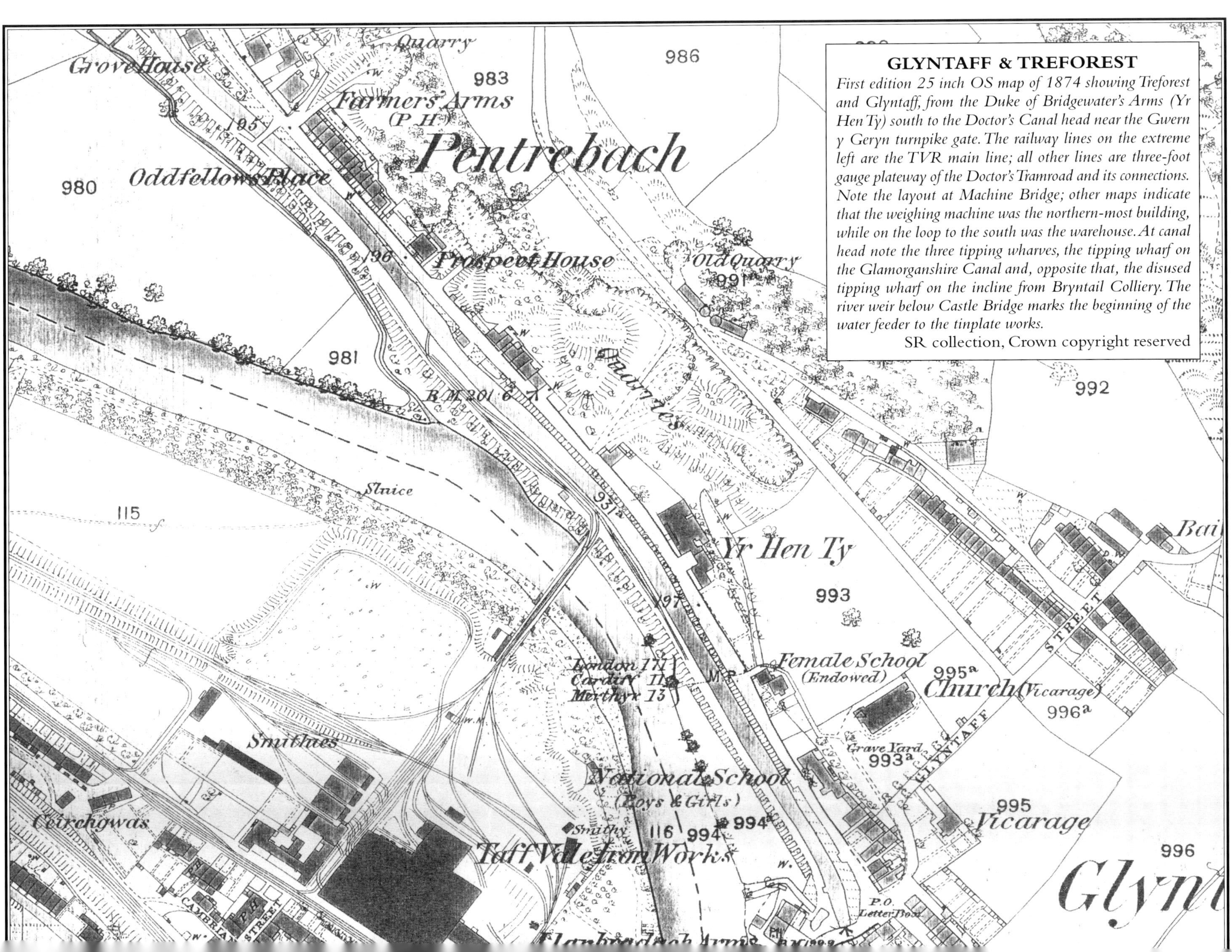

GLYNTAFF & TREFOREST

First edition 25 inch OS map of 1874 showing Treforest and Glyntaff, from the Duke of Bridgewater's Arms (Yr Hen Ty) south to the Doctor's Canal head near the Gwern y Geryn turnpike gate. The railway lines on the extreme left are the TVR main line; all other lines are three-foot gauge plateway of the Doctor's Tramroad and its connections. Note the layout at Machine Bridge; other maps indicate that the weighing machine was the northern-most building, while on the loop to the south was the warehouse. At canal head note the three tipping wharves, the tipping wharf on the Glamorganshire Canal and, opposite that, the disused tipping wharf on the incline from Bryntail Colliery. The river weir below Castle Bridge marks the beginning of the water feeder to the tinplate works.

SR collection, Crown copyright reserved

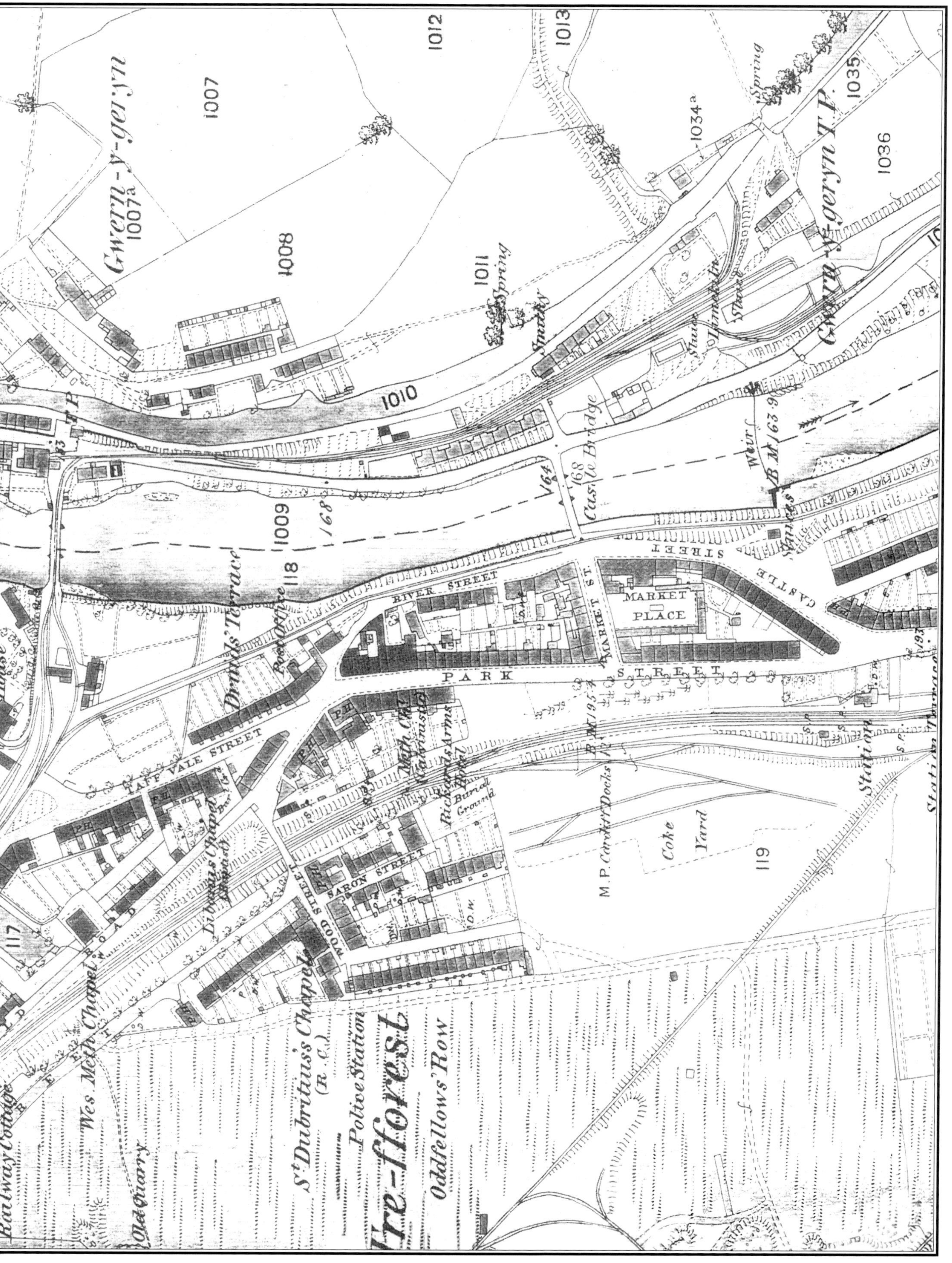
Gwern-y-geryn
Gwern-y-geryn T.P.
1007
1007a
1008
1009
1010
1011
1012
1013
1034a
1035
1036
117
118
119
Spring
Smithy
Castle Bridge
Weir
Druids' Terrace
Post Office
River Street
Market St.
Market Place
Castle Street
Park Street
Taff Vale Street
Saron Street
Wood Street
Richards Arms Hotel
Burial Ground
M.P. Cardiff Docks
Coke Yard
Station
Railway Cottage
Wes. Meth. Chapel
St Dubritius's Chapel (R.C.)
Police Station
Oddfellows' Row
Tre-fforest
Old Quarry

This rare photograph of the head of the Doctor's Canal in dereliction in the 1890s, belies the activity it had known in its working life. The solitary house nearest the canal was quite likely originally occupied by the wharfinger, one of Doctor Griffith's employees. The terrace on the left was known quite naturally as Dip Houses. On one side they faced the coal tips on the Doctor's Canal and on the other they faced the tips on the Glamorganshire Canal at Pwllyhwyad Bridge. Thomas Forrest & Sons photo, courtesy GRO.UD/Pp

and canal has been the Thomas papers in Glamorgan Record Office and the odd newspaper sale notice. The surviving GCC one month down traffic tonnage sheets for August 1863 are a tantalising snippet and contain accounts for four coal traders entering the canal at Dynea.[37] By this time, the main volume of sale coal for export through Cardiff was using the Taff Vale Railway and the Bute Docks, although Pontypridd Colliery, operating as Fowler Brothers, had a coal yard on the wharf at Cardiff as late as 1859.[38] The remaining canal traffic from Pontypridd, Newbridge and Gelliwion collieries was to Melingriffith Tinplate Works, College Ironworks, the coal yards at Llandaff Yard and Cardiff town. On top of this, Pontypridd Colliery was supplying the Patent Fuel works at Blackweir on the outskirts of Cardiff. Most probably this was not to be used in the fuel blocks themselves, which used steam coal not bituminous coal. It is likely that much of the growing house and smiths coal trade in Pontypridd and Treforest, which was not collected from the pit head or level mouth of these collieries, was supplied to the town via the tramroad.

The Doctor's Canal supported at least two boat yards. The one at Blaen y Llyn was strategically placed near the junction at Dynea. It may have been operating on a small scale before 1851, because the 25 year old boatbuilder, Ebenezer Morris from Carmarthen, is recorded at Dynea on the 1841 census. Ten years later he was working as a labourer at Merthyr. In 1861, it was run by the widower David Jones employing four men, including his son James. Like several canal boatbuilders on the Glamorganshire Canal, Jones had originated from the shipwrighting tradition of Cardiganshire, where the 24 year old James had been born. David Jones' two daughters of 22 and 21 were, however, born at Merthyr Tydfil where he had moved to work at the Ynysfach boatyard (at Parliament Lock) in about 1838. The increasing sale coal trade on the canal in the 1850s would have persuaded him to move his business south to Dynea to build and maintain the coal boats on the Doctor's Canal. From the 1870s, he was joined at the yard by his young grandson, David William Gorvett, and together they ran the yard to its closure in the early years of the 20th century.[39] The dock utilised the water from the Glamorganshire Canal overflow weir which joined the Tir Ucha overflow. Jones built the cottages across the canal from the dock and it seems that, by 1902, Gorvett was operating an undertaker's business from the yard.[40] There was no connecting bridge between dock, saw pit and the cottages but the junction towpath bridge was only a few hundred yards away. Thomas Jones, the Llandaff North boatman, told a story that about 1886 he and David Jones both went to Aberfan to buy the same canal boat, available for disposal by Meakin & Dean, railway contractors who had used the canal while constructing the GW&RR joint line. Tom had secured the boat on an earlier visit by paying

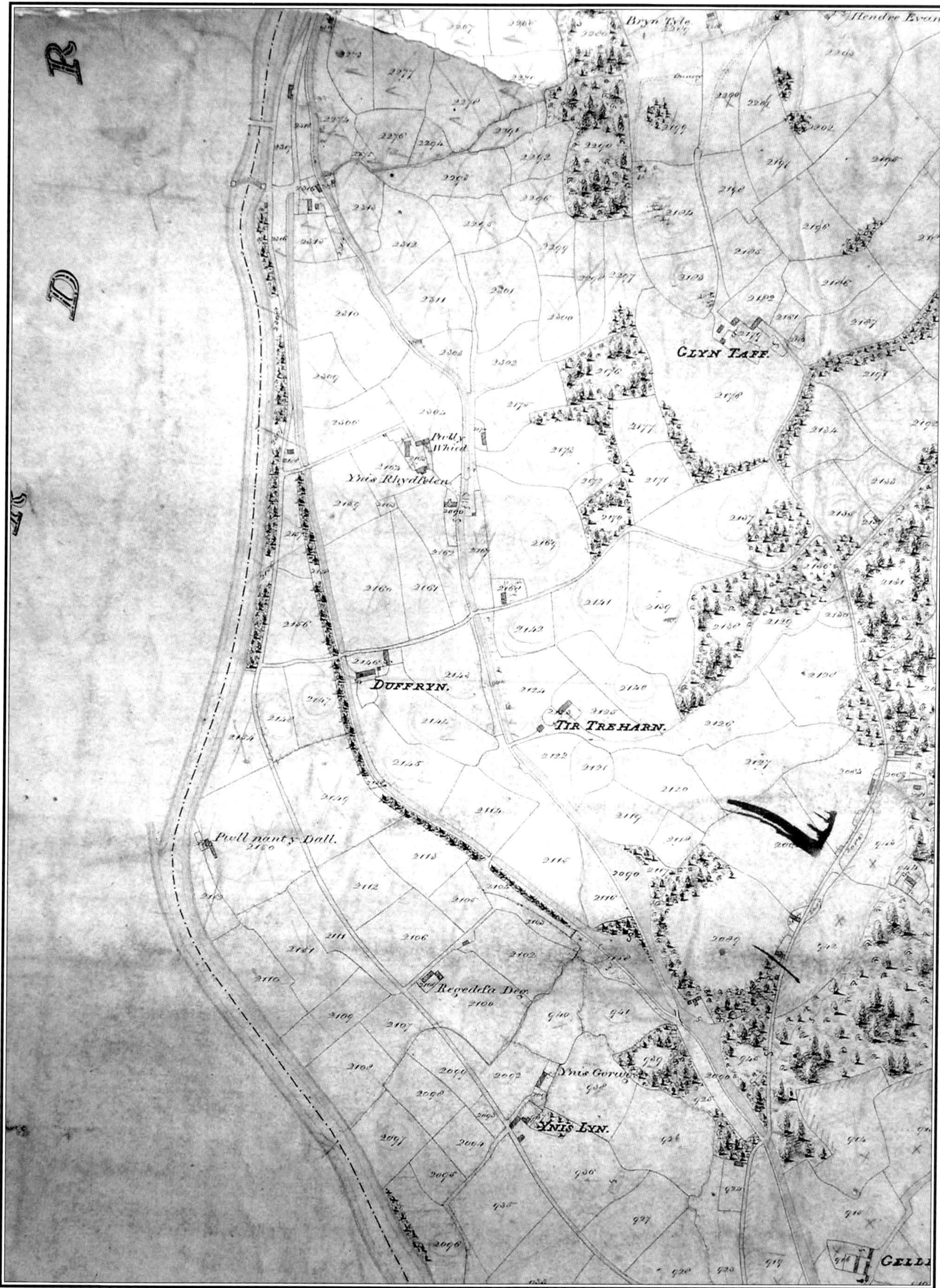

The Doctor's Canal from a copy of the Eglwysilan Tithe map of 1841. At this time it seems that the Julia river bridge from the tinplate works to Rhydyfelin had not yet been built and that the work force was relying on the ford and ferry to get to and from work. As far as the finished tinplate was concerned, the Crawshays must have been using the tramroad connection to the canals. Courtesy GRO

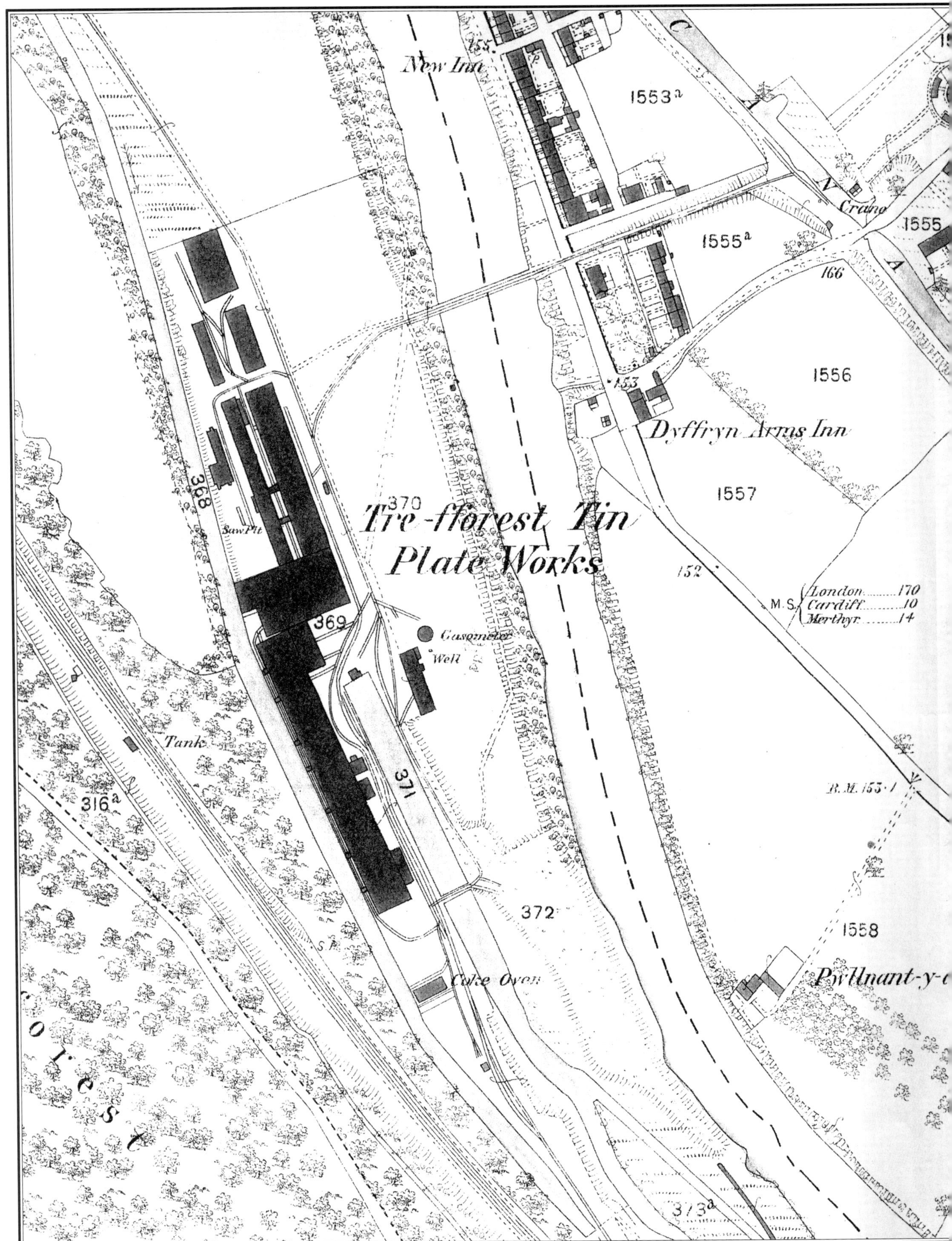

New Inn
155
1553a
1555a
1555
Crane
166
1556
153
Dyffryn Arms Inn
1557
370
Tre-fforest Tin
Plate Works
368
Saw Pit
369
Gasometer
Well
152
M.S.
London 170
Cardiff 10
Merthyr 14
Tank
371
316a
B.M. 153·1
372
1558
Pwllnant-y-
S.P.
Coke Oven
373a

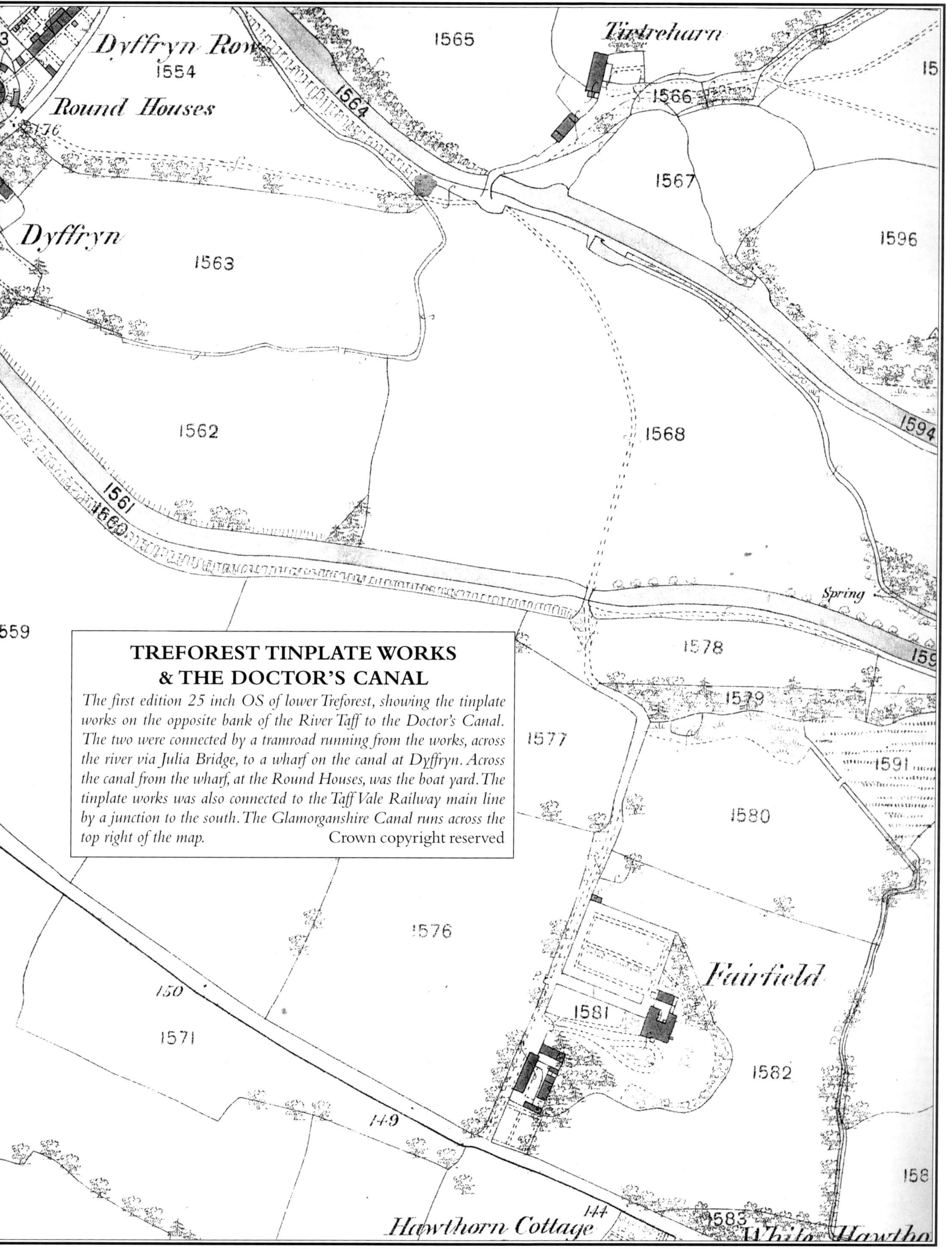

TREFOREST TINPLATE WORKS & THE DOCTOR'S CANAL

The first edition 25 inch OS of lower Treforest, showing the tinplate works on the opposite bank of the River Taff to the Doctor's Canal. The two were connected by a tramroad running from the works, across the river via Julia Bridge, to a wharf on the canal at Dyffryn. Across the canal from the wharf, at the Round Houses, was the boat yard. The tinplate works was also connected to the Taff Vale Railway main line by a junction to the south. The Glamorganshire Canal runs across the top right of the map.

Just downstream from Castle Bridge is the tinplate works weir, shown here from the feeder which took a quite considerable amount of water to drive the Treforest Tinplate Works rolling mills. The Doctor's Canal head was across the river and behind the Hide & Wool Market. This photograph also shows the Pontypridd UD Council's tramways depot, its electricity works, the refuse destructor and the gas works. It was ash from this power station that was used to fill the bed of the Doctor's Canal when it was finally abandoned. SR collection

a deposit. When he saw David Jones at Aberfan, Tom realised why he was there and told him "*you might as well catch the next train home.*" So the disappointed Jones returned to the Dynea dock empty-handed.[41] By that time David Jones was well into his seventies.

The second known yard was situated at the canal bridge at Dyffryn, where the road from the Cardiff to Merthyr turnpike to Glyn Taff crossed the Doctor's Canal. A 55 year-old boat builder, William Thomas, is recorded at Dyffryn in 1841 but the main impetus to the business would have been the building of the river bridge to the Treforest Tinplate Works. The yard with dock was opposite the tinplate works wharf, near Francis Crawshay's Roundhouse and that is where some of the boatbuilders and sawyers lived in 1851. The dock no doubt expanded to service Crawshay's boats. In 1851, the yard may have accommodated two separate businesses. One was the Cornish shipwright John Allen's. In the early 1830s he had worked in the shipyards at Cardiff – quite probably that of Richard Tredwen because Tredwen, Allen and Allen's wife Betsy all hailed from Padstow. The other boatbuilding business at Dyffryn was John James'. He employed three men, all of whom, like James, came from Cardiganshire. Like David Jones, he too had worked in the Merthyr boatyards (on Dowlais boats). Later James was to move his business down the Glamorganshire Canal to Gabalfa. No evidence has been found of the dock Griffiths and Coffin had agreed to build in the early years of the canal. Maps of the Doctor's Canal head at Treforest give no indication of any boat dock there – simply a large winding hole for turning boats.

Despite the superior quality of Coffin's bituminous coal for coking purposes and the 1831 repeal of the clause favouring the Newport traders, it took a long time for Coffin and his fellow traders to break into the monopoly held by the Newport and Swansea markets. The growth of the Aberdare steam coal trade provided the final impetus and in 1835, Walter Coffin joined with Thomas Powell, Josiah John Guest and others to revive the scheme for a Merthyr to Cardiff Railway. This time the arguments for it were overwhelming and it became the locomotive-hauled Taff Vale Railway – opened in 1841 and including branches to Eirw for Coffin's coal and to Llancaiach for Powell's. Coffin quickly made a link from his tramroad to the railway at Eirw and from that time on his coal became transferred from canal to railway, bypassing the Doctor's Tramroad also. At Cardiff, the Marquess of Bute persuaded him to leave his wharf on the Sea Lock pound of the Glamorganshire Canal and move to the Bute Dock. This should have sounded the death knell for Coffin's tramroad but it continued in operation providing a horse-drawn passenger service to and from the market at Treforest. In fact the combined Coffin and Thomas tramroad was the cause of a social shift in focus for Rhondda inhabitants, from the market town of Llantrisant to the new towns of Treforest and Pontypridd. There are records of several types of special vehicle being used for carrying dignitaries and groceries.[42]

The TVR branch was extended to Dinas in 1849 and remained a mineral railway until passenger services were started between Porth and Dinas much later, on 7 January 1863.[43] The first edition 25 inch OS map of 1871 shows Coffin's tramroad to have been lifted. The first steam coal came out of Rhondda in 1855 but none of it was carried on the Glamorganshire Canal. As E.D. Lewis states,

> *'Coffin played no part in the development of the steam coal trade which was the main reason for the striking growth in Cardiff's foreign coal exports to 249,001 tons in 1851, but he had created an extremely profitable French demand for his own bituminous or coking coal.'*[44]

Like many of those who made their fortunes from the mineral wealth of the Glamorgan hills, Coffin had moved his private home to Llandaff city and become a notable figure in Cardiff public life. In 1853 the coal owner

Dyffryn Lock (No 33) on the Glamorganshire Canal was known by boatmen to the end as 'Lock Lewis', after its long-serving lockkeeper William Lewis. This summer scene was photographed about 1910. The well turned out boat, steerer and lady passenger all contribute to the relaxed atmosphere of what appears to be the occasion of a local pleasure trip. All is not well on the maintenance side, however. The picturesque cascades from Lock Lewis's top gate indicate gross wastage of water from leaks and the urgent attention of the carpenters. Hayward photo, Pontypridd

Dyffryn Bridge carried Dyffryn Road across the Glamorganshire and this 1930s view gives a good indication of the full width of the canal between bridges. The long row of houses in the background is Ynys Terrace on Council Street. SR collection

Left: The parapets of Dyffryn Bridge are in a bad state of repair in this 1940s photograph and the canal is derelict. The long house with shop was originally Glyn Taff Cottage and occupied at the time of the 1851 census by James Kidman, a 78 year old retired salt merchant who had operated from a wharf on the Sea Lock pound in Cardiff. Dyffryn Bridge became known to boatmen as 'Kidman's Bridge' and the name stuck.
Jim Rees collection

Below: The round houses were built by Francis Crawshay and, in 1851, the eight properties housed the shipwright and the carpenters who worked in the boatyard on the Doctor's Canal. The bridge in this photograph of about 1914 is carrying Dyffryn Road across the Doctor's Canal, alongside the old boat dock. Here, too, was the tinplate company's wharf. SR collection

withdrew from active involvement in his commercial interests, to further pursue his political career and become MP for the town.

Competition from railways did not stop the lower portion of the Rhondda tramroad continuing to be useful into the 20th century, fulfilling its original purpose of bringing down coal to Treforest for transfer to the Doctor's Canal. It was never converted for locomotive use. The Lan Colliery was opened in 1866 on the line of the tramroad and was offered for sale with five canal boats.[45] In 1875, it sent 15,011 tons down the tramroad but by 1881 this had declined to 3,565 tons.[46] Then, in 1875, Daniel Thomas sank Pwllgwaun Pit under the continuing powers of the old 1812 lease between Griffiths and the Bassett sisters. By 1889, Lan Colliery had stopped production but Pwllgwaun Pit sent 7,263 tons along the tramroad.[47] The pit was always known as 'Dan's old muck hole' and in 1902, as Phillips & Mogford's Pwllgwaun Colliery, it was sending small coal to Cardiff by tramroad and the two canals, the boats being loaded to 15-16 tons and consigned to Jenkins & Scale.[48] It is also said that Pwllgwaun supplied coal to Nantgarw Pottery. Although Pwllgwaun Colliery lasted until 1947, the Doctor's Canal fell into disuse in about 1911, when traffic also ended on the tramroad and in 1913 the Machine Bridge was widened to take motor traffic. In 1918, the Doctor's Canal was listed in Bradshaw as derelict.[49]

Parts of the tramroad may be followed today, notably along the south bank of the river Rhondda at Hopkinstown, along Sardis Road in Pontypridd, and along Broadway in Treforest as far as the Machine Bridge. Nothing remains of the Doctor's Canal. In 1920 powers were obtained by Pontypridd Urban District Council to extend their electric tramways from Castle Inn Bridge to Upper Boat, using part of the course of the canal, which was infilled and purchased by the PUDC for £3,150 in 1923. A light railway order was obtained on 2 September 1927 but the council

In the foreground of this view of Rhydyfelin are the chimneys of the tinning shed at Treforest Tinplate Works. Running diagonally at the left of the picture and beneath the railway viaduct is the Julia Bridge, the original of which was built by the Crawshays to connect their works to Dyffryn Road and to their wharf on the Doctor's Canal, across the river. Dyffryn Road, the Round Houses, Glyn Taff Cottage and the bridges over the two canals can be seen. This image gives a good idea of the relative levels of the two canals as they made their converging ways towards Dynea, off right. On the hillside in the right distance are the spoil tips of the Dynea coal levels, above the line of the A(N&SW)D&R which ran to Caerphilly and Newport. The railway viaduct in the middle of the photograph is that of the Cardiff Railway as it approaches its intended junction with the TVR at Treforest; however, the TVR refused permission to make a permanent junction and, apart from one ceremonial coal train, the viaduct was never used.

SR collection

Dynea Lock (No 34) and lock house, and the family of Ben Jones, the lockkeeper. The junction with the Doctor's Canal was just to the left, off picture. The outlet from the lock by-pass weir can be seen in front of the house. The reason for the very large pool is that clay was extracted here for the canal company's use. For example, the Plymouth accounts show that 64 tons were extracted for them from here in 1829 and a further 59 tons in 1830. (GRO Pl 628) SR collection

Left: *GCC boat No 503 is moored at the claypit below Dynea Lock, in what was left of the canal in 1943. The boat was one of those built for the company in the 1890s and originally had a cabin which carried the name* Castell Caerffili *on the forward bulkhead. The narrow tapering profile of this boat prompted canal workers to call her 'The Needlegun'. No 503 is seen here without a cabin and downgraded to maintenance duties. Caught on the upper side of the Nantgarw breach in 1942. 'The Needlegun' was never able to return to Cardiff and she was left to her fate in this 'wide' in the Three Mile pound at Dynea.* ILW photo 27 March 1943, neg 212

Right: *In September 1986, the infilled junction of the Doctor's Canal with the Glamorganshire Canal was exposed while workmen were installing a long-needed storm drain and flood prevention scheme. This photograph shows the entrance to the Doctor's Canal, over which there was once a towpath bridge.* Mike Morris

did not proceed with the tramway.[50] The course of the Doctor's Canal was obliterated in 1970 by the builders of the A470 Cardiff to Merthyr trunk road, except for a portion of Poplar Road in Rhydyfelin which is built on the line of the canal leading to the junction at Dynea.

Bryn Tail Colliery

One of the more spectacular engineering features associated with the Glamorganshire Canal was the tramroad connecting the level mouth at Bryn Tail with the tipping wharf on the canal bank. The course of most of the steep 800 yard long incline from the level survives, while the lower 300 yards of horse drawn tramroad was obliterated by the laying out of Glyntaff Cemetery. The incline runs through Glyn Taff Wood on a mixture of causeway and cutting and the remains of bridges survive where it crossed access paths to Wood Cottage and Craig-fach farm house.

The colliery was not a success and seems to have operated for only a few years in the 1860s. The reason for its failure was the unwarranted trust which its operators held in their lease with the landowner, Dr William Price.

Cardiff City Library's Kyrle Fletcher collection includes a draft mineral lease, dated 2 Feb 1807, of the 115 acre Bryn Tail Estate, then owned by John Richards of Llandaff. The 21 year lease was to Samuel Harford, Richard Jones Tomlinson, John Harford and Richard Blakemore (*i.e.* the Melingriffith Company) and charged a galeage of 6d per ton, each ton being measured long weight at 21 hundredweight per ton. The Bryn Tail Estate was some miles from Melingriffith, whose closer collieries on the Garth and at Craig yr Allt appear to have been more than adequate for the purposes of their iron and tinplate works. No evidence has come to light that the Bryn Tail lease was completed, nor that any coal prospecting took place at Bryn Tail until 1858.[51]

Dr William Price was surgeon to the Brown Lenox Chain Works but is more popularly remembered as Treforest's notoriously eccentric druid and the man who introduced cremation into modern Britain. In November 1857, he purchased and mortgaged the adjoining estates of Bryn Tail and Craig Alfa from John Rogers the younger, who had inherited the freeholds from the Rev'd Evan Jones in 1835. Rev'd Evan Jones had in turn acquired Bryn Tail and Gwaun Gwern Geryn in 1809 and Craig Alfa in 1813.[52]

In May 1858, the four foot 'Gwenhiolen' seam was struck only 16 yards from the surface on Price's land.[53] This fanciful naming would have been Price's own since he named his daughter Gwenhiolen. His agent was more conservative in the *Colliery Guardian* advertisement where it is described as the Red Ash seam, known in the markets under the name Mynyddisllywn, Maesmawr, Llantwit and Gelligaer.[54] With the mining engineer William Harrison's report, he was ready to lease the mineral rights. William Harris and Charles Davies junior, as partners, took over the coal level and a 14 year term was granted them in the colliery lease of 17 June 1859. Rent would be £500 per annum, together with one shilling per ton for all coal raised in any one year above 10,000 tons.[55] Harris was the wealthy son of a gentleman farmer living at Monmouth. He left Monmouth to live at Bridge House, Bedwas, where he is said to have owned and operated other collieries.[56] Charles Davies relied on the Bristol-based finances of his father Charles Davies, who resided at Claremont House, Abergavenny.

For the Bryn Tail lease to be profitable depended on Dr Price's allocating some of his own land and also arranging for land to be given up by Baroness Windsor and Lord Llanover to enable an inclined plane to be built to the Glamorganshire Canal. There should have been no problem because, even if the other two landowners would not co-operate, Price could have called out the canal commissioners to value the land and force it to be given up under the four mile clause of the Canal Act. In April 1859, Price made a £100 offer to Baroness Windsor for the 2a 3r 17p required of the Plymouth estate. They considered this derisory and decided to await appointment of commissioners.[57] Before Price's own land at Bryn Tail could be given up, he had also to reach an agreement with his mortgagee. Why this proved difficult has not been ascertained but Price would have been ill advised to agree to such covenants in the lease before he knew their exact cost. Characteristically, Price lost interest in fulfilling these responsibilities to his lessees as he left the country to live at Boulogne in France. Meanwhile, the apprehensive Harris and Davies used the delay to develop the level workings towards the brow of Eglwysilan Hill, where the seam thickened.[58] However, in December 1859, with no immediate prospect of Price's furnishing them with the land for the incline, they had no means of getting their coal to market, so they started the slow process of litigation.[59] In December 1860, the lessees filed a bill in Chancery against William Price and his mortgagees to compel him to provide the land, claiming costs and reserving rents and royalties due under the lease until the case was resolved.

In his absence abroad, Price arranged that the mortgage of Bryn Tail and Craig Alfa be assigned to his Bristol solicitor John Griffiths Trenerry. While the legal battle to recover Harris and Davies's costs continued, the estates were sold by auction on 16 August 1862.[60] By this time, the partnership of William Harris and Charles Davies junior could not sustain the continuing lack of income from Bryntail. They filed for bankruptcy. Referring to Charles Davies' mortgage liability to his father of £2,000, the justice remarked, '*It seems to me that while the colliers who go under ground are most reckless of their lives, those connected with collieries above ground are equally reckless of their interests.*'[61] Harris family tradition tells that, even though he eventually won his case, he was never able to recover costs from Price because Price claimed immunity under the Statute of Limitations Act by living in France for seven years. Two of the Harris sons were removed from public schools in England and all four of his sons became miners as the family fell on hard times.

The second partner, Charles Davies junior, was somewhat luckier, as his father continued to back the venture. At the August 1862 auction, it was Charles Davies senior who bought the estate from Trenerry. Whether the mortgage

The short-lived Bryntail Colliery had a spectacular inclined plane to link to its wharf on the canal at Pwllyhwyad Bridge. By the time this photograph was taken in the 1890s, the line of the disused incline had been cut by the embankment of the A (N&SW) D&R. The abandoned colliery workings can be seen on the hillside across the road from Hendre Prosser farm. Bryntail farm is higher up behind the woods. The line of trees past Craig Fach marks the route of the tramroad to the valley floor. The canal wharf was behind the whitewashed cottages and alongside the large dwelling near the gas works. Also shown in this photograph by Thomas Forrest & Sons, are Dip Cottages and the other collection of buildings at the head of the Doctor's Canal. Courtesy Pontypridd Heritage Centre

assignment and sale were an artifice to enable Davies to purchase the land or whether the history of litigation and the conditions of sale put off other possible purchasers is unknown. The old workings, dormant for almost three years, were put into shape and leased by Davies to a new partnership of his two sons (Charles and E.T. Davies) and a Mr Ditchett of Bristol.[62] Davies also proceeded in taking actions against the hapless William Harris to recover monies lost by his son in the first venture.[63] Davies junior was now living at Harris's former home, Bridge House, Bedwas, while Harris is recorded as residing at Rhydyfelin.

Now that Davies owned the land he was able to sanction building the incline to the canal. He also set about evicting Price's common law wife and daughter from Craig Alfa:

> *'Mrs Price and her daughter tenaciously held possession of a tenement upon the estate until they were unroofed, and even then, were with difficulty dislodged after enduring the 'pelting of the pitiless' rain, protecting themselves as they best might by the most impervious of umbrellas.'*[64]

By March 1864, the incline was complete.[65] On Wednesday 4 May, the colliery was formally opened and the first load of coal was transported down the incline to the canal tipping wharf. A party of guests from Bristol arrived by train at Treforest to attend the celebrations which are well described in the *Cardiff & Merthyr Guardian* for Friday 6 May:

> *'... a circuitous route ..., past pendant rocks, through the blooming gorse, o'er flower-spangled grass, over almost inaccessible stiles, and across stepping stones and mountain streamlets – brought us at length to the tip and our destination. At one glance the eye takes in all the great beauty of the Taff and Rhonda* [sic] *Valleys; all the busy traffic of the 'Fothergill' iron works, and that of the rail, road and canal, to which the Bryntail colliery is about to add its useful and, we doubt not, advantageous quota of supply.*
>
> *The first business of the morning was naturally a descent into the 'levels' of the pit, – timid gentlemen peeped curiously into its cavernous depths, shrugged their shoulders and*

hesitated until the ladies led the way to the rough seats improvised in the small iron tram waggons: then every particle of spare room became occupied, the horse was harnessed, everything was speedily arranged for the start, the parties having been considerately supplied with lighted candles stuck into hastily-constructed clay-holders. At the word, 'Go-a-head,' one or two elongated examples of humanity seemed suddenly alive to a conviction of 'Hats!' and the driver instantly obeying a vociferous and gentle shout to 'stop', reined back the horse. The 'chimney pots' were deposited in a place of safety, and some novel head-dresses having been made with pocket-handkerchiefs, the 'trams' were instantly en route. Scarcely, however, had the train entered the tunnel, when there was a 'run-off the rail', and a stoppage – daylight was disappearing, and this little casualty affecting the progress of the party was speedily remedied – but not before one gentleman had made his escape, to await the return of his more adventurous friends where he was menaced with less danger. 'Heads down' are the constantly-repeated warnings that break in upon the happy laugh of the excursionists: but above all, there occasionally comes the monosyllabic call of 'Spraggs', after which the vehicles stop, and the footfall of the horse in the splashy bottom of the pit is no longer heard. A steep descent seems to pitch the occupant of the highest seat almost into the laps of those beneath him – there is more jolting and more 'Spragging', the heads are in very close proximity, and a gust of wind extinguishes the only remaining lights, except the one carried by the driver! At last the headings are reached, and the grotesque-looking visitors have an opportunity of inspecting a remarkably fine seam of the Llantwit coal, varying from 2ft 6in to 4ft 6in in thickness, highly bituminous and suitable for house purposes. A miner shows the process of excavation, and after a pleasant hour of scientific research in 'the bowels of the earth', the party return with almost a repetition of the incidents above specified, most of them carrying specimens of 'slag' or Bryntail coal.

During their absence three trucks of coal containing about four tons, have been got in readiness at the top of the steep incline, three quarters of a mile long, and terminating in a 'tip' at the canal side, where they are at once 'screened' and shipped. The ascending and descending waggons are held in check by a massive chain, manufactured at the works of Messrs Davies (Pontypool). A third of the entire distance is afterwards performed by horsepower, and during the process the empty waggons that have reached the pit mouth are being refilled for a similar descent. The gradient of this declivity is said to be 1 in 9. At the top a number of stalwart collier-men, with brawny arms, honest hearts, and loud voices

– congregated around the waggons, and waited, hat in hand, for the arrival of Messrs Davies's party, who were following the track of the waggons as best they might, and with a variety of ludicrous evolutions.'

The guests then proceeded to the canal-side Grove House at Pentrebach, where a champagne luncheon was served with the hospitality of Mr and Mrs Charles Evans. The party left on the 3.15 train to Cardiff where, at 5 o'clock, Messrs Davies, Ditchett and Davies entertained a select circle of friends at the Angel Hotel.

Thus, after five frustrating years Bryn Tail Colliery was finally sending coal to Cardiff along the Glamorganshire Canal. The 1862 sale notice had given an indication of the kind of profit which could be made. It estimated that several thousand tons could be weekly raised and delivered on board, at Cardiff, at a total cost of 5s 2d per ton when the going rate was some 8 to 9 shillings. The cost breakdown was as follows:

	s	d
Raising	2	0
Dead work, including over ground hauling & tipping into boats	1	0
Canal Tonnage	1	0
Boatage & boats	0	5
Shipping Expenses, Wharfage, etc.	0	9
TOTAL	5	2

Not five months later, Charles Davies senior was advertising for sale the whole of Bryn Tail and Craig Alfa estates, including Bryn Tail Colliery and the Craig Alfa paving and building stone quarry. Now that he, at last, had a working colliery with transport infrastructure (a railway incline with capacity of 300 tons per day), perhaps he felt it was time to cut his losses. Whether a buyer was found who would operate the colliery is not known but what is certain is that the colliery was not a continuing success. Whereas connection to the canal was at last made, most new colliery concerns in the 1860s had long been setting their eyes on railway connections; there was little scope for this at Bryn Tail, although the 1864 sale notice optimistically proposed that '*easy access also can be secured to the Taff Vale Railway*'.[66] The first edition 25 inch OS map of 1875 shows Bryn Tail Colliery and the incline to the canal as disused.

Today, the site of the colliery repays a visit.[67] The ruins of a building near the level mouth probably housed a haulage engine. There are few signs of waste tips, which would point to the colliery's short working life. Nowadays Bryn Tail farmhouse, to the north of the colliery site, is better known as the childhood home of William Edwards the Pontypridd bridge builder; Edwards had been long dead before coal prospecting was attempted and abandoned in his old haunts.

Collieries near the Southern Outcrop

Before the coming of the coke-fired iron industry in the mid 18th century, there was more coal mining activity at the southern edge of the geological coalfield than in the northern hills. At the heads of the valleys there was no significant population to support any ambitious house-sale colliery, as the lack of a decent transport facility prevented selling coal at any distance from where it was dug.[68] When the organised iron industry did come, most of the mined coal was to feed the furnaces and their attendant forges and steam engines. Some independent house-sale levels, such as Thomas Key's at Abercanaid, then started to supply the needs of the growing population and the operators of canal-side limekilns but there was little coal sent down the canal. By comparison, in the southern uplands which formed the hinterland of the market towns of Llantrisant, Caerphilly and Cardiff, there was more opportunity for the entrepreneur coal prospector. Some coal was sent coast-wise from the river quay at Cardiff but the quantity bore no comparison to that carried from the well-established harbours of Swansea, Neath and Newport. In fact enough Swansea and Neath coal was imported at Cardiff in the 1730s to warrant the London authorities considering appointment of a dedicated official to meter it for tax. About this time a proposed plan to regularly ship coal from Cardiff to Bridgwater was scuppered because of the Customs' insistence that it be taxed. Clearly potential coal trade from Cardiff now gathered its own momentum but in 1775 and again in 1782, the local Customs officer reported back to his London superiors that there was still no need to appoint anyone to solely look after metering coal traffic in or out of the river. His report has quite naturally been often quoted in the light of Cardiff's subsequent history as the foremost coal-exporting port in the world:

'We have no Coals Exported from this Port, nor ever shall, as it would be too expensive to bring it down here from the internal part of the country.'[69]

The Glamorganshire Canal was to give the lie to this statement.

Craig yr Allt

In the opening years of the canal period, the main area of coal mining nearest to Cardiff was around the Garth in Pentyrch parish and across the river on the canal side at Craig yr Allt, near Nantgarw, in Eglwysilan parish. These coal levels mostly served William Lewis' Pentyrch Ironworks of 1740 and, to a much lesser extent, Harford, Partridge & Co's Melingriffith Tinplate Works (established about 1757). The two concerns were amalgamated in 1805 and thereafter were jointly run by Richard Blakemore. The tinplate works' requirement was small, since the tinning process used charcoal rather than stone coal and power at Melingriffith was by water rather than steam. Most of its coal seems to have come from Craig yr Allt, although even before the canal in 1790, it was getting some by road from as far afield as William Thomas's Llanfabon Colliery.[70]

The chronology of coal mining on Craig yr Allt is confused by there having been several neighbouring

In the 19th century, the village of Nantgarw supported a mixed population of potters, colliers and boatmen, all overlooked by the Williams family seat at Duffryn Ffrwd, seen here in the centre of this circa 1904 postcard. The village grew up below the canal; the bridge on the road from Caerphilly can be seen crossing the canal at the pottery. The Cross Keys public house is in the centre of the picture, on the main Cardiff road next to the river. Behind it and to the right is the corn mill and the Colliers Arms. Off right would have been the entrance to Craig yr Allt Colliery – always liable to flooding when the river was high. The village suffered twice in the 20th century from the imposition of further transport routes. In 1908, when the Cardiff Railway was built, the river bed had to be moved westward in order to accommodate an intrusive railway embankment. Worse, in the late 1960s, the village was destroyed for the building of the A470 to Merthyr. The road used the bed of the canal but the roundabout and slip road to the Treforest Industrial Estate meant that chapel, mill, inn and dwellings were demolished. The pottery and the Cross Keys survive.

SR collection

landowners through which the workings intersected. We shall deal with them generally, to include also the coal works of Duffryn Ffrwd and Bryncoch. The level at Duffryn Ffrwd was worked in 1790 by William Key, who owned land in the mid Taff Valley and operated a road carrier service for the Merthyr ironworks. His colliery was one of the suppliers to Melingriffith. Soon afterwards, his brother Thomas took on its operation. In September 1794, when the canal had been cut through the land and its potential was becoming even more evident, William Lewis (of Pentyrch Ironworks) took a 21 year coal lease at £10 pa, plus 6d per ton of coal, of Craig yr Allt land from John Goodrich of Energlyn. A few months later, Thomas Key also took a 31 year lease from Goodrich of neighbouring Craig yr Allt land under quite different terms. For a £55 yearly reserved rent, Key was to pay 3/4d for every twenty shillings worth of coal dug, Goodrich being allowed to carry away a sixth of such coal in lieu of galeage.[71] Key shipped from a wharf near Nantgarw Bridge, while Lewis shipped from Graig Bridge, just downstream. Thomas Key's plan was to start a sale-coal business by shipping his coal not coast-wise to Ireland but up the Severn to inland customers in England. As steward to the Earl of Plymouth, he had inside knowledge of a scheme to make a collateral cut from the canal's Sea Lock pound to a shipping wharf on the River Rhymney to the east of Cardiff. The second GCC Act to extend the canal south of Cardiff town to the Sea Lock was to have included this branch. Thomas Key's letter of 24 Feb 1796 to William Taitt is worth quoting at length:

> *'On Monday I rec'd one of the New Canal Bills from Lord Plymouth's attorney. ... I never was so astonished and Thunderstruck in my life as to see the long talked of extension to Rumney River struck out and cut short at the present Tide Lock – And cannot help saying that the Proprietors have very much gone against their own Interest in that point.*
>
> *Surely they might have had a Clause to empower them to extend it there at any time hereafter, if they found it their interest so to do, which it appears to me is not now the Case. Some time ago I had a great scarcity of Coal, owing to my principal works on the Canal side the River* [Duffryn Ffrwd] *being got into a fault. And those on the opposite side* [Maesmawr – see below] *being entirely cut off by continual Floods. But that is not the Case now. My different works are now got into such Order that I can regularly rise 400 tons per week if I had a sale for it – besides a prodigious stock in Hand. And I cannot at present get a Sale in the Country for much more than 100 Tons per week I expect from this time forward.*
>
> *I understood the extension to Rumney was to open an Up*

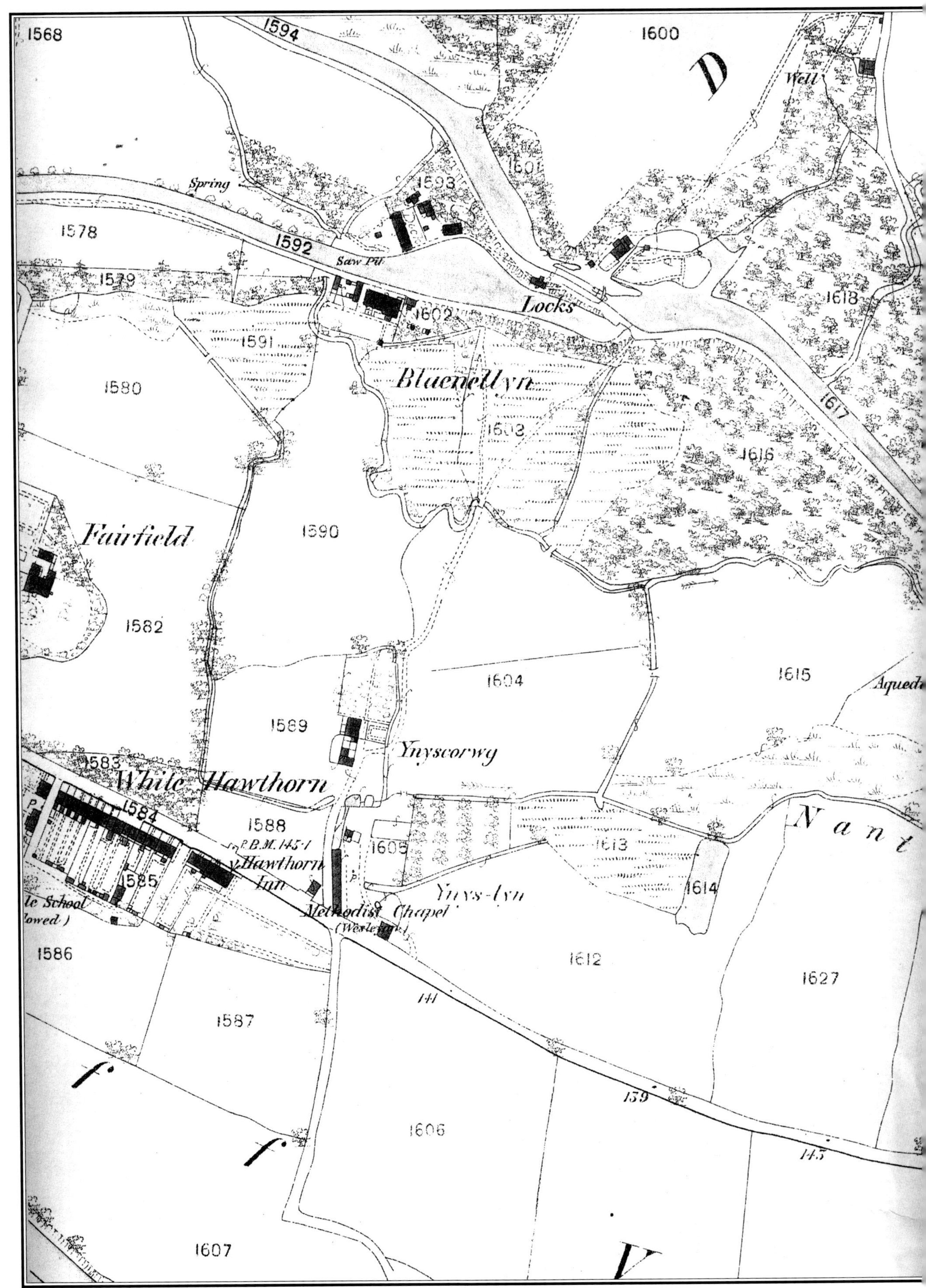
Spring
Saw Pit
Locks
Blaenllyn
Well
Fairfield
Ynyscorwg
White Hawthorn
Hawthorn Inn
B.M. 145·1
Methodist Chapel
(Wesleyan)
Ynys-lyn
Nant
Aqued
le School
lowed)

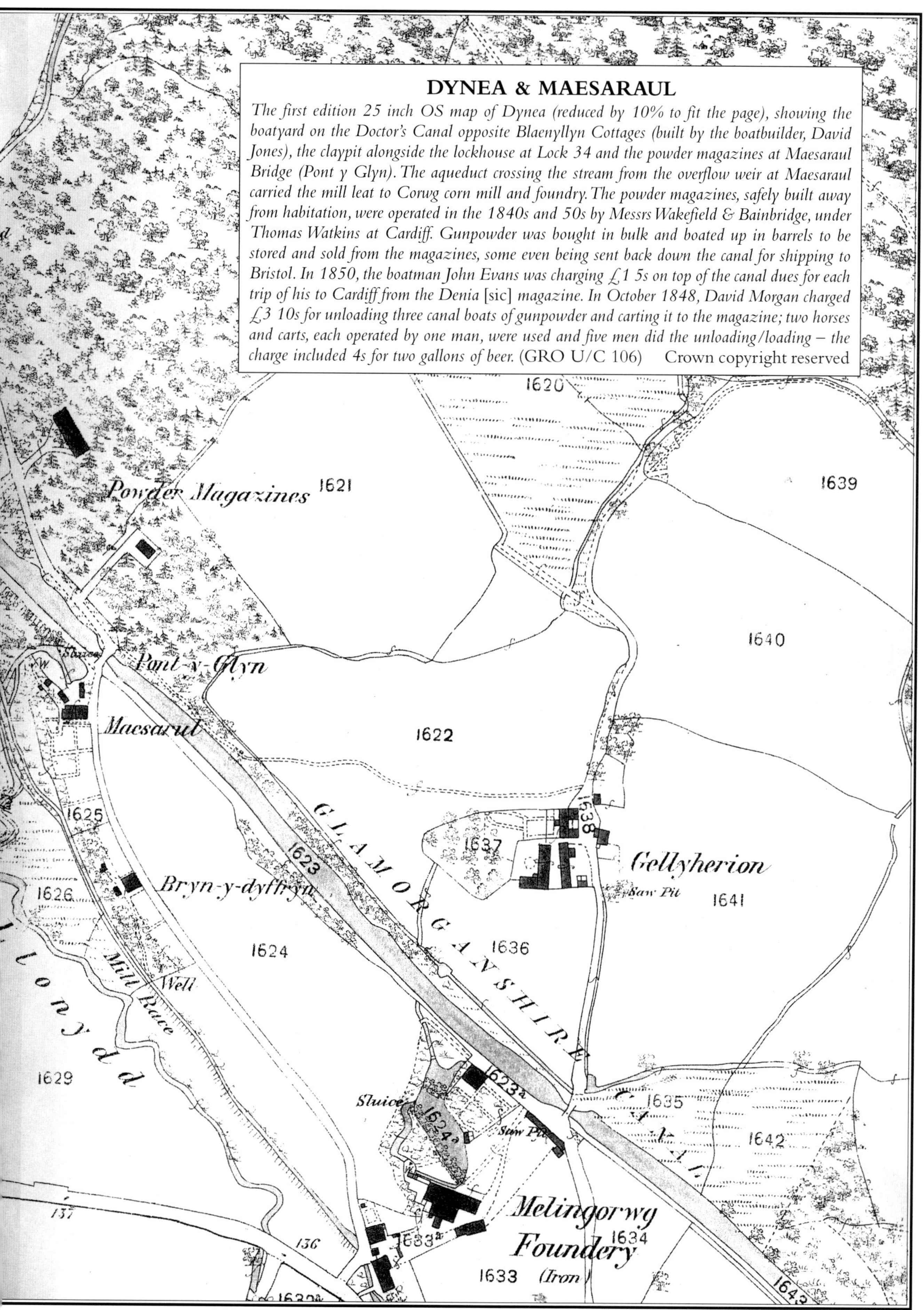

DYNEA & MAESARAUL

The first edition 25 inch OS map of Dynea (reduced by 10% to fit the page), showing the boatyard on the Doctor's Canal opposite Blaenyllyn Cottages (built by the boatbuilder, David Jones), the claypit alongside the lockhouse at Lock 34 and the powder magazines at Maesaraul Bridge (Pont y Glyn). The aqueduct crossing the stream from the overflow weir at Maesaraul carried the mill leat to Corwg corn mill and foundry. The powder magazines, safely built away from habitation, were operated in the 1840s and 50s by Messrs Wakefield & Bainbridge, under Thomas Watkins at Cardiff. Gunpowder was bought in bulk and boated up in barrels to be stored and sold from the magazines, some even being sent back down the canal for shipping to Bristol. In 1850, the boatman John Evans was charging £1 5s on top of the canal dues for each trip of his to Cardiff from the Denia [sic] *magazine. In October 1848, David Morgan charged £3 10s for unloading three canal boats of gunpowder and carting it to the magazine; two horses and carts, each operated by one man, were used and five men did the unloading/loading – the charge included 4s for two gallons of beer.* (GRO U/C 106)

Graig Bridge, looking upstream. The remains of the colliery tipping walls are on the right. S.C. Fox photo

Severn Coal Trade, particularly to the Severn and Thames Canal free of Duty. And the Agent of that Canal would have contracted with me for any Quantity I would name at the present price I sell it for, if it could have been ship'd Duty free, without any Trouble. – which must in time have turned out to great advantage to the proprietors of this Canal – for I know we can do it upon better Terms than the Newport people possibly can – I understood the Estimate amounted to Near £7000 for making that extension which seems to me to be preposterous in the extreme – for there was no Tide Lock wanting or anything of that sort. And I am sure I could make such a Cut as would be necessary for this purpose for £700 or less …'.[72]

At that time, the River Rhymney formed the border between Wales and England, so coal shipped from a wharf on the Rhymney would have been free of duty and so cancel the advantage Newport had in the sale-coal trade. Key gambled on this facility and it may have been the financial blow when it did not materialise that triggered events leading eventually to his being sacked by the Plymouth Estate on the death of the Earl. Thomas's two brothers John and William took over his affairs in 1799 but continued to develop the coal-sale business from Cardiff undaunted by the disadvantage of the export duty. An indication of their intent was their immediate application to the Marquess of Bute for a wayleave

Copied from a glass lantern slide, this view of the canal shows the Cardiff Railway embankment and Nantgarw village, and was taken from Graig Bridge. Part of the colliery waste can be seen on the left. The tall chimney in the distance is the Nantgarw Colliery, sunk in 1911. SR collection

A distant view of Craig yr Allt from across the valley, showing T.W. Booker's coal levels at Gwaelod y Garth in the foreground. The Bryncoch Brickworks buildings can be seen above the leftmost abutment of the TVR viaduct, with the incline from Craig yr Allt Colliery extending up the hill past the Rhymney Railway to the line of the Barry Railway. Above the central arch of the viaduct can be seen the buildings on the canal at Treble Locks. Compare this view with the engraving on page 17.

SR collection

Taffs Well Lock at Glan y Llyn (No 38), with the southern slopes of Craig yr Allt and the waste tips of the Bryn Coch and later Rockwood collieries showing. At the lock, in order to help boatman and lockkeeper alike, a plank bridge has been laid across the canal between the lower lock gates and the stone locktail bridge. SR collection

to enable their two collieries to be connected.[73] The 1797-9 GCC tonnage book records the Keys sending boats of coal from Nantgarw to Melingriffith, Llandaff Yard, Cardiff town and the New Wharf.[74] John Key and his successor, Brockett Grover (see below), in 1828 were said to have formerly worked Craig yr Allt on Goodrch's land for some thirty years, *i.e.* until their lease expired in January 1826.[75]

After the Keys and Grovers, the main independent coal owner in the Pentyrch area in the first half of the 19th century was Morgan Thomas. In November 1826, the GCC were worried that he was opening a level on land owned by the Williams of Dyffryn Ffrwd and tipping on the slope a few yards above the canal at Craig yr Allt. The canal company's clerk, Thomas Reece, wrote to their solicitor, William Meyrick, for a writ to be served on Thomas to prevent him tipping above the canal for fear of landslips causing damage to it.[76] Harrison's 1830 map shows Morgan Thomas's coal wharf at the Graig Bridge, with a short stretch of tramroad leading to it. The tithe map continues to show Thomas in occupation there and his colliery was visited by the Commission for Children's Employment in Mines. At that time (1842), Thomas was employing 46 men, including ten aged under 18 and one under 13. This compared with Richard Blakemore's collieries at Coed y Bedw (Pentyrch) employing 200.

The Blakemore empire had decided to go into the sale-coal business. The coal yard on the turnpike at the canal's Ynys Bridge is likely to have been to sell coal locally from the Pentyrch collieries. Coal stocks would have been ferried across the Taff to the road leading to Ynys Bridge. Alternatively, it is possible that the coal yard was to receive coal by canal from Craig yr Allt for transshipment to the Pentyrch works, although it is more likely that such coal was sent by road and ferried across the river at Maen Milwr or at Taffs Well. Whichever way the coal was going at Ynys, it was made easier from 1808 when Blakemore built the river bridge to replace the ferry there. After Melingriffith and Pentyrch were joined by tramroad in 1815, a branch tramroad from its river bridge at Cilynys took Pentyrch sale-coal to a coal tip at Tongwynlais Lock. At the same time, arrangements were made to receive and ship the coal at Blakemore's wharf on the Sea Lock pound. The tinplate works at Melingriffith continued to receive coal by canal from Craig yr Allt and their June 1853 works accounts record 1,980 tons of small coal delivered from there by John Evans.[77] At Craig yr Allt in 1859, the Melingriffith company was given permission by the GCC to build an incline bridge from their colliery level on the Cardiff-Merthyr road across the canal, not only to the canal tipping wall but to a tipping wall on the newly-built Rhymney Railway. This arrangement is shown on the first edition 25 inch OS map of 1874. After an earlier refusal, in 1863 the colliery was given permission to use water from the canal for its steam engine.[78] The colliery was abandoned prior to 1878.

On the south-western scarp of Craig yr Allt was Bryn Coch Colliery and brickworks. Fireclay and a small amount of ironstone were worked here in the 1850s by John Edmunds, who was son of Edward Edmunds of nearby Penrhos and who, as we have seen, was working Hafod and Pontypridd coal in Rhondda. Edmunds was given permission in 1852 to make a quay wall and passing place for boats on the eastern bank of the canal at Bryn Coch. In 1861, the colliery suffered an inundation of water.[79] By 1863, Thomas Williams & Co of College Ironworks, Llandaff Yard, had taken over the brickworks and colliery and in 1867, the Goodrich land was acquired by the Plymouth Estate, whose account books then start showing the half-yearly volumes of fireclay and ironstone raised (though not the coal whose royalties continued to go to Goodrich).[80] The first edition OS map of 1874 shows a substantial network of rails linking coal level, brickworks and canal wharf. Bryncoch operated until 1905.

Just south-east of Bryncoch there was also an earlier level, situated near where Ty Rhiw cemetery now is. This may have been Taffs Well Colliery said to have been operated by Brown Lenox. A tramroad led from it, alongside the Nant Llywydd, to Brown & Co's wharf and a boat maintenance yard on the canal just above Caeglas Lock. The middle part of the tramroad can still be walked. The minute book reference on 3 April 1856 that '*Mr Williams be authorised to communicate with the canal at a field below Taffs Well Lock*' may be associated with this colliery.

Much of the Craig yr Allt and Bryncoch take was later exploited by the Rockwood Colliery (1906), the Rockwood Slant (1914) and the New Rockwood (1937). The last closed in 1963.

Penygroes

Upstream of Nantgarw at Tynywern were the canal wharves for the collieries on Mynydd Mayo. The earliest of these was Penygroes – one of several collieries operated by the canal company's principal clerk, Philip Williams. His lease of Penygroes was for 21 years from October 1805 and a tramroad incline ran from the colliery down to the canal. In 1801, Richard Crawshay and Watkin George had put up £10,000 security on Williams' appointment as clerk and it seems that Crawshay had lent Williams money to establish his coal mining business. When Williams died in 1808, the impatient Crawshay immediately sent his men to remove as much of value as they could from Penygroes and take it to Crawshay's nail forge at Ynysangharad. He then felt in a bargaining position to recover what money he was owed from Williams' estate through the executor, Williams' brother David, of Beaufort Ironworks. Unfortunately, there was not a single bidder when sale of the denuded colliery was attempted. Solicitors' letters started to fly. Crawshay tried to explain his position in January 1809:

> *'I have paid excessive dear for my connection rather Friendship for Philip Williams – any actual partnership with him I believe never existed but was proposed certainly tho' never carried into execution for as advancing him money – I fulfilled my promise – and after his Decease think I had a right to take what I could find on the Colliery's Books to reimburse me.'*

A sales advertisement appeared in the *Cambrian* in September but must have been unsuccessful too. Crawshay himself then died and his nephew and executor, Benjamin Hall, had to take up the cause. A new advertisement appeared the following July for an auction at the Duke of Bridgewater Arms in three lots – the colliery, the trams and tramplates, and thirdly '*several Coal-waggons, Jenny-ropes, Boring-rods, Sledges, Shovels and various other Utensils for carrying on the trade of a Collier now at Ynis-un-Yarrod Mill* ...'. The colliery was sold to Brockett Grover (see below) and he was able to get it back into production by January 1811. Meanwhile, Thomas Reece, the new clerk to the canal, had to swear an affidavit to David Williams that none of the colliery's tools had been disposed of while in the care of Richard Crawshay.[81]

There is some evidence that Walter Coffin had a colliery near Penygroes. An entry in the Plymouth accounts for 7 June 1814 reads '*paid stamp for contract with Mr Coffin for the colliery at the Upper Boat.*'[82] The tithe map shows Walter Coffin occupying 16 acres and Cae Ty Du farm, where the coal wharves lay. Harrison's 1830 map shows the Penygroes tramroad at Tynywern as 'old incline'. In 1860, a new level was opened near Groeswen chapel with a longer tramroad incline to the canal. It was operated under the collective title of Mynydd Mayo Colliery and in August 1863, the three partners, John Owen, E.C. Downing and Thomas Jones, were all boating coal to the Sea Lock from Tynywern, each under his own name.[83] By the time the 1874 OS map was surveyed, these levels and tramroad inclines all appear again as disused.

Prospecting once again broke out in the area in 1890, when Beddoe & Co opened the Groeswen Colliery but output now went to Newport on the PC&N Railway.[84]

Coed Cae Dyrus

In August 1855, Evan Williams of Duffryn Ffrwd struck coal in Ty Fri Wood, just north of Nantgarw. He laid down a tramroad incline to the canal but then, in 1858, started driving a level under the waterway. This caused the canal company some concern and in December they sent John Lewis to examine it. The inevitable canal breach and colliery inundation happened to the extent that, a year later, the *Star of Gwent* reported that no further effort had been made to reach the lower seams. Williams paid the canal company £658 19s11d damages.[85] The 1874 OS map shows the tramroad incline and level to the upper seam as disused but the lower level close to the canal to be in use as the Coed Cae Dyrys Colliery. It became known alternatively as the Nantgarw Llantwit Colliery but was abandoned in July 1893.[86]

The last colliery in the lower Taff Valley did not use the canal, although its shafts were very close to the canal bank. This was Nantgarw Colliery, started in 1911 but shut from

A view of the Taff Valley at Nantgarw in 1954, looking northwest from near the summit of Graig yr Allt. Upper Boat, Treforest and Pontypridd are in the centre distance. Storehouse Row cottages on the Nantgarw canalbank can just be discerned towards the bottom left of the photograph. The course of the Glamorganshire Canal used to run up the valley a little to the right of centre and then followed the lower limits of the dark woodland seen marking the lower slopes of Mynydd Mayo and Mynydd Eglwysilan (right). This length of the canal was the remote and picturesque Three Mile Pound, which was later to be obliterated by the A470 Cardiff to Merthyr trunk road. The photograph includes the territories of five constituent railway companies absorbed into the former Great Western Railway. On the left, beyond the River Taff is the Taff Vale Railway. In the centre, serving

the National Coal Board's Nantgarw Coking Plant, is the Cardiff Railway, while to the right we see the Newport-bound Alexandra Docks Railway. In the immediate foreground is the Barry Railway, with the Rhymney Railway losing height just below. Duffryn Ffrwd can be seen in a clearing on the right. Today, in 2004, it is only the TVR line that survives; the NCB plant and colliery and the Upper Boat Power Station have been swept away and the A470 trunk road dominates the landscape of the valley. In the left distance, on top of the escarpment near the power station, can just be seen the engine house for Thomas Powell's incline from his Dihewyd Railway at Maesmawr. The engine house survives in use today as a private residence.

ILW photo 13 August 1954, neg 1308

1927 until 1951 because of severe geological problems. The colliery was finally closed in December 1986.

Maesmawr and Maesbach

We have left one of the most productive of the GCC colliery customers until last. Perversely, it lay on the opposite side of the river valley to the line of the canal.

In December 1765, Elizabeth Elton, widow and relict of Jacob Elton, merchant of the City of Bristol, remarried. Being the only child of Robert Matthew and granddaughter of Edmund Matthews, Elizabeth was heir to the Maesmawr and Ynys lands where the Matthews had lived (comprising 82 acres in all). Thus her new husband, the Rev'd Dr John Casberd, vicar of St Augustine the Less, Bristol, came into ownership of an estate which their marriage settlement hinted contained valuable coal reserves.[87] These lands were situated on the west bank of the River Taff in the parish of Llantwit Vardre. Coal mining here is mentioned in Edward Llwyd's *Parochialia*, compiled in 1697.[88]

Eight years later, in February 1774, Casberd was granting a sixteen year lease of much of this land to Edward Williams, described as Yeoman of the parish, at an annual rent of £101 10s. Additional rent of £5 per annum was to be charged for each acre which Williams brought under the plough but the lease also allowed for coals to be dug for a further mineral rent of £24 per annum.[89] It is not known how long Williams worked the coal at Maesmawr and whether his lease was extended into the canal period.

In November 1795, the eldest son of Elizabeth and John's marriage, John Thomas Casberd, who had followed his father's calling and was rector of Whitstanton, Somerset, married Mary Charlotte Jones of Fonmon Castle and the lands of Maesmawr were passed to the son.[90]

No direct references have been found to outlets from coal mining on Maesmawr land in the first years of the Glamorganshire Canal but it is most likely that coal shipped from Weavers Bridge by Thomas Key in 1797-9 was from Maesmawr, which Key himself was working at that time, together with his other collieries along the canal. Maesmawr Colliery is plainly shown on the 1799 plan of the intended dramroad from Carno Mill and Merthyr to Cardiff.[91] When Thomas Key was sacked as Plymouth agent in 1799, his brother John took over his coal mining and canal carrying interests, and these included Maesmawr Colliery.

Maesbach estate adjoins Maesmawr to the south. In April 1791, Melingriffith Tinplate Works is recorded as purchasing some coal from James Jacob at Maesbach.[92] A July 1799 lease of Maesbach Colliery was not certain whether the colliery's output would be carried by the Glamorganshire Canal or by the '*Railroad or Tramroad hereafter to be made by authority of Parliament in the vicinity*'. The dramroad from Carno Mill and Merthyr to Cardiff was indeed intended to cross Maesbach property but was ultimately built only as the Merthyr Tramroad and terminated at Navigation (modern day Abercynon). In 1799, the Maesbach landowner was James Jacob of Caerphilly and his 21 year mineral lease to John Scott of Cardiff charged £30 per annum, plus 3d per ton, for any quantity of coal or culm raised exceeding 2,000 tons in the year. Allowance was made for coal used '*by any ffire or other engine for working or draining the pits*' (but this wording may be purely common form for the lease and is no indication that there were steam engines at Maesbach in these early years – both water and coal were drained from the property by level not by vertical shafts). Tonnage was to be weighed at 21 cwt to the ton and 112 lbs to the cwt. The lease stipulates that for the purposes of calculating galeage it '*would be computed from and by the Gauge or Index of the Boat or Boats on the Canal Index or rate of Tonnage of the Cart or Carts Carriage or Carriages in which the same shall be carried and conveyed*'. Only that coal not conveyed by the Glamorganshire Canal or by tramroad from Maesbach need be weighed on the colliery's premises, the indication being that total production was expected to be carried on the canal or tramroad.[93] This lease was confirmed in October 1800 by Edward Jacob.[94]

The extant Glamorganshire Canal letterbook begins on 13 April 1805 and includes copy letters to freighters demanding tonnage payments. James Morrison was then working Maesbach Colliery but it appears to have been a struggling concern. His erratic quarterly tonnage accounts are recorded as follows:

Maesbach Colliery tonnages

Year	Quarter	£	s	d
1805	Mar			10
	Jun	3	2	0
	Sep	33	11	1
	Dec	24	10	9
1806	Mar	18	12	0
	Jun	5	7	4
	Sep			0
	Dec	5	18	5
1807	Mar	14	9	4
	Jun	14	4	10
	Sep	13	10	9
	Dec	5	1	3
1808	Mar	1	16	8
TOTAL		140	5	3

While James Morrison's Maesbach account for the quarter to Michaelmass 1805 amounted to £33 11s 1d, John Key's combined account (which would have included Maesmawr, Abercanaid, Duffryn Ffrwd and Craig yr Allt) was for £400 4s 10d. The December 1806 quarterly Maesbach account was only £5 18s 5d, whereas Key's was £334. It is dangerous to draw too much from these figures and translate them directly into relative weights of coal, because the total transport charge per ton would differ depending on the destination of each boat-load. Also, these accounts might be for balance amounts outstanding, rather than for the full tonnages charged. Nevertheless, the values of both accounts vary so greatly as to indicate how much the scale of the two operations must have differed. Both Key and Morrison had wharves at the Sea Lock at Cardiff.[95]

During this period, Morrison was slow to pay. By 31 July 1809 he still owed £63 15s 7d of the £140 5s 3d, the

Maesyraul Bridge, looking north, with the canal frozen over in the depths of the 1940-1 winter.
W. John collection

last payment on account having been only five guineas in March 1806. The canal company distrained his two boats, one held by Lewis Evans (at the Sea Lock) and the other by John Rees (at Navigation) and they planned to auction them on 12 August.

Eighteen months later, in February 1811, the canal company was allowing Morrison £25 for his wharf at Cardiff against his debts to them, as the remaining nine years of the Maesbach Colliery lease was auctioned at the neighbouring Rhydhelig public house. The colliery was described as:

'Maesbach Colliery, consisting of complete Iron Tram-roads from the two levels to the side of the canal (without occasion for machinery) extending about one mile and a quarter.

This newly opened colliery has been worked by unskilful tennants, who have left the two levels much injured, but may be opened (as per estimation of a qualified person) for 12 or 15 pounds.

A recent survey having been made by eminent miners, it is ascertained that the very valuable coal called the Maesmawr Vein takes its course through the whole of the Maesbach Estate, consisting of 114 acres and is about 4 feet in thickness, almost of unparalleled good quality, lays under a good rock and to be worked by level, which from its superiority is preferred to any other coal both by captains of vessels and the inhabitants of Cardiff and its neighbourhood.

There are also two other veins called the Great and Little Veins of excellent strong quality and free burning; the rock over not as good as the Maesmawr.'

The two canal boats and trams were offered at a fair valuation.[96] The fact that there were only two boats is again an indication of the small scale operation.

Only two months later, mineral leases were being offered for sale on the 200 acre Ty Main and Lower Duffryn estates which adjoined Maesmawr on the opposite bank of the river and through which the canal passed.[97]

The Maesbach Colliery then appears to have passed for a short period to the Jones family of Bristol.[98]

Meanwhile, Brockett Grover had arrived on the scene. Grover, born at Windsor in Berkshire and like Dr Richard Griffiths described as a surgeon, apothecary and midwife,[99] was a close associate of the Key family and had acted as witness to John Key's Merthyr partnership agreement with William Taitt in 1795 (see Volume 1), and in subsequent agreements between the Key brothers. He married John's daughter Elizabeth and on John's death, aged 62, in 1808 he adopted the name Key and inherited his father-in-law's embryonic coal empire.[100] In the next couple of years, Grover sought to expand the concern. As we have seen, in 1810 he purchased the late Philip Williams' colliery on the opposite side of the Taff Valley at Penygroes.[101] He then bought Maesbach so that by 1813, he was operating at least four collieries with connections to the Glamorganshire Canal and was advertising for labour.[102] None of these collieries operated initially in an area of high population.

From 1813, Grover consolidated his colliery undertakings and became one of the foremost shippers of coal on the canal alongside Smith and Coffin, until his own demise in 1831. He took up residence at an aptly named house, Porth y Glo, close to Weaver's Bridge and next to the Upper Boat public house. The row of dwellings built next to the coal tips there were suitably named Dip Cottages. Here, Grover was able to manage shipments of Maesmawr and Maesbach coal from his wharf below Weaver's Bridge. From this bridge, a road led directly to his Penygroes Colliery, whose own tramroad incline reached the canal a quarter of a mile downstream below Tynywern Bridge.[103]

Porth y Glo was so placed that Grover could watch trams of his coal crossing the river by ferry on their precarious way to the wharf. Upper Boat was so named because it was the site of a ford and ferry across the Taff. The tramroad from both Maesbach and Maesmawr also crossed the river by ferry at this point. It is ably described in J.G. Wood's

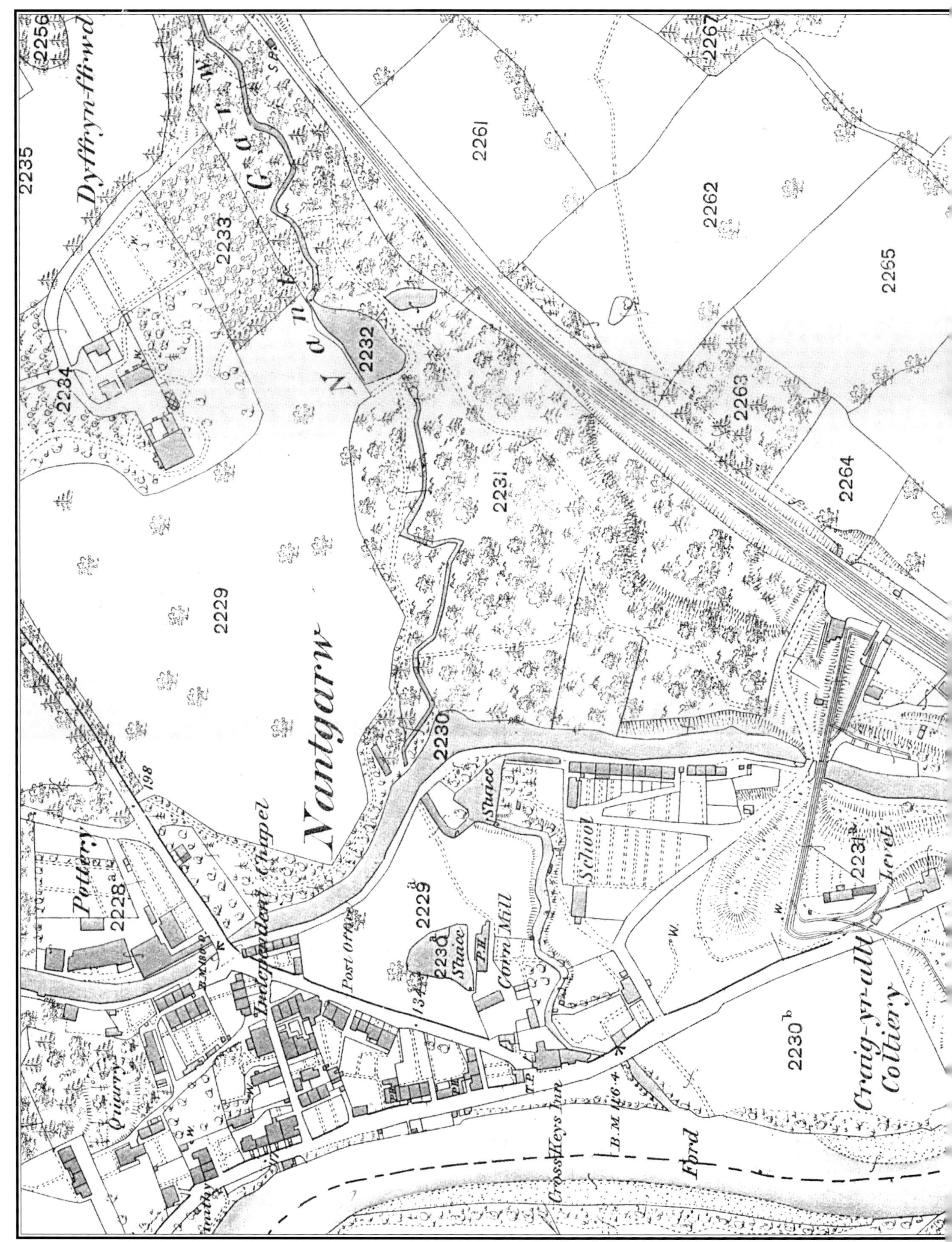

Nantgarw
Nant Garw
Dyffryn-ffrwd
Pottery
Independent Chapel
Post Office
Corn Mill
School
Sluice
Sluice
P.H.
Quarry
Cross Keys Inn
Ford
Craig-yr-allt Colliery
Level
2229
2229a
2228a
2230
2230a
2230b
2231
2232
2233
2234
2235
2256
2261
2262
2263
2264
2265
2267

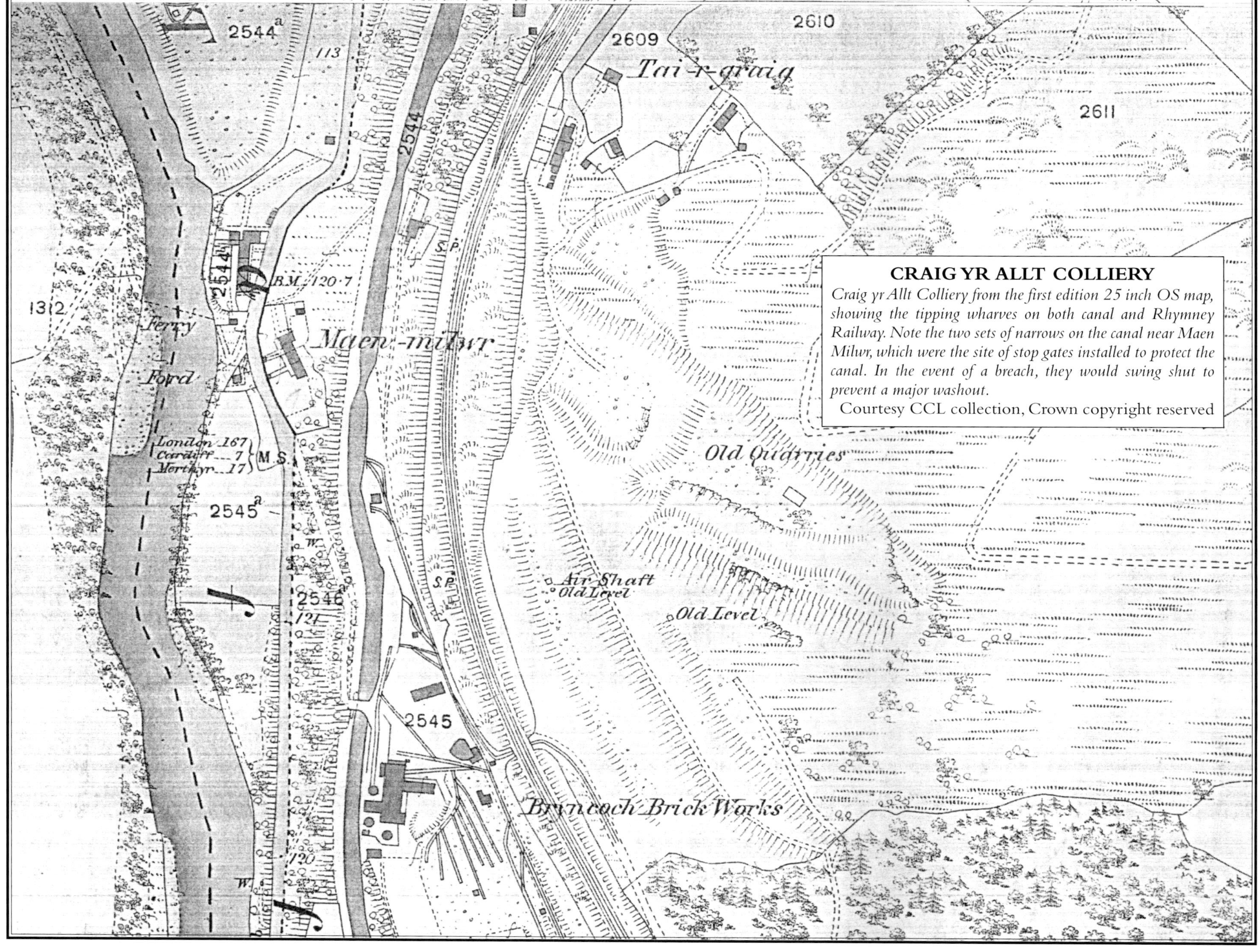

CRAIG YR ALLT COLLIERY

Craig yr Allt Colliery from the first edition 25 inch OS map, showing the tipping wharves on both canal and Rhymney Railway. Note the two sets of narrows on the canal near Maen Milwr, which were the site of stop gates installed to protect the canal. In the event of a breach, they would swing shut to prevent a major washout.

Courtesy CCL collection, Crown copyright reserved

Winter snow sprinkled on Maesmawr Bridge, Upper Boat, in February 1954.
Derek Chaplin photo

Rivers of Wales, published in 1813, and again by William and Samson Sandys in their manuscript account of their 1819 tour:

> *'At a public house upon the east bank of the river, called the Upper Boat, is a curious contrivance for transporting trams loaded with coal, whatever may be the height of the water. A ferry-boat is provided with a stage, which is elevated or depressed at pleasure, by means of iron pins passing into its frame-work, so that this stage may always be kept at the same height from the level of the water, with a platform upon which the trams are conveyed upon it from the bank; the boat being brought exactly to the end of the platform, the trams are drawn on it as upon one plane, and disembarked on the opposite shore by means of a similar platform.'*[104]

> *'About two miles before we reached the inn we crossed a rail road which is carried on also on the opposite side of the river, the carts being conveyed across in the following ingenious manner. A strong boat has a sort of stage or frame work built on it of the same breadth as the rail road, with grooves for the wheels corresponding with those of the road itself; this stage is so constructed that it can be raised or lowered at pleasure, so as to keep it always on the same level as the rail road, whatever the state of the tide may be. One of these boats is joined to the end of the road which is carried out to the very edge of the bank, one or two carts then move into it with as much ease as on the road itself; when thus loaded the boat is detached and ferried to the opposite bank where by similar process it discharges its cargo. A rope goes across the river which passes through a pully attached to the boat and this prevents its being affected by the current.'*[105]

The latter includes a drawing by William Sandys of the ferry, laden with two coal drams crossing the river.

It was not long before the activity at Weaver's Bridge caused its name to be changed by some to Pont Maesmawr. Grover combined the Maesbach and Maesmawr collieries into one concern but it appears that the acquisition of much of the Maesbach lands by the Marquess of Bute curtailed his exploitation beneath that estate. The 1824 Bute Estate survey gives no indication of coal mining under Maesbach.[106] Nevertheless, so successful was Grover's Maesmawr operation that all future plans to drive a railway

William Sandys drawing of the ferry at Upper Boat, used to take waggons of Maesmawr coal across the River Taff to the wharf at Weaver's Bridge. NLW Cwrtmawr Mss 393

A delightful gathering of swimmers on the parapet of Cae Ty Du Bridge in the summer of 1938. Courtesy Caerphilly Local History Society

from Merthyr to Cardiff followed the right bank of the river south of Pontypridd, so that they would directly serve Maesmawr Colliery. First of these was George Overton's 1823 plan to extend the Merthyr Tramroad from Navigation to Cardiff.[107] This abortive scheme was followed by James Green's 1829 report to the Marquis of Bute.[108] Finally came the successful plans for the Taff Vale Railway in 1834 and 1835. These latter plans show the tramroad and its branches at Maesmawr, by which time Grover's mineral empire had collapsed and George Insole was working the colliery.

Grover's output had considerably reduced and it was his turn to be chased by the canal company for tonnage payments. In April 1831, Maesmawr Colliery was put up for sale by John Brockett Key Grover:

> *'From 60 to 100 tons of coal a day may be easily raised. The Tram-plates, Trams, Canal Boats, Horses, &c., now employed in working the Colliery, to be taken at a valuation, and immediate possession will be given if required.'*[109]

In November 1830, the Marquess of Bute's mineral surveyor, Robert Beaumont, prepared draft terms for a thirty year lease of Maesbach coal at 9d per ton to Webb & Co, whose existing collieries in Monmouthshire were shipping from Newport. Two years were to be allowed Webb to prove the coal – an indication of the state that the old colliery was in. Terms included permission to erect a bridge across the River Taff and to lay a tramroad to join the canal, so that they would not need to use the Maesmawr tramroad and ferry. Interestingly, a clause also stipulated that all the coal raised was to be shipped from Lord Bute's own harbour and wharves – the Bute Estate were already forming their own plans to compete with the canal's shipping facilities in the Sea Lock pond.[110]

At this time, the partnership of George Insole and Richard Biddle was being dissolved as their business of Brickmakers and Coal-Merchants, Dealers and Chapmen at Cardiff was declared bankrupt.[111] Insole was clearly vindicated in this concern and continued trading as a coal merchant on his own from the wharf at Cardiff. In November 1832, he purchased Maesmawr Colliery and turned round the ailing business by investing £3,000 in sinking a pit to the four foot seam.[112] He also treated with the Marquess of Bute to work the deeper coal under Maesbach and reopen that colliery. He offered to work 30 tons per working day and pay a royalty of 10d per ton for the four foot vein and 6d per ton for the three foot vein. He planned also to bring much of the Maesmawr coal to bank through the Maesbach Level, for which he offered a wayleave of 1d per ton.[113]

Insole's offer to take Maesbach prompted the Bute Estate to get Beaumont to make another survey. Beaumont recommended that because the colliery was so close to the canal and to Cardiff they could demand higher royalties of 1s per ton for all coal drained by level and 10d for that drained by machinery, *i.e.* drawn up a shaft. Beaumont had a vested interest in keeping the output from his own colliery at Top Hill near Gelligaer competitive, since transport

The Taff Valley, Garth Gap, Walnut Tree viaduct and the village of Taffs Well as seen looking southwest from Craig yr Allt in 1954. At the top left is the wooded Little Garth Hill, where the smoke of limestone burning indicates the position of the Steetley Company's dolomite quarry and calcining furnaces. In the foreground are the screens of the small New Rockwood Colliery, with its sidings on the ex-Rhymney Railway, below the

line of the ex-Barry Railway. The courses of the Glamorganshire Canal and Cardiff Railway are seen threading their way up the valley near the centre of the photograph and the white canal cottages at Caeglas Lock are identifiable. The straight line of the earlier tramroad from Taffs Well Colliery to the canal can be seen passing the small Ty Rhiw cemetery in the centre of the picture. ILW photo 13 August 1954, neg 1309

charges to Cardiff for Top Hill coal were as much as an extra 1s 6d per ton, Top Hill being six miles further up the canal and an extra three miles by tramroad from its canal tipping place at Navigation. At the same time, Beaumont suggested that Casberd should reduce his wayleave from 2d to 1d per ton for using the tramroad and if he did not, then Bute should threaten to make his own direct tramroad to the canal on his own land, by crossing the river immediately opposite the mouth of the proposed new level (at Rhydhelig), as had been proposed in the Webb draft lease. Even this might be unnecessary

> *'in the event of a general line of Railroad being brought down this valley the road from this time would then join it at the nearest point convenient.'*

Insole and Bute could not reach agreement and Insole was left to develop Maesmawr and continue to use Grover's old tramroad and the Upper Boat ferry. We have not been able to ascertain when a bridge replaced the coal ferry at Upper Boat but one is shown on the 1841 Tithe map. It would be remarkable that no river bridge was built here before the 1830s and is surely testament to the efficiency of the ferry that it carried such volumes of coal over so many years.

The success of the Maesmawr operation and the passing of the Taff Vale Railway Act in 1836 brought both parties back into discussion in 1837. Beaumont stuck to the advice of his 1833 report and terms seem to have been agreed with Insole, because a surviving account book shows royalties being paid to the Marquess of Bute from 1840.[114] In 1841, Insole was employing 157 at Maesmawr. The mouth of the new level to the lower coal seams lay between railway and river, and output continued to use the tramroad and be shipped on the canal until after 1846, when a siding was made from the TVR to Insole's Maesbach Colliery.[115] In 1865, T.W. Booker's Melingriffith Company sank Rhydhelig Colliery on Maesbach farm but its total output was intended as sale coal and was carried by rail via the TVR. Any coal required by Booker internally would have been transferred to Booker's own Melingriffith - Pentyrch Railway, which had two junctions with the TVR.

Mention should be made here of the Maesmawr incline, which had nothing to do with Maesmawr Colliery. This was first mooted in 1837 and was opened in 1844 to bring coal from Thomas Powell's Dihewyd Colliery to the Taff Vale Railway at Maesmawr. Powell contrived to build the horse-drawn Dihewyd Railway and incline under the Glamorganshire Canal Company's four mile clause, by continuing the incline under the Taff Vale Railway to the tramroad from Maesbach to Weaver's Bridge.[116] However, it was clear to all that none of Dihewyd's coal would ever reach the canal and would all be loaded onto TVR trains at a junction from the incline to the main line. E.P. Richards wrote to Bute echoing concerns T.W. Booker had expressed to him:

> *'that if the land is taken under the powers of the Canal Act, Mr Powell cannot use it for the purpose of conveying his coal to the Taff Vale Rail Road.'*[117]

Nevertheless, Powell did get away with it!

In 1844, George Insole opened operations at Cymmer in Rhondda to compete directly with Walter Coffin. Coffin refused Insole and his son permission to use his tramroad link to the TVR branch at Eirw, so the Insoles had to send their coal by road to Eirw, until the TVR extended to Cymmer. As far as can be ascertained, the Insoles' Rhondda coal empire never used the Glamorganshire Canal, so it falls outside the scope of this work.[118]

NOTES TO CHAPTER 1

1 For several anecdotes concerning Griffiths, see Morien *History of Pontypridd and Rhondda Valleys*, Pontypridd 1903.

2 J. Charles *Pontypridd Historical Handbook*, Pontypridd, 1920, p18, cited in E.D. Lewis *The Rhondda Valleys*, London 1959. Lewis is required reading on the subject of Rhondda and the birth of the coal industry. See also E.D. Lewis 'Pioneers of the Cardiff Coal Trade' in *Glamorgan Historian* Vol 11 Barry, which covers Walter Coffin and George Insole in detail.See also E.D. Lewis 'The Coal Industry' in E.S. Hopkins (ed) *Rhondda Past and Future*, Rhondda nd c1974.

3 Entry in John Bird's diary, 29 March 1792.

4 GRO D/D G 1806 R. Griffiths to J.J. Guest, 9 March 1806, cited in Chris Evans *The Labyrinth of Flames. Work and Social Conflict in Early Industrial Merthyr Tydfil*, Cardiff 1993, p44.

5 Entries in John Bird's diary, 27 March 1790 and 7 September 1797; see Hilary Thomas *The Diaries of John Bird 1790-1803*, Cardiff 1987, pp167-8.

6 Elizabeth Phillips *A History of the Pioneers of the Welsh Coalfield*, Cardiff 1925. The terms of the Homfray lease are stated in their auction notice following Homfray's bankruptcy; *Cambrian*, 6 November 1813.

7 Volume 1 pp167-8.

8 GCC minute book, 3 June 1807, 1 June 1808 and 22 April 1809.

9 Robert Large *Doctor Griffiths's Tramroad and Canal*, Diploma in Continuing Education (Local History) dissertation, University of Wales Cardiff 1996. The present authors gratefully acknowledge this work.

10 The much smaller two-arch tramroad bridge at Newdale near Wellington, Shropshire beats Griffiths' bridge for age by over forty years.

11 GRO B/C GCa 2 GCC letterbook, 2 August 1809.

12 Volume 1, Chapter 10.

13 Lewis gives his reference variously as *Cambrian*, 10 October 1809 (in 'Pioneers', p26) and 20 October 1809 (in *Rhondda Valleys*, p114) but the paper was not published on either of these dates and neither reference has been found by the present authors.

14 These rates differed slightly from the GCC maximum rates fixed under the Act, where lime and limestone movements were charged the same as coal and iron ore.

15 GRO DD Tho 1044/1 copy memorandum of agreement Walter Coffin to Richard Griffiths, 1 December 1809.

16 GRO DD Tho 1038.
17 GRO B/C Gca 1 Canal Commissioners Minute Book; *Cambrian*, 23 December 1809, 28 July and 15 September 1810.
18 GRO DD Tho 1050.
19 A similar elongated canal basin, the Abergwydden, was built on the Monmouthshire Canal, where Benjamin Hall's tramroad joined the canal to collieries on his own land. Jeremiah Homfray had an interest in a coal level on this canal too (the Crumlin Colliery).
20 GCC minute book, 22 September 1810.
21 GRO B/C GCa 2 GCC letterbook.
22 *Cambrian*, 2 December 1809.
23 For a full treatment of this and '*the pernicious effects*' of the Newport privilege on the Cardiff coal trade, see E.D. Lewis 'Pioneers', pp26-9.
24 GCC minute book, 4 February 1811; GRO B/C GCa 2 GCC letterbook.
25 *Cambrian*, 6 November 1813. Richard Reece, Griffiths' former partner was one of the assignees.
26 Jane was the only sibling of nine who had any offspring. For more details on the family see Morien *History of Pontypridd and the Rhondda Valleys* Pontypridd 1903, pp38-45.
27 *Cambrian*, 22 January 1831; Charles Hadfield *The Canals of South Wales & the Border*, Cardiff 1960, p118 (no source is given).
28 *Cambrian*, 10 October 1829; its tramroad connection is shown on Nichols, Priestley & Walker's map of 1830.
29 GRO D/D Xcv 1 Account and day book of Insole & Biddle 1830.
30 GRO DD Tho 1034.
31 Capt W.H. Smyth *Nautical Observations on the Port and Maritime Vicinity of Cardiff*, Cardiff 1840, p11. These figures are slightly at variance with those published in the *Cambrian*.
32 GRO DD Tho 1035.
33 Insole day account book 1843, cited in E.D. Lewis *Rhondda Valleys*, p46.
34 See table of Rhondda collieries in E.D. Lewis *Rhondda Valleys*, p56; the branch to Eirw is shown on Prujean's map of 1843.
35 See Volume 1, p209. GCC minute book 7 June 1826.
36 David James Rees *Pontypridd South Past and Present*, Risca 1983, pp59-60.
37 GRO D/D x 296.
38 GCC minute book 29 September 1859.
39 Analysis of census returns; Don Powell *Victorian Pontypridd and its Villages*, Cardiff 1996. This book is a valuable source of information on Pontypridd's transport. industrial and social history.
40 GRO D/D Tho 72-80, land for building Blaen y Llyn cottages, 27 October 1875 and subsequent transfers.
41 Related to ILW by Tom Jones.
42 Robert Large *Doctor Griffith's Tramroad and Canal*, p19.
43 TVR passenger train service Pontypridd-Treherbert opened 7 January 1863, D.S. Barrie *The Taff Vale Railway*, Sidcup 1939, pp8 and 12.
44 E.D. Lewis 'Pioneers', p34.
45 *Colliery Guardian*, 31 August 1867, p204. Thanks to Tony Cooke for this reference.
46 GRO DD Tho 1048.
47 DD Tho 1170 cited in Large *Doctor's Tramroad and Canal*, p20.
48 Boat Permit dated 29 July 1902, ILW collection.
49 H.R. de Salis *Bradshaw's Canals & Navigable Rivers of England & Wales*, London 1918 p104.
50 Robert Large *Passenger Tramways of Pontypridd*, Blandford 1977, p22; Large *Doctor's Tramroad and Canal*, p34. The dissertation also gives an account of various schemes to use the bed of the tramroad.
51 GRO (formerly CCL) KF 31, 2 February 1807.
52 Recited in GRO BRA 639, 16 August 1862 (formerly CCL Deeds II 3176, MS D.11.47).
53 *Star of Gwent*, 8 May 1858. Thanks to Tony Jukes for this and other references from the *Star of Gwent*.
54 *Colliery Guardian*, 18 September 1858.
55 Recited in GRO BRA 639.
56 Family tradition recorded in a letter from J.J. Harris to D. Gethin Thomas, 11 September 1968. Courtesy Tony Jukes.
57 GRO D/D Pl 816/1,51 and 52.
58 *Star of Gwent*, 5 November 1859.
59 *Star of Gwent*, 18 February 1860.
60 GRO BRA 639 (formerly CCL Deeds II 3176 MS D.11.47) sale notice and conditions of sale.
61 *Cardiff & Merthyr Guardian*, 21 April 1863 (which refers to Davies jnr as of Pontypridd colliery). *Star of Gwent*, 9 May 1863, records the orders of discharge from bankruptcy, 21 April 1863. Petitions were filed at the Bristol Bankruptcy Court against Davies on 23 January and against Harris on 17 March.
62 GRO BRA 639.
63 *Star of Gwent*, 16 May 1863.
64 *Cardiff & Merthyr Guardian*, 6 May 1864.
65 *Star of Gwent*, 1 April 1864.
66 *Cardiff & Merthyr Guardian*, 30 Sept 1864.
67 The site lies on private Bryn Tail land on the opposite side of the road to Hendre Prosser.
68 See William Rees *Industry Before the Industrial Revolution*, Cardiff 1968, vol.1, pp102-7, for some early references to coal mining in east Glamorgan.
69 Cardiff Collector's Report, July 1772 cited in Edgar L. Chappell *History of the Port of Cardiff*, Cardiff 1939 p73.
70 WIMM 1991 25/3 Melingriffith Stone Coal Account Book 1790.
71 CCL deeds 2581 and 2583. The landowner, John Goodrich, was one of the canal company's commissioners.

72 NLW MS11910E, Thomas Key to William Taitt 24 February 1796.
73 Entry in John Bird's diary 29 March 1800; Hilary Thomas *The Diaries of John Bird 1790-1803*, Cardiff 1987.
74 GRO D/D Art O/21.
75 CCL Bute VII 12, 13 June 1828. See also John G. Owen 'Coal in the Caerphilly Basin' in *The Journal of the South East Wales Industrial Archaeology Society*, Vol 3, No 2, Cardiff 1979.
76 GRO B/C GCa 4/52 letter attached to an unconnected lease.
77 NLW Edgar Chappell papers Box 5. See also CCL MS1.170 Benjamin Haddock's Memorandum Book, where wages at Melingriffith in October 1828 included loading and unloading Craig yr Allt coal in trams.
78 GCC minute book 27 June 1860 and 24 June 1863.
79 *Colliery Guardian*, 4 May 1861.
80 GCC minute book 12 February 1852; GRO D/D X 296; GRO D/D Pl 579/1, 592-4.
81 NLW Maybery 6371, 2563, 2565, 3746, 3769, 2577, 2223 and 3824. *Cambrian*, 9 September 1809 and 28 July 1810.
82 GRO D/D Pl 945/15
83 *Cardiff Times*, 28 April and 23 June 1860, cited in Glyndwr G. Jones *Cronicl Caerffili*, No 6, p9; GRO D/D X 296; *Kelly's South Wales Directory*, 1865, p559.
84 *Cardiff Times*, 21 June 1890 cited in Glyndwr G. Jones *Cronicl Caerffili*, No 7, p32.
85 *Star of Gwent*, 4 August 1855, 24 May 1856 and 5 November 1859 (thanks to Tony Cooke for these references); GCC minute book 13 October and 25 October 1858.
86 Glyndwr G. Jones *Cronicl Caerffili*, No 7, p32.
87 The relevant fields were Kae Nant y Gloe and Kaya yr Lan y Gloe. GRO CL Deeds 2582 (formerly DD424.40) abstract of title of the Rev'd dr Casberd, his wife and others, to Glamorganshire lands. 7 and 8 December 1765. St Augustine's no longer exists but was situated adjacent to Bristol Cathedral.
88 Cited in William Rees *Industry Before the Industrial Revolution*, Cardiff 1968.
89 GRO CL Deeds 1579 (formerly 1193.39) 13 February 1774.
90 GRO CL Deeds 2582 (formerly DD424.40). 23 November 1795.
91 GRO Q/DP 8b.
92 WIMM 1991.25/3 Melingriffith Stone Coal Account Book 1790.
93 GRO CL Deeds 2644. 20 July 1799.
94 GRO CL Deeds 510. 1 October 1800.
95 GCC minute book 18 July, 22 September 1810 and 4 February 1811.
96 *Cambrian*, 12 January 1811. Thanks to Colin Chapman for this reference.
97 *Cambrian*, 2 March 1811.
98 GRO CL Deeds 507, 1 July 1812, has Mary Jones, widow, assigning the lease to Brockett Grover. GRO D/D A 4, 29 March 1813, is a letter from Frederick Jones of Bristol to Brockett Grover, concerning his mother's non-compliance to execute the assignment of the lease to Grover but now indicating her willingness to proceed.
99 *Universal British Directory - Cardiff*, 1795. Even so, he never appears in any document under the title Doctor. John and Thomas Key are recorded as flour merchants, referring to their activities at St Fagans and Ely.
100 First mention of Grover in the GCC letter book is 11 October 1808 and his quarterly account for £208 2s 5d which would be for Maesmawr tonnages.
101 Advertisement in the *Cambrian*, 28 July 1810. First mention of Grover's Penygroes account separate from his Maesmawr account in the GCC letter book is 21 January 1811.
102 *Cambrian*, 14 September 1811.
103 Porth y Glo remained in the Grover family until 1896. See GRO CL Deeds 3539-3544, sale notices, 20 May 1896.
104 J.G. Wood *The Rivers of Wales*, 1813, p64.
105 NLW Cwrtmawr MSS 393, published in Tegwyn Jones 'A Walk through Glamorgan', *Glamorgan Historian*, Vol 11. This also reproduces Sandys' drawing of the ferry.
106 GRO David Stewart's estate map of 1824.
107 GRO Q/DP 24.
108 GRO D/DA/15/45.
109 *Cambrian*, 22 April 1831.
110 CCl Bute VII 4, draft lease and notes 6 November 1830.
111 *Cambrian*, 26 March, 9 April 1831, 14 January and 30 June 1832.
112 E.D. Lewis 'Pioneers of the Cardiff Coal Trade', *Glamorgan Historian*, Vol 11.
113 CCL Bute VII 4, G. Insole to E.P. Richards, 25 December 1832.
114 CCL Bute VII 4, R. Beaumont to Marquess of Bute, 9 Nov 1837; CCL E.P. Richards letterbook, E.P. Richards to Marquess of Bute, 16 December 1837; GRO D/D Xcv 3, Insole rent accounts of Llantrisant Estate (cited in Richard Watson *Rhondda Coal, Cardiff Gold, the Insoles of Llandaff - Coal Owners and Shippers*, Cardiff 1997).
115 PRO RAIL 684.2, TVR directors' minute book 15 May 1846.
116 CCL Bute papers, E.P. Richards' letterbook, E.P. Richards to Marquis of Bute, 21 September 1838; NLW Bute Papers, E.P. Richards to Marquess of Bute, 26 November 1842.
117 NLW Bute Papers, E.P. Richards to Marquess of Bute, 3 December 1842.
118 For a full account of the Insoles, see Richard Watson *Rhondda Coal, Cardiff Gold, the Insoles of Llandaff - Coal Owners and Shippers*, Cardiff 1997.

Chapter 2

MAINTAINING THE WAY

As Percy Harward had pointed out in his Report to the Bute ownership in 1885, 'Two men cannot do much work with a loaded boat when one has to haul and the other has to steer the boat.' *Samuel Fox, out with his camera in the 1930s at Mynachdy Lock, demonstrates that nothing has changed as a maintenance worker takes the towline to his shoulder and bow-hauls his boat from the bank.* S.C. Fox photo, CCL collection

Unlike a natural river, which tends to look after itself, a canal needs constant vigilance to secure its safety and a regular programme of maintenance, to ensure that water levels are kept sufficiently high for boats to be loaded to full capacity. Structures such as lock gates, lock chambers, weirs, bridges, embankments and towpaths must also be kept in good repair for the safe and efficient working of the navigation.

The proprietors of the Glamorganshire Canal were only too aware that their waterway, built along hill slopes among mountains in a region of high rainfall, was particularly prone to bankslips. '*I hear your Canal has given way & no Iron can be got down to Cardiff*' wrote William Hood to the management of the Dowlais Ironworks in January 1817.[1]

By contrast, in the dry August of 1800, before the need for reservoirs had been fully recognised, the GCC Minute book observed, '*Owing to the dryness of the season little or no Trade has been done from lack of Water.*'[2]

The depredations of Nature and the heavy wear and tear on the canal's infrastructure were to occupy the canal company's attention throughout its existence, and it will be remembered that, as early as December 1794, it was a breach in the canal that caused a crisis for the GCC. Thomas Dadford, having been refused payment to repair the breach, removed his workmen and deserted the canal, leaving the company to manage the undertaking themselves.[3]

Dadford's desertion left the company without an engineer and at an emergency meeting of the canal

An almost timeless scene on the canal bank at Nantgarw, as two country characters sweep the towpath neatly with brooms. The canal's picturesque bends winding the hillside above the village were viewed from the lawns of Duffryn Ffrwd – home of the magistrate Evan Williams, a local VIP, which may account for the special attention. S.C. Fox photo, CCL collection

committee in Cardiff on 16 December 1794, no time was lost in ordering that:

> '*the Canal be taken possession of by the Committee on behalf of the Proprietors and that they employ such person or persons as they shall think proper for the repairing, amending, managing and taking care of the same.*'

At the same meeting it was ordered that the canal be put under the care and inspection of a sub committee of proprietors, the canal to be divided into an Upper District (Cyfarthfa - Newbridge) and a Lower District (Newbridge - Cardiff). Inspectors of the Upper section were to be Richard Crawshay, Samuel Homfray, Thomas Williams, Daniel Williams and Watkin George. Overseeing the Lower section were John Bassett, Richard Griffiths, John Williams, Richard Reynolds and Joseph Vaughan. They were a formidable group of ironmasters and industrialists, who could also rely on the expertise of practical men like Watkin George, the remarkably talented engineer of Crawshay's Cyfarthfa ironworks.[4]

It seems the GCC could call in a surveyor when the need arose, for in 1809, the company allowed Tappendens & Scale to erect a bridge (cast iron, or other) on the south of the aqueduct '*under the inspection of our Surveyor.*'[5]

Arrangements to strengthen the supervision of the canal were made in 1839, when William Edmunds was appointed to superintend the upper part of the canal at 21s per week and a house.[6] In 1848, the company was still calling on the engineer of the Cyfarthfa Works for technical advice and in that year, William Williams of Cyfarthfa was sent to Glyndyrus to advise on improvements to the locks. Later that year, he was asked to report on the condition of the Pontyrun engine.[7]

More mundane items seem to have been left to the chief clerk to deal with, as in June 1851, when permission was given to William Milward '*to erect a Bridge over the Canal under the superintendence of the Clerk.*'[8] However, the GCC moved away from dependence on Cyfarthfa's engineers in 1851 by appointing its own engineer, T.E. Blackwell, at a salary of £200, with Henry Hoskins as resident superintendent of the works of the canal at £150 p.a. and the use of the house at Navigation belonging to the company.[9]

Responsibility for carrying out the canal committee's directives rested with the company's Chief Clerk, who, as managing secretary, resided at the Navigation House at Abercynon. Apart from attending meetings, dealing with the freighters, appointing and dismissing staff, and preparing balance sheets, the chief clerk's outdoor involvement with

It is not always appreciated that, in the days when the canal was very active, the towpath (never a public right of way) could be a dangerous place for walkers. Writing in 1973, Mrs Margret Davies (nee Peggy James and granddaughter of John James of Gabalfa boat yard) had this to say: 'When we were children, the canal was busy with barges and we dreaded being caught between locks because the horses always kept close to the hedge and the rope was across the path. We were always warned never to try to get under the rope but we were too frightened to push against the hedge.' *One wonders how Sammy Fox was going to fare after taking this photograph of an approaching boat at Gabalfa.*
S.C. Fox photo WIMM collection

the supervision of canal maintenance was considerable. Thomas Reece, the clerk in 1825 at a salary of £450 plus allowances, was ordered '*to purchase the 8 pieces of timber offered by Mr Henry Jones at 4 shillings a foot delivered at the Co's yard*', for the use of the company's carpenters[10]. Repair and replacement of worn out lock gates must have had a high priority at this time and we find the GCC continuing to buy substantial quantities of hardwood timber. In 1826, Reece purchased 20 tons of oak timber on the best terms he could and in 1828, a further 30 tons went to the Navigation Yard workshops for the skilled job of lock gate making.[11] The GCC put a high value on the expertise of its experienced carpenters and stonemasons. In 1825, Mr Humfrey, a skilled master carpenter, was appointed full time to the company at £6 a month, with an allowance of £6 p.a. for horse keep and the use of the company's house at Nantgarw.[12] The title 'Mister' indicates that this craftsman commanded considerable respect from both management and the workforce. In 1848, the GCC minute book records that William Hale, no doubt used to the hard labour of the sawpit, was kept on as sawyer for another year.[13]

In the early years, with no resident engineer on the canal, how was repair work identified on this busy navigation with its numerous bridges, locks and properties? In common with most canal managements, the committee of the Glamorganshire overcame the problem in the most agreeable way, by setting out by boat on their annual survey of the whole of the canal to see for themselves what needed to be done. The tour of inspection from Cardiff to Merthyr was by horse-drawn boat and lasted for three days in the months of May or June, and no doubt it was a pleasant and convivial occasion for the committee, with food, wines and overnight accommodation provided at the canal company's expense. The 1818 inspection Report[14] provides some interesting detail about the canal and the state of its infrastructure.

There were 83 bridges on the canal; 77 were in good repair but the remaining six should be rebuilt. Of 51 locks, the bottom gates of 42 were in good shape; those of the other nine should be replaced with new ones. Nine new top gates were wanted and the walls of six locks required pointing. Lock No 1 at Merthyr '*should be rebuilt this summer.*'

The Report noted that the canal had 46 feeding weirs and 39 waste weirs and to pass brooks under the canal there were 13 culverts; 29 trunks and screw gates were provided for draining the canal, and '*the Weir and the Aqueduct on the river Taff are in very good repair and also the Banks and Hedges.*'

The 29 trunks and screw gates mentioned in the Report usually drained into the river. A trunk was a hinged door in the bed of the canal, which could be hauled open by means of a chain running to a crab winch on the towpath. A screw gate let out water through a rising door or paddle.

For maintenance purposes, the canal was divided into sectors, then lengths. One such sector ran from Cardiff to Melingriffith under the charge of a foreman. Lengths, usually 2 or 3 miles, were patrolled by maintenance workers or lengthsmen, with a responsibility for keeping the canal banks clear and cutting back hedges. This job was by no means just concerned with a neat appearance. Young trees growing at the towpath edge had to be kept cut to ground level. If not, they would snag the boat towlines. Similarly, mayhem could break loose on the towpath if cattle got through a badly maintained fence or field hedge. A boat for the use of a gang of men was kept at various points along the line for the heavier repair and maintenance duties. Other boats, downgraded from 'main line' revenue-earning turns, were available for day-to-day bank mowing and general maintenance. It was evidently a slow and inefficient procedure and, in 1885, the canal manager, Percy Harwood, reported to the Bute administration, 'Two men cannot do much work with a loaded boat when one has to haul and the other has to steer the boat.'[15]

A countryman of uncommon importance to the canal company was the mole-catcher. Without his skill the burrowing mole could undermine the stability of canal banks on hill slopes, encouraging leaks and possible disaster. In 1810, the man on the Glamorganshire was paid 15s a week for full time mole-catching and was given a house to live in at

Both pages: *Canal engineers in South Wales, a region of heavy rainfall, faced special problems in keeping a stable environment for the waterways. Canal banks terraced on steep hillsides were prone to slip, especially if formed on underlying beds of saturated clay. A particularly bad spot was at Cilfynydd, where the canal suffered several slippages during its lifetime. These four photographs show the breach of 1896 and how it damaged the TVR branch line to the Albion Colliery. A daunting task awaited the canal's engineer – it is on record that upwards of 100 men would be drafted in to repair such breaches. The bank gave way here again in 1915 and this time a decision was made not to repair but to close the canal north of Pontypridd.* WIMM collection

Newbridge.[16] Most of the company's maintenance workers were provided with a house or cottage, usually rent free and with a pension for long service.

In 1825, Thomas Evan, the feeder tender at Abercynon, retired with a pension of 6s a week and in 1828, a cottage was built at the feeder to accommodate his successor.[17] In total contrast, one hundred years later, below Gabalfa Lock, we find a cottage occupied by Frank de Gruchy, who made and repaired tarpaulins for the company's Pontypridd goods boats.[18]

When a particular pound became silted, the water was let out and the canal drained and allowed to dry out. The men attacked the mud bank by hand with spade and shovel, throwing the mud into the grounded workboats. At the end of the job, the gang retired to the bank where, if it was a Sunday operation, the manager and his foreman would supervise the distribution of beer.[19] Meanwhile, the newly cleaned pound would be refilled with water and the loaded mud boats refloated and moored until Monday, when they could be taken away for unloading at the nearest point of disposal. W.T. Watkin-Lewis, who became Engineer to the Bute Docks and Glamorganshire Canal, has described his involvement in what was probably the last major cleaning project to benefit the navigation – in the summer of 1894:

> *'At first we endeavoured to remove the obstruction by means of a small steam dredger, but this proved ineffectual. I had to revert to manual labour by pick and shovel. The work was carried out by a large gang of labourers – as soon as a length was dried out on Saturday. With the summer times the work was kept on for the whole period of light, and the same hours on Sunday. On many occasions an many as 100 men were employed, a great many being casuals ... The work lasted out nearly a year, but was fully justified by the greatly enhanced utility given to the waterway.'*[20]

A company workboat, nicknamed *Alabama*, with lengthened cabin, a cooking stove and seating for ten men, could well have been on duty through that Victorian summer.[21]

By far the most serious dislocation to canal traffic happened when the canal was stopped for the complete rebuilding of a lock chamber. This would be necessary when lock walls were pushed inwards by frost action or, as happened at Dynea Lock in 1822, the stone pitching of the floor of the lock blew up because of ground pressures.

This is the scene of the aftermath of heavy rains at Dynea in October 1908. At least five official photographs exist showing this breach in the embankment and the subsequent stages in its repair. Here, looking south, stop planks have been placed in position in the narrows under Maesyraul Bridge, to allow the canal to refill and boats to be brought from Cardiff to as far as the bridge. A man stares into the chasm from the broken towpath. As with Cilfynydd, this was the site of successive breaches and it should be noted that even the stone wall bank had not been able to retain the flood waters of the Nant Corrwg. ILW collection

Another view of the October 1908 breach at Dynea. Surveyors were brought in and a workmen's hut erected alongside the waterway. In this view taken from Maesyraul Bridge, towards Dynea Lock (just visible in the centre left distance), a gap has been made in the coping stones of the canal bank wall and a giant baulk of timber is ready to be set in place as the first step in building a dam to isolate the breach. ILW collection

With a timber dam sealing off the breach and a pipe installed to maintain a water supply to the canal below the Maesyraul Bridge, the workmen are beginning the task of restoring the waterproof bed and rebuilding the banks. A temporary tramway has been erected to assist in bringing materials to the site. Pontypridd Library collection

In 1824, maintenance work to the canal caused a month-long stoppage.[22] In July 1841, the carpenters and masons were called out to three weeks work at Aberfan. The clerk, George Forrest, wrote to the Dowlais Iron Co:

> *'I beg to inform you that Aberfan Locks, 5½ miles from Merthyr are about to be rebuilt & that the work will commence on Monday the 12th of July; there will be no passing through them for 3 weeks ... but a Tram road will be made past them along which Iron, Goods &c can be conveyed to and from Boats above & below the locks for the first fortnight of the Stop, but during the 3rd week there will be no passing above Navigation House.'*[23]

In fairness to the canal company, the summer season, usually a slacker period in the iron trade, was commonly chosen for stoppages but always after some advanced discussion with the iron freighters.

Keeping the length of stoppages to a minimum relied on the skill of the stonemason. Much of his work was done in the winter months, when stone was cut and dressed in preparation for the summer rebuilding work. To assist the work of the masons, the GCC ordered in 1820 '*a Shed to be built near the Steep Locks for the Masons to dress Stones in the Winter.*'[24]

The company looked after its skilled craftsmen and when the canal's master mason, Hopkin Smith, retired in 1841, he was rewarded with a pension of 10s per week for long service. Edmund Lewis succeeded him and was given a bonus of £25 from the GCC for his exertions and good workmanship at the walls of the Sea Lock. At the same time, the unfortunate ordinary masons and carpenters went home gloomily, with their wages reduced to 3s 6d a day to keep their rate in line with lowered rates of pay in the ironworks.[25]

Continuing this review of maintenance work on the Glamorganshire Canal, we look at what always has been the most serious risk of all on Welsh canals – the problem of major bankslips. Whilst conserving water was an important aspect of lockkeepers work at all times of the year, the canal maintenance staff on patrol in winter knew that rising storm water entering the canal must be released both by day and through the night. The dangers of bank collapse in these conditions was very real. A minor break in the bank could be contained, if the lengthmen could isolate the break soon enough by dropping stop planks into the nearest narrows. Vulnerable places were given extra protection. At Tongwynlais, on a ledge above a bend in the River Taff, was a stop gate in the canal intended to be self-acting in the event of a breach. At Tynygraig Lock in 1885, close to the permanently at-risk Cifynydd length of the canal, Edmund Howell occupied the lock cottage free of rent, specifically for regulating the water at night.[28] Despite these precautions, the GCC suffered heavily from damaging breaches, most recently at Cilfynydd in 1896 and 1915, at Dynea near Treforest in 1908 and finally at Nantgarw in 1942.

It is fortunate that Watkin-Lewis, the Bute engineer in

Dynea breach 1908. A canal company clay boat is seen here unloading clay into wheelbarrows at Maesyraul, to be used in forming the waterproof puddle on the canal bed. ILW collection

G C C
382

Goods being transshipped at Foundry Bridge, Upper Boat, Pontypridd, in October 1908, as a result of the Dynea breach. The men have paused briefly from their task of unloading GCC Boat No 382 to pose for the photographer. The cargo, boxes of provisions bound for Pontypridd, will complete the remaining three miles of their journey by road. The clay boat in the foreground was assisting in the repair work. Note that the number of this boat, 301, is incised on its rudder post. Pontypridd Library collection

In correspondence between the Glamorganshire Canal Co and the Pontypridd civil engineers Thomas & Morgan & Partners, who were called in to advise on the repair of this bankslip, the GCC referred to the incident happening at Ty Sidra, Nantgarw, on 26 May 1942 (Whit Tuesday). However, Tom Frazer and a number of other canal workers put the date a day earlier. This serious breach, which is seen here looking down the valley towards Cardiff in 1944, was never repaired and it gave the GCC a useful opportunity to close down its carrying operation and sell the canal to the City of Cardiff. ILW photo 1 March 1944 neg 258

charge of the 1896 Cilfynydd repair operation, has left his own description of the work. After pointing out the serious subsidences caused by coal workings under the canal, he continues:

> '*One morning Mr Llewellyn called upon me with the grave telephone news that a serious breach had occurred at Pontypridd on a mile length of water which had torn a great cavity in the bank – a ghastly chasm 50 feet deep and 80 feet across in the line of course after a period of heavy rain so that water had accumulated in the hillside.*
> *My ganger on the Cardiff local section was a particularly reliable chargeman and I appointed him foreman of the force of labourers, our own regulars plus a number of temporary navvies, and a few craftsmen – carpenters and masons. Firstly a dam was constructed either side of the hole so that the canal could be filled with water above and below, thus enabling boatloads of materials to be.conveyed to the site. Then the main construction work was proceeded with a massive stone retaining wall 50 feet high.*'[29]

The successful repair of the breach allowed the company's carrying traffic to resume between Cardiff, Abercynon, Merthyr and Aberdare, and the trading of the last few bye traders to continue. However, when another disastrous breach occurred at Cilfynydd in July 1915, the GCC decided that it would be uneconomic to repair the damage and the section to Abercynon was closed beyond Pontypridd. To maintain the water supply for the Cardiff - Pontypridd boats, the company built a wooden trunk or flume to carry water across the gap at Cilfynydd. Latterly, the water was drawn from the Nant Caedudwg, the flume remaining in use until 1943.[30]

Clay was a most important element in forming the puddle to keep the bottom and sides of the canal bed watertight and the company ensured that good supplies were ready at hand in case of leaks. One source of clay was a pit near a low hill formed of glacial drift near Dynea. A minute book entry for 23 June 1858, suggests the GCC were worrying about the charges demanded by a certain Mr David. Letters were read from Mr David. Mr Shepherd (the clerk) was instructed to ask Mr David at what rate he would allow the Canal Co to continue to take whatever clay they may require in future if they were to pay the sums demanded in the two letters. The GCC maintained a number of boats especially for carrying clay and Mr Reece was instructed to have two new clay-boats built in 1827 and another in 1834 to replace a worn out clay-boat.[31]

The glacial deposits in the neighbourhood of Dynea were also good for gravel and in 1846, £20 was paid to Mr Wm Morgan '*for gravel taken from his land near Deniah.*'[32] In 1839, the committee ordered two gravel boats to be provided by the Clerk, to be built by Mr Jenkins or such other person as the Clerk may prefer.[33] Until well into the 20th century, the main use for gravel was to provide a surface for the canal's 25 miles of towpath.

When manager Percy Harwood prepared his Report on the state of the canal undertaking for Lord Bute in 1885, it was clear that the company's maintenance yard at Abercynon, built by Thomas Dadford in 1792, was in a run-down state: '*the Canal Co. Sawpit (covered in), the Smiths' and the Carpenters' and a Fitters' shop also, all out of repair.*' Thomas Edwards, the company's carpenter, occupied the house free of rent. Trying to bring economy to the Navigation yard and saving on maintenance, he earned for himself the nickname 'Tom One Flasher' by removing one of the two top gate paddles from the locks.[34]

In 1893, the GCC purchased the vacant canalside

property of the former Cambrian Patent Fuel works at Gabalfa, north of Cardiff,and transferred all its maintenance activities from the Navigation yard at Abercynon to the Cambrian yard at Gabalfa. That same year, the canal company bought the Preston-built steam tug *Bute* for work on the canal and, until withdrawn in 1913, *Bute* was based and serviced at Gabalfa. It seems that the workshops and dry dock were built by the GCC, since they do not appear on the Cambrian sale plan of 1893.[35]

In one way or another the forces of Nature play a determining role in the operation of canals and those who maintain the way learn to treat these elements with the greatest respect. A dramatic form of traffic dislocation happened in severe winters when the canal was blockaded by ice. Extra labour was drafted in to man the GCC icebreaker and to attend to its four or more horses. In the great freeze of 1895, stronger measures were called for when nine Cardiff patent fuel boats, loaded with urgent export orders for the Bute Docks, were stuck fast in the ice. Assistance came from the steam tug *Bute* which, having been hurriedly fitted with a steel knife, successfully hauled its train of nine boats on an ice-free path to the docks.[26] As for the company's more traditional icebreaker, rocked from side to side by its handrails and an eight man team, it was last seen in action on the Cardiff length of the navigation during the severe wartime winter of 1940-41.[27]

By the early years of the Second World War, the GCC was running only two boats on the canal and the working of traffic to Pontypridd was already difficult for boatmen and horses. Because of the accumulated mud in the channel,

Two dramatic photographs showing the GCC's ice breaker in operation at Mynachdy Lock in the Winter of 1940-1. The vessel was built of oak and the sides were sheathed with iron plates. Manned by a crew of nine, it was their job to hold on to the wooden rails and rock it from side to side as it was drawn along the ice-bound canal by two horses. Not surprisingly, its operation invariably drew a small crowd of spectators.
Carol Sharp collection

the boats, nominally capable of loading to 20-21 tons, could carry only six or seven tons.[36] By 1939, there were no other traders. The final blow to the canal company came on 26 May 1942 at Nantgarw, when, after heavy rain, the bank gave way allowing three miles of water to escape through a huge chasm. The GCC received a survey report and estimate for repairs from Thomas & Morgan & partners, civil engineers of Pontypridd, but the company decided not to go ahead with restoration.[37] Instead, it made arrangements to send the small amount of traffic by road to fulfil its contracts and all movements of its goods boats were discontinued. Thus, the breach at Nantgarw marked the end of the Glamorganshire Canal, except for the Sea Lock pound in Cardiff which remained in use until 1951.

The Marquess of Bute's takeover of the canal had for a time checked the decline of the waterway but had not halted it and by the 1930s the horse-drawn boats working to Pontypridd were perhaps seen by some as a picturesque anachronism, the old Cambrian yard itself epitomising the Glamorganshire Canal's long descent into delapidation and decay. A visit there in 1943 conveyed an overwhelming sense of the past – of life suspended.

After the Nantgarw breach of 1942, the five moored working boats remained afloat at the Cambrian boatyard, with one in place in the dry dock. In the spring of 1943, the canal's faithful retainer, Harry Watts, chose the best boat in the yard and set out with billhook and scythe, on the last of his grass and bramble cutting missions. Shafting the boat from Gabalfa to Llandaff and Melingriffith, he cleared banks and weirs over a few days, then returned stern first with his load of material for burning.[38]

In the wider world away from Gabalfa, momentous changes were taking place that were to affect the future of the waterway and ultimately lead to its obliteration. The year 1943, a year of waiting for the canal and its staff, saw the purchase of the Glamorganshire Canal by Cardiff Corporation and the passing of the Corporation's Act which authorised its abandonment. In the years following these events there was, sadly, no longer a need for maintaining the way.

NOTES TO CHAPTER 2

1 GRO Dowlais Iron Co Letters; Wm Hood (London agent) to Dowlais Works 25 January 1817: see Madeleine Elsas *Iron in the Making*, Cardiff 1960, p153.
2 GCC Minute book 30 August 1800.
3 GCC Minute book 13 December 1794.
4 GCC Minute book 16 December 1794.
5 GCC Minute book 25 August 1809.
6 GCC Minute book 26 June 1839.
7 GCC Minute book 10 February and 7 June 1848.
8 GCC Minute book 25 June 1851.
9 GCC Minute book 31 July 1851.
10 GCC Minute book 1 December 1825.
11 GCC Minute book 7 September 1826, 20 tons; 11 October 1828, 30 tons.
12 GCC Minute book 7 July 1825.
13 GCC Minute book 7 June 1848.
14 GCC Minute book 3 June 1818.
15 GCC Report of P.G. Harwood, dated 31 July 1885; presented to the Committee 12 August 1885.
16 GCC Minute book 18 July 1810
17 GCC Minute book 3 February 1825, 28 July 1828.
18 Information from John Close, GCC foreman, 1948
19 *Pontypridd Observer*, 12 and 26 August 1950. Articles on the canal by John Powell.
20 W.T. Watkin-Lewis *Recollections*, privately published Swansea c1943, pp135-36.
21 Information from John Close, 1948.
22 GRO Dowlais Letters, Thomas Reece to Dowlais Works, 22 April 1822; see Elsas *Iron in the Making*, Cardiff 1960, p153; GCC Minute book 2 June 1824.
23 Dowlais Letters; George Forrest to David Griffiths, 24 June 1841; see Elsas *Iron in the Making*, Cardiff 1960, p158.
24 GCC Minute book 31 August 1820.
25 GCC Minute book 17 September 1841.
26 W.T. Watkin-Lewis *Recollections*, p137.
27 Information and photograph from Harry Watts, 1948.
28 GCC Harwood Report 1885.
29 W.T. Watkin-Lewis *Recollections*, pp140-41.
30 Ian L. Wright observations at the site 1943.
31 GCC Minute book 8 November 1827 and 7 February 1834.
32 GCC Minute book 10 September 1846.
33 GCC Minute book 26 June 1839. Mr Jenkins's dock was on the east side of the Sea Lock pound in Cardiff.
34 Information from W. Gomer, 1949.
35 CCL LC42, 658.82, 662.7, 725.4 Cambrian Fuel Works: Particulars of Sale; Plan, etc., Cardiff, 8 June 1893.
36 Information from W. Gomer, 1949.
37 Copy of correspondence between GCC and Thomas & Morgan & Partners, May and June 1942, Bill Hamlin collection.
38 Ian L. Wright observations on the canal at Gabalfa and Melingriffith, April-July 1943.

Chapter 3

THE GLAMORGANSHIRE CANAL BOAT

An Opportunity Lost

When Cardiff Corporation drained the Glamorganshire Canal between Llandaff and the city centre in 1947, the firmed-up canal bed soon allowed easy access on foot to a number of items of industrial archaeological interest that had formerly been inaccessible. The best preserved of these artefacts were the Brown Lenox boat weighing machine at North Road Lock and the complete Glamorganshire Canal Company's cabin Boat No 451, which had been floated into the weighing dock by John Close, the canal foreman, in 1944.

In a letter to the National Museum of Wales, dated 6 April 1949, Ian Wright appealed to the museum to take urgent steps to acquire and protect the weighing machine and Boat 451, as the boat and the weigh house were by this time the target of local vandals. Nothing happened but in the meantime he decided to make sketches and collect data on board No 451 and so record as much information about the boat as the confined site in the weigh dock would allow.

With the help of Derek Chaplin, formerly of Cardiff and now of Bristol, who brought a useful 70 foot tape on site, No 451 was successfully measured and recorded. Unfortunately, the boat's false floor, keelson and bottom boards could not be examined because they were submerged in an accumulation of rainwater. Ian Wright and Derek Chaplin's examination of No 451 formed part of a paper first published in South Wales in 1976.[1]

The appeal to the National Museum of Wales did eventually have a positive result for the boat weighing machine and in 1955, the British Transport Commission took over and dismantled the machine and placed it in store in Cardiff.[2] As for No 451, the last Glamorganshire Canal working boat, there was to be no future. The boat had been allowed to deteriorate for too long and could not survive. It was an opportunity lost.

Origins

It is widely believed that the design of the South Wales type of canal boat – with its minor regional variations – can be traced to the north west of England, where James Brindley and John Gilbert, serving Francis Egerton, Duke of Bridgewater, had evolved a type of tunnel boat for working underground in the Duke's coal mines at Worsley. These craft could carry coal in containers direct from the mines to Manchester, by way of the Duke's own canal. In turn, this design may have been introduced into the north west by Midlands boat builders from the River Severn.[3]

The Bridgewater Canal – the pioneering wonder of the age – had obtained its Act of Parliament in 1761. The primitive and uncompromisingly practical design of these Brindley-type boats and their later derivatives was to be adopted enthusiastically in South Wales during 1790-1799, by the canal engineer-contractors Thomas Dadford & Sons. During these years, the Dadfords, with others, had introduced the Brindley-type boat to the Glamorganshire, the Neath, the Monmouthshire, the Brecon & Abergavenny and the Swansea Canals, and their use extended to the Aberdare and Tennant canals as these later waterways were opened. Although Thomas Dadford had spent much of his life as builder and engineer to canals in England, where the locks became standardised to take, in the majority of cases, boats of 6 feet 10 inches width and 72 feet in length[4], when he came to the South Wales valleys he built boats that were shorter and wider. On the Glamorganshire, his boats were around 60 feet long by 8 feet 9 inches wide. These dimensions may have been dictated by his choice of lock dimensions – the Abercynon flight would have been very difficult to build round the hillside from Goetre Coed if the locks had been standard English size. What is certain is that one influenced the other and both were down to the canal's engineer. Because of the greater width of the Welsh boats, they required the support of a substantial internal keelson.

The Worsley Boat and the Glamorganshire Connection

Worsley mine boats, as we have seen, came to be built under the direction of James Brindley and John Gilbert – Brindley being engineer to the Bridgewater Canal and Gilbert the Duke's agent. Boatyards established on the Worsley Estate built mine boats in large numbers and to varying sizes.[5] All were simple wood-built craft, constructed to unusually narrow dimensions (48 feet long by 4 feet 6 inches was a common size)[6] and the design is instantly recognisable for its similarity to the Glamorganshire Canal boat. The Worsley boat we illustrate, photographed in 1949

A small mine boat at Worsley Delph, at the entrance to the Duke of Bridgewater's Collieries, which were once served directly underground by James Brindley's Bridgewater Canal. This simple yet ruggedly built type, variously known as an M boat or 'starvationer', was used by the National Coal Board's engineers for periodic inspection of the disused mines. The Worsley photograph is reproduced here to show how compelling is the family resemblance between the South Wales boats and this Brindley type example from the Northwest. ILW photo 23 July 1949 neg 855

at the Worsley Delph exit from the mines, is an inspection boat of the smallest type and used at that time for examining the condition of the subterranean galleries. Perhaps the most compelling feature of the Worsley mine boat is the economical method of building. There was no foredeck, after deck or cabin and the open hold displayed the boat's long rows of prominent internal knees. These 'ribs' immediately reminded the Bridgewater boatmen of hard times and the skeletal knees earned the boats the long standing nickname 'Starvationers'. In the course of time, enlarged versions of the Worsley type boat were developed at boatyards in the north west, many of these wooden craft continuing to carry coal in containers under National Coal Board ownership well into the 1950s.[7]

Turning to consider the Glamorganshire boats, we are struck by a number of characteristics of Brindley design. First of these is the crude wedge shaped bow, as observed from the forward end. This feature is also very reminiscent of the shape of some day boats once commonly in use for coal traffic on the Birmingham Canal Navigations. Glamorganshire boats had a cross planked flat bottom with fairly straight sides, which were held in place by rows of 'starvationer' type knees and which themselves were spiked direct to the boat's bottom boards from underneath.[8] There were usually five hull planks laid end on end and the hull might be given a few inches of sheer – that is, the amount of 'rise' given to the hull towards bow and stern. For reasons already explained, the 8 feet 9 inches wide Glamorganshire boats were built with a heavy keelson. All these features produced a boat of primitive type, which was quite unlike the elegant and sophisticated long distance narrow boat that had evolved a fairly standardised form on the English canal network since the 1770s. At least some of the Glamorganshire boats did have cabins from the outset, as evidenced by Pamplin's drawing of 1802. Others, such as clay boats and stone boats, would have been without cabins. At first, the boats were built to take loads of up to 20 tons but in the early 1820s, when the canal was deepened, boats were rebuilt to take up to 25 tons. This is confirmed in evidence given by the carrier Lewis Williams, who in 1826 operated 20 boats, which he had had rebuilt in the previous four years to take the larger capacity.[9]

So how did the Worsley mine boat design filter through to the South Wales valleys? Undoubtedly, it was the Glamorganshire Canal's builder, Thomas Dadford senior, who introduced it, for the Glamorganshire was the first of the modern canals in South Wales. By 1790, Thomas Dadford had gained formidable experience on canals in the English Midlands and his work as engineer to the Trent & Mersey Canal Co would have brought him into contact with canals and boats of the north west. However, it is worth remembering that Dadford, a Midlands man, had earlier worked for the Staffordshire & Worcestershire Canal Co and had become engineer to that company in 1773. Whilst with the Staffs & Worcester, Dadford would have been aware of the intensive use being made of the short distance day boats of the Birmingham Canal Navigations, which were box-like, cheaply built,

The Glamorganshire Canal boat, as depicted by William Pamplin in 1802, at Canal Head, Merthyr, differs very little from the last GCC boats of 150 years later. This drawing is reproduced again here in Volume 2, because the image became reversed between proof reading and printing of Volume 1.
Cyfarthfa Gallery & Musuem collection

straight sided craft of the Brindley type whose hull planks, one suspects, were pulled together at bow and stern with little or no need for steaming. It is significant that in the Glamorganshire Canal's opening years, until 1794 and before the canal was fully complete, Dadford's son James owned the first boats and ran a carrying service for the iron companies. James would have overseen the building of his boats, probably using expertise imported from the Midlands.[10]

North west mine boat or ubiquitous Midlands day boat – whatever the origin may have been – there is no doubt that the practical and economical Glamorganshire boat was successful. By the time the Taff Vale Railway and the Bute Ship Canal were being promoted in 1836, about 300 of them were said to have been at work on the Glamorganshire and Aberdare Canals,[11] supported by the labour of the 20 or so boatyards that built and repaired them.

Boat Building

Although most of the sites of the Glamorganshire and Aberdare Canal's boat building yards are known, as well as the names of some of the boat builders, we have to

A photograph of rare interest, showing the building of a maintenance boat for the Neath Canal in 1936. The builder is the Neath Canal's foreman, Ben Jones, who is working at the canal company's Tonna yard. Jones has set up the early stages of construction upon a stage or cradle. He has positioned the boat's knees and has fitted the first hull plank and, in order to give stability to the knees during planking up, he has fitted temporary cross spars between the opposites.
Neath & Tennant Canal Society collection

admit that so little is known about the work at these yards that it is not possible to comment with confidence about exactly how a Glamorganshire boat was built. Traditionally, boat builders did not write down details of how this job was done. A few calculations would be referred to in a notebook but, invariably, craftsmen like Evan Davies of the Caeglas Dock, Taffs Well, described by a relative as a master boat builder, simply carried this handed down knowledge in their heads, with the additional help of sets of templates. Insole & Biddle's daybook gives some information on the materials used and the wages paid at their Cardiff boatyard for repairing Dowlais boat No 52 in April-May 1830 and for building a canal lighter for Joseph Davis – but the method of building is not described:

Extracts from Insole and Biddle daybook
[boatbuilding and repairing on the Sea Lock pound]

I
An extensive entry itemises the charge for parts and labour to the Dowlais Company 'To repairs of Boat No 52 Docked April 10th 1830.' The labour is itemised each day per individual involved. The costs of parts are

Apr 14
8 lbs Spikes @ 3d
2 pieces 3in Birch Plank for Lower Strakes (26 x 13 and 26 x $9^{1}/_{2}$)

Apr 16
New Keelson in one piece 57 x 11 x 8 Red deal £5 4s 6d
12 lbs Spikes @ 3d
3 in Birch 39 x $8^{1}/_{2}$
3 in Elm 17 x 17
11 New Knees @ 4/6
110 Treenails @ 8s
4 lbs Spikes @ 3d

Apr 30
Plank for Strakes in Red deal
(1 - 55 x 11, 1 - 37 x 11, 1 - 55 x 13, 1 - 25 x 14)
6 lbs Spikes @ 3d

May 3
14 lbs Spikes @ 3d
300 @ 2d nails
400 @ 4d nails
piece 2in Birch 28 x $9^{1}/_{2}$

May 6
121 ft 1in deal @ 3d
54 ft $1^{1}/_{2}$in deal @ 3_d
72 ft $^{1}/_{2}$in deal @ 2d
$1^{1}/_{4}$in Birch 112 x $6^{1}/_{2}$ @ 4d
2in Oak 24 x 4 @ 10d
300 Plate nails
200 8d nails 6 lbs Striker's
1 Stancheon 1s 100 6d nails
1 in deal 12 x 11 @ 3d

May 7
Dockage 5s

Total cost of repair charged to Dowlais was £52 7s 9d

II
Monday July 5 1830

Offered Mr Josh Davis to build him a
lighter for Canal as follows

3in Elm bottom & lower strake
Oak Stem, Stern Post, Knees and upper
strakes. Other strakes red Pine $2^{1}/_{2}$in
3 red Pine Kilsons of sufficient size
the boat to be 60 feet long and of the usual
breadth & depth of other lighters –
Smiths work complete except plates
to be caulked, coated and launched
for the sum of Eighty Pounds
and old Boat as agreed.

III
1 July 1830

Robert Thomas Merthyr Dr
To New Canal Boat fit for use £90 0s 0d[12]

The last new boats to be launched into the Glamorganshire Canal are believed to have been built between 1887 and 1890, as part of the canal company's new carrying fleet. Five cabin boats were built at various yards, receiving the numbers 501 – 505 and the names of local castles.[13] Unfortunately, too much information from this remote period has slipped away unrecorded and today in South Wales no canal boat builder survives to talk about his ancient craft. Those who later stayed in business as repairers have also left the scene. Repair work at the canal boatyards on the Cardiff end of the canal had been very active into the 1920s, as long as the Maindy and Blackweir patent fuel works were in production but with the closure of the Gueret and the Star fuel works between 1927-29, there was a collapse in the fuel boat trade and the laying off of a whole fleet of boats.

Two casualties resulted from the fuel works closures. Work stopped at the Llystalybont (Maindy) Dock of the Gueret Co, who had always employed their own boat builders. At Gabalfa, John Rhys James was forced to close his dock about 1927 as his hire and repair contracts with the Star Patent Fuel Co of Blackweir were ended. Only the canal company's yard – the Cambrian – survived into the 1930s to keep the few GCC boats serviceable. By 1942, the company's last year in business, the boat fleet had diminished to seven, two of which were maintenance boats. Jack (John) Morgan and Lewis Davies, known affectionately on the canal as 'Jack the Dip' and 'Lew Dock', were the last

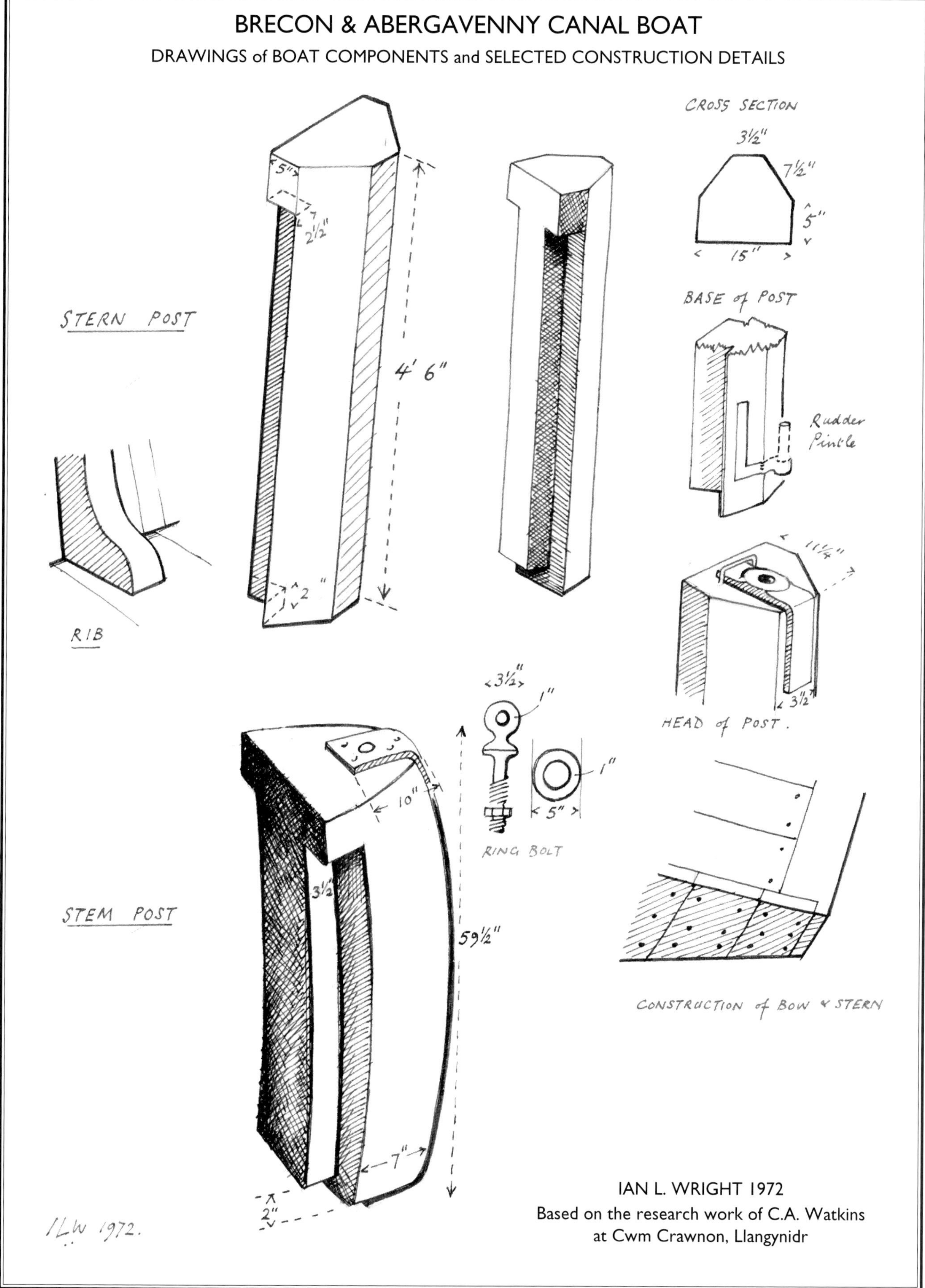
BRECON & ABERGAVENNY CANAL BOAT
DRAWINGS of BOAT COMPONENTS and SELECTED CONSTRUCTION DETAILS
CROSS SECTION
3½"
7½"
5"
15"
BASE of POST
Rudder Pintle
11¼"
3½"
HEAD of POST.
STERN POST
5"
2½"
4' 6"
2"
RIB
3½"
1"
1"
5"
RING BOLT
10"
3½"
59½"
7"
2"
STEM POST
CONSTRUCTION of BOW & STERN
ILW 1972.
IAN L. WRIGHT 1972
Based on the research work of C.A. Watkins
at Cwm Crawnon, Llangynidr

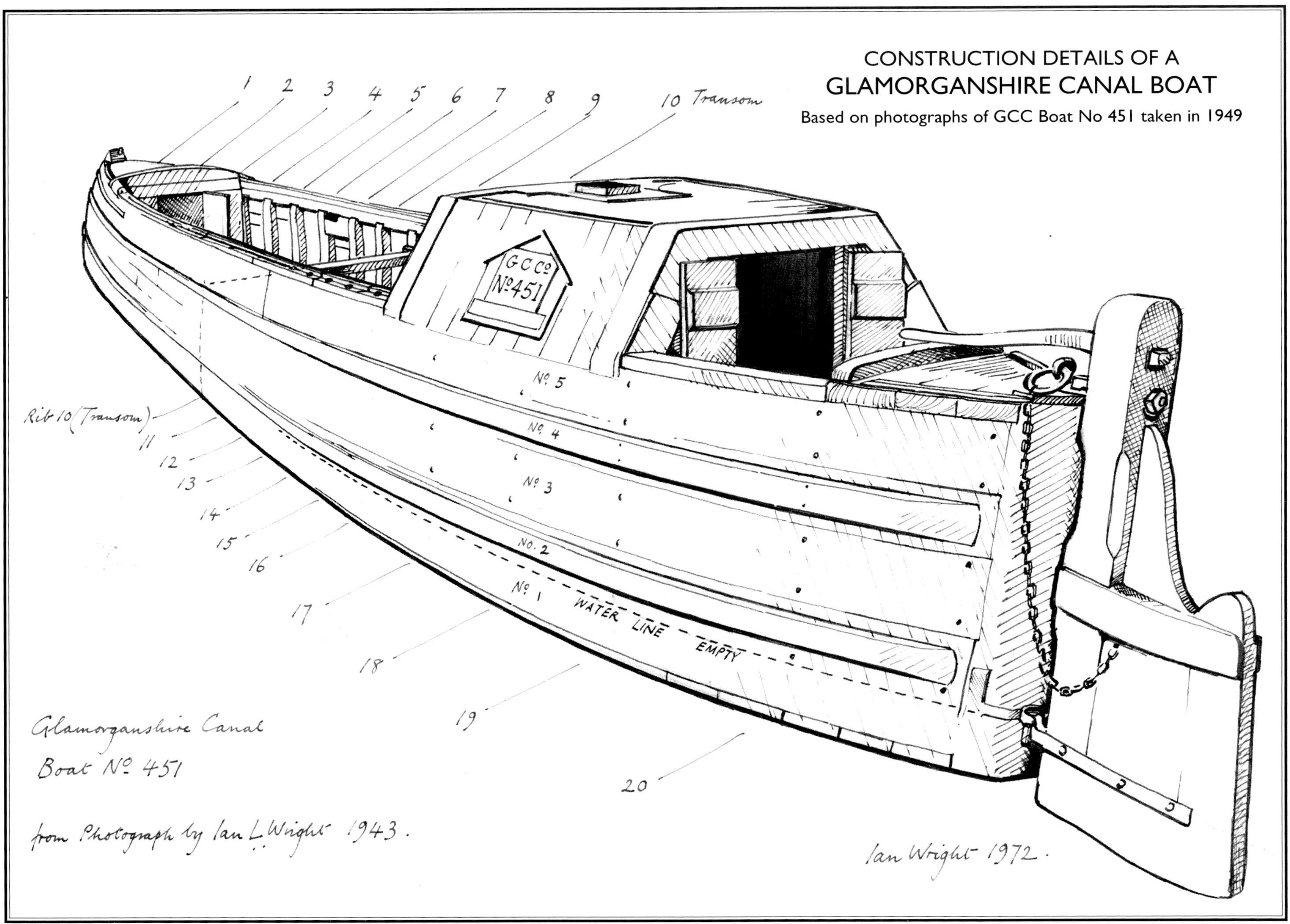
CONSTRUCTION DETAILS OF A
GLAMORGANSHIRE CANAL BOAT
Based on photographs of GCC Boat No 451 taken in 1949
1
2
3
4
5
6
7
8
9
10 Transom
Rib 10 (Transom)
11
12
13
14
15
16
17
18
19
20
GCCo
No451
No 5
No 4
No 3
No. 2
No 1
WATER LINE EMPTY
Glamorganshire Canal
Boat No 451
from Photograph by Ian L Wright 1943.
Ian Wright 1972.

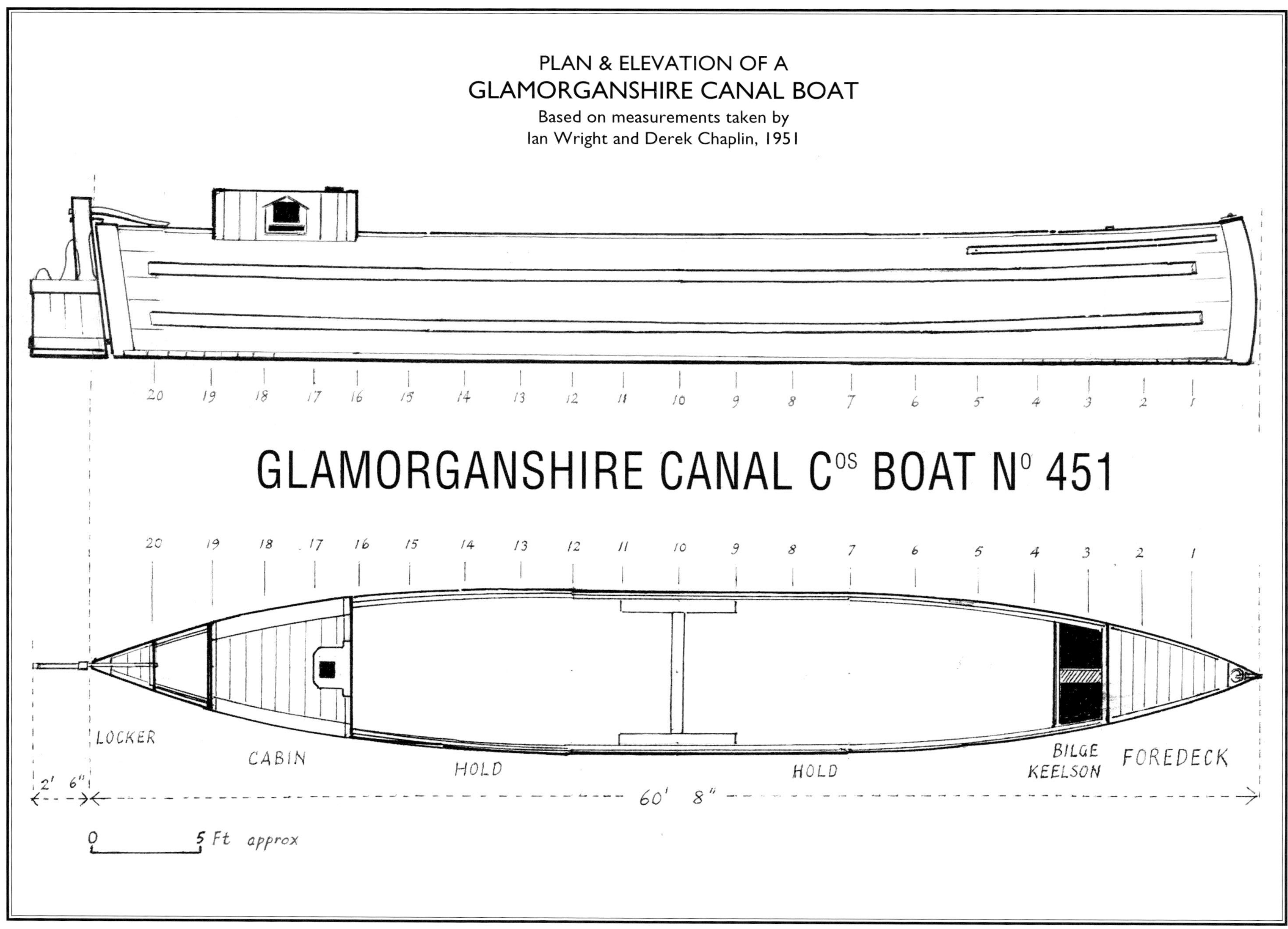
PLAN & ELEVATION OF A
GLAMORGANSHIRE CANAL BOAT
Based on measurements taken by
Ian Wright and Derek Chaplin, 1951
GLAMORGANSHIRE CANAL C^OS BOAT N^O 451
LOCKER
CABIN
HOLD
HOLD
BILGE KEELSON
FOREDECK
2' 6"
60' 8"
0
5 Ft approx

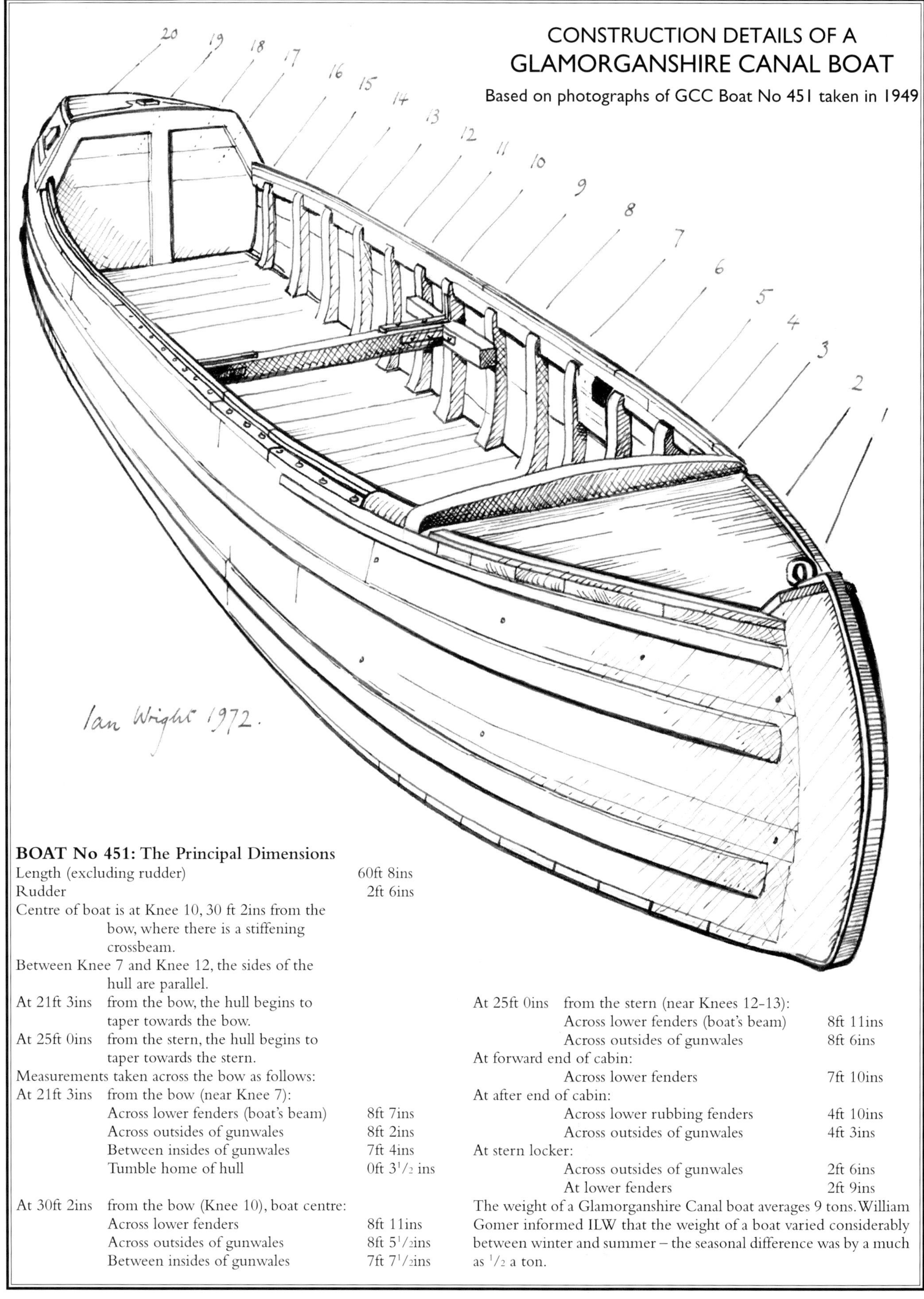

BOAT No 451: The Principal Dimensions

Length (excluding rudder) 60ft 8ins
Rudder 2ft 6ins

Centre of boat is at Knee 10, 30 ft 2ins from the bow, where there is a stiffening crossbeam.

Between Knee 7 and Knee 12, the sides of the hull are parallel.

At 21ft 3ins from the bow, the hull begins to taper towards the bow.

At 25ft 0ins from the stern, the hull begins to taper towards the stern.

Measurements taken across the bow as follows:

At 21ft 3ins from the bow (near Knee 7):

Across lower fenders (boat's beam)	8ft 7ins
Across outsides of gunwales	8ft 2ins
Between insides of gunwales	7ft 4ins
Tumble home of hull	0ft 3½ ins

At 30ft 2ins from the bow (Knee 10), boat centre:

Across lower fenders	8ft 11ins
Across outsides of gunwales	8ft 5½ins
Between insides of gunwales	7ft 7½ins

At 25ft 0ins from the stern (near Knees 12-13):

Across lower fenders (boat's beam)	8ft 11ins
Across outsides of gunwales	8ft 6ins

At forward end of cabin:

Across lower fenders	7ft 10ins

At after end of cabin:

Across lower rubbing fenders	4ft 10ins
Across outsides of gunwales	4ft 3ins

At stern locker:

Across outsides of gunwales	2ft 6ins
At lower fenders	2ft 9ins

The weight of a Glamorganshire Canal boat averages 9 tons. William Gomer informed ILW that the weight of a boat varied considerably between winter and summer – the seasonal difference was by a much as ½ a ton.

boat builder-repairers at the Cambrian yard and when their employment ended in 1942, they were indeed the last of their line. At the Cambrian, the small workforce had also included a blacksmith and 'Whistling Bill Watkins', who had worked as a striker.[14] An elderly member of this community who secured the market boats against the weather was Frank de Gruchy, a tarpaulin maker. All these skilled men, who had seen no changes in life and technology at the dock for 50 years, now went into retirement or took up employment elsewhere.

In spite of the influx of boat builders and shipwrights from Cardiganshire and Cornwall to work at and run yards on the Glamorganshire Canal in the early years,[15] the origins of these craftsmen's expertise in building sea-going craft seem not to have affected the design of the canal boats introduced by the Dadfords. There may have been the odd experiment (such as the iron boat supplied to Dowlais by Neath Abbey Ironworks as early as 1810[16]) but the mainstay remained the 'traditional' wooden canal boat.

Boat Building – Some Evidence and Sources

With only a little information available about boat building on the Glamorganshire Canal, we must examine common practices at other canal boatyards. Three diverse sites on other canals have proved to be particularly instructive:

1. The dockyard at Ladyshore, near Farnworth, in Lancashire, on the Manchester Bolton & Bury Canal.
2. The canal bank at Llangynidr, on the Brecon & Abergavenny Canal in South Wales, where boat remains were deposited after the removal of derelict boats from the canal in 1959 and 1965.
3. Tonna, on the Neath Canal in South Wales, where there is photographic evidence of boat construction in 1934.

Without doubt one of the most revealing sources on canal boat building comes from a booklet written by Alec Waterson, a boat builder at Ladyshore Colliery on the Manchester, Bolton & Bury Canal.[17] At 68 feet long by 6 feet 6 inches wide, the boats on this canal were similar in design to the Glamorganshire boats but they lacked the heavy keelson. Waterson was a rare example of an experienced boat builder who could write with complete authority about every process in the building of wooden canal boats and could supply drawings that made these processes understandable.

Boats at Ladyshore were laid down on a cradle or flat frame, placed on wooden supports standing some 2 feet 6 inches off the ground, so that where necessary the builder could work from underneath. At Ladyshore – as must have happened also on the Glamorganshire – the work took place on a partly covered canal bank site, with a ramp or slip allowing sideways launching of the completed boat into the canal. On the other hand, at John James's dock at Gabalfa on the Glamorganshire, it is probable that a new boat could have been built within one of his three dry docks. At Llystalybont, the remains of a slip formed of four rails where the Gueret fuel boats were winched out of the water for repairs, could still be seen *in situ* in 1948.

Photographs showing a Neath Canal boat in course of construction, demonstrate and confirm that the Ladyshore method of building wooden boats was followed in South Wales – in this remarkable case the photograph was taken as late as 1934. The Neath boat is shown on a cradle at an intermediate stage of building, the hull planks still to be fitted and the wooden knees held rigid in pairs across the boat by means of temporary overhead cross spars, exactly as in Waterson's diagram.

At this point, a brief outline of the boat building processes will help to place the various stages in their correct order. First to be laid on the cradle were the boat's bottom planks. Boat bottoms were of elm boards, 3 inches thick and laid crosswise on the cradle. Elm timber was used universally for boat bottoms because of its long lasting properties when permanently submerged.

The next stage in the building of a South Wales type boat would be the laying down of the keelson on to the bottom boards. An example of a keelson recovered from a derelict boat pulled out of the Brecon & Abergavenny Canal at Llangynidr, during clearance operations in 1965, measured 10 x 10 inches square by 57 feet 10 inches long. The keelson had been scarf-jointed together from two or three shorter sections of timber, which was later identified as pitch pine.

Once the keelson was laid, the heavy oak stem post and stern post were lifted by block and tackle and fixed into position. Waterson describes how these posts were marked out beforehand and rebated to receive the ends of the hull planks. Drawings of stem and stern posts recorded in 1960 at Llangynidr Wharf by Angus Watkins, reveal that the Ladyshore and the Welsh boatyard methods of securing the hull planks at bow and stern were identical. The age-old tool used in boatyards for shaping timber was the adze.

The fastening of the boat's first hull plank (or bottom strake) to the boat's bottom, and to the stem and stern post and rows of oak knees, brings together the emergent outline of the vessel. It should be mentioned that the boat builder initially plots the position of the oak knees by using templates. 'Planking up' of the rest of the hull now follows and the planks, usually of oak or possibly of pitch pine, now require to be steamed in a steam chest to make them hot and pliable. While in this state they are bent to the profile of the supporting knees and kept in position by cramps, or props and wedges, until they cool and set.[18]

Finally, to ensure a watertight boat, all joints and timber seams needed caulking. This was done with 'oakum' – a grassy, root-like substance soaked in oil (Ladyshore), which was forced into the seams as a rope-like thread, using a flat caulking iron and a caulking mallet. Another well known traditional substance used by canal boat builders was 'chalico' – a hot mixture of Stockholm tar and fresh horse manure, which would set solid and was impervious to water. Sam Brain, a pre-war canal worker of Llandaff North, remembered Jack Morgan – Jack the Dip – filling holes in the hull planks of Glamorganshire canal boats at the Cambrian yard with this steaming preparation.

It now remained for two jobs to be completed – the

fitting of the boat's ironwork and the tarring of the hull. These tasks successfully concluded, our Glamorganshire boat took to the water, either by being sent hurtling down a slip with a tidal wave or, less spectacularly, making a sedate exit from her newly flooded dry dock.

The cost of a canal boat, built new at Gabalfa around 1890, has been given as £80 and complete with cabin accommodation, £90.[19] Little had changed over a period of sixty years since Insole & Biddle had charged Robert Thomas £90 for a new boat and Joseph Davis £80 for a new lighter, taking his old boat in part exchange.

No 451

Having discussed the possible origins of the Glamorganshire boat and the craft of the boat builder, it is now the turn of a particular boat, the canal company's No 451, to be examined in some detail.

No 451 survived more or less intact at North Road, Cardiff until about 1950 and was the last working boat to make the run from Cardiff Wharf to Pontypridd before the breach at Nantgarw put the canal out of action and ended the goods service in May 1942. Like all boats on the Glamorganshire, 451 was built for towing by horses. In 1942, the boat was allocated to Tom Frazer of Treble Locks, with his son Cyril acting as his helper or 'butty.' It was Cyril's job to take turns at leading the mare, 'Violet', and to cycle ahead of the boat with a windlass to make the locks ready for the boat[20] – a procedure referred to on English canals as 'lock wheeling'.

No 451 is correctly described as a 'boat' or 'canal boat'. It was not a barge, which is a term generally applied to a vessel of 14 feet beam or over. At 9 feet wide, the Glamorganshire Canal boats were strictly not narrow boats either and John Norris, referring to virtually identical boats on the Brecon & Abergavenny Canal, has nicely described them as 'narrowish'.[21]

The survey on No 451 at North Road, Cardiff in 1949, recorded that this GCC boat was of all-timber construction, 60 feet 8 inches long by 8 feet 11 inches beam (measured across the boat's widest point at the lower rubbing strake or fender, 25 feet from

Top: No 451, originally an open fuel boat belonging to the Star Patent Fuel Works, was bought by the GCC in the 1930s to help maintain the company's Cardiff to Pontypridd goods service. Here the boat is seen on the Cambrian dry dock at Gabalfa, with work in progress as the new owners complete the building of the boat's cabin. This photograph was taken by Philip Oke for Commander H.O. Hill's Society for Nautical Research in 1936. National Maritime Museum, London, Oliver Hill Collection P74091

Above: The bow of No 451 on the same occasion. The incised star and number are proof of its original ownership. National Maritime Museum, London, Oliver Hill Collection P74090

A forward view of the interior of a GCC boat cabin, from a sketch made on board No 451 at North Road, Cardiff, in 1949. Cooking and heating were provided from the central coal fire, placed close to the cabin's forward bulkhead. Either side were the cupboard spaces traditionally used for storage of the boatmen's mattresses, that were rolled out for sleeping at night on the side benches. At the entrance to the cabin, either side of the boat's double doors, were shelves for the boatmen's cups, plates and cutlery, salt box, and meat- and bread-boards. Food was stored outside the cabin, in the small triangular shaped locker space at the stern of the boat. No 451's cabin was added by the company's boatbuilders in 1936. At 7ft 0ins long by 7ft 0 in wide and tapering to only 4ft 0in at the entrance, this design of cabin accommodation was fairly limited but it was sufficient to provide welcome comfort to boatmen in earlier years on the longer 'upalong' runs to Aberdare and Merthyr.

Original sketch by ILW

the stern), this widest point corresponding with the position of the boat's 15th knee. Rebated into the boat's stem and stern posts were the five hull planks, $2^{1}/_{2}$ inches thick by about 9 inches deep, and these hull planks were secured to 20 knees, which tapered to 4 inches square at gunwale level, with spaces of 2 feet 5 inches between each knee. The remains of almost identical boats were examined on the Brecon & Abergavenny Canal by Angus Watkins in 1959 and 1965, revealing that the knees were independent structures made of oak, each attached to the outer edge of the boat's flat bottom and fixed by iron nails driven right through the bottom boards from underneath. It is assumed here that the Glamorganshire Canal boat builders' procedures were the same as those on the B & A.

The discarded stem and stern posts from the boats at Llangynidr and the remnants of knees, were all identified as made of oak, whereas the hull planks, which had been scarf jointed together, were of pitch pine. Boat bottom timber samples taken away for examination were later identified as elm. It is at this point worth noting that boats with iron knees were quite common on the Glamorganshire and the Mon & Brecon system and in the 1940s, a number of this type survived as derelict hulks. An interesting detail revealed at Llangynidr in 1959, was that one of the two boats lying at the lower wharf was constructed with conventional iron nails; the other showed that the builder had used wooden trenails.

It is assumed that No 451 had a keelson probably of scarf-jointed lengths of 10 x 10 inch pitch pine adding up to about 57 feet overall and similar to the dimensions of the Cwm Crawnon keelson measured by Angus Watkins in 1965. Still with the subject of keelsons, some new evidence came from the excavation of a Glamorganshire boat at Merthyr Tydfil in 1982 and photographed in the Cyfarthfa pound in 1983 after lying buried for more than 90 years (see Vol 1 p24). The photograph clearly reveals the complete central keelson with an additional long timber either side to give extra support to the loadbearing hold of the boat. For carrying purposes, No 451 was fitted out with loose removable planks laid crosswise to form the false floor.

Accommodation on No 451 began at the forward end, with a foredeck extending from the stem post as far as knee 3 to form a locker where horse fodder was stowed. The open cargo floor extended from knee 3 through to the cabin bulkhead, which was built just aft of knee 16. The boat's gunwale was formed of a length of 4 x 2 inches timber rebated into the top of each knee. The outside of the gunwale held a row of small rings for securing the tarpaulins and the inside of the gunwale was surmounted by a wooden coaming or rail. A stout beam crossed the boat amidships to strengthen the hull.

The youthful author, Ian L. Wright, poses for an unlikely tobacco advertisement in the stern of the GCC's last boat, No 451, resting on the cradle of the boat weighing machine at North Road, Cardiff. The pipe, incidentally, was de rigeur *for the serious student in 1948, usually accompanied by the wearing of 'Oxford bags' trousers.* Owen Prosser photo

A cabin (exterior fore-and-aft measurement 7 feet 1 inch) extended from behind knee 16 to knee 19. At the forward end, the cabin measured 7 feet 6 inches across the gunwales, tapering to 4 feet 3 inches at the after end. Height of the cabin above the gunwales was 1 foot 4$^1/_2$ inches. Access to the cabin was by two doors opening outwards and an immediate step down from the higher floor of the steerage space. Aft of the cabin was a small triangular decked space, forming a locker for the storage of food. The spartan interior of No 451's cabin, first visited and sketched when still intact in 1948, had been fitted out with side benches either side for seating and sleeping, and with cupboards at the forward end for the storage of bedding and kitchen requirements. Centrally placed at the forward bulkhead was the crew's all-important cast-iron coal stove, with a square iron chimney rising to project slightly above roof level. Originally somewhat taller, the boat stove pipes on the canal were required to be cut down so that they would clear the sagging masonry of some of the canal company's bridge arches.

Two essential components of a canal boat are its rudder and towing mast. No 451's rudder post was slightly inclined to coincide with the slope of the stern post and at its longest point, the rudder blade added to the length of the boat by about 2 feet 6 inches. The boat's wooden tiller, being detachable, was missing from its position by 1949 but our photograph of 451 taken in 1943 (*ILW neg 221*) clearly illustrates it. In the days of the GCC's carrying trade, the horse line was attached to a removable round towing mast, about six feet high, normally stepped into a slot in the keelson in line with knee 7. As can be clearly seen in the Ynysangharad photograph (Vol 1 p201), the mast had to be inclined on an empty boat so as to give clearance under bridges. Other gear carried by a working boat consisted of two or three removable transverse planks fitting into recesses near the gunwale; these supported blocks on which rested the central running planks. Most of these features are clearly identifiable in the Ynysangharad picture, which is an outstanding portrait of the canal at work.

The date and place of building of No 451 are unknown but prior to 1927, it was owned by the Star Patent Fuel Co of Blackweir and used in the fuel trade. In those days the boat did not have a cabin. By 1936, No 451 had passed to GCC ownership and Philip Oke's two photographs, taken in that year, show the boat in the Cambrian yard dry dock at Gabalfa, being overhauled and fitted with a cabin for the Pontypridd goods work.[22]

With favourable water levels and regular canal maintenance, 451 could probably have carried up to 24 tons. Unladen weight was around 9 tons and loading was reckoned as 1 inch to the ton but such was the silted state of the cut in the final years that Frazer and the Bladens

A view of No 451 in the dock of the weighing machine at North Road, Cardiff, showing detail of the stern of the boat and its rudder. The five plank construction of the hull will be noted. Incidentally, the horse-drawn wagon on the towpath is a public works department vehicle for tipping at Grangetown pumping station. ILW photo 10 March 1948 neg 347

could load no more than 6 or 7 tons for Pontypridd.

Boat Decoration, Colour and Owners' Marks

In the wartime year of 1943, an observer on the canal towpath between Mynachdy Lock and Llandaff would have had a good view of all six of the Glamorganshire Canal Company's remaining working boats lying at the Cambrian yard, Gabalfa - five of them moored to the far bank, with one under cover on the dry dock. It was a melancholy scene particularly to anyone who understood that these boats would not be used again.[23] Their drab turnout was unrelieved except for a touch of light blue colour on cabin ends and rudder posts. They carried no names and there was no panelling or colour on the cabin side, the GCC merely complying with its own byelaws by displaying the company's initials and the boat's number on a sheet iron plate.

Since 1887,[24] all the company's cabin boats, and the remaining boats with cabins that belonged to independent traders, became subject to the Canal Boats Acts of 1877 and 1884, which classed such craft as dwellings and required cabin boats to be put on a register to be kept by the local Medical Officer of Health and to be subject to periodic visits by his inspectors. Responsibility for the inspection of Glamorganshire Canal boats under these Acts was taken by the Medical Officer of Health for Cardiff.[25] Thus, after 1887, the cabin boats on the Glamorganshire Canal were to carry a 'registration plate', which adopted Roman figures in white letters on black and, in the case of No 451, the MOH registration plate was inscribed 'CARDIFF REG V'. As for the number '451', this seems to have served both as a GCC fleet number and as a registration number allocated by the company to every boat working on the canal.

The Rhydyfelin Boatmen's Models

As we have seen, the canal company's boats were turned out in the minimum of colour and there were no features on company boats that could be remotely described as boat decoration. It therefore came as a complete surprise

The two Rhydyfelin boat models, representing Glamorganshire Canal bye-traders' craft working in the late 19th and early 20th centuries. The one at the back (503) was built by Richard Williams senior, boatman circa 1880-90 and is now in the Welsh Industrial & Maritime Museum's collection. The model in the front was the work of his son, also Richard, who numbered it 504. This model was made about 1907 but, unfortunately, does not appear to have survived. The main colour on the cabin panels is red, with red and blue for the rudder, and for the quartered diamond on the bow and stern plates. The boatmen had used gold for the ground of the bow and stern plates but, in practice, on full size working boats the ground colour of the plates would have been white. Length of model 503 was 37ins ($39^1/_2$ ins including the rudder; beam $5^1/_2$ ins. Length of model 504 was 39ins (42ins with rudder); beam $5^1/_2$ ins. ILW photo 26 Nov 1949 neg 906

to Ian Wright when he discovered two decorated model canal boats in a boatman's cottage at Rhydyfelin in 1949. These were to provide important evidence of a tradition of boat decoration among owner-boatmen trading on the Glamorganshire Canal – a tradition which seems to have faded into complete obscurity by about 1914, with the disappearance of the last of the independent bye-traders. Tantalisingly, apart from the models themselves, it is a tradition that has left behind not one piece of photographic evidence.

The owner of these Glamorganshire boat models was Richard Williams, of Dyffryn, Rhydyfelin, a boatman who had left the canal in 1939 after working as butty on GCC boats captained by William Thatcher. There were originally two boat models – one, built by Richard Williams, of fairly rugged workmanship and the other of finer lines, which was constructed earlier by Williams's boatman father, also Richard. Ian Wright measured the two boats and recorded some colour notes in 1949 but already some useful information had come to light about the colour and designs on bye-traders' boats through conversation with two boatmen who in their youth had owned and made a living on such boats whilst working as independents.[26]

Of the two models, No 503, the finer built model of the two, made by the senior Richard Williams, is now in the Welsh Industrial & Maritime Museum's collection and is believed to have been made in the 1880s. The junior Williams' model, numbered 504, was not so fortunate and seems not to have survived. Apart from the boats' numbers, which are not authentic when applied to bye traders' boats,[27] the modellers achieved a high level of accuracy over the layout of the working gear – cross planks, blocks, running planks, towing mast and the arrangement of the fully panelled cabin – all these details have the ring of truth about them that is to be expected from men who had spent a working lifetime on canal boats.

Bow Plates and Cabins

It would be a mistake to suppose that boat decoration on the Glamorganshire Canal had ever resembled the flamboyance of the highly developed boat art of the family narrow boats of the English canal system, with their images of roses and castles , abundant colour and lavish signwriting. Nor do we know how widespread was the practice of using colour and decoration on the boats of the bye-traders. If you took a pride in your boat and could afford it, you had the boat docked, painted and decorated and your name lettered out on the middle panel of the cabin side. The work was done at a private boatyard, such as the one owned by John James at Gabalfa – a builder remembered by boatmen as 'a good painter'. At the other end of the scale, a less artistic or less affluent boatman might be satisfied with his name painted on a piece of wood, nailed on to the cabin side.

This picture of a loaded boat approaching a lock was not a particularly common sight in the late 1930s but hardly anyone seems to have recorded such a scene – not even Samuel Fox. The horse is still working hard as the towline is still taut but the boatman is preparing to slip the rope off the mast as the boat nears the lock entrance, in this case Mynachdy Lock. The boat is being steered near to the bank so that the boatman can jump ashore and work it into the lock. This is a characteristically untidy load heading for Pontypridd but the bagged flour is well protected from the weather.
Courtesy Carol Sharp

The most common exterior decoration on a bye trader's boat was the bow plate (sometimes there were stern plates too).[28] It consisted of a rectangular sheet iron plate, with a white ground, on which was painted a quartered diamond set between double crescents, the colours chosen being invariably blue and red. From its leading position at the bow of the boat, this example of folk art could well be traced back to the oculus or eye tradition, still to be found on coastal craft as far apart as Portugal, India and the China Sea, and, further into history, on the fighting ships of ancient Greece.[29] The function of the eye as a talisman on the Glamorganshire Canal was certainly very real to one boatman of the past who insisted "*They are the eyes for the boat to see the stones.*"[30] The canal reference is to debris, usually submerged stones, thrown into the canal at bridge narrows and causing damage to the bottom of the boat. The maritime tradition of the eye has worked similarly for sailors over the centuries, enabling their boat to steer clear of rocks and the dangers of storms at sea, or so they believed.

The two Rhydyfelin canal boat models confirm that some traders' boats had cabin sides set out in three panels, the central panel displaying the owner's name, boat number and 'home port'. The background was red and the framing black or dark blue, the flanking red panels being painted

Another picture of a working boat at Mynachdy Lock, again taken from the off-side of the canal but looking towards the lock. The boat is returning empty from Pontypridd to Cardiff and a taut towline has already been re-attached.
Courtesy Carol Sharp

with a propeller-style motif described by the boatmen as 'the four pears design'.[31] Alternatively, a cabin panel could be decorated with a formalised flower petal design of the type easily produced with a compass.[32] According to Bill Gomer, our principal source of information on the subject, it was usual to see a boat's name painted on the leading bulkhead of the cabin, the structural members of the bulkhead being decorated red and the rest blue. Asked about the use of other colours on the Glamorganshire – red, or green? – Bill repeated that red and blue were the most widely used colours – "*I can't remember any green.*"

A possible explanation for the popularity of red and blue on the boats is that they may relate to the country craft of the wheelwright. Red and blue were common enough colours seen in combination on agricultural farm waggons and it has been established that, over several generations, some boatmen and labourers were recruited to the canal in times of poverty and depression on the farms.

Two Pontypridd canal traders who are known to have owned decorated boats were the quarry owner John Gibbon and the civil engineering contractor Thomas Taylor.[33]

A Folk Art on the Boats

It may seem unlikely that any boat artefacts could have survived from boating days on the Glamorganshire Canal but in the post-war years 1948-49, during visits to interview retired boatmen in their homes, Ian Wright discovered three interesting objects that had been associated with the boatmen's life afloat.

At Llandaff North, the boatman Tom Jones still treasured a decorated meat board in his kitchen, of the type which hangs on a wall, the back being decorated with a geometrical compass pattern in red and blue. In his garden, a much-weathered steerer's tiller hung on the front of a shed. It was carved with a running design of fish swallowing the tail of the fish in front and the carving was the speciality of Walter Morgan, the Abercynon lockkeeper, whose work was much prized by passing boatmen.

At his home in Rhydyfelin, as well as displaying his canal boat models, Richard Williams kept a small salt box which had once hung in a canal boat cabin. It was painted a cream colour with the date 1869 and the owner's initials were fairly crudely added in brown.

Apart from the preserved Richard Williams' canal boat model, nothing is known of the fate of these artefacts and it is presumed that their importance was not recognised and that none of them has survived.

Reconstructions

In 1990, an opportunity arose to make the colour details on Glamorganshire bye traders' boats more widely known and Edward Paget Tomlinson produced colour reconstructions of two such boats in the *Waterways World* series 'Colours of the Cut'.[34] These illustrations serve to show what a decorated boat might have looked like.

In 1993, Tony Lewery, a specialist in the art of the canal boatmen, produced a commemorative series of postage stamps for the Post Office, featuring 200 years of British Canals. The Welsh stamp design was based on a reconstruction of a Brecon & Abergavenny Canal boat cabin and the well-authenticated bow plate motif, all decorative elements being strongly emphasised in the popular red and blue.

Thanks to the recollections of the boatmen, we do have a good picture of how a bye trader's boat may have looked. We live in expectation that one day someone who reads this book will come forward to say "*I have a photograph of one.*"

The Steam Tug *Bute* and the Fire Float *Fire Queen*

The steam tug *Bute* began work on the Glamorganshire Canal in 1893, on the initiative of the company's traffic manager, Lewis Llewelyn, who persuaded the Bute management that the canal had a useful part to play in the carriage of provisions and general goods to the new and rapidly expanding coal mining communities of the Taff and Cynon valleys. The GCC had already itself begun carrying in its own horse boats for the first time in 1887.

Bute had arrived in Cardiff under tow by sea from Preston, Lancashire, where she had been built at the yard of Alsupp & Sons Ltd. Her design was similar to tugs used on the Rochdale Canal. The GCC had intended that steam towage between Cardiff, Merthyr and Aberdare would replace the horse boats but at least two experimental runs over the 12 miles between Cardiff and Pontypridd convinced the company that a tug with a tow of two or three boats, each separately having to be passed through 21 locks, was not a viable proposition. The runs also revealed the canal was so silted up that the depth of water had been seriously reduced.

Bute's engines were originally built amidships but cargo accommodation either side of the engine room was considered too limited and so her engines were later put aft, allowing her to carry about two thirds the cargo of an ordinary boat. Until her withdrawal from service in about 1914, the steamer did useful work bringing down tinplates from Melingriffith for export at Cardiff docks.

Fire Queen, a fire float owned by Cardiff Corporation, was a familiar vessel on the Glamorganshire Canal for over 30 years. Following delivery to Cardiff under tow by sea on 9 November 1912, the vessel was put through its paces on pumping tests at Cathays Park on 18 November, attended at the canal side by the Cardiff Watch Committee and a large gathering of dignatories. Foremost amongst them were Superintendent G. Geen, of the City Fire Brigade, and Isaac J. Abdela, representing *Fire Queen*'s builders.[35]

The float's fire fighting equipment, which included a pump capable of delivering water at 1,400 gallons per minute, had been supplied by Merryweather of Greenwich. Abdela & Mitchell had built the vessel at their small yard at Brimscombe, on the Thames & Severn Canal. Her dimensions of 50ft x 9ft beam and reduced headroom, allowed the fire float's passage through the locks and bridges on the Glamorganshire Canal and through the Queen Street tunnel. Formal acceptance by the City Council came on 4 December 1912 and *Fire Queen* was stationed on the

The steam tug Bute *is seen here in her rebuilt form at her base at the Cambrian Yard, Gabalfa, in 1906. The steel knife at the bow was fitted to the vessel during the severe winter of 1895, when the canal was blockaded by ice. George Sharples, who had helped build the boat in Preston and had delivered her to Cardiff, is seen in charge of the steamer (left) with Walter Tyrrell, the company's locomotive fitter standing next to him. Tom George is at the stern, steering.* Bute *endured for a long time in local memory, her steam whistle sounding to alert the lockkeepers between Cardiff, Llandaff and Melingriffith. A once familiar sight, too, was the lowering of the vessel's funnel, as she passed through the arches of the GCC's low bridges.* Bill Hamlin collection

The fire float Fire Queen *on the canal alongside North Road and Cathays Park, Cardiff. This is one of at least two photographs known to have been taken on the occasion of her delivery, which explains the smartly dressed crew in formal pose and the two city dignataries on the towpath on the right.*
WIMM collection

canal near the timber pond, with a telephone link provided, one man being kept constantly on board, although four crew members were required to get the float under way.

It is recorded that in the following year, 1913, *Fire Queen* was in action at a fire on a steamer in the Bute East Dock, where she did good work. However, due to a blunder on the part of the Fire Brigade and the GCC, the dispatch of the float to a fire at the Exchange Buildings, Mount Stuart Square, on 21 April 1915 was seriously delayed because of the absence of a lockkeeper at Lock 51. Following this incident, a lock windlass was put on board the boat and training given to the fire crews on how to operate the lock. *Fire Queen* remained on duty on the canal in Cardiff until October 1935, being regularly stationed at her mooring near the Central Hotel on West Canal Wharf. She was then withdrawn and sold to a Swansea firm. However, during her voyage under tow for Swansea she ran aground on the Tusker Rock off Porthcawl and her ultimate fate is not known.[36]

NOTES TO CHAPTER 3

1 Ian L. Wright 'The Glamorganshire Canal Boat', in *Journal of South East Wales Industrial Archaeology Society*, Vol 2 No 2, April 1976, pp58-64.
2 Cardiff Corporation Canal Committee minutes, 5 May 1954 and 22 April 1954.
3 C. Hadfield *The Canal Age*, London 1971, p109; see also Hadfield & Biddle, *Canals of North West of England*, Vol 1, Newton Abbot 1970, p27; M. Clarke, 'Wooden Boat Building and the Origins of the Narrow Boat', in *Waterways Journal*, Vol 3, Boat Museum Society, 2001, pp58-59, 67-70. For illustrations of the Worsley Mine boats at Worsley Delph, see E. Paget Tomlinson *Britain's Canal and River Craft*, Ashbourne 1993, pp28-29.
4 C. Hadfield *The Canal Age*, pp109-110.
5 M. Clarke p70.
6 C. Hadfield *The Canal Age*, p109.
7 E. Paget Tomlinson *Britain's Canal and River Craft*, pp28-30.
8 C.A. Watkins, unpublished 'Notes on a Canal Boat abandoned in the Brecon & Abergavenny Canal near Cwm Crawnon, Llangynidr, 1955-65'.
9 Dyfed Archives, Trostre acc 4734/47 p15.
10 GRO Dowlais Iron Company letters folios 141/142, 236/7, 261, 262/3.
11 E.L. Chappell *History of the Port of Cardiff*, Cardiff 1939, p65.
12 GRO D/D Xcv 1 Insole & Biddle daybook.
13 William Gomer in conversation with ILW, 16 September 1949.
14 Mrs Hilda Williams, daughter of George Stone, in conversation with SR, 31 March 1981.
15 See census returns 1841, 1851, 1861.
16 Joseph Tregelles Price to Josiah John Guest, 14 and 18 July 1810, printed in Madelaine Elsas *Iron in the Making 1782-1860, Dowlais Iron Company Letters*, Cardiff 1960, p159.
17 Alec Waterson *Recollections of Boat Building at Ladyshore on the Manchester Bolton & Bury Canal*, Bury 1982.
18 L.T.C. Rolt *Inland Waterways of England*, London 1950, p134.
19 Thomas Jones of Llandaff North in conversation with ILW, 15 December 1948.
20 *Pontypridd Observer*, 23 May 1996, interview with Cyril Frazer, pp28-29.
21 John R. Norris *Guide to the Brecon & Abergavenny Canal*, Hurstpierpoint 1994, p7.
22 National Maritime Museum, Oliver Hill Collection photographs P74090-91 by Philip Oke, 1936.
23 Ian L. Wright. Notes from personal observation, 1942-44.
24 *Western Mail*, 7 April 1893, interview with Lewis Llewelyn.
25 Cardiff Medical Officer of Health Reports. Thanks to Bill Hamlin for transcriptions of the local Canal Inspector's reports.
26. Thomas Jones of Llandaff North and William Gomer of Rhydyfelin in conversation with ILW, 1948-49.
27 GCC boats Nos. 503 and 504 were built new for the canal company about 1890, for the GCC's Cardiff to Merthyr and Aberdare carrying service. They were given the names *Castell Caerffili* and *Castell Llandaf* respectively and must have been regarded as something special by the canal management and the boatmen. The model makers Richard Williams junior and senior probably thought so and this may be the reason for the choice of the prestigious numbers 503 and 504 for their bye-trader boat models.
28 Bow and stern plates were common on traders' boats working on the Monmouthshire and Brecon & Abergavenny Canals and plenty of photographic evidence on these canals survives. The arrangement of the central diamond and flanking crescents is almost identical to those on the Glamorganshire boatmen's models.
29 James Hornell *Water Transport: Origins and Early Observation*, Newton Abbot 1970, facsimile of the 1946 edition.
30 William Gomer in conversation with ILW, 16 September 1949. As a boy, William had asked his father (also a boatman) the reason for the decorated plates on the bow of the boats. William's father had said that boatman John John, known in Rhydyfelin and on the canal as 'Shon Twm Shon' and then a very old man, had told him "*They are the eyes for the boat to see the stones.*"
31 The four pears or 'tear drop' motif is to be found decoratively in various parts of the world. Allied to the swastika, it often carries a mystical or magical meaning. On the inland waterways, the 'bunch of pears' was to be found on the trading wherries of the Norfolk Broads, both at the base of the mast and at the mast head. See Robert Malster *Wherries and Waterways*, Lavenham 1986, p52 and front endpaper. Also note illustration on the preserved wherry *Albion*.
32 William Gomer: six-petal flower motif sketched from memory, 1949, in ILW collection.
33 William Gomer in conversation with ILW, 16 September 1949.
34 'Colours of the Cut', No.29, *Waterways World*, March 1990, p121.
35 Bill Hamlin, notes.
36 C.P. & C.R. Weaver *Steam on the Canals*, Newton Abbot, 1983, p39.

At least three generations of the Frazer family worked as boatmen on the Glamorganshire Canal. Here, John Frazer (right) poses with his butty and boat horse at Treble Locks circa 1905. The butty may well be one of Frazer's sons but it does not look like Tom who appears in a photograph, taken at this same location, on page 107.
Bill Hamlin collection

Chapter 4

THE CANAL BOATMAN

SOME ASPECTS OF WORKING LIFE AND TRADE

An Introductory Note

Merthyr Tydfil's local historian of the 1920s, F.J. Pedler, remarked that a description of a journey along the Glamorganshire Canal in one of the coal or iron barges would be most interesting and he considered it surprising that no writer had left us an account of canal life in those busy earlier days.[1] Perhaps everyday life on the canal boats of industrial South Wales may have been too commonplace a topic to interest a 19th century reader. Time has moved on and today the Glamorganshire Canal is completely lost and the way of life on the boats and canal banks has gone forever. Fortunately, the canal company's records and documentary evidence help to bring those working days to life.

A source of more direct information about canal life has come from conversations with retired boatmen. No recording equipment was available to the authors in those days. It was all done with notebook and pencil but a boatman's story can be very immediate and where it has seemed relevant,. we have used the men's own words in the text.

Two boatmen of the past, Thomas Jones of Llandaff North and William Gomer of Rhydyfelin, were particularly helpful and their recollections conclude this chapter. An unusually well informed writer on local canal tradition was John Powell of Lock Lewis, Rhydyfelin, who did much to stimulate local interest in the canal through articles and illustrated lectures in the1950s. We have made free use of material in his Pontypridd newspaper contributions, which are full of humour, understanding and affection for the boat people.

Some Suggested Origins

As early as 1792, men were needed to work the boats in the canal trade that had been generated by the opening of the Glamorganshire Canal from Merthyr Tydfil as far as Newbridge (Pontypridd). About this time, there must have been a few boatmen engaged in moving construction materials for the canal builders. A GCC document for March 1797-March 1798 shows payments to Thomas Key for boating stones. Key probably employed more than one boatman on this work.[2] Not much is known about this first generation of canal boatmen but it seems reasonable to suppose that many of them were local men, perhaps transferring to the new canal from employment as road hauliers on the Cardiff turnpike, as more lengths of the waterway were opened for traffic. Some may have come on to the canal as sons of local farmers. Others were perhaps canal construction labourers or hauliers, who stayed on after it was completed to work boats for the new iron freighters. The evidence of the census of 1841 is rather late in date to be conclusive but does show that the overwhelming majority of boatmen's names in the Merthyr and Taff Cynon registration districts are Welsh and that almost all of them were born locally. Finding the manpower for the boats was probably not an enormous problem, since the iron industry was attracting to Merthyr a considerable inward migrating population. Some of these people were rural workers from agriculturally depressed parts of mid and west Wales in search of a better living and it is possible that a number of them may have been attracted to life on the boats:

> *'The promise of high wages and a relatively continuous employment drew in labour from agriculture. Although there is evidence that some Irish labour was used to build the Glamorganshire Canal it seems that the districts surrounding the coalfield, in particular the rural counties of Carmarthenshire, Breconshire and Cardiganshire, provided the main external source of labour.'*[3]

Mainly on the evidence of 19th century census returns for the registration districts through which the canal passed, the present authors have concluded that this inward migrating labour continued to find employment on the Glamorganshire Canal and to supplement local sources of labour throughout the period 1790 – 1914, not only in building the canal but in operating it. To the maintenance gangs, lockkeepers, masons, carpenters and boatbuilders required to run the waterway, must be added the heavy demand for boatmen.

A working boatman could learn his trade with no great difficulty. The primary need was for a man to be physically tough and accustomed to working with horses.

A Boating Tradition

In the course of time, there emerged a tradition of land-based boating families on the Glamorganshire Canal, where it was common for the sons of boatmen to follow

Far left: *Tom Frazer. Boatman, of Treble Lock Cottages, Glan y Llyn. He took the last loaded boat from Cardiff to Pontypridd in May 1942 accompanied by his son Cyril as his butty.*
ILW photo 1 Sept 1970 neg 2230

Left: *Sam Brain. Canal maintenance gang worker in the 1930s. He occasionally assisted as relief Sea Lock keeper. Called up for military service in 1939. On release in 1945 he discovered that the canal had ceased to function. He lived at Llandaff Lock.*
ILW photo 16 Apr 1971 neg 2248

their fathers on to the boats. This custom grew out of the GCC byelaw requiring every boat master to employ a helper or butty to lead the horse and assist with the boat.[4] This rule had obvious incidental advantages for recruitment and was good for the continuity of the boating way of life.

According to the evidence of the Taff Cynon and Merthyr census returns, it is clear that boatmen lived with their families in canal bank cottage communities or in terraced streets close to the canal in Merthyr.[5] Other canal settlements along the line were at Treforest, Nantgarw, Tongwynlais and Llandaff. In general, the canal company did not reckon to build housing for boatmen and it was usual for the unmarried man to find lodgings somewhere close to the canal bank, as for example the census returns show that boatman James Rowlands had done at Glyndyrus in 1881.

Charles Hadfield, referring to the Glamorganshire Canal's activities around 1836, wrote that it was thought there were over 200 boats at work on the canal during this time of almost full capacity.[6] Even if all 200 boats were not manned at once, it can be seen that a very large number of boat masters were passing through the canal at any one time, each one of them working with his assistant or 'butty.' A canal of only 25 miles in extent may sound of small consequence but the geography of the passage to Merthyr required the boatcrews to raise their boats over 540 feet between Cardiff and Merthyr through 50 locks, a prodigious amount of work and effort for men and horses. The working time of this journey was around 20 hours, to which has to be added the time for an overnight stop. So great has been the change of pace that, for example, a heavy lorry of the present day loaded to 20 tons on the A470 trunk road, can complete the same journey to Merthyr in 40 minutes.

We now pause to look at some incidents recorded in the past which draw attention to the life of the boatman. Perhaps the most extraordinary occasion was recorded by John Bird of Cardiff, when an unnamed boatman conducted Judge Hardinge down the canal on his way to Cardiff Assizes in August 1793: '*He came from Merthyr to Newbridge in one of the Canal Boats, accompanied by Mr Samuel Homfray, with a Harper.*'[7] It should be added that the canal was still not complete to Cardiff in 1793 and so Judge Hardinge rode down from Newbridge the rest of the way on horseback – a more rapid but less comfortable mode of transport.

An unusually high profile event in the life of the boatmen was the celebratory arrival of the first boats into Cardiff, on the opening day of the Glamorganshire Canal between Merthyr Tydfil and the port on 10 February 1794. After steering their fleet of boats into the town, behind '*the first barge finely decorated with colours*',[8] the crews sat down to a festive treat which was paid for by the canal company, who ordered their treasurer to '*pay to Mr John Bradley £5. 7s. 9d the amount for his Bill for an Entertainment given the Boatmen on the Boats first coming down to Cardiff.*'[9]

Fragments of information from the past are often recorded in newspapers, letters and minute books because of accidents or other incidents when things went wrong. It was a very serious matter for a boatman's livelihood if a man's boathorse was killed and in 1807, a boatman who lost his horse at the swing bridge at Melingriffith, perhaps through drowning or severe injury, was given £5. 5s. 0d by the Melingriffith Company by way of compensation. Similarly, Mrs Lewis, who lost her boathorse near the Treble

Lewis Llewelyn. Chief weigher at the boat weighing machine at Cardiff in 1880. He was appointed GCC Traffic Manager under the Bute administration and gave evidence to the Royal Commission on Canals in 1906. Lewis died in 1912. Courtesy Jeanne White

Locks in 1811, applied to the GCC for reimbursement and received £5. 5s.0d from the treasurer.[10] Mrs Lewis is thought to have been an owner and not a boatwoman, since the tradition on the Glamorganshire Canal was for all-male operation of the boats.

There were occasional breakdowns in law and order. Chaos ruled at the Treble Locks one day in October 1836, according to a letter to the Dowlais Company written by George Forrest, chief clerk to the GCC. He complained that he scarcely knew of *'one Boatman so determinedly bad in his Conduct on the Canal.'* Forrest was referring to the misdemeanours of William Meredith, who pushed his boat into the Treble Locks out of his turn and caused a build up of 16 boats, an indication of the massive congestion of traffic on the canal at this time.[11] Perhaps it was an indication, too, that such a man could win a fist fight with all 16 stranded boat captains if it came to it. It may have been the same William Meredith, boatman, who was sent to trial in 1840 for stealing clothing from a boat lying opposite the Union Bridge public house at Newbridge.[12] As a Llandaff boatman once put it, *'They were not all parsons' sons on the canal in my time, you know.'*

Some of the more light-hearted moments of a boatman's brief leisure time, in the canal village of Tongwynlais, are recorded by E.L. Chappell. Chappell must be thinking of a period before 1900 as he describes the annual Ton Fair and Market held in the second week in August. It extended over two days, the local works being closed and on the third day, the boatmen had a holiday for the Boatmen's Fair. During the long period of waiting turns to pass through Tongwynlais Lock, the boatmen used to while away the time in horse dealing, gambling, drinking, or performing a popular dance called the Boatmen's Jig.[13]

We now look in more detail at the boatmen's way of life, recording where we can some of the memories the men themselves have passed on to us. Boatmen were the most visible of the workers on the Glamorganshire Canal and to some degree their way of life set them apart from others who earned a living on the waterway. More often than not they were on the move and linking three worlds – the maritime world of the Sea Lock Pound in Cardiff, their own close-knit canal communities in the semi-rural world of the towpath, and the industrial life of the furnaces and coal pits. To the observer leaning on the parapet of the canal bridge, the quiet horse-drawn progress of the boatman at the helm presented an idyllic picture, as he moved through quiet waters towards his home in the hills. Perhaps the elements of water and of movement from place to place contributed to this romantic image. It was soon clear to anyone in touch with the reality of the boatman's life, however, that there was nothing romantic about working on the boats, especially in winter when mornings were dark and frost gripped a boat's ropes and made the lock margins treacherous. It is hard to see anything romantic either, about manhandling 280 lb sacks of flour into a boat or having to spend half a morning hand-loading 20 tons of paving stone at the quarry. *"I've been up at 4 and gone to bed at midnight to try to get a living"* one owner-boatman explained, *"and if you worked for the company on the Merthyr boats then 16 hours was considered a working day. Only after that would you get your bonus."*[14]

Mr. Ivor Llewelyn, last manager of the Glamorganshire Canal.

Ivor Llewelyn. Canal manager of the GCC following the death of his father, Lewis. He served the company until the canal was taken over by the City of Cardiff in 1944. His employment continued in the City's Estates department, until his retirement in the 1950s. *Cardiff Times*, 14 Jan 1950

Harry Watts, the last boatman at work on the Glamorganshire Canal in 1943, was small of stature and not very much different in appearance from any worker of the 1930s, with his flat cap, collarless shirt done up to the neck, waistcoat, baggy trousers with leg bottoms tied close with string and his jacket slung on the cabin roof of the boat, where he kept the lock windlass. He lived at the long-gone Three Cups Row between the Gabalfa and College locks. As a boy, in about 1889, he had boated to Merthyr with Johnny Mynachdy.

Gilbert Randall, the Cilfynydd

Left: *John Bodger. Born in Somerset, he was lockkeeper at Mynachdy Lock in 1861 but by 1881, when he was 50, had moved to Canal Cottage, Gethin, where he remained as foreman in charge of the Merthyr length of the canal through to 1898. His son William took over from him at Mynachdy.* Courtesy Maureen Perkins ***Right:*** *Noah Fletcher and his wife Sarah. Son of a boatman and brought up on the Glamorganshire Canal at Glyntaff and Coedpenmaen, he became the Aberdare Canal Company's last lockkeeper and foreman. He died at Canal Cottage, Cwmbach in 1917, aged 65.* Courtesy John Fletcher

foreman, remembered the more distinctive outfit of a boatman called Rimrun. A bearded man, Rimrun sported white moleskin trousers and a blue jersey. John Powell, who remembered the Rhydyfelin towpath as a boy before the First World War, also mentions the white moleskin trousers, the corduroy jacket and, around the neck of the more extrovert among the boat captains, the eye-catching red kerchief. John Powell continues:

> *'Travelling between Merthyr or Aberdare and Cardiff in days when most parts were out of touch with events, boatmen were regarded as very knowledgeable people carrying news and gossip as well as cargo. Away from home, bargemen slept in their boat cabins. These cabins were marvels of compactness. At the front of the cabin was a little fireplace with chimney. Each side of the grate was a cupboard out of which a bed could be brought across a longitudinal seat running along both sides of the cabin. In racks above the seats shone knives and forks. Brightly polished brass, usually horse trappings, were usual adornment; and prints (usually cigarette cards of boxers, horses or actresses) gave the shrewd visitor a reliable clue as to what subject he might safely talk about.'*[15]

For the boatman leaving home on Monday morning and perhaps not returning until Saturday, food on the boat was of the simplest. Eggs, bacon, potatoes, home-made bread, butter and cheese were common items in the larder, which was located in the small compartment under the tiller in the stern of the boat. Tea without milk, from large billycans was popular. Washing-up was done along stretches of the canal where the water was clear though the boatmen never drank canal water. Bill Gomer carried a stone pitcher on his boat for drinking water: "*We liked to fill up with spring water at Aberfan. There was another mountain spring, at Pontygwaith but that one dried up in summer*" he recalled.

Bill Bladen of Llandaff North acted as butty to his father Bert in the final years. He recalled that they were up at 4.30 in the morning and off by 5: "*Five hours to Ponty and four hours down empty. When conditions were bad we were out til 7.30. We cooked our own food (bacon, eggs and chips) in the cabin in the 3 mile pond from Treble Locks to Rhydyfelin, where the gypsies were.*"[16]

Before leaving the topic of eating and drinking on board, it must be mentioned that the boatmen carried a reputation for 'living off the land' and many a farmer is said to have found his field short of a few potatoes in the season, while occasional vegetables disappeared late at night from a lockkeeper's garden. There was also the traditional barter that went on in exchange for a few lumps of coal or some other tempting item in his cargo.

The vast majority were honest men but the reputation

FEATURE

PONTYPRIDD OBSERVER, MAY 23, 1996

PONTYPRIDD OBSERVER, MAY 23, 1996

FEATURE

29

Memories of a vanished way of life

BY STEVE DIXON

on it at a time.
member Fred Perry, a big bloke on
ntain, who used to work in the
farm in a small way and, sum-
he had a stream running at
house and he would be out
ower all year round."
the barges could travel
ypridd and back in 10
s the first in Cardiff,
ndy Lock.
way down and
weather. In the
d we would be
Brown Lenox
ers at Taffs
y back to
father in
ttle white
to call
he stone
as first
e hors-
anding
orning
barge
n my
oat to
canal

at that time, two Blaytons, Thatcher from Rhydyfelin and us.

"In my grandfather's time, it was very busy with 30 boats on the canal."

The locks used to need many thousands of gallons when they were filled up. The water came from a lake measuring one mile around and half a mile across.

"This area was lovely before the war. You could walk all around here tidy, and swim in the canal and ice skate in the winter.

"The roads have spoilt it.

"I do sit down in the house and think about those days sometimes."

Working on the canal was not without its occasional dangers, Cyril also recalled.

"The only trouble we had was during the war with the Captain's Cafe, which backed on to the lock in Cardiff.

"The Germans bombed it during the night and when we got there, there were stones from the building behind the lock and we couldn't get through."

Cyril and his father had another wartime scare when they were travelling past Llandaff Fields and bombers dropped flares.

"We took a chance and carried on," said Cyril.

When the canal froze over, it would take 14 horses and a dozen men to wield the icebreaker.

Sadly, there is little trace of the canal left to see and only the memories of people like Cyril keep its place in history.

"I am the only one left that was on the canal," he said wistfully.

Pictures reproduced with the kind help and assistance of the Maritime and Industrial Museum, Cardiff, and Cyril Frazer.

CANAL HAND: Cyril Frazer reflects on his life on the locks

HORSEPOWER: Thomas Frazer, Cyril's father, pictured aged 16 at the turn of this century, holding a canal horse, with a barge and the canal gasworks in the background

TREBLE LOCKS: The mighty treble locks at Glan-y-Llyn, which took many thousands of gallons of water from a nearby lake to fill

BREACHED: Workmen repair a breach of the canal at Upper Boat in the 1890s

GOODS SUPPLY: Barges carried grocery supplies to destinations such as Hopkin Morgan's warehouse in Trallwn, Pontypridd, and brought loads of chain back to Cardiff from the Brown Lenox and Forgemaster sites

Above: *Cyril Frazer. He was a boatman butty to his father, Tom, until the end of canal carrying on the GCC in 1942. He lived at Treble Locks cottages and in 1996 claimed to be the last surviving Glamorganshire Canal worker. He died in 2000.*
Pontypridd Observer, 23 May 1996

Right: *Cyril's father, Tom Frazer, as a boy of sixteen in the summer of 1906. He is posed with his boat horse by the Treble Locks at Taff's Well.*
Bill Hamlin collection

Portrait of a retired Glamorganshire Canal boatman. Tom Frazer at Treble Locks circa 1970.
Bill Hamlin photo

Our second style of boatman is the man under contract to the GCC, who worked on the canal company's boats to regular schedules between Cardiff Wharf and Merthyr or Aberdare. The GCC had taken on the responsibility of carrier on its own canal in September 1887.[17] Bill Gomer, who had helped on these boats as a boy, described the arrangement succinctly: "*You bought a contract and asked the company for a boat*". The Bladen brothers, Bill and Bert, with their respective sons Bert and Bill as butties, were managed by their widowed mother, who had the boat contract with the GCC and paid her sons and grandsons wages from the monthly income. While the GCC supplied the boats, they used their own horses – in 1981 they recalled 'Bonny', 'Captain', 'Violet' and 'Dick'. Tom Frazer took over 'Violet' from the Bladens.[18]

In the third category were the boatmen who owned no boats but who worked for industrial traders like the Star Patent Fuel Co of Blackweir and the L. Gueret works at Maindy. The fuel works boatmen worked an intensive traffic during and after the 1914-18 war, with some 60 boats between them. North Road Lock was kept open for them between 6 in the morning and 11 at night, so that orders could be completed and shipped to the Bute Docks.[19]

With the help of the reminiscences of two retired boatmen, Thomas Jones and William Gomer, it is possible to see what life and work was like on the canal over a hundred years ago. We have to be reminded of course that by the late 19th century, the fortunes of the Glamorganshire Canal were at a low ebb. However, the purchase of the canal by the Marquess of Bute (with effect from 1885) was seen to be bringing improvements to the waterway and a new, if short-lived, boost to its traffic.[20]

stuck fast. "*Bring the ducks in Mother. Here's the boatman coming*" was the cry in Rhydyfelin in the days of the boats, according to a group of pensioners Ian Wright met on a canal bridge in the 1940s. For others, reeling from some severe loss and looking for someone to blame, the finger of suspicion would be directed towards '*Y Badwr, yr Hen Ddiawl*' (that Old Devil the Boatman).

On the Glamorganshire Canal we are able to identify three broad categories of boatman. Firstly, we find the independent owner-boatman or bye trader, who had been the mainstay of canal carrying since the 1790s. The canal boatmen's name for the independents was 'hobbler' and as Bill Gomer once said, "*If you weren't working for the Company you were a hobbler.*" On English canals the independent trader was called a 'Number One'. On the Glamorganshire, the last independent owner-boatman was Ben Gould of Treforest, who was best known for his connection with the Pontypridd engineering works of Brown Lenox, bringing down anchors and chain cables to Cardiff.

Thomas Jones of Llandaff North, born 1863[21]

Thomas Jones was a bye trader on the Glamorganshire Canal who had started work on the boats at the age of 13. In 1879, when he had reached the age of 16, he bought a boat of his own and started bringing down coal to Cardiff from '*Davis Blaengwawr*'. Blaengwawr Colliery was near the head of the Aberdare Canal and a tram road

Walter Morgan and Tom Thomas. Photographed as the two 'oldest inhabitants' of Abercynon – in their day called Navigation. Walter, of the canal company's Tollgate House near the Aqueduct, was lockkeeper at the Aberdare Canal junction in the 1890s. Tom Thomas, on the right, kept a shop serving the canal and tramroad community at the Basin. Harry Rogers collection

***Right:** Harry Watts. His work as a butty on canal boats began when he was 10 years of age. He became an independent boatman and then lockkeeper at Mynachdy Lock in the 1930s. During World War One, he checked the heavy Patent Fuel traffic passing through North Road Lock in Cardiff.*
Courtesy Carol Sharp

connected the pit to a wharf at Canal Head, Abernant. In 1948, when he was 85, Tom recalled bringing up imported cog wood (pitwood) to collieries at Mountain Ash.

He had also loaded Bridgwater bricks in the Sea Lock pound (which had come in by sea from the River Parrett) and vividly remembered arguing his right not to be charged tonnage on them for the first mile. "*The ship captain has already paid for the first mile*" said Tom. "*The issue has never been raised, Tom*" replied the man in the office. "*Then it's time it was raised*", responded Tom, "*and I'm raising it now.*" The question was settled eventually in the boatman's favour.

Tom Jones was proud to remember a church outing he had organised, for 600 adults and children, down the canal in boats from Merthyr, perhaps about 1880. The organisation of Sunday school treats like these was direct and personal, the vicar turning up at Abercanaid where boats were loading coal at the Plymouth Basin (the Upper Abercanaid Dock). "*Wait until tomorrow*", the boatmen told him, "*and Tom Jones will be up.*" The deal was put together the following day. "*Oh, you'll need four boats for the 600*" Tom explained. "*It will cost six pounds altogether. Four pounds for the four boats and two pounds for waiting around until tomorrow.*" The four boats set out '*under the Parliament*' (below Parliament Lock) for a day of sports, picnics and singing in a favoured field down the valley. "*Shame on you, Tom Jones, you ought to be horsewhipped*" called the daughter of the White Hart, Abercanaid, as she viewed the impressive four boat turnout. "*You with the best horse and best boat coming down last!*"

At one stage, Tom Jones discovered that a sawmill at Aberfan '*needed a regular*' and so he boated timber from Cardiff to Aberfan in the 1880s. By 1885, the railway contractors Meakin & Dean were completing their building work on the Quakers Yard & Merthyr Joint line of the Great Western and Rhymney railways, which ran parallel to the canal and Tom arranged to buy one of the boats the contractors had been using to carry materials for building the railway. As well as purchasing their boat, Tom came in useful to the contractors in another way: "*After Meakin & Dean had finished the railway I loaded all the furniture and belongings of the clerk of works into my boat and took it down the canal to Cardiff where it was loaded up at the Great Western Railway and forwarded on to his home.*"

During the late 1880s the Glamorganshire Canal Company was still doing its best to enforce its byelaws and from time to time, it was the habit of Percy Harwood, the canal manager, to take the train to Taffs Well or Treforest and walk the towpath to keep an eye on what was going on. "*There were not many lock keepers around in the later years of the canal*", Tom explained, "*and one day I jumped on to the coal as we left Portobello Lock and let the horse walk on by himself. Just then Mr Harwood appeared up the bank and tackled me about not being on the towpath leading the horse. "There are no lockkeepers around nowadays," I said to him, "and we're having to do the lockkeeper's job as well as ours.*" From that time

John James, boat builder, Gabalfa Dock circa 1890. He came to the Glamorganshire Canal from a shipbuilding community in Cardiganshire. He was running the boat yard on the Doctor's Canal at Rhydyfelin in 1851, before moving down to take over William Beynon's yard at Gabalfa. His son, John Rhys James, ran the yard until it closed in 1927. ILW collection, copy neg 2349

George Stone and Bill Watkins. George was an engineer who started work at the canal's pumping station, then moved to Cardiff for a time to Sea Lock Cottages, where he was locomotive driver on the canal company's railway. Finally he moved to College Lock but was also in charge of the weighing machine at North Road, to which he cycled when he was needed. The Government's Southern Canal Control Sub-Committee excused him from serving in the First World War because of this work. George died in 1969. The photograph shows him with 'Whistling' Bill Watkins, right, blacksmith's striker, at Cambrian Yard. SR collection

onwards Mr Harwood did not challenge our boatman again.

In 1898, Tom Jones was involved in an unusual assignment for the canal company. "*I set out with my horse and the company's 10 ton work boat fitted up with seats and an awning for a three day tour of inspection of the whole of the canal to Merthyr and to Aberdare. On board were some officials, the canal engineer, and two important engineers from London. At night times I stabled the horse and went home to Llandaff by train and I arrived back on the canal to take the party on next morning.*" Tom Jones's passengers, his '*engineers from London*', were indeed the eminent consulting engineers Sir Douglas Fox, then president of the Institute of Civil Engineers, and Sir Leader Williams, the distinguished creator of the Manchester Ship Canal. They both confirmed to Watkin-Lewis, the canal company's engineer travelling with them, that the mining subsidence made closure of the Merthyr section of the canal imperative. Reassured by expert opinion, the GCC now felt free of the risk of legal action and could go ahead with its plan to close the unstable length of the upper canal to Merthyr, on the grounds of public safety.[22]

Perhaps Tom Jones already knew that his summer voyage of inspection with the VIPs foreshadowed the end of the water to Merthyr. "*By Christmas they had shut the Merthyr side up*" he recalled 50 years later. Tom now realised that there was little future for him as a trader on the canal. Remarking that "*the canal went too quiet*", he added with feeling, "*I loved the old canal but I wanted a living out of it.*" Reluctantly, about 1900, he left the boating life behind and took a job "*on the land.*"

Bill Gomer. As a young Rhydyfelin boatman he traded between Cardiff, Merthyr and Aberdare in the 1890s. He was GCC warehouseman at Treforest from 1912-41 and a canal caretaker/patrolman in the 1950s. ILW photo 25 Sept 1950 neg 1074

William Gomer of Rhydyfelin, born 1882

William (Bill) Gomer was only a boy of nine in 1891 when he began buttying with his father. He distinguished himself on his first day by falling off a coal boat, into the canal in the Abercanaid Dock. Like Tom Jones of Llandaff, Bill was able to buy a boat of his own at 16. His time as a hobbler was to prove quite short however, because of the closure of the Merthyr portion of the canal in 1898. This was followed in 1900 by the end of trading between Abercynon, Mountain Ash and Aberdare when colliery subsidence in the Cynon Valley caused the closure of the Aberdare Canal. Nevertheless, Bill Gomer's nine years on the boats still remained the clearest of recollections for him over 60 years later, when he passed on his memories to Ian Wright. In 1899, Bill was driving horses for the Pontypridd merchants, Lewis the Cornstores, who traded from a canal-served warehouse at Trallwn. In the following year, he was boating stone for Gibbon, the quarry owner at nearby Pentrebach and in 1901, he was put in charge of the Graig & Hafod chain horse, delivering shop goods with the canal company's drays to the hillier parts of Pontypridd.[23] "*I've brought a haulier for you, Missus*" his mentor said to Mrs Thomas, the canal company's local agent at Trallwn, on his first day. At about this time, the Glamorganshire Canal Company was using six horse drays for deliveries from its wharf in Pontypridd.[24]

Bill began his long association with the Treforest warehouse of the GCC in 1912, where he worked for the company for 29 years until it was closed in 1941. The main commodity handled at Treforest and Pontypridd was bagged flour, which Bill was keen to point out came in "*real 280 pound sacks.*" These huge sacks, weighing 2½ hundredweight (or 125 kilos in metric), were moved easily enough out of ships by derrick and chain but the final positioning of the sack into the canal boat was the skilful and agonising work of men's backs. "*You would take on 140 sacks of flour in Cardiff and that would load your boat to 17½ tons,*" Bill recalled from his days working the GCC goods boats to Merthyr and Aberdare in the late 1890s. "*I remember Ned Skine at Cardiff Wharf making me take 18 tons to the Aberdare Canal, where the low water levels made it hard to make the boat swim. The worst place for bumping along the bottom was in Newtown* [Mountain Ash]. *Coming out of a lock in low water like that you would have to be careful. A loaded boat could easily ground on the top sill of the lock and if the water level dropped she could easily break her back.*"

Looking back to the traffic in the mid 1890s, Bill Gomer mentioned that the canal company's goods boats were scheduled to work three turns in a week and for many years there were four boats running on each turn. The services ran between Cardiff Wharf and Pontypridd, Merthyr and Aberdare. As the new mining community of Abercynon expanded, a daily boat brought up shop goods to new transit sheds that had been built there. Bill Herbert, Bill Thatcher, William John, John Frazer and Bertie Parry all worked on the Abercynon boats at about this time. A number of Bristol Channel traders were familiar visitors to the Glamorganshire Canal's Sea Lock pound in Bill Gomer's youth, all of them keeping up the long tradition of trade between Bristol and Cardiff. An owner, Jane Davies, ran an import business in market goods, assisted by various sons and relatives. She ran boats on the Glamorganshire Canal and hired others. She maintained her own boat dock at Maesmawr Bridge, where her craft were repaired.

Associated with Jane Davies were the sea-going vessels *Ceres*, *Flora Belle* and *Bee*.

"*R. Burton & Sons had two wharves on the Sea Lock pound*", Bill Gomer remembered, "*one by Lock 51 near the timber float and the other by the Testing House.*" Later, Burtons moved to the Little Dock where the canal company's Pontypridd boats used to load. Burtons traded into the canal with the steamers *Isca*, *Enid*, *Ethel* and *Moderator*, which brought in market goods from Bristol.

"*I must not forget to tell you about the little sailing ship* Electric. *She was owned by J. Stoate of Watchet and in the days when I was boating* [1890-1900], *I would see her unloading sacks of flour at the warehouse just above the Sea Lock on the towpath* [east] *side.*"[25]

"*The Cardiff - Pontypridd boatmen got a monthly wage from the company for making their three trips a week whatever traffic had to go. On the up-along work we did not get the monthly wage, because the Aberdare and Merthyr runs were too long a distance. The company paid us 1s 8d a ton for boating goods to Aberdare or Merthyr. They would pay you a bonus. Suppose I left West Wharf in Cardiff at 5 pm. They would pay me a bonus of 2s 6d if I could get the boat to Merthyr by 7 o'clock tomorrow night. It was not all easy going and there were places on the Merthyr side where it was hard to make the boat swim but when you got to Aberfan the water was so deep that you could drive on the gallop!*"

Even as late as the 1960s, the old course of the Glamorganshire Canal just below the site of the deep locks at Aberfan remained a quiet and pretty place among beech trees and well sheltered from the wind. So it was no surprise to hear Bill Gomer remembering the place with pleasure from his boating days in the 1890s. "*Delivering to Merthyr, I'd try to get back to Aberfan to moor up for the night. I'd leave again about five o'clock next morning and work through the Abercynon Fives and Elevens and get to Gibbons* [quarry, Glyntaff] *at ten. I'd be loaded by dinnertime and if all was clear it would take me around six hours to get to Cardiff.*" With working hours like these, one is left to wonder when a young boatman found time to cook, eat or sleep!

Some of the more practical aspects of working horse boats were clearly recalled by Bill Gomer, as well as the never-to-be-forgotten Arctic winter of 1895. "*You got your son or your brother or a nephew to help you with your boating*" continued Bill. "*On the canal your mate was called a butty. When my father was boating to Merthyr he gave work to an old pedlar to help as his butty. Everybody on the Merthyr end of the canal called him Tom Blackberry Cake and he was a well-known character on the towpath. Your butty would be on the bank leading the horse and he would need to go on ahead to set the lock, taking the windlass with him for winding up the paddles. He'd get the gates open for the boat. If you were going into an empty lock going up, you'd steer for the entrance and give the horse a good 'gee up' then take off your towline so you could pass under the bottom gates platform. Open the Jack head paddle a bit* [the ground paddle] *and the water would bubble under your boat and stop her nicely. You then closed the bottom gates, opened up the top paddle and wound up the top gate flashers* [paddles] *- gently at first or you'd flood the front of the boat. That's why we'd keep a tarpaulin sheet over the front of the cargo. When the lock was filled and you'd made a level you could put the towline back on the mast, open the top gate and get the horse going again, remembering to roll the top gate flashers down again or you'd be in trouble with the bosses for emptying the canal.*"

In February 1895, much of the country was affected by a long period of severe weather, which put the Glamorganshire Canal out of action for up to 16 weeks. The low temperatures brought hardship to the boatmen, who were unable to work because the boats were blockaded by ice over many weeks. Ice breaking crews were faced with such solid conditions that they could make no impression and the GCC helped the stranded boatmen by opening soup kitchens.[26] Just before these Arctic conditions began, Bill Gomer's father was locking down to the Aberdare Junction on his way home to Rhydyfelin. It was a cold evening and getting late. "*Tom Blackberry Cake wanted my father to moor for the night at the Junction. "No," said my father," We must keep on going. Perhaps by the morning the ice will be behind the gates.*"[27] It seems the Gomer's boat got home safely but the spring of 1895, for everyone on the canal, was a very long time in coming.

Bill Gomer was brought up in a culture that did not understand the concept of waste. In his day, local resources were carefully conserved and equally carefully exploited and, because economic necessity directed it, ways of converting opportunities into earnings were never overlooked by the boatmen. An interesting initiative at Merthyr is worth recording.

"*The water coming out of the feeder at Jackson's Bridge used to wash a lot of ash and gravel into the Penydarren pond*" Bill recalled. "*At weekends the work gang would let the water out of the canal and remove the shoals of gravel. We would get the gang to put a few boatloads of this gravel on to the landing place under the warehouse.*[28] *We'd load this stuff into my boat and I'd take it down to Abercynon or Cilfynydd, places that were then being built, and I'd trade the gravel to the builders who were putting up streets of houses there. They'd use it for making mortar.*"

Again, it was a common practice among the boatmen at the end of the summer to harvest a free crop from the hillsides. "*We used to cut fern* [bracken] *from the mountain slopes and boat it down the canal to Cardiff, where we would sell it for bedding for the horses.*"

One last memory of the boating life concludes Bill Gomer's story. It is a recollection of a call once commonplace on the boats and along the miles of towpath. As he is rounding a bend and approaching the lock a boatman calls ahead to alert the lockkeeper, "*Whoo Up, Boat comin' up!*" And as if to underline how close-knit was the world of the canal communities, retired boatmen, years after they had finished boating, would greet one another as they passed in Rhydyfelin's small streets and terraces and call, "*Whoo, Dan!*" and "*Whoo Dai.*" As Bill explained, "*That's what they'd call Whooping.*"

As John Powell of Lock Lewis once remarked, these strong and original characters of the boats put more into life than they got out of it. Certainly, theirs was not just a job but also a way of life – one that unfortunately was to run at too slow a pace for the modern world.

The horse remained the principal motive power on the Glamorganshire Canal for 150 years. However, some boatmen and horsekeepers, particularly those hiring to the Maindy and Blackweir fuel works, favoured the use of mules. In this photograph of 1917, a boat mule and its driver are dressed for a special occasion – the annual works outing by boat for employees of the Star Patent Fuel Works of Blackweir. The boat mule or horse exerts his effort against the collar to which the side chains are attached. These lead to the rear of the animal where they are kept apart by passing to the ends of a wooden 'spreader' called a swingletree. Beyond the swingletree, the haulage chains are exchanged for rope lines, which converge into a single towline running to an attachment at the top of a moveable 6ft mast towards the front of the boat. When shown this photograph in 1973, Tom Frazer named the canal characters as, from left to right: Tom Francis, nicknamed 'Eggy', John Birch and the bowler-hatted driver Tom Birch (with whom no horse or mule would argue!). The location is the Long Wood below Tongwynlais.

ILW collection

One of the finest photographs ever taken of a Glamorganshire Canal boatman at work. In idyllic summer conditions around 1910, a 21 ton load of Star Patent Fuel leaves North Road Lock (Lock No 49) and is about to skirt the walls of Cardiff Castle, bound for the docks. The boatman, shirt-sleeved in the warmth of the sun, drives the horse, whilst his butty guides the stern of the boat from beneath the footbridge The lockkeeper appears to be lowering the paddles on the top gate, which would suggest that he has just 'flushed' the boat out of the lock. This was a common practice on many canals, particularly at awkward locations such as this, where the footbridge hindered the passage out of the lock, although it was officially proscribed at certain locks on the Glamorganshire, where water shortages were often a problem as other industries competed for the resource. Once the bottom gates were open, the lockkeeper would ease the top gate paddles and allow a flow of water to flush the boat on its way, where, clear of the

bridge, the horse could take the strain. The effort for the horse was all in getting the boat under way and once this was achieved, the vessel largely kept going under its own momentum, the animal just having to maintain a steady plod. With the little bit of help from the lockkeeper, the horse is just beginning to take the strain on the rope here. The rope is connected to the towing mast in the centre of the boat and the boatman is pulling back on the swingle tree, so as to keep the harness and chains clear of the horse's flanks and to counteract the tendency for the animal to be dragged towards the canal by the weight of the laden vessel. Also of interest in this view, directly behind the lockkeeper can be seen the Canal Company's weighing machine, which is covered in detail in a later chapter. The cast iron bridge spanning the lock entrance, which gave access to the castle grounds, is shown in good detail, whilst behind it, the white-washed thatched-roofed building beneath the trees is the Castle Lodge. Neil Parkhouse collection

NOTES TO CHAPTER 4

1 F.J. Pedler *History of the Hamlet of Gellideg*, Merthyr Tydfi 1930, p32.

2 GRO QAW 35, GCC balance account March 1797 – March 1798.

3 Chris Baber 'Canals and the Economic Development of South Wales', in Colin Baber & L.J. Williams (eds.) *Modern South Wales: Essays in Economic History*, Cardiff 1986, p34; Trevor Boyns & Chris Baber 'The Supply of Labour, 1750-1914', in G. Williams & A.H. John (eds.) *Glamorgan County History, Vol V Industrial Glamorgan*, Cardiff 1980, pp316-20.

4 GCC Bylaws Nos 6 and 8, 3 June 1826.

5 Census returns 1881.

6 Charles Hadfield *The Canals of South Wales and the Border*, Cardiff 1960, p108. Hadfield was probably quoting from evidence of the Taff Vale Railway Bill.

7 Entry in John Bird's diary, 17 August 1793; see Hilary Thomas *The Diaries of John Bird 1790 -1803*, Cardiff 1987, p88.

8 Phillips *General History of Inland Navigation*, 4th edition 1803, p585.

9 GCC minute book 5 June 1794.

10 GCC minute book 9 May 1807 and 29 August 1811.

11 George Forrest (Navigation House) to Richard Davies (Dowlais), 28 October 1836, in Madeleine Elsas (ed) *Iron in the Making: Dowlais Iron Company Letters 1782-1860*, Cardiff 1960, p157.

12 *Cardiff & Merthyr Guardian*, 29 February 1840.

13 Edgar Chappell *Old Whitchurch*, Cardiff, p234 and 236.

14 William Gomer in conversation with ILW 4 January 1956.

15 John Powell article in *Pontypridd Observer*, 12 August 1950.

16 Bill Bladen in conversation with SR at Llandaff North, 6 September 1981.

17 *Western Mail*, 7 April 1893.

18 The cousins Bill and Bert Bladen in separate conversations with SR at Llandaff North, 6 September 1981.

19 See chapter on Patent Fuel.

20 Hadfield *Canals of South Wales*, pp116-7 and *Western Mail*, 7 April 1893.

21 Thomas Jones in conversations with ILW at Llandaff North in 1948.

22 W.T. Watkin-Lewis *Recollections*, privately published c1943, p147.

23 A chain horse is put in front of the horse in the shafts, to assist him.

24 Royal Commission on Canals, 1906; evidence of Lewis Llewelyn, para 10784. Information from William Gomer.

25 *Electric* was registered in Bridgwater, 46 net reg. tons and was wrecked off Watchet in 1903. G. Mote *The Westcountrymen*, Bideford 1986, p34.

26 W.T. Watkin-Lewis *Recollections*, p137.

27 Lock gates will not fold back if solid pack ice has formed behind them.

28 See Volume 1, Chapter 4. The landing place under the warehouse was still intact when ILW examined it with William Gomer in September 1950.

Chapter 5
THE WATER SUPPLY TO THE CANAL AT PENTYRCH & MELINGRIFFITH

The Melingriffith Pump

The Pentyrch Ironworks, so called because it was situated in Pentyrch parish on the west bank of the Taff, was established in 1740 by the Lewis family of Llanishen; it drew water from the Taff to drive its forges and rolling mills. On the opposite side of the valley, a little further down the Taff, in 1749, the Melingriffith Tinplate Works was established on the site of a former corn mill; it also relied on water from the Taff for its power, its weir being below where the Pentyrch tailrace emptied back into the river. Thus the same water effectively powered the works at both Pentyrch and Melingriffith.[1] At the time of the first Glamorganshire Canal Bill, both were still independent concerns but Melingriffith did rely on Pentyrch for much of its iron. In fact the companies utilised the river and their respective feeders for inter-communication too. Boats may have been loaded in the tailrace below the Pentyrch forge but they would have had to ride the rough water in the river bend to Tongwynlais, so Chappell believes they were loaded from waggon or pony further downstream near Cilynys. The boats must have been guided across the river by oars, skilful use of a rudder or by a rope. At Radyr Weir there was a canal lock, by which the boats entered and returned from the Melingriffith feeder. Remains of this lock, including the stone recess for the gate, can still be seen just north of where the sluices regulate the feeder's water intake.

Whilst the owners of these works keenly supported the building of the canal, they made sure to safeguard their individual water supplies. Two clauses were included in the Act for that purpose.

Clause VII stipulated that an overflow weir be erected on the canal below the Nant Garw Brook, to let surplus water into the river above the Pentyrch weir; the lock below this overflow weir had to be kept in constant repair to prevent any unnecessary leakage to the lower ponds, thus ensuring that the maximum volume of water was diverted into the river for Pentyrch's use. Clause VI similarly protected Melingriffith's supply but in their case, the canal overflow weir discharged directly into the Melingriffith feeder upstream of the works. The canal passed so close to Melingriffith that, additionally, clause V of the Act protected the lands of the proprietors of the tinplate works, Harford Partridge & Co, from the canal encroaching on them.

Such arrangements should have worked well for the Pentyrch and Melingriffith companies, because they sought to restrict the water used by the canal company to that necessary to pass boats through the locks. Any surplus water entering the canal in the upper reaches would be made available to the iron and tinplate works for them to continue in business. However, from the canal company's point of view, it left them little scope for supplying the canal with further water below Melingriffith to make up for the inevitable wastage from leaks and evaporation. Only the Whitchurch Brook, at Gabalfa, could contribute in some small way to topping up the canal south of Melingriffith. What no party realised when the bill was being formulated was just how much leakage there would be between Melingriffith and Cardiff. This was the final section of the canal to be completed. In the Dadfords' anxiety to finish the canal within budget and under pressure from Richard Crawshay to get the canal opened as soon as possible, they skimped on the depth of excavation and on the amount of puddling clay used.

Although boats had reached Cardiff and the canal was opened officially in February 1794, William Taitt wrote from Cardiff to Robert Thompson at Dowlais on 25 February, that the canal would be out of operation for a fortnight because of a breach and again on 30 March, that the canal leaked so much below Melingriffith that the boats could not navigate and a further breach near Cardiff would take two days to mend.[2] Again, in May, boats were prevented going further than Melingriffith for lack of water.[3] In September, Thomas Dadford was pressing for yet more money, having already been paid upwards of £17,000 more than the original contract price.[4] Finally, in December 1794, there being no more money available, the Dadfords unceremoniously stopped work on the canal, paid off their workmen and handed the canal over with the breach unmended.[5] The proprietors were left to organise the management of the remaining work and its maintenance themselves, whilst they sought to sue the absconding engineers. On 1 January 1795, the canal waters broke through once again at the same spot and the carriers were forced to take their iron around the breach.[6]

Taitt's letters to Thompson show how serious was the

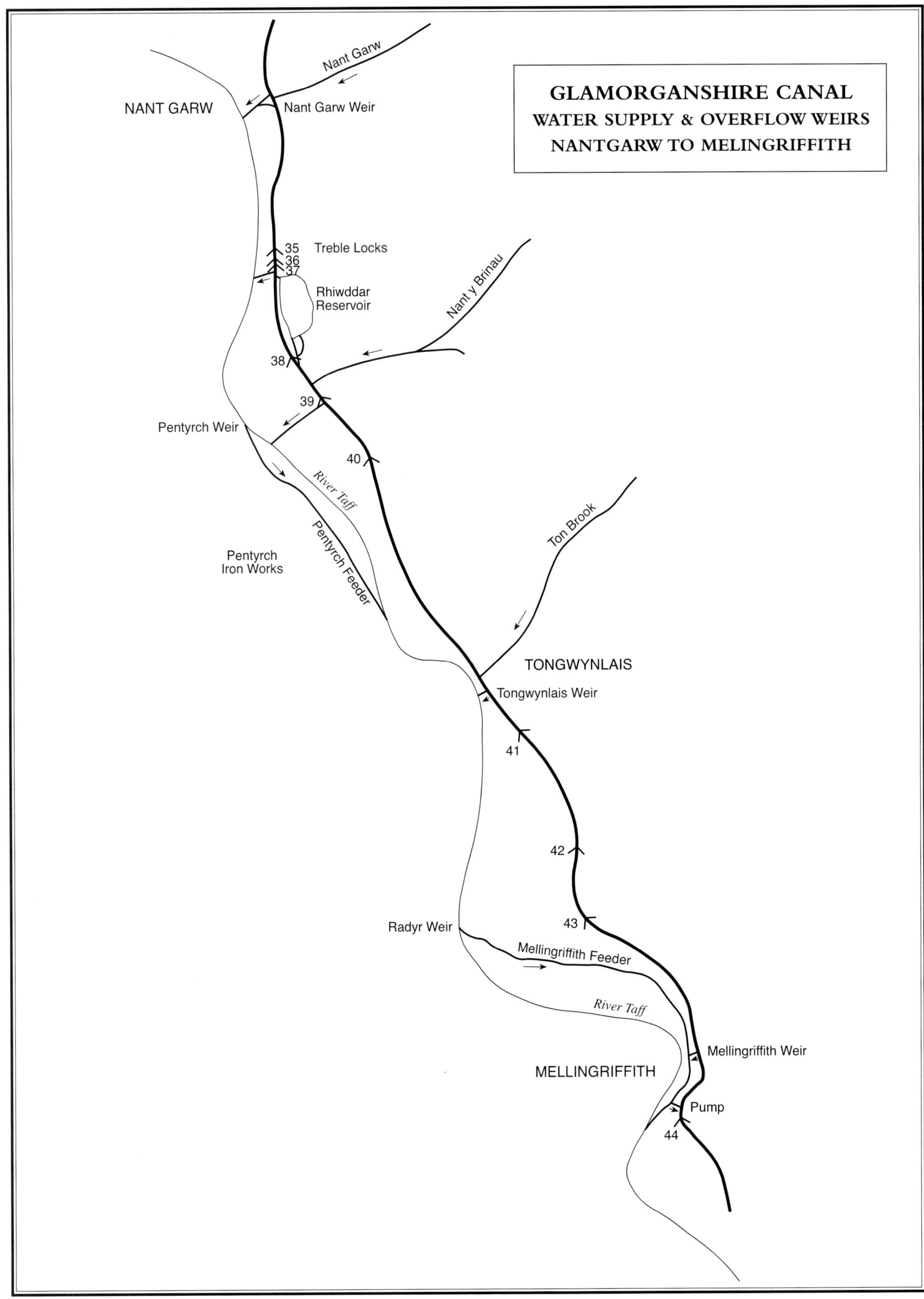
GLAMORGANSHIRE CANAL
WATER SUPPLY & OVERFLOW WEIRS
NANTGARW TO MELINGRIFFITH
Nant Garw
NANT GARW
Nant Garw Weir
35
36
37
Treble Locks
Rhiwddar
Reservoir
Nant y Brinau
38
39
Pentyrch Weir
40
River Taff
Pentyrch Feeder
Pentyrch
Iron Works
Ton Brook
TONGWYNLAIS
Tongwynlais Weir
41
42
43
Radyr Weir
Mellingriffith Feeder
River Taff
Mellingriffith Weir
MELLINGRIFFITH
Pump
44

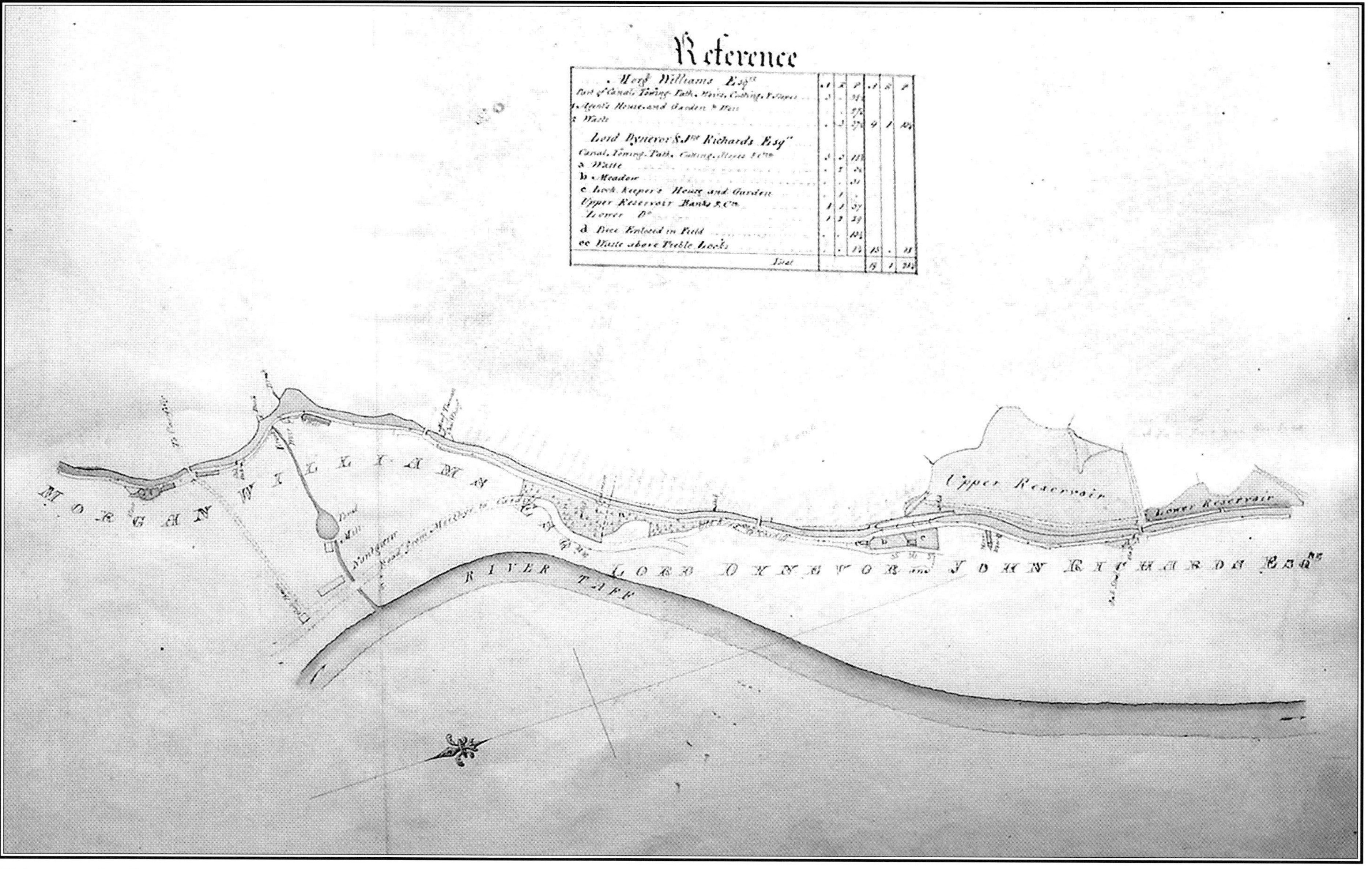

This portion of William Harrison's 1830 survey of the canal shows the stretch between Coed Cae Dyrus and Taff's Well Lock. Note the agent's house and warehouse at Nantgarw, opposite the pottery, Edward Edmund's boat dock and the Nant Garw Brook feeding the corn mill. While the Melingriffith Company's boat was being repaired here for a month in 1807, it used boats from a variety of sources, sometimes using its own horse and man and sometimes contracting directly with a boatman [see WIMM 1991.25/6]. *The turnpike gatehouse is shown where the Caerphilly road leaves the main Merthyr to Cardiff road. Further along the three mile pound is Morgan Thomas's coal wharf at Craig yr Allt, followed by Bryn Coch Bridge, then Treble Locks and John Hodgkinson's Rhiw Ddar reservoirs of 1820. The large weir below Treble Locks is the site of John Llewellin's boat dock, first mentioned in the canal minutes of 1818.*

Courtesy Glamorgan Record Office

When the Derby man William Billingsley and his Worcester son-in-law, Samuel Walker, built their pottery, the village of Nantgarw already supported a population of colliers and canal boatmen. Edward Edmunds of Penrhos had been agent to the iron and tin-plate companies since before the coming of the canal and ran a carrying business from Nantgarw where he had his own boatyard and dock. Edmunds sub-leased the canal-side property to Billingsley in 1813 and the establishment of the pottery caused the canal company to build a warehouse opposite the works and lay a public wharf there for the convenience of the local corn mill too. A bridge crossed the canal at this spot, carrying the main road running from Caerphilly to the Taff Valley and onward to Llantrisant. SR collection

water position in only this first year of operating the canal. The Dowlais Company had, against William Lewis's advice, moved all their traffic from the road to the canal carriers. They now had to put their own waggon back on the road and transfer horses from the Dowlais Railroad to operate it.[7] Taitt believed the canal would be closed again for a good month after the frosts, since Crawshay and Griffiths had drained it (presumably to mend the breaches) but that this would allow the frost to open up the sides and bottom to create more leaks.[8] The letters also show how much an ironmaster had to direct his agents in navigation strategy, to plan the movement of boats in order to make the most of available water in competition with other users of the waterway.[9]

It was in this climate of water shortage and continuous leakage below Melingriffith that, on 11 April 1795, a special meeting was held of the canal proprietors in charge of managing the Lower Section of the canal, below Navigation. The committee, comprising Richard Crawshay, Richard Griffiths, John Bassett, Joseph Vaughan and Watkin George, resolved

'*to erect an Engine at the Tail of the Melingriffyd Mill race for the purpose of conveying water into the Canal and the Proprietors of the Melingryffyd Works consenting thereto. It is ordered that Mr Watkin George immediately proceed to erect the same the expense whereof it is presumed will not exceed Three Hundred Pounds.*'[10]

It was fortunate for the canal company that it was on good terms with Harford Partridge & Co, the owners of Melingriffith, for this agreement to be possible. During the first three years of its existence, until the June 1793 annual general meeting, James Harford had been Treasurer, whilst Joseph Vaughan continued to represent them on the committee and assist in management of the lower section.

The plan was to pump water from the tailrace of the Melingriffith feeder and channel it into the canal at the Melingriffith Lock. The pump, driven by the flow of water from the tailrace itself, was designed by Watkin George and incorporated castings made by him at Cyfarthfa, other materials being supplied on the spot by Melingriffith. Work proceeded and payment of bills was authorised at canal company committee meetings in October (£160 13s 7d to Harford Partridge & Co and £104 3s 8d expenses to Joseph Vaughan) and December (£72 10s 10d to Crawshay George & Co and £53 4s expenses to Joseph Vaughan).[11]

Having made this concession to the canal company, the

Billingsley and Walker's intention was to manufacture soft paste porcelain to rival the French Sevres article. They used the services of the decorator, Thomas Pardoe, who was also working for the Swansea pottery from his base at Bristol. With limited Quaker capital from William Weston Young and Lewis Weston Dillwyn of Swansea pottery, the team struggled with their experiments for some years. Although they were successful in producing a very fine product, the amount of rejected output was substantial. The concern lasted only until 1820, when Billingsley and Walker were persuaded to move to work for Rose at Coalport. Thomas Pardoe continued at Nantgarw painting the unsold stock until his death in 1823. After this the works were reopened and managed by successive generations of the Pardoes. They did not manufacture porcelain, however, but made rich brown earthenware and also clay pipes. It was the Pardoes who built the third kiln. The business finally closed in 1921 but the premises remained in the Pardoe family long enough for the last to witness the restoration of Nantgarw House and the china works museum to open on the site. Both of these views of the pottery date from about 1904. SR collection

management of Melingriffith were vigilant to prevent excess water passing through the lock. February 1797 gives the first hint of the many complaints that were to come, when the canal company minutes record Harford & Co's request for redress for water being taken by the canal.[12] The boatmen were in the habit of flushing their boats out of the locks by opening the paddles of the upper lock gates when the lower one was open, a practice which was clearly against the spirit of clause VI of the Act.

The investigation resulted in the canal company being obliged to issue a bye law:

> '*that when any Boat passes through any Lock on the Canal the Lock Keepers and Boatmen be not allowed to flush any water after any such boat and particularly that they do not in future Suffer any waste water to run from the Melingriffith pond into the lower cut.*'[13]

At the annual general meeting held on 5 June 1797, Joseph Vaughan was not re-elected to the canal company committee and from that time Melingriffith ceased to have a representative.

Next month, during a time of canal closure either from drought, breaches or planned maintenance, John Harford (James Harford's brother and the managing partner at Melingriffith) sought '*to heighten the Machine for raising Water for their Company's convenience*', to which the canal company's response was:

> '*We are mending the ponds effectually as fast as we can if raising the Machine will benefit the Melingriffyd Company they are welcome to do so provided no injury is done to this company.*'

Why the Melingriffith company should wish to heighten the pump is difficult to understand, since the lower it was the lower the head of water (even for an undershot wheel) required to turn its wheel and hence the less effect would any backwater have on the efficiency of the Melingriffith machinery. This decision was to have important consequences for the Melingriffith company in the years following.

The Nant Garw Brook supplied water through a succession of holding ponds to the corn mill in the village, the stream being culverted under the canal. The supply was supplemented by this long overflow weir from the canal. The photograph dates from around 1905. SR collection

It is questionable whether the pump operated effectively to provide sufficient water for the lower ponds. In an attempt to supplement the water supply to the last few locks at Cardiff, in March 1800 it was recorded that '*a feeder from the River Taff to Crockerton Locktail is agreed to be done by Mr George's order and contracted for by him.*'[14] However, the canal company were probably frustrated by the Marquess of Bute, whose land would have been required and nothing came of this proposal. Years later, this route was used for the Bute Docks feeder which passed under the canal near the Castle at North Road Lock and is still in use today to maintain the level of the Bute East Dock for modern industrial purposes.

The Disputes Begin

In spite of the Melingriffith pump, the canal continued to suffer from water shortages. John Bird's diary of 30 August 1800 records '*owing to the dryness of the season little or no trade has been done on the canal from want of water.*' It was inevitable that every opportunity would be taken to overlook the agreements with Pentyrch and Melingriffith – at the very periods of summer drought when those

The dramatic structural forms of the Treble Locks staircase are enhanced by afternoon sunlight in this 1930s photograph by Samuel Fox. Note the pitched horse-way forming a steep ramp for the towpath. The ivy-covered building on the right was the disused gas house, which had supplied gas for lighting at the locks from the 1830s. S.C. Fox photo CCL collection

A general view of Treble Locks from below, taken from a position on the reservoir side of the canal. The lock house, of pennant sandstone and yellow brick dressings, was built in 1908 to replace the earlier structure which was demolished to make way for the Cardiff Railway which squeezed between canal and road at this point. In the 1930s, two families occupied the lock house – on the left were the Frazers, who were boatmen, whilst to the right lived the elderly David Williams who was a toll collector. The earlier building had also consisted of two separate properties, housing the families of the two lockkeepers. S.C. Fox photo WIMM 73.17

concerns themselves were desperate to keep their machinery turning. Crawshay was quite prepared for the Glamorganshire Canal Company to take these risks, firstly because of the sort of man he was and, secondly, because the 8% dividend ceiling meant that the canal company was conveniently flush with money which it could use to spend on defending its actions in court, should it come to that. And come to that it certainly did.

William Lewis of Pentyrch Ironworks was the first to bring a case against the canal company, in 1802. The lack of water at Pentyrch in dry seasons he blamed on the canal company's building their second feeder at Quakers' Yard. The two feeders, he claimed, enabled almost the whole of the River Taff's waters to be extracted for the canal's use. The canal proprietors had then been illegally granting leases to themselves as controlling shareholders for sites for works to be supplied with water from the canal. The canal company acted as if they owned the waters of the Taff.[15] These facts might not have mattered provided the water was being returned to the river above Pentyrch's weir but no water was passing over the Parliamentary Weir at Nantgarw because the canal company had built another weir at the head of the next lock (Treble Locks), with a watercourse around the locks and into the pond below. This weir was four inches lower in the crown than the Parliamentary Weir and *'not content with that they have made a skrew gate or sluice in this weir which draws up 9 inches and is three feet wide and is always kept up or opened in dry seasons, so that not a drop of water can escape over the weir intended for the benefit of the Pentyrch Works.'*[16] Harford Partridge and Co joined William Lewis in the expense of bringing the case to a special jury at the Great Sessions at Cardiff. To help argue Lewis's case, they employed an engineer, Weldon, who produced a model of Treble Locks and the weirs. Lewis won and was awarded a nominal £100 damages '*with a view to settle the question of right*', although his claim had been for damages of £1,500.[17]

Harford Partridge & Co then prepared their own similar action and the name of Richard Blakemore, twenty-seven year old nephew of John Partridge, first appears on the scene, as he started to take an interest in Melingriffith whilst he was managing another of the partnership's concerns - Monmouth Forge. For the next thirty years, Blakemore was to develop into an art the bringing of legal actions against the Glamorganshire Canal Company. Like Lewis, Blakemore challenged the legality of the canal company's building its second feeder at Quakers' Yard. He wondered whether it was possible to fit gauges on the two weirs so that the water the canal company extracted could be restricted. He was also seriously considering prosecuting Hopkin David, the lockkeeper at Melingriffith, for perjury in the previous case, presumably in the hope that he would be forced to be more truthful when next called as witness.[18] The plea of trespass was heard before a special jury at the 1803 Summer Assize in Hereford and again a nominal award of £100 damages was given in acknowledgement that

The view from the top of Treble Locks was equally dramatic, as this study of circa 1904 shows. The gas retort seems to be still in working order to illuminate the locks and enable round-the clock operation. There is no sign of any need for that, however, and no evidence of the traffic congestion of earlier decades. The upper reservoir also is in good condition but unnecessarily so because, by this time, the Pentyrch Forge needed little water and the reservoir was redundant. There was a boat dock here on the right, in the field between the locks and the Parliamentary Weir. It is mentioned twice in the minutes of 1818 and is shown on Harrison's map of 1830 but by the 1870s it had gone. On the canal bend, in line with the reservoir dam, is Rhiw Ddar Bridge. In the far centre distance, the Barry Railway's Walnut Tree Viaduct can just be made out, spanning the Taff gap. SR collection

Real excitement, as a party of picnickers aboard the steam tug Bute *prepares to enter Lock 37, the bottom of the Treble Locks, with the assistance of a boat horse.* CCL collection

Melingriffith had been wronged.[19]

However, even as Richard Blakemore was remitting the legal fees for the case to their solicitor, John Powell, in August 1803 he was commenting that the canal company were contemplating making some alteration to the weirs at Melingriffith but did not intend to take in the tailwater nor to improve the engine. A month later he was proposing further litigation.[2]

On 26 October, Richard Crawshay inspected the canal at Melingriffith, accompanied by the canal company's clerk, Philip Williams and committee member Thomas Bourne (who was also Clerk to the County of Glamorgan). There followed a correspondence with John Harford. Crawshay, of course, had made sure he had witnessed the regulating planks on the (illegal) Melingriffith Lock bypass weir as being three inches higher than the level of the Parliamentary Weir, which conveniently resulted in a steady stream of water from two to three inches deep across the full seventeen feet width of the weir. With all this water entering the Melingriffith feeder, Crawshay, disregarding his obligations under the Act and deciding that attack was the best method of defence, concluded that the engine was of little use to the canal company, because it was not able to return that same amount of water to the canal below the lock. Harford had intimated that he was keen

Treble Locks, standing derelict two years after the last boat had passed. The reservoir is empty. ILW photo 1 Mar 1944 neg 257

to have the engine removed because of its inconvenience and he claimed that it was always intended that '*after a certain time*', the engine would be given up for the benefit of his works. Crawshay therefore instructed Williams to write to Harford on behalf of the canal committee, consenting to the removal of the engine and its use by Melingriffith '*at a fair valuation*' but advising that really such action would not be in Harford's best interest. He recommended, as an aside, that Melingriffith would do well to harness the power of the overflow at its Parliamentary Weir, where the head was about four foot higher than further down the feeder, where the water was actually used by the works' waterwheels. This was clearly easier said than done, even if the overflow supply could be guaranteed – which Harford knew it could not because it was the very subject of dispute. Harford, his partners and Richard Blakemore did not find this advice at all helpful and they must have realised that nothing was to be gained by reducing the canal company's water supply by removing the pump; it would simply encourage the canal company to continue to run water past Melingriffith Lock.[21]

Negotiations predictably broke down as a result of Crawshay's disingenuous advice. At the following summer's assize at Hereford, a special jury once again found in favour of Harford Partridge & Co and this time £300 damages was awarded.

Melingriffith's complaints were unending as their works were continually at a standstill at times of low water, the cause of which they always placed at the canal company's door. The canal company, for their part, were spending money in keeping the lock at Melingriffith in the most watertight condition possible but opening the bypass sluices whenever they too suffered from low water. Not much had changed in ten years.

On 30 March 1805 and again on 5 April John Harford served notices on the canal proprietors. He proposed that his company take over the operation of the canal lock at Melingriffith. The committee's

The ghost of Treble Locks remains as the A470 rises past the surviving lock house, on its way to the Nantgarw interchange. ILW photo 1 Sept 1970 neg 2229

(*i.e.* Crawshay's) response was an emphatic No! but

> '*if the Melin Griffith Company wish to propose any plan which may be less objectionable, the Committee will give it their serious attention. Not that they are convinced of the real injury the Melin Griffith Co. complain of, but from a real wish to prevent animosity and litigation.*'[22]

Both the canal company and Harford Partridge & Co used the same solicitor, John Powell of Brecon. Crawshay visited Powell to discuss how the two concerns could settle their differences. It seems that Powell suggested that both companies retain independent engineers to act as joint consultants. Crawshay must at this time have regretted the recent departure of his former partner and inventive engineer Watkin George to Benjamin Hall's Union Iron Works at Rhymney. John Harford and Richard Blakemore were invited to attend the next canal committee meeting on 7 May, at which it was recorded:

> '*It is hereby agreed between the parties that Mr Rennie shall be applied to on the part of the Canal Co to meet Mr Jessop the Surveyor on the part of the Melin Griffith Co that from the Surveys & Reports of those Gentlemen a foundation may be laid for an amicable adjustment of all matters in dispute.*'

They hoped both engineers would have completed their task and be able to present their written recommendations to the GCC Annual General Meeting on 5 June23.

William Jessop and John Rennie were the foremost water engineers in the country. Jessop was sixteen years Rennie's senior and, in 1805, was sixty years old. In earlier years, he had been accustomed to reviewing many of Rennie's schemes but for the past ten years or so both engineers were considered to be of equal status. Jessop had been Chief Engineer of the Grand Junction Canal and, in 1796, had proposed locks over Blisworth Summit supplied with water by steam engines; the committee asked for a second opinion and chose Rennie's and Robert Whitworth's alternative of a tunnel. Both Jessop and Rennie had worked with James Watt, Jessop in his scheme to drain the Fens with steam engines and Rennie actually being employed by Watt in 1784. In 1800, Jessop and Rennie had worked together in recommending steam power as the only certain way of draining Deeping Fen.[24] Richard Crawshay had taken advice from Jessop when he was promoting the Glamorganshire Canal in February 1790.[25] Rennie was to be appointed not just for Melingriffith but to help resolve the company's other major water dispute – with the Plymouth Ironworks.

The 5 June target was wildly optimistic but, on 22 August 1805, the canal company committee meeting was attended by Samuel and John Harford and Richard Blakemore, and heads of agreement were drawn up between the two parties. These are worth quoting in full:

> '*That the present Water Engine in Messrs Harford Partridge & Co's ditch at Melin Griffith shall be given up to them to be applied as they may think fit and the Canal Co at Messrs Harford Partridge & Co's request & expense to make any alterations or improvements therein which they shall*

Previous page: *A lock house was ordered to be built at Portobello in June 1815 but a structure does not appear on the 1830 map. Further evidence that it had not been built comes from the minutes of 1834, when a second erection order was given. One assumes this circa 1908 postcard view shows the lockkeeper's family lined up against the balance beam of the top gate. The stone tiles on the roof had been recently pointed and their garden is something to be proud of.*
SR collection

Above: *Portobello Lock and lockkeeper's cottage in 1944. Forest Row and the Portobello limestone quarry are seen beyond the lock. At the time, the cottage was occupied by the widow of a canal pensioner. It was one of the few buildings still roofed with stone tiles, possibly obtained from Llantwit Fardre. Note that the porch to the cottage has been re-designed since the 1908 view.*
ILW photo 31 March 1944, neg 254

Right: *Another study of Portobello Lock (Lock 40) and lock house. Note the stone steps on the lock house side, which allowed access to moored boats on the bank opposite the towpath. The bridge in the background carried the former Rhymney Railway line.*
ILW photo 1946, neg 335

This 1906 view from the Barry Railway's Walnut Tree Viaduct shows quite a lot of canal- and railway-related activity. The canal swings in from Cae Glas Lock, in the left distance, and at Portobello Lock is crossed by the Rhymney Railway, nearing the end of its long descent from Penrhos to its junction with the Taff Vale Railway here at Walnut Tree. From the time it opened and until Caerphilly Tunnel was driven, this was the RR's route to Cardiff, with running powers over the TVR from Walnut Tree Junction. The RR's locomotive shed, to the left of the works, still survives. The works which dominates the centre of the photograph started in 1864 as the Garth Anchor & Chain Works. It had its own canal basin whose entrance (hidden in this view by the bend of the canal) was spanned by a surviving cast iron towpath bridge, dated 1865. For a ten year period from 1884 it was a Patent Fuel works, after which it reverted to being an iron foundry. Across the canal and behind Forest Row are the Portobello limestone quarries; they had a tramroad connection to the canal between the two terraces of housing. At this time, during the building of the Cardiff Railway they also had a railway connection to the RR, via a zig-zag junction and across the wooden canal bridge, to supply stone for the building of Queen Alexandra Dock at Cardiff (see Vol 1 pp216-222). The substantial building in the right foreground is the Walnut Tree Inn, facing the main Merthyr road where it crossed the canal. SR collection

require. That the Canal Co shall on the first day of January next pay Messrs Harford Partridge & Co the sum of £700 for setting up a Fire Engine to throw into the upper level of the Canal the Water of the Taff after passing Melin Griffith Works & the Canal Co shall pay Messrs Harford Partridge & Co during the continuance of their interest in the Melin Griffith Works the yearly sum of £90 for working the said Fire Engine on every first day of January & the first payment thereof to be made on the first day of January 1807.

In consideration of the premises Messrs Harford Partridge & Co to relinquish all claims for damages already sustained or hereafter to be sustained by the Water taken for the necessary supply of the Canal between Melin Griffith and the Sea & that the manner securing such supply at Melin Griffith by means of the said Fire Engine or otherwise shall be referred to the determination of Mr Rennie & Mr Jessop & that Mr John Powell shall apply to them for that purpose & take all other necessary steps for carrying this agreement into full execution & effect that proper Instruments be prepared and to be executed by the parties accordingly with all convenient speed after Messrs Rennie's & Jessop's determination & specification shall be received.'[26]

All that was awaited was the design of the fire (or steam) engine to replace the existing water-driven pump – or so it seemed.

Rennie seems to have been playing hard to get and it is unclear whether he had visited Melingriffith before the August heads of agreement meeting, or even had accepted the commission. Crawshay had written to him on 9 May and again on 8 June. Having received no reply, on 3 Sept Philip Williams sent Rennie a copy of the heads of agreement requesting '*that the business should be settled as soon as possible your engagements and Mr Jessop's will admit. An early answer to this will much Oblige.*' Williams' further letter of 14 November at last elicited a favourable reply. Both Jessop and Rennie were then informed that the week of 13-21 December was the most convenient for Harford Partridge & Co and the canal company committee to receive them. Rennie and Jessop attended the 21 Dec GCC meeting '*having viewed the Canal & Works at Melingriffith & from thence to the Sea and having rec'd all necessary information to enable them to make their report.*' They both had to leave by 6 o'clock next morning but undertook to deliver their report to John Powell within two months.[27]

In fact the report was not completed until 1 March 1806 and was laid before the committee meeting on 11 March.[28] Powell was instructed to draw up the proper deeds of agreement. He had completed it by 29 April and Benjamin Hall was sent a copy for his opinion (perhaps he in turn sought Watkin George's comments from Rhymney).[29]

Just when progress seemed to be being made, the uneasy peace was broken again. On 29 March, it was reported that Richard Blakemore had written to both Jessop and Rennie with his own suggested amendments to their award. The canal committee instantly disapproved; they themselves were so pleased with the engineers' report that they refused to entertain any discussion. A nervous correspondence

The cast date of 1865 on the towpath bridge which crossed the entrance to the Garth ironworks basin. ILW photo, neg 2260

ensued throughout the summer but Melingriffith would not accept the report as it stood and the canal committee would not consider any amendments. At one point, Williams had to write to John Powell (still solicitor to both canal company and Melingriffith) to warn him never to let the award and associated papers out of his hands but to keep them in his possession for the use of both parties.[30]

A lengthy draft copy of the articles of agreement survives in the Maybery papers at the National Library of Wales, the source of which was the practice of William and John Powell of Brecon. It would appear to be a combination of the 22 Aug 1805 heads of agreement and the Jessop and Rennie Award, which Powell had begun to draft as instructed by the canal company committee on 11 March 1806.[31] The main additional provisions to the 22 Aug 1805 agreement are as follows:

'i) the Melin Griffith Company should by iron pipes 18 inches in diameter and a culvert of the same dimensions convert water for 24 hours on every Saturday and Sunday, or either of those days, from the Mill Head of Melin Griffith works into the pond immediately below Melin Griffith lock and the Canal Co should make, at the expense of Melin Griffith Co, a watercourse from the tail water of the pond below the third lock below Melin Griffith lock exclusively, to be 4 feet in width at bottom and not less than 3 feet in depth with the necessary slopes;

ii) if an obstacle should arise to making the cut, the Melin Griffith Company should make the culvert and iron pipes of 3 feet in diameter, and if there is a deficiency of water during the week in any of the ponds between Melin Griffith and the tideway, the Melin Griffith Co should allow the sluice of the culvert to be drawn so that the Canal Company should not suffer inconvenience through want of water;

iii) if the Melin Griffith Company feared that the occasional supply of water in the week should prove inconvenient, they should be permitted to lay down the 18 inch culvert for Sunday water and raise the additional water by means of a steam engine into the pond below Melin Griffith lock equal to the said supply, or by an engine of greater power into a

The lower section of the canal competed for water with the Pentyrch Ironworks. This ironworks had been founded in the 1740s, to the west of the River Taff and using water from the river to drive its rolling mills further downstream. (The sixteenth century ironworks and ordnance foundry is believed to have stood in the tributary valley to the left, between the Little and Greater Garths.) This panoramic photograph shows the whole of the derelict Pentyrch Ironworks complex, in 1906. The view is looking up the Taff Valley from the side of the Little Garth, where the limestone and ironstone were extracted. The line of houses on the Greater Garth hillside marks the southern outcrop of the South Wales Coalfield. Here, coal was worked from levels and delivered into the mining and iron workers village of Gwaelod y Garth via several long tramroad inclines. From Gwaelod, the main connecting tramroad ran south to bring the coal to the brickworks and the coke ovens. The building catching the sun and looking like a church tower is the fan house of the Lan Colliery, a drift mine to the lower seams and provider of most of the on-site coal in the works' final years. Between the two Garths, the quarry on the left was the source of clay for the brickworks (centre), which operated independently as the Glamorgan Brick Works after closure of the ironworks.

In the foreground is the focus of all these concerns – the remains of the coke ovens, the three blast furnaces, the boiler houses, the blowing engine house and the casting houses of the Pentyrch Ironworks. The two earlier stone-clad furnaces survive today in truncated form, buried beneath the housing estate that now occupies this site; the third furnace of 1874 had been ironclad and was just a pile of rubble alongside the other two when this photograph was taken.

The wide feeder can be seen clearly, running from the river weir (across the river from the village gas works and the stone hut covering the hot spring which gave the settlement its name), past the low-lying terraces of workers cottages at the Lan Level near the brickworks, then behind the furnaces and on its way to the forge (out of picture).

Across the river, in the parish of Eglwys Ilan, are Taff's Well and Glan y Llyn. Far in the distance are Treble Locks and the Rhiw Ddar reservoirs. Contractors' locomotives work on completing the route of the Cardiff Railway near where it crosses the canal at Taff's Well Lock. Still further north, a plume of smoke rises from Craig yr Allt Colliery.

The route of the TVR can also be made out as it passes through Taff's Well, crosses the river and turns north past Ynysgau Junction and signal box, where the Pentyrch railway (successor to the tramroad) joined the main line. The TVR superintendent's report of 16 September 1845 records the connection made here at Ynysgau Colliery. As a final aside, this panorama is assembled from two E. T. Bush picture postcards, Nos. 2329 and 2330.

SR collection

small reservoir capable of 5 or 6 locks full of water above the level of the upper pond to be made on the east side of the Melin Griffith lock, so that by means of a culvert and draw gate through the side wall of the lock they might fill the locks for the passage of boats without drawing any water from the pond above Melin Griffith lock, except for reasonable waste, such reservoir to have a waste weir for discharging the necessary water into the pond below the lock;

iv) that the Canal Co should raise the banks of the Canal between the Melin Griffith lock and the lock next below so as to hold water in the pond between the said locks 12 inches higher than the present level.'

The old term Fire Engine (at one time used to denote a Newcomen engine as compared to a Boulton & Watt Steam Engine) was that used by the Melingriffith representatives and the canal committee in their 1805 heads of agreement, and this term is perpetuated in Powell's draft articles, alongside the term Steam Engine in that part which comes from the engineers' award. The canal company minutes similarly referred to the Pontyrhun engine as a Fire Engine.[32] Blakemore's suggested amendments are not known. It is quite apparent, though, that these articles do seek more to safeguard the canal company's water supply below Melingriffith than to safeguard the supply to the tinplate works. Perhaps this is why Blakemore could not bring himself to accept his own consultant's recommendations. There is no mention of Melingriffith in the otherwise comprehensive volumes of John Rennie's reports now held at the Institute of Civil Engineers. If the 3 October 1806 letter from Philip Williams to the Melingriffith company is to be believed, it was Jessop himself who contributed most to the scheme:

'We adopted the plan & employed the persons suggested

The Barry Railway's Walnut Tree viaduct (1901-1969), which was part of a direct route between Barry Docks and the collieries of the Rhymney Valley, dominates this view of the Taff Gap, towering above the buildings of Pentyrch Forge, which was driven by the waters of the Pentyrch feeder. Iron, smelted at the furnaces, was refined into bars here at the forge and then carried further down the valley to Melingriffith to be rolled and made into tinplate. Sam Allen, in his Reminiscences *(pp167-8), tells how he decorated the 1866 chimney stack with two eagles in red brick and a bottle of porter from The Lewis Arms at Tongwynlais for each eye. At the time this photograph was taken, circa 1908, the site was occupied by Waterhouse Bros, manufacturing iron hollow ware. In its last years as a foundry, it was run by T.A. Lawrence & Son, producing railway points, crossings and railway chairs. Their manhole covers and drain covers too, are still to be seen serving their original purpose in the locality. Lawrence's foundry continued until after the Second World War but was probably last to use the Pentyrch Railway to Ynysgau in the late 1930s. They ran two locomotives,* Verdun *and* Princess Mary*; the locomotive shed was on the right, just out of picture.*
SR collection

This late 19th century photograph by Harvey Barton & Sons of Bristol is dramatic proof of how low the river level could get, through the combined diversion of its summer waters by the Pentyrch Ironworks and the Glamorganshire Canal. The stepping stones carried the route to Pentyrch but also gave access to the ironworks from the settlements at Portobello and Walnut Tree (later to become part of the enlarged village of Taff's Well). The cinder tips of the ironworks, on the left, were later taken to Cardiff for use in land reclamation during the building of Queen Alexandra Dock.
SR collection

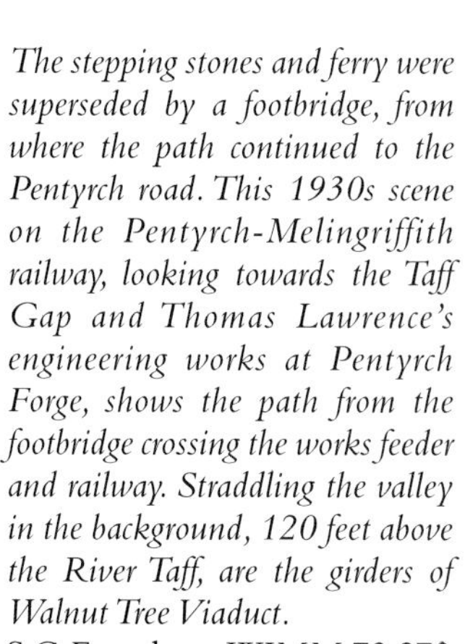

The stepping stones and ferry were superseded by a footbridge, from where the path continued to the Pentyrch road. This 1930s scene on the Pentyrch-Melingriffith railway, looking towards the Taff Gap and Thomas Lawrence's engineering works at Pentyrch Forge, shows the path from the footbridge crossing the works feeder and railway. Straddling the valley in the background, 120 feet above the River Taff, are the girders of Walnut Tree Viaduct.
S.C. Fox photo, WIMM 73.273

and recommended by yourselves and have every reason to believe your Engineer Mr Jessop had the forming the award which you have had the address to persuade him to abandon.'[33]

Jessop's own papers have not survived.[34]

The canal company felt there was no need to negotiate and they continued to press for Blakemore to accept the award unaltered. Meanwhile, so pleased was the GCC with him, that Rennie was retained to make proposals to improve the water supply to the upper section of the canal at Merthyr and, late in October, he presented his interim report to the canal company committee.[35] At that meeting, they discussed with him the Melingriffith scheme and agreed to pay the £700 cash in order to press Melingriffith into acceptance. A note of the minute was sent to Melingriffith.[36] Three days later, Williams was reminding Crawshay by letter that Charles, their banker, had not yet received Crawshay's cheque to enable him to pay the Harfords.[37] Had Crawshay had second thoughts or had Harford and Blakemore already refused to accept the money?

We are therefore left to wonder whether anything did take place on the ground as a result of Jessop and Rennie's award. What is certain is that the water engine was not replaced with a steam engine, nor were the weekend bypass pipes and culvert constructed, nor were the storage reservoir and steam pump built, and it is doubtful that the enlarged lock bypass watercourse was built at Mynachdy (the lock below the third lock from Melingriffith). Yet scholars of the canal and of Melingriffith persist in referring to the water pump (which still survives) as being of John Rennie's design of 1806. The sources of this conclusion probably all stem from John Lloyd's incompletely quoting the 1806 draft articles of agreement[38] and the fact that Rennie went

A similar but later image to that in Volume 1, p216. In the foreground are the lower forges of the Pentyrch Ironworks but behind is the locomotive shed for the Pentyrch railway. The river bridge here was only built in 1808. Before that a ferry connected Pentyrch Forge with its wharf on the canal at the Ynys Bridge. From the lower right, the road crosses the tailrace of the Pentyrch feeder, the Pentyrch to Melingriffith railway, the River Taff, the Taff Vale Railway and the Glamorganshire Canal, before reaching the turnpike road a short distance across the valley. The river makes a wide bend and can be seen reappearing at Tongwynlais, where a high retaining wall has been built to protect the canal from the newly-constructed Cardiff Railway. SR collection

on to design a more sophisticated water driven pump at Claverton on the Kennet & Avon Canal in 1811. These writers all conveniently ignore the term Fire Engine and take it to mean Water Engine! Who is to say that the engine at Melingriffith today is not the original Watkin George design of 1795?

When the following year's dry season loomed, Crawshay reverted to their original agreement and made a new offer to John Harford that the canal company would pay £350 and £45 a year towards the support of an engine, '*otherwise both parties are liable to the Expd of the award made by Messrs Rennie & Jessop and it must be submitted to.*' Harford rejected the offer.[39] The only evidence the present writers have found that the Watkin George engine was possibly replaced at this time, is in a rough draft of evidence prepared on behalf of the Melingriffith company in the autumn of 1810, which states '*the Canal Co … fit up an Engine four Years ago in the Tail race of the MG Works to raise Water into the Canal and in order to obtain a Head of Water to Work this Engine they put a dam or floodgates quite across the Melingriffith Tail race.*'[40] This work is not recorded in the canal company's minute books and no special item for a new engine is recorded in their accounts. It is possible that, whilst working on the Glynduris and Pontyrhun scheme, John Rennie took some time to visit the Melingriffith site and advise on a realignment of the existing engine, all parties being reconciled to the fact that his and Jessop's award would never be implemented.

It should not be assumed, because of the continual disputes over water rights, that good business relations were impossible between Harford Partridge & Co and the Glamorganshire Canal Co. Bird's *Guide to Cardiff* of 1796 states that '*Not less than 13,000 boxes annually of the very best tin plates are sent from the town to Bristol*' and in 1803, Malkin observed that Melingriffith was perhaps the largest tinplate works in the world.[41] Not only was this output sent down the canal to Cardiff but the raw materials were also imported via the canal and coal was delivered by canal boat from the company's levels at Craig yr Allt. Melingriffith was one of the canal's main traders (after the much larger ironworks at Merthyr and some collieries) and its partners continued to hold shares in the canal company.

Another indication that sense could prevail is that, amid the frustrations of the Jessop and Rennie affair, in 1807 both companies agreed to exchange land so that the canal towpath could be diverted to the opposite side to the works at Melingriffith. Initially, a swingbridge took the towpath across the canal upstream of the works.[42] Its awkwardness caused the death of at least two horses falling into the water. Boatman E. James was paid 5 guineas compensation by the Melingriffith Company to which was added a further 9 guineas by the canal company. William Jones, a boatman

The Pentyrch and Melingriffith works lay more than two miles apart and were on opposite sides of the River Taff. To improve communications between them, Richard Blakemore built a tramroad in 1812-5, which followed the river and works feeders and crossed the Taff at Cilynys Farm. When the TVR was built in 1840, it had to cross the horse-worked tramroad on the level near Ty Nant. On 4 May 1847, the TVR directors authorised a railway siding to a limestone quarry near Pentyrch, to be worked by Thomas Morgan. We assume that this was the Ty Nant Quarry, once prominent against the Little Garth opposite Castell Coch. Its new standard gauge siding, on leaving the TVR would have reached the quarry by sharing the same formation as the tramroad. In 1871, the Melingriffith & Pentyrch Company converted its tramroad to a standard gauge railway and built an iron bridge for it to cross the Taff. The TVR directors minutes of 15 September and 13 October record agreement that the railway company would execute the work at the Ty Nant crossing on its behalf. The through route from Melingiffith to Pentyrch was cut after the closure of Pentyrch Ironworks but the Taff's Well quarry owners, Thomas Edwards & son, were taking out roadstone from their Ty Nant Quarry via the TVR at this point as late as the 1930s. These two photographs of the crossing and Pentyrch exchange siding were taken on 16 April 1954. In the bottom view, looking north towards Castell Coch, a Down coal train from Rhondda Fach passes the TVR's former Pentyrch Station on its way to Cardiff docks. The locomotive is No 5608, of the GWR '56XX' Class of 0-6-2 tanks, built for service in South Wales. The top picture shows an Up empty wagons train, hauled by another '56XX' Class 0-6-2, No 6643. Booker's Road (as the TVR called it) was still in use between this point and Melingriffith; the exchange siding is on the right. Just along the Melingriffith line to the left is Cilynys Farm. With the final closure of Melingriffith, the crossing was removed by British Railways in 1961.

Both R.J. Doran

The canalside village of Tongwynlais, here seen from Castell Coch, marks the River Taff's and the canal's exit from the coalfield and the beginning of their final stretch to the sea. The canal would never again get so close to the river until they met at the Sea Lock, below Cardiff. The canal meanders past Ivy House (see Volume 1, p247), through the high, straight Cardiff Railway embankment, round the old village to Ton Lock and then plunges into the Long Wood, making for the tall chimney of Melingriffith Tinplate Works in the left distance. From the right, with the same goal in mind, the Pentyrch railway (former tramroad) passes through the Elizabethan Cilynys Farm and crosses the river on Iron Bridge. While the main line of the tramroad followed the river bend to Melingriffith, the line of its branch to Ton Lock cuts right across the photograph along Ironbridge Road. Perched on top of the railway embankment, left of centre, is the platform of Tongwynlais Station. SR collection

from Canton, was similarly compensated 8 guineas.[43] Harford Partridge & Co agreed that the swing bridge could be removed and for their own bridge to be shared with the canal company for horses and boatmen to cross.[44] The 1849 cast iron replacement of this bridge survives but was removed in 1990 and re-sited near the renovated pump by members of Oxford House Industrial Archaeology Society of Risca and the Inland Waterways Association.

Only another year was to pass before battle lines began to be drawn again. The canal company made a point of minuting '*Messrs Harford & Co having altered their Mill Tail Race by which the Water is taken from our Engine ... in consequence of which we shall be under the necessity of supplying the Canal with water by taking it through the Paddles at the Melingriffith Lock ...*'.[45] The man who bore the brunt of this decision was Hopkin David, the loyal lockkeeper, who must have undertaken his duties uneasily in the shadow of the tinplate works. For working the engine, David received an annual allowance of 5 guineas.[46] Thomas Reece (who replaced Philip Williams as Clerk in June 1808, following Williams' death) wrote to David with an attempt at reassurance:

> '*Whenever the Canal betwixt M'Griffith and the Sea Lock is in want of a supply of Water and there be no prospects of obtaining the same from the Engine, you are desired to take through the Melingriffith Lock as much water as will be necessary for the purpose of the Canal. I do not wish you to run Water for every single boat but whenever there are three or four boats together you will run through the lock enough to Navigate, taking good care that no water is wasted & the Boatmen by no means be suffered to flush Water in any Lock below M'Griffith. As to Mr Blakemore's threats to send you to Gaol you need not be under the least Fear on that head, for the Canal Co will always protect their Servants from receiving any harm by doing their duty. I beg you will attend to the above & not suffer the Boats to be detained as they were last Week.*'[47]

Hopkin David would have wisely kept that letter in a safe place.

Pentyrch and Melingriffith Under Single Management

By this time, from 1 July 1808, the partnership of Harford Partridge & Co had been dissolved. Richard Blakemore, with Joseph Reynolds and two of the old partners, Thomas Prichard (of Ross on Wye) and Richard Jones Tomlinson (of Bristol), took over the Melingriffith Company, which since 1804-5 had also included the Pentyrch Iron Works, and operated under the name of Reynolds Blakemore & Company. Blakemore adopted full managerial control and over the years he acquired the interests of his fellow partners.[48]

Where its former proprietor, William Lewis, may have

Tongwynlais Village

Two contrasting views of Tongwynlais showing the changes which took place in the fifty years that separate their taking. In the top view, which dates from around 1900, the canal snakes its way through the village, with only the River Taff on the right for company. By 1902, the Cardiff Railway had reached Tongwynlais, pushing its way through the village on an embankment which bordered the canal at this point. By the time the later photograph was taken on 12 April 1951, however, the canal was abandoned and the railway, temporarily retrieved, was the outlet for coal and coke for the new NCB plant at Nantgarw. This section of the Cardiff Railway was abandoned in 1952; today the line terminates at Coryton, a couple of miles south of here. Top SR collection; bottom ILW photo neg No. 1098

This lovely circa 1905 view, from a glass lantern slide, is looking north along the canal towpath at Tongwynlais, with the Marquess of Bute's Castell Coch high up on the right. The River Taff can just be seen down on the left, whilst the Merthyr Road runs above the canal in the centre background.
S.C. Fox collection, courtesy WIMM

been somewhat reticent in fighting for Pentyrch's water rights,[49] Richard Blakemore relished the prospect and he increased the pressure on the canal company to honour its obligations to maintain an adequate water supply to both Melingriffith and Pentyrch. A further lawsuit was prepared in 1810.

At this time, Melingriffith Works consisted of four mills, two forges, cold rolls and a shearing machine all powered by ten water wheels. The three forges at Pentyrch Works were powered by five water wheels.

Mindful that the canal company were bound to use as their defence his refusal to honour the Jessop and Rennie award, Blakemore chose to attack the underlying causes of their continual dispute. In the preamble to his case he asked why the canal company should persevere in open defiance of the verdicts already found in his company's favour. Richard Crawshay died in 1810, perhaps to the relief of even his most Christian of business rivals. Blakemore gave as the main cause of the dispute:

> '*That the entire & uncontrolled management of the Concern & near a moeity of all the Shares in the undertaking unhappily for the Plts & for the Country at large got into the Hands of Mr Crawshay the Ironmaster of Cyfarthfa in Merthyr of whom being but a few weeks dead and leaving immense wealth behind him (an infallible protector to its possessor) we will forbear to speak further than that he was a man of the most overbearing tyrannical Disposition with whom every effort for redress & for an amicable accommodation which was unceasingly tried Year after Year & even to the Hour of his Death failed altho the means were easy & practicable on terms that would afford to both Parties the most ample enjoyment of their respective Concerns & at a small expense much less than has already been spent in the Court of Law between them.*'

With respect to the award, the case states '*Mr Jessop … acknowledges that he had done an act of Injustice to the MG Co in consulting to it.*' This statement does undermine Blakemore's argument that he and Harford had been expecting to be able to discuss the engineers' report but which Crawshay and the canal company were prepared to accept unchanged.

The subject of the two 1810 cases in the Court of Exchequer is little different from the previous ones. The

The desolation is clearly evident at Ivy House in this 1962 photograph. The former canal-side warehouse still stands on the right bank, beyond the broken parapets of one of Dadford's fine bridges. The Ton Brook pours into the canal bed, washing away the untidy work of fly-tippers, before disappearing beneath the towpath and into the River Taff. The whole scene is overlooked by the equally redundant stone parapet of the Cardiff Railway bridge.
Roger Peakman

heads of complaint concerning the Melingriffith case were:

i) The head of water required to operate the engine reduced the efficiency of Melingriffith's own water wheels by washing back on them and restricted the further development of water power in the works. Blakemore wanted the engine removed;
ii) Excess water was being allowed through the Melingriffith Lock in contravention of the Act;
iii) The canal and locks below Melingriffith were in a poor state of repair resulting in water wastage.

The heads of complaint concerning the Pentyrch case were:

i) The 'fraudulent' weir on the three mile pond below Nantgarw was lower in level than the Parliamentary Weir, thus allowing the water to run round the Treble Locks instead of over the Parliamentary Weir to the Taff;
ii) The Treble Locks were in a poor state of repair so allowing water to leak through them;
iii) Boatmen flushed their boats through the locks.

Blakemore now invited John Rennie to give evidence but he declined '*on account of prior engagements*' and recommended Bryan Durkin, who was brought in to survey the state of the canal. Among his findings was that there was a steady stream of water one inch deep over the whole length of the 27 foot cill of the sea lock. This was used to imply that the canal was wasting water.

It was said in evidence that the arrangement at the Melingriffith engine required pounding back the tail water of their water wheels to a depth of 2ft 3in, instead of allowing it to run away freely. James Stevens, a former forgeman at the works, frequently had to go down to the engine and, against threats from the canal employees, draw up the flood gates to release this tail water so that his hammer wheel could work. The blades of the wheel often became broken under the strain of the backwater and he estimated that he often lost four to five shillings a week in his work by such hindrances.

Further evidence on the state of the canal and water wastage was given by the Penydarren Company's agent, Edward Edmunds of Nantgarw, who had been an active trader on the canal since the start. His boatman for seventeen years, William Morgan, and another boatman, David Evans, were scathing. The College Pond would empty from leakage in 24 hours if no supply of water were brought in additional to that required for navigation. Thomas Rowland, a navvy employed under Dadford in cutting the canal, claimed that 4-500 yards of the Great House pond (that between Melingriffith Lock and Llandaff Lock) had been neither lined nor puddled. Charles Phillips, Llandaff lockkeeper, and Christopher French, the lockkeeper between Llandaff Lock and Cardiff, were seldom to be seen, so that boatmen were at liberty to draw water from pond to pond and to flush their boats out of the locks.

Blakemore claimed damages of £10,000 to cover lost output from both works and also the 'play wages' which had to be paid to retain his employees when the works were idle through lack of water power. The case also states that the canal company had spent upwards of £15,000 in law suits in twenty years, of which more than £3,000 had been with the Melingriffith alone and £6-8,000 with the Plymouth Iron Works.[50] The profitable canal company, limited in what dividend they were allowed to declare, could afford these costs.

This new case prompted the canal company to make a waste weir below Treble Locks for the benefit of Pentyrch.[51] They were adamant in not removing the engine at

The tollhouse building on the course of the Pentyrch-Melingriffith tramroad at Cilynys river bridge. This interesting building may have been provided for the tramroad as early as 1815. Its position near the eastern approach to the tramroad bridge at Ironbridge Road, Tongwynlais, suggests a bridgekeeper's lodge where tolls were taken from members of the public using the bridge. Its siting in the V-junction of two tramroads would have been convenient for controlling the turnout to the branch tramroad leading to the Ton canal wharf. Again, the lodge may indicate a position where tram waggons were weighed before being hauled to the canal because the tramroad was used by the stone quarry owners as well as the Pentyrch & Melingriffith Company. The Melingriffith Works Accounts for 1853 include paying Mary Howell for collecting tolls at the 'Tramroad and Tramroad Bridge'. The 63 year old widow is described as Gatekeeper in the 1851 census returns. In the photograph, Ironbridge Road is seen passing to the left of the building and in 1951 a number of stone sleeper blocks were still visible in the lane. The lodge has since been demolished.

ILW photo 12 April 1951 neg 1099

Melingriffith and Melingriffith continued to attempt to limit the effect of the backwater on their own machinery. Blakemore's repeated demands for compensation were out of the question.[52]

Again Blakemore won the law suit at Hereford but did not win the compensation. On 4 Feb 1811, we find the treasurer being ordered to pay the sum of £487 4s 4d to Messrs Wood, attorneys for the Melingriffith Company, being the awarded damages and taxed costs. Church's bill for representing the canal company amounted to £258 10s 10d.[53]

At this time, also, the Aberdare Canal was being built and was to form a junction with the Glamorganshire Canal at the lock flight at Abercynon. Blakemore sought to limit the amount of water which would pass from the Aberdare Canal into the Glamorganshire, by stipulating that the overflow weir at the stop lock between the two canals should discharge its water into the River Cynon, rather than bypass the lock and enter the Glamorganshire Canal. He argued that water from the Cynon was more likely to reach his works at Pentyrch than by flowing round the canal system.[54]

Although the law suits did no party any good, in June 1811, Richard Blakemore served yet another notice on the canal company's clerk, concentrating on his claims for compensation for water used and demanding that the engine be removed. In August he actually had a wall built to divert water from the engine, to which the canal company quickly protested.[55]

In 1813-14, Blakemore prepared affidavits to apply for a mandamus to the Court of King's Bench, which would direct the canal commissioners to award compensation to his company for even legally taken water. The canal's increase in traffic had made the water situation desperate for Melingriffith. Thomas Reece had to attend the proceedings in London and Benjamin Hall's capacity as Member of Parliament seems to have swung the case for the canal company, for a vote of thanks was given him at the committee meeting in June 1814. The canal company ensured that they retained the report by Maull, the barrister, of the proceedings and judgement.[56] Blakemore's claims for compensation remained frustrated.

During these years, Blakemore set about consolidating the combined operation of Pentyrch and Melingriffith. In 1808, the Ynys Bridge was built by Harford & Co across the Taff. This connected Pentyrch Works with the canal and the turnpike road as they passed through the Taff Gap near Castell Coch. In 1812, the old route by water between both works began to be replaced by a connecting tramroad, which S.W. Allen records as being opened in 1815. The tramroad crossed the Taff by a wooden bridge at Cilynys and then followed the bank of the river to Melingriffith. Here, Blakemore had planned a transshipment basin for Pentyrch below Melingriffith Lock, for which he was given authorisation by the canal committee. However, this must have proved impracticable, for the necessary bridge across the wide feeder tailrace seems never to have been made. Instead, the tramroad made it possible for Pentyrch to connect with a coal wharf at Ton Lock. The branch left the main line at Cilynys Bridge where a toll house was built, probably to collect tolls from members of the public using the bridge. In 1816, Blakemore installed a tip at Ton Lock for shipping coal from the basin there. Also, in November 1812, the Melingriffith company was given permission to expand its premises at the Cardiff wharf and build a new warehouse.[57]

Despite the critical shortage of water, the canal company persisted in acting as if it had the rights to all water in the Taff Valley. In January 1815, it allowed its committee

This superb view of Tongwynlais Lock dates from around 1910. Taken from one of the tail gates, it clearly shows the iron rack and pinion paddle gear and windlass on the gate. Two wooden tying up posts are installed on the towpath side, one for within the lock and one beyond the head gate, where boats would have needed to queue before taking their turn to pass through the lock. Lockkeeper Morgan Morgan is seated on some drainage pipes on the right and behind him can be seen the boat weighing dock, dating from 1836. The weighing machine, built by Brown Lenox to a design similar to that already in use on the Monmouthshire Canal at Newport, was moved to Cardiff – but the dock remained. James Israel's 1817 corn mill was also situted at Ton Lock (see Volume 1, p236), just behind the photographer on his left. It suspiciously derived its power from the canal's precious water. By 1825, it was operated by Rowland Thomas who was behind in his rent to the canal company.

SR collection

Lockkeeper Morgan Morgan leans on the beam of the upper gate in 1910. He had succeeded his father, also Morgan, at this lock. SR collection

Tongwynlais was an interesting lock, in a picturesque valley setting and watched over by Castell Coch. The lock house was set back at an angle to the canal, as shown here, giving an excellent view of what was going on at the lock. Sporting lean-to extensions on each side, it nevertheless shows its pedigree with the whitewashed walls. Note the headless cast iron lamp standard on the right, a relic of the days when the canal was so busy that night-time working was instigated, necessitating lighting of the locks. S.C. Fox photo, CCL collection GC17

member, Dr Richard Griffiths, to divert waste water to irrigate his farm at Blackweir.[58] In May 1817, it granted a lease below Ton Lock to James Israel, for erecting a corn mill and to utilise water from the canal. This was made at the very same meeting where a reply was made in person to Richard Blakemore's complaint that Pentyrch was being starved of water and waste water was bypassing Treble Locks. This would be the very water which Tongwynlais Mill would use to supplement the supply from the Ton Brook. Such action must have incensed Blakemore, who set about intimidating Israel to prevent him from building the mill. On 13 September, the canal company minuted their firm support for James Israel's mill and the conveyance was signed on 25 October.[59]

The Reservoirs at Treble Locks

The canal company did have some sense of responsibility in water conservation and the committee set about enforcing its bye-laws. In the summer of 1818, several boatmen were convicted for flushing water on the canal.[60] This did little to placate Richard Blakemore who, in February 1819, had already started another suit in Chancery.[61] However, at long last the canal company felt they were pushing their luck and William Crawshay junior, back on the committee (though not as chairman) following the death of his father's son-in-law Benjamin Hall, offered a more conciliatory approach. Crawshay and Richard Hill would meet Blakemore and his close friend John Scale (of Aberdare Ironworks) and discuss how their differences could be resolved out of court. Crawshay's skilful use of the independent Hill resulted in a frank report, with recommendations being placed before the June Special General Assembly of the canal company. Hill had experience of water disputes, when he was actively involved to the point of fighting the lockkeeper at Merthyr in support of his late father's campaign to preserve the water rights of his Plymouth Ironworks. After many years, that dispute had been resolved by John Rennie's proposals to make Glyndyrus

The Cardiff Photographic Society took a trip on the canal on 9 June 1894, in the steam tug Bute. *She is seen emerging from Ton Lock, under its locktail bridge and into the stretch of canal which passes through the Long Wood. On the left is the corn mill but who is that in the foreground waiting patiently away from the bustling lockside crowd? Is he the boat's engineer, moustachio'd, dressed in moleskin breeches tied up beneath the knee, with a tam o'shanter on his head and a smoking clay pipe in his mouth? On the left, some of the fortunate members of the CPS are seen on the deck and hold of the* Bute *– and not a camera in sight.*

Both CCL collection

Middle Lock, Lock Canol or Llwynmallt Lock, (Lock 42), giving a clear view of the top gate 'flasher' paddles operating mechanism. The ground paddle jack head has a protective iron rod bent over where the rack will rise, so preventing fouling of the tow rope. This was scenically one of the most attractive places on the canal. Certainly it was a favourite spot for Samuel Fox, who came here many times to photograph it. This is now the northern end of the Melingriffith to Tongwynlais Nature Reserve, where the canal water supply is culverted through an embankment carrying the road to Forest Farm industrial estate. The lock still exists but can no longer be seen from this viewpoint. S.C. Fox photo WIMM 73.85/60

One of the ubiquitous 0-6-2 tank engines hauls a coke train from Nantgarw across the Glamorganshire Canal at Middle Lock, on the former Cardiff Railway. The locomotive is ex-GWR No. 41, which was built in 1921 as Rhymney Railway No. 45. The abutments of this bridge survive on an inaccessible length of the canal sandwiched between the M4 embankment and the Forest Farm industrial estate access road embankment.
ILW photo 3 Jan 1952 neg 1176

Forest Lock and the lockkeepers house in the 1930s. The overflow weir ran behind the cottage, which appears to be part way through the process of receiving a new coat of whitewash. S.C. Fox photo

An evocative image in the Long Wood south of Forest Lock, near Whitchurch, as GCC boat No 504 passes empty on its way back to West Canal Wharf, Cardiff for loading. Note the square chimney on the cabin. The most likely boatman at the helm is Bill Thatcher of Rhydyfelin, who worked with Richard Williams of Dyffryn in the same village. As butty to Thatcher, Richard is out of the picture to the right and walking the towpath in charge of the horse. Both these men retired in 1939, leaving only two boats at work on the Pontypridd run. There seems to be a passenger seated in the hold, behind the mast. S.C. Fox photo WIMM 73.142

The water supply for the Melingriffith Tinplate Works was taken from the River Taff at Radyr weir. Just upstream at the feeder house is the entrance lock through which boats laden with iron from Pentrych Works entered the feeder and delivered their loads to the tinplate works. This method of communication probably stopped soon after the tramroad connection between the two works was established in 1815. In 1871, when the railway replaced the tramroad, the lock chamber was bridged and this now carries the Taff Trail cycle track across the lock remains. A TVR passenger train comprised mostly of 6-wheeled stock heads up the valley on the left of this circa 1906 view. SR collection

reservoir and install the Pontyrhun pumping engine. Perhaps this was a model upon which to base a renewed attempt to resolve the Melingriffith dispute. Furthermore, Blakemore may have been particularly relaxed in Hill's adjudicating, just as Blakemore himself had been called earlier in the year to resolve a dispute amongst the partners of the Merthyr Tramroad, on tonnages due from Hill.[62]

Hill's and Crawshay's report, without prejudice, recited Blakemore's perennial complaints but went on to propose:

> '*a reservoir should be made below the Treble Locks capable of containing 500 Locks of Water and that such reservoir should be discharged in the course of the Week from Sunday night to Saturday night into the pond below the Lock next below the Treble Locks at such times and in such manner as might be necessary for the supply of the Navigation from the said Lock to the Canal pond below Melin Griffith and that a Waste Weir should be made in the pond below the Treble Locks to discharge all the Water taken into the Canal (except on Sundays) into the River Taff above Pentyrch Weir – and that a side paddle should be put in the Lock below the Treble Locks for the purpose of discharging the Water thereof into the Aqueduct to be made for conveying the Water from the said Lock into the River Taff above the said Weir and that the paddles in the Tail Gate of such Locks should be stopped up.*'

In essence, the proposed reservoir was meant to store up excess water flowing around the canal on Sundays (when Pentyrch's rolling mills were standing) so that it could be used by the canal during the week. This would then allow Pentyrch use of the waters of the river during weekdays. To provide an adequate supply of water which would fill the reservoir on a Sunday, the report recommended that Tappendens' old feeder from the Clydach at Newbridge be brought back into use.[63] The report also recommended that canal water from Treble Locks to the Sea be used solely for navigation (to deter the canal company from further granting others rights to its water).

With regard to the Melingriffith pump, it recommended that the channel from the wheel to the river be deepened, which would enable the canal company to lower its water wheel by two feet and so remove the necessity for the sluices which currently dammed back the tailrace from the tinplate works and interfered with the effective operation of the works' machinery.

Blakemore accepted these recommendations and, prior to the presenting of the report, had acceded to contribute one half of the expense of the alterations at the wheel and watercourse, to the extent to him of £200. It was adopted by the Special General Assembly and Blakemore withdrew his latest legal proceedings, awaiting its implementation. Reece called out the commissioners to value the necessary purchases of land from Lord Dynevor and John Richards, and advertisements were placed in the *Cambrian*, *Gloucester Herald* and *Bristol Mercury* for contractors' proposals to be

The Quaker influence of the Harfords caused this terrace to be built at Sunnybank for Melingriffith workers. It comprised two sets of habitations, one built on top of the other. The upper houses were accessed from the path on the bank behind. On the night of the 1851 census, these 13 dwellings were occupied by a total of 66 people.
S.C. Fox photo, WIMM 73.141

Below: *The 1851 cast iron towpath bridge spanning the Parliamentary weir, as the canal left the Long Wood on its approach to Melingriffith. On the left is the feeder to Melingriffith Tinplate Works and on the right is the canal. The weir allowed excess water from the canal to overflow into the feeder to help drive the wheels and turbines in the works. Beyond the works, having served its purpose, the waste water from the feeder drove the canal company's pump to return water back to the canal. Behind the figure and alongside the canal is the site of the demolished Sunnybank housing.*
Derek Chaplin photo 1948 neg 483

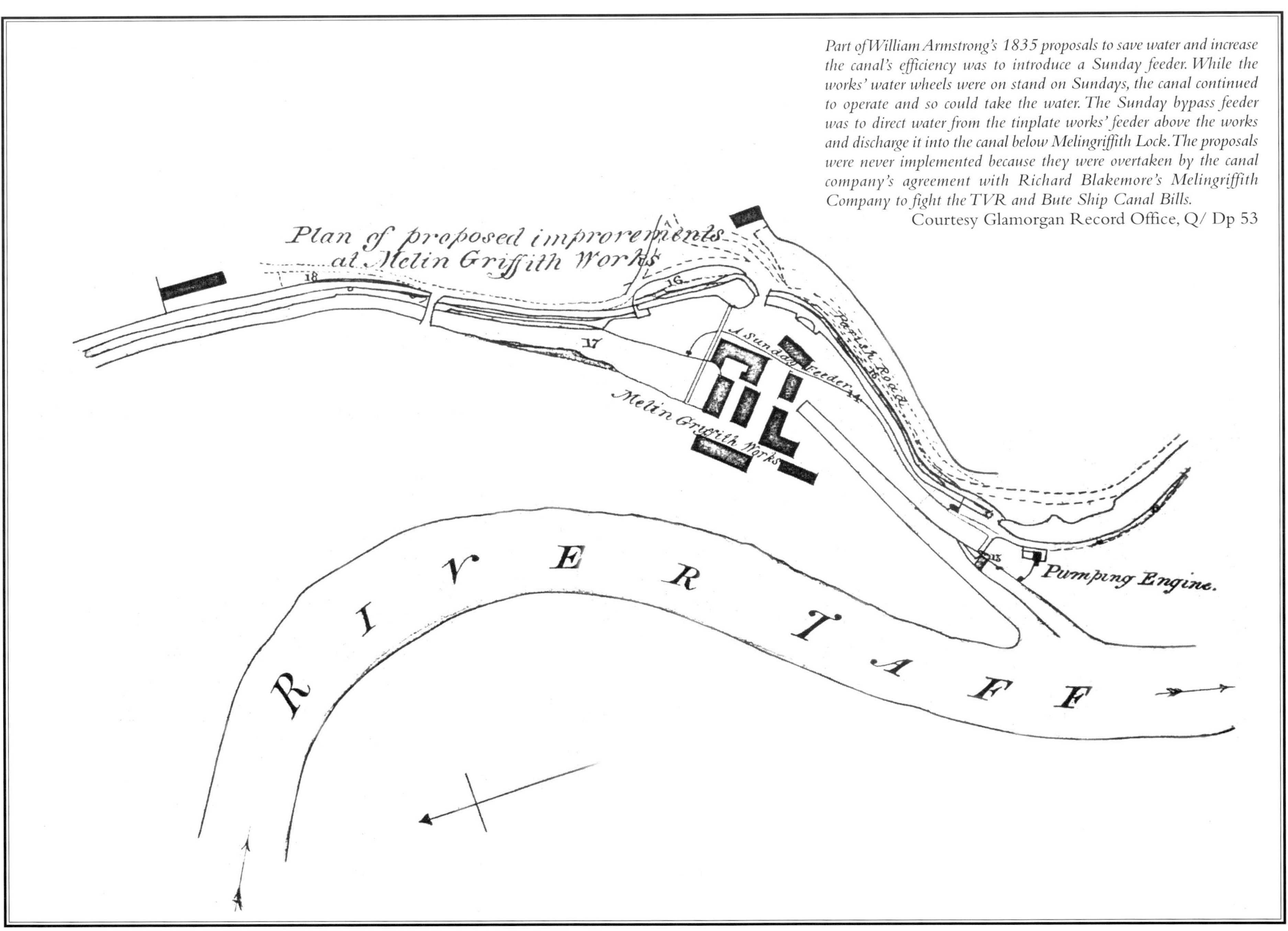

Part of William Armstrong's 1835 proposals to save water and increase the canal's efficiency was to introduce a Sunday feeder. While the works' water wheels were on stand on Sundays, the canal continued to operate and so could take the water. The Sunday bypass feeder was to direct water from the tinplate works' feeder above the works and discharge it into the canal below Melingriffith Lock. The proposals were never implemented because they were overtaken by the canal company's agreement with Richard Blakemore's Melingriffith Company to fight the TVR and Bute Ship Canal Bills.

Courtesy Glamorgan Record Office, Q/ Dp 53

An aerial view of Melingriffith Tinplate Works in 1927. The wide feeder runs into the centre of the works, between river and canal. It left the works through the two arches in the lower centre of the photograph, where it then drove the canal pump, hidden in shadow next to the lower lock gates. Water raised by the pump from the feeder tailrace entered the canal above the lock. The process of tinplate making can be understood in outline from studying this photograph. Bar iron arrived from Pentyrch Ironworks at the top left (by boat on the feeder until 1815, then by tramroad until the 1870s and by rail thereafter). The first long shed alongside the river is the bar shed. Between that and the boiler house (marked by the tall chimney) was the main rolling mill, where the bar iron was rolled and cut into black plate. Until the 1850s, the rolls were totally water-powered and the turbine house was situated at the point where the feeder entered the works. Beyond the rolling mills and past the boiler house was the black pickling room, at the bottom end of the works near the feeder tail race. The production line then turned 270 degrees and worked back through the annealing room, the cold rolls, the tinning machines and the finishing/packing rooms next to the canal. A railway branch crossed the open feeder from the packing and loading rooms to return the finished tinplate, that was not being transported by canal or road, back to the railway junction with the TVR.

Photo courtesy WIMM

The canal towpath crossed to the right bank at Melingriffith and the waters literally washed the walls of the tinplate works as boats made their steady way to Cardiff. The tight bend here was the cause of many a lost horse and it is a sobering reminder that all Merthyr and Aberdare coal and iron tonnages had to pass this way, in loads of just 20-25 tons. There was a small loading basin beyond the road bridge into the works, hidden round the bend and behind the buildings in this view. Additionally, there were two wharves, of which part of one can be seen here in the foreground. Coal arrived at the tinplate works from the company's own mining operations near Taff's Well. In 1913, when this view was taken, Melingriffith was part of the Richard Thomas & Co empire, which operated tinplate works throughout South Wales, from Carmarthenshire to the Forest of Dean. The two railway wagons in the yard would have arrived on the private Melingriffith railway. SR collection

Two of the Richard, Thomas & Baldwin locomotives that worked the final years of the Melingriffith railway to Pentyrch crossing. Above, Peckett 0-6-0ST Emerald Isle *(Works No 1424 of 1916) is seen on 15 May 1952 on the sylvan approach to the works. On the right, this unnamed outside cylindered Manning Wardle 0-6-0ST (Works No 1936 of 1917) was captured at the weighbridge in wintry conditions in January 1955. The closure of the Melingriffith Tinplate works brought an end to operations on the private railway in the late 1950s.*

Above: R.C. Riley; right: R.W.A. Jones

received by 6 September.[64]

John Hodgkinson, the ubiquitous tramroad engineer, won the contract for building the reservoir, having previously been called upon by the committee to survey a possible deviation of the canal at William Price's limestone quarry at Ivy House, Tongwynlais, in 1813.[65] David Morgan won the contract for deepening the Melingriffith watercourse. Contracts were drawn up and neither project lost any time in getting started.[66] Morgan's work was complete by January, when his bill of only £41 5s 7d was paid together with a gratuity of twenty guineas. This did not stop the canal company's billing Blakemore the agreed maximum of £200.[67]

Hodgkinson at first proceeded quickly and the canal company minutes record stage payments of £200 (Nov), £100 (Dec), £130 (Jan 1820) then £155 (May). In January 1820, it was agreed for him to make a second, smaller, connecting reservoir below the main one at Treble Locks and to raise the canal banks from Rhiwddar Bridge to the lock below (Taffs Well Lock) at an additional cost of £70. True to Hodgkinson's reputation, he was slow to complete and, in February 1821, the canal company threatened legal

An aerial view of the Melingriffith Works in its final years, from the opposite end of the works, taken in the 1950s after the canal had closed. The photograph clearly shows the river dropping through the rapids, as it turns the bend towards the former TVR bridge – this loss of height would have been the reason for the original corn mill being sited here before the tinplate works took over in 1749. The bridge at the bottom of the picture carries the road from Fforest Farm across the feeder and canal. A hundred yards downstream, the canal leaves the feeder to wind round the smiths, machine and fitting shops, to pass under the bridge carrying the road to the works entrance. The canal basin is hidden by these fitting shops. The prominent building in the centre, with the hipped roof, is the works offices and the carpenters' shops are behind it. By this time the feeder had been covered here by a box shed. The canal bed winds round the Whitchurch escarpment and passes under the railway at Primrose Hill. in the top left of the picture, out of Whitchurch and into Llandaff North.
Photo courtesy WIMM

action at the approaching Quarter Sessions. This must have had the desired effect because Hodgkinson met Reece on site on 9 April, presumably to survey the completed work. When the reservoir was filled it leaked and, in June 1822, compensation of one guinea was paid to David Morgan whose potato garden had been damaged. Finally, in April 1823, we read that the canal company was still withholding the balance of Hodgkinson's account (£18 10s 5d), until he raised the banks of the reservoir to the height specified in the contract.[68]

Attempts to Enlarge the Sea Lock Pound

The cost of this additional work came out of the General Fund, *i.e.* from revenue income, but Blakemore still had to honour his £200 contribution. After being billed in August 1820, it took several threatening letters before he paid up finally, in May 1822.[69] The canal company should by then have been relieved that their problems with Richard Blakemore were over. At that time the banks were being raised throughout the canal's length from the South Gate Bridge at Cardiff to Merthyr, in order that boats could carry an

An art student's drawing of the Melingriffith Works office building as it existed in 1950. The architectural style suggests a date at the end of the 18th century.
Barbara de Salis

In the afternoon sun, GCC boat No 128 rounds the bend in the Melingriffith narrows. It seems that the towline is attached to the stem post rather than the mast. When the canal was first built, the towpath stayed on the right past Melingriffith; it is no wonder that boatmen had difficulty leading horses round the bend.
S.C. Fox photo WIMM collection

The works bridge at Melingriffith, as photographed by Samuel Fox during one of his towpath walks in the 1930s. Brick was a rare building material on the Glamorganshire Canal and this brick arch is probably a later rebuilding. Here the canal was confined between the tinplate works and the steep bank leading to Velindre. The route past the tinplate works was undoubtedly the most tortuous section of the whole canal and through the bridge, the towpath made a sudden 90 degree turn which caused many a boathorse to end up in the water. S.C. Fox photo, CCL collection

increased load of 25 tons. The committee, now under the chairmanship of William Crawshay junior, following the death of Dr Benjamin Hall, was also considering preparing a Bill to allow it to make a call to widen and deepen the Sea Lock pound. Relations with Blakemore remained nervously polite and when the Melingriffith pound had to be drained to erect a wall, the canal committee sought permission from Blakemore as to when would be the most convenient time for his company.[70] A letter arrived from Blakemore in June. Crawshay and Hill promptly agreed to meeting him. Blakemore was now objecting to the enlargement of the canal, claiming it would reduce the surplus water that could be available to his works. The committee were aghast and they responded with their minute of 19 July 1822:

> '*Ordered that after the most mature consideration of the conduct of the Melingriffith Co since the establishment of the Reservoir at the Treble Locks that all further use thereof be immediately suspended and that the Canal Co henceforth revert upon the powers of their Act of Parliament for the supply of the Canal with Water.*'[71]

This response may have brought Blakemore to his senses, for he appears to have backed off for the time being. What was concerning everyone more at this time was the projected extension of the Merthyr Tramroad from Navigation to Cardiff and it was a pleasant surprise to the canal committee that Richard Blakemore offered to join them in their campaign to fight the Bill. They willingly accepted his support.[72]

At this time, also, Hopkin David, the long-serving lockkeeper at Melingriffith, died. John David (his son?) moved from Deniah Lock to replace him and probably live with his widowed mother. She was awarded £5 for funeral expenses in consideration of her husband's undoubted faithful service.[73]

Having found a new angle by which to tease the committee, Blakemore could not resist placing an injunction on the company to prevent their proceeding with the enlargement of the canal. The canal company was also forced to abandon their Bill to widen and deepen the Sea Lock pound because the Marquess of Bute was starting to take an interest in the growing port of Cardiff. He not only objected to giving up more land for the widening but claimed manorial rights to the waters of the Taff, which would be called upon to maintain the supply to the enlarged pound. The 1823 report by his engineering surveyor, David Stewart, advised Bute that he, '*not Mr Blakemore*', should be the one to claim compensation for water used by the canal company. From that time it would be more difficult for any industry within his Lordship's manor to extract water from the rivers.[74]

This unique photograph of the Melingriffith pump at work is also the oldest we have of it, dating from the late 19th century. With a ladder against one of the A-frames and the clean look of the timbers, it seems to be fresh from a major overhaul – perhaps even a full replacement of its oak timbers. The sheerlegs on the opposite side of the feeder spoil what is a dramatic image, with the paddles a blur on the slowly turning wheel. The log in the water trough is possibly to prevent the water freezing. The pump mechanism consists of two cylinders of 2ft 8ins bore and 5ft 0in stroke. The connecting rods are 18ft 5ins long and of cast iron 4ins by 5ins section. The frame was built of 12ins x 12ins American oak. The twin rocking beams are of 17ins x 14ins oak, 22ft long with cast iron cappings and lifted water 12ft into the timber trough. By the time of this photograph, Pentyrch Ironworks had ceased production and Melingriffith was getting its coal and bar iron from elsewhere. On the works railway siding in the background stand a selection of private owner wagons, with several from Rhondda's Standard Colliery bringing in steam coal, whilst the bar iron wagons are from Dowlais. Photo courtesy Llandaff Diocese Dean and Chapter

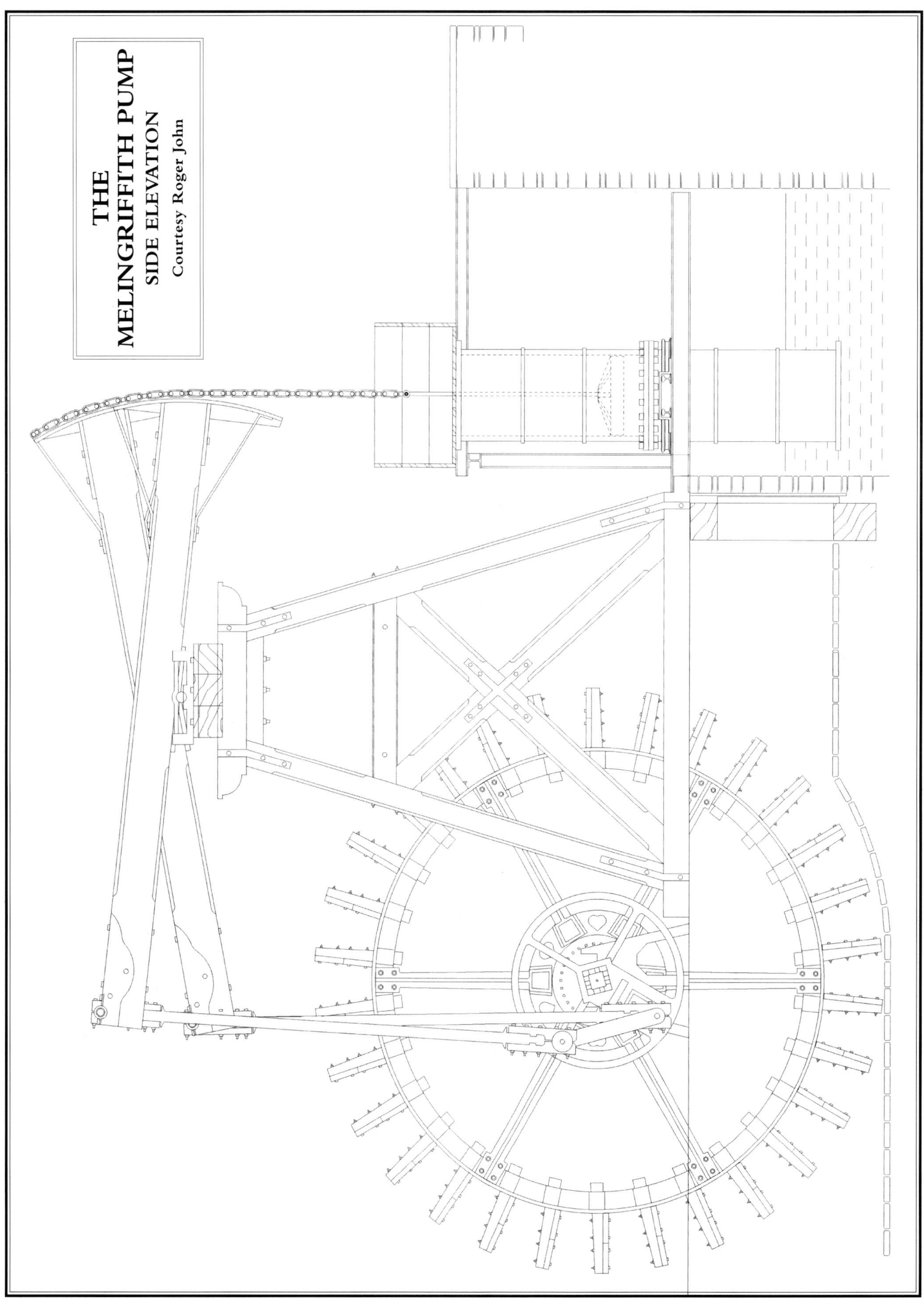
THE
MELINGRIFFITH PUMP
SIDE ELEVATION
Courtesy Roger John

The Bill having failed to reach Parliament, work still continued in places on raising the canal banks to take boats with 25 tons loading. Blakemore was requested to either raise the sides of the Melingriffith loading dock or install a stop gate across its entrance; he naturally refused so the canal company retaliated by threatening to dam it up, '*expressing the Company's hopes that he will not allow them to proceed to so unpleasant an extremity.*'[75]

The canal company's opposition to the Cardiff Tramroad Bill reached a successful conclusion with the dubious help of Richard Blakemore. The Bill was withdrawn by its promoters after representatives from Dowlais, Penydarren and Plymouth were allowed onto the canal committee, having agreed to finance improvements at the Sea Lock pound in return for further cuts in the canal tonnage rates. Preparations were made to fight Blakemore's injunction[76] and while the canal company waited impatiently for the trial, they were careful not even to allow the dock at Richard Tredwen's new boat-building yard at Cardiff to be connected to the canal.[77] This whole process delayed by several years the canal's being able to accommodate the heavier loads. Carriers such as Lewis Williams, who in 1825-6 had 20 boats

***Above:** The Melingriffith pump photographed from the works side of the tail race in 1948, by which time it had not been in use for 20 years. Note the iron strappings on the farside rocking beam. Mrs Close, wife of the canal company's Cardiff foreman, was daughter of the Melingriffith lockkeeper who was in charge of working the pump. She remembered the pump in action and had childhood memories of the excellent sewin (Welsh: sea trout) her father caught in the tail race at the bottom of the lockkeeper's garden.*

ILW photo 12 April 1948, neg 487

***Left:** The 18 ft 6 in diameter paddle wheel of the Melingriffith pump is 12 ft 6 in wide. It has cast iron spokes and had a solid oak axle. Originally there were 30 blades but when the wheel was recorded in derelict condition in 1958, only a few remained.*

ILW photo 14 April 1958 neg 1921

Melingriffith Lock and Oak Cottage in the late 1880s when the works were taken over by Richard Thomas of Lydbrook to start his twenty-year acquisition of South Wales tinplate concerns. The photograph was taken by G.H. Bedford of the Cardiff Photographic Society and shows, in the background, part of the works prior to its final phase of rebuilding. CCL collection

carrying Cyfarthfa iron from Merthyr to Cardiff, had had their boats rebuilt to take the increased capacity. However, the boats were continually grounding at places below Melingriffith. The worst places were in the Cathays pound and in the Tunnel below Crockherbtown Lock. Crockherbtown was the last lock before the sea lock itself. In the summer of 1826, its lockkeeper, Thomas Collins, recorded boats needing re-floating there almost every day – in one day there were as many as 15 that had to be eased off the canal bed by Collins raising the 'flasher' (the top paddle of the lock) to let water through the tunnel. The company installed a stop gate at the South Gate Bridge (Custom House Bridge), to allow the water level between it and the tunnel to be maintained at an adequate level. Even ships in the Sea Lock pound were going aground.[78]

This was a period of significantly heavier expenditure on legal costs. Church, whose offices were in Brecon, had been replaced as solicitor by the Merthyr based William Meyrick. Meyrick was already Cyfarthfa's solicitor and lived at Gwaelod y Garth House, purchased for £2,500 from William Crawshay when the latter moved into his newly-built and ostentatious Cyfarthfa Castle. In appointing Meyrick, Crawshay's canal committee made a point that this was purely for convenience now that Merthyr was able to support its own legal experts '*and the claim of a legal gentleman highly qualified and materially interested in the Canal.*'[79] However, in the years that followed, Meyrick's charges became so exorbitant that, at one point, the canal company had to declare enough was enough, as they insisted on Meyrick's bills being independently audited.[80] They continued to retain him through the 1830s, however, even though his daily charge rate was as much as eight guineas. It was Meyrick, in 1831, who was instrumental in the prosecution of Dic Penderyn, scapegoat of the Merthyr riots, which resulted in Dic being sent to the gallows.[81]

In June 1828, Blakemore was withdrawing water from the engine at Melingriffith and this prompted the canal company themselves to threaten litigation in the Court of Chancery but then to propose a negotiated settlement which was concluded in April 1829.[82] This did not stop Blakemore rediscovering his taste for litigation and he spent the years of the early 1830s arguing that the canal had had no legal rights to enlarge the cut so many years after such powers of its Act of Parliament had lapsed. Judgement was made in Blakemore's favour and the canal company failed in its writ of error at the House of Lords in 1831.[83] A team of five committee members was formed to represent the canal's interest in November the following year at the Court of Chancery in London; they were William Crawshay, Richard John Hill, Josiah John Guest, Rev'd George Thomas and Thomas Reece.[84] The case then went to the courts at Gloucester in 1834, where Blakemore again won. Although the canal company appealed, an agreement was finalised with Blakemore on 30 June 1835, with William Crawshay, Rev'd George Thomas and Richard Franklen.[85] At long last this tedious dispute was over and he was entitled to regular compensation for water taken, as long as he allowed the expansion of the canal and the increase in traffic to proceed.

This had taken too long for the other three Merthyr ironworks. Blakemore received his judgement while the

The canal widened out quite dramatically after rounding the tinplate works, as this view looking across the bend in the waterway to the substantial lock cottage at Melingriffith shows. Unusually for canal company property, it is not whitewashed in this 1913 picture postcard scene. On the night of the 1851 census there were six people living in this house with the Irish lockkeeper, Edward Liston. SR collection

canal company was once again preparing to fight the resurrected Cardiff Tramroad, now being enacted in the modern guise of the Taff Vale Railway. As in 1823, Blakemore offered his support in opposing the railway Bill.[86] He attended the proceedings in London and even had the effrontery to claim expenses from the canal company – a claim which was summarily rejected by the committee. This time the railway promoters had the upper hand and to remove the joint opposition of the canal company and Richard Blakemore, they drew up a tripartite agreement between canal, railway and ironworks. This included confirmation of the 1835 agreement for water compensation. In this, the canal company was to pay Blakemore £1,500 per annum from 25 March 1834 to 25 March 1839. In return, the canal company was entitled to take up to 10 tons of water per minute past the Pentyrch and Melingriffith works in time of short water, without paying any additional consideration to the extent of 15 tons. Any additional use was to be paid to Blakemore at a rate of £100 per annum per ton per minute beyond 10 tons, provided it did not prevent the canal continuing to supply the reservoir at Rhiwddar. The opposition was effectively removed and the TVR got its Act.[87]

In January 1831, the reservoir at Rhiwddar had been breached when Benjamin James of Rhiwddar Farm was paid ten guineas for injury done. In 1834, major repairs had been necessary and the contract was executed by Thomas Davies.[88]

Too late, in 1835, the canal company retained the services of the Bristol-based engineer, William Armstrong, to investigate how to conserve water and improve traffic flow by replacing all the staircase locks with single locks separated by small pounds. The proposed improvements included a Sunday bypass weir at Melingriffith. At a Special General Meeting in January 1836, the canal company resolved to push a new Bill through Parliament to effect these alterations in direct opposition to the Taff Vale Railway Bill. Against Bute opposition, the Bill failed and was withdrawn in May.[89] When the Annual General Meeting met in August, the committee was resigned to the building of both the new Bute Ship Canal and the Taff Vale Railway; Armstrong's final invoice was approved and that was an end of the matter.[90]

After passage of the Taff Vale Railway Act, Richard Blakemore disappeared from the scene as he retired back to Monmouthshire. Management of the Melingriffith and Pentyrch concern passed to his adopted nephew, Thomas William Booker-Blakemore. Richard died in 1855. While Thomas had attended many of the court hearings in the 1820s and 30s on the Melingriffith company's behalf,[91] he seems not to have had the inclination, nor indeed the need, to continue his uncle's struggle to maintain his works' supply of water power. From 1803 until 1836, Blakemore had waged a relentless battle against the Glamorganshire Canal Company, initially as a foil to the ignorantly autocratic Richard Crawshay but then not stopping after Crawshay's death, as if he were constantly seeking revenge for

Melingriffith Company boats moored on the off bank and framed by the arch of Ty Mawr Bridge.
S.C. Fox photo, WIMM collection

Crawshay's contemptuous treatment of his company. In one of the hearings of the 1835 case it was stated that, during this period, Blakemore had spent over £20,000 on litigation with the canal company.[92]

Less water power was needed at Melingriffith and Pentyrch as both works gradually installed steam power to drive their new rolling mills.[93] In 1840, William Cubitt was advising the canal on how it could improve its facilities at Cardiff, to compete with Bute's first dock and the Taff Vale Railway. One option was to take the agreed 10 tons of water per minute past Melingriffith in a Sunday bypass feeder. However, these plans came to nothing as the canal company found great difficulty in getting its schemes past the combined opposition of the Marquess of Bute and the Taff Vale Railway.[94]

The canal company relied on water from the Melingriffith pump almost until the end. It became particularly necessary when the patent fuel trade became established at Maindy (between Melingriffith and Cardiff). This meant that more boats were plying to and from the docks than were bringing water through Melingriffith Lock, much of the raw material for patent fuel manufacture arriving by rail to the largest of the works. Lionel Heath remembered his father, in the 1920s, regularly sending a man from his Star Works to Melingriffith to set the pump working in order to have sufficient water to send a consignment of boatloads to the sea.[95] Residents of Llandaff North recall the monotonous rhythm of the simple machine. It was able to pump at a rate of 360 cubic feet per minute.[96]

A final note on the pump. In 1891, when both the Glamorganshire and Aberdare Canals were owned by the Marquess of Bute, a report recommended that the redundant Aberdare steam pumping engine of 1846 be moved to Melingriffith to replace the water wheel.[97] If this had been done, we should have lost the most important artefact of the Glamorganshire Canal which survives today, a relic which arguably dates from the first years of the canal's operation.

The pump lay derelict from the 1920s. After canal closure the lock was obliterated, the lock house demolished and the canal bed gradually removed from the Melingriffith landscape. The rotting pump remained in its ditch. In 1963, it was subjected to a detailed survey and plan[98] but by 1974, the structure had seriously deteriorated and it became clear that the future of this important example of canal technology was far from certain. Fortunately at this point, concerned voluntary groups from Oxford House Industrial Archaeology Society of Risca and members of the Inland Waterways Association joined forces to initiate the pump's rescue. Over the next fourteen years, the huge task of restoration went on at weekends as volunteer manpower and grant assistance became available. During this time all the massive timber components were replaced, the mill leat and tail race were cleared of mature trees and debris and a number of replacement engineering parts for the wheel and engine had to be replicated and reassembled including the wooden axle of the wheel being replaced by one of steel. When a housing estate was to be built on the cleared tinplate works site, a grant from the Welsh Development Agency enabled the old works feeder to be perpetuated below ground and so provide a continuing water supply for possible future operation of the restored pump. After all this work, however, the future of the pump remains in doubt as no public body is prepared to adopt its maintenance.[99]

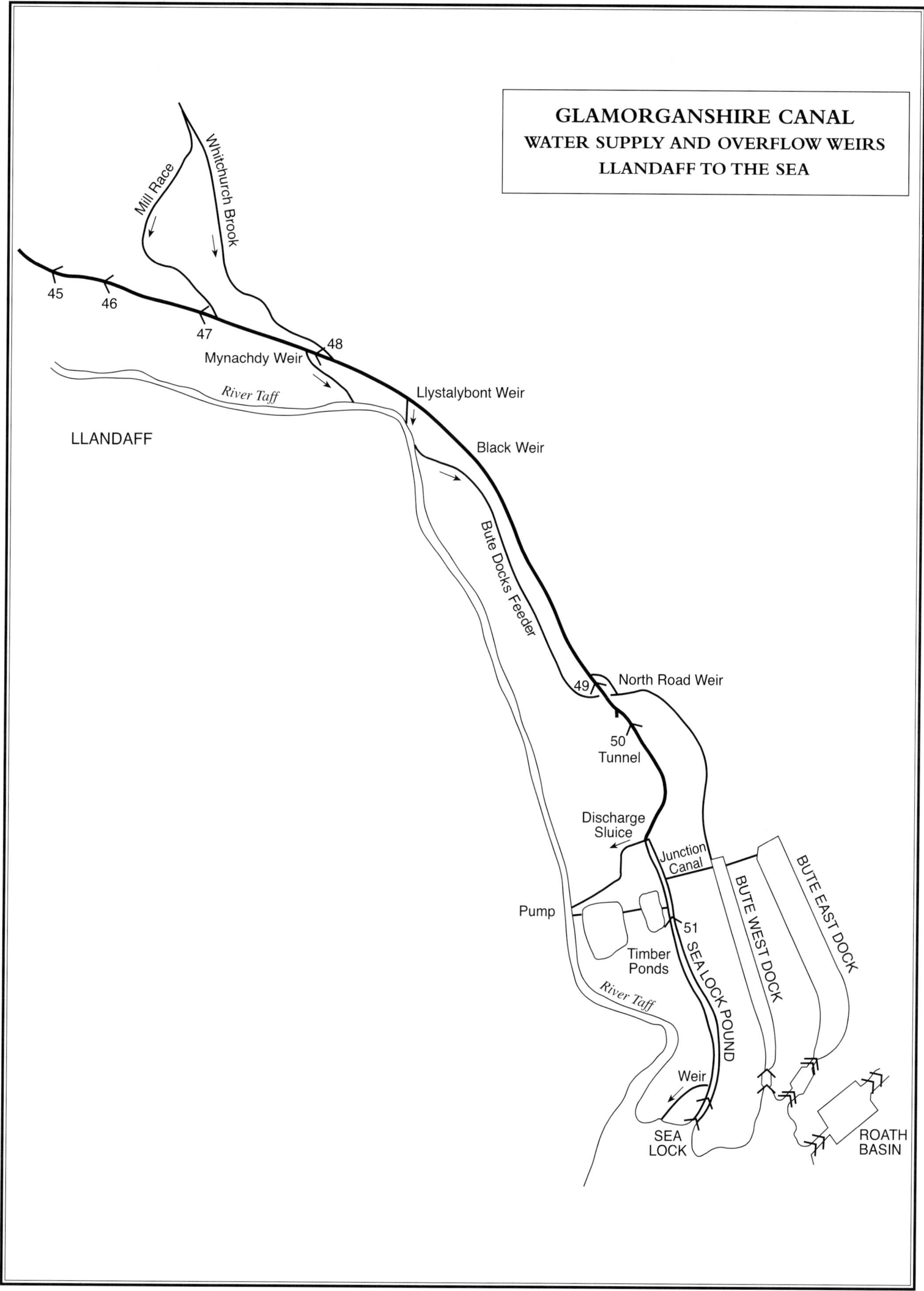
GLAMORGANSHIRE CANAL
WATER SUPPLY AND OVERFLOW WEIRS
LLANDAFF TO THE SEA
Mill Race
Whitchurch Brook
45
46
47
48
Mynachdy Weir
River Taff
Llystalybont Weir
LLANDAFF
Black Weir
Bute Docks Feeder
49
North Road Weir
50
Tunnel
Discharge
Sluice
Junction
Canal
Pump
51
Timber
Ponds
River Taff
SEA LOCK POUND
BUTE WEST DOCK
BUTE EAST DOCK
Weir
SEA
LOCK
ROATH
BASIN

NOTES TO CHAPTER 5

1 For the history of both Pentyrch Ironworks and Melingriffith Tinplate Works see Edgar L. Chappell *Historic Melingriffith*, Cardiff 1940, (a facsimile edition was published in 1995).
2 GRO Dowlais Iron Company (DIC) letterbook folios 156/7 and 177/8.
3 GRO DIC letterbook folio 308, 28 May 1794.
4 GCC minute book 30 September 1794.
5 GRO DIC letterbook folio 261, 10 December 1794 and CCL GCC minute book 13 December 1794.
6 GRO DIC letterbook folios 366, 1 January 1795 and 387 8 February 1795.
7 GRO DIC letterbook folio 338, 6 January 1795 and 366, 1 January 1795.
8 GRO DIC letterbook folio 368, 4 January 1795.
9 See especially DIC letterbook folio 403, 9 April 1795.
10 GCC minute book 11 April 1795.
11 GCC minute book 22 October and 5 December 1795.
12 GCC minute book 11 February 1797.
13 GCC minute book 25 March 1797.
14 GCC minute book 1 March 1800.
15 These were granted and are itemised in GCC minute book 6 June 1798.
16 NLW Maybery 187.
17 CCL Bute I 20 and the diary of John Bird 4 September 1802.
18 NLW Maybery 2705.
19 NLW Maybery 1917 and 191.
20 NLW Maybery 3827 and 3935.
21 GCC minute book 17 November 1803.
22 GCC minute book 11 April 1805.
23 GCC minute book 7 May 1805 and GCC letter book 1, 5 and 8 May 1805.
24 For Jessop see Charles Hadfield and A.W. Skempton *William Jessop, Engineer*, Newton Abbot 1979. For Rennie see Cyril T.G. Boucher *John Rennie 1761-1821. The Life and Work of a Great Engineer*, Manchester 1963 and Wallace Reyburn *Bridge Across the Atlantic. The Story of John Rennie*, London 1972.
25 Gwent Record Office D2.162, letterbook of Richard Crawshay 1788-1797.
26 GCC minute book 22 August 1805.
27 GCC letter book 3 September, 14 November, 4 and 21 December 1805.
28 A certified copy of the agreement signed by Jessop and Rennie and dated 1 March 1806 was made by the Powell solicitors in December 1808 and is in GRO B/C Gca 4/60.
29 GCC minute book 9 and 11 March and 29 April 1806.
30 GCC minute book 29 March, 10 July and 3 Sept 1806. GCC letter book 4 May, 30 August and 3 September 1806.
31 NLW Maybery 192.
32 GCC minute book 27 October 1807.
33 GCC minute book 3 October 1806.
34 For a discussion on the reasons surrounding the missing Jessop papers see Charles Hadfield *Thomas Telford's Temptation*, Cleobury Mortimer 1993.
35 This is dealt with fully by us in Chapter 4 of Volume 1.
36 GCC minute book 24/25 October 1806.
37 GCC letter book 28 and 29 October 1806.
38 John Lloyd *The Early History of the Old South Wales Ironworks (1760 to 1840)*, London 1906, p109.
39 GCC minute book 18 July and 15 August 1807, and GCC letter book 20 July 1807.
40 CCL Bute I 17.
41 Quoted in Chappell *Historic Melingriffith*.
42 GCC minute book 10 July and 3 September 1806.
43 GCC minute book 9 May and 15 August 1807, and CCL Bute I/9.
44 GCC minute book 4 June 1807 and GCC letter book 9 June 1807.
45 GCC minute book 2 September 1808.
46 GCC Minute book 13 October 1814 ratified the continuing payment of this sum to David.
47 GCC letter book 23 July 1809.
48 CCL Bute I 20; GRO former CCL deed 5183 copy assignment of lease of Pentyrch Works and farm from William Lewis to John Harford and Richard Blakemore (Harford Partridge & Co), 20 August 1805 and Chappell *Historic Melingriffith* p54.
49 NLW Maybery 2195, letter from Wyndham Lewis to Messrs Powell, 16 March 1803.
50 CC Bute I 8, 17-20 and 35.
51 GCC minute book 24 April 1810.
52 GCC minute book 29 August 1811 and 26 July 1813, and GCC letter book 5 September 1811.
53 GCC minute book 4 February and 26 June 1811.
54 GRO D/D Art O/24 and GCC minute book 18 January 1810; for a fuller account of this Aberdare Canal water dispute see Volume 1 Chapter 6 pp117-9.
55 GCC minute book 26 June, 29 August and 27 September 1811.

56 GCC minute book 29 November 1813, 1 March, 16 April, 22 June and 13 October 1814.
57 GCC minute book 1 June 1808, 3 April and 16 November 1812 and 6 January 1816; S.W. Allen *Visit of the Cardiff Naturalists' Society to the Tin-Plate Works of the Melingriffith Company, Ltd, May 7th 1913*, Cardiff 1913; S.W. Allen *Reminiscences*, Cardiff 1918.
58 GCC minute book 12 January 1815.
59 GCC minute book 3 May, 10 May and 13 September 1817, and GRO B/Ca 4/67.
60 GCC minute book 7 August 1818.
61 GCC minute book 4 February and 1 April 1819.
62 NLW Maybery 116. Hill had built a private tramroad between his works and the Merthyr Tramroad and his partners in the tramroad claimed he was avoiding the full tonnage dues.
63 See Volume 1 Chapter 10.
64 GCC minute book 2 and 16 June, 1 July and 5 August 1819.
65 GCC minute book 22 April 1813.
66 GCC minute book 6 September, 7 October and 2 December 1819.
67 GCC minute book 6 January and 31 August 1820.
68 GCC minute book 4 November, 2 December 1819, 6 January 1820, 4 May, 7 June, 15 February 1821, 2 May 1822, 5 June 1822, 29 March and 17 April 1823.
69 GCC minute book 31 August 1820, 20 September 1821, 7 March 1822 and 2 May.
70 GCC minute book 13 December 1821.
71 GCC minute book 5 June and 9 July 1822.
72 GCC minute book 2 October 1823.
73 GCC minute book 11 December 1823.
74 NLW Bute 104.
75 GCC minute book 2 June, 10 June and 16 July 1824.
76 GCC minute book 14 September 1824, 7 July 1825, 3 November 1825, 6 April 1826 and 8 November 1827. NLW Maybery 194 and 195.
77 GCC minute book 7 July 1825.
78 Evidence of witnesses on behalf of the GCC given at the Hereford Summer Assizes 1827, Dyfed Archives Trostre Acc 4734/47 and Canal Memoranda of Charles Price 1826-7, Dyfed Archives Trostre Acc 4734/46a.
79 GCC minute book 2 October 1823.
80 GCC minute book 6 February and 6 March 1835.
81 For more on William Meyrick see several references given in footnote 3 of Gwyn Alf Williams 'The Merthyr Election of 1835' in *The Welsh History Review,* Vol 10 No 2, Cardiff, June 1981, p360 and Gwyn Alf Williams *The Merthyr Rising*, London 1978.
82 GCC minute book 4 June 1828, 30 January 1829 and 2 April 1829.
83 NLW Maybery 419. *The Cambrian*, 21 November 1829 and 10 September 1831.
84 GCC minute book 13 July and 12 September 1832.
85 GCC minute book 6 August 1834, 25 August, 24 October and 3 June 1835.
86 GRO D/D AN 11/1.
87 D.S. Barrie *The Taff Vale Railway*, Sidcup 1939.
88 GCC minute book 21 January 1831, 30 December 1834 and 6 February 1835.
89 Charles Hadfield *Canals of South Wales and the Border*, Cardiff 1960, p111.
90 GRO QDp 53 and GCC minute book 13 January, 1 and 22 June, 13 July and 23 August 1836. Armstrong is best remembered as one of the entrants to the competition to design the Clifton suspension bridge. He lived in Clifton and undertook several public services contracts in Bristol and Bath.
91 See for example December 1828 and January 1829 entries in the Melingriffith Cash Book for 1822-31, WIMM 30/M/B2 Acc. 1991.25/7.
92 *Monmouthsire Merlin*, 9 May 1835, cited in Chappell *Historic Melingriffith*, p57.
93 See, for example, *Cardiff & Merthyr Guardian*, 1 October 1851, when three such mills were being installed at Melingriffith.
94 GCC minute book 16 November 1838, 26 June 1839 and 3 June 1840.
95 In discussion following lecture on Patent Fuel by J. Homer at the SE Wales IA Society.
96 NLW Bute Box 141 Parcel 6. Report relative to the water power of the River Taff, 1842.
97 GCC minute book 26 August 1891.
98 Survey for WIMM by R.V. Bayliss, September 1963.
99 Various reports 1974 onwards by Robin Williams, Chairman OHIAS.

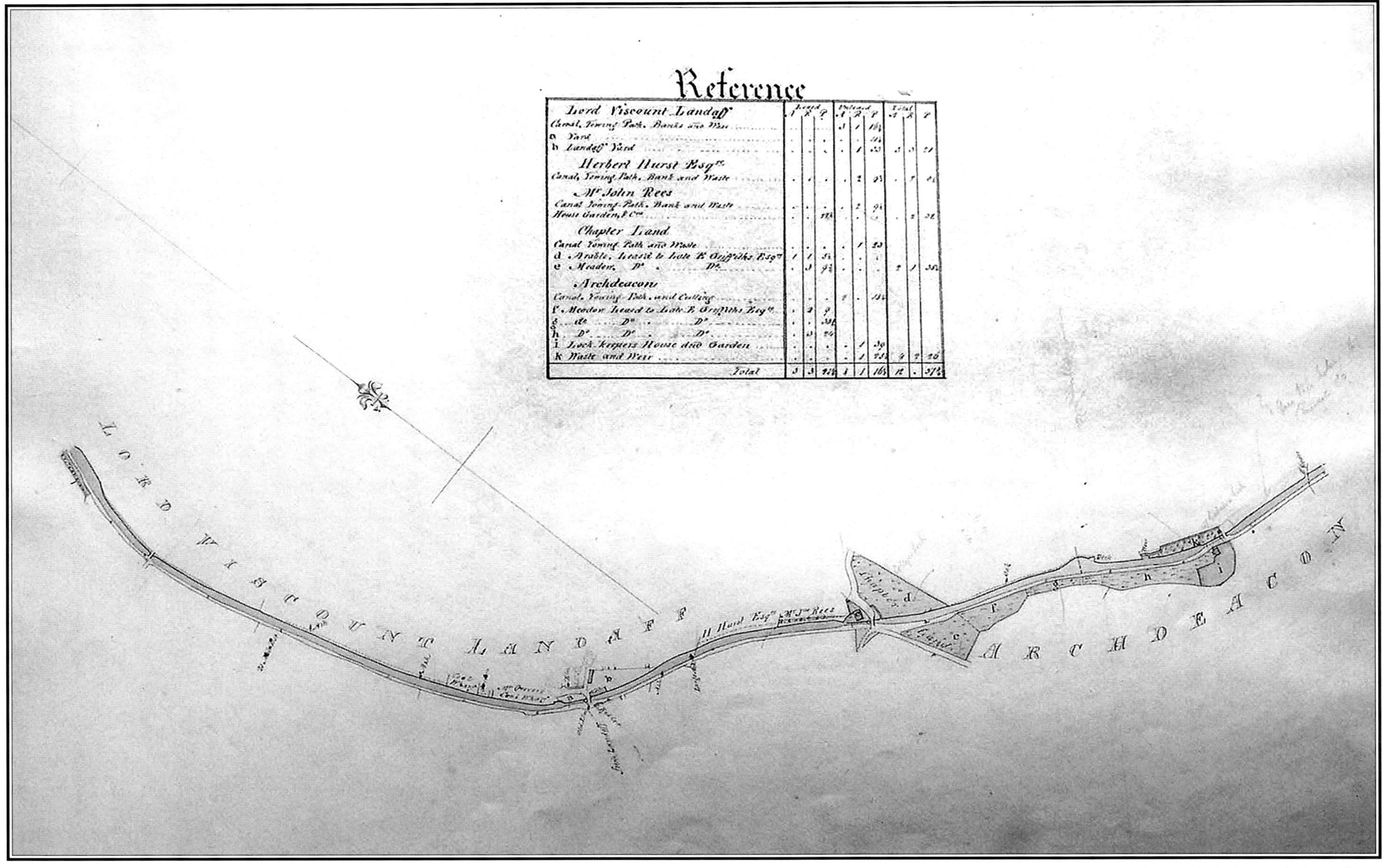

The canal survey of 1830 between Ty Mawr and Gabalfa shows the coal wharves and warehouse at Llandaff Lock. This was an important location which served the cathedral city of Llandaff, across the river, the main road to Merthyr crossing the canal at this point. In the 1820s and 30s, Coffin and Grover were supplying house coal from their own wharves there, Grover's yard being the original coal yard of John Key. The next lock is College Lock, where the ancient pilgrim route from Whitchurch to Llandaff crossed the canal to the old river bridge. The house here had been built in 1814, not by the company but by a canal boat owner and operator, William Beynon, who ten years later built a dock at his boat yard shown here above Gabalfa Lock. In the year this map was produced, Beynon sold the College lock house to the canal company but he continued to operate his business at the boat yard. Courtesy Glamorgan Record office

Chapter 6

WHITCHURCH, LLANDAFF AND GABALFA

South of Melingriffith, the canal entered the flood plain of the Taff on its final five leisurely miles to the sea. Through this area of lowland farming, between Melingriffith and Cardiff, Thomas Dadford needed to provide five locks – Melingriffith, Llandaff, College, Gabalfa and Mynachdy.

Llandaff Yard

The road from Llandaff city to Merthyr (via the new Llandaff river bridge) crossed the canal at Llandaff Lock. This gave communication to the rich farmlands of St Fagans and the Vale of Glamorgan. It was an obvious place to establish a wharf and the spot became known immediately as Llandaff Yard. From here, the hungry iron towns in the hills would be serviced with farm produce from the fertile lowlands. The Key brothers, Thomas and John, were among the first to exploit this opportunity. Their other brother, William, was already a carrier (by road) before the canal was built and, collectively, they were quick to use the new form of transport to service their markets. Thomas Key concentrated on mineral movements of coal and limestone and in 1795, he leased land above the lock at Llandaff Bridge (between road and canal) from Lord Llandaff and laid out a coal yard. Meanwhile, from the same year, John Key had a partnership agreement with William Taitt of Dowlais works, to supply merchandise to Merthyr from his farm and grist mill at St Fagans; their warehouse at Merthyr was managed by John Brown.[1]

No mention is made in the canal minute books of leasing land for a wharf at Llandaff but rather of providing a public wharf. In July 1798, the canal committee '*ordered that the Lands purchased by the Proprietors of the Chapter of Llandaff and now occupied by the Rev'd Powell Edwards or his Tenant to be appropriated to the purpose of a public and free Wharf.*'

The canal company's tonnage account book survives for the year September 1798 to September 1799. It gives summarised details for up and down movements on the canal in that first year of full through operation to the Sea Lock. In September 1798, for example, Thomas Key was delivering coal to Llandaff Yard from his collieries at Maesmawr and Abercanaid, totalling 85½ tons and taking 532 bales of straw back to Merthyr from Llandaff.[2] John Key was sending flour, bran, butter and malt to the Merthyr warehouse at Lock 1.[3] John Steel, Rees James and Lewis Thomas were also operating separate services between Cardiff and Merthyr, and occasionally worked from Llandaff Yard. In that month, Steel took over a ton of sacked flour from Llandaff Yard to Lock 1. Rees James took flour to the Dowlais Wharf in Merthyr, whilst Lewis Thomas took malt, flour, potatoes, apples and pears to the same destination. An indication that not all manufactured tools were imported into Cardiff from Bristol is given by an entry on 8 September, when two gates with four posts and a plough and harrow were loaded at Llandaff, consigned to Dowlais.

Also in September 1798, the Penydarren Works delivered 10 tons of bricks and John Key delivered 17 tons of building stone from Pentrebach to Llandaff Yard. Already the Pennant sandstone quarries along the route of the canal were serving the needs of builders in the north of Cardiff.

In 1803, the Cathedral, in the guise of the canal company's very own Dr Benjamin Hall, was let a wharf at Llandaff and in the next few years the canal company, realising the growing importance of this facility, made several investments at their public wharf. On 7 December 1804, it was ordered that a small dwelling house be erected there at a cost of no more than £35. In 1807, the canal company enlarged the wharf and in 1814 they extended the warehouse.[4] In these early years, wharfage income at Llandaff was significant enough to be itemised separately in the published GCC accounts alongside Sea Lock Dues, Sundry Rents and Tolls at the Aqueduct.[5] It seems that Llandaff was the canal company's only public wharf.

The land around Llandaff Lock was farmed by the Llewellin family – William and his son Evan. In the 1820s, they were letting land alongside the canal to the Cardiff Hunt for their kennels. The hunt comprised some familiar names such as Hill, Homfray and Lewis, second generation ironmasters, who had moved away from the source of their wealth in the hills to enjoy life at Llandaff, close to the genteel life of Cardiff and the Vale of Glamorgan. Also nearby was Gabalfa House, seat of Sir Robert Lynche-Blosse from 1809. The road from Llandaff turnpike gate to the Merthyr turnpike gate in Whitchurch became an important through route and was turnpiked in 1826.[6] The

An aerial view of the canal and river passing through Llandaff North in 1931, looking north. At the very top is the bridge under the TVR main line at Primrose Hill. The canal then passes the derelict brickworks and claypits near the Gelli Bridge. This brickworks had a limited life, being built by the Cardiff entrepreneur, Solomon Andrews; the new stack was erected in 1889 but the works was abandoned by 1904. Gelli Bridge carried the old road from Gelli Farm to Radyr church, crossing the river near Radyr Quarry by ford where the river bed consists of natural slabs of Radyr stone. The community housing of Llandaff North, seen here on the eastern side of the canal, grew up to house commuters after the opening of the Taff Vale Railway, Llandaff station (top right) being over a mile from Llandaff proper and in a different parish. It eventually connected with the canalside community at Llandaff Yard and the whole area became known as Llandaff North from the early years of the 20th century. When the moribund canal was taken over by Cardiff Corporation in 1943, the Parks Committee considered proposals for a four mile stretch from Llandaff Lock through Melingriffith and the Long Wood to become a public amenity. The length alongside Hailey Park, shown in this photograph, was to have been used for boating. Sadly, that part of the scheme came to nothing.

CCL collection

Samuel Fox captured this scene at Primrose Hill, Llandaff North in the 1930s, as local children play on a maintenance boat loaded with a harvest of towpath cuttings and brambles. Rightly or wrongly, such a scene today would horrify most parents, with fears of falling in and drowning; it was a different age. The cottages were built by the Melingriffith Company. The prominent house on the horizon is Ty Mawr, after which a local road and canal bridge were named and whose farm once encompassed the whole of the present Hailey Park. S.C. Fox photo, CCL collection

The brickworks chimney at Gelli Bridge is prominent in this rainy afternoon's view of the stretch of canal behind Hazelhurst Road, looking north. On the horizon, the Garth Hill marks the canal's entry to the coalfield. S.C. Fox photo, WIMM collection

Typical of the numerous iron foundries that operated close to the bank of the urban canal was David Evans' Eagle Foundry in Llandaff North. It was established in 1861 on a site between the canal and Whitchurch Road (now Station Road), above Llandaff Lock and near to the Pineapple public house. Here, sometime in the late 19th century, five foundrymen pause for the photograph while preparing a charge for the furnace. The simple lift would raise the material to the platform so it could be tipped into the cupola furnace. Casting would have been done into sand moulds in the casting shed behind. Many items of street furniture made at Evans' Foundry, especially drain covers and manhole covers, survive throughout Cardiff. Photo courtesy Llandaff diocese Dean and Chapter

activity at Llandaff Yard and this crossing of communications created a focus that Evan Llewellin exploited by opening his house for the sale of beer. In Harrison's map of 1830, it is shown as the Red Cow but soon afterwards it became the Cow & Snuffers. Despite stories of happy drinkers vying with each other to come up with the most outlandish combinations, this unusual name almost certainly has its origins in Ireland. It is likely to be an anglicisation of the gaelic '*An Cúr ar Snámh*', meaning the Swimming Dog or Otter, a name known to have been used for several public houses or inns in that country. The earliest reference found for the change of name at Llandaff is 1832.[7] Its proximity to the Glamorganshire Canal was also something of a hazard for the well-imbibed, with numerous documented instances of drinkers falling in the lock and drowning, almost up until the canal closed. Other signed beer houses close to the canal were the Exchange, the Pineapple, the Gardener's Arms, the Three Cups and the Roller's Arms. The last two named served the College Ironworks, which rolled iron into small bar and made wire for use in nail making; in its last years it was also supplying plate to Llantrisant Tinplate Works.

Gabalfa

It is a sobering thought that, although Llandaff and Gabalfa were some twenty miles from Merthyr Tydfil, the tens of thousands of tons of canal-borne iron and coal destined for the Sea Lock pound at Cardiff had to pass through the area, and the canal boats had to return the same way with their various back loads. It is not surprising, then, that small industries sprang up all along the route either to service the waterway's multitude of needs or to directly profit from the benefits of communication. Alongside Key's former coal yard at Llandaff Yard (subsequently taken over by Grover and Coffin to continue to supply house and smith coal), David Evans' foundry was opened in 1861. Downstream from College lock, William Beynon began a boat repairing business which flourished into a boat

The warehouse at Llandaff Lock (shown here, pine-end on, in the 1920s) survived in use as a scout hut until its demolition in 1959. It dated back as far as 1804 and was extended by 40 feet in 1814, serving as a granary to store produce destined for the working populace at Merthyr. Even before that, however, John Key was sending produce from his farm at St Fagans to Merthyr by canal from this spot. Christopher James, the Merthyr businessman, rented part of the warehouse from 1817 to 1820 and Lewis Williams, the canal carrier, also had a lease through the 1820s until 1838. The several farms at Gelli and Gabalfa sent hay by canal for Merthyr's large population of horses and combined their occupations of hay merchant and boatman. One of these farmers was Hugh Steel, who had two boats at the time of his death in 1840 when the business was inherited by his son William, who also ran the coal yard. As the area's population grew, Anglican services began to be held in the granary, until All Saints church was built on Gabalfa Road in 1890. The old granary then continued as a community reading room and institute, finally becoming a scout hut.

SR collection

Across the canal from the warehouse at Llandaff Lock was the Cow & Snuffers public house, seen here in 1906 after a substantial extension had been added to it. It was built perhaps as early as 1812 and operated by the main local farmer, Evan Llewellyn (whose daughter Jane, incidentally, married Hugh Steel the hay merchant). Harrison's map of 1830 names it the Red Cow but it was certainly called the Cow & Snuffers by 1839, when the GCC minute books mentioned it by name. Isambard Brunel made an oblique reference to it in his diaries too. The pub lay on the main road from Cardiff to Merthyr via Llandaff city and its claim to fame is of Disraeli having stopped there on his way to Greenmeadow, Tongwynlais, whilst he was courting his dead friend's widow Mary Ann Lewis in 1838-9. The new building incorporated a carved stone bust of the Victorian prime minister over the larger ground floor window, which is still there today. One can only guess that the two men in the foreground are lockkeepers and/or boatmen. In the far distance, and across the river, is the spire of Llandaff cathedral. SR collection

building yard under John James and his son. Another boatyard, near Mynachdy Lock, was Parry and Williams'. Lewis Williams ran a carrying service on the canal, naturally using his own boats. By the time of the 1851 census, his son William was operating a soap works on the site, while the other brother was an iron and brass founder employing ten men and boys. As well as these industries, boatmen lived the whole length of the canal and were not confined to particular 'canal villages'.

The Cambrian Patent Fuel works at Gabalfa is dealt with in the chapter on Patent Fuel. In 1893, the vacant premises were offered for sale and this gave the new owners of the canal the opportunity to move their boatyard from Navigation. The canal was already being administered from Cardiff and Navigation House had been taken over by James Hurman to be converted into a public house.[8] The patent fuel works became the Cambrian Yard, with its dry dock, saw pit and manager's house. The parts of the fuel works that the canal company could not utilise, they just left to decay further. Some fifty years later, when the canal finally closed at Gabalfa, remnants of the fuel works could still be recognised. Very quickly, the whole length of canal from College Lock to Mynachdy Lock was swallowed by the Gabalfa housing estate.

The Whitchurch to Tongwynlais Nature Reserve

Towards the end of 1942, there was speculation in Cardiff about what the city might want to do with the Glamorganshire Canal if Cardiff Corporation were able to acquire it. The city's Parliamentary committee had already been at work on the legal framework of the Bill leading to the Cardiff Corporation Act of 1943, which would enable the canal to be abandoned. At a meeting of the Parks Committee, the chairman, Alderman Hill-Snook, made an inspired suggestion that the stretch of water from Llandaff North to Tongwynlais should be used for boating. Also, commented the *Cardiff & Suburban News*, there was an idea that the taking over of the canal may assist in the creation of that green belt which was the dream of post-war advisers.[9]

In January 1943, the Parks Committee's proposals for

Page right, bottom: *GCC boat No 451 alongside the Three Cups, Llandaff Yard, with College Lock in the distance. The field on the right is the site of the College Ironworks. The dwellings on the right were formerly part of the ironworks properties and may originally have been Thomas Evans' Roller's Arms public house, closed in 1868, apparently on the orders of Richard Lumley, the Methodist partner in the works. The whitewashed property is William Beynon's house of 1814, finally demolished in 1956. Across the lock, on the towpath side is the lockkeeper's house of 1834.* ILW photo 15 April 1943 neg 221

The lockkeeper's house at College Lock, with Elizabeth Stone, the lockkeeper's daughter, holding baby Reg Williams. This is the 1834 lock house, built by the canal company on the opposite side of the lock to William Beynon's house of 1814. SR collection

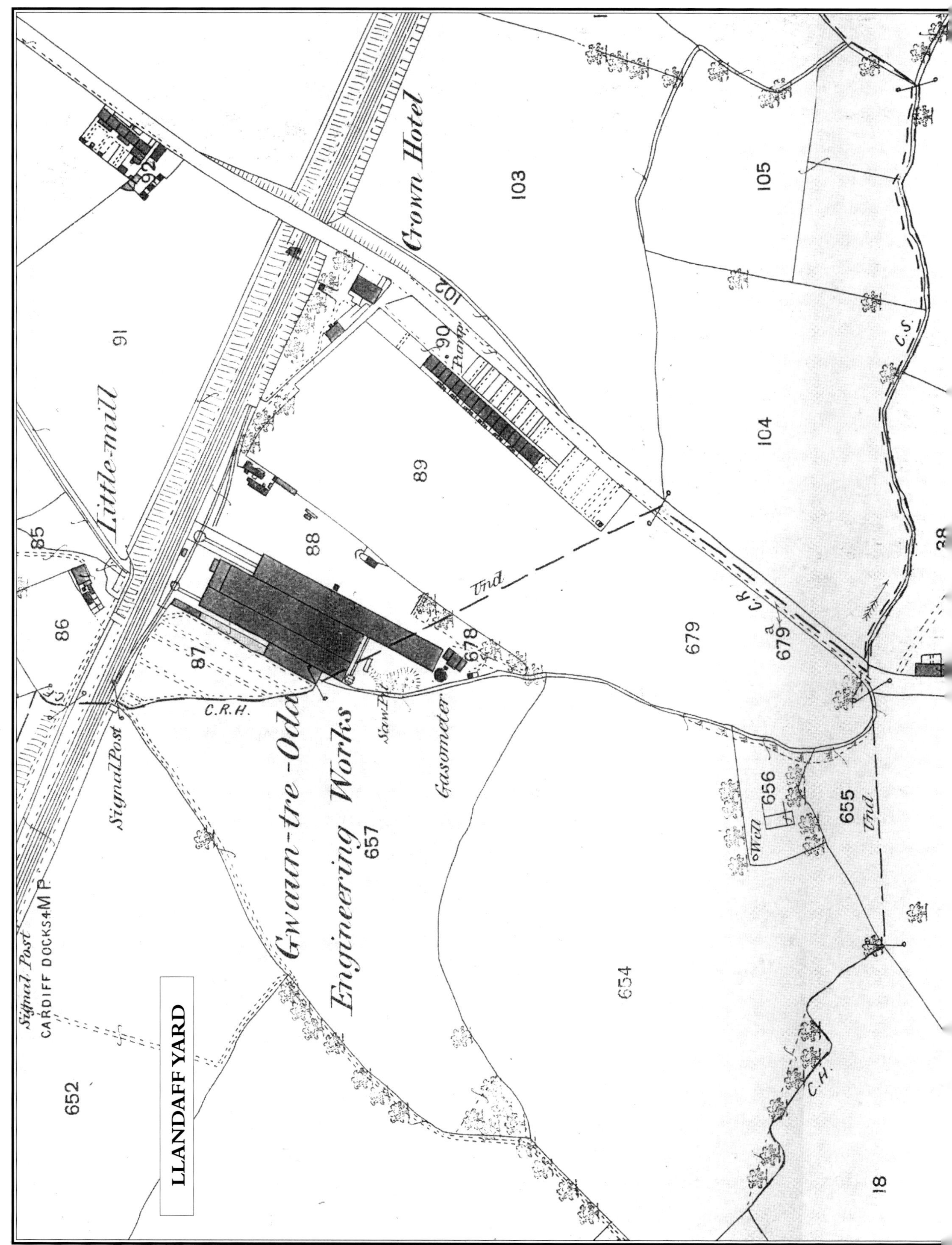
LLANDAFF YARD
Gwaun-tre-Odd
Engineering Works
Crown Hotel
Little-mill
Gasometer
Signal Post
Signal Post
CARDIFF DOCKS 4 M P
Pump
Well
C.R.H.
C.S.
C.H.
Tnd
652
654
655
656
657
678
679
86
87
88
89
90
91
92
102
103
104
105
18

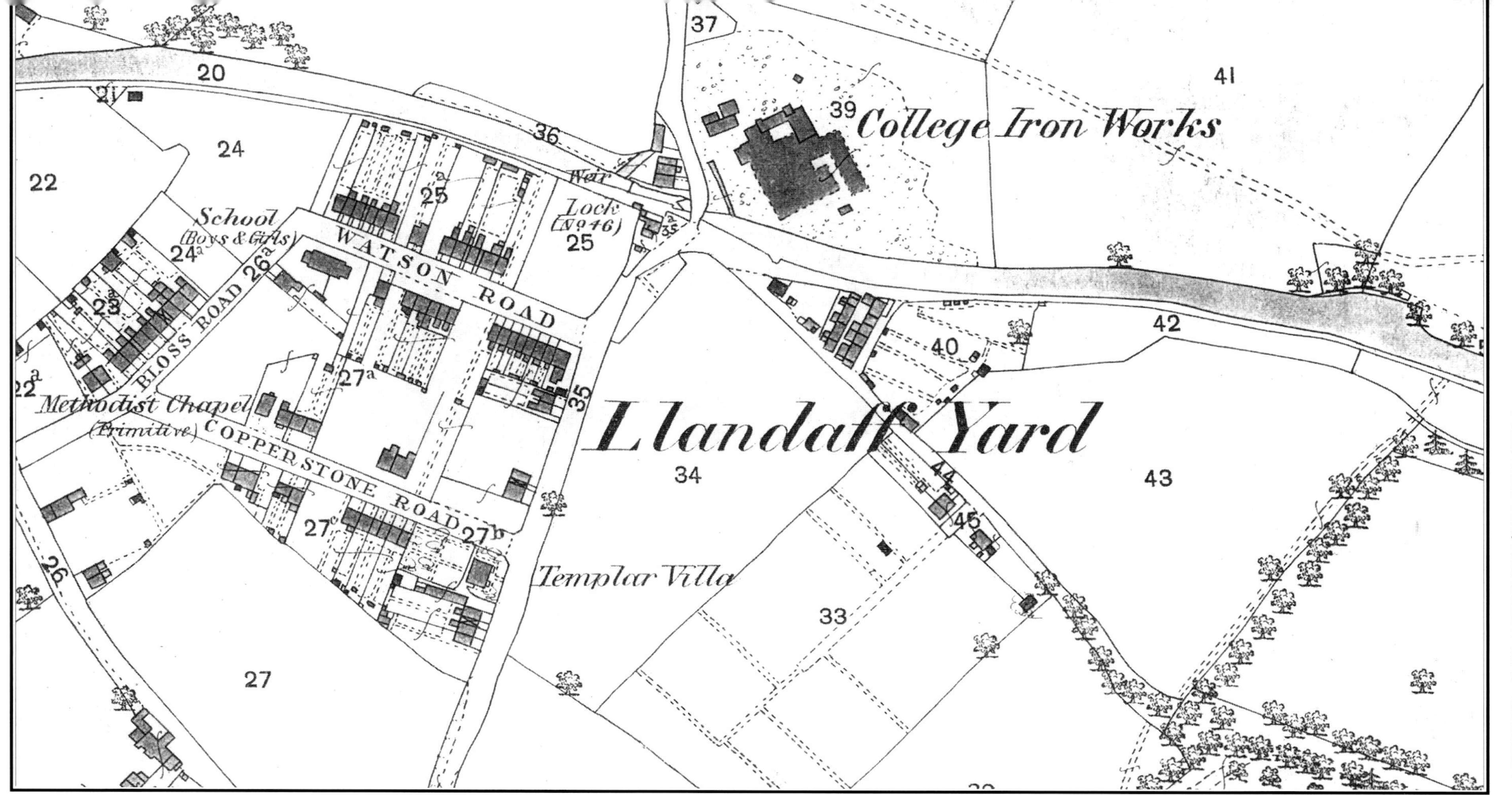

The first edition 25in OS of Llandaff Yard was surveyed in 1875 and 1879. This portion shows the so-called 'freehold' properties near College Lock (Blosse Road and Copleston Road have been mis-spelt by the map makers). College Ironworks rolled iron into small bar and made wire for use in nail making; in its last years it was also supplying plate to Llantrisant Tinplate Works. It was on Chapter Land (where the tithe barn originally stood), leased to Evan Griffiths then sub-leased by his descendants, the Thomas brothers, to William Price in 1848. It seems that Price founded the works and in turn sold it to David Davis of Merthyr and Thomas Williams of Aberdare (later of Gwaelod y Garth house, Merthyr) who turned it into a going concern in the mid 1850s. In early January 1857, its two newly-erected stacks were blown down by the hurricane. From 1861, it operated as Lumley & Williams, the Rev'd Richard Lumley having taken the place of David Davis who ceased to have an active involvement and had become manager of the Gadlys Ironworks. In 1863, Davis and Williams bought the disused Penydarren Ironworks in a vain attempt to get it working again (see T.F. Holley & J. Brynmor Jones 'David Davis, Galon Ucha 1813-1894', in Merthyr Historian *Vol 12, Merthyr 2001). College Ironworks was on stand in the late 1870s but in 1880, the re-opened works had 12 puddling furnaces and 3 rolling mills. By 1901, when the leases expired, the works was in dereliction (see* GRO D/D Tho 1091 B/4).

In September 1858, the Cardiff Local Board of Health were inviting tenders for the removal of the town refuse by canal boats to College Green, probably for spreading as fertilizer. By 1864, the area was known as the 'Llandaff Nuisance', with twelve houses where 'doctors did not like to go'. The other works on this map is of interest, although not connected to the canal. This is the Waen Treoda Engineering Works on the TVR. In 1871, as Charles de Bergue's Ironworks, it had the contract to build the first Tay railway bridge. With the death of Charles de Bergue in 1873, the contract ran into problems and it was re-assigned to Hopkins, Gilkes & Co (Ltd) of the Teeside Ironworks, Middlesborough. Even so, some of the Cardiff management stayed on to complete the ill-fated project. Note the Whitchurch Brook driving John's Little Mill (a corn mill), supplying water to the Bridge Works and then turning south-east to pass under College Road. This stream was the last external water supply the canal had before it reached Cardiff; the stream entered the canal below Gabalfa Lock.

Courtesy CCL, Crown copyright reserved

Left: *Joseph Welch, publican from 1897 to 1909, poses with his dog outside the Three Cups, Llandaff Yard. It ceased to be a licensed premises in 1935 and was demolished along with the rest of Three Cups Row when the Gabalfa housing estate was built in 1947.* SR collection

Below: *An empty working cabin boat has just come up Gabalfa Lock and is bound for College Lock as it passes two fuel boats at James' boatyard – still busy in the early 1920s. The buildings are the covered dock and the workshops, with the lower dock entrance just out of picture on the right. As well as boat building and repairing, James kept a fleet of boats which he hired to timber importers on the Sea Lock pound and the Bute Docks. Ten John James boats were also on loan to the Star Patent Fuel Works. In addition, James worked a small holding to the north of the dock.*
S.C. Fox photo, CCL collection

this new public amenity (in the event of the city's purchase of the canal) were approved by the Parliamentary committee. A 4-mile stretch of the canal and towpath, which had not been earmarked for road development, was to be set aside. Referring to the Alderman's scheme for boating, Mr W. Nelmes, the city's Director of Parks, had added that the existing lock '*could be replaced by a stone sill, with a boathouse whence the boats could be taken for use on the upper or lower reaches.*' [10]

The passing of the 1943 Act authorised the abandonment of the Glamorganshire Canal with a clause directing that between Melingriffith and Tongwynlais the canal should remain a waterway. Meanwhile, the purchase of the canal by the city of Cardiff became effective from 1 January 1944 and the Long Wood section of the canal passed to the administration of the city's Parks Department. The length of canal from Llandaff Lock to Melingriffith, originally proposed to be part of the amenity area, was not included in the scheme and was later unfortunately lost.

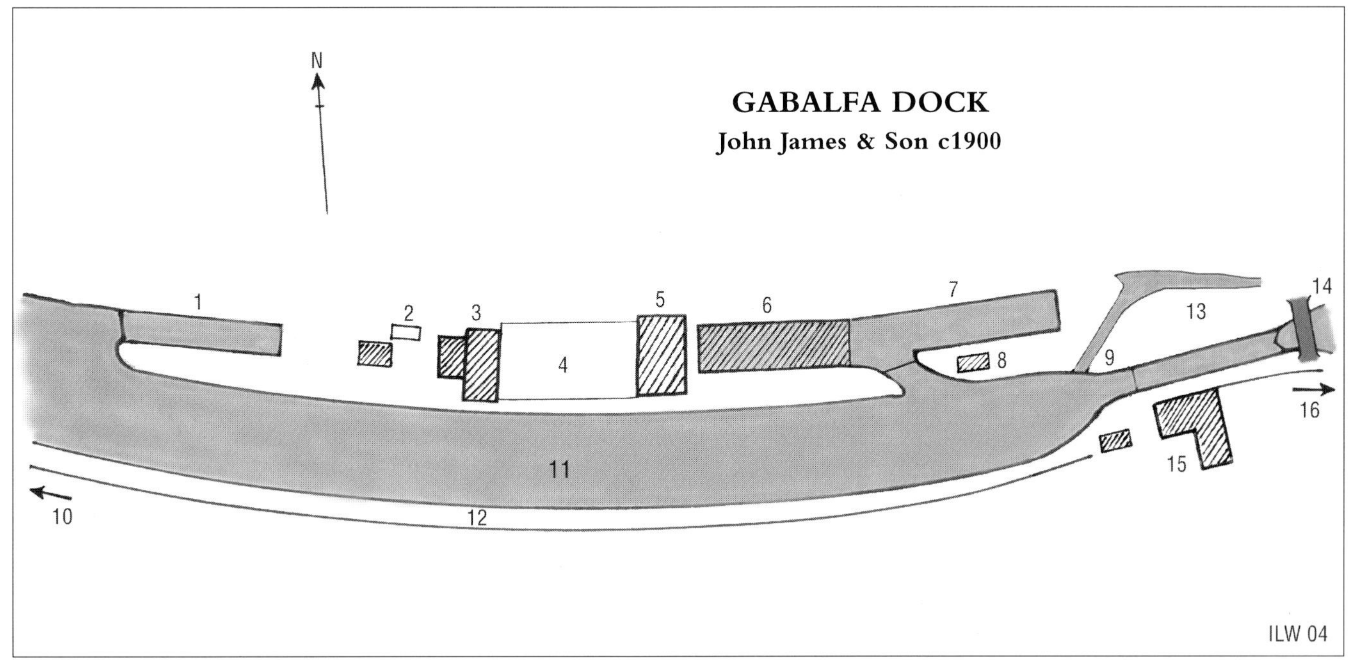

KEY

1. Open dock
2. Saw pit
3. Dock house
4. Garden
5. Workshop
6. Covered dock
7. Open dock
8. Blacksmiths shop
9. Bypass weir
10. To Llandaff
11. Canal
12. Towpath
13 Gabalfa Lock (Lock No 47)
14. Footbridge
15. Gabalfa Lock house
16. To Cardiff

Below: *The abandoned masons' boat marks the entrance to the upper dock at James boatyard. The white washed dwelling is the dock house and beyond is Gabalfa Lock house, the lock being just out of sight around the corner. This view again emphasises the rural nature of the canal on the outskirts of Cardiff.* S.C. Fox photo, WIMM 73.180

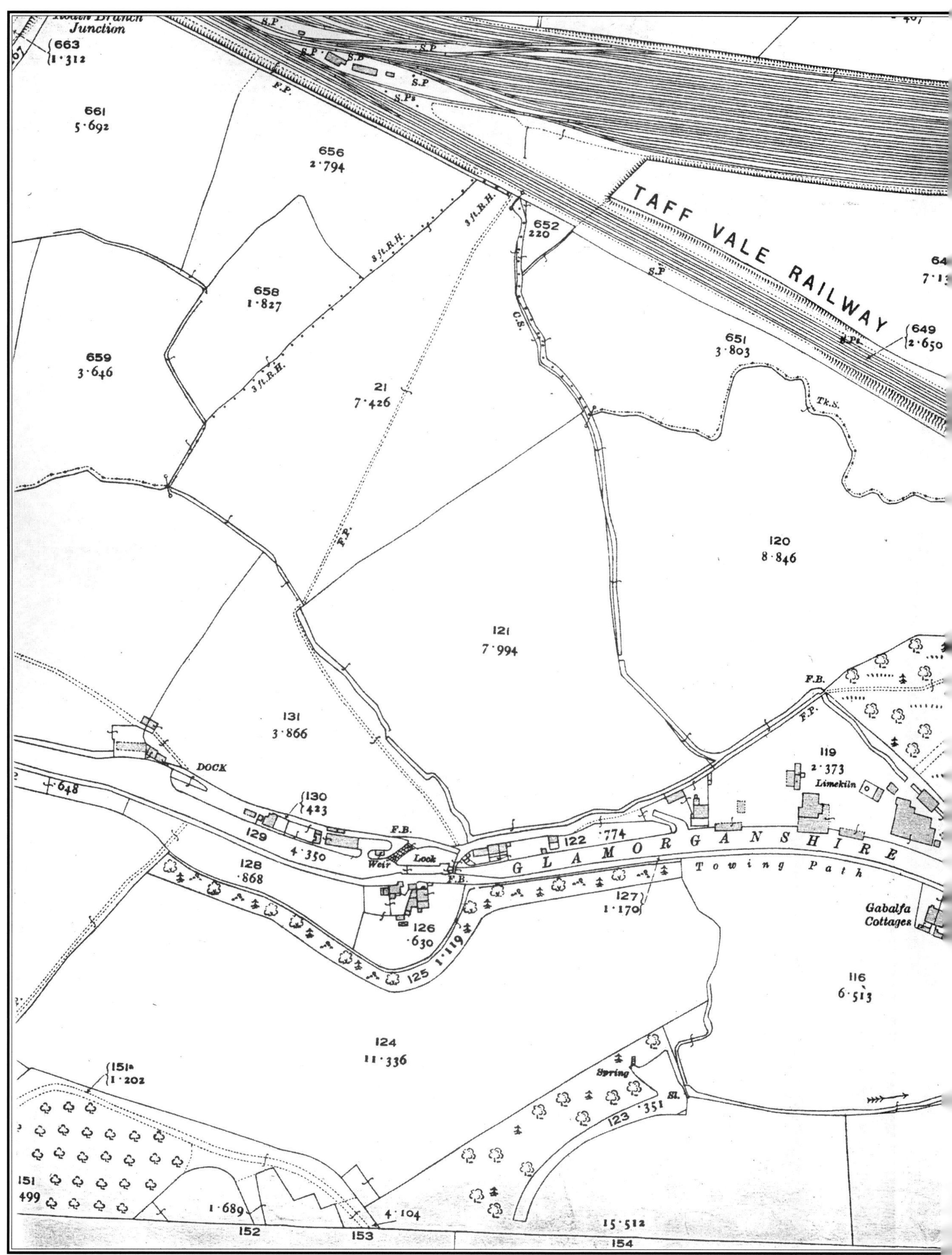
Junction
TAFF VALE RAILWAY
GLAMORGANSHIRE
Towing Path
DOCK
Weir
Lock
F.B.
Limekiln
Gabalfa Cottages
Spring
Tk.S.
F.P.
S.P.
C.S.
661 5·692
656 2·794
658 1·827
659 3·646
21 7·426
652 220
651 3·803
649 2·650
120 8·846
121 7·994
131 3·866
130 ·423
129 4·350
128 ·868
122 ·774
127 1·170
126 ·630
125 1·119
119 2·373
116 6·513
124 11·336
123 ·351
151a 1·202
151 499
152
153 4·104
154 15·512
663 1·312
·648
1·689

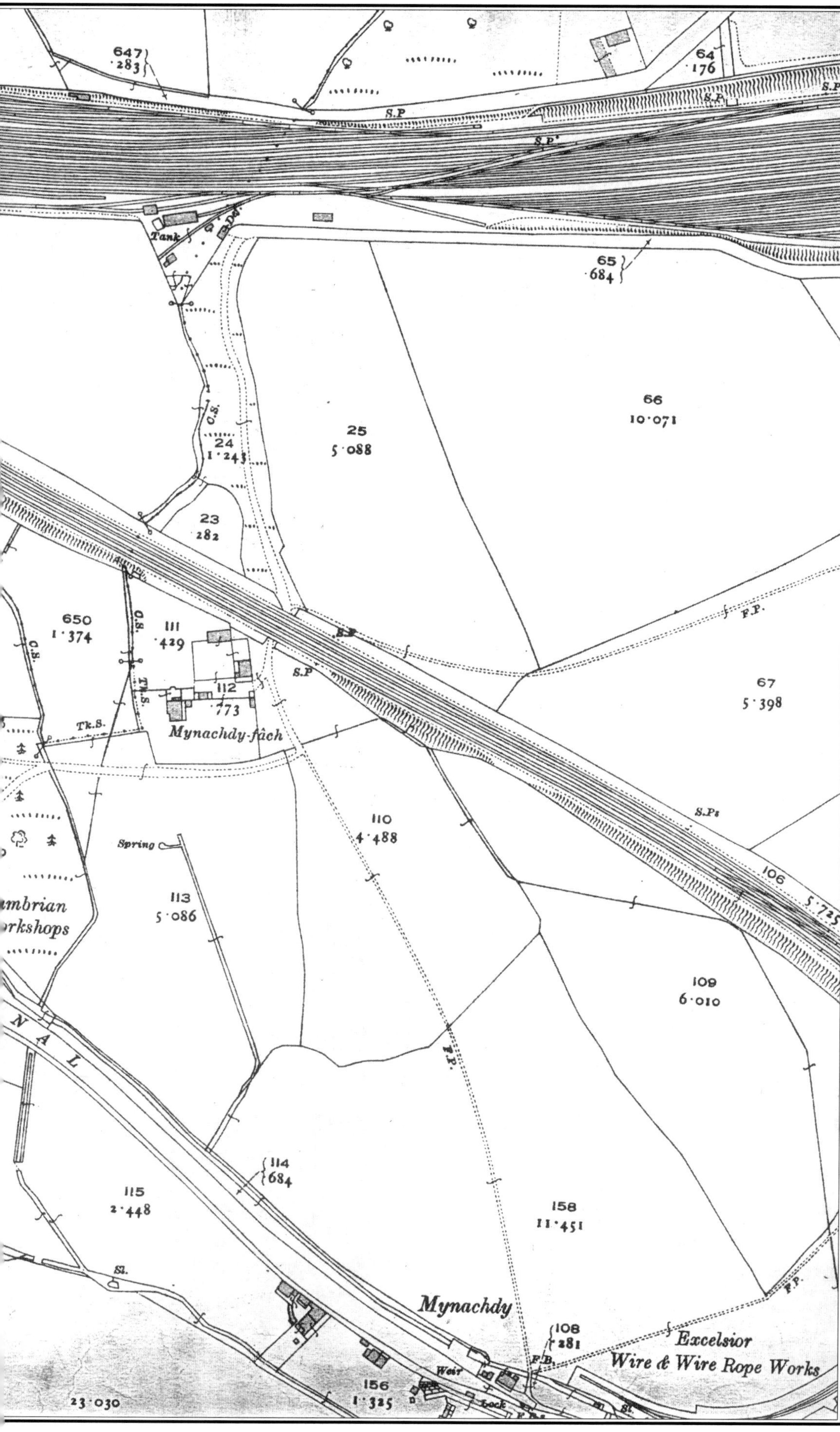

GABALFA LOCK & the CAMBRIAN WORKSHOPS

This portion of the third edition 25in OS of 1920, shows James' boatyard, Gabalfa Lock and the canal company's Cambrian Workshops on the site of the old Cambrian Patent Fuel Works. Also just creeping into view, bottom right, is Mynachdy Lock and the Excelsior Wire Works. James's boatyard by this time had three docks – an upper open dock and two lower docks near to the lock bypass weir, one of which was a covered dock. John James was from Cardiganshire, first moving to Dowlais but then setting up his own boatyard on the Doctor's Canal at Dyffryn. He moved finally to Gabalfa to take over operation of William Beynon's old boat yard. He and his son John Rees also ran a building business and several houses in Llandaff Yard were their work, including Hafodarthen Terrace in Copleston Road. Running diagonally across the map is the TVR main line into Cardiff. The plethora of tracks at the top of the map are holding loops for coal wagons on the TVR's Roath Dock Branch, a small indication of the huge tonnages of coal which were brought down the valleys every day. The two routes meet at Roath Branch Junction, with a further fan of dead end sidings continuing just off the page, top left. Note the map has been reduced by 15% to fit the page.

Courtesy CCL,
Crown copyright reserved

James' Dock House awaits its fate as the Gabalfa housing estate closes in. ILW photo 23 Dec 1948 neg 741

The natural beauty of the Melingriffith - Tongwynlais length of the canal, bound tightly on the east by a mile-long steeply sloping wooded hillside and on the towpath side by level meadowland leading towards the Melingriffith feeder and the River Taff, had long been appreciated by walkers. Midway between Sunny Bank and Tongwynlais, the waterway narrowed to pass through the picturesquely-placed Forest and Middle Locks. However, it seemed that in the years following the Second World War, popular interest in boating had largely evaporated and as a result no elegant mahogany skiffs of the kind seen on Roath Park Lake were ever transferred for hire on the city's canal.

Whilst walkers and naturalists in the post-war world enjoyed the rural tranquillity of the Glamorganshire Canal, the appreciation of the canal as an asset of industrial historical interest appeared to be nil. The canal suffered considerably from the activities of Cardiff Corporation over the years. Brick weirs replaced top gates at Forest and Middle Locks in 1945 and the remaining gates were removed soon afterwards. The lock cottage and locktail bridge at Forest Lock were demolished and at Middle Lock the whole lock wall was destroyed.

During the 1970s a growing countrywide interest in the waterways as a national heritage was becoming more clearly apparent to the city's Parks Department and by 1975,

Gabalfa Lock house and the photographer's bicycle. ILW photo 21 June 1947 neg 473

Harry Watts has been out with GCC goods boat No 451, downgraded to grass cutting and towpath hedge maintenance duties between Gabalfa and Melingriffith during the spring of 1943. In one of the last boat movements on the Glamorganshire Canal, Harry has brought the boat down from Llandaff stern-first with the rudder tied in the fixed position. He has filled Gabalfa Lock but before he can open the top gate to admit the boat, he has to remove the accumulation of submerged sacking and ashes from the top gate hollow quoin before he can swing the gate. This traditional mixture was used on canals to plug leaky lock gates. ILW photo 15 April 1943 neg 222

One of the few known close-up views of a boat in a Glamorganshire Canal lock. Harry Watts has raised the bottom gate paddles at Gabalfa and the boat is just about to be lowered in the lock. It will then continue its journey stern-first to the Cambrian Yard. ILW photo 15 April 1943 neg 223

official attitudes to the surviving Melingriffith - Tongwynlais length of the canal had changed. Between 1975 and 1978, in a complete reversal of policy, the Parks Department was making efforts, aided by Manpower Services Commission Job Creation Schemes, to clear fallen trees and to '*put the locks back again*'. The west wall of Middle Lock was duly reinstated but the structural modifications to Forest Lock (the stone floor of the lock chamber now has a step in it) can only serve to confuse future archaeologists.

Although the canal and towpath had been owned by Cardiff City Council since 1944 and the Melingriffith - Tongwynlais length had been scheduled as an amenity area, it was not until 1 April 1967 that the wider district came under the jurisdiction of the Council, through extension of the city's boundaries northward beyond Tongwynlais. The way was now open to secure the whole route and adjacent lands as a conservation area and, following discussions between Glamorgan Naturalists' Trust and the Cardiff Naturalists' Society, Cardiff City Council designated the area as a Nature Reserve in June 1967. In November 1967, Cardiff City

Above: *Boat No 451 floats cabin-first out of Gabalfa Lock, aided by a push from Harry Watts' boat hook. This lock was always known by canal people as 'Lock French', after Charles French, a lockkeeper there in 1829.*
ILW photo 15 April 1943 neg 224

Right: *Harry Watts is seen shafting his boat stern-first to the Cambrian Yard, with a load of hedge cuttings for disposal by burning.*
ILW photo 15 April 1943 neg 214

Quiet waters and derelict boats at the Cambrian Maintenance yard, Gabalfa, in the 1930s. GCC No 504, formerly Castell Llandaf, lies against the wharf. Moored on the outside is the work-boat No 277, nicknamed 'Alabama'. Her enlarged cabin with door at the forward end could seat a work gang of ten men. Originally a coal boat, the Alabama had belonged to the owners of Coed Cae Dyrus Colliery at Nantgarw. A relic of the old Cambrian Fuel Co is the loading canopy still overhanging the wharf. The house was the manager's and in the last years of the canal, it was occupied by Walter Tyrrell, the canal company's engineer. In front of the house is the ice breaker.

S.C. Fox photo, WIMM collection 73.205

Left: *Although the Cambrian fuel works was closed and up for sale in 1893, the old factory buildings remained in a dilapidated state long after the GCC had taken over the site for its boatyard. It was not finally cleared away until 1948. In this evocative scene at the boatyard, recorded on Christmas Eve 1943, five of the GC Company's boats are moored at the old factory to await their fate. Gabalfa Lock is in the distance.* ILW photo 24 Dec 1943 neg 244

At the same location, this view was taken from on board GCC No 455 – 'the Newport boat'; according to Harry Watts, this boat had come from the Monmouthshire Canal. It was among several owned by the Star Patent Fuel Works and purchased by the GCC in the 1930s. The canal company docked them at the Cambrian Yard and fitted them out for the Pontypridd carrying work. ILW photo 24 Dec 1943 neg 242

At the Cambrian Yard, Gabalfa, between the wars, some precarious work is taking place on the lower pintle that holds the rudder on boat No 499. S.C. Fox photo, CCL collection

Parks Department and Cardiff Naturalists' Society agreed to form a joint management committee to run the Reserve.[11] Described as '*a sanctuary for birds and a haven for wild plants*', the Reserve is of course a place of peace for the enjoyment of people in much the same way as the canal had been in the last days of the boatmen. In 1981, the Reserve, including the railway cutting, was declared a Statutory Local Nature Reserve,[12] but not before a series of onslaughts by the modern world had reduced the length of the reserve by almost a third. Between Middle Lock and Tongwynlais, the way is blocked by a road embankment, an M4 motorway interchange and the A470 Cardiff to Merthyr Trunk road. Progress northwards from Middle Lock to Tongwynlais is by a series of diversions along waymarked footpaths which, like the canal towpath walk, are alternative ways up the valley broadly forming part of the mainly off-road cycle path and footpath known as the Taff Trail. As it exists today, the Reserve is nearly 3/4 mile long and represents the last substantial remnant of the Glamorganshire Canal.

NOTES TO CHAPTER 6

1 CCL deeds II 2584 and 2586-7.

2 Glamorganshire Canal tonnage account book September 1798-9, GRO D/D Art O/21. Thomas Key's return journeys from delivering coal to the Sea Lock at Cardiff consisted mainly of Aberthaw limestone and bagged lime.

3 John Key was also sending shop goods and porter from Cardiff to Merthyr.

4 GCC minute book 13 January, 17 November 1803, 7 December 1804, 4 June, 18 July 1807, 22 June 1814.

5 GRO QAW 2/37, 1814-15, for example.

6 GRO Q/DP 31c.

7 For a discussion on the origins of the name Cow & Snuffers see Stephen Rowson 'The Glamorganshire Canal at the Turn of the Century' in *Archive - The Quarterly Journal for British Industrial and Transport History*, Witney 1994, Issue 1, p51 and Issue 4, p51.

8 GRO B/C Gca 4/113

9 *Cardiff & Suburban News*, 30 January 1943: editorial report and comment on Cardiff City Parks Committee meeting 25 January 1943 and Cardiff City Parliamentary meeting, 26 January 1943.

10 *South Wales Echo*, 26 January 1943 and *Cardiff & Suburban News*, 30 January 1943.

11 Mary E. Graham 'A New Nature Reserve – the Glamorganshire Canal between Tongwynlais and Whitchurch and the Long Wood', in *Transactions of Cardiff Naturalists' Society*, Vol XCIV, 1966-68, Cowbridge 1969, pp4-13.

12 Cardiff City Council Leisure and Amenities Department *Visitors Brief Guide to Glamorgan (sic) CanalLocal Nature Reserve*, Cardiff 1987.

By 29 June 1947, when this photograph was taken, the canal bed was dry at Gabalfa and the Cambrian Yard was awaiting clearance for building the Gabalfa housing estate. Boat No 488 awaits its certain fate. ILW photo neg 475

Chapter 7

PATENT FUEL

In 1841, Lieutenant Dornford transferred his allegiances from the Glamorganshire Canal, where he had been harbourmaster, to Lord Bute where he took on similar but what he must surely have expected to be more exciting, duties as dockmaster to the new Bute Dock. On 13 June 1843, Lieutenant Dornford wrote a letter marked 'Private' to Thomas Collingdon, the Marquess of Bute's secretary:[1]

> *'I had an interview with Mr Locket yesterday. He appears very anxious to establish the parties who are to make the 'Patent Fuel' and at the same time not wishing any person to see he is anxious to benefit himself! he told me the parties would require about 200 feet of square ground to erect their Machinery, Steam Engine etc upon and he thought it would be to Lord Bute's advantage! to let them have the ground at a very small Rent the first year and then to increase it if they found it answer. As if the Rent was too high they would establish themselves at Newport or further up the Canal, the fact is he wants to get them here as he is afraid of the Tredegar Coal cutting him out. I see of course it ended in all talk. I gave him to understand the depth of Water I expected would be £1-0-0 per foot. However he wished that I shd mention this to you (as I suppose as a sounding rod) and said he should not leave Cardiff till the end of the Week when he should like to know what you thought about it.'*

Dornford's personal expectations were slow to materialise as the new dock company struggled in the first years to take trade from the 'Old Canal'. His letters abound with reports such as '*Trade is very slack*' and '*I am sorry to say all continues very dull & very little doing.*' Perhaps it was the Bute management's pre-occupation with these matters and (for example) with persuading the Dowlais Company to move its import/export business from the Taff Vale Company's Little Dock on the canal to the new Bute Dock that caused them to ignore Locket's proposals and lost them this early opportunity to set up a Patent Fuel works at Cardiff.

It is generally believed that the first works for manufacturing Patent Fuel using coal-tar pitch as a binding agent was established in 1842, near St Etienne in France, the first in England following in 1846 at Newcastle upon Tyne[2] and the first in South Wales in 1847 at Swansea.[3] The works were erected at Tir Llandore by the firm of Warlick & Co, government contractors of Deptford, presumably to supply the Royal Navy. It was not until 1857 that the first was built at Cardiff – on the bank of the Glamorganshire Canal.

Patent Fuel (occasionally known as Preserved Coal) is a compound of small coal and a binding substance (invariably pitch) that has been intimately mixed together, heated to the melting point of the pitch and subjected to considerable pressure in moulds so as to produce rectangular blocks of a definite size and shape. The blocks were allowed to cool slowly in contact with the air and were then fit to be used for the same purposes as large coal.[4] This artificial product retained the name of Patent Fuel, because the stages of the manufacturing process (washing and drying the coal, crushing and disintegrating the pitch, mixing coal and pitch, heating the mixture, pressing the blocks and automating the whole process to include stacking and loading the blocks into boats and wagons) continued to be the subject of a string of patented inventions to improve their efficiency.[5]

The industry made use of previously wasted small coal obtained not only from collieries but also from the dockside screenings where the coal was tipped into the colliers' holds. Steam coal proved the best type of coal for Patent Fuel and this was available in abundance in Cardiff. In the early days, the huge quantities of coal dust on the dockside could be purchased at a nominal price, its removal being treated as a favour to the dock authorities. Pitch, too, was readily obtainable, as it was a by-product from gas works and coke works.[6] The process of manufacture sealed the coal into a block which preserved its calorific power even when it was exposed to the weather (a significant factor in tropical climates). This was particularly so when the dry heat process replaced the steam presses – so reducing the moisture content of the blocks. The economies of stowage and its capacity for minimal breakage compared to virgin coal made the fuel ideal for the world's navies as, from the 1840s, they rapidly adopted the steam ship in place of sail. First to use Patent Fuel extensively were the packet boats which carried the Royal Mail.[7] The British Navy, who from 1851 were using Welsh steam coal exclusively, were also experimenting with Patent Fuel. From the outset it was an advantage for the manufacturing works to be sited at or near to port. By the late 1890s, well over 90 per cent of

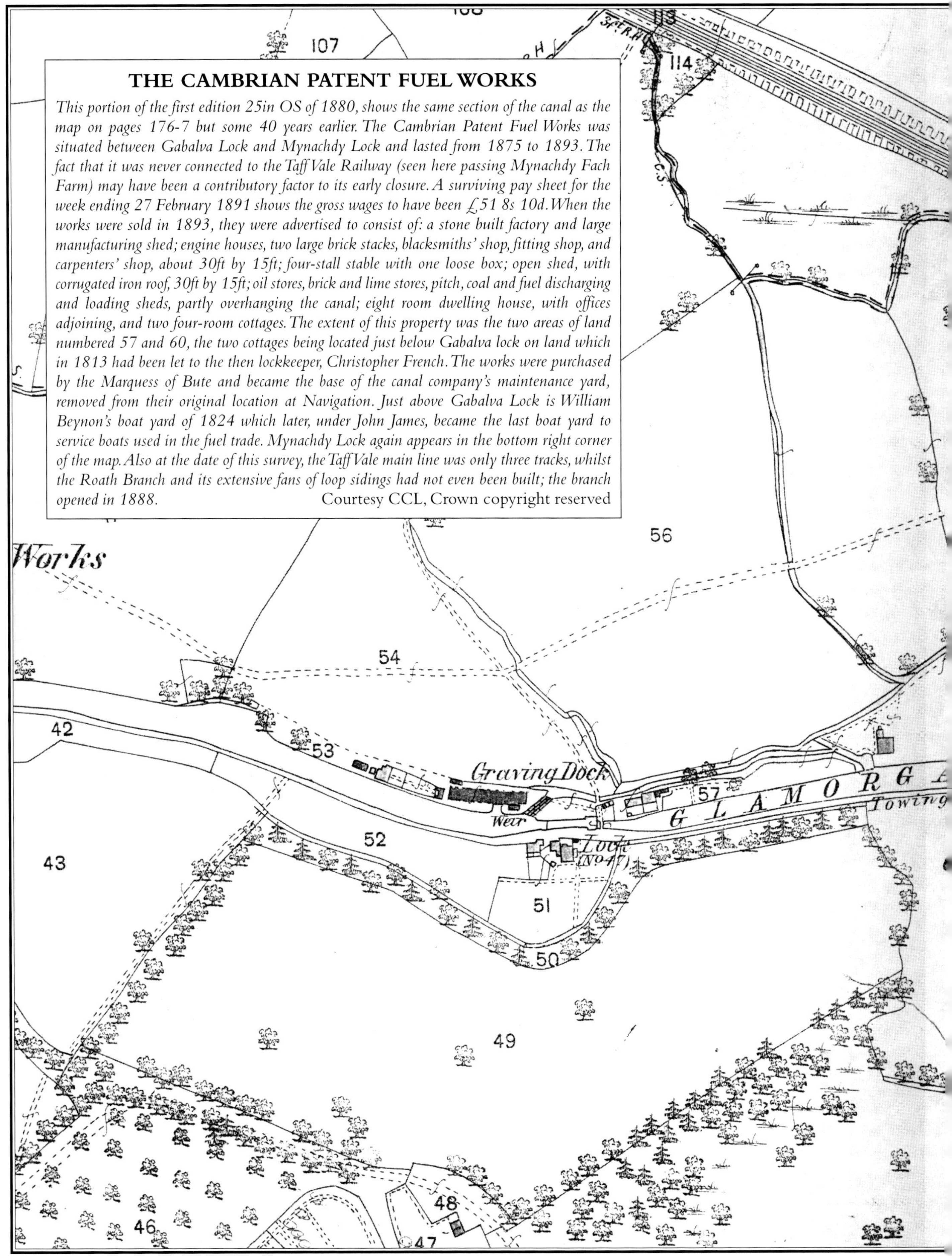

THE CAMBRIAN PATENT FUEL WORKS

This portion of the first edition 25in OS of 1880, shows the same section of the canal as the map on pages 176-7 but some 40 years earlier. The Cambrian Patent Fuel Works was situated between Gabalva Lock and Mynachdy Lock and lasted from 1875 to 1893. The fact that it was never connected to the Taff Vale Railway (seen here passing Mynachdy Fach Farm) may have been a contributory factor to its early closure. A surviving pay sheet for the week ending 27 February 1891 shows the gross wages to have been £51 8s 10d. When the works were sold in 1893, they were advertised to consist of: a stone built factory and large manufacturing shed; engine houses, two large brick stacks, blacksmiths' shop, fitting shop, and carpenters' shop, about 30ft by 15ft; four-stall stable with one loose box; open shed, with corrugated iron roof, 30ft by 15ft; oil stores, brick and lime stores, pitch, coal and fuel discharging and loading sheds, partly overhanging the canal; eight room dwelling house, with offices adjoining, and two four-room cottages. The extent of this property was the two areas of land numbered 57 and 60, the two cottages being located just below Gabalva lock on land which in 1813 had been let to the then lockkeeper, Christopher French. The works were purchased by the Marquess of Bute and became the base of the canal company's maintenance yard, removed from their original location at Navigation. Just above Gabalva Lock is William Beynon's boat yard of 1824 which later, under John James, became the last boat yard to service boats used in the fuel trade. Mynachdy Lock again appears in the bottom right corner of the map. Also at the date of this survey, the Taff Vale main line was only three tracks, whilst the Roath Branch and its extensive fans of loop sidings had not even been built; the branch opened in 1888.

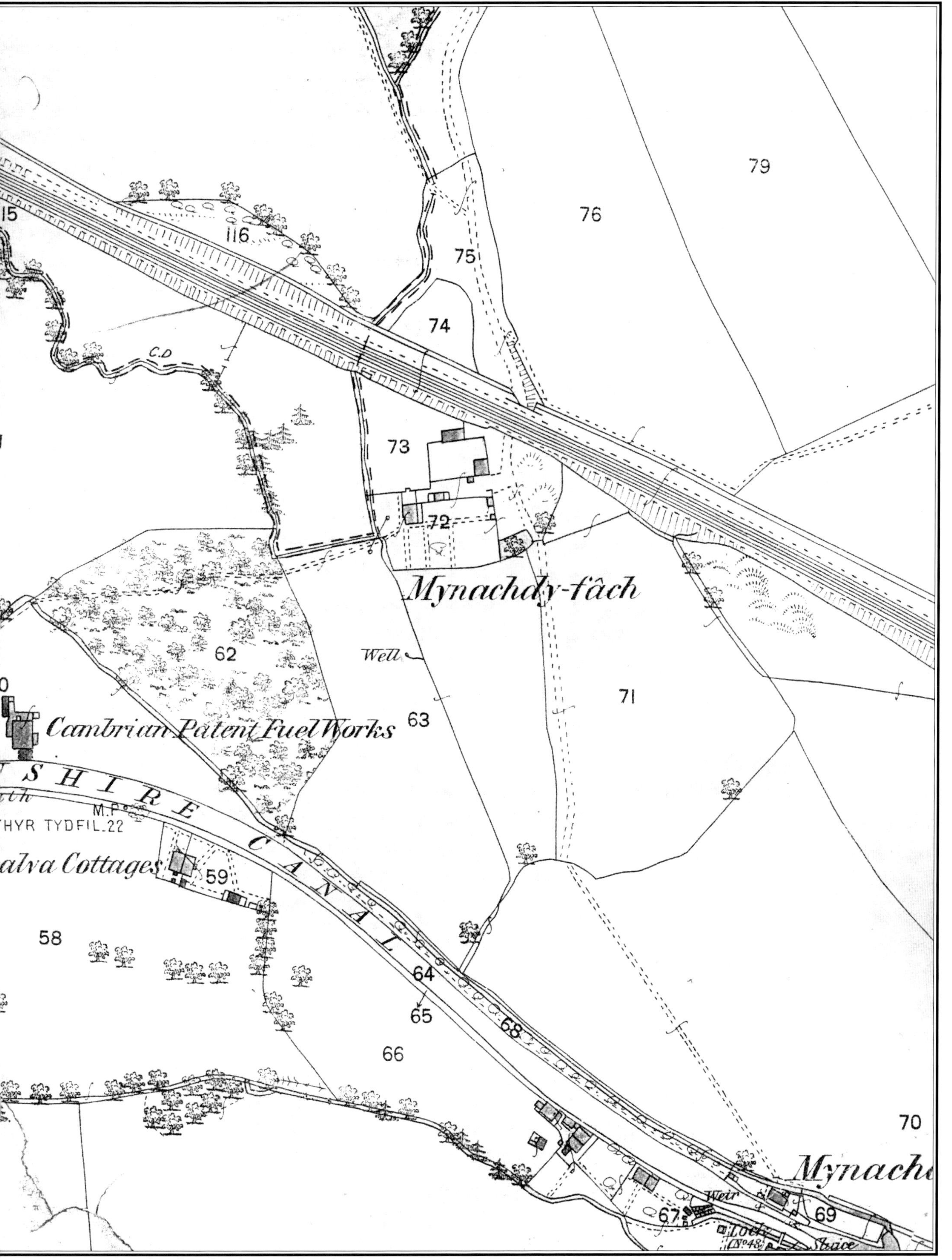
79
76
75
74
116
115
C.D
73
72
Mynachdy-fâch
Well
62
71
Cambrian Patent Fuel Works
63
S H I R E
M.P.
HYR TYDFIL 22
C A N A L
alva Cottages
59
58
64
65
68
66
70
Mynach
Weir
67
69
Lock
(No48)
Sluice

Sammy Fox has caught a busy scene at Mynachdy (Lock 48), where a boat is being lowered to the pound which passed the British Rope Works and the three Patent Fuel works at Maindy. The crane at the rope works wharf can be seen beyond the lockkeeper, who is closing the upper gate.
S.C. Fox photo, WIMM 73.228

Patent Fuel from South Wales was exported for use by the world's navies and railway companies.

As far as the Glamorganshire Canal was concerned, four factories were established by rival companies on its banks in north Cardiff, another at Taff's Well and two others on the Aberdare Canal.

The Works at Maindy

In June 1857, the Cardiff Preserved Coal & Coke Co (Ltd) were building on a five acre site with a 1,000 ft frontage to the Glamorganshire Canal, just below Llystalybont Bridge. The works was founded by Henry Walker Wood of Briton Ferry, who had been operating a fuel works at Port Talbot since 1851 and in the mid fifties had supplied ships of the British Navy for the war against Russia in the Crimea. (In 1896, some blocks of Crown fuel made at the Port Talbot works were salvaged from the wreck of HMS *Prince*, which had gone down in Balaclava Bay in 1854.) By February 1858, the company, perhaps as part of a recruitment drive to attract local labour, announced it was holding a regular night school and Sunday school for children and adults of the neighbourhood at Maindy.[8] As production commenced, the canal company resolved that the tonnage rate for this new commodity would be the same as for coal.[9]

Wood's patented process at this first of Cardiff's fuel works was very labour intensive and within three years, the company needed financial restructuring and was sold to new shareholders operating as the Crown Preserved Coal & Coke Co Ltd. Wood retained a minority shareholding and his son, T.H. Wood, was allowed to remain as manager. Compensation claims from creditors and minority shareholders against the old company continued until as late as 1868.[10] Following the sale, production was immediately increased and then again in 1863, when a third factory was erected at the Maindy site, which was then reported to be operating night and day.[11] In 1862, 13,550 tons of Patent Fuel left the Bute docks, rising to 17,250 tons in 1863.[12] This would not only have comprised output from Crown but may also have included a contribution from the short-lived Aberdare Patent Fuel Company. This works had sprung up on the Aberdare Canal at Cwmbach in 1859 using Werfa coal and, according to a sale notice in 1863, had a capacity of 100 tons per day

Mynachdy Lock waste weir, cottages and the lockkeeper's cabin. S.C. Fox photo, WIMM 73.714

utilising manager George Ashcroft's patent process for operating the hydraulic press.[13] The works' 120 ft long wharf on the Aberdare Canal would have been suitable to accommodate two boats (see Volume 1 p128). It is probably not a coincidence that Ashcroft also had workshops on the Glamorganshire Canal at Blackweir.

The environmental effect of these Patent Fuel works is illustrated by a test case, brought against Messrs Wood and the Crown Works at the 1863 Glamorgan Summer Assize. Charles Lloyd, tenant of a cottage at Maindy (with the encouragement of his speculating landlord, George Morten), complained of the damage done to his property and garden by the soot and dust spilling from the extended works. The defence pointed out that the Crown Works did not have a monopoly on this nuisance and pollution also emanated from the nearby Maindy Foundry, the soap works and from passing trains of coal trucks on the railway. Most of all, the defence argument ran:[15]

> *'Go to Whitmore Lane or to any place near the docks where there would be little difficulty in finding plenty of wives who would complain about the coal dust arising from the coal tips near the docks. They would say that they would not hang out their clothes without getting them covered with dust. They would say, then put down the coal tips, put down the docks … If they allowed such an action as this to claim damages there was not a single house in London that would not be liable. What indeed would become of the manufactures in such towns as Birmingham and Manchester?'*

Schoolboys fish for sticklebacks and tadpoles in the moribund canal below Mynachdy Lock in the 1930s. Across the water, the wharf alongside British Ropes is well overgrown. S.C. Fox photo, CCL GC112

Mynachdy Lock, north Cardiff. John Frazer's boat, returning empty from Pontypridd, threatens to overtake the horse as the driver slows up for the photographer on a hot summers day in the 1920s. Bill Hamlin collection

Needless to say, the jury was persuaded to find for the defendants. And what of Lloyd's family and their neighbours in the terrace that became known as Crown Cottages? This judgement paved the way for them to be subjected to the filth from two more Patent Fuel works, the Anchor and the Star, which were to be built within a stone's throw of their doorsteps.

T.H. Wood seems to have been something of a crank. Following the lead of T.W. Booker at Melingriffith, he imposed his zealous patriotism on the workforce at the Crown Works by insisting they all join the volunteers – the A and B Battery of the Royal Glamorgan Artillery, which he had founded, providing them with a gun shed at Blackweir and a regular instructor paid for by the works. It was a common thing to stop the whole works for big gun drill. He also forbade his thirsty men from drinking at the nearby Maindy Inn, run by Josiah Oates. Early in 1865, the company saw fit to replace the eccentric Wood as managing director with the coal owner, Thomas Edward Heath, who had been managing John Nixon's Werfa Colliery at Aberdare with his engineering partner Tom Evens. In 1851, Heath was already a coal proprietor and shipper based in Crockherbtown, Cardiff. By the time he was 31, in 1857, he had built an impressive pile, Northlands, in North Road and was living within easy walking distance of the Crown Works. His inventiveness gave new impetus to the concern. By the time of his appointment, there were 240 men and boys employed producing an output of 800 tons per week, all of which would have been sent down the canal.[16]

The Patent Fuel industry was more mature in France at this time and 1866 saw the opening of the Anchor Patent Fuel works by Tinel & Co, who, for their works at Le Havre, already sourced most of their small coal from Cardiff. The works were situated on Dr Richard Griffiths's former property at Maindy Bank, a few hundred yards up the canal from the Crown Works and next to the continuing soap works and Parry & Williams' old boat building yard.[17] The Anchor Works were managed by Louis Jean Baptiste Guéret from 1868 and by 1879 the firm relinquished this Cardiff Patent Fuel business solely to Louis and his brother Henri.[18] The Anchor used the existing 1859 Couillard patent process for hydraulic presses,[19] a steam heating process which had also been operated by the Pentreguinea Fuel Company in Swansea since 1860.[20] When Henri died in 1895, the Anchor was formed into the limited company of L. Guéret

Looking back towards Mynachdy Lock from opposite the rope works wharf. The Excelsior had their own boat (No 63), which delivered raw materials from their stores on the Sea Lock pound. Output was mostly by rail and the TVR. S.C. Fox photo, WIMM 73.258

Four young girls play on the sunken remains of two boats alongside the rope works at Maindy. The boat in the foreground has iron knees and has been strengthened with a cross-member to prevent its hull from spreading. S.C. Fox photo, WIMM 73.271

252
THE EXCELSIOR WIRE ROPE CO., LTD.
Cardiff, July 5th 1912
Messrs Glamorganshire Canal Co
Cardiff
Please receive the following Wire Ropes, viz :—

	Tons	Cwts.	Qrs.	lbs.
Please Permit our Boat To Pass from Stores To Works with 104 Bails of Yarn	5	0	0	0
3 Cask of Oil		10		
2 Wooden Reels		2		

Excelsior Wire Ropes boat permit No 252, July 5 1912. ILW collection

Ltd and in 1909, by this time also operating eight other Patent Fuel works in mainland France, it purchased a considerable share of the Albion Colliery at Cilfynydd.

Meanwhile, from the Crown Works, T.P. Balls, who had been recruited by Heath from the hydraulic engineers William Armstrong, left the company to install his own patents and reopen the Cwmbach Works on the Aberdare Canal. Again in 1872, Heath himself failed to have his patents for a dry heat process accepted by the Crown Works, so he left to start the Star Patent Fuel works with his partner Tom Evens, still engineer of the Werfa Colliery, Aberdare. Machinery built to their new patents was able to press 500 tons of materials into blocks in 24 hours. Heath also patented a system of wire rope carriers and roller shoots to enable the blocks to be carried all over the stocking yard with no labour.[21] A constituent part of the Star Company's machinery, installed in 1874, was the redundant Great Western Railway broad gauge locomotive *Nelson*, adapted for re-use as a stationary engine and surviving long enough to be photographed by T.E. Heath's grandson, Lionel Heath.[22]

The Star Works were erected on the site of the old Maindy Forge and foundry of 1854, just down the canal from the Crown Works.[23]

Then, in 1875, the Cambrian Patent Fuel Works too were established – just north of Mynachdy at Gabalfa, on a three

When the Star Fuel works were established in 1874 it was only two years since the South Wales lines of the GWR had been converted from the broad gauge. T.E. Heath acquired a redundant broad gauge locomotive, Nelson, *in 1874 and installed it at the Star Works as a stationary engine. Built at Swindon in 1853,* Nelson *was one of Gooch's 'Ariadne' Class standard goods 0-6-0 tender engines. All the company really required was the boiler but, supposedly, when* Nelson *first arrived, it was hooked up to the machinary and driven from the footplate, like a locomotive. Later, it was extensively adapted for stationary use as seen here. It is seen connected to the gear drive to the factory, powering an 8ft 2in diameter spur wheel.*
Country Life, Dec 1972

acre site with a substantial 1,165 ft frontage to the canal.

The Cambrian attracted a number of small share holders but significant amongst them was the colliery proprietor William Davies (of Holly House, Pontypridd), who may have supplied the works with its small coal. By 1883, Davies is recorded as '*Boat Owner*', with a £600 share of the widely distributed £12,440 capital. Another shareholder was Noah Rees, hay merchant of Working Street, Cardiff – a family business which survived at the same premises into the second half of the 20th century.[24]

So by the mid 1870s, there were three Patent Fuel works operating within a mile of each other, in the area variously known as Maindy, Llystalybont and Blackweir, and another less than a mile away from them. All relied on the canal for their raw materials and for sending their finished product to Cardiff. Traffic was shipped exclusively through the Bute Docks rather than through the canal Sea Lock pound, this being enforced by a clause in the leases of the works at

Above: *Louis Gueret's Patent Fuel Works when still in operation and looking towards Llystalybont. The rail wagons from Cwmaman and Lockets have brought in small coal from the Dare Valley. Patent Fuel blocks are stacked behind the coal wagons.*
S.C. Fox photo, CCL GC203

Left: *This view from the other side of the Anchor Works clearly shows the conveyors and slides used to load fuel blocks onto the boats. The rake of wagons this time is from Bwllfa – also in the Dare Valley.*
South Wales Coal Annual for 1913

Gueret's Anchor Works being demolished in the 1930s while the company's boats are left to rot in the silent canal. The boat in the foreground is LG Ltd No 20. In 1949, Cardiff Corporation infilled the canal with domestic rubbish, which buried some 30 boat hulks between Blackweir and Mynachdy Lock. Although the corporation's bulldozers probably did a good deal of damage to what was left of the boats, future archaeologists might think it worthwhile to excavate parts of the site to re-examine these relics of our industrial past.
S.C. Fox photo, WIMM 73.272

Maindy which lay on Bute land.[25] All traffic when it reached Cardiff therefore passed from the canal through the Junction Canal into the West Dock. To ease movement of fuel to the docks, and the collection and delivery of small coal and pitch, a new fleet of boats was built. Such was the eventual volume of trade that at least one boat builder was able to concentrate solely on the supply and maintenance of fuel boats for the canal. Cabins were unnecessary on the short two mile route. There were just three locks for the canal boats to negotiate below Maindy and this included the Junction Lock between the canal Sea Lock pound and the Bute West Dock. The Cambrian's boats had one extra lock to negotiate – that at Mynachdy.

The increasing competition and the loss of key technical management may have been the reason for a second voluntary liquidation of the Crown Works in 1877. However, the works was immediately sold as a whole to William Butler of Bristol, who placed the management of

Boat No 502, loaded with flour for Pontypridd, has just passed beneath Llystalybont Bridge and is approaching the Anchor Works on its way north. On the right is the site of the entrance to the old Parry & Williams boat dock and the soap works. S.C. Fox photo, CCL GC204

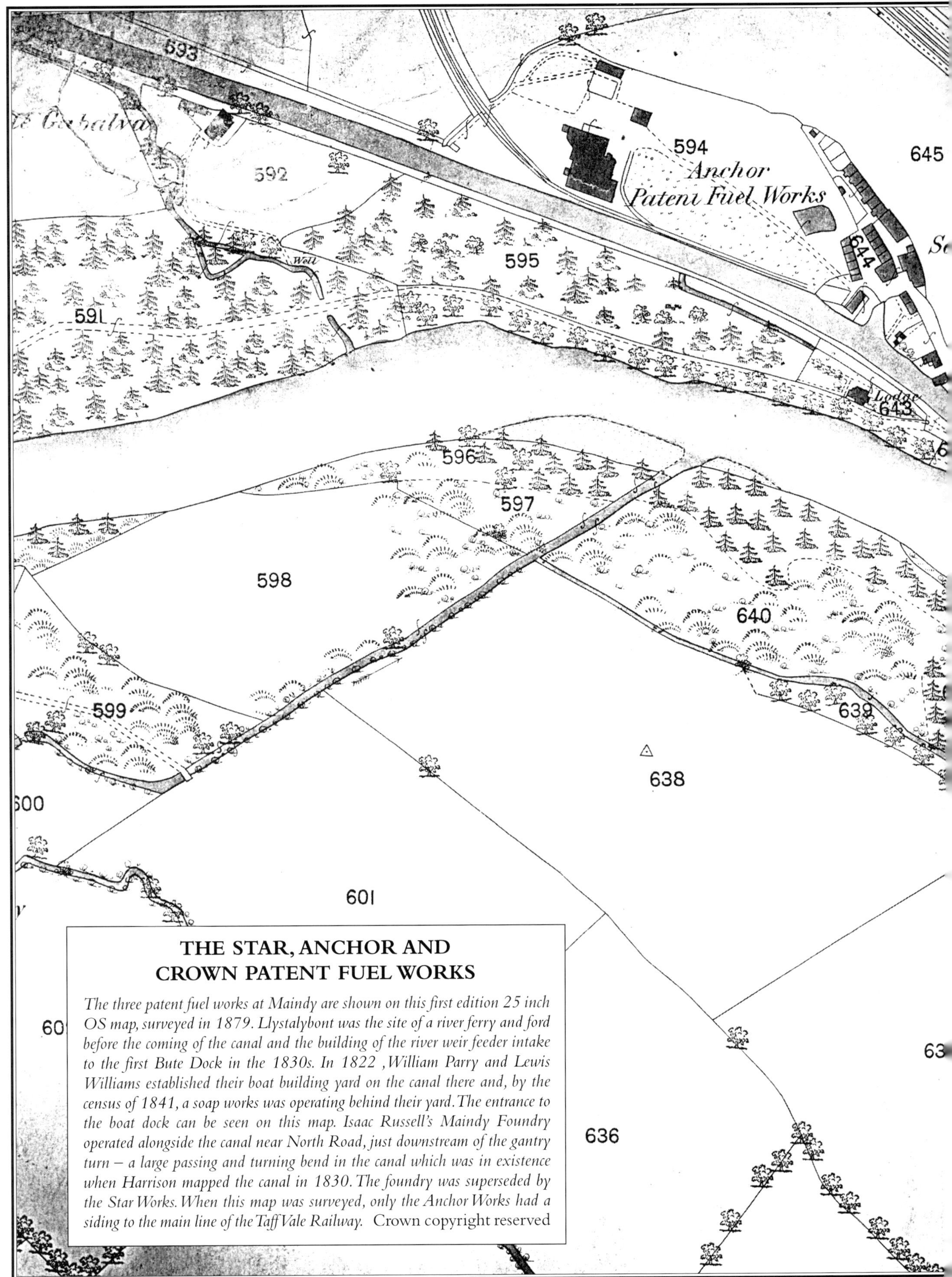

THE STAR, ANCHOR AND CROWN PATENT FUEL WORKS

The three patent fuel works at Maindy are shown on this first edition 25 inch OS map, surveyed in 1879. Llystalybont was the site of a river ferry and ford before the coming of the canal and the building of the river weir feeder intake to the first Bute Dock in the 1830s. In 1822 ,William Parry and Lewis Williams established their boat building yard on the canal there and, by the census of 1841, a soap works was operating behind their yard. The entrance to the boat dock can be seen on this map. Isaac Russell's Maindy Foundry operated alongside the canal near North Road, just downstream of the gantry turn – a large passing and turning bend in the canal which was in existence when Harrison mapped the canal in 1830. The foundry was superseded by the Star Works. When this map was surveyed, only the Anchor Works had a siding to the main line of the Taff Vale Railway.

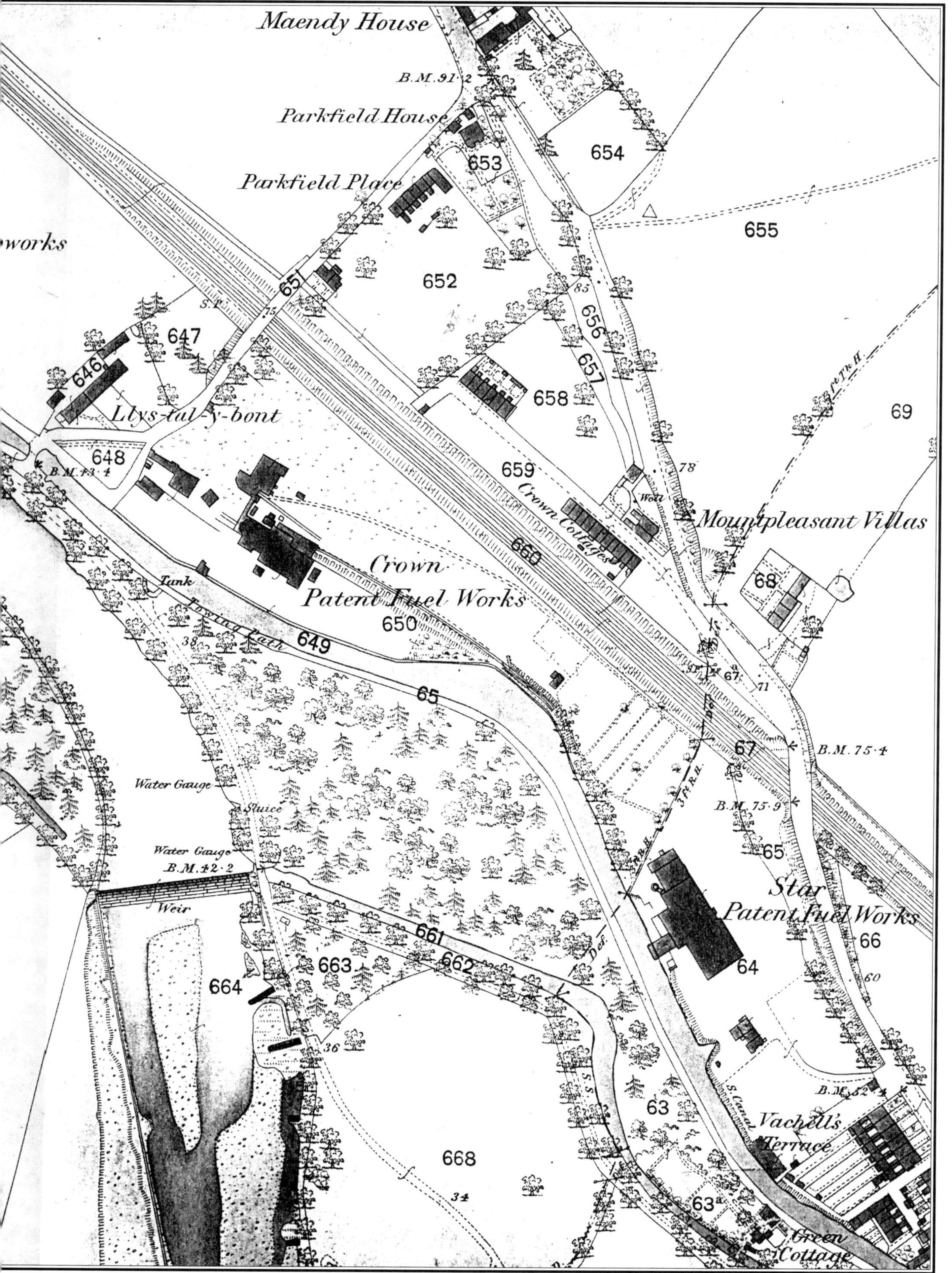
Maendy House
B.M. 91·2
Parkfield House
Parkfield Place
works
Llys-tal-y-bont
B.M. 43·4
Crown Cottages
Mountpleasant Villas
Crown
Patent Fuel Works
Tank
Towing Path
Water Gauge
Sluice
Water Gauge
B.M. 42·2
Weir
B.M. 75·4
B.M. 75·9
Star
Patent Fuel Works
B.M. 52·4
Vachell's Terrace
Green Cottage

The subject of this 1946 aerial view is the Cambrian Wagon Works, which was built on the long-vacated site of the Crown Patent Fuel Works. The site of the Anchor Works, at the very top of the photograph, has also been cleared but fuel boats remain to rot in the derelict canal. The old cottages at Llystalybont survive to this day. Powell Duffryn Review, January 1947

it in the hands of his son Samuel.[26] Butler remodelled the works and adopted his own patents, substituting steam pressure with hydraulic. A siding was put in to the TVR so that coal could be brought in by rail, whilst retaining the canal route to the docks for the finished product. William Butler also ran a small fleet of mainly barges and tugs, collecting tar from various places on the River Severn, the Bristol Avon and the Kennet & Avon Canal. This was brought back to their works at The Parting in Gloucester and Crews Hole in Bristol, for refining into pitch. The main destination for the pitch was the Crown Patent Fuel Works, which explains Butler's interest in acquiring it. A number of vessels were purchased for transporting the pitch from Bristol to Cardiff, including the steam barge *William* and three trows, *Aurora*, *Mary Ann* and *Willie*. Having unloaded at Cardiff, the vessels were able to backload coal, for use in the production process at Crews Hole.[27]

The Anchor Works had been the first to connect to the railway a few years before.[28] By the turn of the century, the Star too had rail access. Only the Cambrian relied totally on the canal for transport. The Cambrian also differed from the others by owning its freehold, part of which was land that, from 1813 to 1876, had been leased to Christopher French and his son (also Christopher), lockkeepers at Gabalfa Lock. At the end of 1882, the Cambrian Works was re-capitalised as the Cambrian Patent Fuel Company Ltd and put in its best year by shipping 53,634 tons through the Junction Lock – for the first time more than the Star (53,305) and the Anchor (42,616) but, by 1893, the company had ceased production. Being totally reliant on the canal for transport, it may never have recovered from the eight month Sea Lock pound closure of 1886, when Lock 51 was being put in.[29]

Each new works maintained a tradition of having its own distinguishing motif stamped into the fuel blocks – along with the Crown, the Anchor and the Star, the Cambrian adopted the Harp as its logo. Elsewhere, at Newport, the Cardiff & Newport Patent Fuel Company was known by the Arrow and, at Swansea, the Pacific Patent Fuel Company used a representation of a two-funnelled steam ship. Other companies in South Wales were the Swan, the Castle, the Phoenix, the Atlantic, the Reliance, the Diamond and the Eclipse. Each also appears to have marketed a particular size fuel block. Some of the

138 "ANCHOR" PATENT FUEL. MAINDY WORKS, 5th Nov 1919.
Messrs. THE GLAMORGANSHIRE CANAL CO.,
Please Pass our boats until 10 O'clock
& Oblige
GUÉRET, Ld. H. Brown

Order No 305
CAMBRIAN FUEL WORKS.
To

116 "ANCHOR" PATENT FUEL. MAINDY WORKS, 14th Nov 1919
Messrs. THE GLAMORGANSHIRE CANAL CO.,
Pass our Boats tonight
10 o/c & oblige

347 14. 4. 21
CARDIFF, 19
To the Glamorganshire Canal Co.
Please pass Boat No. 386
with Tons of "Star"
from our Works to the Docks.
For the "STAR" PATENT FUEL
Western Mail Limited, Cardiff, 3193.

No. 363
GLAMORGANSHIRE CANAL.
PERMIT L. GUERET, LTD., Boat No.
Master, to pass this day of 191
UP.

SPECIES.	T.	C.	Loaded.	Landed.
PITCH.			BUTE DOCKS.	MONACHDY.

Machine Weight. C.
Tolls— Paid. £ s. d. To Pay. £ s. d. Signed by
Wharfage at Loading
Wharfage at Landing

GLAMORGANSHIRE CANAL.
L. GUERET, LTD., Boat No.
UP.

361
"Anchor" Patent Fuel Works,
CARDIFF,
13 - 3 - 1929
Boat No. 17
Charge Tonnage on one Boat Load of Fuel.
L. GUERET & Co., Limited,
"Anchor" Patent Fuel Works.

1637
Works,
5 1929
Boat No. 455
Charge Tonnage on one Boat Load of Fuel.
GUÉRET, LLEWELLYN & MERRETT, LTD.,
"Anchor" Patent Fuel Works.

A selection of boat permits from the Cambrian, Anchor and Star fuel works, including an unused permit from the Anchor Works for delivering pitch from the Bute Docks and also two permits to enable their boats to work from 6 am through until 10 o'clock at night in November 1919. The Star and Anchor works kept the canal busy in the years up to and through the First World War and even into the 1920s but appearances were deceptive. The canal's decline could not be halted by the Patent Fuel loadings, which contributed only low tonnage payments to the canal company on the carrying distances of barely 2½ miles. There was no longer any revenue coming to the canal company from the small coal formerly boated to the works from Abercanaid and from the Aberdare Canal. Both works were receiving their coal requirements via the private sidings put in to connect them with the Taff Vale Railway.

All ILW collection

This aerial view of 1927 shows the Star Works in its last year of operation. The small 19th century settlement of Blackweir, situated between the canal and Cardiff's North Road, owes its existence to the life of the Glamorganshire Canal and the associated Patent Fuel works. The social life of this self-contained community centred around its two public houses, the Machen Forge (in existence in 1858 but rebuilt in 1872) and the Hope (first licence granted 1853), and the little church of St Alban (just out of picture). Another canalside beerhouse at Blackweir in 1850 was the Homfray Arms. Alongside the railway, on the extreme right of this photograph, can be seen part of the Great Western Railway's Cathays carriage sheds. CCL collection

The Star Patent Fuel Works, Maindy. Several heavily-laden boats await their trip to the Bute Docks while the canal bank holds a large stock of blocks. The three laden boats are distinguished by having wooden bollards protruding either side of an apron at their sterns. These would have been used in lashing boats together in the docks at Cardiff. They are identifiable as Nos 40, in front, 273, to its right, and 169, beyond. The Star logo can also be seen alongside the number on the latter. The photograph was taken in 1903 by Oswald Milne, then a student but who later went on to become an architect of some renown, speicalising in designs for large country houses, schools and hotels. Royal Institute of British Architects

dimensions available from the Cardiff Works were:[30]

Brand	Size (inches)	Weight (lbs)
Anchor	10 x 6$^1/_2$ x 4$^1/_2$	12
Anchor	12 x 8$^1/_2$ x 5$^1/_2$	28
Crown	10 x 8 x 6$^1/_2$	24$^1/_2$
Crown	8$^1/_4$ x 6$^1/_4$ x 5$^1/_4$	12$^1/_2$
Star	11 x 7 x 7	22$^1/_2$

The writers have not been able to ascertain the dimensions of the Cambrian's Harp brand but a report[31] of trials made with this fuel by Her Majesty's Ship *Sirius*, in December 1878, remarks that the blocks were '*about three times the size of Graigola Merthyr Patent Fuel*'. The latter was another Swansea-manufactured fuel, which came in 9lb blocks measuring 9$^1/_2$ x 5$^1/_2$ x 4.

A ton of fuel required 33 cu ft storage room, compared to about 44 cu ft for a ton of coal. Although the squared shape of the blocks made for efficient use of stowage space, the down side was that this did demand much labour (compared to coal tipping and trimming), so proprietors turned their talents to inventing methods of automating as much as they could. At the Anchor Works, blocks were moved around the yard and onto canal boats by conveyor belts. At the other end, where boats unloaded onto the quay and ships were loaded from the quayside stacks, cranes were used with swinging trolleys. But ships could also be loaded directly from canal boat using a crane hulk and this became the normal method. When the Cambrian Works at Gabalfa were up for sale in 1893, their crane hulk, *The Breeze*, was an additional item on offer.[32] The Crown Works extended their use of Patents to a steam-operated elevator, installed in a barge operating alongside ship and canal boat in the open dock. While coal was traditionally delivered free on board, the cost of stowing Patent Fuel on board was passed on to the customer (from 9d to 1/- per ton in 1909).[33]

The year 1886 saw the building of Roath Dock and the by now highly successful Crown Works decided to open a brand new custom-built fuel works at the dockside, with a capacity of 3,000 tons per week. Negotiations with Bute Docks started in 1889 and the demand of the world's shipping and railway companies was so great, that the plant which eventually opened in 1891 had a capacity of twice that and this was again increased, by 1896, to 7,500 tons per week. The canalside works at Maindy remained open. These were heady days in the South Wales steam coal trade. Small coal for the Patent Fuel works was abundant at the shipping tips and the dockside location of the new works reduced the company's costs of importing the other main raw material – pitch. The Crown Company determined to do the same at Port Talbot, where new docks were being built by the Port Talbot Dock & Railway Company. As at Cardiff, the new Port Talbot works was designed as a

In 1917, the personnel of the Star Patent Fuel Works and their families were treated to their last annual works outing by boat. This surviving photograph of the occasion shows the happy voyagers on the canal at the Long Wood, Tongwynlais. Over 100 persons are assembled on Star boat No 460 with, so it is said, a barrel of beer and a piano. ILW collection

Empty Patent Fuel boats and dock lighters fill the foreground of this circa 1880 view of Cardiff West Dock, apart from one which appears to be loaded with gravel or possibly ballast. The scene is entirely sail, with the exception of the brand new paddle steamer on the left, in the process of being fitted out, with shear legs erected possibly for lifting the heavy steam machinary into position. WIMM collection

modern integrated manufactory by William Hammett, who had started with the company in 1865. This increased the capacity at Port Talbot by 2,570 tons per week and when it opened in 1898, production at the old Maindy Works finally ceased.[34] The Maindy site became the Hall, Lewis & Co Wagon Works which by 1935, were part of the Powell Duffryn Associated Collieries' Cambrian Wagon Works. This company were building, repairing and leasing railway wagons but were not, as far as is known, making use of the Glamorganshire Canal.[35]

From 1888 until 1900, the Crown Co also had a Patent Fuel works and stores canal-side at the northern end of Harrowby Street, with a branch railway line from the GWR Clarence Road Riverside line crossing Dumballs Road to service it. They advertised in November 1888 in the local press: '*Patent Fuel made from House Coal (230 Blocks to ton) 9 shillings at works; or by load 11s 6d per ton delivered, Crown Works, Old Sea Lock, Cardiff.*'[36] This appears to be a quite separate concern from the main company and was perhaps an attempt by Butler to supply the home market – either small industry or domestic. It was also quite probably where Butler received his consignments of pitch for the Maindy works and the solid pitch may have been broken down here before sending up the canal. The premises are shown on the 1901 OS map but by that time they had been sold to the Barry Railway Company.[37]

The Garth Works

The last company to open a Patent Fuel works on the bank of the canal was another with French roots – inappropriately styled L'Agence Maritime Anglaise. The Garth Anchor & Chain Co had gone into liquidation in 1876 and its assets were sold at auction in 1881 to William Pearson Strawson, a chain and anchor maker from Cradley Heath, the centre of chain making in the Black Country. The premises were assigned to the Garth Estate in the names of Frank Montagu Morgan and Joseph Gibbs in 1884 and they commenced negotiations with a Parisian, Charles Audouy, to establish a Patent Fuel works in the vacant premises at Walnut Tree.

An important aspect of the negotiations before the lease could be signed, was the transport arrangements both for receiving raw materials and for distributing the finished product. Although the works inherited the canal basin of

A magnificent scene of sail and steam in the Roath Dock, which shows two ships being loaded with Patent Fuel using the Butler Patent elevator machine. Eight canal boats are lined up awaiting their turn alongside the barge holding the steam-operated elevator. Note how the fuel blocks are being stacked on the canal boats in readiness for passing to the elevator. This was a slow manual process compared to coal loading but was outweighed by the other advantages of Patent Fuel, such as the stowage space required. In the extreme right foreground, a lighter or canal boat is receiving sacks from another vessel. WIMM collection

This highly atmospheric photograph of the Bute West Dock was taken by H.J.B. Wills as one of a series for the Cardiff Railway Company (as the Bute Docks Company was renamed following their Act of 1897), to illustrate their dock facilities at Cardiff. In the foreground, a number of boats laden with Anchor Patent Fuel blocks contrast with the buoyant empties awaiting their return trip to Maindy. The way of loading the boats into two stacks leaving a central gap 'amidships' is clearly shown. We are also given a good indication of the draught the canal had to provide for a full load of 25 tons – it was 2ft 9ins. The boat on the left of the loaded fuel boats, carrying a load of timber, is one of Robinson David's. The location is at the northern end of the dock; the junction canal entered it from the right and the building on the far right is Spillers Flour Mill.

H.J.B. Wills photo, S.K. Jones & SR collection

A poor quality but rare close-up of the Crown's elevator, which graphically shows how labour intensive was the transshipment from canal boat to ocean-going ship. Two gangs of four load fuel blocks onto the elevator from the canal boat, whilst two pairs of men unload them onto the vessel's deck. From the deck, there were probably slides to carry the fuel blocks into the holds, where another gang of four (probably the men on deck on the right) would have been needed to stack them neatly – sixteen in total. CCL collection

1865, their major outlet was to be by rail. The works were sited where the Rhymney Railway's old line to Cardiff joined Taff Vale Railway metals. A connecting siding had to be put in from the Rhymney Railway, who had to carry the product just a short distance to Walnut Tree Junction, whence the TVR took the trains of fuel onward to Cardiff Docks for shipment.

Surviving correspondence shows that effecting such an agreement with two rival railway companies was no simple matter. At one stage, Morgan had to write to Cornelius Lundie, the Rhymney Railway's general manager, that Audouy was threatening to accept an offer to move to De Bergue's old Bridge Works on the Taff Vale Railway, closer to Cardiff at College Road, Llandaff Yard.[38] This seems to have done the trick and, on 1 September 1885, Lundie wrote to Morgan that the Rhymney Railway would charge 1d per ton for coal delivered by the TVR at the Garth works and $^1/_2$d per ton for Patent Fuel taken out from the works to the TVR. He also agreed with Audouy's demands that the charge made by the RR in any one year would be a maximum of £500; for coal carried by the RR over Rhymney lines to the Garth Works there would be no terminal charge.

Heads of Lease from Morgan and Gibbs were granted from 1 Jan 1886 at £200 per annum for the first two years and £400 pa thereafter, all subject to successful exchange of lands with the RR. A ledger account was opened with the RR from 1 March and a formal agreement by the RR to put in sidings is dated 2 June.[39] A draft traffic agreement with the TVR, dated 29 Dec 1885, states that all traffic from the works to Cardiff should be over the TVR lines

'... except 33% of the Patent Fuel manufactured at the said works which may be sent by the Glamorganshire Canal but not otherwise and also until the Rly Co shall have access to Messrs Heath & Co's Fuel works excepting such traffic as may be destined for those works.'[40]

It is not clear what this link between the Garth and Star works was. No volumes are stated in the TVR draft but their charge was to be 1d per ton per mile.

The type of fuel made at the Garth Works was different from the pressed block fuel of the Maindy works. Audouy's patent of 2 November 1886 is for ovoid briquettes '*in the form of bullets*'. The process was based on two wheels containing the moulds moving in opposite directions and touching each other. The letters to Lundie indicate that the capacity was to be 600 tons per day.

Further patents for screening and washing the coal were taken out by Robert Le Las at the works in May 1888 and by Audouy in January 1889 for a portable fuel press. Production seems to have continued through a change of ownership from L'Agence Maritime to Powley, Thomas & Co in 1890.[41] On 30 August 1892, Audouy and Alfred Lusty purchased the premises from the executors of Joseph Gibbs and in 1894, Audouy (now recorded as being of Antibes, France) surrendered the works to Maurice Le Las, civil engineer of Walnut Tree Bridge. By 1914, Le Las too had assigned the works to Thomas Gregory, a metal founder from Hopkinstown, at which time it is assumed that Patent Fuel production ceased and the works reverted to being a steel, iron and brass foundry. The works continued until, as South Wales Forgemasters, it closed in 1987.

Whether the Garth Patent Fuel works used the canal is not known but they are not included in W.T. Lewis' statistics (see table overleaf). The agreement with the Taff Vale Railway, as with all colliery companies at that time, was that the works should provide its own railway wagons. How many canal boats the Garth Works owned, if any, is not known.

Statement showing the Quantity of Patent Fuel passed through the Junction Lock, West Dock

Name of Merchant	1882	1883	1884	1885	1886	1887	1888	1889
Crown Preserved Co	74,550	93,159	96,778	94,836	92,757	101,199	113,904	124,908
Heath & Co (Star)	60,837	53,305	55,473	47,842	42,880	44,208	58,233	64,995
Maindy Patent Fuel Co (Anchor)	39,960	42,616	32,080	56,880	67,009	75,075	48,820	62,223
Cambrian Patent Fuel Co	37,381	53,634	39,830	31,120	33,893	11,949	4,578	7,686
Totals (tons)	212,728	242,714	224,161	230,678	236,539	232,491	225,535	259,812

The source of this table is W.T. Lewis' handwritten book of dock statistics in the Bute collection, Cardiff Central Library (Bute XI 56)

Last of the Canalside Fuel Works

As for the steam coal industry, the peak period for the fuel works was the decade before the outbreak of the Great War. At that time, the Star was producing about 200,000 tons of fuel annually and total Cardiff output for the Star, Anchor and Crown peaked in 1913 at 716,899 tons (it should be remembered that by that time the Crown had removed from the canal and was manufacturing at Roath Dock). The war and post-war depression in shipping drastically reduced the main overseas markets, as oil replaced coal as a power source for shipping.

In 1887, following the death of its founder, Thomas Edward Heath, the family owned Star business was converted into a limited liability concern, the Star Patent Fuel Co Ltd, where the main shareholders and directors were still members of the Heath family but with the coal owner James Harvey Insole, son of George Insole, taking fifteen of the 250 £100 shares. Another restructuring took place in 1909, during the boom period. However, in December 1927, the company closed. When their assets were taken over by British Briquettes in 1929 they had no stock in trade.[42]

During the years when the company was working to capacity, about 1,000 tons of fuel a day were carried to the docks by fifty Star boats. Ten boats were on hire from the boat builder John James of Gabalfa, who would also do repairs as the company did not have their own capacity. Before the days of the railway sidings, they had a couple of cabin boats which went up to the Aberdare Valley for small coal. The *Jubilee* and *Jubila* were built in 1887, the last two boats for the Star Patent Fuel Works. The pitch came occasionally from the docks in boats but more usually by rail. The Canal Company's weigh bridge at North Road was very rarely used, just sometimes as a check. The Star supplied the Canal Co with the weight, by weighing a certain number of blocks and taking the average. The number by boat was counted by a mechanical counter. The Star had an icebreaker boat built by Thomas Spittle of Newport. Reminiscing about the works, Lionel Heath told the tale that by law the cabin boat had to have a window but the men did not like this so they painted a picture of a window, showing a red faced man holding a mug of beer.[43]

In 1919, the assets of the Anchor Works were transferred to a new L. Guéret & Co Ltd but Patent Fuel was not a main activity of this large steam coal business. A further reconstruction followed as Guéret, Llewellyn & Merrett Ltd, before it was absorbed into British Briquettes in 1929 and closed down.[44]

British Briquettes Ltd was formed in 1929 to effect an amalgamation of the briquette and Patent Fuel industry in South Wales, taking over Crown Preserved Coal Co Ltd, Rose Patent Fuel Co Ltd, Graigola Merthyr Co Ltd, Pacific Fuel Co Ltd, Star Patent Fuel Co Ltd, Guéret, Llewellyn & Merrett Ltd, Arrow Fuel Co Ltd and all the issued shares of Abertillery Pitch & Benzol Co Ltd. The new company had a wide range of activities in addition to Patent Fuel and in 1936, was absorbed into Powell Duffryn Associated Collieries Ltd – but by that time it was six years since Fuel had been carried on the Glamorganshire and Aberdare Canals.[45]

Waiting Turns – A Postscript on the Patent Fuel Trade Through North Road Lock

The crucial importance of an adequate water supply for the operation of the Glamorganshire Canal has been clearly demonstrated in a number of chapters of both volumes of this history. We have also seen how the demands of the canal for the finite waters of the River Taff had placed the GCC in constant competition with the proprietors of water-powered industry who were competing for the same resources. Although circumstances were not exactly parallel on the river navigations of Britain before the Canal Age, we are reminded of the bitter opposition of millers to the building and operation of locks at mill sites on the navigable rivers of 17th and 18th century England.

On the canals, water, a precious commodity, was collected by means of feeders from rivers and streams; the commonest form of water conservation, however, was to regulate the passage of boats through the locks, by the practice of 'waiting turns'.

In this procedure, a lockkeeper saves a lock of water by firstly allowing an up boat into the empty lock, then filling the lock to raise the boat and pass it on its way at the higher level. A waiting down boat is then admitted into the full lock; the water level is lowered and the lock is emptied. The down boat then leaves the lock at the lower level and proceeds on its way. Thus by this method two boat movements through the lock could be achieved with the use of only one lock of water. By the same token, a second boat wanting to lock down might be asked to wait a short while for the appearance of another up boat if

This 1909 scene at North Road Lock illustrates the practice of 'waiting turns', which was so necessary in order to conserve water in dry summers when the traffic was so great. Here, two Star Patent Fuel boats are passing. The loaded boat is just leaving the lock and the horses have crossed so that the empty boat can take its turn to enter the lock. Photo by Sargent, Cardiff

there was not one already queueing.

A late example of waiting turns in daily lock-keeping on the Glamorganshire Canal was to be found operating in North Road and Crockherbtown – the two locks in central Cardiff where a heavy boat traffic in Patent Fuel between Maindy and the Bute Docks had significantly increased water use on the Cardiff end of the canal between the years 1858 and 1928.

The canal company kept monthly records summarising the daily traffic passing its locks at Abercynon, Trallwn (Pontypridd), Treble Locks, Melingriffith and North Road with Crockherbtown. A number of these traffic sheets were rescued for preservation in 1948. The examples relating to North Road Lock are of particular interest, as they provide figures for water use from which the water conservation savings of waiting turns may be calculated. From the seven monthly samples reproduced in the accompanying table, it will be noticed that the number of loaded and empty boats passing the lock is almost evenly balanced but most interesting is the calculation that the water saving derived from waiting turns (7 samples over the years 1908 – 1919) averages 31.46 per cent.

Selected monthly totals of traffic passing through North Road and Tunnel Locks, Cardiff

	Up boats	Down boats	Total	Lockage	Saving	% Saving
Jan 1908	1691	1693	3384	2244	1140	33.68
Aug 1908	1303	1309	2612	1700	912	34.91
Dec 1910	978	981	1959	1401	558	28.48
Jan 1913	1705	1703	3408	2306	1102	32.34
Feb 1913	1279	1281	2560	1767	793	30.97
Jun 1913	1442	1438	2880	2011	869	30.17
Oct 1919	929	942	1871	1313	558	29.82

NOTES TO CHAPTER 7

1 GRO D/D Xjo Cardiff Dockmaster's letters, 1841-5.

2 Philip R. Björling *Briquettes and Patent Fuel - Their Manufacture and Machinery Connected Therewith*, London 1903, pp3-4.

3 *Cambrian*, 13 August 1847, cited in William Henry Jones *History of the Port of Swansea*, Carmarthen 1922, pp349-50

4 W. Galloway 'Patent Fuel' in Ivor James (Ed) *British Association Handbook for Cardiff and District*, Cardiff 1891, p141.

5 See Björling *Briquettes and Patent Fuel* for many of the patents.

6 From the 1860s, pitch from the Midlands was being supplied to the fuel works at South Wales ports by trow from Gloucester, having originated at gasworks on the Staffordshire & Worcestershire and the Worcester & Birmingham canals; Hugh Conway-Jones 'Severn Carriers in the Railway Age' in Tony Burnip (Ed) *Waterways Journal Volume Three*, Ellesmere Port 2001.

7 Although the source of fuel is not discussed, see Basil Greenhill and Ann Giffard *Steam, Politics & Patronage – The Transformation of the Royal Navy 1815-54*, London 1994.

8 *Cardiff & Merthyr Guardian*, 20 June 1857, 15 and 27 February 1858. For the Wood family and the Briton Ferry Ironworks, see C.W. Roberts *A Legacy from Victorian Enterprise – The Briton Ferry Ironworks and the Daughter Companies*, Gloucester 1983.

9 GCC minute book 23 June 1858.

10 Various reports in *Cardiff & Merthyr Guardian*, including 18 August 1860, 1 May, 26 June and 7 August 1863, 11 January 1868.

11 'The Crown Preserved Coal Co Limited' in *The South Wales Coal Annual for 1909-10*, Cardiff 1909; *Cardiff & Merthyr Guardian*, 21 March and 22 May 1863.

12 *Cardiff & Merthyr Guardian*, 24 June 1864. Note that these figures differ from those in W.T. Lewis's book of handwritten statistics (GRO Bute XI 56 pp6-8) which give 24,379 and 17,078 tons passing through the Junction lock in 1862 and 1863 respectively. The high figure of 24,379 for 1862 is suspect when compared to 11,209 tons for the previous year.

13 *Cardiff & Merthyr Guardian*, 3 January 1863; PRO BT31/524/2100.

14 *Cardiff & Merthyr Guardian*, 11 August 1860.

15 *Cardiff & Merthyr Guardian*, 24 July 1863.

16 *Coal Annual 1909-10.*

17 21 year lease 21 Jan 1870 to Pierre Jacque Tinel and Pierre Ernest Couillard, GRO D/D Tho 206. The 14 year boatyard lease and plan of 14 June 1822 to Lewis Williams and William Parry is in GRO D/D Tho 204 and the yard and saw pit continue to be shown on William Harrison's 1830 survey of the canal. The site had been taken over by the soap works by the time of the census of 1851, although the canal company's Table of Distances still celebrated it as Llystalybont Boat Dock.

18 David Evans 'L Guerét Ltd' in *The South Wales Coal Annual for 1913*, Cardiff 1912.

19 T.E. Heath 'Artificial Fuel' in John Ballinger (Ed) *Cardiff: an Illustrated Handbook*, Cardiff 1896.

20 *Cardiff & Merthyr Guardian*, 31 January, 7 March and 31 July 1863 for Pentreguinea Works.

21 T.E. Heath *Artificial Fuel.*

22 Reproduced in Mary Corbett Harris 'Fuel for Austria's Navy', in *Country Life*, December 21, 1972. Lionel Heath was a founder member in the late 1960s of the erstwhile South East Wales Industrial Archaeology Society and will be remembered for his outstanding engineering models, several of which are in the collection of the National Museum of Wales.

23 See *Cardiff & Merthyr Guardian*, 1 July and 5 August 1864 for details of Isaac Russell and R.J. Towne's steam forge.

24 PRO BT31/2070/9159 and BT31/3107/17828).

25 NLW Bute B143, cited in Martyn J.L. Bishop *The Patent Fuel Industry of Cardiff*, Diploma in Continuing Education (Local History) dissertation, University of Wales Cardiff, September 1995.

26 *Coal Annual 1909-10.*

27 *The Story of William Butler & Co (Bristol) Ltd*, Bristol 1947, p49. Thanks to Colin Green for this reference.

28 The first edition 25in OS shows only the Anchor connected to the railway.

29 This Cambrian Patent Fuel Company Ltd should not be confused with the anthracite using company of identical name, formerly the Lansford Syndicate Ltd, which operated at the Prince of Wales Dock, Swansea from 1918 to 1926 (having adopted the name Cambrian after the end of the Great War in 1919); see PRO BT31/24127/151016.

30 *The South Wales Coal Annual for 1914*, Cardiff 1913.

31 Björling *Briquettes and Patent Fuel*, p237.

32 Cambrian Fuel Works sale notice for 8 June 1893, CCL D518.45 (p).

33 *Coal Annual 1909-10.*

34 *Coal Annual 1909-10.*

35 GRO GB214 D/D CWW A/1 – E/1.

36 Information on advertisement from Bill Hamlin, source not recorded.

37 Stephenson & Alexander auctioneer records, GRO D/D SA12/698. Thanks to Keith Edwards for these references.

38 GRO D/D NLE 6/5. The De Bergue operation at Llandaff Yard had closed following Charles de Bergue's death in 1873 and their subsequent failure to complete the contract to build the Tay railway bridge for the North British Railway.

39 GRO D/D NLE 6/1, 6-7.

40 GRO D/D NLE 6/3.

41 GRO D/D NLE 6/17; Jackson Powley, E. Franklin Thomas and Alfred J. Lusty.

42 PRO BT31/3820/23980. Grateful thanks to Philip Riden for his notes from this and some of the other PRO references.

43 Lionel Heath in conversation with Bill Hamlin August 1972.

44 PRO BT31/15474/43886.

45 PRO BT31/33116/241691.

Chapter 8

THE GLAMORGANSHIRE CANAL LOCKS

Crockherbtown Lock, in central Cardiff, was also known as Tunnel Lock. It is seen here in dilapidated condition in 1949, with nature beginning to invade. It is hard to imagine the peak days of the Patent Fuel trade in 1913, when this lock was passing an average of 150 boats, loaded and empty, every day. At this point on the canal, the lock lowered the boats nearly 10 feet, so that boatmen and horses could pass under Queen Street. The remains of the weighing machine dock and weigh house will be noted on the far side of the lock. The debris in the background is from World War Two, when the adjoining Carlton Restaurant was bombed in a Cardiff air raid. ILW photo May 1949 neg 810

The canal company's locks have already been noted briefly in Volume 1 and photographs have illustrated some of the fifty-one lock sites. The discussion that follows is intended to bring the locks into closer focus and to help identify the simple components of a lock and how they functioned.

In the opinion of the authors, the most interesting features of the canal in landscape (often with the greatest visual impact) were the locks, with their massive stone ramparts. This is particularly true if they were seen rising in multiple, as at Pontypridd, or even in a staircase of three, as at Treble Locks, Taff's Well.

A lock begins with a stone-built chamber, which is closed at each end by gates. These gates were built of oak, the top gate being a single one mounted on top of the lock's breast wall and resting against a timber sill (or cill), which helps to keep the lock watertight when empty. The breast wall on which the top gate operates is, in effect, the lock's 'step'. At the bottom end of the lock chamber were deeper double gates which mitred together when closed, to form the shape of a 'V'.

Expressed in the simplest terms, a lock is a gated enclosure for raising or lowering vessels to higher or lower levels on a canal or river. In filling a lock, water is first

Above: *The top gate at Crockherbtown from outside the lock at the upper end and photographed from the heel post side of the lock. The lock had been out of use since 1942-3, so the position of the two paddles, or 'flashers' (normally submerged), is clearly revealed in the drained canal bed. The paddles rose together vertically through a mechanical movement which may be unique on British canals. The initial pull was by near-horizontal rack and pinion action on the gate arm. The rod will be seen to connect to a yoke which, when drawn sideways, raised the paddles vertically through the movement of bell cranks. It will be noticed that the paddle on the left side of the gate has been disconnected and is missing. The gate and paddle rodding were protected from damage by a timber and iron guard, which also acted as a narrow walkway for the boatman.*
ILW photo 26 Dec 1950 neg 1078

Top right: *The top gate seen from outside the upper end of the lock and from the opposite side of the dry canal. To the left of centre is the heel post pivoting in the 'hollow quoin', with the iron collar seen holding the post in place. The iron anchor which holds the collar is let into the horizontal face of a huge block of Pennant sandstone masonry. On the extreme left is part of the jack post and the recess in the wall for the ground paddle. Although this photograph of Crockherbtown Lock emphasises the poor condition of the structure, it does bring into focus the importance of all three of the traditional craft skills which are still alive on the canals – those of the mason, the carpenter and the blacksmith.*
ILW photo 26 Dec 1950 neg 1079

Bottom right: *A view looking towards the heel post as seen from the interior of the lock chamber. The gate is resting against a rather battered timber sill, which is secured across the top of the breast wall, just visible at the lower edge of the photograph.* ILW photo 26 Dec 1950 neg 1081

admitted through a ground paddle, which is located upstream of the top gate and worked with a windlass. The paddle is raised by rack and pinion gear, attached to a cast iron mounting or a timber post called a jack head. Water passing the ground paddle is conveyed to the lock chamber through a subterranean stone conduit, which emerges below water level at the base of the breast wall. The boat rises in the lock as the water level increases and the filling of the lock is finally speeded up by opening the top gate paddles with a windlass. On the Glamorganshire Canal, the gate paddles were called 'flashers'.

To lower a boat in a full lock, the top gate is first closed, the gate paddles and ground paddle are fully lowered to the closed position and then the bottom gate paddles are raised. A triangular wooden platform at the lower end of the lock enabled the boatman to cross to attend to the lower gates. [1]

Gates on the Glamorganshire Canal were oak framed. The pivoting upright member, operating in a recess in the lock wall, was called a heel post and the outer gate timber was known as the head post. To allow a gate to swing easily, the heel post's pivoting surface was rounded, so that it could revolve within a hollowed masonry cavity in the lock wall called a 'hollow quoin'. Lock gates were kept in place at the lock floor by pin and socket at the base of the heel post. At the top of the lock wall, the heel post became fully rounded so that it could be held in place by an iron collar.

The two extended ends of this collar were secured into

Water gushing through the top gate at Caeglas Lock (Lock No 39), at Taff's Well, on a postcard view by Ernest Bush from circa 1908. The gate is obviously in need of some remedial work but the lock house behind looks very spruce. SR collection

Left: *The Forest Lock site on the Whitchurch - Tongwynlais nature reserve, 'remodelled' by Cardiff City Parks Department in 1974. No atmosphere of preservation existed in 1945 when the same Cardiff Corporation weired the top gate and demolished the locktail bridge and lockkeeper's cottage.*

David Gould photo 1980

Below: *The lower gates of Middle lock. Note the wooden platform to allow the lockkeeper to cross the lock in order to open each of the mitred gates in turn. The ashlar on the approach masonry to the lock bears the marks of many years towrope wear from boats leaving the lock.*

S.C. Fox photo, WIMM collection

the projecting studs of land anchors, which were themselves let into the top surface of the lock's heavy masonry.[2]

A very common feature of the traditional timber lock gate on the canals, is the heavy projecting gate arm. The ability of a lock gate to swing easily, is greatly enhanced by the outward extension of the top beam of a gate frame and the purpose of the long arm is to act as a counterbalance to the weight of the gate – hence the name 'balance beam' or, more commonly on the Glamorganshire Canal, the 'balance pole'. As experienced users of canal locks will already know, the boatman's back pressed hard against a balance beam is the time-honoured way of opening a lock gate.

In 1950, some eight years after the last boat had passed, one of the locks in Cardiff that still remained intact (Crockherbtown Lock, No 50) was visited and some details recorded. The captions to the photographs taken on that occasion have been included to make clear how the top gate operated.

The Lower Gates

The lower gates of Glamorganshire Canal locks were fitted in pairs and were deeper than the top gate, because they extended to the full depth of the lock. Their operating gear was of the simplest – a long rod working vertically on each gate to lift a single paddle, which was raised by a rack mechanism mounted on the gate and worked by

Mynachdy Lock (Lock No 48), with the whitewashed lock house alongside and rudimentary footbridge over the lock tail. Note the pitched stone facings to the canal bank as it drops down from the lock. S.C. Fox photo, WIMM neg 73.242

A charming study of the waste weir above Mynachdy Lock, looking north west with the recently built Western Avenue in the background. Note the slots, called 'rabbets' (a local corruption of rebates), at the weir edge, for putting in stop planks to raise the water level in the canal when necessary. S.C. Fox photo, WIMM neg 73.713

Right: *Part of the 'furniture' of the Glamorganshire Canal was the Jack Head or Paddle Post, an important towpath feature which held the rack and pinion gear for raising the submerged door or paddle that released water in times of flood. The paddle would also be raised to empty a particular pound for maintenance purposes. This cast iron example, probably cast at Cyfarthfa, was recorded at Cilfynydd in 1971, where it released flood water into Nant Elen Deg (Nant Caedudwg) which passed under the canal in a culvert.*
ILW photo 16 April 1971 neg 2240

Below: *The abrasive action of a wet towrope impregnated with fragments of gravel could do a great deal of damage when in contact with walls and bridges – even iron bridges (as seen in Volume 1, p230). To minimise the formation of deep grooves worn away by contact with horse towlines, the GCC provided this cast iron post to protect a stone wall on a sharp turn in the towpath at Melingriffith Lock.*
ILW photo 2 April 1972 neg 2282

windlass, carried by the boatman.

An interesting feature of all GCC lower gates was the wooden hanging block or 'fender', which was suspended by chains (see photograph of Llandaff Lock). This served the dual purpose of protecting the gate and iron rodding from damage when the gate was folded back into its masonry recess in the lock wall.

The Treble Locks

The Treble Locks, Nos 35, 36 and 37, were referred to by the canal company in its early years as 'the Steep Locks', a very appropriate description of a massive structure which ended the long lockless reaches of the 'Three Mile Pond' and lowered the canal thirty-three feet without intermediate pounds, one lock running directly into another to form a staircase. A lock is only as good as the strength and quality of its masonry and, in 1809, some shoddy work to the walls of Lock 37 came to light in a spectacular way. Two letters of Thomas Reece, the canal company's clerk, to Richard Crawshay, the chairman, explain the GCC's predicament and how the company's masons set about their emergency programme of repairs:[3]

> *'I am exceedingly sorry to have bad news to communicate to you. Lock No 37, one of the Steep Locks, has given way, must be taken down immediately – it's so bulged, that no Boat can possibly pass – a fleet of Boats had gone through a few hours before and not the least appearance of anything*

It was a parliamentary requirement that canals and railways be marked out at intervals of 1/4 mile along the line of course, so that toll rates could be clearly assessed. Wooden markers were originally put in place along the towpath but these cast iron examples replaced them. 7 1/2 came from the Powder magazine on the Merthyr section at Cefn Glas. 22 1/4 was on the towpath at Mynachdy Lock. Probably cast at Cyfarthfa, they are now preserved at the Welsh Industrial and Maritime Museum, Nantgarw. Bill Hamlin photo by permission of WIMM

wrong. I should be glad if you would have the goodness to permit Mr Bailey to come down, that we may contrive the best plan of proceeding with the Lock, as well as taking the Iron down etc.'

and

'*I should have written to you before this but I expected that Mr Bailey would have been down. We are taking down the lock with all possible despatch. I hope to get to the foundation by Thursday Night, by which time we shall be fully prepared with Materials to begin to rebuild having the Limekiln on fire and 10 Masons preparing Stones, of which we shall want at least 400 tons for the old Wall consists of nothing but mere pebbles put together with Mortar, the greater part of which consists of Earth. The Tram Road that we made around the lock answers the purpose very well, we have taken down 100 tons of Iron since Wednesday morning & hope we shall take from 180-200 Tons weekly, till the Lock is finished.*'

The lock that failed was of course the bottom lock of the Treble Lock staircase. The congestion of traffic caused by a three-week stoppage for repairs can well be imagined. Thomas Dadford, the canal's builder and contractor who left the canal in 1794, must ultimately carry the blame for this failure to supervise his sub-contractor. A clue as to who this sub-contractor may have been appears in the Table of Distances, published by the GCC in 1809. This identifies these locks as 'Jackson's Treble Locks' and the question arises – is this the same James Jackson of Ledbury who did the masonry work for the canal company's 1795 Jackson's Bridge, crossing the River Taff at Merthyr and who built the walling for the GCC's extension to the Sea Lock in Cardiff in 1796-98?

In spite of the unhappy consequences of building earth and pebbles into the walls of Lock 37, it should be said that much of the masonry work seen in the Glamorganshire Canal's lock chambers was of the finest quality – superbly squared and laid sandstone courses and the finest jointing. The east wall of Middle Lock at the top end of the Melingriffith to Tongwynlais nature reserve is an excellent surviving example of the mason's craft and is certainly worth a visit. This lock is one of two which can be seen on the reserve. Neither lock retains its original gates and visitors need to be reminded that Cardiff's Parks Department has made some alterations to Thomas Dadford's masonry which the observer may find puzzling.

This cast iron sign was recovered from Gabalfa Lock. ILW photo 1946 neg 2116

NOTES TO CHAPTER 8

1 See Volume 1, p159 for a photograph of the lock platform, illustrating part of Lock 21 in the Abercynon flight.

2 See Volume 1, p159 which illustrates the iron anchor and studs let into a heavy block of masonry together with the ends of the collar holding the heel post of Lock 21, Abercynon.

3 GRO B/C GCa 2 GCC Clerk's letter book, 23 and 30 September 1809.

The later type of boundary marker was of cast iron. This one could be found near the Abercynon flight of locks. Gordon Rattenbury

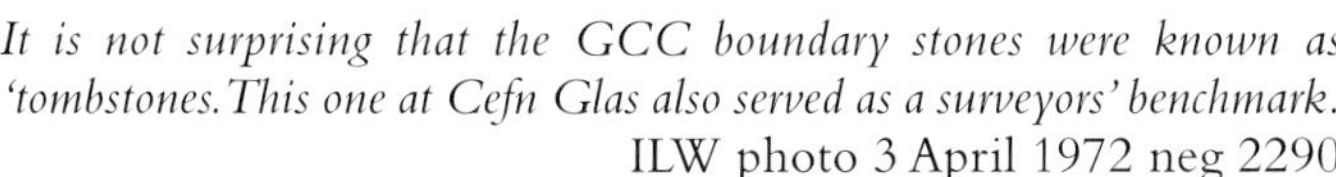

It is not surprising that the GCC boundary stones were known as 'tombstones. This one at Cefn Glas also served as a surveyors' benchmark.
ILW photo 3 April 1972 neg 2290

Cast iron bollard at the entrance to the lock leading to West Dock, circa 1958, showing grooves worn by boat ropes.
Stan Vickery phoro, neg 28-29

The boat weighing machine and weigh house at North Road. Although the GCC committee ordered a machine 'similar to that at Newport', it is unlikely that the design was identical to Whitmore & Son's machine, which the Monmouthshire Canal had been using since 1816. The elegant cast iron design seen here is typical of Brown Lenox' work. The boat dock had a gate at both ends, so that after it had been weighed, the boat did not have to be backed out. At the previous two sites (Tongwynlais and Crockherbtown) this was not so. The sluice for draining the dock was operated from within the weigh house.

ILW collection

Chapter 9

THE BOAT WEIGHING MACHINE

'Every Boatman to permit his boat, whether laden or unladen, to be weighed at the Company's Weighing Machine, whether required by the Agent or Clerk of the Company, or the Lock-keeper at the Ton Lock.'

GCC Bye Law No 39 4 June 1834

The Northamptonshire village of Stoke Bruerne, a canal settlement some seven miles south of Northampton, is an unlikely resting place for a Welsh canal relic that began life around 170 years ago on the Glamorganshire Canal at Tongwynlais, near Cardiff. Stoke Bruerne lies at the summit of a long flight of locks on the Grand Union Canal between London and Birmingham and is well known for its Waterways Museum, where collections of models, relics, documents, photographs and paintings housed in a converted warehouse, evoke the waterways past. Since being opened by British Waterways in 1963, the museum has extended its display area beyond the wharf to a disused lock near the Boat Inn. Here, set up over the empty lock stands the largest structure on the site – the Glamorganshire Canal Company's boat weighing machine.[1]

Boat weighing machines were a rare phenomenon on British canals and only four examples appear to have been built. These were at Newport on the Monmouthshire Canal, Tongwynlais (later moved to Cardiff) on the Glamorganshire Canal, Brimscombe on the Thames & Severn Canal and at Midford on the Somersetshire Coal Canal. Provided the appropriate tolls were paid, any person could trade with a boat on a canal and the canal companies charged tolls to freighters on the basis of tons carried per mile. In order to check fraudulent declarations of cargo, a system of 'gauging' boats had to be adopted. Every new boat was turned into a dock and the draught carefully measured when empty. Next, the vessel was loaded with one ton weights up to full capacity, the draught being measured at each ton of loading. Using 'tonnage plates' fixed on either side of bow and stern to graduate the boat's 'dry inches', it was possible to record this information in a register, copies of the record being distributed to each toll house along the canal. With every suspect cargo, the long-winded process of measuring, checking with the book and calculating the weight of the cargo had to be undertaken. Clearly it was easier to take the boat master's word for it.

The period 1830-1840 was a time of enormous pressure of traffic on the Glamorganshire Canal, much of it consisting of iron and coal from Merthyr and Aberdare for shipment at the port of Cardiff, and the canal company decided to bring in a more efficient method of checking cargoes. On 1 February 1834, the company's clerk, George Forrest, inserted a notice in the *Cambrian* advertising for

'A Machine for Weighing Canal Boats and their Cargoes similar to that at Newport belonging to the Monmouthshire Canal Company.'

As a consequence, on 7 Feb 1834, the canal company resolved to place an order with Brown, Lenox & Co of Pontypridd to build a Weighing Machine, Weigh House and Dock, for the sum of £550. The firm of Brown Lenox & Co had a long and interesting history in engineering. The Pontypridd works was established in 1816 by Samuel Brown, an officer in the Royal Navy, who was a talented engineer and inventor, in partnership with his cousin Samuel Lenox. The extension of the company's business to South Wales became necessary when increasing demands for chain cables outstripped the capacity of the firm's Millwall works in London. Brown Lenox & Co held excusive contracts for the supply of chain cables to the Royal Navy and the firm provided the cables for such suspension works as the Union Bridge near Berwick Upon Tweed, the Trinity Pier at Leith, the Hammersmith Bridge, and the Chain Pier at Brighton, which was completed in 1825. Later, at their Pontypridd works, they forged the great iron cables for Brunel's *Great Eastern*.[2] On 24 October 1834, the GCC committee ordered that Brown Lenox be paid '*£450 on account of the Weighing Machine and Dock at Ton Lock.*' The total cost of the machine seems to have been £643 including the dock, since the canal company's minutes authorised payment of £193 balance due for the dock of the weighing machine at the committee meeting of 9 March 1838.

The Ton Lock site was at the southern end of the village of Tongwynlais, some six miles north of Cardiff, where the towers of Lord Bute's Castell Coch overlook the Taff Valley. By 1838, the Glamorganshire Canal was being worked day and night close to full capacity and, in the absence of trade union hours in those days, the canal company ordered that '*Morgan Morgan be kept constantly at the Weighing machine.*'[3] Although the machine was later removed from Tongwynlais, the present author (Ian Wright) was able to discover traces of the walls of the weighing dock on the east side of Ton Lock when he examined the site in 1945.

Once capable of weighing up to 40 tons, the weighing machine consists of six classically proportioned cast-iron columns supporting a superstructure and an overhead system of levers, from which a cast-iron cradle is suspended on four radial rods from the four corners of the massive yoke. The canal boat was floated into the lock and the gate closed. A paddle was then raised to empty the lock and the boat settled down on the suspended cradle. The weight was then taken on the weighbeam, which was so poised on a fulcrum that the leverage exerted was 112 to 1. The counterpoises inside the weigh house took the form of convenient weights, which could be placed on the suspended pan up to a total of 800 lb and equal to 800 cwt or 40 tons on the cradle.[4]

In 1850, the machine was dismantled and moved to Cardiff, where it was set up next to Crockherbtown Lock, just north of the present-day Queen Street.[5] There was a second move in 1894, when the machine was reconditioned and rebuilt on a site close to Cardiff Castle. This was a fortunate decision for the future of the machine as it turned out, for had the structure remained at Crockherbtown, it would almost certainly have been destroyed or seriously damaged by a bomb which fell on the Carlton Restaurant nearby during the Second World War. In a paper on the weighing machine which he read in 1929, Harry Eddins, Cardiff's Chief Inspector of Weights & Measures at the time, recalled assisting with the repair work during his apprenticeship in 1894. Referring to the knife-edges forming part of the yoke from which the cradle is suspended, Eddins remarked that these were secured in the slot in the casting by means of oak liners. These oak liners were shown to be in a remarkable state of preservation, being extremely hard, and that much hammer and chisel work was needed to remove them. On completion of the overhaul, the machine was verified by the local inspector of weights and measures and found to be sensitive to 14 lbs – a figure Eddins says that "*compared very favourably with some of our modern weighbridges.*" Regular daily weighing continued at the machine until about 1914, after which time it seems to have fallen into disuse.[6]

In 1944, the Glamorganshire Canal was purchased by the Cardiff Corporation and, by a circumstance of unusual interest to the industrial archaeologist, the canal company's last working boat found a resting place in the North Road weigh dock, having been put there after failing to get through to the West Wharf for the official takeover ceremony on 1 January.[7] Concerned for the future preservation of the weighing machine, the National Museum of Wales pointed out its great interest '*as a mechanism in quality and character, illustrative of the invention, skill and technique which were associated with the Industrial Revolution in this country*"[8] and put in a plea to the City Council that it should be preserved in situ. No action was taken until 1955. In this year the Cardiff Corporation presented the weighbridge to the British Transport Commission, and it was dismantled and carefully stored away in a dockland warehouse. Unhappily, however, no attempt was made to save the Glamorganshire Canal Company's last boat.[9]

On permanent exhibition for the past 40 years, the Cardiff weighbridge has enjoyed a favourable climate of interest in our early industrial heritage. Not without honour, except perhaps in its own country, it was host in the 1960s and 70s to the beautiful Grand Union narrow boat *Northwich* – a companion exhibit marooned in the

From 1850 until 1894, the boat weighing machine operated at this boat dock alongside Crockherbtown Lock (Lock 50). This photograph of the heavily overgrown remains in May 1949 shows the sluice gate at the rear of the boat dock. This was used to empty the dock and so leave the boat hanging in the cradle for weighing.
ILW photo May 1949 neg 811

Boat No 451, moored alongside the boat dock at North Road after it had failed to negotiate Crockherbtown Lock to attend the canal's hand-over ceremony to Cardiff Corporation on 1 January 1944. Later, the boat was placed on the cradle in the dock and, in that position, was destined to be the final surviving GCC boat.

ILW photo 2 Jan 1944 neg 236

The weighing machine was situated just upstream of North Road Lock (Lock 49). The scene, with the thatched entrance lodge to the castle grounds adding to the canal's picturesque, was often photographed and is particularly busy here. The whitewashed wall attached to the right of the lodge supports a lockable door entrance to a path leading to the weigh house. Bill Bladen is watching the towline being re-attached to the towing mast as he begins to lead his horse 'Dick' away from the lock, returning an empty boat to the wharf. Also, what seems surely destined to be a short-lived game of cricket is taking place on the towpath. ILW collection

dock like some inland *Cutty Sark*.[10] Apart from the appeal of its uniqueness, the Brown Lenox weighing machine demonstrates the character of so many industrial artefacts of the 18th and early 19th centuries, such as water wheels, beam engines, cranes and cast iron bridges – a forthright and economical use of material and a simplicity of form that admirably expresses function.

Unfortunately, as we write, the continued existence of the entire museum at Stoke Bruerne is under threat. The weighing machine is again unwanted by its custodians and it is down to a new generation of enthusiasts to fight to safeguard its future.

NOTES TO CHAPTER 9

1 This chapter is an updated revision of Ian L. Wright 'A Canal-age Relic on View' from *Country Life*, 12 September 1974, p689, with permission of the editor, Clive Aslett.

2 For more on Brown Lenox see Volume 1.

3 GCC minute book 9 March 1838.

4 H. Eddins *Incorp Society of Inspectors of Weights & Measures Monthly Review*, November 1929 pp190-2. Thanks to Mr O. Barnes and Bill Hamlin.

5 GCC minute book 5 June 1850.

6 Eddins *Monthly Review*, 1929.

7 Information from John Close, canal foreman, 1948.

8 Letter to Ian Wright 1949.

9 Cardiff Corporation minutes 26 February and 5 May 1954; canal sub committee minute 8548 22 April 1955.

10 *Northwich* was later removed for restoration and was paired with the Fellows Morton & Clayton steamer, *President*, in active operation on the waterways.

Chapter 10

CARDIFF TO THE SEA – THE EARLY YEARS

Cardiff from the south by Paul Sandby, painted in 1776, some twenty years before the coming of the canal. Until 1850, the river flowed along the line of what is now Westgate Street. The vessel on the right of the painting is tied up at the riverside shipyard (the site of the present-day Great Western Hotel). Further upstream, round the bend, another vessel lies at the town quay. CCL collection

The Canal Comes to Cardiff

In March 1790, John Bird's diary records that the Corporation of Cardiff was pressing for the canal to be cut past the westward side of the town. It is difficult to see how this could have been done without the canal crossing the river, or using the bed of the river past the town quay. Perhaps they expected the canal to terminate at the existing river quays of the Merthyr iron companies. What is more likely is that some were considering that Penarth was a safer place than Cardiff to establish a floating harbour. However, the engineer, Thomas Dadford, intended keeping well distant from the river and planned to take the canal through the White Friars land to the east of the castle. From there he would use the town ditch from the East Gate to the South Gate and thence through part of the Moors, to the mouth of the Great Pill on the River Taff, about a mile below the town. The pill bank was the site where, over the years, vessels had dumped their stone ballast as they prepared to sail the final couple of miles upstream to the iron companies' wharves near the town quay. At the Bank, the canal basin was to be erected and from here larger vessels of 150 tons burthen would be able to go every tide.[1] This was the route delineated on the plan which accompanied the Glamorganshire Canal Act passed on 9 June 1790.[2]

That summer, Lord Bute's men completed the sea wall to protect his land on the foreshore and the following year, under the critical eye of these employees, Dadford's men did their first work below Cardiff by stopping up the pill. Richard Crawshay was forced to reassure Bute personally that his wall would be safe from these works and he tested whether Bute would give the canal company the additional

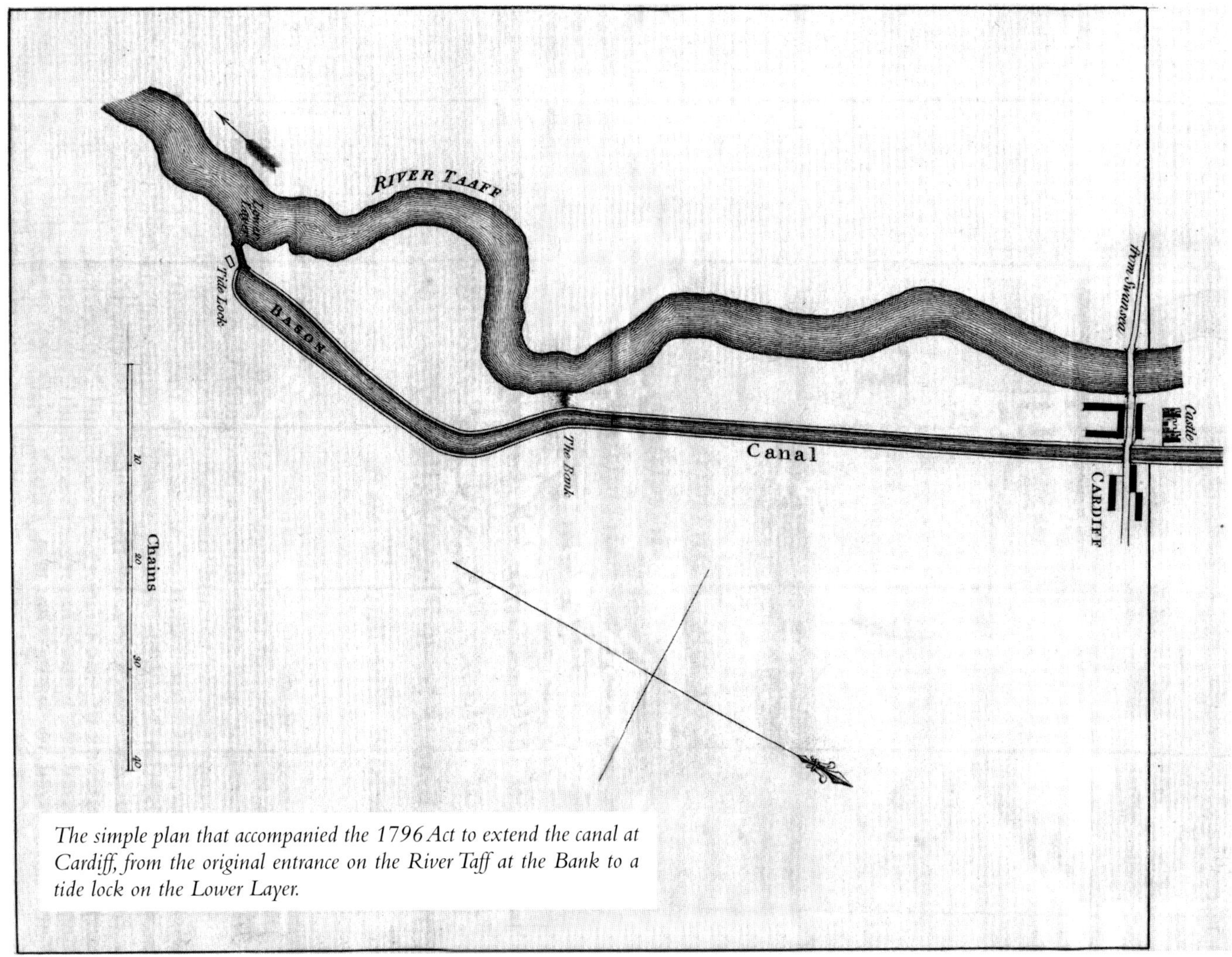

The simple plan that accompanied the 1796 Act to extend the canal at Cardiff, from the original entrance on the River Taff at the Bank to a tide lock on the Lower Layer.

land it would require if the canal were later extended across the salt marshes to the sheltered harbour at Penarth.[3] Dimensions for the basin and Sea Lock were agreed with Dadford in June. The basin was to contain sixteen feet depth of water and be not less than forty feet wide. The tidal lock was to be not less than thirty feet wide and ninety feet long, the entrance to the lock being not less than thirty-six feet wide.[4]

In April 1793, the last call was made on subscribers to the full £60,000 authorised by the Act. The canal had been built from Merthyr southward and only reached the Friars Green in Cardiff in 1793. The proprietors and freighters had had three years to consider what shipping facilities should finally be provided. It was decided that the canal should be extended some 700 yards from the basin and that the Sea Lock now be situated at the Lower Layer, closer to the sea and on the river estuary. Joseph Vaughan of Melingriffith, a committee man, confided in Bird that he estimated it would cost £30,000 more to complete.[5] The canal committee began making preparations for an application to Parliament for more money and in March 1794, Dadford, who had not finished the first contract, was instructed to make the survey.

The framing of the Bill was closely scrutinised by the freighters, led by Richard Hill (of Plymouth Ironworks) and William Taitt (of Dowlais Ironworks), who feared that this second Act might force tonnage rates to be increased, since Crawshay proposed a clause to give the proprietors full power to alter the rates.[6] Hill was already in dispute with the canal company over its commandeering his works' water supply at Merthyr. Taitt, although a member of the Glamorganshire Canal committee, may have been still smarting over the abandonment of the canal's plan for a Dowlais branch. The triumvirate was completed by Samuel Homfray (of Penydarren Ironworks). These three prime freighters set about organising petitions against the Bill. Hill was a committee man on the Aberdare Canal Company, whose freighters would use the Glamorganshire Canal for the sixteen miles to the wharves at Cardiff, from its proposed junction with the Glamorganshire north of Navigation. The Aberdare Canal Company expressed their firm opposition at their own committee meetings in January 1794 and again in October 1795, and James Dadford (son of Thomas and committee member of the Aberdare Canal Company) prepared their petition against the Bill.[7]

The Glamorganshire Canal was officially opened from Merthyr to Cardiff in February 1794. John Bird sent an account of the opening to the *Gloucester Journal*:

'*The Canal from Cardiff to Merthir-Tidvil* [sic] *is completed,*

The canal company's offices and former offices of the Merthyr iron companies, set back from the wharf itself, present a decrepit appearance in this 1893 official photograph. The man is believed to be the GCC's general manager, Lewis Llewelyn; compare his stance to his identical pose in the view at Trallwn in Volume 1, p192.
CCL collection

Below: *The canal offices and the old Cyfarthfa iron warehouse survived into the 1980s and they are seen here in March 1972. Between 1882 and 1963, this road was also occupied by the northern extremity of the Glamorganshire Canal Railway.*
ILW photo neg 2281

and a fleet of canal boats have arrived at Cardiff laden with the produce of the iron-works there, to the great joy of the whole town ... The first barge that arrived at Cardiff was finely decorated with colours, and was navigated from the Molingriffield [sic] *works by Mr. Bird, sen. Water-bailiff of Cardiff.'*

By September that year, the basin and sea lock had not been completed and Lord Bute's land taken by the canal company could not yet be accurately surveyed for valuation.[8] Nevertheless, if we are to believe his dates, John Phillips suggests that the Sea Lock had been in use from 29 June 1793, because, in a remark dated November 1794, he records that 245 vessels had passed through the lock from 29 June to 15 April.[9]

In December 1794, when Crawshay was refusing to advance any more money to Thomas Dadford, the engineer abandoned his contract as complete and retired to his home in the Midlands. The canal proprietors suddenly had a not-entirely complete 25 mile canal on their hands. They set about appointing two sub-committees to manage the upper and lower sections, that of the latter comprising John Bassett, Richard Griffiths, John Williams, Richard Reynolds and Joseph Vaughan.[10] In order that a case could be brought against Dadford, the engineer Robert Whitworth[11] was retained to inspect the workmanship and the state of the canal as Dadford had left it. Charles Hassall and William Pitt were appointed as surveyors in the Dadford case.[12] While this was in progress in the summer of 1795 it was minuted that:

'*workmen be stopped from making any further new cutting below the South Gate until after the referee's award is made except the new work now doing near the Bank for the Landing Ore or other goods at an expense not exceeding Thirty Pounds.*'[13]

In October, the canal company took Whitworth's advice to protect the Sea Lock workings from flood and tide by dumping a large quantity of stone against the river bank.[14]

The Second Act and the Canal's Completion

The delay caused by the Dadford case gave more opportunity for discussion on how the connection with the sea would be effected and what extra could be included in the new Bill. Colliery owners such as Thomas Key had been quick to recognise the value of cheap transport and the canal was already carrying significant quantities of coal. Key hoped to open an up-Severn coal trade to markets on the Thames & Severn Canal. He argued for a branch canal from the basin, eastward across the Moors to the River Rhymney. If the canal's entrance were on the Rhymney (in Monmouthshire), then up-Severn coal would not have been subject to duty and so Key's superior Maesmawr product could have competed with the well-established Newport coal trade. As it was, from a Customs viewpoint, Cardiff was considered to be on the Bristol Channel not the River Severn and so its exports from the Sea Lock on the Taff would be taxable. This situation was made worse by being formalised the following year in the Monmouthshire Canal Act, which the Glamorganshire coal owners failed to prevent.

Key was not to get his way. Charles Hassall surveyed a branch to the Rhymney to take a route outside Bute's sea wall. His total estimate for completing the canal to the Lower Layer and cutting this branch was £21,364 19s 2d.[15] Richard Crawshay, who ultimately had little interest in coal exports but primarily in shipping his Cyfarthfa iron, was under great pressure to keep the Bill simple and seek as little additional capital as possible. The idea of the Rhymney branch was dropped even though Taitt, who seems to have been playing on all sides, suggested that tossing a sop to Key, who was also Lord Plymouth's agent, might persuade Lord Plymouth to look kindly on an amendment in the canal company's favour to the Plymouth water clause.[16] John Wood, the canal company's clerk and solicitor, advised Crawshay against such complications and the Bill went to Parliament solely to authorise more capital for extending and completing the canal to a sea lock on the Lower Layer.[17]

January and February 1796 were worrying days for Crawshay, as petitions against his Bill from the Aberdare Canal Company, the landowners and the freighters were received in the Commons.[18] When he heard from his friend John Kemeys Tynte, that Samuel Homfray was putting it about that he was prepared to finish the canal under the present Act for under £10,000, Crawshay was moved to respond angrily and sarcastically. He quoted Hassall's estimates of £21,000 and challenged Homfray:

'*Now Sir, if you can put the Compy in the way to do all this for £10,000 they will be very much obliged to you or if you & your Friends will find the sum wanted at 5 per cent it will be thankfully received.*'

His irritation and unease were betrayed when he added:

'*What the Aberdare Canal Compy have to do with us I can't find out, when the Bill goes into Committee they will of course be attended as their demands will merit.*'[19]

Homfray and the other petitioners won the day, for when the Act was finally passed through the Lords on 26 April 1796, it gave the canal company powers to raise only a further £10,000 and not the £21,000 of the original draft. The maximum dividend on this extra capital was also set at only 5% compared to 8% on the capital raised under the first Act. No clause was included to empower the company to extend the canal to the River Rhymney but solely to the Lower Layer. The offending clause for the proprietors to vary tonnage rates was also removed.[20]

It was only after the Act was passed and the Monmouthshire Canal Bill was going through Parliament, that Crawshay seemed to realise the importance of what constituted river traffic as opposed to sea traffic. Then he sought advice from the Thames Navigation Office from

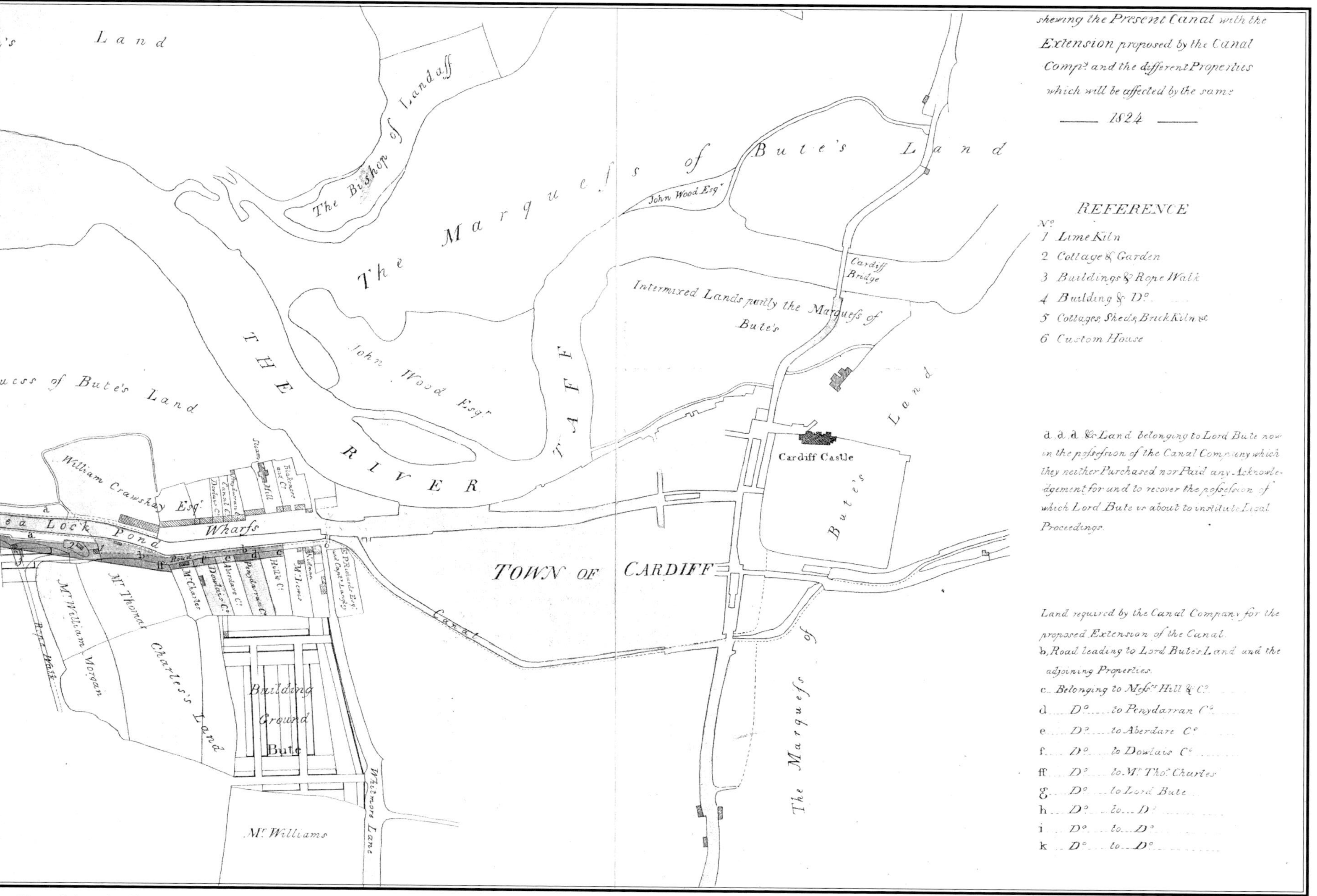

Plan of the wharf lettings at the northern end of the Sea Lock pound in 1824, showing the land on the eastern bank that the canal wanted to take to widen the pound. The figure 6 marks the South Gate Bridge and the new Custom House. Note how close the River Taff came to the canal at that point; the river bank just north of Blakemore's wharf marks the site of Joseph Davies' and Richard Tredwen's shipyards.
CCL collection

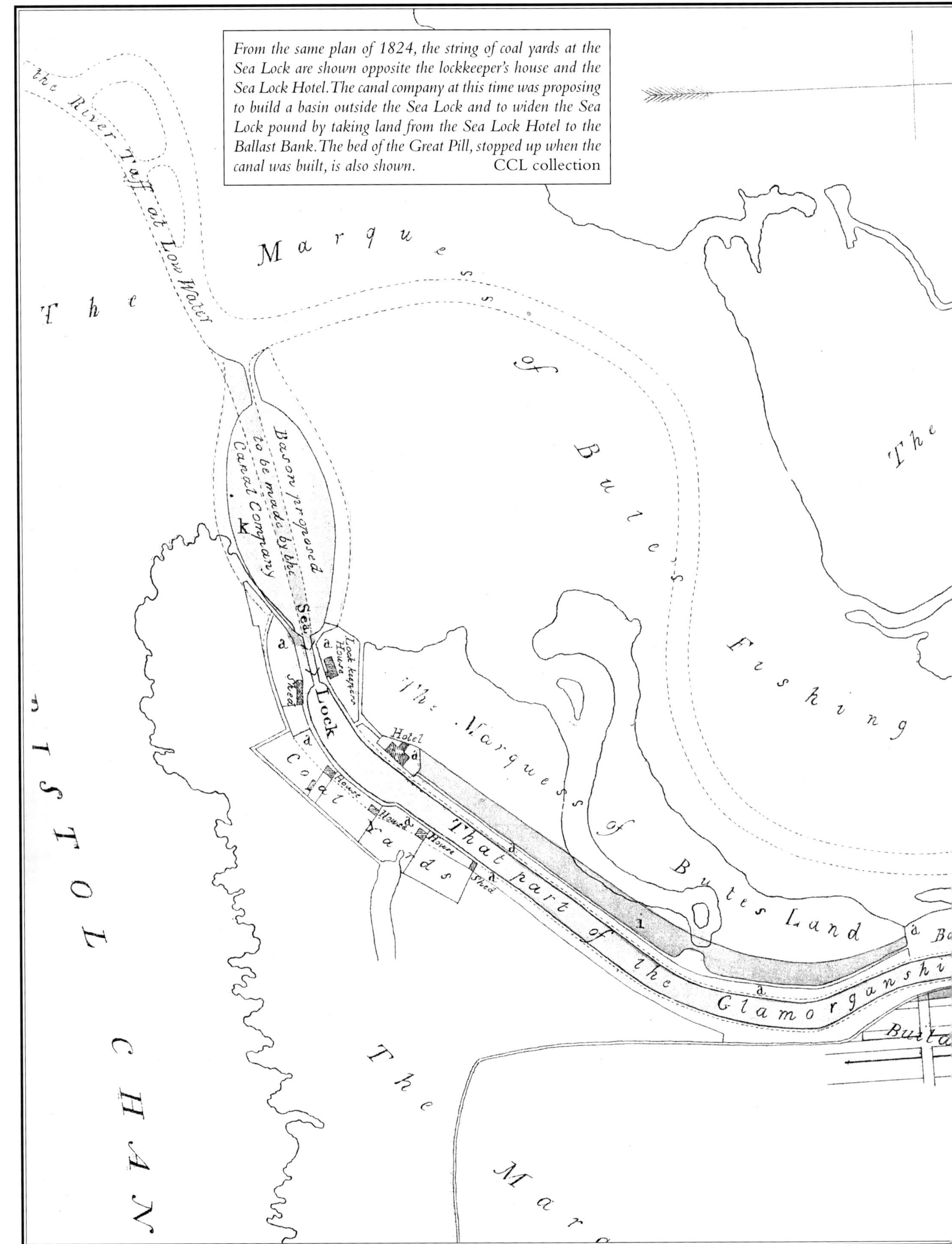

From the same plan of 1824, the string of coal yards at the Sea Lock are shown opposite the lockkeeper's house and the Sea Lock Hotel. The canal company at this time was proposing to build a basin outside the Sea Lock and to widen the Sea Lock pound by taking land from the Sea Lock Hotel to the Ballast Bank. The bed of the Great Pill, stopped up when the canal was built, is also shown. CCL collection

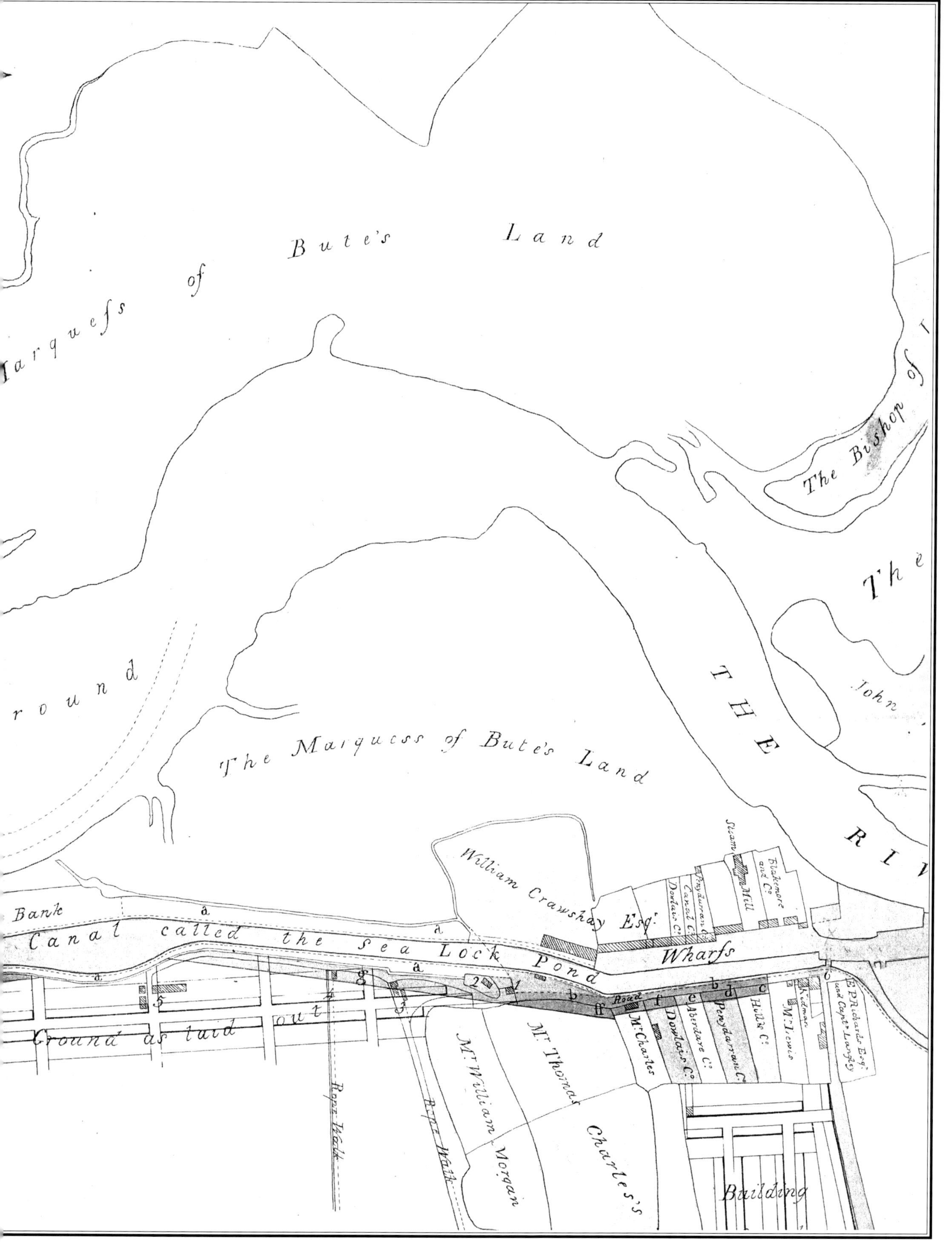

Marquess of Bute's Land
The Bishop of
The
THE RIV
John
round
The Marquess of Bute's Land
William Crawshay Esq.
Steam Mill
Blakemore and Co.
Penydarran Co.
Canal Co.
Dowlais Co.
Bank
Canal called the Sea Lock Pond
Wharfs
Road
Mr. Charles
Dowlais Co.
Aberdare Co.
Penydarran Co.
Hills Co.
Mr. Lewis
E.P. Richards Esq. and Capt. Langley
Ground as laid out
Rope Walk
Rope Walk
Mr. William Morgan
Mr. Thomas
Charles's
Building

In May 1817, the GCC permitted Thomas Nichols to make a dock to repair boats near the Brick Kiln. Subsequently, the lease was taken up by Insole & Biddle. The next tenant was Thomas Jenkins, who continued the building and repair of canal boats at this dry dock but which he also enlarged for the building of sea-going vessels. Between 1832 and 1833, Jenkins launched two schooners of 120 tons from this dockyard. When Thomas Jenkins died in the 1840s, his son William seems to have taken over operations. Later it was being run by William Jenks, whose family had come to Cardiff from the River Severn in Worcestershire. In 1878 it was still known as Jenkins Dock. The photograph shows a canal boat being fitted with a new cabin in the dry dock in 1891. The site of the dockyard was on the east bank of the Sea Lock pound, at the southwest corner of Loudon Square. At this time, according to a pencilled note on a GCC property plan, the yard was known by the name 'Chaddock's Dock'. Robert Chaddick and Edward Pinner operated a ferry at the Sea Lock. The dock appears to have closed during the early years of the 20th century and to have been filled in soon afterwards.

CCL, Mrs McMinn collection

Cyfarthfa's iron yard in the City of London.[21] Years later, the descendants of John Kemeys Tynte considered building a tramroad and establishing a shipping place at the mouth of the Rhymney, for exporting coal from his pits at Rudry[22] but the opportunity of raising the necessary capital through the Glamorganshire Canal Act of 1796 had been lost and these plans too came to nothing.

The Act did include an unusual additional clause which was inserted in March when the Bill was in Committee.[23] It prevented the canal company proceeding with any part of the extension until the written consent had been received from Bute – who that month had been granted a marquessate[24] – who was sole owner of the land through which the extension was to pass. Throughout the period the Bill was in Parliament, Lord Bute was abroad as His Majesty's Ambassador in Madrid. It was not until December 1796, after he had resigned the post and returned to Britain, that the signed agreement was forthcoming.[25] Meanwhile, tonnage receipts continued to fund completion of the canal from the South Gate to the Bank. James Jackson, a mason from Ledbury, contracted in June 1796 to complete the 240 yards of walling on the west bank of the canal, which was intended for the iron companies' wharves.[26] In November, this work was still in progress. To assist access to gunwales of sea-going vessels, the walling on the Sea Lock pound from 50 yards below the South Gate Bridge was to be higher above the water level than the normal six inches on the canal itself.[27] Elsewhere, the banks were completed in turf.

Richard Tredwen, a builder of small sea-going coastal vessels, managed a shipyard on the River Taff at Cardiff. He later moved his business to a dry dock he had built on the east side of the Glamorganshire Canal, where he was assisted by his nephews, Thomas and John Hodge, who took over management of this yard by the time of Tredwen's death in 1857. There were two dry docks, radiating from a common entrance. The photograph shows the remains of the larger dry dock, taken from the dry bed of the Sea Lock pound on 1 August 1957. The masonry had supported a single set of lock-type gates, so that a boat could enter the dock from the canal, the gates would close and the water would then be let out of the dock. The second dock led off to the right. A drawbridge on rollers carried a path across the common entrance. The 1861 census records that Thomas Hodge employed 18 men and 24 boys at this shipyard. A small vessel was in for repair when Ian Wright visited the Sea Lock pound of the canal in 1947 but by the following year, Cardiff Corporation had succeeded in permanently closing the James Street swing bridge to navigation. ILW photo neg 1842

Bute's agreement to the extension through his lands was confirmed by his steward Henry Hollier, at the committee meeting of 17 December 1796. The only proviso was that the Marquess's employees, horses and other beasts (but not carriages) be allowed to use the towpath and canal to move freely between his lands on the east and west of the canal below the South Gate. At the same meeting, it was ordered that trees be planted each side of the canal from the South Gate to the Sea Lock.

Wharves are Let

Work now moved on apace. So that iron and tinplate could be stocked at the Sea Lock pound, wharves of 120 yards length (room enough for six moored canal boats) were let for 99 years to each of the main works (Dowlais, Pentyrch, Penydarren, Melingriffith and Plymouth) – at annual rents of five guineas.[28] Fields on the opposite bank, behind the towpath and road to the moors, were similarly let by Cardiff Corporation and the Marquess of Bute. It must be remembered that the canal Acts had allowed for compulsory purchase of the bare minimum of land to allow for the canal, towpaths and wharves; landowners were therefore guaranteed a healthy income from letting adjoining property to the freighters and operators whose businesses were attracted to the canal. In Cardiff the prime landowner so to benefit was the Marquess of Bute.[29]

Early Management

The contractor selected to cut the canal from the Bank to the new Sea Lock was Lewis Evans. His £650 tender for completion by 1 November 1797, included an eighteen month maintenance agreement.[30] At a cost of £80, a lockkeeper's house was built at the Sea Lock by William Pritchard, whose claypit and brickyard lay below the canal bank on the East Moors.[31] It may have been the same ageing, but versatile, Lewis Evans, who, seeking continued employment with the canal company, was appointed the lockkeeper at a guinea a week rent free.[32] By June 1798,

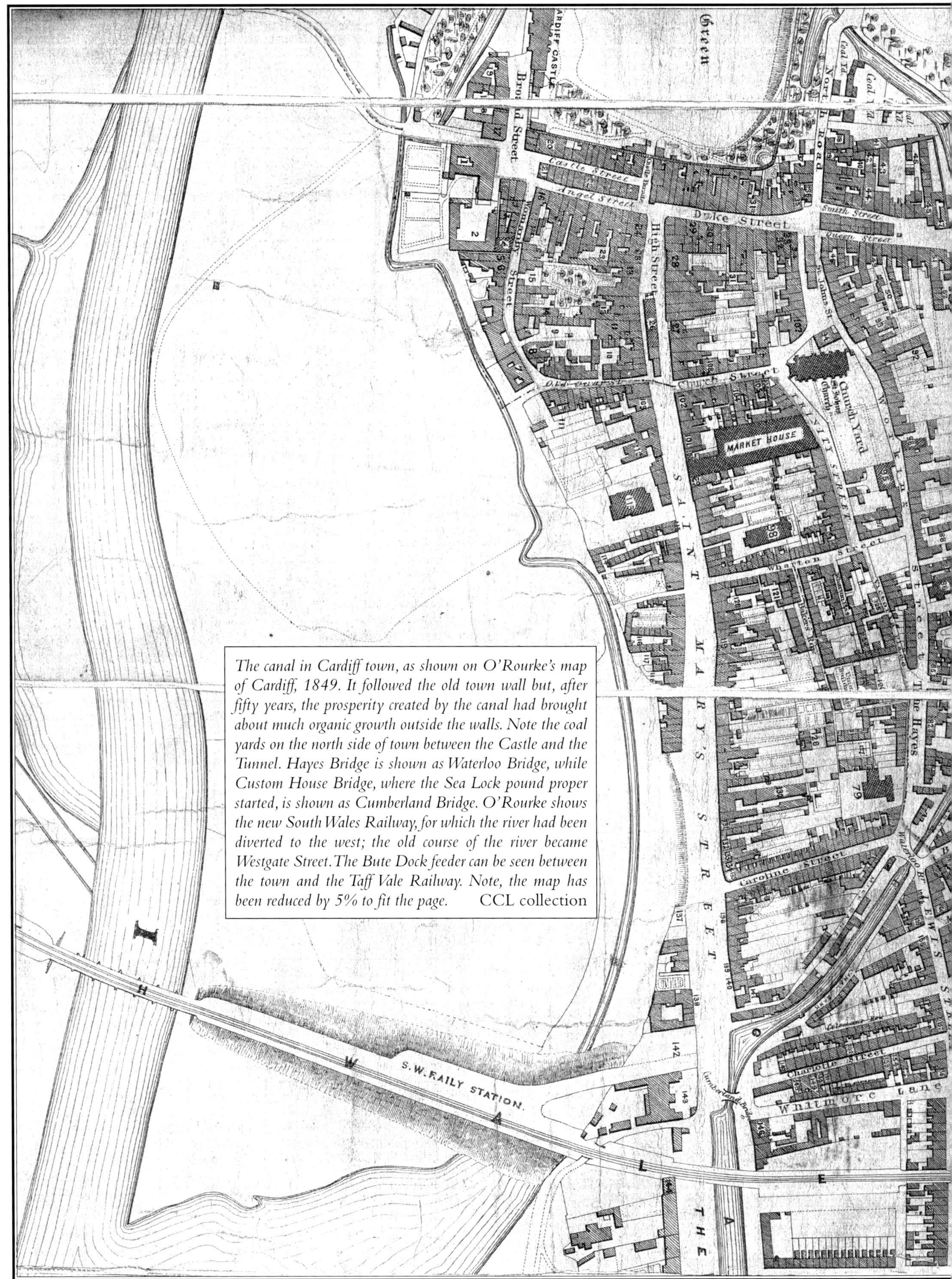

The canal in Cardiff town, as shown on O'Rourke's map of Cardiff, 1849. It followed the old town wall but, after fifty years, the prosperity created by the canal had brought about much organic growth outside the walls. Note the coal yards on the north side of town between the Castle and the Tunnel. Hayes Bridge is shown as Waterloo Bridge, while Custom House Bridge, where the Sea Lock pound proper started, is shown as Cumberland Bridge. O'Rourke shows the new South Wales Railway, for which the river had been diverted to the west; the old course of the river became Westgate Street. The Bute Dock feeder can be seen between the town and the Taff Vale Railway. Note, the map has been reduced by 5% to fit the page. CCL collection

Woodfield House
Longdike
INFIRMARY
Gaol Lane
COUNTY
GAOL
Nursery
RAILWAY STATION
NEWTOWN
DOCK FEEDER
Wellington Terrace
Nelson Terrace
Little Frederick Street
David Street
Charles Street
Wesleyan Chapel
GAS WORKS
CROCKHERBTOWN
Paradise Place
Play Ground
Barrack Lane
Union Street
Ebenezer Street
Mary Anne Street
Rodney Street
Rupertra Street
St Marys
Church School
Friars
Thomas St.
Hills Terrace

A circa 1897 snow scene alongside the walls of Cardiff Castle, where the canal ran in the former castle moat just below North Road Lock. S.C. Fox photo, ILW collection

the Sea Lock was ready and the pound was filled for the reception of vessels. The old basin adjoining the original site for the Sea Lock at the Bank remained wider than the rest of the pound and enabled boats to turn freely. Bye-laws were issued to control its use and the canal was opened throughout – more than eight years since Parliament had passed the initial Act.[33] Just as he had four years previously, when the canal had been opened to Cardiff, John Bird wrote an account of the opening and sent it to the *Gloucester Journal* for publication:[34]

> '*The Sea Lock of the Glamorganshire Canal at Cardiff, was opened this afternoon at six o'clock, and the* Castle of Cardiff, *a fine sloop of 80 tons burthen, very opportunely arrived from Bristol, and was navigated into the Canal amidst the acclamations and rejoicings of numerous spectators. The Bason* [sic] *and Canal for the space of a mile is of sufficient depth to admit of more than 100 brigs, sloops &c to ride in perfect safety, and constantly afloat for loading and unloading, an advantage which must strike every person trading to this port, as no delay can arise from the shoals in the river, but a free communication be carried on during the Neap as well as the Spring tides.*'

Once the final costs of completing the canal were known and in order to settle for the land purchases, the first call was then made on the shareholders under the 1796 Act. The Act authorised calls totalling £10,000 yet only £3,600 was necessary.[35] No further call was ever made under the Act. In 1807, when the canal company was next in need of more capital, the two year deadline for completing work under the Act had expired and this lapse prevented it from raising any of the remaining £6,400.[36]

It was soon realised that the privilege granted the Marquess of Bute was inconvenient to all. To avoid cattle being driven over the public wharves, the canal company built a cattle road from the South Gate towards the marshes, around the back of the company's houses, a route which became known as Dumballs Road. To open up access from town to wharves, Cardiff Corporation was asked, in March 1799, to take down the South Gate and repair the connecting road from St Mary's Street, although the corporation did not grant permission until November 1802.[37] The opportunist John Bird was already informing the Marquess of Bute that here, at the meeting of town and dockland, was an excellent situation for his Lordship to build an Inn.[38]

The operation of what was Cardiff's first floating dock required fairly minimal management on the part of the canal company. Bye-laws were set and then evolved, as the pond's usage grew and more rules became necessary. It was down to the canal freighters and ship owners to abide by these rules, while the canal company simply collected the tolls and harbour dues, and maintained the fabric of the canal.

To return to the canal employees at Cardiff, from 1790 John Wood, the Cardiff solicitor, had been clerk to the proprietors, the equivalent of company secretary, at a salary of £40.[39] Lewis Morris was clerk at Cardiff; his main job was to issue and collect boat permits. As the volume of work increased, his annual salary was advanced in July 1795 to £42 and in June 1797 to £50.[40] In 1801, he was paid an additional £20 gratuity for his valued services and in 1802, along with Lewis Evans and John Knowles, the Merthyr clerk, he was paid a £10 gratuity.[41] From June 1796, many of John Wood's responsibilities were passed to Patrick Copeland, who was appointed company clerk with overall charge of managing the canal, reporting directly to the committee. On a salary of £100, Copeland was based at Navigation but when the Sea Lock was opened in 1798, a bedroom in the clerk's (Lewis Morris's) house near the South Gate was appropriated for his use when at Cardiff. In July, Copeland moved his books of account to this new office.[42]

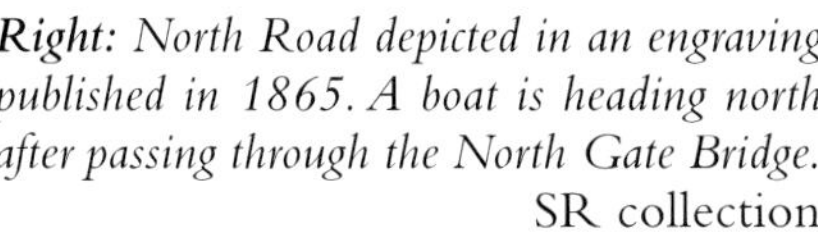

***Right:** North Road depicted in an engraving published in 1865. A boat is heading north after passing through the North Gate Bridge.*
SR collection

***Below:** A slightly later engraving of North Gate Bridge, published around 1880, with a boat seen heading south to the docks. Today, Kingsway runs across here.*
Bill Hamlin collection

Wood retired at the 1799 general meeting and Copeland took over completely as clerk, and in 1800 also briefly assumed the post of treasurer, with the resignation of Jeffreys Wilkins. Come the 1801 general meeting, Patrick Copeland himself resigned completely from the Glamorganshire Canal Company; Philip Williams was promoted from clerk at Merthyr to become the new company secretary and Thomas Peirce became treasurer.[43]

In these first few years, it was already apparent that coal shipment was an important function of the canal. Sea-going ships were loaded directly from canal boat and a bye-law was issued in September 1803 for tarpaulins to be used between boat and vessel, to prevent coal from falling into the canal. To minimise congestion and interference near the iron wharves, coal transshipment was banned above the Bank and was allowed only between the Bank and the Sea Lock. A vessel awaiting a cargo of iron would discharge its ballast on the Bank and would then moor in the old basin, or Pool, until the respective wharf was ready to load it. All boat movements were manually worked by rope, oar or sail, horses not being allowed to draw boats below the South Gate Bridge.[44]

It was not long before Lewis Evans' job of lockkeeper at Sea Lock was naturally widened to include Pool Master and his salary was increased at the June 1806 general meeting to £100 per annum, including a £5 allowance for coal and candles. It is quite possible that, out of this salary, Evans had to pay his own assistants. The Sea Lock remained closed on Sunday, unless a special application was sanctioned in writing by the committee.[45]

Richard Hill, having his own mines in Cumbria, was the first of the Merthyr ironmasters to import red iron ore to mix with the local iron stone, or mine. Reference to landing ore in 1795 has already been mentioned. The outcome of an application by Hill in May 1807, for an

At the beginning of the 20th century, Cardiff Corporation installed some fine decorative cast iron balustrades on several of its city canal bridges. This official photograph shows the Kingsway Bridge after completion and widening. Sadly, all cast iron has long since been removed but the original 1794 stone arch of this bridge still survives, in the pedestrian subway to the modern even wider road.

Bill Hamlin collection

iron ore wharf separate from his iron wharf, is not recorded but in August 1809, a 50 yard wharf adjoining the ballast bank was let at 2 guineas per annum to the Hills of Plymouth Works for their iron ore imports.[46] Here, they effectively enlarged their wharf frontage by building a loading/unloading dock similar to their later dock at Abercanaid, near their works.

Coal

It was not many years before the enforced transshipment of coal directly from canal boat to sea-going boat became an inconvenience in the Sea Lock pond. Although coal should not be stored for long in the open, colliery proprietors and coal merchants were demanding their own yards on the canal. From 1807, the canal company began letting coal wharves on the left bank near the Sea Lock. John Key (who had taken over his brother Thomas's colliery activities from 1799) was the first to apply, followed by Brockett Grover, his own successor at Maesmawr, in 1809.[47] James Morrison and Mary Jones, Maesbach, had the 80 feet wharf nearest to the Sea Lock.[48] Morgan Thomas, Craig yr Allt, was shipping from his own yard at Cardiff in 1813.[49] These next few years saw a dramatic rise in coal exports from the canal, as it began to carry traffic from three new sources. Doctor Richard Griffiths' canal was joined to the Glamorganshire at Dynea and brought down coal from the lower Rhondda. Sir William Smith's tramroad connected with the Glamorganshire at Navigation and brought down coal from Llanfabon. The Aberdare Canal was joined to the Glamorganshire above Abercynon and brought down coal from the Cynon, together with iron from Hirwaun, Abernant and Llwydcoed.

Although the iron wharves were let on 99 year terms, the canal company decided that coal wharf leases would be for only 21 years. The colliery business was not operated on the same scale as iron making. Colliery proprietors came and went. Pits and levels were opened and closed. The committee acceded that '*leases at their expiration should be renewed to the present proprietors on the same terms provided that they are then in possession of their collieries.*' Coal wharves situated on the east bank from the Sea Lock were let to Sir Jeremiah Homfray (Gelligaer and Rhondda), who took over Morrison and Jones' wharf, Walter Coffin (Rhondda), Brockett Grover (Maesmawr), Dr Richard Griffiths (Rhondda), and Sir William Smith and William Bray (Llanfabon).[50] Iron wharves on the west bank, below the ballast bank, were granted to Tappendens & Co (Abernant), Bouzer & Co (Hirwaun) and Scale & Co (Llwydcoed, Aberdare).[51] Excepting Homfray's, each of the wharves had a 190 feet frontage onto the canal and the rent was 2 guineas per annum.

With this traffic increase came a welcome rise for the clerk at Cardiff. From February 1811, Lewis Morris' salary was £100, with £5 for coal and candles. A gauging dock was ordered to be made, between the iron wharves and the Sea Lock, at which Morris was to gauge and index all the canal boats on the canal. In return for the increase he agreed '*on no account to take any other employment.*'[52]

In April 1812, a frontage of 140 feet on the West bank, conveniently close to the Sea Lock, was let to the sea captain, James Walters, where he built the Sea Lock Hotel. The initial lease ran for 42 years at £5 per annum.[53]

By 1812, the canal at the Sea Lock pound was in need of a good clean out. A complete closure was planned for two weeks in June 1813, when the pound was drained. Because there was no lock between the sea and the tunnel lock at Crockherbtown, the Sea Lock pound was emptied by first placing stop planks across the canal where it narrowed at the South Gate Bridge. This method was also applied to empty the pound above the South Gate Bridge into the river, which was close to the canal at that point and this was done in 1817, so that the town ditch could be

Tom Frazer emerges from Crockherbtown Lock (Lock 50) with a loaded boat in about 1936. On the right is the former weigh dock and cabin. In its last years this was one of the more forbidding locations on the canal. Hemmed in on three sides by the high walls of the Friary, Queen Street and the Carlton Restaurant, the canal and towpath descended abruptly to pass under Queen Street's masonry arch. In this black cavern, which boatmen called 'The Ole', it was just possible for two boats to pass. The canal then narrowed for the Tunnel, whilst a paved passage rose to the surface to allow boat horses to be led up to street level and over the top of the tunnel. The boats were manhandled through. ILW collection

cleaned. This unpleasant operation was effected by gangs of men using wheelbarrows, planks and trestles. Accumulated mud, slime, coal and other jetsam were shovelled out and wheelbarrowed away from the site. While the canal was drained in 1813, it was decided to excavate it further and so extend the deep water area towards the South Gate Bridge. At the same time, the Sea Lock gates were repaired. The following summer, the bottom gates were renewed and the lock lengthened as far as it could be, to the inverted masonry arch.[54] In August 1818, it was agreed to put in a double stop gate at the South Gate Bridge, to be used as a lock in periods when the Sea Lock pound might be under level but this does not appear to have been actioned.[55] Throughout the canal's life, there was a continued need for cleansing because of the high level of suspended particles which passed through the Sea Lock gates with each tide, even though the canal was not a tidal pound but was fed by fresh water.

In August 1815, Lewis Evans gave notice and was replaced as pool master by John Morgan.[56] Evans would have witnessed remarkable changes in his 20 or so years of employment with the Glamorganshire Canal in Cardiff. At the time of his retirement, the canal scene below the town was altering from a bleak windy saltmarsh, where cattle grazed undisturbed, to one of constant activity on land and water. Lessees were building permanent warehouses and offices on their wharves. Cranes were being erected and docks were being dug. Engineering works were beginning to sprout up to service the visiting ships and the growing town. In March 1815, the Dowlais Company installed a steam engine at their wharf and was allowed to lay a pipe and use water from the canal.[57] It was on this side also that the canal company's carpenter was based.[58] In October 1815, Edward Davis was allowed to make a wharf alongside his mill. In November the following year, the pound was let out in order to raise a sunken canal boat belonging to Davis. This same month, Thomas Nichols was applying to build a boat repairing dock near Pritchard's brick kiln, although permission was not granted until May 1817.[59] Also on that east bank, Thomas Charles, Henry Charles' son and successor as agent to the Merthyr Ironworks and a committee man since 1802, was privileged with a 99 year lease, at 5 shillings per annum, on a 110 feet wharf for expanding his inherited timber business. This extended his land holding, after he had already taken a 42 year lease, for 2 guineas per annum, of corporation land stretching from his field to the canal and as far as the lime kiln.[60] Here, also, James Parry lived in a cottage alongside his lime kiln, where he burnt lime for over thirty years from the building of the canal. Parry owned his own sea-going vessels and brought in limestone from Aberthaw, from which the best Cardiff lime was burnt and transported into the country in special canal boats.[61] In November 1817, the salt dealer and builders merchant, James Kidman, was erecting a house and warehouse on the east wharf, just below the bridge, from which he carried provisions and materials to his warehouse at Merthyr.[62] In 1827, Thomas Kidman continued the salt trade at this wharf (probably from the Severn via Gloucester) in his 18 ton sloop *Gleaner*, built at Berkeley.[63] Kidman retired to live at Duffryn, where boatmen came to call the canal bridge there 'Kidman's Bridge'. In the 1820s, two rope walks were also laid out between the lime kiln and Pritchard's brick works.

With the collapse of the iron industry on the Aberdare Canal in 1813-4, the abandoned wharves were re-let to Dowlais and to William Crawshay, who had bought up the bankrupt Hirwaun and was planning to reopen the works.[64] At the same time, the Abernant Ironworks was bought by the Aberdare Company and so they consolidated the wharves of the two companies at Cardiff.

Crockherbtown Lock (No 50) was where the canal dived under Cardiff's east-west thoroughfare, which was originally known as Crockherbtown and later became Queen Street. This early 1950s photograph of the derelict lock and weigh dock places the canal in a modern context – the fine building with the clock tower is the Friary Buildings of the Principality Building Society. V. Hardacre photo, CCL collection

Employees

Despite the post-Napoleonic War slump, traffic on the Glamorganshire Canal continued to grow steadily. On 3 June 1818, it was recorded that two men were assisting John Morgan and that they should be constantly at their post night and day. Morgan was allowed 6s per week for accommodating them in his Sea Lock keeper's house. At the two locks in the town, George Collins replaced lockkeeper Thomas Lewis Hugh, who was ordered to work on the banks under John Morgan's direction. The following year, Morgan was awarded an annual allowance of £5 for coal and candles, then from 1821, the canal company paid him £15 to keep a horse. At that time, too, the company authorised that a shed and privy be placed at the Sea Lock.[65]

After several drownings, in 1819 a petition by '*many respectable inhabitants of Cardiff*' resulted in a causeway being made along the wharf, which was lit at night. As well as extending the working day, this would have enabled sailors to return safely to their ships from the ale houses and brothels in the lower town. In 1821, Cardiff's first gas works and gasometer were built alongside the canal in the town.[66]

In May 1820, a new bye-law was issued, to impose a charge of 1d per ton registered tonnage on incoming vessels for wheeling out their ballast.[67] The lock still remained closed on Sundays.[68]

Schemes to Widen the Sea Lock Pound

The first Marquess of Bute died in 1814 and was succeeded by his grandson. From 1819, the twenty-five year old second Marquess of Bute started taking more

A graphic view of 'The Ole'. This is the southern portal of the tunnel near Hills Terrace, as seen on 17 March 1944. Boats were unable to pass in the tunnel and there was no towpath except for 23 yards at the northern end. Boatmen had to pull their boats through by means of the chain fixed to the tunnel wall. Historically, the site of this 115 yard tunnel formed part of Cardiff's medieval town moat. At the present time (2004) it is the location of the St David's Shopping Centre. ILW photo neg 266

than a passing interest in the development of Cardiff's shipping facilities. It was he who now owned most of the land below the town, in fact most of Cardiff as a whole. His interest was kindled by his newly appointed surveyor, David Stewart. Stewart made it his business to advise the young Marquess whenever the Glamorganshire Canal Company encroached on his lordship's inherited powers. This encompassed not only land at Cardiff but the whole issue of water supply in the Taff Valley.[69] Stewart encouraged Bute to provide his own shipping facilities at Cardiff and he put forward a grand scheme to divert the River Taff to join the River Ely to the west. The new channel would pass through Lord Plymouth's land on the Grange. The Ely would be straightened after the Taff had joined it, to form a floating harbour with flood gates to the sea near Cogan Pill. This harbour would also be connected to the Glamorganshire Canal above the ballast bank, by a long canal parallel to the diverted Taff.[70] In 1821, Thomas Telford's expertise was brought in to add weight to the proposal and a revised scheme transferred the floating harbour away from the united rivers to a dock at the Cogan end of the connecting canal.[71] The new canal was to be eight feet deep for 32 of its 56 feet breadth and was to be protected from flooding on the low Grange Moors by eight feet high banks on both sides.[72] The scheme proved prohibitively expensive and the next decade was spent with Bute and his advisers considering various plans for dock developments from other such illustrious engineers as James Green and William Cubitt.

The ironmasters who were the committee of the Glamorganshire Canal, were made to realise that they now had limited scope to develop their own shipping facilities. In May 1821, they themselves appointed George Overton to survey the port and propose how, within the canal company's constraints, it could be improved to better accommodate the increased trade. Overton reported within the month.[73] His full report is inserted in the committee minute book.

Apart from questioning whether even the projected trade could stand the cost of implementing the grand schemes

This 1890s image of the canal between the tunnel and Hayes Bridge gives some idea how buildings present themselves across an industrial canal. The scene has been described as the remains of Cocks Tower on the town wall, probably referring to the square stone-built section in the centre. Beyond that may well be the Hayes Foundry or the malthouse at Dowson Bros Brewery.

W. Booth photo, ILW collection

of Stewart and Telford, he counselled against disturbing the beds of the two rivers and diverting the course of the Taff, since he feared that the approaches to the existing Sea Lock would then become silted and would injure the canal company's position. He confined his recommendations to the canal:

> '*viz, the widening, deepening and straitening of the pond from the Sea Lock to the Wharfs, which would not only do away with the expense of lighterage from the Wharfs to the Sea Lock but also produce that dispatch so desirable to large vessels which are required to be sent off speedily, the depth of the water on the upper Sill of the Sea Lock being 5 feet more than at the Wharfs, this being one of the greatest evils will be removed as vessels of 300 Tons burthen can afterwards take in the whole of their cargoes at the respective Wharfs.*'

He went on to propose a basin below the Sea Lock which

> '*would not only enable Vessels of large burthen to come into the Lock at all times but the Water such basin would contain being loosed out rapidly would undoubtedly scour the settlement from the Channel and always keep it open.*'

To effect the depth of water in the channel and to divert it more directly to the mouth of the river, Overton proposed the building of a breakwater and he referred to his recent visit to Devon, to view John Smeaton's Plymouth Breakwater and his having attended evidence at the London Bridge Committee – a John Rennie scheme. He suggested the traders would '*submit to a general tax upon the whole of their Trade*' to pay for the benefit of being able to pass boats in and out of the canal at any time regardless of tide.

As a contingency for when the lock was being repaired and '*in order to Ship Coals more readily from the Canal above the Lock*', Overton recommended a branch be taken from the south of the basin to the canal. In essence, he was proposing a narrow lock for coal ships and a wide lock for iron-carrying vessels. It is clear from this that coal shipments, whilst significant in volume, were still in small coastal vessels, in comparison to the London-bound iron exports, that were being carried in larger vessels which would use the basin.

Finally, the recommendation to enlarge the pond from the wharves to the Sea Lock was accompanied by placing

> '*a Stop Gate in the middle of the pond and another about the Wharfs with large flood gates to flush a considerable quantity of water down at once to carry off the Mud at convenient times which gates would be useful when casual repairs may be required at the Lock it may also be well to take into consideration whether a Culvert near the Wharfs and another near the Old Pill would not be servicable to carry off such mud into the River the inconvenience of mud gathering is very apparent and it will be observed that after the pond is made level the difficulty of scouring the mud the whole length will be increased.*'

While the work was in progress, transshipment from canal to sea-going vessels would continue by use of a temporary tramroad along the wharf.

Several times in the report George Overton admits his limitations and states that he was prepared to bow to the experience of more able water engineers. Overton was, after all, more at home engineering tramroads than docks

A sketch of Hayes Bridge (also known as Milkmaid's Bridge) as it appeared in 1859. The work of Sam Allen, it appeared on page 18 of his 1918 book of reminiscences.

and harbours. He had surveyed the route of the Stockton & Darlington Railway, when that committee was undecided whether to build a canal or railway. In the published argument for Overton's railway, in 1818, he quoted Thomas Reece's experiences on the Glamorganshire Canal: '*I have had, for the last eight years, 15 boats of twenty tons each, constantly trading from Myrthyr* [sic] *to Cardiff, a distance of 25 miles, 550 feet lockage. They have scarcely averaged five trips a month.*'[74] This is an interesting remark, for it suggests that since becoming the GCC's Chief Clerk, Reece either had his own business or the canal company itself was running a carrying business between Cardiff and Merthyr. Fifteen boats was a considerable fleet.

The minute book does not record how Overton's report for the GCC was received. It must have generated some favourable discussion, for Overton was then requested to report upon the practicability of raising the banks and locks of the canal throughout, in order to allow boats to carry 25 tons as opposed to the current restriction of 20 tons. Robert Stevenson, the Scottish dock engineer, was brought in to amplify Overton's recommendations into a practical and costed proposal. Overton's separate estimates to raise the banks and locks were presented to the 12 July committee meeting and were accepted at the special assembly of 20 September, when it was resolved that the most convenient time for the freighters to cope with the disruption would be the following May and June. A call of £10 13s 4d per share was to be made upon the proprietors.[75]

Stevenson's report was carried at a further special assembly in November, when it was resolved that

> '*the present line of Canal from the Sea Lock to the highest Wharf below the South Gate Bridge be deepened, widened and otherwise improved so as to enable all vessels that can enter the Lock to come up to the respective Wharfs and take in their full Cargoes.*'

For their services, the two engineers Overton and Stevenson were paid £50 and £115 11s respectively.[76] All that remained now was to seek the Marquess of Bute's permission to sell to the GCC the land required for the widening. Benjamin Hall tried first in November, followed by William Crawshay in December, who wrote to Bute through Colonel Knight. A non-committal letter was received in January, which, after pressure was again applied by Crawshay, resulted in refusal by the Marquess in February to give up the land. The canal company was obliged to call out the commissioners to value the land and attempt to enforce the Act by compulsory purchase. When tenders were received for the work from George Overton himself, Messrs Pinkerton & Pearce and others, they all exceeded the original estimates. The canal company sought a meeting with Bute during his visit to Cardiff in March, after which they strangely concluded that the work could possibly be done without taking more of his land at Cardiff after all.[77]

While attempted negotiations continued at Cardiff, work started on the bank raising from the South Gate Bridge all the way to Merthyr, using money from the general funds.[78] Perhaps it was this major project, taking up the full length of the canal, which caused the company to move its carpenter and timber yard from Cardiff to Navigation. Already, since 1817, Dr Richard Griffiths had been making use of the carpenter's garden.[79] Thomas Charles was able to expand his own timber business below the South Gate Bridge, by renting the vacated canal company's carpenter's house and yard for £30 per annum.[80]

The committee needed to pay for raising the banks throughout the length of the canal from Cardiff to Merthyr.

CHAMBERLAIN & SONS
WINE & SPIRIT MERCHANTS
SINGLE BOTTLES SUPPLIED

A circa 1912 view from Custom House Bridge, which emphasizes just how much a part of the city centre the Glamorganshire Canal was. Cardiff Corporation's single-decker electric tramcar No 48 makes its way along Mill Lane, whilst a boat load, probably of bagged flour, moves sedately up the canal towards Hayes Bridge. The boat horse can just be seen on the towpath and the boatman pushes hard on the tiller, to drive the boat closer to the bank as it takes the bend. Bob Marrows collection

Looking the opposite way to the previous picture, the canal is seen approaching Custom House Bridge, with Mill Lane on the right. This is one of the photographs commissioned by the council when it took possession of the canal in 1943, the sandbags in the doorway as a protection against blast damage giving the clue to the fact that it was wartime. CCL collection

To achieve this, they got the agreement of the June 1822 general assembly to apply to Parliament for new powers to raise the £6,400, which they could claim was outstanding from the authorised £10,000 capital of the 1796 Act but whose two year deadline had well and truly lapsed. The plan for widening the Sea Lock pond was deposited with the Clerk of the Peace in September 1822. It sought to take in the Plymouth, Penydarren, Aberdare and Dowlais Iron Companies' respective lands opposite their wharves below the South Gate Bridge. It was also to take the adjoining land of Thomas Charles (including that only recently let to him), together with the lime kiln. However, the whole plan still included Bute land either side of the original basin opposite the Ballast Bank, as well as Bute land from the Ballast Bank to the Sea Lock Hotel.[81]

The Custom House, which in earlier days had been in the High Street near the town quay, was transferred in 1821 to the east side of the Sea Lock pond, immediately below the South Gate Bridge and next to Kidman's premises. From here, customs men could control traffic on both river and canal. The land required for the planned widening lay south of Kidman's wharf. From that time the South Gate Bridge began to be referred to as the Custom House Bridge.

The Cardiff Tramroad Scheme

While the canal company felt stalemated by Bute's stranglehold at Cardiff, the old triumvirate of main freighters (Dowlais, Plymouth and Penydarren) brought further pressure by coming out with their own proposal for alternative shipping facilities at Cardiff. The plan was to extend their Merthyr Tramroad from Navigation, to a basin near the right bank of the River Taff, south of Cowbridge Road. From this basin, a canal would be excavated across Lord Plymouth's land of the Grange and across the meandering River Ely, to a sea lock near Cogan Pill. In favouring Penarth as a shipping place, the proponents were avoiding having to use Bute land. The courses of the two rivers were to remain unaltered. By this scheme, the three Merthyr ironworks in competition to Cyfarthfa were resurrecting their vision of 1798, to build a tramroad from Merthyr to Cardiff and so divert all their traffic from the Glamorganshire Canal. The survey was made by David Davies, from the line drawn out by none other than George Overton, the man who had built the Merthyr Tramroad twenty years previously and who, as we have seen, had recently surveyed the canal's own proposals.[82] Overton and Davies had returned from Durham, where they did not have the strength of character to stand up to George Stephenson's counter-proposals for the Stockton & Darlington Railway. Stephenson's argument for a locomotive assisted edge railway had won the day against Overton's horse-powered plateway. Overton had not been impressed by Trevithick's one-off experiment at steam railway propulsion on his Merthyr Tramroad back in 1804 and he was still not ready to accept the steam locomotive.[83]

The added complication of having to oppose this latest scheme for a Merthyr to Cardiff Tramroad may have caused

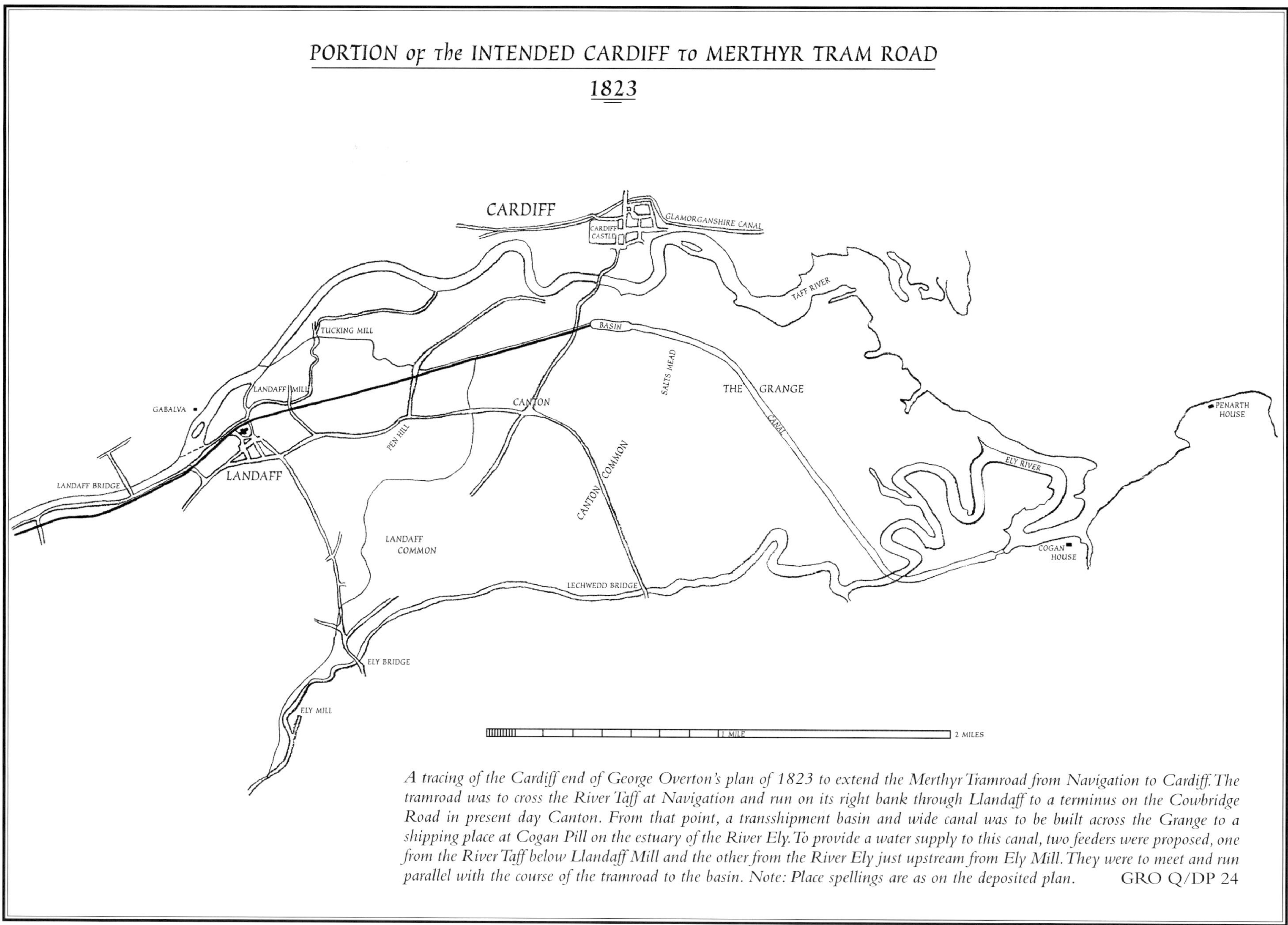

A tracing of the Cardiff end of George Overton's plan of 1823 to extend the Merthyr Tramroad from Navigation to Cardiff. The tramroad was to cross the River Taff at Navigation and run on its right bank through Llandaff to a terminus on the Cowbridge Road in present day Canton. From that point, a transshipment basin and wide canal was to be built across the Grange to a shipping place at Cogan Pill on the estuary of the River Ely. To provide a water supply to this canal, two feeders were proposed, one from the River Taff below Llandaff Mill and the other from the River Ely just upstream from Ely Mill. They were to meet and run parallel with the course of the tramroad to the basin. Note: Place spellings are as on the deposited plan. GRO Q/DP 24

the elderly Rev'd Dr Benjamin Hall to be thankful he had given up the chair of the GCC committee in June 1822. He had outlived his son and been chairman of the GCC since Richard Crawshay's death in 1809. There may have been friction between the Halls and Richard Crawshay's son and grandson, the two Williams,[84] but Hall's influential support for the Glamorganshire Canal had been invaluable since the time of Dadford's survey and the framing of the first Bill. William Crawshay junior was now chairman and it was down to him to organise opposition to the Cardiff Tramroad Bill, whilst also seeking to push his own canal Bill through Parliament.

Attempts to Widen the Sea Lock in the 1820s

The Cardiff Tramroad scheme may not have been as serious as the canal company supposed, for as soon as it was made public, its proponents were preparing terms for the canal company to persuade them to abandon it.[85] By the late summer of 1823, William Crawshay completed negotiating the deal with Richard Hill on behalf of the projectors of the tramroad. The tramroad Bill was dropped, in return for one proprietor of each of the three ironworks receiving five shares in the canal company, to enable them to be elected onto the committee. Tonnage rates would be reduced and, collectively, they would support the canal company's Bill to raise £15,000 to improve the port at Cardiff.

The plan was that vessels drawing fourteen feet of water should be able to be admitted into the Sea Lock at all tides and be able to come all the way up to the wharves. At a special general meeting in February 1824, the GCC's new solicitor, Meyrick,[86] was instructed to draft the Bill and Sir Christopher Cole would support it through the House of Commons.[87] Young's deposited plan of the intended widening of the Sea Lock pond and the intended basin is in Glamorgan Record Office. It is almost identical to the plan of eighteen months previously, except for the addition of the intended basin below the Sea Lock.[88]

Yet the combined forces of the Merthyr (and Melingriffith) ironmasters could do little against the force of landed property which was the Bute Estate. David Stewart's surveys even suggested that the canal company had for some years been encroaching on Bute land it had not purchased.[89] Bute's manorial claims to the waters of the River Taff were the last straw and the canal company were forced to trim their plans and abandon the Bill. At the annual general assembly on 2 June 1824, the accumulated balance of £5,502 18s 9d was voted to be divided amongst the freighters in proportion to their total tonnage paid during the previous three years. The four iron masters and principal freighters forewent their rebate, in return for being elected to the committee for a fourteen year term and so that the canal company could improve the Sea Lock pond as best it could.[90] The clerk, Thomas Reece, was once again instructed to mark out immediately the lands required above the ballast bank for widening and deepening the Sea Lock pond and Meyrick was directed to arrange purchase of the land under the existing Acts.[91]

Reece must have persuaded the committee of the futility of this order if it were to take in Bute land, for the very next day the committee convened again and:

> '*Mr Reece represented that to give immediate relief to the trade it would only require such partial widening and deepening of the Canal opposite and near the Limekiln as would be compatible with the extent of the land near the property of the Canal Company and that such improvement might be effected in the course of four weeks.*'

The committee gave Reece his month and ordered that freighters be informed that the stoppage would commence from 1 August.[92]

The iron companies gave up their 190 feet wharves on the eastern bank below the Custom House, in consideration of which, generous lettings were made of new wharves on the western bank. Hills' Plymouth Ironwork's existing 150 feet wharf was increased to 400 feet, adjoining and above the Ballast Bank, and the lease was extended to 99 years at 5 guineas per annum; Crawshay's Hirwaun Ironworks was allowed 400 feet, adjoining Crawshay's existing Cyfarthfa wharf, for 99 years at 5 guineas per annum; Guest's Dowlais Ironworks was leased 600 feet, between the Ballast Bank and the Sea Lock, for 99 years at 7 guineas per annum. It was also agreed that the Hills would be paid two thirds the cost of building the wharf wall, if within two years the canal was not deepened to enable vessels to take in their full cargoes at the new wharf. Thomas Charles also lost his wharf in return for an annual rent of 15 guineas. The 190 feet wharf surrendered by Dowlais was re-let to Guest for his newly established glass works, the Cardiff Glass Bottle Company, for 99 years at 2$^1/_2$ guineas per annum.[93] The land on which the glass works were built, behind its wharf, was leased from the Bute Estate for 61 years at an annual rent of £31 10s. The Estate retained power to resume possession of any part of the land should it be needed for improvements – perhaps an indication that development of the first Bute Dock was already being contemplated by the Bute Estate.[94]

Dr Griffiths and Thomas Charles were required to surrender their adjacent leases on the former premises of the company's carpenter and the land was re-let to Edward Bird, to give him a wharf in front of his iron foundry.[95] This lease was confirmed the following year at £25 per annum with six month notice.[96] Bird had taken over the iron foundry from the Dowlais Company and in 1823, had been granted use of water from the canal at 2/6d per annum, although for the same privilege in 1815, William Taitt had had to pay one guinea.[97]

GCC Employees in the 1820s

The extended operating hours from February 1825 required the canal company to overhaul the job specifications of its servants. Lewis Morris was finding the combined jobs of Harbour Master and Accountant at Cardiff too arduous but the canal company's response, far from being sympathetic, was to give him notice from 1

July 1825 and to appoint William Day as the Check Clerk at Cardiff, at £100 per annum. John Morgan's redefined role of Harbour Master and Sea Lock Keeper had the required result of confining his services to the Sea Lock and pond below the Tunnel. As a consequence, his £15 allowance for keeping a horse was removed, leaving him a salary of £120 per annum. Morgan continued to have two men to assist in passing vessels at the Sea Lock and the company now permanently divided the Sea Lock House into three, for the three men's separate accommodation.[98] In September 1826, it was reported that William Day was to have the same powers at the Sea Lock as John Morgan but whether this meant that Morgan had resigned is not clear. By January 1827, Day was collecting cash on behalf of the company and banking it weekly through the iron companies' agent, James Henshaw, but in June, William Churchill Dempsey, who had been bookkeeper and Clerk at Navigation since 1 May 1825 at £100 per annum, moved to become Clerk at Cardiff at a salary of £120 per annum.[99] Dempsey was to remain in that post until his retirement in 1858 on a pension of £75. On his death in 1864 he was aged 83.[100] Also in 1825, William Humphrey was appointed Master Carpenter under Thomas Reece at £6 a month and an allowance of £6 per annum for the keep of a horse. He had the use of the company's house at Nantgarw. The following November his wages were increased to 2 guineas per week but on 22 April 1829, he is reported as having died and of John Morgan being '*removed to the situation lately held by William Humphrey.*' Whether this is the same John Morgan who a few years earlier was Harbour Master and was now turned Master Carpenter is difficult to say but, at this same meeting, came the significant additional announcement that Mr Dornford was appointed Harbour Master. In October of that year, at the meeting where Reece gave the committee notice of his own retirement, Reece was instructed to agree with John Morgan for '*the house*' to be built at the Sea Lock for £20 (presumably as accommodation for Dornford).

Dornford's was a propitious appointment and he was to lead activities at the Sea Lock through a momentous decade for the canal company, until his recognised services were poached eventually by the Marquess of Bute; in 1841, he became Dock Master for the GCC's rival – the Bute Docks. The canal company was now paying a total of almost £900 to salaried staff, whereas in the decade to 1820 the corresponding total averaged a steady £520. In that same year (1828), the total wages paid to its 20 lockkeepers was £629 8s.[101]

Ship-Building and Timber Yards

River activity had not ceased with the building of the canal. As late as 1850, it is recorded that Matthew Pride's Bristol traders would use the Old Town Quay, when the canal Sea Lock pound was closed for cleaning or repairs to the lock gates. It was, though, unusual for vessels carrying more than 90 tons to go up river past the ship yards and iron foundry.[102]

Ship-building, in particular, was a growth industry on the tidal river. Certainly from 1816 and possibly as early as 1788, Joseph Davies' timber and ship-building yard was at the south end of St Mary Street, alongside the canal overflow drain to the river and where the Great Western Hotel and the blocked off entrance to Penarth Road now stand (2004). Edward Bird's iron foundry and Richard Tredwen's riverside shipyard were next to and south of it. Davies' ship-building business was acquired by and continued under William Jones from 1823. (It was possibly a different Joseph Davies who was refused a wharf on the canal the following September and who was coal agent to Thomas Powell at the end of the decade from his yard at Crockherbtown. Insole and Biddle actually tendered to build a lighter for this Davies in 1830, the cost of £80 including Davies giving up his old boat in part exchange).[103]

For the next twenty years, William Jones and his son ran an extensive business from here, being ship builder, ship owner and shipping agent. They also ran the steam saw mills. Their imports included regular loads of timber from Canada. In 1833, it was reported that their ship *Pilot* had completed its sixteenth trans-Atlantic voyage to Quebec in nine years, taking twelve weeks per round trip.[104] They kept a timber stock at the bonded yard near the Sea Lock Hotel. In 1825, it is recorded that their yard supplied timber for new balance poles of the Sea Lock gates.[105] In 1843, William Jones senior retired and his son took over Ely Mills. John and Sidney Batchelor bought and expanded the riverside ship-building and repairing business until, in the late 1840s, they were forced to move into the Bute Dock, when the South Wales Railway required the land for its station approach and for the river to be diverted.[106]

The limited widening of the Sea Lock pond did not take place and in September 1824, Richard Blakemore, fighting for restoration of a full water supply to his Melingriffith Works, filed an injunction which delayed deepening the canal from Cardiff to Merthyr.[107] The yards on the east of the Sea Lock below the Custom House were left vacant. While the canal company fought the Blakemore case, they even delayed granting Richard Tredwen permission to connect his new ship-building dock to the canal. Tredwen, who had operated the oldest shipyard on the river, was the first ship builder (as opposed to canal boat builder) to move onto the canal and he took a lease from Bute of land on the east bank of the Sea Lock pond, where he built two dry docks. Tredwen, who maintained regular contact with his shipbuilding kinsmen at Padstow, was a well-respected Cardiff citizen and was a town councillor in 1835, when aged 44. After his death in 1857, the business was taken over by his nephews John and Thomas Hodge (both originally from Lostwithiel, Cornwall). The 1861 census records them employing 18 men and 24 boys. Hodge's drydock continued in use almost until the closure of the canal in 1951 but building of sea-going vessels ceased in 1876.[108] The boat repairing business was taken over by John Thomas of Llanegwood, Carmarthen, whose family, through three generations, ran a thriving cooperage from the premises, retaining the whole of Richard Tredwen's original land stretching from the canal

The extreme lower left of this view shows the Terminus Hotel, on the corner of Mill Lane and St Mary Street, which has been a Cardiff landmark since 1862. Shortly after it was built, the row of buildings opposite it were demolished so that Mill Lane could be widened to reveal the canal below and to accommodate the horse tramway to Bute Street and Pier Head. The subject of this photograph, however, is the housing which lay on the south-east bank of the canal. For twenty years, from the mid-1850s to the 1870s, this was the infamous 'red light' district of Cardiff – serving sailors, dock workers and canal boatmen alike. The editors of a Cardiff directory of 1858 felt obliged to warn its readers against venturing into Charlotte Street: 'The fact of an excessive number of beer shops, as is observed from the addresses, speaks most truly of the vitiated moral atmosphere inhabitants of this street breathe.' *The area was the province of the notorious Jack Matthews, landlord of the Flying Eagle in Charlotte Street, which was linked by a passageway to his several brothel houses in Whitmore Lane. Throughout the 1860s, Matthews was continually in court charged with violence against his clients, the police and, latterly, the press, who waged a relentless campaign against his empire. Matthews was always able to pay his fines of up to £100 a time, yet he was never convicted of any of the many robberies which occurred at his establishments. In 1868, during the celebrations of the coming of age of the Marquess of Bute, the police estimated there were 160 prostitutes at work in these few streets. The area was completely redeveloped following the Cardiff Improvement Act of 1875. The low terrace of houses running across the centre of the photograph is Court Coleman Row. Behind this are the rooftops of the opposite terraces of Charlotte Street and beyond, and parallel to them off picture, is Whitmore Lane which, on demolition, allowed Custom House Street to be widened. New Street, also leading to the Custom House, was laid over the demolished houses and warehouse of Canal Bank. The tall chimney in the background marks the gas works. The gap in the canal bank between the houses and the warehouse might be a horse slip but it marks the site of the sluices for draining the canal pound; until the New Lock (Lock 51) was built, this long pound extended from Crockherbtown Lock to the Sea Lock gates but stop gates existed under the Custom House Bridge.* Courtesy WIMM

almost as far as Bute Street. There was enough land for several cooperages and smithies, the family residence and an orchard of 28 apple trees.[109]

Another ship-building yard established a few years after Tredwen's was that of Thomas Jenkins, on the site of Thomas Nichols' yard of 1817. George Insole and Richard Biddle first took over Nichols' lease and William Pritchard's adjoining brickworks in 1827. From there they ran a general business supplying timber, bricks and coal to the town. Their customers included the gas company, public houses, tradesmen, shops, cabinet makers and carpenters. Their surviving account and day books also record sale of a canal boat to the coal owner, Walter Coffin, for £100, another to Robert Thomas (who was opening his own colliery at Abercanaid) for £90 and regular repairs to Dowlais Company boats. The partnership was short-lived as Insole & Biddle were declared bankrupts and their premises were put up for auction in April 1831. The auction notice describes:

> *'a Dry Dock, capable of taking in for repair Vessels not exceeding 80 tons burthen, and well adapted for the repair of Canal Barges, with convenient Sheds, good Wharf for landing and stocking Timber, Saw-pit etc; containing a frontage to the said Canal of 100 feet, by 400 feet deep.'*

Fifty years were unexpired of a 61 year lease from the Marquess of Bute, at a ground rent of ten guineas per annum. The brick yard was described as:

> *'containing about seven Statute Acres … with the Kilns, Sheds, and other conveniences for making Bricks, Fireman's Cottage etc.'*

Fifteen years were unexpired of a 21 year lease from Bute,

at a rent of £35 8s per annum. The advertisement adds, honestly: 'The premises in this lot are on the line of the intended Canal.'[110] The Act for the Bute Ship Canal had by that time received Parliamentary assent.

Insole & Biddle's account books show them supplying timber to Thomas Jenkins, Shipwright, in June 1827. Bird's 1829 directory does not mention Thomas Jenkins but Pigot's 1830 directory has him as a ship builder at Broth Lane (in the town, the older name for Working Street in the Hayes). His premises backed onto the canal at the aptly named Carpenter's Arms, where Harrison's 1830 canal plan tellingly shows a slipway into the canal. This short basin had been authorised in 1819, in response to the application from a Mr Wood (possibly John Wood, the Town Clerk) to ship and receive goods for the town.[111] Following Insole & Biddle's bankruptcy in 1831, Jenkins took over their lease and moved to the Sea Lock pound proper. There he enlarged his acquired boat dock to be capable of taking

'THE CUSTOM HOUSE BRIDGE: SIR, – May I beg the favour of your inserting this letter in your paper of this week. Whilst this town is vastly increasing in its trade, commerce and importance, it is not only a matter of universal astonishment, but annoyance and regret, to the inhabitants, as well as to strangers, that the streets' pitching should be permitted to continue sunken in holes and ruts. Added to which – and the most justifiable complaint - is the great elevation of the stone bridge over the canal opposite the road to the South Wales Railway Station. Here may be constantly witnessed inhumanity to horses, who are forced to draw heavy loads up the steep ascent to the crown of the bridge, and then hold back down the sudden and great descent on the other side; and unavoidable accidents and annoyance to horse and foot passengers are continually occurring. Here, too, perched on the side walls of this bridge may be daily seen idlers, to witness and discuss the powers of Messrs. Spiller & Browne's fine majestic horses taking wagon-loads of flour over this bridge in capital style; and then the less powerful horses in their turn; and many of them, sometimes, cannot get to the crown of the bridge, and the loads draw them back and throw them down. I have heard that it is contemplated by the Town Council to remove this dangerous bridge, and to erect another of light and elegant structure, of less difficult ascent and descent, and I sincerely hope, for the sake of humanity, that they will lose no time in doing so. The idlers, however, might in the meantime be removed by the order of a policeman. Cardiff, Sept.3, 1857. AN INHABITANT' *(*Cardiff & Merthyr Guardian, *Saturday, September 5 1857). This rare photograph shows the bridge that resulted from such campaigning letters. It was, in turn, replaced in the 1890s. Interesting, too, is the original Brunel-designed cast iron girder bridge of the South Wales Railway, spanning the canal in the background. The two smaller bridges allowed access to West Canal Wharf. The roof of the South Wales Railway Inn of 1851 can also be seen where George Godfrey, with his wife Ellen, was landlord from 1868 to 1876. The building survives today (2004) as part of Jacobs Antiques Market.* WIMM collection

sea-going vessels. Probably the earliest ship built by Jenkins at his new yard was a 120 ton schooner, built for Captain David Lewis to sail out of Liverpool, launched on 6 October 1832. A year later, the 120 ton schooner *Diana*, intended for the Irish and coastal trade, was launched from Jenkins' yard.[112] Whilst Jenkins had taken over Insole & Biddle's boatyard, the 1844 tithe map shows Joseph Davies occupying their former brickyard. Jenkins' yard lasted into the 20th century but not quite as long as Tredwen's.

In August 1833, John Davies was inexplicably refused permission to break through the canal bank to his newly-built boat dock '*near the Glasshouse*'.[113] A dock is shown on the northern corner of the glass works premises on O'Rourke's 1849 map and as '*Old Dry Dock*' on the 1851 public health plan of Cardiff. This would be the Davies dock but it is absent from Wood's 1835 map, which may have been surveyed before Davies built the dock.

In June 1839, the canal committee authorised that another dock, situated in Miss Hill's field on the towpath side in the town, be connected to the canal.[114]

Cardiff Iron Foundry

In September 1826, Mr Towgood was refused permission to float timber in the canal. A bye-law had been introduced the previous year to prevent this practice.[115] In January, Towgood's application for land was refused and the storage of timber or ore on the eastern bank within twenty feet of the canal bank was prohibited. He briefly held the wharf near the trunk, later to become the bonded timber yard of William Jones.[116] His fortunes with the canal committee had not improved by July 1828, when he was given six months' notice to pay £50 rent for the premises lately occupied by Edward Bird at the iron foundry. William Bird's 1829 *Cardiff Guide* and Pigot's 1830 *Cardiff Directory*, both record Moggridge and Towgood at the foundry. Stephen Towgood was a prominent solicitor of the family of Cardiff bankers; John Moggridge lived at Gabalva House, north of Cardiff. Their attempts to operate the Cardiff Iron Foundry ended in failure. After advertising throughout 1833 they finally gave up the foundry in 1834 to Morgan Lisle.[117]

Canal Shipments from the River Taff

From February 1825, the Sea Lock was opened to pass vessels on Sundays and from July, there was a general order to all lockkeepers to admit the passage of boats from half an hour before sunrise to half an hour after sunset. In that month, the Marquess of Bute was informed that the canal company felt liable to replace the trunk on the Sea Lock pond (between the ballast bank and the Sea Lock Hotel) and so be able to abandon the use of ditches to carry away excess water onto Bute's land.[118]

In November 1826, two years after the other major ironworks had extended their wharves, the Aberdare Iron Company (whose output had much increased following its purchase of the Abernant Ironworks in 1819) was leased 400 feet of territory on the west bank where Dowlais had been, opposite Guest's glass works and '*adjoining Mr Coffin's wall*.' From this it can be concluded that Walter Coffin, the coal owner and committee member from 1825, already had the yard on the site of the trunk, in addition to his coal yard across the canal and nearer the Sea Lock.[119] Green's 1828 report to the Marquess of Bute shows this yard let to another committee man, Thomas Charles, as does Harrison's 1830 plan. Yet Coffin must have used this yard, for the opportunist was building coal staithes on Bute land, at the river across the channel bed leading from the trunk and planned to ship his coal from there to ships on the tidal river. On 6 June 1832 it was minuted that

> '*in consequence of the Works now carrying into effect by Mr Coffin for the purpose of shipping coal into Vessels outside the Sea Lock direct from his Wharf – ordered that the Solicitor give him notice to quit the land he now occupies under the Canal Company at the expiration of his tenure in September 1833.*'

John Wood's map of circa 1835 shows a boat dock on the Coffin site (which was opposite the glass works). By 1844, the Tithe map shows no yards south of the Aberdare Iron Company's wharf and the 1851 public health plan defines the area of the old trunk as an old gravel pit, where there is a house and garden and the unnamed outline of the boat dock.

Coffin was not the only one to ship from the river. Thomas Powell's first shipments from the Glamorganshire Canal were from his Gelligaer Colliery. His advertisement in both the *Cambrian* and the *Cardiff & Merthyr Guardian* on 13 November 1830 advised:

> '*From facility of conveyance and other advantages, T P is enabled to offer his Coal at Cardiff sixpence per ton under the price of Newport Coals and to give 21 cwt weight to the ton with the usual gratuity and a bonus or present in addition to every Master of Vessel for the first cargo, whether taken on freight or his own account.*
>
> *The Coals are shipped by crane into vessels in the Canal and by shute from the Jetty Heads into vessels in the River, where there is the same depth of water as at the Lock Gates and no canal dues charged the vessels loading from the Jetty Heads.*'

Powell had applied for land at the Wharf for building offices in December 1829. His 318 feet wharf, leased from Bute from March 1830, was just below the ballast bank. Here he had a substantial basin dug for his canal boats to unload into trams, which were then horse-drawn across the yard to his river-side coal staithes.[120] The yard also had its own boat dock which connected to the canal. As with Coffin, the canal company initially took exception to Powell shipping coal from the river and the GCC solicitor was given instructions on 6 June 1832 to give him notice to quit. Coffin retained his Sea Lock yard until 1842 but Powell's river business continued at least until 1850 – long after the opening of the first Bute Dock but shipping from there only a fraction of his total output. For example, in September 1844, Thomas Powell persuaded the canal committee to concede to allowing him tonnage between his wharf and the Sea Lock, on the understanding that the coal loaded on his river wharf did not exceed 30 tons per day.[121] Already, in the year ending 30 June 1844, Powell had shipped 60,644 tons from his wharf on the west side of the Bute Dock and Coffin had shipped 48,920 (while the Taff Vale Railway itself had shipped 64,471 tons). In 1845, Powell agreed to ship through Bute's Dock at least three quarters of his coal brought to Cardiff – whether by canal or railway.[122]

As well as their shipping wharves, in 1829 both Coffin and Powell let from the council canal-side coal yards on the town wall. From here they supplied coal to the town populace and small businesses. It was probably these yards that they had to give up to satisfy the canal company's notice of June 1832. In November 1834, the council put them up for sale in order to raise money to pay for their new Cardiff market.[123]

Water Bailiffs

Control of shipping in the channel approaches to Cardiff was the responsibility of the town council, who employed a water bailiff for that purpose. When the canal opened in 1798, that post was occupied by John Bird. As shipping volumes increased over the years, this became a more onerous and responsible task. The council minutes of 30 September 1825 record receipt of a petition of ship owners '*and others concerned in the Navigation of the River Taff from the Sea Lock Gates to the said river Mouth ... for the want of Perches*

***Above:** The replacement for the Brunel-designed cast iron bridge carrying the South Wales main line of the Great Western Railway over the canal into Cardiff General Station was this massive wrought iron girder deck bridge, which is still in place today although the canal has long been filled in. A GCC boat loaded with bagged flour for Pontypridd sits under the warehouse awning on the left, with an empty boat sitting almost broadside across the canal in the foreground, providing a nice study of its carvel construction. Custom House Bridge features once more in the background. The photograph was taken by Philip Oke.*
National Maritime Museum, Oliver Hill collection, neg No. P7 4088

***Right:** An 1890s panoramic view of the lower end of St Mary Street and the industrial area leading to the docks. Custom House Bridge and the GWR bridge can be seen in the centre, with the canal heading off in the distance as the Sea Lock pound. Note the stacks of timber alongside the canal on the East Wharf, beyond the railway bridge. Prominent landmarks include the twin towers of St Mary's Church, in the centre background, with the bulk of Spillers flour mill rising above its surroundings on the left.* SR collection

being planted and Mooring Buoys laid down in proper situations.' On 1 January 1836, a committee was appointed, to include the shipyard owner Richard Tredwen (who was an elected councillor), '*to report on the duties of the Water Bailiff and Conservation of the River Taff, particularly with reference to the necessary buoys to be placed or preserved outside the Sea Lock.*'[124]

Formerly, the unloading of ships' ballast was undertaken by the canal company's employees but on 15 June 1825, it was agreed to put an end to the canal monopoly and open it to the labourers '*upon such terms as the Captains or Agents may agree, the Sea Lock Keeper taking care that it is not improperly placed.*' Nevertheless, the bye-laws were changed so that the canal company would maintain its income by levying a tonnage charge for all ballast disposed of.[125] This was obviously a continuing issue in 1830 and prompted Thomas Powell to include in his advertisements the following advice to masters of vessels: '*To prevent imposition, Captains are requested not to agree for taking out ballast until their vessels arrive at the Wharf.*' The dumping of ballast in the channel approaches was a constant concern of the town council and in August 1853, the council resolved to purchase a boat and employ two men and a boy, based at Penarth, to be constantly on watch between the Glamorganshire Canal, the Bute Dock sea gates and the limits of the port, in order to detect such practice. Their work was overseen by a succession of the corporation's Water Bailiff/Harbour Masters – John Hurry Riches (1850s), Jenkin Jones (throughout the 1860s) and Henry Fraser (1870s) – whose task was to keep the channel free, not only of ballast but of lost anchors, chain cable and even wrecks.[126]

The Bute Ship Canal and the Development of Butetown

In 1828-9, the engineer James Green submitted his reports to the Marquess of Bute, presenting options which were open to the Marquess for improving shipping facilities in the port.[127] Green, whilst retaining employment as Surveyor of Bridges to the county of Devon, had undertaken a number of successful freelance canal surveys in the West Country, including the Exeter Canal and the Bude Canal. Following his work for Bute, he undertook large projects in South Wales for the Kidwelly & Llanelly Canal and for Newport Docks. His chief criticisms of the existing Glamorganshire Canal were that it had been terminated too far up the River Taff from low water and could accommodate ships of no more than 200 tons. The canal's depth inside the Sea Lock was 14 feet 8 inches but higher up at the principal iron wharves it was no more than10 feet. Even ships in the canal could take on only part of their cargo at the wharf and the remainder was loaded below the wharves by lighter, or even outside the lock in the roads. On 15 February 1828, Green had witnessed an event concerning the *Canada* of North Shields (burden 400 tons):

> '*She had received her cargo of Iron firstly on the outside the Lock gates & the remainder on the Roadstead but for want of sufficient water in the Channel she was detained three weeks, having at length sailed & met a contrary wind she received damage at sea and was obliged to return & take out her cargo under the same disadvantage of want of water in the Channel and she being unable to enter the Canal & therefore compelled to discharge into lighters.*'

Green repeated the view of others before him, that the canal should have been made west of the Taff and the port developed at Cogan Pill in the shelter of Penarth.[128] This conclusion would not have pleased Bute, because Penarth was Lord Plymouth's land; Bute's intention was to extend port facilities on his own land at East Moors, Cardiff.

Because of the problems of the high tidal range, Green proposed that the Bute Dock be approached from the Eastern Hollows, near the mouth of the Taff (less than a

East and West Wharves and the Sea Lock pound in 1905. The building on the left is the Custom House, next to the rebuilt York Hotel of 1890. An empty coal train is crossing the canal on the GWR main line, just to the east of Cardiff General station. Beyond the railway, on the west bank is the canal company's wharf and offices. The Glamorganshire Canal Railway can be seen between the wharf buildings and the canal company offices. The new lock (No 51) of 1887 can just be seen in the same gap, whilst the timber pond is off to the right. Across the canal, on East Wharf, are the buildings of Thistle, Hall & Co (builders merchants and ironmongers), then the Glendower Hotel and the

houses of Crichton Street, before the Junction Canal is met and the East Wharf Bridge crossing it, with timber yards and steam sawing and planing mills on both sides. Some Patent Fuel boats lie on the canal, near to the Junction Canal entrance, no doubt awaiting their next turn to the Maindy fuel works. The twin towers of St Mary's Church mark Butetown; the closer dark tower to its left is the Bute Dock Brewery and in the left distance are the flour mills at the Bute West Docks, rebuilt after a disastrous fire in 1882. The Central Hotel in the right foreground is, at the time of writing (2004), gutted following a fire. SR collection

mile from low water), by a high-walled entrance canal with towpath, built across the roads and stretching for almost $1^1/_2$ miles to the dock entrance proper. This idea went through several designs, including one where the entrance canal was tidal to a sea lock at the basin and one where there was a sea lock at its southern end, with another lock at the entrance to the dock basin. The latter was the form which went to Parliament. The surface water in the entrance canal was to be maintained at 41 feet above low water level at spring tide in the outer harbour and the depth of water in the canal was to be 33 feet. The basin, or dock, was to be 1,500 yards long and 20 feet deep.[129] The canal company naturally opposed the Bill, because the dock would be in competition to its own shipping business. Richard Blakemore also objected because he feared it invalidated his most recent arrangement with the canal company for Melingriffith's water supply – even though Green's plan to supply water for the dock was to take a feeder from the River Taff near Blackweir, well downstream of the lowest water intake for the Glamorganshire Canal and below Llandaff Weir. Further opposition came from the Monmouthshire Canal Company, because it would affect its own shipping business at Newport. Bute, with Green, commanded the additional support of Thomas Telford and the Bill received Royal assent on July 18 1830.[130]

Although the Bute Ship Canal Act was passed in 1830, building did not commence straight away. It has been stated that the Bute Estate had difficulty in finding a contractor to build the entrance canal[131] but, what is more likely, is that Bute's advisers were concerned whether this private venture (the Marquess was to put up all the capital himself) could be a financial success when the GCC and its ironmasters would not co-operate. Eventually this impasse was broken by the impatience and obvious impotence of the ironmasters, who realised that development of the port could proceed only with the Marquess's approval. As 1833 was drawing to an end, William Crawshay wrote to the Marquess, '*Indeed, my lord, something should be done for the port of Cardiff. The power is in your hands alone now and we all earnestly hope that you will use it or delegate it to those who will.*'[132] Such lobbying statements gave Bute the confidence to proceed at last – but not before another engineer, William Cubitt, was retained to review Green's plans. Cubitt advised that an entrance channel should replace the ship canal but that the re-surveyed feeder from Blackweir should supply fresh water to a large reservoir situated alongside the dock, which was to be used periodically to scour the basin and entrance channel. These changes required an amending Act that easily passed through Parliament in May 1834. The dock was opened on 8 October 1839.

To coincide with the building of the Bute Dock, the Bute Estate planned a community housing development, on the strip of land south of the town between the Glamorganshire Canal and the dock wharves. The roads were to follow a grid pattern and a somewhat stylised but undated '*Plan of the Intended Improvements in the Port of Cardiff*' is contained within the Bute papers at Cardiff library.[133] It shows four proposed branch canals leaving the Glamorganshire Canal at right angles, whose purpose was presumably to serve the community and create a 'little Venice' south of Cardiff, as well as to drain the area. The plan (which is likely to be James Green's plan number 2 of April 1828) shows that the low water channel beds of the rivers Taff and Ely were to be straightened and the Glamorganshire Canal was to be extended downstream, from the Sea Lock to the river bed by a new basin 1,780 feet long and 400 feet wide. As already stated, a reservoir on the western side of the old Sea Lock would be constructed, to help to scour the sediment build-up out of the new basin at low tide. A narrow canal is also shown running parallel with the main Glamorganshire Canal, from the Wharf through the Dumballs, to connect again with the main canal nearer the reservoir. The intention of this narrow canal was to serve a 2,800 feet long stone quay, to be built on the straightened tidal river. Green felt that, with the building of the Bute Dock, most remaining coal shipments from the canal could be dry-shipped from this river quay and so relieve the pressure on the canal Sea Lock.

Green's reports were made to the Marquess of Bute and we wonder what the proprietors of the canal company would have made of his proposals regarding the canal itself. At that time, there was not yet any suggestion of the Taff Vale Railway and Green's plans for the Bute Ship Canal relied on the Glamorganshire Canal being the sole means of transporting iron and coal to Bute's Dock. Yet the Bute schemes were secretive and did not directly involve the ironmasters on whose freight his success depended. The result was a continued air of suspicion by the canal company and it is not surprising they opposed the Bute Ship Canal Bill in Parliament. With regard to coal shipping on the river, we have already seen that this notion was immediately taken up by Thomas Powell and Walter Coffin but without the need of Green's additional narrow canal.

A communication canal, to run from the southern end of the dock, outside the old sea wall to the Glamorganshire Canal close to its Sea Lock, was suggested by Green in 1828 as an option but one which he did not think would be much used. Nevertheless, it was included in the Bill and is shown in pencil on the later but undated '*No 1 General Plan of the Bute Ship Canal*', which is probably William Cubitt's 1833 amendment to James Green's 1830 plan.[134] This lower junction canal is also shown in a map reproduced in Captain Smyth's *Nautical Observations of the Port and Maritime Vicinity of Cardiff* ..., published in 1840 and which has led many observers to assume that it was built. Only an upper junction canal was built; Bute's contractors began cutting the lower canal prematurely in June 1840 but were forestalled by the canal company and never re-started.[135] A detailed plan of circa 1840, numbers twenty-five separate wharves on the west side of the Bute Dock being served at their rear not only by the Marquess of Bute's private branch railway but by a branch canal and towpath linked to the upper junction canal (the lower junction canal is not shown).[136] Again, this branch canal

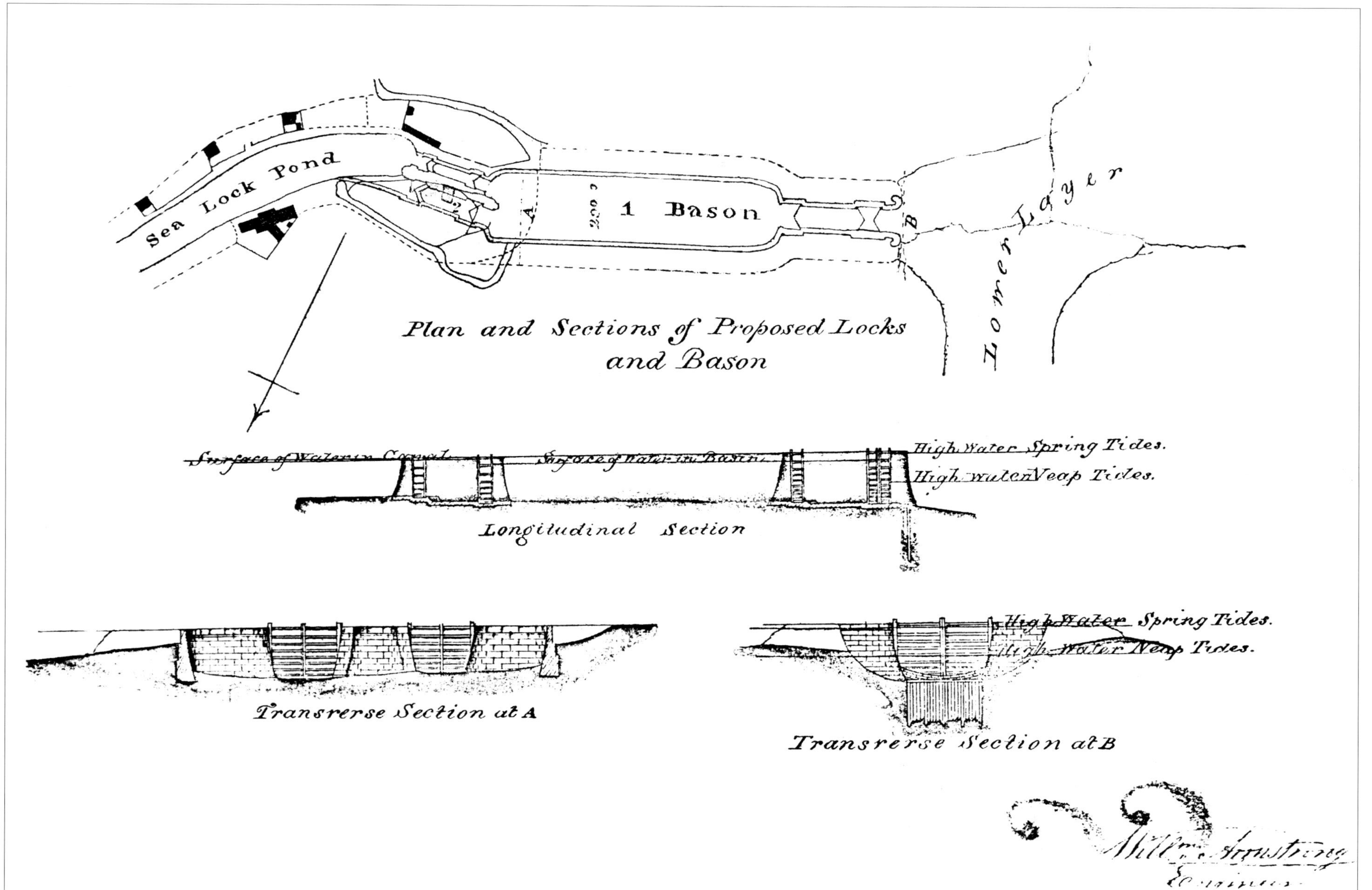

The abortive 1835 canal Bill was based on William Armstrong's plans to reduce bottlenecks and reduce water requirements, by replacing all staircase locks with single locks and intervening ponds. It also included a new basin (1) and wider entrance lock (B) from the sea. The existing Sea Lock was to be augmented by a second larger lock (2) alongside. The Marquess of Bute poured scorn on the proposals and the Bill was thrown out of Parliament in the year that the Taff Vale Railway got its Act.

GRO Q/DP 53

Typical of the Bristol Channel sailing vessels that entered the Sea Lock basin in the 1880s are those seen here, moored alongside the Old Sea Lock Hotel and adjacent premises. The two young men in the foreground demonstrate how the hobblers manoeuvred their boats in the canal. The sloop in the foreground is a Cardiff registered vessel but the faded lettering on her stern is otherwise unreadable. Beyond is another sloop, Annie of Clevedon, *owned by T.R. Egelstaff & Sons, quarry owners at Bristol. This is an interesting vessel (to our publisher!), one of the handful of ships to be built at Lydney and she appears in Mercantile Navy lists as simply* Annie. *The bold lettering on the stern proclaiming her ownership and name is quite unusual. The* 'of Clevedon' *was probably added to distinguish her from the various other* Annies *sailing around the Bristol Channel. This* Annie *was built in 1884 by Joseph Brinkworth and registered at Gloucester, offical number 87606. She was of 38 tons and is the only vessel he is ever recorded as building; by the following year a William Egelstaff is listed as the shipwright at Lydney. Perhaps Brinkworth got into financial difficulties and the Egelstaff family bought the vessel and took over the lease on the tiny shipyard at Lydney for a time. The vessel has probably brought in a load of stone and may be waiting to backload coal before heading back across the Channel. She looks quite new here, which would date the photograph to around 1885. In 1898, she was recorded in the Mercantile Navy lists as damaged and there was some debate as to whether she was worth repairing or should be broken up. Her register was also noted as being closed. However, in the event she was repaired and was recorded as being sold to W. Hickory of Bristol in 1900. Nothing further is known of her.* CCL collection

had been proposed by Green in 1828[137] but there is no evidence it was ever cut on the line of Collingdon Road (now, in 2004, inappropriately renamed Lloyd George Avenue). This map also shows the site proposed for the new St Mary's Church as being to the north of the junction canal; in fact it was to be built to its south. St Mary's opened in 1843, to serve the population of the new Butetown housing development and was in time to appear on the 1844 tithe map of St Mary's Parish. The tithe map is a useful reference for land ownership and lettings at the Sea Lock pound, at a time when the canal company was having to take stock of its position against the newcomer dock and railway companies.

The first of the roads to be built in Butetown (in about 1830) was the main highway, Bute Street, commencing in the town centre at the Hayes, cutting across the old rope walk and terminating at the Sea Wall (present-day (2004) James Street). Although Bute Street was intended to form an axis to the grid pattern, the TVR Bill was soon to take up the land bordering its eastern side. The railway was to run on a low embankment to the Dock passenger station at the southern end of Bute Street. The road therefore became the eastern border of Butetown, ready to allow the rest of the grid to be developed piecemeal, avoiding such obstructions as the old clay pits and brickyards on Davies's and Tredwen's land, the Glass House, the new Little Dock (see next chapter) and the new TVR workshops at West Yard.

After laying down Bute Street, no further road making took place in the 1830s, except at its northern part behind Watson and Richards' timber wharves and the Custom House. The Bute Estate wanted to be sure of the exact siting of its first dock, its wharves and connecting railways, and of the communication (or junction) canal at its northern end, which provided for through boating from the East Wharf of the Glamorganshire Canal. The level of Bute Street was raised at the point where it had to bridge the junction canal. The housing development only got started in 1846, when the streets north of the TVR Little Dock were laid out over the old brick yards and claypits.[138] One occasion when the Marquess did not get his way, was in trying to get the Custom House moved from the Glamorganshire Canal to a site on the outer basin of the new Bute Dock. The Commissioners of the Board of Customs declined his offer.[139]

The Cardiff and Bristol Steam Packet

The supply of practically all manufactured goods to South Wales was traditionally through Bristol.[140] When Cyfarthfa Ironworks was being built in the 1760s, orders for equipment, ironmongery and imported provisions went to the Bristol dealers. However, even as late as 1833, there seems to have been no reliable frequent service to bring goods from Bristol to Cardiff, in spite of the advertisements for John and Matthew Pride's sloop *Amity* suggesting otherwise. Parcels put on board at Bristol could lie there over a week before the ship set sail. The same applied at Cardiff. Even though Christopher James and Lewis Williams advertised a daily carrying service on the canal between Cardiff and Merthyr, their boatmen would, as often as not, wait until they had a full boat. An alternative route for articles and cloth from the manufacturing districts of Birmingham, Lancashire and Yorkshire, using the English canal system, was for them to be unloaded at Worcester and thence be carried overland to Merthyr, rather than continuing down the Severn from Stourport to Bristol. More recently, with the opening of the Liverpool & Manchester Railway, cloth from Lancashire mills was being shipped out of Liverpool directly to Cardiff.[141] But these were exceptions and Bristol continued as the *entrepôt*.

For the Merthyr shopkeepers and traders, who by the 1830s were a well established middle class community, delays at Bristol were no longer to be tolerated. On 3 July 1833, fifteen Merthyr traders met to conclude an agreement with Richard Jones Todd, agent of the new 60 horse power steam packet ship *Nautilus* (powered by Neath Abbey engines) and the four carriers on the Glamorganshire Canal – James Noble, Lewis Williams, Matthew Pride and Christopher James. The *Nautilus* was timetabled thereafter to make three round trips a week between the Cumberland Basin at Bristol and Cardiff, to the river wharf above the ballast bank. The traders collectively resolved to use the lock-up boats of the four carriers, in order to encourage them to meet the packet for immediate transport of their products into the hills. Goods requiring storage, to await a special conveyance, were deposited in the warehouse which had been built on the canal side of the packet station. Two wherries (as they were described in the newspaper) conveyed passengers for the town of Cardiff, along the canal to the Custom House Bridge. The road to the Dumballs from St Mary Street, around the iron companies wharves, was extended to the packet station so that coaches for Merthyr, Cowbridge and Bridgend could collect passengers and small parcels from the paddle steamer. Waggons also met the packet, to take goods by road to other towns in the hinterland of Cardiff.[142] In this way, a timetabled water-borne trade was organised between Bristol and Merthyr.

In 1843-4, after the first Bute Dock was constructed, the packet station was moved from the river to a slip at the southern end of Bute Street, a location which became known as Pier Head. Dornford's letters make clear his difficulties in forcing this change on the commercial life of Cardiff, in the same way as he struggled to persuade ships' captains to use the new dock rather than the old canal. The old river and canal wharf was taken over by Brown Lenox & Co, for shipping chains and anchors made at their Newbridge Works.[143]

The 1830s, 40s and 50s – Coal and Competition

As we have shown, coal had been exported through the Sea Lock since the opening of the canal but the 1820s saw much larger volumes being shipped. Thomas Powell and Walter Coffin were followed closely by George Insole and Robert Thomas. Insole, after extricating himself from his partnership with Biddle, began to concentrate solely on selling coal from his new yard near the Sea Lock. His main supplier was Robert Thomas of Waun Wyllt who, after at first being declined, was awarded his own coal yard also. Insole then went into colliery ownership himself and bought up Maesmawr Colliery from Grover. The consequent increase in coal traffic prompted the canal committee, whose combined interests were still in iron rather than coal, to take advice on whether its Acts allowed them to raise the tonnage rates on coal without, at the same time, advancing the rates on iron and other goods. From 30 September 1833, a general 10 per cent reduction of rates was ordered which brought the rates down to be only 15 per cent of those stated in the Act of some forty years earlier. From 31 March 1834, the rates were then adjusted with the confidence of the legal opinion the committee had received. This resulted in rates on iron and pitwood being kept down to $^{3}/_{4}$d per mile but with rates on all other goods, under the 5d rate category per the Act, being advanced to $2^{1}/_{2}$d per mile. The rate on all goods under the 2d rate category was also increased to $^{1}/_{2}$d per ton per mile.[144]

Coal movements on the canal were now of major significance and it was decided to install a boat-weighing machine, similar to one already in use in Newport, on the Monmouthshire Canal. The machine did away with gauging and allowed any boat and its cargo to be weighed if fraud was suspected. The canal was now to be navigable day and night and the new Clerk, George Forrest, was instructed to appoint a double set of lockkeepers and to light the locks, the tunnel and the Sea Lock. For this purpose it was necessary to build lockkeepers houses at College, Forest, Upper, Portobello and Coedpenmain locks[145]. The

A Bristol Channel pilot cutter, Frolic, *with crew, pose at the Sea Lock gates on what looks like a leisurely occasion. Behind the boat is the canal company dockmaster's house, built in 1855 to Scott & Cornwall's design for Captain Samuel Mercer. The sign on the yard next to the house advertises the Penlee & St Ives Stone Quarries Ltd, whose agents were at Bristol.* WIMM collection

weighing machine was built by Brown Lenox and installed, not at the Sea Lock as in the 1811 proposal but in a dock alongside Tongwynlais Lock. Morgan Morgan was the weigher at Tongwynlais. William Edwards' wages were advanced from 13s to 15s per week, for granting coal permits '*on condition that he pass any boats which may be required during the night*.' At the General Meeting on 4 June 1834, the canal company presented a new set of Rules, Bye Laws and Orders under which the canal was to operate. Finally, to round off this air of modernisation on the Glamorganshire Canal, on 30 December 1834, the minute book notes that the new Weights & Measures Act had decreed there to be 112lbs to one hundredweight and that the GCC would conform.

The 1844 Tithe map shows Coffin's old coal wharf next to the Sea Lock to be unlet, Coffin having by that time completely removed his shipping facilities to the Bute Dock. For a while, the GCC refused a number of applications to take up the vacant wharf.[146] This was while they considered a new plan to improve their shipping facilities and compete with the new Bute Dock's capacity to admit larger ships than the canal could. William Cubitt was the latest in a long line of advisers dismissed by Bute and he offered his services to the rival GCC in 1838. His proposals took shape in 1843, when Edward Scott Barber, a civil engineer based at Newport, produced plans for a second and larger entrance lock to the canal, to be built through the coal wharves on the canal's left bank. The GCC inserted notices in the *London Gazette*, advertising its intentions to present another Bill before Parliament, being at pains to explain that the work would be '*within the limits of the land in* [its] *possession*', *i.e.* it would not require any of the Marquess's land. Even so, the Bill was unsuccessful, as the opportunity to amalgamate canal, railway and dock seemed a possibility.[147]

This proved a very stressful period for the, already irritable, second Marquess of Bute. In 1841, Maria, his wife of 23 years, died childless. The man had sacked a succession of technical consultants and management, including James Green, George Turnbull, William Cubitt, Captain Smyth and Abbott, his dockmaster. His closest advisers were questioning the wisdom of investing in this private dock development. In this light, there were concerns for the

Marquess's health and his physicians pressed him to be free of his troubles and lease the dock to the TVR and GCC.[148] The threat of a new canal Bill to rival his barely-used dock facilities forced the issue. Talks took place in 1843-4, with a view to amalgamating first the TVR and GCC, and then all three concerns – dock and all. Yet nothing came of it and the TVR blamed William Crawshay, who apparently expected some large personal monetary compensation on top of his dues as shareholder.[149] This hiatus was enough to halt the canal company's plans, however, and nothing more was heard of the new Bill.

From the 1840s, the canal company had two rivals – the TVR as alternative carrier and the Bute Dock as alternative shipper. All three managed to grow together and encouraged the opening of many new collieries in the Taff, Dare, Cynon and emerging Rhondda valleys. In spite of the major coal owners, Powell and Coffin, being founding directors and shareholders of the TVR, coal continued to be brought to Cardiff by canal and shipped from its wharves. Growth in traffic was such that boats were scarce and were advertised for in the local press.[150] So much coal was coming down the Aberdare Canal, that John Nixon questioned the continuing practice of passing only every other boat to this canal at the junction. The canal committee felt it a fair arrangement but offered to erect a shed jointly with the ACC, at which to stable the horses while they were delayed there.[151] As colliery proprietors like Duncan & Co (Llancaiach) vacated their canal wharves, others such as William Simons and Fowler Brothers (Pontypridd) took them on.[152] David Davis (Blaengwawr) took over the wharf of D. & J. Thomas.[153] In the 1850s, too, the canal company erected its own hydraulic cranes, for shippers to load coal directly from canal boat to sea-going vessel (see next chapter). It was not all boom though and there were periodic slumps, which became exacerbated by colliery strikes; 1856 and 1857 were particularly bad years for the coal industry. Agents had difficulties in selling canal boats at this time – in early 1857, eight boats (Nos. 100, 225, 429, 430, 431, 437, 438 and 439) remained moored below Watson & Richards' timber yard, unsold after a month's advertising. In August there were fifteen (Nos. 92, 96, 99, 129, 134, 150, 281, 288, 313, 333, 338, 339, 341, 362 and 365) being offered at a bargain, lying at Aberdare.[154]

At the opposite end of the Sea Lock pound, on the side next to the Custom House (which was enlarged in 1857), was the canal wharf from which agents of the ironworks and collieries landed articles from Bristol, Gloucester and further afield, and sent all sorts of supplies by canal to the ironworks and collieries in the hills. Builders' merchants such as James Savage, Stowe & Slocombe, were based here, bringing in cement, bricks and stoneware from Bridgwater, roofing slates from North Wales and guano from Peru. J. Sessions had his enamelled slate and marble works here on the East Wharf.[155] Here, too, were the timber merchants, clustered round the junction canal with the Bute Dock. In 1854, Charles Hurry Riches, son of the Corporation's harbourmaster, was granted a wharf opposite the iron companies' wharves for £20 per annum but he had been there from at least 1851 and was there until at least 1863. As ship owner and agent to the Crawshays, his name is found in account books of the Hirwaun Ironworks for example.[156] Charles' son Tom was an engineer and in 1873, when aged only 27, became Locomotive Superintendent of the TVR, while his son in turn became Locomotive Superintendent of the rival Rhymney Railway[157].

The Marquess of Bute married again in 1845 and, six months before his death in 1848, his only son and heir was born. For the next twenty-one years, a board of trustees managed the third Marquess of Bute's estate on his behalf. The building of Butetown caused the trustees to resurrect claims in 1858-9 that the Glamorganshire Canal Company had taken more of Bute's land than it was entitled to under its two Acts. The dispute resulted in the GCC being obliged to wall off the canal, on the whole length from the Junction Canal to the TVR West Yard, leaving entrances only for the boat yards of Jenkins and Tredwen. On Bute's part, the trustees agreed to remove much of the now-substantial ballast bank on the west bank of the canal, so that the estate could extend the Dumballs Road southward to the Sea Lock. The ballast must have proved very useful for building purposes in Butetown and the dockland area. In 1853, the Glass House lease was surrendered and the land was taken back by the Bute Estate for laying down Mount Stuart Square. Any ambitions the GCC entertained for extending its property eastward were completely thwarted. Only the coal yards near the Sea Lock had direct access to the East – so that they could supply Bute's tenants with their household fuel.

Personnel Changes

When Lieutenant Dornford resigned as Dock Master in 1841, his salary with the GCC was £150 plus 2% Sea Lock dues. He was succeeded in September by another lieutenant from the Royal Navy, Richard Danbery Hyde, who in June 1842 was awarded 25 guineas '*for his zeal and activity in management of the Sea lock*.' At the same annual meeting, George Forrest the company Clerk was awarded a butt of sherry '*for his exertions and energies in the work done in repairing the Sea lock*.' By 1848, Hyde's salary was a flat £250 without any percentage on Sea Lock dues '*in consideration of the increased trade*' and Dempsey's salary, as Clerk at Cardiff, was £160. By contrast, James Lewis's salary as Clerk at Merthyr was advanced in 1849 to £130 '*which salary will be considered as the future maximum of the Clerk at Merthyr Tydfil*.' In 1850, Lewis was replaced at Merthyr by Joseph H. Smith at £100 per annum and the company's house.

At the June annual meeting of 1851, Thomas Shepherd took over as Clerk from John Forrest (George's nephew and Clerk since George's death in February 1848), who had resigned with ill health. Shepherd, not the first former Cyfarthfa cashier to hold the post, had already been a committee man since 1848, when he had been receiving 2 guineas per meeting for examining the accounts. The committee now decided that it was time to concentrate the Clerk's duties on book-keeping and accounts, and to create a new position of Out-door Superintendent, whose duties would consist in looking after the maintenance, repair and improvement of the locks and other works of the canal. The new post would have no responsibility for expenditure, accounts and payment of wages but would need to supervise the practical men employed by the company. The role would command a salary of £300 per annum maximum, with the company house below Navigation House. By the following month, two appointments had been made instead. T.E. Blackwell, engineer of the Kennet & Avon Canal, was appointed Superintendent Engineer at a salary of £200 but residing at Bristol so that he could continue in his position on the K&A. Henry Hoskins was appointed Resident Engineer under Blackwell at £150 per annum and accommodation at the house at Navigation.[158] As well as the nature of these appointments, the minute books during this period show a particular interest of the committee in improving the canal's facilities and in finding out what others were doing to counter the railway and dock effect. Hydraulic coal hoists were ordered (see next chapter), a representative was sent to Scotland to report back on the Monkland Canal's inclined plane,[159] enquiries were made to borrow the Gloster & Berkeley Canal's dredger[160] and in 1853, the bye laws were repealed and replaced with a completely new set of 43 laws – laws which remained in force to be renewed and confirmed in 1890. Blackwell's and Hoskins' appointments were short-lived – Hoskins resignation is recorded on 12 February 1852, while Blackwell's name never appears again in the GCC's story. Even so, the salary account stayed at a consistently high level of around £1,700 between 1852 and 1857.

In June 1852, R.D. Hyde resigned and the vacancy was advertised in the *Cardiff & Merthyr Guardian*,[161] where, from 36 applications, Captain Samuel Mercer was selected and appointed Dock Master at £250 per annum. A new house, designed by the London architects Scott & Cornwall, was built for him at the Sea Lock (and insured for £1,000).[162] At this time, his deputies, the two Sea Lock keepers, were being paid 19s per week and a £16 grant was made available for purchasing a boat for Mercer.[163] Mercer had a stormy career with the GCC. In November 1856, he is recorded as being too greedy and persistently requesting a rise, to which the committee responded by giving him notice but, in June 1857, they decided to keep him on for another twelve months on probation. When that period was up they offered him another year at the reduced salary of £250 with another deputy. Finally, in June 1859, he was given six months notice and required to vacate the house on 1 January 1860. In June 1861, the minute books record that Mercer was making a claim against the company.

In 1853, after the building of the second Bute Dock had commenced, the company started becoming increasingly concerned with keeping the approach channel clear of mud. Francis Crawshay took this on as his personal project. The committee retained Joseph Green in June 1854, to prepare plans to straighten the gut from the River Taff to the Sea Lock gate.[164] In April 1856, there were real problems in keeping the channel dredged and in June 1856, the GCC entered into an agreement with a firm of local contractors, Hemingways & Pearson, for widening and deepening the gut or approach channel from the river to the Sea Lock. For the next few years, they had continual difficulties using the dredging machine and could not provide a satisfactory service. The canal committee several times threatened to sue. Ultimately, Hemmingways & Pearson were released from their contract in June 1860 and the final payment to them was authorised at the following year's AGM.[165] Dredging within the Sea Lock pond was a constant cost to the company and was itemised separately in the accounts from 1846, amounting to about £250 per annum. Meanwhile, the Bute East Dock had opened and the Rhymney Railway had joined the TVR in bringing coal to the docks by train. Brunel's broad gauge South Wales Railway had also arrived at Cardiff and crossed the canal between the Custom House Bridge and the Wharf. Anthony Hill and William Crawshay agreed to put together a joint proposal for a railway branch to the back of their respective wharves but nothing came of it at that time.[166]

The 1850s saw peak trade on the canal. Thereafter, the canal began to experience a steady decline. It became hemmed in by competing railways and docks. It had to seek alternative clientele, as its staple custom of iron and coal deserted it for the faster railways and greater capacity shipping facilities. In 1856, the Ely Tidal Harbour & Railway got its Act and this diverted coal trains from the TVR at Radyr to coaling staithes on the eastern bank of the Ely River estuary. This was an independent concern from the TVR but several of its promoters were common to both companies. They are also familiar as having been significant former players on the Glamorganshire Canal – they included Thomas Powell (Duffryn, Aberdare and Gelligaer), Rev'd George Thomas (Gyfeillon), William Cartwright (Llancaiach), James Insole (son of George, Rhondda), Thomas Wayne (Cwmbach, Aberdare) and John Nixon (Werfa, Aberdare).[167] At last, in 1857, the long-recurrent idea of a dock at Penarth became reality with the passing of the Penarth Harbour Dock & Railway Bill and the opening of Penarth Dock in 1865. The Penarth Company obtained additional powers, through their 1861 Act, to build a road from Pier Head, Cardiff to the dock railway at Ferry Road. It was to cross the canal's Sea Lock by swing bridge and then the River Taff by a further swing bridge.[168] The canal company naturally objected to the inconvenience of the bridge over the lock and, in February 1861, they sought the services of the engineer, John Fowler, to give evidence on their behalf against the Bill. Following the GCC's unsuccessful opposition, their lawyers, Crowder & Maynard, submitted an invoice for their expenses. William Crawshay enquired pointedly whether it included fees from Fowler '*after his statement that he could not give any evidence against the crossing our Sea Lock but that which would strengthen the application of the Penarth Co. and injure the Case of the Canal Company.*'[169]

In 1864, the Powell Duffryn Coal Company, formed after the death of Thomas Powell, made proposals to Crawshay to purchase the canal. Their idea was to convert it into a railway and control their own coal transport to

A photograph of 1902, showing what by then was the former course of the Taff Vale Railway's old Ferry Road across the Sea Lock to the foreshore past the Hamadryad Hospital to Penarth. On the right is the dockmaster's house of 1855. The road was abandoned, and the swing bridge removed, when the Clarence Road Bridge was opened over the Taff.

H.J.B. Wills photo, CCL collection

Cardiff to rival the TVR. Negotiations broke down, apparently, when Crawshay demanded preferential wharfage.[170] At the GCC AGM in June 1864, the 76 year old William Crawshay resigned the chair and his son Robert Thompson Crawshay took his place. William had been Chairman of the canal company for forty-two years. That same month, the *Cardiff & Merthyr Guardian* announced that Captain Dornford was leaving the position of Dock Master of the Port of Cardiff, a post he had held for twenty-two years, since leaving the similar position on the canal which he had held for twelve years. The newspaper sought contributions to a testimonial collection for purchasing a silver service for Dornford. The fund had already collected almost £150 and the listed subscribers included many of the greatest captains of industry, who owed much of their wealth to the canal and the Bute Docks. Seventeen companies and individuals contributed £5 a piece; Robert Crawshay was the only Cyfarthfa donor and he pledged £2.[171]

NOTES TO CHAPTER 10

1 CCL MS 2.716 Diary of John Bird, 13 March 1790.
2 See Volume 1, p26.
3 CCL MS 2.716 Diary of John Bird, 6 March, 13 May, 1 October 1790 and 12 April 1791; Gwent Record Office, Richard Crawshay letterbook 1 and 8 July 1791 to Lord Mountstuart.
4 GCC minute book 1 June 1791.
5 CCL MS 2.716 Diary of John Bird, 10 April 1793.
6 NLW Maybery 2475, Richard Hill to John Powell, 9 December 1793.
7 GRO Aberdare Canal Company Minute Book 18 January 1794 and 21 October 1795; NLW Maybery 2503, Richard Hill to John Powell 2 October 1795.
8 CCL MS 2.716 Diary of John Bird, 6 September 1794.
9 John Phillips *The General History of Inland Navigation; containing a Complete Account of all the Canals of the United Kingdom …,* 4th editon, London 1803.
10 GCC minute book 13 and 16 December 1794.
11 Robert Whitworth was one of the great canal engineers and surveyors, having trained under James Brindley. He worked on numerous canal and river navigation schemes including the Birmingham with Dadford.
12 GCC minute book 1 April 1795. Charles Hassall of East Wood, Narbeth, Pembrokeshire and William Pitt of Pendsford, Staffordshire. Pitt was later paid £63 for his work (minute 15 July 1795) and Whitworth £84 (£42 moiety paid 22 October 1795). There appears to be no record of Hassall's charges but a suggestion that he received a 'present' from the canal company through the copper works owner, John Morris of Clasemont, Swansea (Crawshay letter book 1 December 1795 and 2 December 1795).
13 GCC minute book 15 July 1795.
14 GCC minute book 22 October 1795.
15 GRO Q/DP 7.
16 NLW MS 11910E. Thomas Key to William Taitt 24 February 1796; Wm Taitt to John Wood 25 February 1796. See Volume 1, chapter 4.
17 GCC minute book 14 January 1796 for details of the Bill.
18 NLW MS11910E William Taitt to John Wood 12 February 1796 describes three petitions against the Bill.
19 NLW MS11910E Richard Crawshay to Samuel Homfray 18 February 1796.

20 Geo III CAP. LXIX. There are records of various parties receiving expense payments for attending proceedings in London: Henry Hollier, Bute's chief Steward and Clerk of the Peace for Glamorgan was paid 20 guineas for attending the House of Lords (GCC minute book 1 October 1796) and Richard Griffiths was likewise paid £45 (GCC minute book 17 August 1796). Mr Biggs bill to the Aberdare Canal Company for conducting their opposition was £119 4s 4d and James Dadford's expenses for attending as witness in London were £30 (ACC minute book 14 July 1796).
21 Gwent Record Office D2.162 Richard Crawshay's Letterbook 1788-97. Richard Crawshay to Sir Charles Morgan 15 December 1796.
22 Information from Tony Jukes.
23 House of Commons Journal 3, 8, 23 February, 16 March 1796; House of Lords Committee Book 21, 22, 24 March and 8 April 1796; GCC Minute Book 30 April 1796; Gwent Record Office D2.162 Richard Crawshay's Letterbook 1788-97, Richard Crawshay to Lord Auckland (London) 5 April 1796.
24 John Davies *Cardiff and the Marquesses of Bute*, Cardiff 1981.
25 GCC minute book 17 December 1796.
26 GCC minute book 30 April and 25 June 1796. Jackson was probably the same Jackson who in 1791 had built the canal company's river bridge to carry the Dowlais Railroad at Merthyr. He was probably also the contractor who built the Treble Locks at Taff's Well.
27 GCC minute book 12 November 1796.
28 GCC minute book 25 March 1797.
29 For a thorough account of the origins of Bute land ownership see John Davies *Cardiff and the Marquesses of Bute*, Cardiff 1981.
30 GRO B/C GCa 4/42.
31 GCC minute book 9 December 1797. Pritchard's kiln suffered several floods from the canal and in 1809 the dimensions of the canal trunk were ordered to be increased to be able to drain the canal more effectively and so prevent further incursions. Another flood occurred in 1810 but he was awarded no compensation.
32 GCC minute book 28 July 1798.
33 GCC minute book 28 July 1798 for the Sea Lock bye laws.
34 GCC minute book 27 June 1798; CCL MS2.716 Diary of John Bird 30 July 1798; *The Glocester Journal*, 2 July 1798.
35 GCC minute book 5 June 1798.
36 See Volume 1, chapter 4.
37 GCC minute book 28 July 1798, 27 March 1799; Cardiff Corporation Council minutes in *Cardiff Records* Vol IV.
38 CCL MS2.716 Diary of John Bird 24 February 1798. The South Gate was at the southern end of St Mary Street where the Custom House was later built. After 1821, the name South Gate Bridge gradually gave way to Custom House Bridge.
39 GCC minute book 30 June 1790.
40 GCC minute book 15 July 1795 and 7 June 1797
41 GCC minute book 25 June 1801 and 3 September 1802.
42 GCC minute book 1 June 1796, 27 June and 28 July 1798.
43 GCC minute book 26 June 1799, 4 June 1800 and 24 June 1801. See Volume 1, p122 for Thomas Peirce.
44 GCC minute book 29 September 1803, 5 June 1805 and 4 June 1806.
45 GCC minute book 4 June 1806 and 11 April 1805.
46 GCC minute book 9 May 1807 and 25 August 1809.
47 GCC minute book 9 May 1807 and 25 August 1809.
48 GCC minute book 18 July, 22 September 1810 and 4 February 1811.
49 Ridd's *Cardiff Directory* 1813.
50 GCC minute book 22 September 1810, 4 February, 23 November 1811, 3 April and 24 June 1812.
51 GCC minute book 23 November 1811.
52 GCC minute book 4 February and 29 August 1811.
53 GCC minute book 18 April 1812.
54 GCC minute book 22 April, 23 June 1813 and 22 June 1814.
55 GCC minute book 7 August 1818.
56 GCC minute book 17 August 1815.
57 GCC minute book 31 March 1815.
58 GCC minute book 16 January 1817.
59 GCC minute book 13 October 1815, 30 November 1816 and 10 May 1817.
60 GCC minute book 3 May 1817; Cardiff Corporation Council minutes May 10 1816 in *Cardiff Records* Vol IV.
61 GRO D/D Art O/21 GCC Tonnage Book 1798-9; Ridd's *Cardiff Directory* 1813; Pigot's *South Wales Directory* 1830.
62 GCC minute book 1 November 1817; Pigot's *South Wales Directory* 1830. In minute of 8 January 1821, John Williams and James Kidman were given leave to erect a crane at their yard on the third pond (at Merthyr) at one shilling per annum rent. The Kidmans seem to have been the last in a tradition of salt dealing in Cardiff.
63 Bill of lading, private collection.
64 GCC minute book 7 August 1818 and 6 May 1819.
65 GCC minute book 3 June, 7 August 1818, 7 October 1819 and 8 January 1821.
66 Cardiff Corporation Street Commissioners minutes 14 April 1821 in *Cardiff Records* Vol IV.
67 GCC minute book 4 May 1820.
68 GCC minute book 3 December 1818, 7 January, 4 March, 1 April 1819 and 20 September 1821. Letter 22 February 1819 (exhibit 8 of NMW resource pack on canals, source not stated).
69 For example Stewart's 'Report on the River Taff and Fisheries' NLW Bute 104 (see chapter on water supply to Melingriffith and Pentyrch).

70 Cardiff reference library plan P/15.
71 GRO Q/DP 22.
72 Cardiff reference library plan P/16.
73 GCC minute book 10 May and 6 June 1821.
74 *Observations on the proposed Rail-way or Tramroad from Stockton to the Collieries, by way of Darlington*, Durham 1818, pp13-4. This pamphlet also includes Overton's experiences in South Wales on the Monmouthshire Tramroad and Samuel Homfray's Sirhowy Tramroad, arguing the superiority of tramroads over canals. Although Overton won the battle against a canal, in the end it was George Stephenson's, not Overton's, survey that the S&D adopted, the edge railway winning the argument over the tramroad.
75 GCC minute book 12 July, 20 September, 1 November 1821.
76 GCC minute book 1 November 1821 and 7 March 1822. At the earlier meeting which authorised Overton's payment, the committee also authorised payment of £40 to a Mr Young '*for surveying and plans*'. Stevenson's report and plans have not been located.
77 GCC minute book 1 November, 13 December 1821, 10 January, 7 February and 7 March 1822.
78 GCC minute book 5 June 1822.
79 GCC minute book 16 January 1817.
80 GCC minute book 19 July 1822.
81 GRO Q/DP 18.
82 GRO Q/DP 24 and WIMM 87.160I.18.
83 Maurice W. Kirby *The Origin of Railway Enterprise - The Stockton and Darlington Railway 1821-1863*, Cambridge 1993, pp39-41.
84 See J.D. Evans 'The Uncrowned Iron King', in *The National Library of Wales Journal* Vol VII No 1, Summer 1951.
85 NLW Maybery 2259, 10 January 1823, John Guest to John Jones, solicitor, Brecon.
86 Meyrick was previously clerk to the canal commissioners and was paid £21 17s 4d when the commissioners were called out in August 1819 and February 1822. GCC minute book 2 January 1823. The reasons for replacing the Brecon-based Church with the Merthyr-based Meyrick in October 1823 were given as both his proximity to the canal and his material interest in the canal. The GCC were to regret his appointment, when bills for his professional fees started to be presented.
87 GCC minute book 27 February, 4 June, 4 September, 2 October, 11 December 1823, 24 January, 11 February 1824.
88 GRO Q/DP 25 March 19 1824. See also the copy plan in CCL P/9.
89 CCL P/27 plan of the land taken by the canal company between the town of Cardiff and the Sea Lock.
90 GCC minute book 2 June 1824.
91 GCC minute book 10 June 1824.
92 GCC minute book 11 June 1824.
93 GCC minute book 16 July 1824.
94 *The Inner Harbour*, Survey of Cardiff 1989, p65.
95 GCC minute book 3 March and 1 December 1825.
96 GCC minute book 26 February 1826.
97 GCC minute book 2 October 1823 and 31 March 1815.
98 GCC minute book 10 June 1824, 7 April, 15 June and 7 July 1825.
99 GCC minute book 7 September 1826, 4 January, 27 June 1827. Day moved to Swansea where he worked as an accountant and general agent. At a parish meeting in 1833, a man called Tittle accused Day of embezzlement whilst with the GCC but Day won the slander case, calling as character witness Thomas Reece, who by that time had himself retired from the GCC and was a magistrate for the county of Monmouth. Day was awarded £40 damages and Tittle became insolvent as a consequence. See *Merthyr Guardian*, 20 July 1833.
100 *Cardiff & Merthyr Guardian*, 10 July 1864.
101 GRO QAW 2/52-63.
102 *Cardiff & Merthyr Guardian*, 8 November 1851.
103 Insole & Biddle daybook GRO D/D Xcv 1, 15 June 1830.
104 *Merthyr Guardian*, 23 November 1833.
105 GCC minute book 3 November 1825.
106 *Cardiff & Merthyr Guardian*, 8 November 1851; Cardiff Corporation Council minutes December 14 1846 in *Cardiff Records* IV. For a detailed history of the quays and river traffic on the Taff, see Edgar L.Chappell *History of the Port of Cardiff*, Cardiff 1939, and for a reliable description of shipbuilding in Cardiff see D.E. Jeffreys *Maritime Memories of Cardiff*, Risca 1978.
107 GCC minute book 14 September 1824.
108 D.E. Jeffreys *Maritime Memories of Cardiff*, Risca 1978, p32.
109 SR conversation with Muriel Hawarth, great grand-daughter of John Thomas, 14 August 2001.
110 *Cambrian*, 9 April 1831.
111 GCC minute book 4 February, 2 June and 2 December 1819.
112 *Cambrian*, 13 October 1832 and *Merthyr Guardian*, 23 November 1833. Jeffreys has the tonnage of *Diana* as 90.
113 GCC minute book 14 August 1833.
114 GCC minute book 26 June 1839. The application was made by a Mr Vachell (probably Charles or William) and the occupier may have been Miss Elizabeth Hill (see TVR Act of 1836 p140).
115 GCC minute book 1 June 1825.
116 CCL Bute XI 3, James Green's report 19 May 1828.
117 GCC minute book 7 September 1826, 4 January 1827, 28 July 1828, 24 October 1834 and 13 January 1836.
118 GCC minute book 3 February and 7 July 1825.
119 GCC minute book 2 November 1826.

120 NLW Bute mss , Box 31X, cited by E.D. Lewis 'Pioneers of the Cardiff Coal Trade', *Glamorgan Historian* Vol 11 Barry nd. An oil painting by Alexander Wilson of Powell's staiths is in the possession of Cardiff City Council. It is reproduced in Edgar Chappell *History of the Port of Cardiff*, Cardiff 1939, p45.
121 GCC minute book 11 September 1844.
122 CCL Bute XI 44 and 14.
123 *Merthyr Guardian*, 22 November 1834 and Cardiff Council minutes reproduced in *Cardiff Records* Vol IV.
124 *Cardiff Records* Vol IV, quoting the Cardiff Council minutes.
125 GCC minute book 15 June 1825 and 7 July 1826.
126 Cardiff Council minutes reproduced in *Cardiff Records* Vol IV; former Cardiff Corporation archive, water bailiff reports transcribed by SR. GCC minute book 15 February 1854.
127 For Green see Charles Hadfield 'James Green as Canal Engineer', in *The Journal of Transport History* Volume 1 No 1, University of Leicester, May 1953, pp44-56 and Brian George *James Green – Canal Builder and County Surveyor (1781-1849)*, Exeter 1977.
128 CCL Bute XI 3 James Green's report 24 April 1828.
129 Edgar L. Chappell *History of the Port of Cardiff*, Cardiff 1939.
130 I William IV, cap CXXXIII.
131 Edgar L. Chappell *History of the Port of Cardiff*, Cardiff 1939, p81.
132 Crawshay to Bute 19 December 1833. NLW Cyfarthfa papers Box III, cited in John Davies *Cardiff and the Butes*, p250.
133 CCL Bute XIII 12. James Green's plan No 2 is referred to in his report to the Bute Estate – CCL Bute X1 3.
134 Associated British Ports archive ABP3312 (formerly 106A).
135 GCC minute book 3 June 1840.
136 Associated British Ports archive ABP3316.
137 A large coloured original of James Green's plan which shows this branch canal is in the ABP archive, numbered 40. A second copy is held at NLW and was used for the dust jacket to John Davies *Cardiff and the Marquesses of Bute*, Cardiff 1981.
138 Bute XI 35, 10 October 1846.
139 Bute XI 55/9 6 June 1839.
140 See Walter Minchinton *Bristol: Metropolis of the West in the Eighteenth Century*, Transactions of the Royal Historical Society, 1954.
141 See, for example, advertisement for the *Adelaide* in the *Cambrian*, 26 May 1832.
142 *Merthyr Guardian*, 6 and 13 July and 26 October 1998. *Cambrian*, 15 June 1833.
143 Dornford's Dockmaster letters GRO D/D Xjo. Tithe map 1844 and O'Rourke's map of 1849.
144 GCC minute book 14 August, 25 October 1833 and 7 February 1834.
145 GCC minute book 13 December 1833.
146 GCC minute book 7 June (John Edmunds) and 25 October 1843 (William Richards).
147 GCC minute book 16 November 1838, 5 and 26 June 1839. Deposited plan GRO Q/DP83. *London Gazette*, 16 November 1843.
148 John Davies *Cardiff and the Marquesses of Bute*, Cardiff 1981, p252.
149 GRO D/D AN 10 11/12, 18 Dec 1843; *Railway Times*, 23 December 1843; CCL Bute V 9, 14-15 May 1844; TVR Directors Minutes 16 August 1844 PRO RAIL 684.2.
150 See for example *Cardiff & Merthyr Guardian*, 1 November 1851.
151 GCC minute book 1 June 1853.
152 GCC minute book 23 June 1858 and 29 September 1859.
153 GCC minute book 7 November 1850.
154 *Cardiff & Merthyr Guardian*, 17 January, 7 February, 14 February and 29 August 1857.
155 *Cardiff & Merthyr Guardian*, 4 August 1860.
156 GCC minute book 20 April 1854. 1851 Census returns; Slater's *Cardiff Directory* 1852; Hirwaun cash ledger 1855-7, private collection; Wakeford's *Cardiff Directory* 1863. Also private correspondence SR with Sylvia Murphy.
157 Charles Hurry Riches is buried in Adamsdown cemetery. His large slate gravestone is at the north-westerly corner and contrasts with the vast majority of sandstone grave markers in the cemetery.
158 GCC minute book 25 June and 31 July 1851. *Cardiff & Merthyr Guardian*, 12 July and 8 August 1851.
159 GCC minute book 31 July 1851.
160 GCC minute book 4 December 1851 and 12 February 1852.
161 *Cardiff & Merthyr Guardian*, 26 June 1852.
162 GCC minute book 20 April and 9 November 1854.
163 GCC minute book 23 June and 28 July 1852, 1 June 1853.
164 GCC minute book 7 June and 27 July 1854. Joseph was James Green's son.
165 GCC minute book 19 February 1857, 13 October and 30 December 1858, 18 August 1859, 27 June 1860, 26 June 1861.
166 GCC minute book 27 June 1860.
167 Eric Mountford and Neil Sprinks *The Taff Vale Lines to Penarth*, Headington 1993, p7.
168 The wrought iron canal bridge was made by the de Bergue Foundry, College Road, Whitchurch. It turned on a circular roller set in one side of the Sea Lock. ABP collection, Cardiff.
169 GCC minute book 19 September 1861.
170 *The Cardiff Times*, 25 November 1864.
171 *Cardiff & Merthyr Guardian*, 24 June 1864. The presentation to Dornford is described in the edition of 26 August.

Chapter 11

THE TAFF VALE RAILWAY COMPANY'S LITTLE DOCK

By the summer of 1836, construction had started on the Bute Ship Canal (later to become Bute West Dock). To facilitate the unloading of imported building materials, the Marquess of Bute's resident engineer, George Turnbull, applied to the canal company for permission to erect a crane and wharf wall on the Glamorganshire Canal's bank, near the glass works (the site of the present Mount Stuart Square). Whilst it was agreed that the position was the best possible to minimise interruption of the canal company's trade in the Sea Lock pond, it was minuted that the committee

> '*much prefer so long & continued a landing of stone as that expected for the Marquess of Bute's Ship Canal should be carried on in a Dock or Slip in the Marquess's land cut through the Towing path communicating with the Canal which the Clerk is directed to urge very strongly for Mr Turnbull's adoption.*'[1]

Thus was a small dock – the Little Dock – built, through which materials and plant necessary for the construction of both the Ship Canal and the Taff Vale Railway were received via the canal.

Under the powers of the Taff Vale Railway Act of 21 June 1836, the TVR leased a large area of land from the Marquess of Bute, lying to the east of the canal and north of the coal yards and the kilns of the Guest-owned glass works. The area included the land on which the Little Dock was constructed. The canal company consented that the valuation of the small amount of their land required by the railway company be left in the hands of John Llewellyn, Benjamin Hall's agent at Abercarn and chairman of the canal commissioners.[2] On Bute land, the TVR built their workshops adjacent to the Little Dock, where a limekiln also was built so that the dock and railway companies could burn their own Aberthaw lime.[3] By June 1840, no compensation for any of the land taken by the TVR had yet been received and the Clerk, George Forrest, was instructed to write to the railway company's Secretary for its prompt payment.

The first section of the Taff Vale Railway opened on 8 October 1840, from Cardiff to Navigation. No coal shipping facilities had yet been installed in the Bute Dock and on 20 October, the TVR Board instructed their resident engineer, Bush, to '*prepare an estimate of the cost of making conveniences at the Docks on the Company's land near the glass houses for shipping coal and iron.*'[4] It was not a foregone conclusion that the TVR and the coal and iron shippers would use the Bute Dock. The TVR now saw the Little Dock as a potential outlet for its traffic. On 2 November, the railway was opened down the west side of the Bute Dock.[5] This also served the Little Dock; wagons were turned and hauled by horse across Bute Street to the dockside. On 3 November, Bush was authorised by his Board '*to make the necessary alterations in the present Dock according to the plan produced.*'[6] By the following month, Walter Coffin is reported to have been shipping coal and coke from the dock, while a great quantity of iron ore was also being landed there.[7]

Regular traffic of iron and coal started on the TVR in June 1841. Coal transshipment from wagon to ship at both docks, in the first couple of years, was effected by shovel and wheelbarrow but in a report to the TVR Board on 14 March 1842, their General Superintendent, George Fisher, stated:

> '*With proper machinery and attention on* [the] *South you may ship from four to five hundred tons of coal leaving* [the] *North side for red ore and merchants goods – in fact the quantity of coal may be increased by any extent by having inclines and tips and if allowed and necessary the same stages could be continued down the canal.*'[8]

They had the same idea for shipping iron from the canal, rather than use the more expensive Bute Dock. Lieutenant Dornford, the dockmaster who the previous year had defected from the canal company to Lord Bute, communicated this message via the Marquess' secretary, Thomas Collingdon: '*I find the Dowlais Co are determined to do all they can to thwart the 'Bute Docks'. I hear they intend to erect a Jetty & ship into the old Canal from the Railway Terminus! This will be a sad blow to us for the present.*' The next day, he wrote further:

> '*I had a peep behind the curtain yesterday. The Iron Masters are all up in Arms at the 1/- per ton being put on & are*

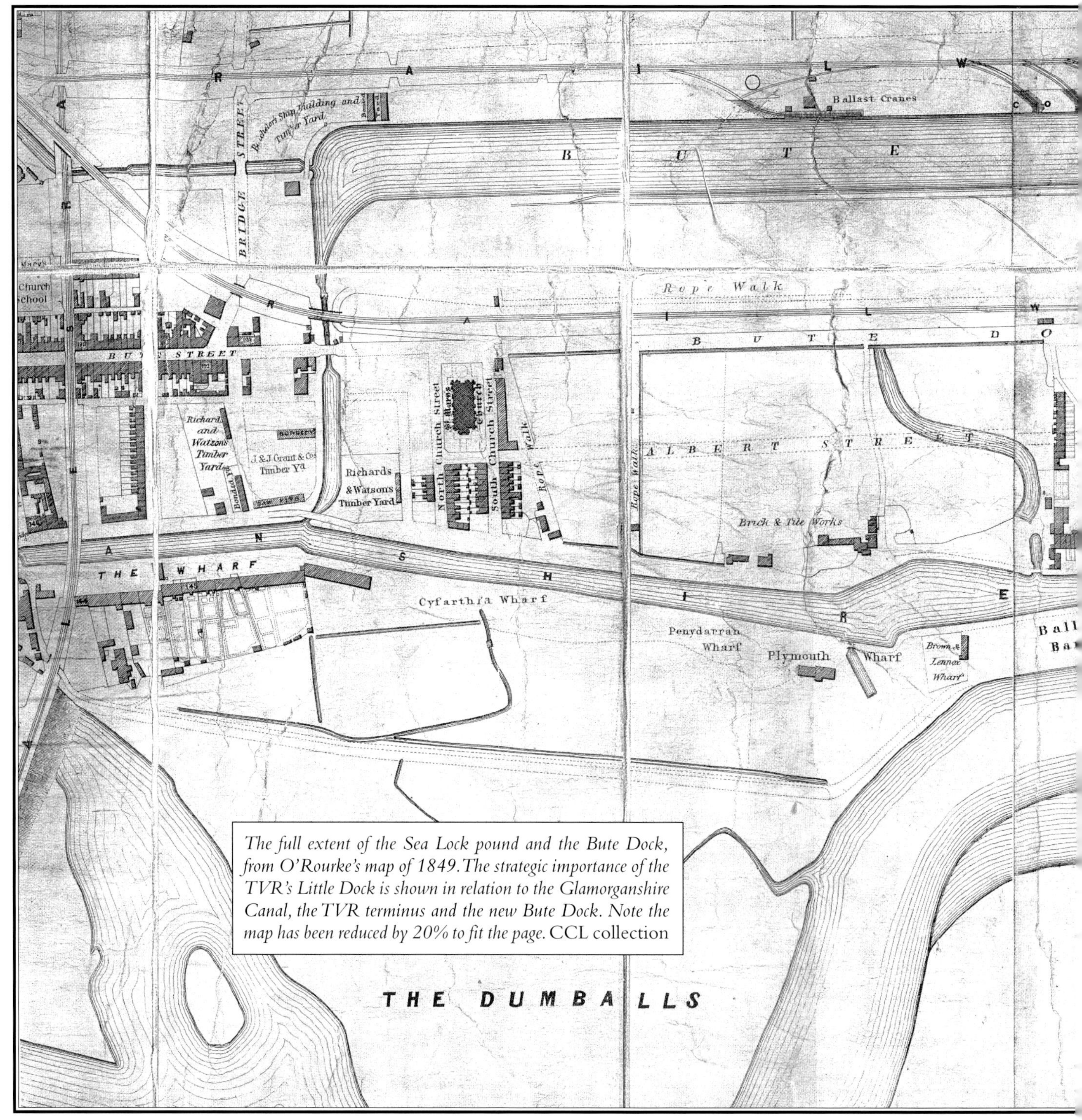

The full extent of the Sea Lock pound and the Bute Dock, from O'Rourke's map of 1849. The strategic importance of the TVR's Little Dock is shown in relation to the Glamorganshire Canal, the TVR terminus and the new Bute Dock. Note the map has been reduced by 20% to fit the page. CCL collection

determined to go hand in hand to do all they can to resist & oppose poor Bute Docks. They positively say not a Ton of Iron shall be shipped from the Bute Dock in fact it is their intention to make wharfs at the Old Ballast Bank & where they can on the Eastern side down to the Gates.'

The canal company were, of course, keen to encourage this battle and there is more than a hint of panic in Dornford's correspondence with his London paymasters. The TVR now resolved to enlarge the Little Dock. On 9 April, he wrote, '*Is it not possible to make those Rail Road gentlemen pay handsomely for taking the Iron, Coal etc across Lord Bute's ground from their Terminus to the Little Dock?*' and the following week, '*among the numerous reports plying about, one is the Taff Vale folks intend to enlarge their 'Little Dock', another the Canal Co means to join them & finish the Ely Branch – in short anything against the Bute Docks.*'[9] On 30 April, the TVR advertised in the *Cardiff & Merthyr Guardian* for tenders to excavate some 8,000 to 9,000 cubic yards and construct some 900 to 1,000 cubic yards of masonry dock walling.

Notwithstanding their threat to build their own dock on the River Ely at Penarth, the TVR proceeded with installing the first hydraulic wagon lift and tipping appliance, to Robert Stephenson's recommendations, at the south-

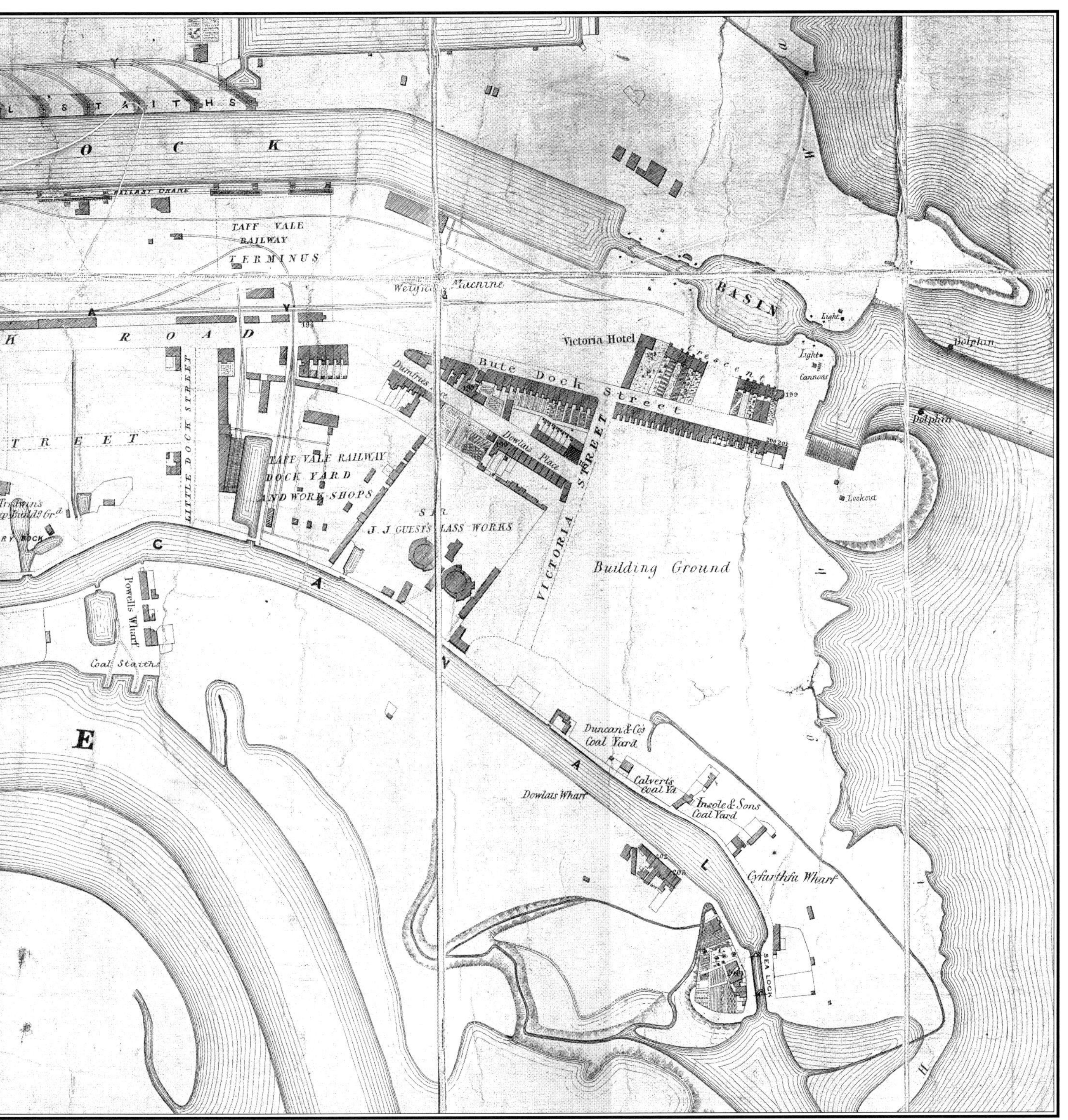

west of the Bute Dock. It was ready in December 1842, while the Bute Dock's own coal tip was not operational until the following summer. In January, Dornford remarked sarcastically, '*Mr Stephenson I hear is in Tuscany.*' And in February he despaired, '*Do come and shew us how to erect a Coal Tip!*' By the time the Bute Docks tip was complete, a second had been installed by the TVR and Thomas Powell was erecting one on his wharf in the Bute Dock, for discharging directly from canal boats into shipping vessels.[10] Shipment at the enlarged Little Dock remained manual. When Bute and the TVR finally reached agreement on terms of Bute's lease of the west of his dock to the TVR, the railway company agreed to pay him wharfage and lockage dues for all exports through the Little Dock as if they had been exported through the Bute Dock.

During the tense period of 1842, the Dowlais Company's shipping agent, David Griffiths, took advantage of the relative proximity of the Little Dock to Dowlais's new wharf on the Bute Dock, by being able to ship its iron from the 'Old Canal' even though it had arrived by rail. Sir Josiah Guest's Dowlais Company may have been the first to move its wharf to the Bute Dock, where it would be served by the TVR of which Guest was Chairman and a major shareholder, but circumstances arose which caused Griffiths

The canal basin, on 14 April 1883. The wharves on the right had once served the yards of a succession of pioneer coal owners of the Taff, Cynon and Rhondda valleys. In the distance, through the canal's open safety gates, the tall chimney marks their full extent and the site of the former hydraulic engine, provided by the canal company to assist transferring coal from canal boat to sea-going vessel. On the left is the Old Sea Lock Hotel. The entrance to the TVR's Little Dock is just out of sight on the right of the basin, as it bends to the left in the far distance.

GRO collection

to continue using the canal. Some vessels, not chartered exclusively to Dowlais, might load part Plymouth or Cyfarthfa iron and part Dowlais and so, having loaded at the Plymouth or Cyfarthfa canal wharf, their masters would refuse to take their vessels round to the Bute Dock for the Dowlais consignment. As a result, Griffiths had to tram the iron across Bute Road to the Little Dock for shipment. Another example occurred on November 25, when the Captain of the *Hope*, bound for Rouen with an urgent order of Dowlais rails for Paris, would not enter the Bute Dock but insisted on being loaded in the canal. The Marquess put pressure on the Dowlais Company to desist from this practice and it responded politically by sacking the unfortunate Griffiths. However, in the following few years Dowlais was still finding opportunist reasons for using the Little Dock.[11] There was even some Dowlais iron which, having arrived by rail at the dockside wharf, was then shipped by canal boat to ironmongers in Cardiff town.[12]

Examples of imports received through the Little Dock in the mid 1840s were flour from Bridgwater, Watchet and Carmarthen for Spillers, potatoes from Kinsale and the Scilly Isles for Driscoll, sundries from Southern Ireland (Kinsale, Wexford and Cork), salt from Gloucester, tin from Liverpool for the Melingriffith Company, slates from Portmadoc, pitwood from Chepstow, timber from Inverness and Bristol, bricks from Bridgwater and Newport, and regular shiploads of iron ore from Cornwall (Charlestown, Pentewan and Fowey) and Cumbria (Whitehaven and Barrow) for the Dowlais Company. The Bristol Packet also occasionally unloaded there, although from February 1844 the new packet slip was open at the Bute Dock entrance.

Coal was shipped from the Little Dock during this same period by Thomas Powell, George Insole, Walter Coffin, Edward Edmunds and Duncan & Co but, most of all, by the Dowlais Company. A typical week would see twenty ships either discharged or loaded there, the largest vessels being of 100 tons burthen.[13]

The Bute papers in Cardiff Library include an 1844 comparison of the expense in discharging a vessel of 150 tons of iron ore at the Bute Dock and the Little Dock. At the Bute Dock, the ore was discharged directly from Vessel to Railway Trams at 3/4d per ton (9s 5 1/2d). At the Little Dock, the ore was initially discharged from Vessel to Wharf at 1/2d per ton (6s 3d), then from Wharf to Barge [*sic*] at 1 1/2d per ton (18s 9d), then from Barge to Trams at 1d per ton (12s 6d). This final operation represented transshipment from canal onto the Merthyr Tramroad at the Basin at Navigation. The final destination of the iron ore would have been Dowlais, one of the three iron works east of Merthyr who jointly owned the Merthyr Tramroad. Therefore, the cost difference in favour of the Bute Dock was 2 1/4d per ton (£1 8s per vessel). An additional TVR wharfage charge of 2d per ton on iron ore landed at the Little Dock, was in lieu of the similar wharfage charge at Bute Dock.[14] Even so, Dowlais preferred to continue to use the Little Dock to receive its imported ore for some years to come.

In these years, shipments from Little Dock grew to such an extent that the GCC could not be sure whether to be happy or sad. On 25 October 1843, the canal company's solicitors, Maynard and Davis, were asked to take counsel's opinion on the legality of the TVR's having the dock. There is an air of resignation in the wording of the minute and nothing more is recorded until 6 June 1850, when Messrs Crowder and Maynard were again to be consulted '*upon the subject of the Dock used by the Railway Co and to report their opinion upon the power of the Canal Co to prevent the use of the same by the Railway Co.*'[15] Again, this resulted in no action by the GCC. Their concern, this second time, was probably prompted by the TVR's decision to transfer one of its old hydraulic rams of 1842 from the west wharf of Bute Dock to the south wharf of the Little Dock, part of the TVR's arrangements in abandoning the west wharf for their new high-level tips on the east bank of Bute Dock.[16] The hydraulic ram proved a success and, from 1850, the volumes of coal and coke shipped from Little Dock were sufficiently great to warrant separating them from the Bute Dock shipments in the TVR accounts.[17]

The hydraulic ram is described by Sam Allen in his *Reminiscences* of 1918 (pp42-3):

> '*... the visitor will see a huge iron tank, perched high above the roof, on a tower ... Sunk into the ground in the centre of each tip, was a very large cylinder and ram, on the top of which was a cradle, on which the laden trams rested. Pipes of large diameter communicated with these rams and the bottom part of the big elevated tank, so that the simple weight of the water, due to its height and the large diameter of the rams, was quite sufficient to provide the necessary power to lift the laden trams the required height in order to allow the coal to slide out into the vessel's hold.*'

The GCC's Own Hydraulic Hoists

The extended use of machinery to ship coal at the Bute Dock and now at the TVR's Little Dock, caused the canal company at last to consider how it should assist its own coal freighters. Despite being open for ten years, the TVR and Bute Dock could not cope with the huge growth in the steam coal trade from Aberdare. The canal was still holding its own and tonnages carried by it were still increasing. On 6 June 1850, the canal company committee ordered that an advertisement be inserted into several newspapers throughout the country,[18] that '*they are desirous of adopting a Plan or Device for loading coal into Vessels lying afloat in the Canal from Barges alongside, and that they will give a premium of one hundred Guineas for the best Model or Exposition.*' William Crawshay invited the principal coal freighters to attend the meeting on 31 July. That meeting is described by John Nixon's biographer. Of the models exhibited, William Armstrong's was selected but Vincent suggests that Nixon proposed an alteration to the design before it could be accepted. They had to be sure there was some vertical movement in the device, so that it could reach ships' hatchways without fouling the rigging.[19] On 17 October, '*the Chairman was requested to write to Messrs Armstrong and Burlinson for the Ground Plan of their Machines*

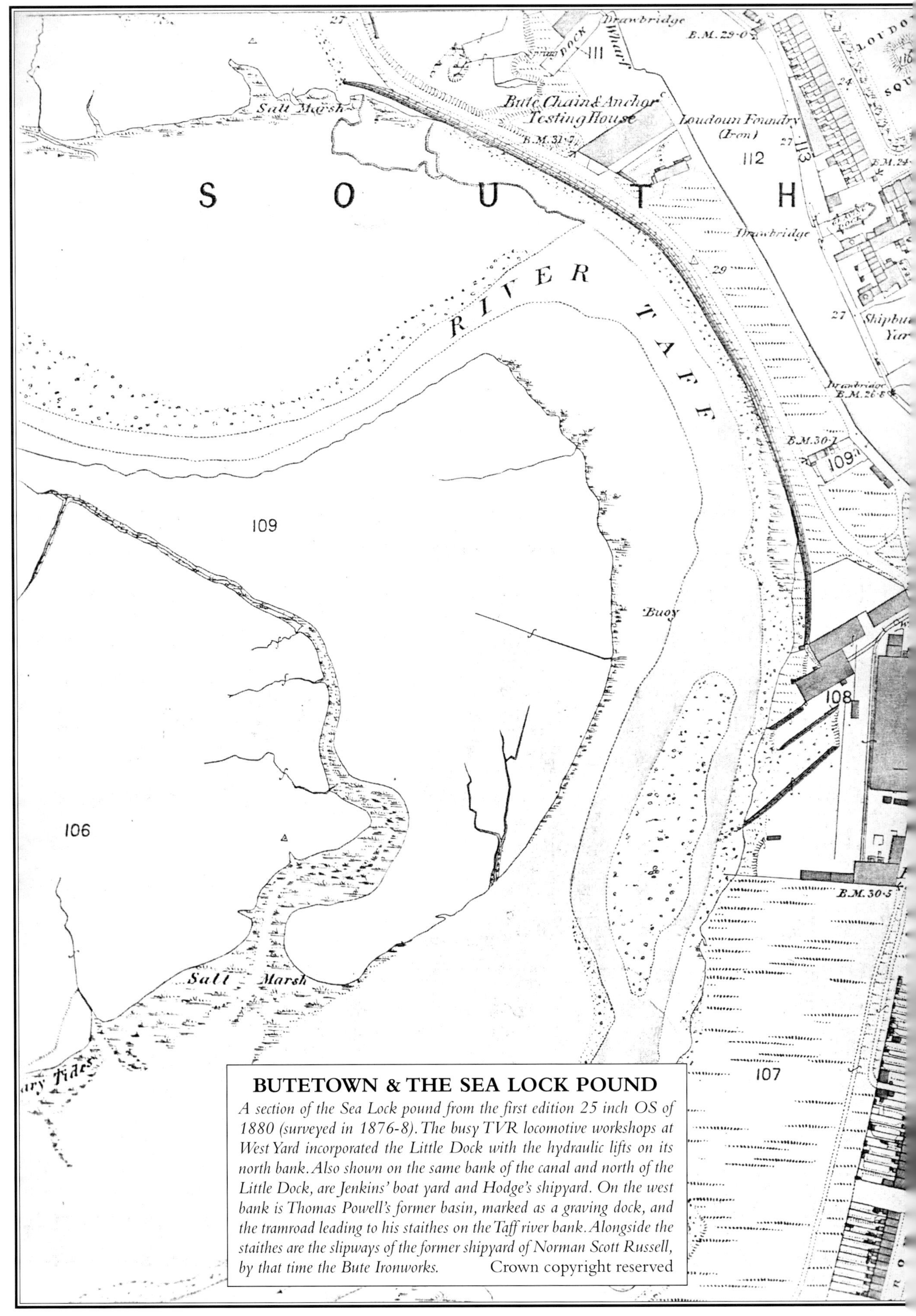

BUTETOWN & THE SEA LOCK POUND

A section of the Sea Lock pound from the first edition 25 inch OS of 1880 (surveyed in 1876-8). The busy TVR locomotive workshops at West Yard incorporated the Little Dock with the hydraulic lifts on its north bank. Also shown on the same bank of the canal and north of the Little Dock, are Jenkins' boat yard and Hodge's shipyard. On the west bank is Thomas Powell's former basin, marked as a graving dock, and the tramroad leading to his staithes on the Taff river bank. Alongside the staithes are the slipways of the former shipyard of Norman Scott Russell, by that time the Bute Ironworks. Crown copyright reserved

W A R D
DOCK
St Paul's Free Church
Independent Chapel
Midland Wagon Works
Timber Yd
Saw Mill
Hotel
Sig! Box
HANNAH STREET
HENRY STREET
ALICE STREET
PATRICK STREET
Iron Foundry
Foot Bridge
Butetown
Reservoir
Hotel
B.M. 28·7
TRAMWAY
LITTLE DOCK
115
Drawbridge
Bute
on Works
West Yard
(Taff Vale Railway)
Branch Bank
B.M. 28·2
Dock Chambers
Scandinavian Chapel
Smithy
Hotel
B.M. 28·8
B.M. 26·6
School (Boys & Girls)
B.M. 25·8
Hotel
Branch Bank
115a
MOUNT STUART
Siloam Chapel (Welsh Par. Bap.)
SQUARE
WEST BUTE STREET
Rothesay Terrace
116a
School (Boys)
Baptist Chapel (General)
Independent Chapel (Welsh)
JAMES STREET
B.M. 26·8
B.M. 26·9
Hotel
TRAMWAY
Church
ADELAIDE PLACE
SOUTH WILLIAM
LOUISA
GEORGE STREET
116
BUTE WEST DOCK
BASIN
Bute

with a Sketch of Boats and Vessels loading before the Company determine the sites.' Both Armstrong and Burlinson were leading figures in shipping machinery in the North East of England, Burlinson on the Wear and Armstrong on the Tyne. On 7 November, the Clerk was instructed to write '*to the chief Coal Proprietors asking their opinion as to the site they would suggest as most convenient for the Shipping Machines.*' The canal company's minute book is then silent on the subject for a whole year.

Coincidentally, a report in the 8 February 1851 edition of the *Cardiff & Merthyr Guardian*, records the death in Cardiff of Richard Williams, son of Thomas Williams, having been struck by a piece of timber while employed '*in raising a large crane for Mr Nixon, coal merchant.*' The report goes on, tantalisingly, to state, '*the deceased was employed erecting an engine for Mr J. Nixon ... for the purpose of loading coal.*' Could this have been Armstrong's appliance, being erected in the yard of John Nixon rather than at some neutral location on the canal? Nixon, who also came from the North East of England, was shipping from his Werfa Colliery on the Aberdare Canal and, as well as Powell, is known to have used coal boxes. The TVR also had wagons to carry coal boxes. Judgement had just been found against the Aberdare Canal Company, who were preventing Nixon from bridging the canal so that he could finally connect his colliery to the Taff Vale Railway. In early 1851, Nixon may have been preparing his yard on the Bute West Dock for the increased traffic the railway connection would produce; it seems too early to be a reference to erection of the GCC coal tips and it is unlikely they were placed within Nixon's own canal yard.

At the meeting of 4 December 1851, it was ordered '*that Mr W.G. Armstrong & Co's application for part payment of the Hydraulic Machine be complied with and that two thirds of the amount be paid him, say £800, and that he be informed ~~considerable injury has occurred to the Machines in the transit here and also~~ that the Building will be ready in one month from this date for the erection of the Machines.*' What is the significance of the crossed out words? Do they explain the delay of a year? Nothing more is minuted on the subject.

The Armstrong machine was probably a hydraulic crane capable only of derricking a coal box from canal boat to sea-going vessel.[20] As we have shown, coal boxes were used from 1842 by Thomas Powell on the Aberdare Canal and on the Vale of Neath Railway to Swansea.[21] In 1843, Powell was erecting a crane at Bute Dock (see above). Further evidence of use of coal boxes on the Glamorganshire Canal is provided by Sam Allen, who records the memories of George Williams, a Cardiffian born in 1832:

> '*Nixon's Jibs which were the first hydraulic arrangement in Cardiff for the shipment of coal, which was brought down the canal in barges fitted with eight or nine iron tubs filled with coal. The barges were moored close to the quay. The vessel to be loaded lay further out in the canal. Each tub was lifted from the barge and lowered outwardly until over the hatchway. The bottoms of the tubs had hinges, and when the catch was withdrawn the coal fell out into the hold, the empty ones being replaced in the barge.*'[22]

When John McConnochie presented his paper on 'The Bute Docks, Cardiff', to the Institute of Mechanical Engineering in August 1874, P.G. Westmacott, in the audience, recalled '*the application of hydraulic hoists on that* [the Glamorganshire] *canal*' but no details are given.

Vincent says that two of these '*improved cranes were erected on the Glamorgan Canal Company's Sea Lock Pond*' and that they '*did their work for a long time until Messrs. Nixon and Powell established special apparatus of their own for transferring coal from barge to vessel.*' It is strange that no bye-law was introduced to govern their use (the bye-laws were completely revised in 1853 but there is no mention of shipping appliances). The idea of the coal shippers (the major ones, who each still had their own yards on the Sea Lock pound) sharing a fixed appliance at a neutral location would have demanded a co-operative spirit – there would have to have been some rules laid down on how it operated and under whose supervision. The minute book is silent but there is more evidence that the hoists were built, how they worked and exactly where they were located.

An historical article on the Glamorganshire Canal, said to have been taken from the *Cardiff Standard*, was printed in the *Cardiff & Merthyr Guardian*, 27 May 1864. It recounts the 100 guineas premium offered by the canal company in 1850 and continues:

> '*That constructed by W.D. Burlinson, of Sunderland, was approved; it consisted of a lever, 33 ft long, fixed on an axle, about two-thirds from the upper end, on which a leading pulley revolves; this machine to be worked by a steam-engine of 2-horse power, on the shafts of which rope rolls are fixed, and flat ropes attached, and carried over the ends of the pulleys, on the end of levers. When the loaded tub or box is raised to the required height, the lever descends to the level of the ship's deck, by means of brakes and wheels attached to the main axles of levers; when the coals are discharged from the tub, a counterbalance brings them to their former position by the coal-trams. Two of these machines were immediately ordered, and have formed the ground-work of others.*'

The description lapses into referring to coal trams rather than canal boats but is the closest we have found.

The August 1863 down tonnage accounts for the canal include separate charges to the coal companies for '*Engine Dues*' at 1s per boat. In three weeks of that month, the engine was used by David Davis (2 boats), Lletty Shenkin (7 boats), Nixon, Taylor & Cory (30 boats) and Thomas Powell & Son (9 boats). All these represent steam coal collieries situated on the Aberdare Canal. This suggests that all were using coal boxes to tranship their coal directly from canal boat to sea-going vessel, using the fixed hydraulic cranes on the Sea Lock pound at Cardiff.[23]

In Hugh Bird's *Cardiff Directory & Handbook* for 1858, James Street is described as leading '*to the Canal by the passage to the Hydraulic Coal-machine.*' In the *Cardiff & Merthyr*

A glimpse of the TVR's West Yard, dating from circa 1900. The view is looking east, with the ship's masts visible in the background in Bute West Dock. This cramped site was the TVR's main locomotive build and repair facility, and was closed in 1926 by the GWR after the Grouping when the Rhymney Railway's works at Caerphilly was adopted as the GWR's main locomotive works in South Wales. The Little Dock is just out of view, behind and to the left of the building in the foreground. Neil Parkhouse collection

Guardian for 1 March 1862, the drowning of Joseph Casson, master of the schooner *Elizabeth* of Whitehaven (probably arrived with a load of iron ore), is reported. His body '*was picked up in the Glamorganshire Canal, by the company's coal-tips, near the end of James Street.*' James Street terminated at the canal and formed the northern limit of the series of coal yards leading from the Sea Lock. Although there are many maps of Cardiff for the 1850s and 1860s, the authors have not been able to find one which actually shows the hydraulic machines. By the time of the first edition of the 25 inch OS map in the mid 1870s, the old coal yards were built over and all coal exports were to all intents and purposes the monopoly of the Bute Docks. When giving evidence to the House of Lords Select Committee for the Glamorganshire Canal Dock Bill in March 1878, Thomas Shepherd said '*We have no* [coal] *tip on the canal.*' The schedule to the deposited plan for that Bill shows the site of the machines as plot 164 '*Old Engine House*', with Pattison Brothers as occupiers.

The Final Years of the Little Dock

At Little Dock, the peak year for coal shipment was 1857 (58,122 tons) and although in 1870 shipment was still a healthy 33,817 tons, this was now a small proportion of the TVR's total shipment through the Bute Docks. The drastic reduction in tonnage in 1872 is mainly due to the coal strikes of that year but by 1873, wagon size had increased from eight to twelve tons and the hydraulic ram could not raise the wagons to a sufficient height for tipping. The costs required to improve its efficiency proved uneconomical. After ensuring that under their Acts of Parliament they had no legal obligation to ship coal from Little Dock, the TVR decided to cease such operations from 1 September 1873.[24] The dock was retained in a fit and proper state for the receipt, shipment and delivery of goods under sections 31-33 of the TVR's 1846 Act, until these sections were repealed in their 1900 Act.

Sam Allen records one use of the Little Dock, which shows that the TVR continued to make use of it for its own departmental purposes. Before the opening of the Wye Valley Railway (from Chepstow to Monmouth in 1876), a redundant TVR locomotive was loaded onto a schooner in the Little Dock and despatched to Tintern, where it did further work as a stationary engine at a rolling mill on the west bank of the River Wye.[25]

William Gomer, a boat boy and boatman on the Glamorganshire Canal from 1891, recalled that Burton & Sons, provision merchants at Newport, Cardiff and Bristol, used the TVR dock for loading the Pontypridd market boats.[26] So much did the canal company now rely on the dock, that it actually petitioned against the TVR's 1900 abandonment Bill. After the Bill's passing R. Burton were granted a lease of premises elsewhere on the Sea Lock pond at East Wharf.[27]

In March 1903, it was decided to fill in the Little Dock for the purpose of extending the TVR's West Yard locomotive works. The statutory six months notice was given by section 8 of the company's Act of 1900. The dock was to be filled at a cost of £750, the canal bank made up at a cost of £138 and siding laid down for the reception of traffic from the canal at a cost of £100.[28] At the 1922-3 railway groupings, the GWR absorbed the TVR and they closed the West Yard works in 1926.

The memory of the TVR dock lived on in Bute Street for some sixty years, until redevelopment in the area obliterated the street named 'Little Dock Street'.

COAL AND COKE CONVEYED BY THE TAFF VALE RAILWAY TO THEIR DOCK[29]

Year	Tons	Year	Tons	Year	Tons
1850	30,794	1860	48,841	1870	33,817
1851	40,949	1861	42,708	1871	29,052
1852	44,334	1862	47,780	1872	14,585
1853	56,893	1863	35,361	1873	17,143
1854	58,751	1864	45,518		
1855	56,206	1865	42,543		
1856	58,031	1866	45,706		
1857	58,122	1867	39,825		
1858	55,681	1868	33,536		
1859	50,849	1869	33,803		

NOTES TO CHAPTER 11

1 GCC minute book 23 August 1836.
2 GCC minute book 6 June 1838.
3 The limekiln is shown on an undated map of c 1839-40 in Associated British Ports archive, Cardiff ref 3316. It is the only map so far found which shows the Little Dock before its enlargement of 1842.
4 Cited in Terry Powell, *The Taff Vale at Cardiff Docks* The Welsh Railways Archive, Vol II No 6, November 1997.
5 Eric Mountford *The Cardiff Railway* Oxford 1987 p10.
6 TVR Directors Minutes PRO RAIL 684.1. Thanks to Colin Chapman for this and other TVR references.
7 GRO D/D Xjo Cardiff Dockmaster letters, Dornford to Collingdon 23 and 28 December 1841.
8 Cited in Terry Powell.
9 GRO D/D Jo Dornford to Collingdon 20, 21 March and 9, 17 April 1842.
10 GRO D/D Jo Dornford to Collingdon 5 January, 6, 14 and 26 February and 19 April 1843.
11 Correspondence contained in CCL Bute XI 55 (23, 24, 27 and 28).
12 GRO D/D Jo Dornford to Collingdon 12 March 1843.
13 CCL Bute XI.
14 CCL Bute V 7.
15 See also TVR minute of 6 May 1850 in which Mr Bushell reported an interview with Mr Crawshay and Rev'd George Thomas when they had intimated that the Canal Company were determined to take measures to close the entrance into the Little Dock. PRO RAIL 684/3 TVR Minute Book.
16 TVR Directors Minute Book, 25 September 1850. PRO RAIL 684.3.
17 CCL Bute V 41.
18 *The Cardiff & Merthyr Guardian, Herepath's Railway Magazine, The Builder, The Mechanics Magazine, The Artisan, The Newcastle Advertiser* and *The Mining Journal.*
19 James Vincent *John Nixon pioneer of the Steam Coal Trade in South Wales a Memoir* London 1900 p201-5.
20 Author's correspondence with Terry Powell 10 October 1997. For a good detailed monograph on the development of coal hoists see Terry Powell *From Staith to Conveyer*, London 2001.
21 Volume 1.
22 S.W. Allen *Reminiscences*, Cardiff 1918, p172.
23 GRO D/D X296.
24 TVR Engineers Report 13 June 1873, PRO RAIL 684.47. Directors Minutes 13 June, 3 July, 25 August 1873, PRO RAIL 684.7. *The Western Mail*, 25 August 1873.
25 S.W. Allen *Reminiscences* p195.
26 William Gomer conversation with Ian L Wright, 2 December 1949.
27 GCC minute book 31 March 1900.
28 TVR Directors Minutes 17 and 25 March 1903, PRO RAIL 684.11.
29 CCL Bute V 41.

Chapter 12

THE GLAMORGANSHIRE CANAL RAILWAY

Dock and Railway Competition

The 1850s represent the peak decade for traffic carried on the Glamorganshire Canal. From that time, the competitive pressure was on from all sides. Isambard Kingdom Brunel's broad gauge railway line was opened through Cardiff in 1850 as the South Wales Railway. The Bute Trustees' second dock at Cardiff was opened partly in 1855, followed by extensions in 1858 and 1859. This new dock became the Bute East Dock while the old dock became known as the Bute West Dock. The SWR and the new Rhymney Railway were both given preferential access to the East Dock. The aggrieved directors of the TVR, being forced by Bute to stay at the West Dock with its already inferior facilities, got together and promoted the rival Penarth Dock – opened in 1865. Also in 1865, while the third Marquess of Bute was still a minor, the trustees promoted a Bill for a further dock of limited proportions – the Roath Basin.[1]

In this frantic climate of growth, collieries were being opened on the assumption that the shipping capacity at Cardiff would follow. The canal company, at some expense, opposed all the Bills and in turn prepared plans for its own dock and to set up a new company to run it. The Bute trustees now offered to purchase the canal shares. In most circumstances, a canal's committee would have sold but the Crawshays were still reliant on the canal's cheap rates as freighters. The Canal Acts limited the shareholder dividend to a maximum of 8% on the original £100,000 of shares and 5% on the £3,600 raised by the second Act – so the company returned all surplus profits to its freighters (those who used the canal) by way of substantial reductions in rates. For example, in 1862 out of a tonnage income of £123,419 the company returned £106,315 to the freighters, while the shareholders received only the annual total of £8,180 in dividend.[2] The retiring father, William, wrote to the new chairman, Robert Thompson Crawshay, '*I do not see how we can secure the present low tonnages, if we sell the canal.*'[3] The offer was duly refused but the canal company failed in its dock proposals. The consulting engineers, John Hawkshaw and Samuel Dobson, were involved in preparing these plans and in providing expert opinion in the GCC's opposition to the Bute Docks Bill and the Brecon & Merthyr Railway Bill. Charles H. and Frank James, trustees of the deceased William Meyrick's estate, inherited Meyrick's role as solicitors to the Glamorganshire Canal Company and continued where he left off, in deriving a healthy income from conducting the GCC's opposition to Bills of every railway and dock that proposed coming close to the Taff Valley.

Percy G. Harwood, who had been the Clerk at Cardiff since 1858 at £100 per annum, had his salary advanced in 1867 to £150 and was allowed to live at the Sea Lock house.[4]

The Glamorganshire Canal Dock Bill 1878

The Bute Roath Basin, sanctioned by Parliament in 1866 was not opened until 1874. It provided only a modest addition to coal shipping capacity because it replaced the tidal harbour with its coal hoists and railway connections. In the year it was opened, the Marquess of Bute obtained a new Act to construct the Roath Dock to connect with this Roath Basin. However, the Bute Estate again took their time in commencing construction and the collective frustration of coal owners, shippers and timber merchants (the latter who were lobbying for more timber floating acreage) persuaded the canal company to prepare what was to be its last great bid to oppose the Bute Estate's control over the port of Cardiff.

From 1875 to 1878, the GCC minutes refer to canal dock and timber pond schemes in Cardiff, with proposed railway connections to the Great Western Railway. The initial proposal was for the Sea Lock pound, Sea Lock, wharves, properties and land for the railway to be let to a new company for building a dock and providing a railway. It was estimated that the works would take three years to complete, during which time dividend payments would be suspended, as the amount of trade on the canal in Cardiff would be severely affected. From the fourth year, the expected annual rental income would be £4,000.[5] Although this proposition was carried unanimously at the Special General Meeting in November 1875, by 1877 the GCC had dispensed with the idea of renting to an outside company and announced a grand scheme of:

> '*Docks and Railways sufficiently comprehensive to accommodate the shipment of about one and a half million tons of coal a year, it appearing to your Committee after the result of the several*

A very busy view of the wharves, looking north from the East Wharf Bridge approach and taken, perhaps, in the 1880s. Every inch of waterfront is occupied and the canal boats are two abreast on both sides. In the foreground, on Watson's timber wharf, the gauntree is at work and behind it is one of the typical stacks of timber it was used for making. The inefficiency is obvious if the timber that was needed first happened to lie at the bottom of the pile. It was for this reason that timber merchants preferred to float timber in the canal. Their lobbying paid off in 1886, when the Bute Estate made two very large timber floats between the canal and the river, off Dumballs Road. It was across the canal from here, at the West Wharf, that the canal company's railway was being constructed in 1883. CCL collection

Alexanders' timber yards, and saw and planing mills, on the former Penydarren Wharf in 1904. Several lighters are seen being loaded with sawn timber. By this time, the yard had already been connected to the Glamorganshire Canal Railway for some twenty years. WIMM collection

East Wharf Bridge seen from the Junction Canal, which linked the Glamorganshire Canal with the Bute West Dock. The steam crane, operating from a wharf at the Bute saw mills, is lifting timber from the canal. Across the water was Watson's timber yard. The long shed beyond the bridge is the former Cyfarthfa iron warehouse on the West Wharf, where a wagon can just be glimpsed indicating the position of the Glamorganshire Canal Railway. Bill Hamlin collection

meetings held in 1875 for the same object that it would be unwise to go in Parliament for a lesser scheme.'

Surveys and plans were prepared by Richard Hassard, for which he charged £400. The Sea Lock pound was to be replaced from the ballast bank southward with a 2,000 foot long dock, deepened to 20 feet and widened to 400 feet, and equipped with modern coal-handling equipment and connecting rail facility. The River Taff was to be diverted westward, so that this new dock, its wharves and connecting railways could be built between the existing Sea Lock pound and the new river course. It would involve demolishing the housing on Harrowby Street and Dumballs Road and the (already closed) shipyard of Maudslay Sons and Field.[6] A tidal basin, 400 feet by 300 feet, would be situated on the foreshore south of the TVR road to Penarth and its sea entrance would have a 30 foot depth over the sill at high water of neap tides. A junction lock between the tidal basin and the dock (on the site of Thomas Hodge's boat yard) was to be 220 feet long by 50 feet wide, again with a depth of 30 feet over the sill. A graving dock 350 feet by 60 feet was planned for the site of the existing Sea Lock entrance basin. The dock was to be connected to the upper part of the Sea Lock pound by a lock, over which was to pass the railway to the eastern wharf. Above this lock, a timber float was to be made on the west of the Sea Lock pound, taking up some of Crawshay's and Penydarren's former iron wharves between the canal and Dumballs Road, and to the north of Alexander's timber yard.

The railway connection to the new dock was to be made from the Great Western Railway (the former SWR), from a junction (Riverside Branch Junction as it became) just west of the River Taff. The railway was to cross the Taff by its own bridge and then cross Penarth Road on the level.[7]

The plans were deposited in November 1877 and the estimated total cost of building the dock and timber float was £312,043 3s 9d.[8] The Glamorganshire Canal Dock Bill failed in the House of Lords in March 1878. No reason was given. The Marquess of Ripon, in the chair of the Select Committee, simply announced, '*The Committee have very carefully considered the question raised by this Bill and they are unanimously of opinion that the Preamble is not proved and that the Bill should not be proceeded with.*'[9] The canal company

An aerial view of the Sea Lock pound, Dumballs Road and the GWR Riverside Branch in 1927, looking north. Lock 51 is at the top. The entrance to the timber float was just north of the lock. There was then a connecting channel, passing under Dumballs Road and the railway, to another timber float – supplied with water from a pumping station on the river. The numerous sidings to be seen in the photograph, including those immediately adjacent to the Riverside Branch, were all part of the Glamorganshire Canal Railway. The line running across Dumballs Road, at the northern end of the warehouse bottom left, was the physical connection with the rest of the GCR system, which ran down the side of the canal to the Sea Lock. Near the top left of the picture can be seen Riverside North Signal Box, opened in 1894, which controlled the northern end of the loop (the third track to the right of the twin tracks of the Riverside Branch) by which the Glamorganshire Canal Railway connected with the GWR. Below the timber float, on the site of the old Penydarren Wharf, are John Bland's creosote works, Robinson David's yard, and saw mills connected with the timber industry. Further south is Burton & Son's bonded warehouse on the former basin of the Plymouth Ironworks, the sheds of the Lloyds Bute chain and anchor testing house, and Brown Lenox's wharf. Across the canal, the Butetown community is cut off from the canal bank by a high wall, where several small industries run the length of Canal Parade. At the foot of the photograph is the filled-in site of the 1817 Thomas Nichols' boat yard, which had operated under George Insole around 1830 and then passed to Thomas Jenkins. The recreation ground with the fountain at its centre is Loudon Square.

CCL collection

had had a great deal of support from all areas, who criticised Bute for not proceeding with his Roath Dock after he had received the powers; it was said that the passing of the Act had induced coal owners to sink more pits but then Bute chose not to build the dock. Timber merchants urged for timber floats in the port, it being far easier for them to store timber on a float than having to stack it on dry land in fifty-log piles with a gauntree. Even Cardiff Corporation, after initially petitioning against it, had supported the Bill. Others underlined the need for a modern graving dock at Cardiff. Yet with all this support they again could not succeed against the combined opposition of the TVR and the Bute Estate.

The Glamorganshire Canal Railway Act 1882

It was not until 1882 that the canal company was enabled to obtain Parliamentary sanction for a railway to connect its wharves with the GWR. The company's hopes for a dock were never to be realised. The Great Western Railway Act 1880 gave the canal company hope, for it

SHIP BUILDING YARD, CARDIFF.

The riverside Bute Iron Works had become Edward Curran's engineering works in the early 1900s but had not been rebuilt by 1927, when this second aerial view of the Sea Lock pound was also taken. River-launched iron steamships had been built here from the 1860s (as shown in the inset view taken from an 1891 advertisement). A passenger train, comprised of bogie clerestory roofed stock, waits at Clarence Road Station, terminus of the GWR's Riverside Branch, at the bottom of the photograph. Just up from the train can be seen Clarence Road Signal Box, opened in 1894. At the bottom right of the picture was the site of the Crown Patent Fuel Co's works and stores, opened in 1888 and closed in 1900. It was also served by a private siding running across Dumballs Road from a connection adjacent to Clarence Road Signal Box. The siding was not removed until 1912. Towards the top left of the picture, at the end of the sweeping curve, is Riverside Branch South Signal Box, also provided in 1894. It controlled the south connection with the Glamorganshire Canal Railway, which is the third track branching off just past the box. The line running back down the side of the canal and the sidings at bottom right, are all part of the Glamorganshire Canal Railway system. At the very top of the picture are the filled-in Jenkins' boat yard and Hodges' boat yard, with a small steam vessel in dock. On the opposite bank, Phyllis Bowles' houseboat can be seen at its mooring. The cluster of houses between both boat yards predated the building of Butetown and were built before 1830. In the mid 19th century, they housed a community of shipwrights and carpenters, several of whom came from Padstow to work with Richard Tredwen. On the extreme right can be seen the filled-in Little Dock and part of the TVR's West Yard workshops, immediately opposite the oil stores of James Arnott & Sons. Between there and the James Street canal bridge are a collection of small engineering workshop premises and builders merchants, which typified the final decades of the Glamorganshire Canal Sea Lock pound. Clarence Road Station closed to passengers on 16 March 1964, whilst the rest of the Riverside Branch was closed piecemeal between 1965 and 1968. CCL collection

included, as Branch Railway No 5, the Riverside Branch. With the GWR muscle providing this branch, it was only left to the canal to connect to it across Dumballs Road. The engineer William Clarke was asked in 1881 to prepare plans.[10]

Under the resultant Glamorganshire Canal Act 1882,[11] the canal company was empowered to make its own railway and sidings to connect the canal with the GWR Riverside Branch, which the Great Western had opened for goods traffic on 14 September 1882. The Act gave it power to raise up to £27,500 on mortgage. Carriage of passengers on the railway would not be allowed. Clarke's estimate was £10,520 and, in the end, £15,000 was sufficient.[12] Construction work started in 1883, the rails being bought from the Dowlais Company.

Bute Buys the Canal

Tenders were opened for the building of the railway at the same meeting where

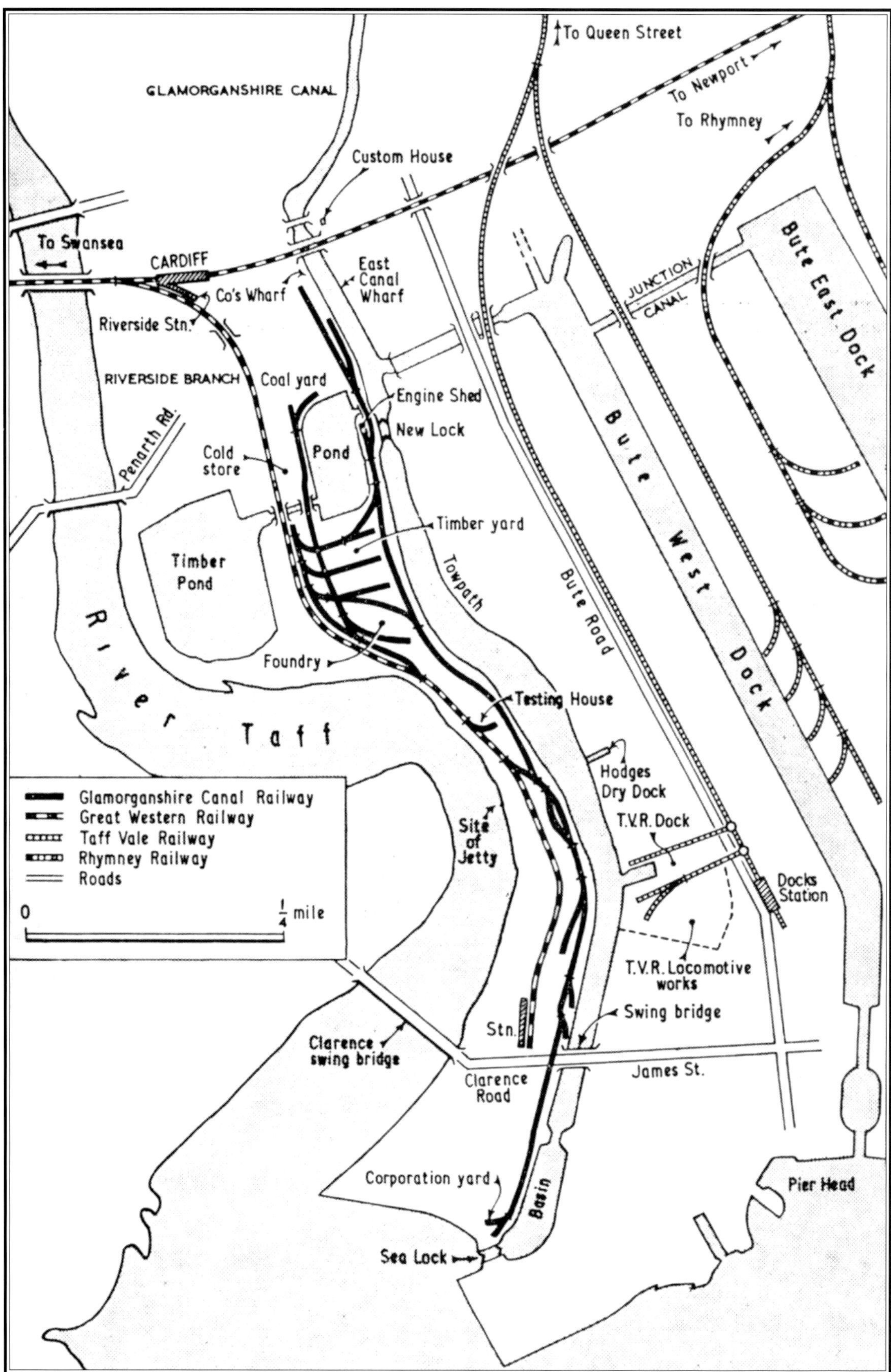

The Glamorganshire Canal Railway, adjacent lines and the Glamorganshire Canal Sea Lock pound. For plans of all the railways serving the Cardiff Docks, including the lines of the canal railway system, see Track Layout Diagrams of the GWR and BR(WR) Section 43A: Cardiff Main Line & Penarth Dock *and* Section 43B: Cardiff Docks *(R.A. Cooke, Harwell, 1998 & 1990).* ILW, courtesy *Railway Magazine*

the company finally gave in and accepted the Marquess of Bute's latest offer to purchase the whole of the canal company's shares.[13]

The agreement was that Lord Bute would acquire all shares of the Glamorganshire Canal and pay interest on the £100,000 original capital at 6½% and on the £3,600 share capital under the 1796 Act at 4% per annum. The Crawshay objection to sale no longer pertained. Robert Thompson Crawshay had died in 1879 and although his sons Richard and William were modernising Cyfarthfa as a steel works, following several periods of closure in the previous decade, they would no longer be using the canal. The Crawshays had reached agreement with the Great Western and Rhymney Railways that the Cyfarthfa coal railway through Gethin, which had pushed as far south as their Castle Pit at Troedyrhiw, would be extended further south to Cefn Glas and cross the valley to a junction with the Taff Vale Extension Railway at Quakers Yard. By this means, the Crawshay brothers would ship steel out of South Wales by rail and would cease to be reliant on the canal – brainchild of their great great grandfather. When control of the Glamorganshire and Aberdare Canals passed to Lord Bute at the beginning of 1885, the Crawshay brothers left the committee and Bute management took their place. Compensation was arranged for the outgoing canal servants – Thomas Shepherd was to receive £1,000, P.G. Harwood £300, Henry Williams £75 and F. Firney £50.[14]

Harwood stayed with the Bute-owned canal company and, on 12 August, he presented to the new committee a detailed and depressing report on the state of the canal. It was resolved to put the canal in order and to let Navigation House and adjoining premises to William Jones, late of Cyfarthfa works. W.T. Lewis proposed, on behalf of the Bute Trustees, that a new lock be put in towards the upper part of the Sea Lock pound, which would then allow the junction lock with the Bute West Dock to be left open and the level of the water in the canal and docks to be maintained, regardless of the level of the canal's Sea Lock pound. He also proposed that a timber float with canal connection be made in the same location as that which had been included in the abortive Bill of 1878. The Bute trustees would pay for the new lock and would allow the GCC land required for the timber float, part of the land belonging to the Crawshay brothers to be exchanged for the first 193 feet of canal at Canal Head, Cyfarthfa, which the Crawshays had already applied for with the intention of filling it for their own use.[15] With Bute now owning the canal, there was no need for a new Bill. The timber pond and lock were the last significant engineering works executed on the Glamorganshire Canal.

The Glamorganshire Canal Railway connected to the GWR's Riverside Branch, which joined the South Wales main line at Riverside Branch Junction, at the west end of Cardiff General Station. All GCR rail-borne goods traffic worked through this junction. The photographer, E.J. Miller of London, was standing on the end of Cardiff Riverside Station Up platform when taking this circa 1921 view. Passenger services on the branch were generally through trains from places such as Barry and Pontypridd and, up until the 1960s, were well patronised. Neil Parkhouse collection

The Glamorganshire Canal Railway

The Glamorganshire Canal Railway was built to serve the wharves, warehouses and industrial properties on the western side of the canal, and to make connection with the Riverside Branch. This double track railway diverged from the GWR South Wales main line west of Cardiff General Station,[16] to run southwards parallel with the Dumballs Road, on the narrow tongue of land formed by the Sea Lock pound of the canal and the River Taff. From 1893, the branch became a useful commuter route also for Barry and Taff Vale Railway passenger trains, after the GWR agreed running powers over the line with the two companies bringing dockland workers and business people to the cramped and rather ramshackle terminal station at Clarence Road.[17]

Goods traffic to and from the canal railway was worked on to a long access loop on the eastern side of the Riverside Branch. The 1901 25 inch OS shows a signalbox at each end of the goods loop (Riverside North and South) and another at Clarence Road to control train movements at the station and the Patent Fuel works siding.

The GWR put in a junction and level crossing over Dumballs Road, to give the GCC access to its railway in accordance with the canal's 1882 Act. This link to the GWR was just south of the Lloyds Bute Testing House. Further north on the loop, a north-facing connection ran on to the canal company's lines, which served various industrial premises, a cold store and the Dumballs Road coal yard. Connections to sidings serving industry on the canal's western wharves required six fully gated level crossings over the Dumballs Road. Among the works so served were Beal's, Brown Lenox and the Titan Foundry.

The canal railway included a direct line running north to south along the western bank of the Sea Lock pound, between the company's West Wharf and the Sea Lock. On its way south, the railway crossed the entrance to the small timber float, where the company's locomotive shed was situated. At the Testing House, the through line then passed over four 90 degree sidings in close succession, each one gaining access to the works by one of a battery of four hand-operated wagon turntables.

At its southern end, the railway crossed Clarence Road by a level crossing, which was operated by the man in charge of shunting. The line then terminated at the Sea Lock, where it served the Corporation yard, HM Royal Engineers Submarine Mining Establishment and the reclaimed metals yard of J. Ford. The GCC weighbridge for road and rail traffic was located in Harrowby Street, close to the canal swing bridge. Further to the west, at the crossing of the River Taff, was the Clarence Road swing bridge. This bridge, named after the Duke of Clarence, had been built under the Corporation's Act of 1887, to extend James Street as Clarence Road into the new suburb of Grangetown, on Lord Plymouth's land. The creation of Clarence Road river swing bridge and the canal swing bridge allowed closure and abandonment of the old TVR road of 1865, from Eleanor Street across the Sea Lock and the river to Ferry Road.

Locomotives

Seven steam locomotives are known to have worked on the canal railway, although the dates when a number of them operated on the system is a matter for conjecture.[18] All seven are listed in the table below, which includes the currently known details of each locomotive's working history. With the exception of *Kitchener*, they were all of the 0-4-0 wheel arrangement, the short wheelbase of such locomotives being ideal round the many tight curves to be found on the sidings running into the various works served by the system. *Kitchener* was also the only engine with inside cylinders to have worked on the canal railway.

Glamorgan was supplied new to the GCC for use on the railway in 1899 and was the mainstay of locomotive power on the system until 1935, when the company acquired *Delwyn*. It seems likely that the other five locomotives noted as working on the GCR were hired in at various times to cover periods when *Glamorgan* was unavailable whilst away being serviced or repaired. *Cornwall*, for instance, was quite possibly borrowed from Robinson David & Co on such an occasion, the company being users of the canal in the docks area in any case.

During the earlier years of the railway, the GCC also

Name	Type	Builders Details	Notes
Glamorgan	0-4-0ST	Hawthorn Leslie 2419/1899 oc 10ins x 15ins	Sold c1938 to A.R. Adams & Son of Newport. Rebuilt 1939 and sold to Partridge Jones & John Paton Ltd, Waterloo Tinplate Works, Machen. Transferred 1953 to Pontnewynydd Sheet & Galvanising Co. Thought scrapped c1961 when works closed.
Rhymney	0-4-0ST	Believed Hunslet 380/1886 oc	Identity not finally confirmed. New to T.A. Walker, contractor, for Llanishen reservoir contract, Cardiff Corporation. Believed then to Walker's Manchester Ship Canal contract. Sold c1912 to Taylor's Navigation Steam Coal Co, Nantgarw. By 1920s, with Provincial Coal Co, Merthyr, at closed Cyfarthfa Works (removing slag?).
Cornwall	0-4-0ST	Hudswell Clarke 645/1903 oc 12ins x 18ins	New as 3ft 6ins gauge to S. Pearson & Son Ltd, contractors, Gunnislake Quarry, No 111 *Cornwall*. Rebuilt HC 1908 to 4ft 8½ gauge. 1921 to P. Baker & Co, Cardiff. Resold to Robinson David & Co Ltd, Cardiff.
Star	0-4-0ST	Avonside 1613/1911 oc 8½ins x 12ins	On loan from A.R. Adams & Son 1938. Bought by Adams from Cordes (Dos Works) Ltd, Newport. Hired to Admiralty at Machen. Later sold to George Cohen, Sons & Co Ltd, London. Resold to Wilson's Forge Ltd, Bishop Auckland c1946.
17	0-4-0ST	Fox Walker 200/1874 oc 11ins (later 12ins) x 18ins	Cardiff Railway No 17, apparently on hire. Sold by CR c1916-7 for government service. Recorded at Brunner Mond, Winnington Works, Northwich, named *Cardiff* and sold 1930.
Kitchener	0-6-0ST	Manning Wardle 781/1881 ic	Hired 1925 from L. Gueret, Anchor Patent Fuel Works, Cardiff. Scrapped c1927 following closure of works.
Delwyn	0-4-0ST	Avonside 1565/1911 oc 14ins x 20ins	As *Finetta*, had worked at various West Country quarries, latterly with Roads Reconstruction Ltd, Conygar Quarry, Clevedon. Bought and rebuilt by Adams 1931. Acquired by GCC from Adams 1935.[19] Sold to James Mahoney & Co, 1947, for £500. As *John L. Deuchar*, it worked at the Salt Union Ltd, Winsford, Cheshire, 1948-53. Scrapped 1953.

The Glamorganshire Canal Co's 0-4-0 saddle tank locomotive Delwyn *(Avonside 1565 of 1911), the company's last steam engine, is seen outside its first shed next to the timber float in the 1930s. Originally named* Finetta, *it was acquired by the War Department in 1915 and later worked at the Sandford Quarries and Clevedon Quarry, both in Somerset. It was rebuilt by Adams of Newport and, according to Ivor Llewelyn, the canal's manager, was purchased by the GCC in 1935. In 1948, it was with the Salt Union Limited and named* John L. Deuchar. *The little Avonside went for scrapping in 1953.*
George Alliez photo

owned a number of open wagons and covered vans, probably 'for internal use only.'

The City of Cardiff's Railway

When Cardiff Corporation took possession of the Glamorganshire Canal from 1 January 1944, it also became owner of the railway. The decision was taken to continue to operate the railway traffic.

In 1945, the Corporation took delivery of a new 4-wheel battery electric locomotive from Greenwood & Batley of Leeds (Works no 2002/45) at a cost of £1,570. It was fitted with two 20 hp 200 volt series wound traction motors and weighed 14 tons. The engine worked successfully for the next eighteen years and allowed the Corporation to dispose of the 0-4-0ST *Delwyn* in 1947. Known unofficially by everyone on the railway by its maker's trade name 'Greenbat', the shunter was smartly turned out in the same crimson lake livery used on the lower panels of Cardiff Corporation's municipal trolleybuses and motorbuses. As a further mark of distinction, the Greenbat's cabsides were emblazoned with the City of Cardiff's coat of arms – a Welsh dragon, a shield, heraldic animal supporters and the declaration: '*Deffro maen ddydd, Y Ddraig Goch ddyry gychwyn*' ('*Awake 'tis day! The Red Dragon is stirring*').

A new engine shed was built at the southern end of the railway at Harrowby Street to house the Greenbat locomotive. Included in the accommodation was a battery charging plant, supplied in 1945 by the Electrical Construction Co at a cost of £210.[20]

The Glamorganshire Canal Railway, like its parent canal, was not included for nationalisation under the Attlee government's Transport Act of 1947, so the undertaking remained in municipal ownership until closure in 1963. At first sight it might appear remarkable that the railway kept working for twelve years after the final disappearance of the canal and the Sea Lock pound. Its principal freights, carried to or from the GWR, were coal, timber, sand, gravel, building materials, scrap, foodstuffs and animal feeds. Unfortunately for the city treasurer, the railway was unable to cover its running expenses and its balance sheets show a deficit in every year of Corporation ownership between 1944 and 1962. Sample figures are:

	1957-8	1958-9	1961-2
Expenditure (£)	3,107	3,175	3,768
Income (£)	1,644	1,162	686
Tonnage carried	28,317	13,566	6,192

Reduced activity on the railway was almost certainly the result of increasing competition from road transport and the relocation of business and warehousing away from this part of dockland.

Looking back to 1944 and the Cardiff Corporation's first years as a railway operator, we can detect only one reason why the City continued to work this loss-making undertaking year after year. Working the railway avoided the potentially more damaging compensation claims of traders whose businesses could be affected by the closure of the line. The railway had served 59 industrial firms in 1924 but was being used by only 19 traders after the Second World War and immediately before closure, the number had dropped to 9.[21]

End of the Line

By 1963, with mounting deficits and low income from the few remaining traders using the railway, the Corporation decided to discontinue railway operations on 23 February 1963, to coincide with the retirement of the railway's foreman, L. Callaghan. The other two men employed on the railway – the locomotive driver, E. Jones, and a platelayer, J. Gallivan – were transferred to alternative work with the city's Public Works Department.

So ended the eighty year career of the Glamorganshire Canal Railway. Although its length, including the various

Clarence Road station in 1921. Although the Riverside Branch belonged to the GWR, both the Taff Vale and Barry railways had running powers over it by agreement. Here, a Taff Vale passenger train, probably bound for Penarth, waits to leave in the charge of 'A' Class 0-6-2T No. 410. In the background, on Clarence Road, can be seen the Avondale Hotel. Neil Parkhouse collection

On 1 January 1944, the canal and its railway were vested in the Cardiff Corporation for the sum of £44,000. On that day, members of Cardiff City Council and the Bute Estate pose for official photographs at West Canal Wharf with the locomotive Delwyn. ILW collection

The last steam locomotive, Delwyn, *was sold in 1947 and the GCC's four-wheeled battery-electric locomotive, supplied new by Greenwood & Batley in 1945 (Works No 2002), took over all work on the canal railway. In this view, recorded in 1957, the 'Greenbat', as it was affectionately known, is on the level crossing over Clarence Road, just to the west of James Street swing bridge, with a single wagon in tow which it has brought from Ford's yard at the southern end of the railway. The buildings on the right are in Harrowby Street and the New Sea Lock public house can be seen in the distance, behind the crossing man's head.* ILW photo 2 Aug 1957, neg 1840

The clearly abandoned timber float looking north towards the city in about 1950. The battery locomotive can be seen standing just in front of the bridge that linked the float with the canal and alongside the original engine shed for the canal's railway. Stan Vickery photo, neg 28-25

Another view of the 'Greenbat' with its Corporation staff, waiting at the crossing gates at James Street swing bridge. The tall building in the left background is the bridge control cabin. The locomotive was painted in the same maroon livery as the corporation's buses. By this time, the canal was completely closed and all that remained in operation was its railway. ILW photo 2 Aug 1957 neg 1841

The Glamorganshire Canal Sea Lock pound looking north towards the, by then, abandoned wharf, taken from Lock 51 about 1950. On the left is the entrance to the timber float under the GCC Railway. On the right is the entrance to the Junction Canal, leading to the Bute Docks.
Stan Vickery photo, neg 28-26

***Right:** By the late 1950s, the canal had been filled in. This view is looking north, circa 1958, showing the railway still in use amidst a scene of dereliction and decay.*
Stan Vickery photo, neg no 28-24

***Below:** On the same occasion, the base and crown post of one of the canalside cranes recorded for posterity. The large ruined building on the right is Hodge's house, between the two old boatyards.*
Stan Vickery photo, neg no 28-23

sidings, was officially recorded as only 1.48 miles, there is no doubt that during those years the line had made a modest contribution to the commercial life of Cardiff.

Dismantling of the railway followed soon after closure and had been virtually completed by 1965.[22] Today, redevelopment on the site has almost obliterated the route but one link with the past remains. The engineering and testing works of Beal & Son, formerly connected to the railway, is still on site in Dumballs Road and is now (2004) modernised and trading under the name Lloyds Beal. As in the past, ships' anchors and cables can still be seen in the Beal yard, though today the firm is also very much concerned with the testing requirements of a wider, non-maritime world of engineering,

NOTES TO CHAPTER 12

1 Eric Mountford *The Cardiff Railway*, Oxford 1987, pp14-21.
2 GCC Accounts GRO QAW 2/43.
3 NLW Cyfarthfa papers Box 6, letter 28 May 1864, cited in Charles Hadfield *The Canals of South Wales and the Border*, Cardiff 1960, p115.
4 GCC minute book 11 January 1865, 6 June 1866 and 5 June 1867.
5 GCC minute book 16, 17 and 30 November 1875.
6 This shipyard had been founded on the River Taff in 1863 by John Scott Russell for his son Norman. Several large steamships were built here. For Russell see George S. Emmerson *John Scott Russell – A Great Victorian Engineer and Naval Architect*, London 1977.
7 GCC minute book 6 June, 5 and 19 October 1877; GRO QDP 398.
8 House of Lords – deposited plan and schedule.
9 House of Lords minutes of evidence 12 March 1878.
10 GCC minute book 8 August and 26 October 1881.
11 45 and 46 Vict.
12 GCC minute book 9 February, 13 April, 23 May and 27 June 1883. House of Lords deposited plans and schedule.
13 GCC minute book 9 August, 23 October, 15 November and 19 November 1883; Hadfield, p116.
14 GCC minute book 21 March 1884.
15 GCC minute book 12 August, 21 November 1885 and 6 February 1886.
16 The present day Cardiff Central station.
17 *Railway World*, August 1964, p281.
18 The information regarding the locomotives has come from several sources: *Industrial Locomotives: South Wales*, Birmingham 1951, p268; *Industrial Locomotives of Gwent*, Geoffrey Hill & Gordon Green, London, 1999, pp133 & 252-5; personal correspondence G. Alliez to Ian Wright 18 August, 19 and 28 October 1965. Notes supplied by John Fletcher and Russell Wear, 2004.
19 According to Ivor Llewelyn, Canal Manager, who produced the information from a diary when interviewed by Ian Wright, 30 December 1949.
20 E.C. Roberts, City Engineer, locomotive sale schedule February 1963. E.C. Roberts figures provided to Ian Wright via S. Tapper-Jones, Town Clerk.
21 Railway Clearing House *Handbook to Stations and Sidings*, London, 1925 edition; E.C. Roberts, report of City Surveyor on Glamorganshire Canal Railway – eight point response to Ian Wright's request for information about the railway, 12 November 1964.
22 The canal and railway were the subject of an article by the present author in 1965 (Ian L. Wright 'A South Wales Canal and its Railway' in *Railway Magazine*, October 1965, pp592-96) and certain material is reproduced here by permission of the editor of *Railway Magazine* with acknowledgement.

A Glamorganshire Canal Railway points lever. Stan Vickery photo, neg 28-31

Chapter 13

THE SEA LOCK POUND IN THE 20TH CENTURY

As the 19th century gave way to the 20th, no event of particular importance seems to emerge in the life of Cardiff's Sea Lock pound. However, as we shall see, a considerable number of industries and trades, some of them maritime, had been attracted to its banks, to take the place of the wharves and warehouses occupied by the ironmasters. The loading places of the pioneer coal exporters had gone the same way. In comparison with the bustling Bute Docks to the east, the Glamorganshire Canal looked like a quiet backwater.

Before looking at some of the canal's changed patterns of waterborne trade, it may be useful to be reminded of the movements shipping and canal boats could make in and out of the 'maritime mile'.

Since the opening of the Bute Docks, two routes had become available to canal traders:

i) Trade in and out of the Sea Lock by small sailing vessels, steamers and canal boats acting as lighters.

ii) A lateral trade via the Junction Canal between the Sea Lock pound and the West Bute Dock. The Junction Canal could accommodate craft of canal boat dimensions only and was also used to float rafts of imported timber between the Bute Docks and the Dumballs Road timber floats. The East and West docks were joined by a communication canal when the East Dock was opened in 1859.

From the evidence of a few photographs, mostly dating from the 1890s, it seems clear that the Sea Lock pound of the Glamorganshire Canal was still playing a useful part in the commercial life of Cardiff. Evidence of the old order survives in a photograph of the Sea Lock (see page 296) where the wooden sailing vessel *Elizabeth Ann* of Porlock, a West Country ketch, is unloading sacks across high wooden staging into the Eleanor Street warehouse. Another little ship in the same trade was Stoate & Son's *Electric*, of the Somerset port of Watchet.[1] A regular visitor to the canal, she was sadly wrecked in 1903. This lower mile of Cardiff's waterway, which had served as a floating harbour for the town since 1798, continued to be an intimate place of family shipowning captains, seamen, boatmen, lockkeepers, publicans, hobblers[2] and shopkeepers – and, of course, sailing ships and small steam vessels – well into the 1920s. Some extracts from surviving Sea Lock registers for 1915–29 will be looked at later, to throw light on the variety of business being brought into the canal by these vessels, both sail and steam.

Trade through the Sea Lock was small and continued to diminish as the 20th century progressed, the canal's use as a dock having become hopelessly outclassed by the superior facilities offered to shipping by the Bute Docks. The last of the Bute Docks to be built – the Queen Alexandra Dock, capable of berthing the largest ocean-going ships of the day – was opened by the Cardiff Railway Company in 1907. (See comparative table at top of next page.)

Trade card for Leyshon's steamers. While a succession of larger and larger docks were built at Cardiff for the main export and import trades, the canal continued to provide a useful service for trade within the Bristol Channel and with the Port of Bristol itself. Kyles *later went into the sand trade.* Bill Hamlin

Comparative Measurements of the Bute Docks and the Glamorganshire Canal

Name	Acreage	Dimensions (ft x ft)	Quayage (ft)	Depths on Cills
Glam Canal Float	12	5,500 x 100	11,000	18ft 9ins springs
Glam Canal Basin		485 x 130		8ft neaps
West Dock	18	4,000 x 200	8,800	28ft 8 1/2ins springs
West Basin	1 1/2	300 x 200		18ft 8 1/2ins neaps
West Lock		152 x 36		
East Dock	44	1,000 x 300	9,360	31ft 8 1/2ins springs
East Basin	2 1/4	380 x 250		21ft 8 1/2ins neaps
East Lock		220 x 55		
		200 x 49		
Roath Dock	33 1/2	2,400 x 600	7,520	35ft 9ins springs
Roath Basin	12	1,000 x 550	2,700	25ft 9ins neaps
Roath Lock	1 1/2	350 x 80		
		600 x 80		
Queen Alexandra Dock	42	2,600 x 650	7,460	42ft springs
Queen Alexandra Lock	2 1/2	700 x 160		32ft neaps
TOTAL	169 1/4		45,840	

Source: John Ballinger Cardiff: An Illustrated Handbook, *Cardiff 1896, p45*

The canal may have been eclipsed but it was certainly not dead and we find that the trade through the Sea Lock had begun to follow a trend where imports through the lock exceeded exports – in 1905 by more than three times the export figure. The canal was not alone because, by 1896, the West Dock only dealt with 8 per cent of Cardiff's coal shipments but by 1911 was receiving nearly 60 per cent of the port's imports.[3] The canal was still dealing with consignments of foodstuffs via the Bute Docks and the communicating Junction Canal. This was a longstanding traffic, with strong traditional connections with Bristol, which could be traced back to the earliest days of Cardiff as a river port. The Sea Lock also found useful work to do in accommodating the Cardiff builders' merchants and provided a base and wharves for the sand dredgers engaged in the Bristol Channel sand trade.

Coal and Patent Fuel

The last significant exports of coal through the Sea Lock had been in the 1870s, in vessels loaded in the Taff Vale Railway's dock on the canal. By 1905, the limited tonnages in general trade through the Sea Lock are unlikely to have included any movements of coal. However, the Patent Fuel trade, using canal boats from Maindy through central Cardiff to the Junction Canal and the Bute Docks, is shown to be surprisingly vibrant. This busy traffic through the top part of the canal was generated by some 80 canal boats in a trade which was to reach a peak of performance in 1913. In that year, in one period of 16 1/2 hours, the two patent fuel works sent 208 boats loaded and empty through the canal between Maindy and the Bute Docks – an outstanding achievement in horse boating and in water conservation.[4] The Patent Fuel trade on the canal gradually declined after 1913 and came to an end in 1928, both the remaining canal-based fuel works closing as a joint result of the post-war slump in shipping and oil fuel taking over from coal worldwide as a fuel.

Tonnage figures for canal borne Patent Fuel passing to the Bute Docks for export are available for 1905 and are given in the table below, with the inward and outward tonnages for all classes of merchandise through the Sea Lock.[5] However, against the formidable Bute Docks coal exports of 7 1/4 million tons in the same year, which we include for comparison, the Glamorganshire Canal's performance appears insignificant.

Bute Docks	Tons
Export of coal through docks	7,294,020
Glamorganshire Canal	**Tons**
Imports through Sea Lock (all classes)	49,402
Exports through Sea Lock (all classes)	14,226
Patent Fuel to East & West Bute Docks	180,101

The Sea Lock Pound in 1901

Although the Sea Lock pound had originally been considered to extend from Crockherbtown Lock to the Sea Lock, for all practical maritime purposes its beginning was at Custom House Bridge in Cardiff, at the lower end of St Mary Street. Of course, with the construction of New Lock in 1886 during the Bute regime, the pound had become divided into two. Just below the Custom House Bridge, where the GCC had its West Wharf and warehouses, the canal had been bridged by the South Wales Railway in 1850, which later became part of the GWR. The railway was to have a marked effect on Cardiff, physically and culturally isolating Cardiff's dockland from the rest of the town for 150 years; only in recent years is

The Sea Lock inner gates and shipping in the basin of the Glamorganshire Canal in the 1880s. Note, at this time the gates had no balance beams and relied on windlasses (out of picture); the enclosed mechanisms on both ground and gates are for lifting the paddles to allow water into the lock. On the left, behind the tree, is the old lockkeeper's house of the 1790s, which had been extended in the 1820s to accommodate the lockkeeper and his two assistants. CCL collection

this barrier breaking down.

The 25 inch Ordnance Survey of 1901 informs us of numerous changes in the occupation of the wharves since the days of O'Rourke's map of 1849. Remarkably, the shape of the canal had remained unchanged since 1798, a result of Lord Bute's implacable opposition to the canal company's efforts to enlarge and improve the waterway and make it more attractive to shipping

There were timber importers leasing wharves on both sides of the canal's upper end, whilst on the east side the two small dockyards with dry docks remained. Chaddock's dock, the upper of the two dockyards and formerly Jenkins' dock, is shown at the southwest corner of Loudon Square. It does not appear on more modern maps and is assumed to have been closed and filled in by the First World War. Thomas Hodge's (formerly Tredwen's) dry dock, a little to the south of Chaddock's, had a longer life. At 140 feet long, $27^1/_2$ feet wide and 11 feet deep, the main dock had a second dock radiating from a common entrance marked by a drawbridge in the towpath. Boats had to enter and leave the docks

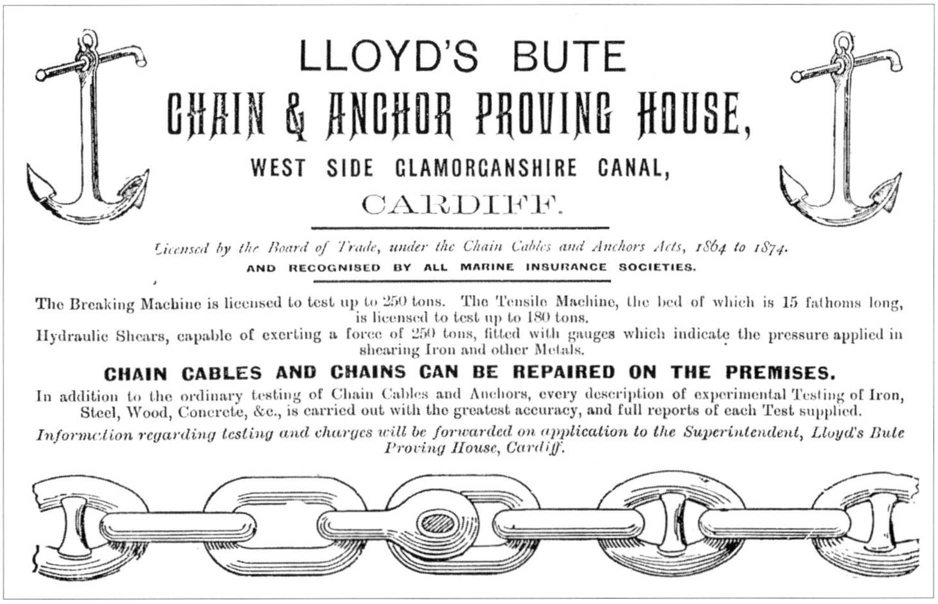

LLOYD'S BUTE

CHAIN & ANCHOR PROVING HOUSE,

WEST SIDE GLAMORGANSHIRE CANAL,

CARDIFF.

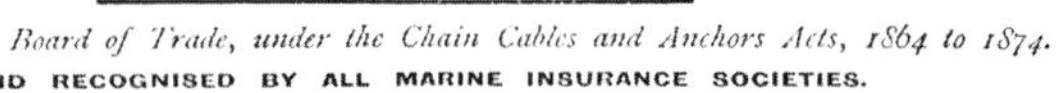

Licensed by the Board of Trade, under the Chain Cables and Anchors Acts, 1864 to 1874.

AND RECOGNISED BY ALL MARINE INSURANCE SOCIETIES.

The Breaking Machine is licensed to test up to 250 tons. The Tensile Machine, the bed of which is 15 fathoms long, is licensed to test up to 180 tons.

Hydraulic Shears, capable of exerting a force of 250 tons, fitted with gauges which indicate the pressure applied in shearing Iron and other Metals.

CHAIN CABLES AND CHAINS CAN BE REPAIRED ON THE PREMISES.

In addition to the ordinary testing of Chain Cables and Anchors, every description of experimental Testing of Iron, Steel, Wood, Concrete, &c., is carried out with the greatest accuracy, and full reports of each Test supplied.

Information regarding testing and charges will be forwarded on application to the Superintendent, Lloyd's Bute Proving House, Cardiff.

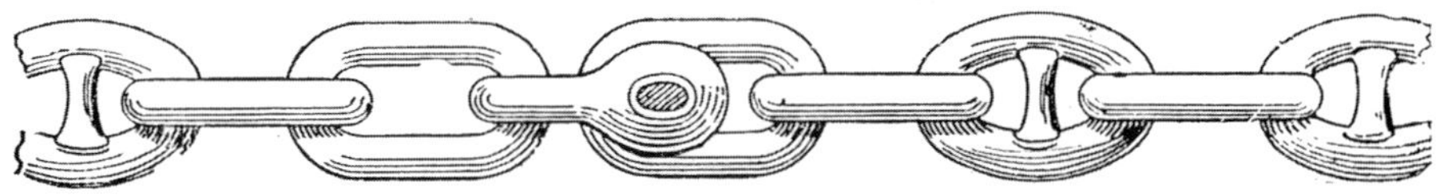

Advertisement for Lloyds proving house, from the Cardiff Tide Tables & Almanack, *1900.*

Above: *Brown Lenox chain cable and attachments at the Lloyds Bute chain and anchor testing wharf in 1912. They are destined for the Argentine battleships* Moreno *and* Rivadavia, *and are being admired by representatives of the Argentine government, the American builders of the vessels and J.B. Richardson, managing director of Brown Lenox. The canal boats on the left would have brought the chain down the canal from the Ynysangharad Works. The crane is standing on the turntable; the track on the inside, nearest the sheds, is part of the Glamorganshire Canal Railway.*

H.J.B.Wills photo, Stephen K.Jones collection

These two photographs were taken on the same occasion, with the view ***above*** *illustrating the steam crane in more detail, whilst that on the* ***right*** *is of the Admiralty anchors which were also bound for the Argentinan vessels.*

Both ILW collection

The first Spillers flour mill in the mid 1860s, with a horse-drawn wagon-load of sacks of flour waiting to depart. The photograph is taken from the road bridge over the Junction Canal and is looking south along Collingdon Road. The railway wagon is standing at the end of the Bute Dock Company's line serving the Public Wharf on the west side of West Dock. The dress of the little group in the centre by the bridge parapet are indicative of the early date of this photograph. Joseph Collings photos, CCL collection

from the 'upstream' direction. Still known after the Second World War as Hodge's Dock and shown as disused on the 1941 OS map, it was observed carrying out repairs to small craft until about 1947.

Following the canal's east bank in the direction of the Sea Lock, the 1901 map marks the TVR dock and West Yard, the James Street swing bridge and the Trinity House buoy store, which was for many years the regular mooring for the Bristol Channel pilot boats.

Making use of railway connections with the GWR's Riverside Branch, a number of heavier industries were established along the canal's west bank and Dumballs Road. Amongst those appearing on the 1901 OS were Lloyds Bute Testing House, to which anchors and ships cables were brought by canal boat, notably from Brown Lenox of Pontypridd. The Testing House had been established on the west bank of the canal in 1865. Also on this west side, the canal served an asphalt works, a tin works and a branch of the Crown Patent Fuel establishment. One small basin – the Plymouth Dock – was still in existence in 1950, a long-lived remnant of Hill's Plymouth Iron Company and the great days of the iron trade. Opposite the TVR Little Dock, on the bend in the River Taff, the large buildings and yards of the Bute Shipbuilding & Engineering Works are prominent. Marked 'disused' on the 1901 map, they point to an earlier phase in industrial history. Established in 1864 by Norman Scott Russell, son of the builder of Brunel's *Great Eastern*, the yard seems only to have built one ship (the *Mallorca*) before it was sold to Maudslay & Son, who operated it for a short time from 1869. Then, after a period of lying idle, in 1883 it became the Bute Shipbuilding & Engineering Company Ltd. Here, in 1889, was launched the SS *Cardiff Castle,* one of the last vessels to be built in Cardiff. She was of 1,965 tons gross register, with a length of 265ft 4ins and beam of 36ft 2ins. This yard was situated below the site of Thomas Powell's canal basin and his coal staiths on the bank of the Taff. All the ships were launched into the river and the *Cardiff Castle* had the misfortune to strike Clarence Road Bridge, which was under construction at the time.[6]

Another view of Spillers mill at the head of the Bute West Dock during building operations on the mill in the 1860s. Two canal boats and a lighter are helping deliver building stone and remove rubble. On the right is the Junction Canal, leading to the Glamorganshire Canal, by which Spillers delivered flour to its markets in the Taff Valley. Note also the timber floating in the dock and canal; this was prior to the building of the timber ponds.

Joseph Collings photo, CCL collection

A final view of Spiller's mill, taken from near the entrance to the then recently built East Junction Canal – which linked the new East Dock to the West Dock. This mill was destroyed by fire in 1882. Joseph Collings photos, CCL collection

The Canal Company as a Carrier

Just below the GWR bridge on West Canal Wharf was the GCC wharf and office, from which, in 1916, three loaded goods boats left for Pontypridd and four Down boats arrived in Cardiff empty, this arrangement alternating daily. There were three turns working during the week, with usually four boats on each turn. Around twelve GCC boats were available for the Pontypridd carrying work, which amounted to about 50 tons daily. All were horse boats loaded to a maximum of 16 tons, although frequently carrying less.[7] The Up traffic was in shop goods and provisions, mainly bagged flour for Treforest and the Pontypridd bakeries. There was no back traffic to Cardiff and boats returned empty.

When the GCC began carrying in 1887, flour, corn and meal for Aberdare, Merthyr and Pontypridd came into the canal by trow from Tewkesbury.[8] Later, it arrived in the West Dock from Avonmouth but flour was also loaded from Spiller's Mills at the top of the West Dock. Spillers & Browne were established there in 1854 and their steam mill turned out 1,200 sacks of flour a week. The firm had originated with Joel Spiller at Bridgwater in 1838, where he later took Samuel W. Browne as partner, in 1852. Their Cardiff mill, built in 1854 and rebuilt in the 1860s, was destroyed by fire in 1882, forcing the partnership to become a limited company before they rebuilt and extended the mill at a cost of £311,000. In 1890, the firm amalgamated with William Baker & Son (Bristol) to become Spillers & Bakers Ltd, building a second mill in the East Dock costing £98,477. By 1898, Cardiff had become the fourth largest port in the UK for importing grain and flour, and in the early years of the 20th century Spillers & Bakers owned their own steamers. At this time J. Hibbert & Co and James Tucker Ltd, both corn merchants, were also operating in the West Dock and, as Cardiff Milling Company Ltd, later moved to the East Dock. Using the junction and communication canals from the East and West docks, canal boats were able to deliver bagged flour to the valleys bakeries.[9]

The canal company's carrying was in the hands of a small number of land-based boating families, whose male members purchased a contract and provided horse haulage, boatman and a mate. In return, the company provided the boat and paid a weekly wage. The names of Thatcher (Rhydyfelin), Bladen (Llandaff) and Frazer (Treble Locks) occur repeatedly on GCC loading bills and boat passes over a period of nearly fifty years. In 1924, only around 30 tons in two boats daily were being loaded for Pontypridd[10] and in 1942, Tom Frazer and the Bladens were the only boatmen left. They left West Wharf on alternate days with

This photograph of the inner Sea Lock was taken in 1891, after balance beams have been re-introduced on the gates. Just inside the basin, the Elizabeth Ann *of Bridgwater is unloading into the Eleanor Street stores. Built in 1853, this West Country trading ketch had been lengthened in 1866. The Alma Hotel and the Torbay Hotel, on opposite corners of Margaret Street and Eleanor Place, are visible and, at the far end of Margaret Street, are the sheds of the Mount Stuart dry dock (now, 2004, the site of Techniquest). Sixty years earlier, this area was the site of the coal wharves for all the major colliery proprietors who shipped from Cardiff.*

G.H. Wills photo, CCL collection

The earlier cast iron East Wharf Bridge, which was replaced in 1903. The photograph would appear to have been taken as work to replace it was in progress, as the stonework on the left looks new and the buttress does not fit with the rest of the bridge. SR collection

only 6 or 7 tons on board, so badly silted had the canal become.[11] Final closure was on 25 May of that year, due to a breach in the canal bank at Nantgarw but when the end of the canal company's carrying came that day, it made no commercial impact at all.

The Building Trade

The expansion of Cardiff as a port and commercial centre continued apace into the 20th century and assured useful business for the building trade. Probably before 1900, trading on the East Canal Wharf had been discontinued and the quays tidied up and railed off from the street. Photographs of the 1905-10 period show the East Wharf had become a collecting point for empty Patent Fuel boats, waiting to be returned to the Maindy and Blackweir fuel works. The East Wharf had formerly been the base for Watson & Co's two timber yards of 1826, John Bland's timber yard (successor to J.J. Grant & Co[12] on the north bank of the Junction Canal) and for one of the more enduring names in the Cardiff builders merchant trade – Sessions & Sons; the founder, Jesse Sessions, had come to the canal in 1857, having established his main business in Gloucester in 1838.[13] Sessions had two wharves on the west side of the Sea Lock pound in the 1920s. These dealt with roofing slate, cement, marble, slate slabs and timber goods. Their sand wharf, later occupied by J. & R. Griffiths, lay below the swing bridge at Harrowby Street. Another merchant, T.G. Williams, had a yard close to the canal company's own West Wharf, receiving bricks and earthenware pipes from Bridgwater sailing vessels and slate by sea from North Wales – though it is doubtful if any such craft were seen trading into the canal after 1920, having completely lost out to rail competition. It should be remembered that all the firms leasing west side wharves were linked to the GWR over the sidings of the Glamorganshire Canal Company's own railway of 1883.

Sand

Trading in sand may be as old as the Sea Lock pound itself and it is probable that flat bottomed sailing vessels such as Severn trows were brought up on to Glamorgan beaches, loaded with sand as the beach dried out and floated off again on the rising tide. Recalling the West Bute Dock in the 1860s, S.W. Allen writes of another origin of the trade:

> *'At that time nearly all the ships entering the port of Cardiff were ballasted with sand or gravel, and this was generally heaped up on large mounds at the head of the West Bute*

dock, and from which the sand merchants obtained their supplies.'[14]

One particular vessel in the sand trade, affectionately recorded by Allen, was the diminutive sand suction dredger *Britannia*:

> "*Visitors to the lower end of the Glamorganshire Canal can occasionally see a queer little craft, with bow and stern very much alike.....The great City Hall and the Law Courts of Cardiff [1906], owe much to this little old friend of the writer. Her name is the* Britannia.'[15]

The canal had always suffered from the disadvantage of its sea exit – the Sea Lock itself being too far up a rather tortuous tidal pill or creek on the Taff that dried out at low tide. The average high tide gave a depth of only 12-14 feet of water over the sill and at neap tides the depth could be as low as 5 feet. Nevertheless, in the 1920s the Sea Lock pound saw increasing use by sand and gravel businesses, which were established at the west side wharves close to Harrowby Street and the James Street swing bridge. In view of the restrictive measurements of the Sea Lock – 131 feet 10 inches from the breast wall to the mitre of the lower gates and a width of 28 feet 9 inches reducing to 24 feet 5 inches at the bottom[16] – the dimensions of the sand traders' steamers were critical, as the firm of F. Bowles & Son Ltd, owners of the *Deloraine*, were to find out in 1944 when the new owners of the canal, the Cardiff Corporation served Messrs Bowles a ban on all movements through the Sea Lock of this dredger. The story of the *Deloraine* case will be taken up later on.

Bill Hamlin of Cardiff, whose dockland boyhood revolved around the Sea Lock pound and the family sand business of Sandridge & Co, passed on to us a number of reminiscences of life and work in this part of Cardiff in the 1920s and 30s.

The family firm purchased the small coaster *Kyles* in 1921 and converted her to a sand suction dredger, the sand and gravel trade in the Bristol Channel having started some years earlier. Based in the Glamorganshire Canal, the *Kyles* worked out of the Sea Lock to shoals in the Bristol Channel, pumping sand and gravel at the East and West One Fathom buoys and at grounds near the island of Flat Holm. She was discharged by grab at the shore terminal, which was usually the canal but could be the West Dock, Newport, Bristol or Bridgwater. In a remarkable career dating from her launching at Paisley in 1872, the *Kyles*, with her many associations with the Glamorganshre Canal, now enjoys honourable retirement in preservation back on the Clyde in Scotland.[17]

Apart from his 1920s memories of life with the *Kyles*, Bill Hamlin recalled the hills of sand on the Sandridge Co's wharf and the huge attraction they proved to the dockland children of the time, as soon as work stopped for the weekend. There was no need to go to the beach at Barry Island. Excitement of a different kind surrounded the passage of a sand vessel through the James Street swing bridge, with gates closing and warning bells ringing on the control tower. A sea-going ship passing so close to the street was a continuing source of wonder, especially if you were not used to ships and the sea. Sand dredger movements were linked to times of high tides in the Taff and the closure of the bridge at evening rush hour train times could prove irritating to office workers, likely to miss their train home from Clarence Road Station.

The 1903 East Wharf Bridge as seen in 1969, crossing the entrance to the filled-in Junction Canal to the West Dock. The vigorous mediaeval design of the cast iron parapet is one of several that were provided by Cardiff Corporation for canal bridge widenings in the city and the commemorative plaque is a mark of civic pride.

David Thomas photo, 8 April 1969

Perhaps the most remarkable fact about Kyles, *a small steam suction dredger based in the Sea Lock pound in the 1920s and 30s, and seen here in the River Avon in 1947, is her survival. Built at Paisley as a steam coaster in 1872, the vessel, as we write, is now 132 years old and, although much altered in appearance over the decades, back on the Clyde in retirement as a floating exhibit at Clydebuilt, the Scottish Maritime Museum on the river bank at Braehead, Glasgow. Having passed through the ownership of various merchants, traders and contractors, both in Scotland and England,* Kyles *was sold in 1901 to the Pontypridd corn merchant and grocer, J. Leyshon, who operated from the east wharf at Canal Parade, Cardiff.* Kyles *then joined Leyshon's other vessel,* St Davids, *in maintaining a daily goods service between Cardiff and Welsh Back, Bristol. After yet more changes of ownership,* Kyles *was bought by George John Hamlin of Cardiff in 1921 and converted to a sand suction dredger. In this form, she worked for the family firm of Sandridge & Co (Hugh Hamlin, manager) bringing in Bristol Channel dredged sand to the firm's canal wharf at Harrowby Street and also making trips up the Avon to the Port of Bristol. The vessel was out of use and laid up in the Glamorganshire Canal between 1939 and 1942, Sandridge & Co having acquired* Catherine Ethel *(formerly* Mistley*) in 1939, converting her to a sand suction vessel to replace* Kyles. *Two owners later, in 1960,* Kyles *was converted to a tanker and it is in this form that the updated veteran, diesel engined since 1953, survives in preservation today. Throughout her life, the little vessel has never changed her name. (John Curdy 'The* Kyles *Story' in* Ships Monthly, *April 1990).* Courtesy the Keen collection, Bristol City Museum & Art Gallery

Unloading sand at the Harrowby Street wharf was still quite primitive at first, Bill remembered. The firm relied on the casual labour of dock hobblers, who were called in to hand shovel sand into large iron buckets, which were swung ashore between the ship's hold and the wharf using the ship's own gear – a time consuming process. Later, an electric crane and grab speeded up the work. As a boy it was Bill's job to walk up Dumballs Road to present the GWR consignment note at the railway office – then a mere hut where the business of incoming and outward wagonloads at the canal sidings were dealt with. Not all rail and road consignments from Harrowby Street ended up in builders' yards; Bill recalled that Sandridge on one occasion supplied sand to Rolls Royce for their bowling greens. His verbal picture of the Glamorganshire Canal Company's office in the 1920s is worth recording:

> *'Monthly, I went to the Canal office on West Wharf to pay the dues and sign the* Kyles *in. That office was like going back to Dickens' time with the regulations on the wall and the heavy counter. Behind was a little man who sat at a high desk entering accounts in a ledger.'*

As for the other Cardiff importers and their ships, Sessions & Sons landed sand at Harrowby Street from their dredgers *Duke of Edinburgh*, *Manley*, *Bloodhound*, *Kendy* and *Lyndale* before moving to a new wharf in the West Bute Dock. Their place along the canalside was then leased by J. & R. Griffiths, whose terminal was over the years supplied by the little *Britannia*, *Isabel*, *Skary* and *Indium*. Meanwhile, above the swing bridge, Bowles had maintained their canal business with the *Thomand* (1919), *Alexandra* and *Tarv* (both from 1925), and *Deloraine* from 1928.

Ceres, one of John Davies' (D.W. Davies warehouse, Cardiff) boats, is seen here apparently discharging her cargo outside the Sea Lock without the need to enter the Glamorganshire Canal. Behind is the hulk of the Hamadryad, *which served as a seamen's hospital until a shore-based replacement was built nearby in 1902. The photograph dates from the 1880s.* CCL collection

Sea Lock Registers

From the 1930s until 1951, navigation of the Sea Lock pound became increasingly the province of the Bristol Channel sand trade and, at this point in the story, it makes a pleasant contrast to look back to the more colourful maritime years of steam and sail as they are revealed in the canal company's Sea Lock registers. Unfortunately, records survive only for 1915-29 and for 1950-51 but the variety of the vessels arriving in the canal – many of them of great character and full of history – is of considerable interest, whilst of equal interest is the merchandise they brought with them.[18]

Possibly the oldest of the traders was *Good Intent* of Bridgwater, coming into the canal from the River Parrett with bricks and tiles. She had been built at Plymouth in 1790. *Lucy* and *Frances* are recorded as arriving from Portmadoc with slates, either for T.G. Williams or Sessions, and *Bessie Clark* of Bideford brought in gravel, quite possibly loaded from shoals in the River Torridge. Also, the now preserved ketch *Garlandstone* (at Morwellham, on the River Tamar, close to where she was built) came into the canal with stone chippings. Amongst the visiting Severn trows were the Severn & Canal Co's *Taff*, unloading flour and *Brothers* of Gloucester (built at Brimscombe in 1847), with cargoes of wheat.

There were at least two West Country traders called *Enid* and the 'Enid *of Avonmouth with apples*' is most probably the steamer belonging to R. Burton & Sons. Another steamer, *Ceres*, is recorded in the Sea Lock register as carrying sugar loaded in Bristol. There was also *Moderator* with chains and the ketch *Julia* with explosives. In addition, the register records the pilot boats *Chimaera*, *Anita* and *Providence* entering the Sea Lock for repairs at Hodge's dry dock, as well as the tug *Earl*. In 1917, the steamer *Ethel* was in the canal with 40 tons of soda from Bristol. There is a possibility that this was connected with the 'British Oxygen Dissolved Acetylene Compressing station' which was built on the east side of the Sea Lock in 1916, for making acetylene gas. The gas was compressed into tubes for use in Cardiff's nearby ship repair yards, for metal cutting and welding. The process now uses the cheaper technology of propane gas. The acetylene station received direct supplies of calcium carbide out of the 'carbide boats' in the Sea Lock for many years, the lease eventually being given up in 1944.[19]

Finally, we must mention *Black Dwarf*, an ex- Clyde puffer in the ownership of William Jones of Lydney, which entered the Sea Lock pound on 28 and 31 May 1919 with cargoes of butter from Avonmouth.[20] *Black Dwarf* generally traded out of Lydney with coal or tinplate and had probably discharged such a cargo in Bristol first. Although butter at

When the Bute East Dock was opened in 1859 it included its own junction canal, linking it with the West Dock and providing a through route from the Glamorganshire Canal. This photograph was taken in 1968 and records the run-down and derelict area at the head of the East Dock, before the massive Cardiff Bay regeneration programme transformed these sites in the 1980s and 90s. The canal is seen looking east, with its exit into the East Dock in the distance where there was once a stop lock for regulating levels (its open gates can just be seen at the second narrows). On the right is Spillers & Bakers' biscuit factory of 1893 – today (2004) one of the few surviving original buildings in Cardiff's former dockland, having been converted into living accommodation. Straddling the canal are the remains of the multi-arched Bute Viaduct, which gave the Rhymney Railway's coal trains access at high level from Tyndall Street to the coal tips on the west side of the East Dock. Anyone wishing to learn more of the tangled complex of lines serving the various docks at Cardiff is recommended to study Track Layout Diagrams of the GWR and BR(WR), Sections 43A *and* 43B, *by R.A. Cooke. The Junction Canal, once so important to the Cardiff Patent Fuel trade, still functions as a feeder to the water areas of the former East Dock. It enters the dock in an area of prestigious waterfront redevelopment, now marketed under the name Atlantic Wharf.* David Thomas photo, 14 April 1968

this period in time was transported in wooden barrels, it is still an image which would make a modern day food standards inspector shudder.

Although by this time it was an export traffic connected with the Bute Docks rather than the canal, it is worth mentioning the Melingriffith Company's continuing use of the canal and part of the Sea Lock pound for their tinplate trade. For some years, the canal company's steam tug *Bute* was employed to bring tows of three or four boats down the canal, on to the Junction Canal and through to the docks, where their cargoes of tinplates were hoisted directly into waiting ships. These canal boats were specially fitted with covered hatches and the towing service probably continued through to the Great War. In 1919, *Bute* still remained the only self propelled vessel registered on the canal but in 1920 it was reported '*This boat has not been in use since the outbreak of war.*'[21]

A measure of the decline in the level of horse boating on the canal (the Patent Fuel boats short distances excepted) is indicated by the diminishing number of cabin boats on the Cardiff Inspector of Canal Boats' Register. From a peak of 59 boats in 1896, the number had decreased to 36 in 1901, to 19 in 1913, to 14 in 1920 and finally to 6 in 1942. The last of the independent bye-traders is believed to have given up boating by 1914.

The Timber Trade

Since construction of the East Bute Dock, there were two ponds lying between the East and West docks. The more southerly, covering 2³/₄ acres, was a reduced version of the original West Dock scouring reservoir, for supplying water to clear accumulated silt from the West Dock Basin and entrance channel. The northerly one, of 5¹/₄ acres, was used by the timber merchants as a float for

The bridge carrying Bute Street over the Junction Canal again, viewed from the opposite side also in December 1922. The lock was actually sited beneath the railway bridge by which the Taff Vale Railway's Cardiff & Merthyr line crossed over the canal on its way down to Bute Road Station, off to the right. As a single track solely used by passenger trains, this is the only line in the Cardiff Docks area still surviving today.
Bill Hamlin collection

There was a lock where the Junction Canal crossed under Bute Street. The lock was intended to keep the level of the Glamorganshire Canal above that of the West Dock but it had gates to maintain differential water levels in the opposite direction too. After Bute took over ownership of the canal, in 1886 a new lock (Lock 51) was put into the Sea Lock pound and this enabled the Junction Lock to be kept open permanently, to allow easy passage of timber between the timber floats and the docks. In this December 1922 photograph, looking westward from the Junction Lock, the stop gates are also shown. These worked automatically, in the event of a breach in the canal. Bill Hamlin collection

A later view of the lock on the Junction Canal, taken circa 1950. Stan Vickery photo, Neg No 29/35

The GCC West Wharf and the Great Western Railway bridges at the head of the mile-long Sea Lock pound, photographed in 1936 by Philip Oke. Company boat No 499, viewed almost broadside, demonstrates the lengthy hull of a 60 foot boat.
National Maritime Museum, Oliver Hill collection p74087

huge logs of imported timber, being joined to the East Dock by a culvert through which the logs were floated. Following the Marquess of Bute taking control of the Glamorganshire Canal Company in 1885, and as part of his plans for integrating the waterway into his dock facilities, two more floats or ponds were constructed to the west of the canal, one either side of Dumballs Road. These ponds were linked together by a bridge beneath Dumballs Road and to the Sea Lock pound by a bridge beneath the canal towpath.[22] Under the same powers, the canal and ponds were to be held at the same level as the water in the West Dock by the building of New Lock (No 51) in the canal's Sea Lock pound. This large wide lock, with its minimal rise and fall, divided the pound into an upper and lower level and was brought into use on 1 January 1887. The timber ponds covered some 15½ acres and 6¼ acres respectively and were opened for traffic on 31 October 1889. Pumps were installed on the River Taff bank to pump water into the Dumballs Road timber pond and so via the canal through to the West Junction Canal and the docks. The old timber float was filled in by the dock company in 1913. The two canalside timber floats were leased by Bute to the Great Western Railway from 1 January 1922, at a cost of £1,500 per annum for 99 years. As part of the terms of this lease, the Cardiff Pure Ice & Cold Storage Co had the right to extract up to 18,000,000 gallons per annum. During winter months, the firm returned 40,000,000 gallons to the ponds from a well on their premises.[23]

The Bute Docks were all supplied with water from the original West Dock feeder from the River Taff at Blackweir, surveyed by James Green in 1830. The Bute Docks (Transfer) Act of 1886, stipulated that the Marquess of Bute was to retain ownership of the weir and feeder, so the Bute Docks Company and later the Cardiff Railway Company had to pay Bute £1,112 10s per annum for its water. The maximum feeder capacity for a 24 hour period, according to tests taken immediately after cleansing it in 1919 and 1920, was 87,637,956 gallons and in the year 1934 was 89,400,000 gallons. With the successive construction of docks, the maintenance of water level, lockage water and the provision of 4,400,000 gallons of water to the Dowlais-Cardiff Iron & Steel Works, the supply from the timber pond pumps was welcome. The pumps remained in position until June 1938, when the larger timber pond was filled in. By that time, the problem of water was eased by the falling away of traffic in the West and East docks, particularly when the heavy Patent Fuel traffic ceased coming down the canal and through to the

*Cardiff Corporation was authorised, by its Act of 1887, to extend James Street as Clarence Road and cross the Taff to serve the new community of Grangetown. This also necessitated providing a bridge across the canal. James Street swing bridge was supplied by Messrs A. Handyside & Co of Derby. (*The Engineer*, 7 Aug 1891, pp105-7.) New electrical equipment was installed in 1920 by Sir William Arrol & Co and the bridge was then operated from the tall signal box, seen here in 1957, as a Cardiff trolleybus crosses the abandoned canal. The bridge had a footpath on both sides. The purpose of the upright steel extensions on the girders is not clear but may relate to the introduction of the trolleybus service after the bridge had been closed permanently. Maintenance of a continuous electrical connection across the swing bridge was a difficulty and was another reason that the Corporation were keen on its closure. Today, the bridge is commemorated in some community sculpture on the site of the crossing.* ILW photo 1 Aug 1957, neg 1848

West Dock. Spillers too moved from the West and East docks to Roath Dock in 1933.[24]

Timber importers had for the most part moved their operation to the Bute Docks by the beginning of the 20th century, where there was access for modern shipping and up-to-date discharge and rail facilities. The movement of pitwood inland to the Aberdare Canal had faded by 1890 and so had deliveries of timber to local merchants in the mining valleys. Independent owner boatmen had lost this business to the railways. Timber wharves had not entirely disappeared from the Sea Lock pound, however, and the firm of John Bland was a strong presence on the west canal bank in the 1930s, with yards, sawmills and a creosote works near the timber pond served by canal, by road and by the Glamorganshire Canal's railway. Here, too, was the firm of Alexander & Co. Other importers similarly placed were Sessions & Sons, Meggitt & Jones Ltd of 1884 (who in 1924 had taken over Watson & Co), Robinson David and Denny, Mott & Dickson.

By 1944, Robinson David seem to have been the only users of Lock 51 and in November 1944, a lockage charge of 4 shillings was payable for timber. 'Lock Float' was perceived by the lockkeepers to take a very long time to fill and so came to be known also as 'Lock Patience'. Three men were required to be on duty to operate the lock – two canal men and one from the GWR. The 20th century brought new and more convenient methods of importing and handling timber and the need for timber ponds faded. However, Robinson David, operating yards in the West Bute Dock, were still floating timber in the canal in 1949-50, on payment of a rental to Cardiff Corporation of £3 per week.[25]

Cardiff Corporation Takes Over

As the clouds of war gathered over Cardiff in 1939, the story of the Glamorganshire Canal moved a step closer towards its end. As far as the Sea Lock pound was concerned, the great finale would be delayed by the

West Wharf at the turn of the century, with a Bridgwater ketch and GCC boat No 491 (formerly owned by John Davies, who traded to Bristol with the Ceres, Flora Belle *and* Bee*) lying at T.G. Williams' wharf, the upper limit of navigation for sea-going vessels. The ketch has probably brought in a consignment of bricks, tiles and pipes from Bridgwater on the River Parrett. Several of the Glamorganshire Canal Company's own railway wagons can be seen standing in the siding behind the yard wall. Views of them are extremely rare; they appear to be lettered* 'G. CANAL CO'*, although the bottom half of the wagons is not visible. The centre one has an end door. This large photograph used to hang in the offices of this builders merchant.* Bill Hamlin collection

war and by legal problems of its aftermath. The event that precipitated change was a small natural disaster – the collapse of the canal bank at Ty Sidra, Nantgarw, on 25 May 1942,[26] after a period of heavy rain – and not reported in the media because of wartime security. Civil engineers were called in to report on how the breach could be repaired but no restoration work was done.[27] The Nantgarw slip marked the end of canal carrying between Cardiff and Pontypridd, and for a short period the canal company fulfilled its obligations to Pontypridd customers by delivering bagged flour by road.[28]

The opportunity to acquire the canal undertaking was not lost on the City of Cardiff and in April 1943, it was agreed to purchase the canal from the GCC for £44,000[29] – an extraordinarily good bargain for the corporation and its ratepayers. The purchase secured for Cardiff Corporation the whole of the waterway between the Sea Lock and Abercynon, which also included the valuable lands in the town and the whole of the lands and properties beyond. The exception was the length of canal in Cardiff from Kingsway to Blackweir, sandwiched between North Road and the Castle grounds, which was to be sold for £2,000 to Mountjoy, the company set up to manage the former property of the Marquess of Bute. That portion of the canal was filled in and is used to this day as a linear car park for the city. The authorising Cardiff Corporation Act of 1943 had received the Royal Assent on 5 August that year and the canal was vested in the Corporation on 1 January 1944. Under the powers of the Act, the GCC carrying business was closed down, the Cardiff-Pontypridd boats, as we have seen, having ceased to operate in May 1942. However, a clause in this wartime Act would cause the canal's new owners considerable frustration in the years to come and result in the Sea Lock pound remaining in active operation by the sand traders until 1951.

During 1943, Cardiff Corporation set the stage to begin realising the potential of its property for development. It looked at the Sea Lock pound and found it had purchased a working harbour. Anxious to re-use or sell its assets without delay the City Council was far from enthusiastic about running a decrepit and loss-making canal and it was examining ways of ridding itself of responsibility. An early move in that year was to try to remove the sand traders and in August, J. & R. Griffiths and Sandridge were given 12 months notice to withdraw their businesses from the canal.[30]

This action by the Corporation seems to have prompted a letter from the Ministry of War Transport:[31]

> '*4 November 1943*
> *I am directed by the Minister of War Transport to*

This aerial view was taken in 1951, the last year of the canal, and shows the whole of the Sea Lock pound from the wharf to the lock gates. It can be seen that the canal is totally devoid of boats. The sand wharves of Bowles and Griffiths are visible either side of the James Street swing bridge and it is also clear from this photograph that the safety gates alongside the New Sea Lock Hotel have been removed from the narrows. Had the gates been in place and operational when Catherine Ethel *was entering the lock from the sea on 5 December 1951, then only the lower basin would have been emptied of water, rather than the whole canal. These safety gates had been installed in 1872 but seem to have been removed by the 1930s. There is much else of interest to be seen in this view. The road to Grangetown, having passed over the swing bridge, becomes Clarence Road, then crosses the River Taff on Clarence Road swing bridge. Grangetown itself occupies the top left corner of th photograph. Almost the whole of the ex-GWR Riverside Branch can also be seen. Clarence Road station can be made out, by the road between the two bridges, with a passenger train in the charge of one of the ubiquitous 0-6-2 tanks rounding the final curve on the approach to the station. The six coaches of the train gives an indication that the branch was still well used at this date. Towards the centre top of the picture, a similar length north-bound train can be seen approaching Cardiff Riverside Station, which was amalgamated with Cardiff General Station, alongside it on the main line, in 1940. The massive engineering works of E. Curran & Co Ltd has expanded onto the area of land between the branch and the River Taff since the 1930s. The works was partly built on land reclaimed from the timber pond. The company, established by Edward Curran, began with the manufacture of reverbatory furnaces in 1909, later graduating into heavy engineering and also enamelled ware. Much of the works was established during the Second World War. Following the cessation of hositilities, E. Curran & Co Ltd were wound up in 1947 but a new company, E. Curran Engineering Ltd, was formed to carry on operations on the site in 1948. Much of the Glamorganshire Canal Railway system can also be seen in this view, with the Corporation Siding which formed the southern terminus of the line visible bottom left. Note also the second siding here, alongside the canal and running to a shed partly hidden beneath some trees. This was the later engine shed for housing the railway's locomotive.* WIMM collection

***Above:** Bowles Wharf, above the James Street swing bridge and looking seawards, in April 1943.* CCL collection

***Left:** The sand wharves of Sandridge & Co (left) and J. & R. Griffiths (right) below the James Street bridge, also taken for the 1943 survey by Cardiff Corporation. Spot the barrage balloon.* CCL collection

***Below:** The two sand wharves as seen from Harrowby Street.* CCL collection

Leyshon's steamer St Davids *(featured on their trade card illustrated on page 291) unloading hemp rope at J. Ford's marine stores in 1915. In the foreground is the windlass for opening the inner Sea Lock gates. Ford had taken on this stores and adjoining premises in 1906, from John Wesley Hambly and John Pomeroy Hambly, who had a boat building and repairing yard close to James Street from 1887 and had planned to move closer to the Sea Lock.* (GRO B/C GCa 4/157, 108/1, 108/2, 169 and 171; GCC minute book 23 June 1887 and 12 Jan 1889)

SR collection

A Newport-bound Great Western Railway express can be seen leaving Cardiff General station, bottom left of this circa 1930 aerial photograph, and is about to cross the canal. Although the canal wharf is shown, prominent on this wet day are the gas works gasholder and the sheds of Robinson David's timber yard, in a line alongside the dock feeder where the rails of the Taff Vale Railway diverge on their way to the coal tips at the Bute West Dock (off picture to the right). SR collection

refer to the Cardiff Corporation Act 1943 and to say that in accordance with his powers under Section 27 of that Act the Minister requires your Corporation on and after 1 Jan 1944 to keep open and navigable until the expiration of six months after the termination of the war period that part of the Glamorganshire Canal between Crockherbtown Lock at Queen Street and the Lock giving access to the Bristol Channel.'

The letter made it clear to the City Council that it could not legally close the canal '*until six months after the war period*' and so the Corporation's plans to remove the traders and eliminate the Sea Lock pound were, theoretically, put on hold. In 1943, no-one could have predicted that the end of the war would come on 8 May 1945 and perhaps it was a surprise to the City Fathers to learn that *'the termination of the War Period'* referred to in the Act carried the meaning '*termination of the War Emergency*' – another amorphous date even further into the future. It would in fact be another seven years to the end of the War Emergency (8 October 1950) and another six months after that (5 April 1951) before any notices could be served on the sand traders. Meanwhile, in the Sea Lock pound itself, life went on much as before. In 1939, at his wharf next to the New Sea Lock Hotel in Harrowby Street, Hugh Hamlin of the Sandridge Co had purchased the *Catherine Ethel*, a small steam coaster which he had converted for work as a sand suction vessel to replace *Kyles*. Formerly called *Mistley* and owned by W.H. Muller for trading between London and Paris, she had been built in 1906.[32] As we shall see, *Catherine Ethel* would, in a few years time, be involved in a drama that would bring the whole history of the Glamorganshire Canal to an end.

In 1943 meanwhile, managerial control of the canal had passed to the City Treasurer, whilst the City Engineer had taken responsibility for maintenance of the waterway from Market Street, Tongwynlais to Abercynon. In July, the Corporation had set up a canal sub committee to be responsible for the canal's affairs and particularly to negotiate agreements with traders. Ivor Llewelyn, the canal's last manager, was re-engaged for twelve months at a salary of £425 and the old company Sea Lock keepers, C. Hunt, J. Woolacott and R. Price, were similarly re-engaged on a temporary basis. The company's six cabin boats lying idle at the Cambrian Yard, Gabalfa were offered for sale, together with any machinery at the yard not required by the City Engineer. The Engineer's attention was soon turned to the dangerous state of the western Sea Lock top gate. The lock was closed for repairs, which were estimated to cost the City £1,900, plus £350 spent isolating the pound by stanking across the old stop gate narrows.[33]

On 1 January 1944, the day the Glamorganshire Canal was vested in the City of Cardiff, the Lord Mayor, Alderman Frederick Jones, along with the Town Clerk, S. Tapper Jones, and members of the City Council, donned overcoats and turned up on the West Wharf to array themselves around the steam locomotive *Delwyn* for a commemorative photograph to mark the occasion. On the one side they were joined by Ivor Llewelyn and his canal representatives and on the other side by Robinson David's canal boat and boatman. A canal company boat was intended to be present but had had to turn back at Queen Street when it was found that Crockherbtown Lock had become impassable. A splendid photograph was nevertheless taken and it was minuted that a framed copy should be hung in a corridor of the City Hall. A small event symbolic of the transfer was the order to remove the canal offices on West Wharf and install them in more prestigious accommodation in the City Hall. The Corporation's intention with regard to maintenance of its boats and the canal locks was clear to all, with its decision to terminate the tenancy of Cambrian Yard. It was also resolved to lower the water level in the canal north of Tongwynlais and to terminate the tenancy of land on which the now redundant Glan y Llyn reservoir lay. As a gesture to recreation, the Corporation decided to allow fishing in what was left of the canal, the Bute Angling Club to pay one guinea per annum for the privilege. Canoeing would be strictly prohibited.[34]

The *Deloraine* case

Throughout the long history of the Glamorganshire Canal, there is ample evidence that the canal company was seldom free from dispute and litigation, involving itself and its freighters. In 1944, this tradition seemed as alive as ever when Cardiff Corporation became involved in legal action brought against it by the sand trader F. Bowles & Son, owners of the steam sand dredger *Deloraine*. Action had been triggered by the City Engineer's report to the canal committee of the relative dimensions of the *Deloraine* and his decision – upheld by the committee – that the ship would '*not in future be permitted to use the Sea Lock*.'[35]

The response of Bowles & Son took the form of a Writ of Summons served on the Town Clerk, claiming a declaration that they were entitled to navigate the Sea Lock of the Glamorganshire Canal with their steamer *Deloraine* and an injunction restraining the Corporation from

On 1 January 1944, the canal and its railway were vested in the Cardiff Corporation for the sum of £44,000. On that day, members of Cardiff City Council and the Bute Estate pose for official photographs at West Canal Wharf. They include Ald. Frederick Jones, Lord Mayor of Cardiff, and Henry Morgan of the Bute Estate. The locomotive is Delwyn *but the boat is a lighter from the timber merchants, Robinson David – canal boats could no longer reach the Sea Lock pound because of debris in Crockherbtown Lock.* ILW collection

Robinson David's timber yard, Herbert Street. The lighter was used for moving cut timber to and from the canal, the Bute Docks and the timber yards. It is not so heavily built as the boat in the next picture. This particular yard lay on the dock feeder at the northern end of the West Dock, near to where John Batchelor had his ship yard from 1850 to 1857. WIMM collection

prohibiting such navigation.

The matter of the restriction of trade in 1944 was finally settled after a four day hearing in the King's Bench Division, before Mr Justice Lynskey, on 24 January 1947. In evidence it was stated that *Deloraine* had passed through the Sea Lock in and out at least 2,200 times between 1928 and October 1944. The Act of 1796 Sect 53 stated that:

> '*All persons shall have free liberty to use ... and also navigate upon the said Canal with any such ship, boats or other vessels as the locks would permit.*'

Citing the notice the Ministry of War Transport had served on the Corporation in November 1943, his Lordship noted that the Order in Council ending the emergency had not yet been made and therefore the provision of the Act of 1796 remained in force. He was satisfied that the *Deloraine* was a vessel which the Sea Lock would permit to navigate upon the canal. If the locks did not prevent the navigation of any particular vessel it seemed to him that they permitted it. The Judge granted Messrs Bowles a declaration that they were entitled to navigate the canal with the *Deloraine* but thought this was not a case for an injunction. Bowles were awarded costs and damages and the Corporation did not appeal.[36] Messsrs Bowles had used a new wharf at the Ferry Road on the River Taff as an alternative to their wharf on the canal. Settlement with access to the wharf from Avondale Road was for £31,000.

A Strategic Swing Bridge

In taking over the Glamorganshire Canal in 1944, the City of Cardiff's motive had not been to promote the life of a working waterway and it is certain that the story of the sand importers in the Sea Lock pound, and of the canal itself, would have ended in 1944 if Cardiff Corporation had been able to have its way.

Unfortunately for the new owners, as the Bowles case had proved, the legal provisions of the 1790 and 1796 Acts had upheld the right of navigation through the Sea Lock and the 1943 Act had delayed the Sea Lock's destruction. However, in 1945 in a parallel move calculated to curtail use of the Sea Lock and the James Street swing bridge, the Corporation, probably illegally, prohibited the passage of small boats through the lock and minuted a resolution:[37]

> '*... that the Sea Lock be not operated solely to permit passage*

In 1936, photographer and researcher Philip Oke visited the Sea Lock pound, to record canal craft on behalf of Commander H.O. Hill of the Society for Nautical Research. This photograph is of the unmarked Robinson David & Co lighter moored at the timber firm's yard on the west side of the canal, below the timber float at Dumballs Road. Across the canal to the east is Peel Street, with St Mary's Church just visible above the end of the stone-built shed. Although this craft is very similar in design to the conventional 60 foot Glamorganshire Canal boat, it was much more heavily built in order to withstand the rigours of loading and carrying massive uncut logs between the Bute Docks, the Sea Lock pound and Robinson David's sawmills. It has four wrought iron strengthening knees on each side. Notably, too, this boat is double-ended; it has no rudder and movement was by some form of towing or shafting from the bank. National Maritime Museum, Oliver Hill collection p74089

of any boat not classified in any Register of Shipping.'

In June the following year, 1946, a report was received from the City Engineer on the condition of the swing bridge and the canal committee resolved:

> '... *in view of the danger of damage to James Street swing bridge the Town Clerk be authorised to negotiate with Messrs Bowles & sons with a view to providing them with an alternative wharf in order to obviate the opening of James Street bridge.*'

As we have already briefly noticed, the negotiations about an alternative wharf for Bowles were high on the Corporation's agenda, following Mr Justice Lynskey's judgement in favour of the sand trader in January 1947. Now adopting a conciliatory tone, the Corporation entered lengthy negotiations with the company in 1947, with the result that Bowles agreed to vacate their wharf above the swing bridge, to surrender their lease and to cease to use the canal, and instead to take up additional accommodation made available to them next to their Ferry Road wharf on the River Taff.[38]

Thus, at some considerable cost, the Corporation had succeeded in dislodging Messrs Bowles from their wharf on the wrong side of the James Street bridge and could concentrate at last on getting the bridge closed permanently. The closing of the swing bridge was effected in May 1948, following representations to the Ministry of Transport, the canal committee minuting:

> '... *the City surveyor be asked to arrange that the James Street Swing Bridge is not opened in the future and the Transport Committee be informed accordingly.*'[39]

Meanwhile, the City Council was getting complaints in the newspapers about the insanitary condition of the drained canal course through the city. Filling in the canal between Queen Street and Mill Lane took place at this time, allowing Mill Lane eventually to be widened and the open air fruit and vegetable market in the Hayes to be removed to the Mill Lane site. The canal was in water (1948) only between Custom House Bridge and the Sea Lock, and its water supply came entirely from the West Bute

Clarence Road swing bridge, spanning the River Taff in the bottom left corner of this 1920 aerial view, connected Grangetown with Cardiff's dockland. As it then crosses the canal, on the right of the picture, the road becomes James Street and enters what was at this time the business centre of the city. The coal exchange and Mount Stuart Square were built on the site of the Guest Glass Works of the 1830s. In the distance, beyond the TVR West Yard and Bute Street, can be seen the, by this date very antiquated coal staithes on the Bute West Dock and the more up-to-date coal hoists on the East Dock. As each dock

opened with better facilities, the Bute Company was continually faced with the problem of how to keep shipping profitable in its older docks, whilst the sheer scale of these facilities is a clear indication of why the canal had become little more than a backwater in comparison. CCL collection

Dock, which had passed to the British Transport Commission's Railway Executive on 1 January 1948, following the Attlee government's Transport Act 1947. As described earlier, there was no navigation for shipping above the canal swing bridge after May 1948.

The Sea Lock Basin

The Corporation now turned its attention to the Sea Lock basin – the active portion of the canal between the James Street swing bridge and the Sea Lock – and inconveniently occupied by the two surviving canal sand traders. Having just disposed of the swing bridge problem, the Corporation found itself immediately frustrated by another.

The Town Clerk and the chairman of the City Council's Canal Sub-Committee attended a meeting in London at the Ministry of Transport and were informed that the Sea Lock Basin at Cardiff could be included for nationalisation under a scheme being considered for the Docks and Harbours of Cardiff; '*Failing such inclusion the Cardiff Corporation would be enabled to continue to utilise the basin.*' The Corporation therefore decided to leave further negotiations with the sand traders in abeyance and so, in an apparently endless atmosphere of uncertainty, the little ships of Sandridge & Co and J.R. Griffiths continued to bring in their cargoes of sand through the Sea Lock.[40] A period of waiting ensued and it eventually became known that the Sea Lock Basin would not be transferred to a Cardiff Docks and Harbours scheme. In 1949, the British Transport Commission's Railway Executive transferred responsibility for running the former railway-owned South Wales docks to a new Docks & Inland Waterways Executive. Perhaps because of its minimal commercial importance, the Glamorganshire Canal was left out of this second BTC reorganisation.

The dock-owning D&IWE would appear only infrequently in the canal company's minutes at this late stage in the canal's history but in December 1949, the Town Clerk reported an application from the D&IWE for permission to close permanently Lock 51, to save the Executive the expense of maintaining the gates in an operative condition. In a new agreement, the Corporation would take the lock out of use and recognise that the timber floating area would be reduced. The Executive would agree to indemnify the Corporation for the consequent loss of rental.[41]

Earlier in 1949, the City Surveyor reported a complaint from sand trader J.R. Griffiths that one of their vessels had fouled an obstruction in the canal's entrance channel on 27 April 1949 and had broken a propeller. Photographs and a plan had been submitted but the canal committee recommended not to accept liability.[42] Again in 1950, Griffiths complained of silting in the channel but in a reply they received assurances that they had heard a number of times before – '*The traders will not be required to transfer their businesses from the canal without receiving 12 months notice in writing from the Corporation.*'

It will be remembered that a clause in the Cardiff Corporation Act of 1943 had underlined the City's

An aerial view of the Sea lock at low tide one day in 1927. The line of the 1865 TVR road from Eleanor Street, which crossed the lock and the foreshore, can be discerned. The vessel moored against the gate narrows opposite Harrowby Street is probably Sylvia, the steam pilot. In the far distance is the Dowlais Steelworks, built on the East Moors in the 1880s. CCL collection

In 1950, after permanent closure of the James Street swing bridge, there were two remaining Bristol Channel sand and gravel firms on the west bank of the Sea Lock pound at Harrowby Street. Pictured here are the sand suction vessels Catherine Ethel *(Sandridge & Co) and, in the foreground, the diminutive* Britannia *(J. & R. Griffiths), both seen moored at their respective wharves. The New Sea Lock Hotel can be seen between the two boats. There is no hint, in this tranquil scene, of what was to transpire at the end of the following year, when all would be dramatically changed as , on 5 December 1951,* Catherine Ethel *was in collision with the Sea Lock inner gates, bringing a disastrous end to the canal as the city's dockland had known it.* ILW photo 7 September 1950 neg 1058

responsibility to keep open and available for navigation the Sea Lock pound of the canal, until the expiration of six months after the termination of the Emergency. A letter had been received from the Ministry of Transport informing the Corporation that the Emergency had come to an end on 8 October 1950 and that notice could therefore be served after 5 April 1951 on the Docks & Inland Waterways Executive, of the Corporation's intention to stop the supply of water to the lower reaches of the canal. At the canal committee meeting on 5 June 1951, considering these matters the committee seemed indecisive and it was minuted that no action was to be taken.

A Fateful Night

It was now time for other forces to settle the future of the canal and on the night of 5-6 December 1951, Fate took a hand at the Sea Lock Basin, staging a scene that appeared nothing short of cataclysmic to those who were witnesses to it and dealing a mortal blow to the fortunes of the canal.

Just before midnight on 5 December, in pouring rain, the loaded steam suction dredger *Catherine Ethel*, of 154 tons gross and owned by Sandridge & Co, entered the Sea Lock and collided with the inner lock gates, with the result that they collapsed. The whole of the water in the canal from the Sea Lock to Lock 51 – extending for almost a mile – was suddenly released with the force of a tidal wave, sweeping the Sea Lock gates and *Catherine Ethel* out into the estuary in a wall of water. It was fortunate that the accident caused no loss of life or injury and no other vessel had been present in the canal at the time.

The *Catherine Ethel* had effectively and permanently put the canal out of action, in an act of destruction that Cardiff Corporation could never have hoped to match. In a number of ways the incident had helped to settle long drawn out issues and many problems. The canal was never repaired. On the morning of 6 December, many dockland children decided not to go to school but spent their time recovering scrap metal from the canal and disposing of it profitably at the canalbank scrapyard of J. Ford. Elsewhere, a crane was brought in to remove a mud-caked car and two bicycles. A deep hollow layered in mud and the castoffs of ages was all that remained of the canal on that depressing morning.[43]

So it was that iron from Merthyr had brought the

The drained bed of the canal on the morning following the Catherine Ethel *disaster. The view is looking north, with James Street swing bridge in the middle distance and the sand wharves of J. & R. Griffiths and Sandridge & Co on the left.* Stan Vickery photo, Neg No. 27

Glamorganshire Canal into being, whilst it was to be sand that would keep it alive in its last years and, coupled with somebody's mistake, it would be sand that finally extinguished it.

Not surprisingly, the *Catherine Ethel* accident was to have its own legal implications. Sandridge & Co, owners of the vessel, brought an action against Cardiff Corporation for breach of contract or duty and damage to their vessel and the Corporation counterclaimed alleging damage to the lock and denying liability.

The law case, picturesquely styled '*Catherine Ethel* versus the Lord Mayor, Aldermen and citizens of the City of Cardiff', was heard before Mr Justice Willmer in the Admiralty Division of the High Court and lasted from 19-29 January 1954. The action failed and judgement was awarded to the Corporation on a counter claim that there was negligence on the part of the owners of the vessel in colliding with the lock gates.

Catherine Ethel survived the accident and carried on working for Sandridge & Co until 1962, when she was sold to Llanelly Quarries Ltd. Found to be too large to operate successfully for this company, she ran only four or five cargoes and was then laid up at Llanelly, where she was finally broken up in 1964-5.[44]

The remains of the canal as seen looking north from the swing bridge in the late 1950s. Filling in of the channel is in progress, with the top end from just past the bend here on up almost completed. The wagon is on the Glamorganshire Canal Railway system, which still remained in operation although the canal had closed.
Stan Vickery photo, Neg No. 29/33

A late afternoon view of the entrance channel to the Glamorganshire Canal in April 1943. This photograph gives a graphic indication of just how far from the sea the canal's entrance was and also the tidal nature of the channel.
CCL collection

A similar view to that above but taken after the Catherine Ethel *had collided with the Sea Lock gates, showing the swept out remains of the entrance channel.* Stan Vickery photo, Neg No. 29/33

NOTES TO CHAPTER 13

1 William Gomer, personal memory of the ship in the Sea Lock pound 1891-1900. In conversation with ILW in 1949. See also Gordon Mote *The Westcountrymen*, Bideford 1986, p34 and 86.
2 In the maritime Sea Lock pound and the ports of the Bristol Channel and the South West, a hobbler was a casual worker at the docks and particularly a man working with a boat. On the Glamorganshire Canal, a hobbler was an independent owner boatman.
3 D.G. Hoppins *The History of Cardiff Docks*, 1947, manuscript copy in private collection.
4 The peak of this canal traffic was reached on 10 January 1913, as recorded in a North Road Lock register and a lockkeeper's boat book, ILW collection.
5 Royal Commission on Canals 1906.
6 John Ballinger *Cardiff: an Illustrated Handbook,* Cardiff, 1896, p50; David Emrys Jeffries *Maritime Memories of Cardiff*, Risca 1978, p36 and p85; George S. Emmerson *John Scott Russell – A Great Victorian Engineer and Naval Architect*, London 1977, p251.
7 Information from contemporary GCC loading bills and permits, ILW collection.
8 *Western Mail*, 7 April 1893. Interview with Lewis Llewelyn.
9 Ballinger *Cardiff*, 1896, p50; Hoppins *Cardiff Docks*, 1947.
10 Information from contemporary GCC loading bills and permits, ILW collection.
11 Information from Tom Frazer and William Gomer in conversation with ILW.
12 See O'Rourke's map of 1849.
13 Ballinger *Cardiff*, 1896.
14 S.W. Allen *Reminiscences*, Cardiff 1918, p59.
15 S.W. Allen *Reminiscences*, Cardiff 1918, p53.
16 Evidence *F. Bowles v Cardiff Corporation*, Admiralty Division of High Court, 1947.
17 *Ships Monthly*, April 1990, pp28-31.
18 Sea Lock Registers 1915-29 GRO B/c GCa 3.
19 CCCC minutes 17 March 1944; GCC lease to The Acetylene Illuminating Co Ltd, 20 Dec 1916, GRO B/C GCa 4/189.
20 It is from this small steamer of 44 tons reg which the publishers of this book have taken their name.
21 Canal Boats Acts 1877 and 1884; Cardiff Medical Officer of Health's Canal Boat Inspectors Report 1920.
22 The 1886 plans and elevations for the lock gates and wrought iron lattice towpath bridge over the entrance lock to the timber pond are contained in ABP 3301. The lock was 30ft long, the bridge 22ft 8ins wide and the canal entrance under the bridge was 15ft wide. The bundle also includes sections of the timber pond.
23 D.G. Hoppins *The History of Cardiff Docks*, 1947, manuscript copy in private collection.
24 D.G. Hoppins *The History of Cardiff Docks*, 1947, manuscript copy in private collection.
25 CCCC minute book 21 Dec 1949 and 23 June 1950.
26 25 May 1942 (Whit Monday) is the date received from canal workers who were immediately affected by the event. In correspondence with the civil engineers, the GCC quotes the date 26 May 1942, Whit Tuesday.
27 Report prepared by Morgan Thomas, civil engineers Pontypridd; information from Deputy Town Clerk W.G. Hopkins via Bill Hamlin.
28 Information from Tom Frazer.
29 CC minute 9 April 1943. Thanks to Bill Hamlin for notes taken by him from the Corporation minutes and made available to ILW.
30 CCCC Minute Book 9 August 1943.
31 CCCC Minute Book 18 November 1943.
32 Information from Bill Hamlin.
33 CCCC Minute Book 25 Nov 1943 and March 1944.
34 CCCC Minute Book 25 Nov 1943, 7 Feb, 17 March and 15 December 1944,
35 CCCC Minute Book 29 September and 15 Dec 1944, 6 June 1945. In evidence at the High Court Kings Bench Division hearing F. Bowles v Cardiff Corporation January 1947, the dimensions of *Deloraine* were given as length 125 feet $1^1/_2$ ins and beam 22 feet 2 ins.
36 *F. Bowles v Cardiff Corporation*, January 1947.
37 CCCC Minute Book 6 June 1945.
38 CCCC Minute Book 30 Jan, 10 April and 26 April 1947.
39 CCCC Minute Book 28 May 1948.
40 CCCC Minute Book 28 May 1948.
41 CCCC Minute Book 21 Dec 1949.
42 CCCC Minute Book 7 July 1949.
43 *South Wales Echo*, 6 December 1951 has a report of the incident. See also the Evidence in *Catherine Ethel v Cardiff Corporation* heard in the High Court Admiralty Division, 19-29 January 1954.
44 Information from Bill Hamlin.

Appendix A
Samuel Coupe Fox 1864-1953
The Cardiff amateur photographer

Samuel Coupe Fox was born in Sutton in Ashfield, near Mansfield, Nottinghamshire, in 1864. On growing up, he became apprenticed to a printer in the town, Henry Chaney, and later married Chaney's daughter Alice. Having moved to Burnley in Lancashire, the couple's only child, William Chaney Fox, was born there in 1889.

Samuel moved to Cardiff in 1890 where he was to live for over sixty years until his death at the age of 89 in 1953. It was in Cardiff that his career as a journalist took off, firstly with the *Western Mail* and later as a reporter on the *South Wales News*. Later still, he become leader writer for the *South Wales Echo* and music and drama critic for the *South Wales Daily News*. He was also editor of the weekly *Cardiff Times*. Samuel was a retiring and self-effacing man. His regular article 'Man About Town' was published anonymously and there was never a credit line for anything else he wrote.

The same private approach prevailed when Samuel indulged in his passion for photography – at least when confronted by people inhabiting his outdoor world. He would go to great lengths to disguise his activities, so that those around him would not be aware of his camera and thus act naturally. His output as an amateur photographer was considerable and yet, excepting perhaps in his own city of Cardiff, he is still a comparatively little known name. A large proportion of his work is a record of sailing ships and the sea, and on Samuel's death in 1953, his son William, recognising their value to maritime research, deposited over 3,000 negatives and prints for safe keeping in the National Maritime Museum at Greenwich.

S.C. Fox became interested in photography in about 1895 and from those early years, he rarely set off on his excursions without a camera. His photography – he seems to have been content with a variety of lightweight hand-held cameras – extended over fifty years and for the most part his work displayed considerable artistic and pictorial merit. Samuel used glass plates and various sizes of roll film, which he processed and enlarged himself. A number of subjects he reproduced as lantern slides. In the interests of economy, he also went in for the rather perilous activity of cutting his glass quarter plates in two!

Samuel had an eye for the beauty of the local rural scene around Cardiff, now largely lost under suburban and light industrial development, and the relentless road building that goes with it. During holidays, he visited many coastal towns, villages and harbours, mostly in Devon and Cornwall. Sail was captured also at Scarborough and Whitby, which were visited in 1909 and 1910. One of his favourite places in Cardiff was Roath Park, which was within easy walking distance of his later home in Llanishen Street in the Heath district of the city.

For the present authors, the most valuable legacy S.C. Fox has left to us is his archive of almost 250 photographs of the Glamorganshire Canal, images recorded almost entirely between North Road Lock in Cardiff and the Three Mile Pond at Nantgarw, over the best part of fifty years.

Fox was not a canal enthusiast in the sense we would use the term today. It was simply that the Glamorganshire Canal satisfied his need to be in the countryside and provided him with added interest and incident along the towpath during his quiet waterside walks.

During his leisure hours with a camera, Samuel probably paid little regard to his photographs as records of a passing age. This may account for his failure to date or label any of his hundreds of prints or negatives. As far as the Fox Collection's canal photographs are concerned, this anonymity did not turn out to be a problem. In January 1983, the authors visited Cardiff Central Library and were able to identify and caption every S.C. Fox photograph depicting the canal – all 250 of them!

In 1985, William Fox, then living in Golder's Green, London and at the advanced age of 96, decided to donate the remainder of his late father's collection of Cardiff photographs and negatives to the care of the Welsh Industrial & Maritime Museum, Cardiff, and David Gould of East Grinstead, who had helped to secure their future, took charge of the transfer. By July, WIMM had received 445 negatives relating to the Glamorganshire Canal, plus other railway, maritime and Cardiff subjects, all of which David Gould personally entered into the museum's negative register. As David Gould has written: '*If we owe a debt of gratitude to S.C. Fox for taking such evocative and beautiful photographs, we surely owe an equal debt to his son, William Chaney Fox, for ensuring their preservation for all time.*'

The authors are indebted to David Gould for much of this biographical information. As a child, he was brought up in Cardiff, in the same Llanishen Street home as Samuel Fox, his mother Rachel Gould having been housekeeper to the elderly Mr Fox between 1947 and 1953.

Appendix B
A VIEW FROM THE BOAT

This lovely study of the canal at Nantgarw circa 1910, with the one of the bottle kilns of the pottery visible in the background, is again the work of Samuel Fox. It is thought the lady might be Kitty Chaney, sister of Fox's wife Alice. S.C. Fox photo, Neg No 73.146, courtesy WIMM

This appendix continues our description from Volume 1, of how the canal would have looked to a boat crew travelling south. This part of the journey takes us from Pontypridd down to the Sea Lock in Cardiff and is now set in 1914.

A late 19th century view of the bridge over the River Taff at Llandaff. The line of the canal is visible in front of the houses in the right distance and the chimneys of Melingriffith Tinplate Works can be seen above the bridge, with the Taff gap on the horizon. CCL collection

Ynysangharad

Beyond Trallwn Wharf, the navigation curves away to the south and east, running parallel with the Berw feeder. The deep staircase locks at Ynysangharad lower the canal 20 feet 5 inches and stand alongside the famous Newbridge Chain and Anchor works, established by Samuel Brown in 1818. One or two boats can usually be seen in the lower basin, loading chain and shackles for carriage to Cardiff.

Pentrebach and Glyntaff

The hillside here is remarkable for its precipitous quarries. John Gibbon, with a quarry by the Farmer's Arms, still sends Pennant stone from his wharf. Further to the south, at a higher level, the boat passes the Duke of Bridgewater's Arms. A wharf opposite was once used for loading iron from the Taff Vale Ironworks at Treforest, which began sending iron across the river to the canal in 1853.

Viewed across the river to the west from the boat's vantage point is Treforest's well populated hillside, with the White Tips left behind by the dismantled Forest Iron & Steel works.

Treforest

The main Cardiff - Merthyr road crosses the canal over the Gwern y geryn Bridge by the Llanbradach Arms and the Pontypridd trams cross this bridge to reach their depot. The boat's crew must take care here, to pass a slackened towline over any boats that may be unloading at the company's store which is at the bridge. Up to four market boats may call here daily on their way to Pontypridd.

The three arched bridge over the river near here is the Machine Bridge, or Pont y Doctor, which carried Dr Griffiths' coal tramroad to the Doctor's Canal.

The navigation now turns away from the river and heads for open country and the valley widens. On the way, it passes under Pwllyhwyad Bridge and runs close to the abandoned Doctor's Canal basin, which lies 20 feet below the level of the Glamorganshire.

Rhydyfelin

It is pleasant to be cruising past fields and farms again, as industry is left behind. Rhydyfelin's cottages and newer streets relate mostly to the main road. The village, dominated by the steelwork of the Cardiff Railway's viaduct, is home to a number of canal boatmen.

At Dyffryn, is a large round house – an architectural curiosity.

Dyffryn Lock, usually called Lock Lewis, is the focus of a small canal community. Mynydd Mayo, with its patchwork of hill farms, is a pleasant backdrop.

Dynea

At Dynea Lock, the lockkeeper's cottage nestles under a low flat-topped hill, a popular venue for Sunday school picnics by boat from Pontypridd. Just below the lock is the junction of the Doctor's Canal with the Glamorganshire. The embankment which follows was the scene of a breach in 1908, which disrupted traffic for two months.

Main Street, Rhydyfelin, circa 1908, with the River Taff on the right and the Cardiff Railway viaduct beyond. SR collection

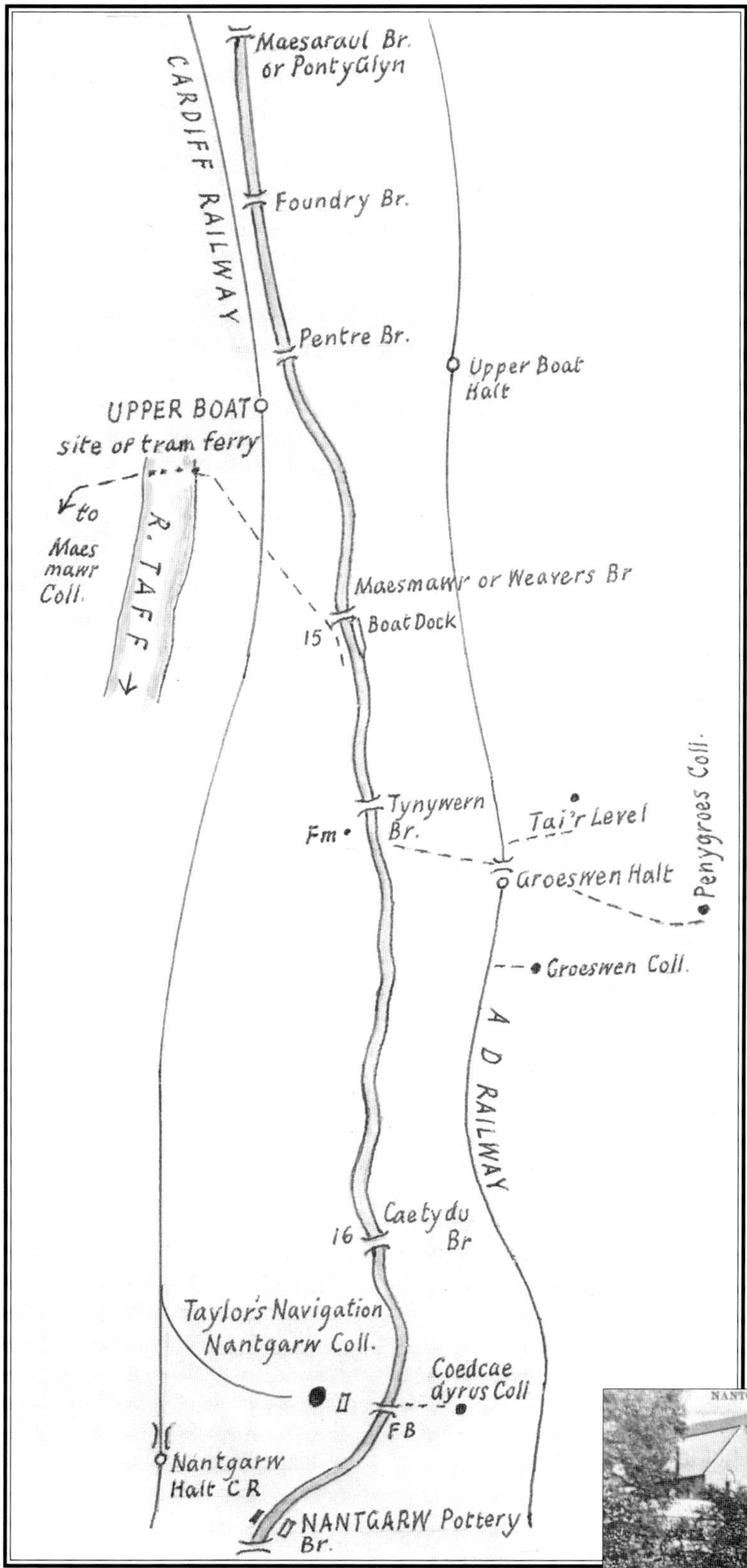

The 3 Mile Pond

Leaving Dynea Lock, the boat enters the Three Mile Pond, where quiet rural reaches evoke an atmosphere of complete remoteness from the working world. Woodlands border the canal along the lower slopes of Mynydd Mayo and cover long-abandoned inclines, where tramways once brought coal down to the boats.

The canal follows the contour above the fields of Tynywern Farm, eventually passing Thomas Taylor's Nantgarw Colliery, where sinking began in 1911.

Nantgarw

An attractive village with cottages and a storehouse on the wharf. The renowned pottery, with its pot kilns, lies opposite. Here, between 1813 and 1822, Joseph Billingsley produced the world famous porcelain. Under the bridge, the canal loops past the grounds of Dyffryn Ffrwd and passes Graig Cottages, the homes of colliers who worked in the coal levels of Craig yr Allt, which rises to 888 feet.

The stone bridge over the canal at Graig once carried the Craig yr Allt Colliery tramroad up the steep hillside to a coal siding on the Rhymney Railway. The boat crew will see evidence of a tipping wall on the off side below the bridge.

Other signs of colliery activity here are some banks of coal waste which are rapidly returning to nature.

The canal, which is built on a ledge around the hillside, passes some narrows once holding stop gates. At Bryncoch Brickyard, the Three Mile Pond ends abruptly at the top of Treble Locks.

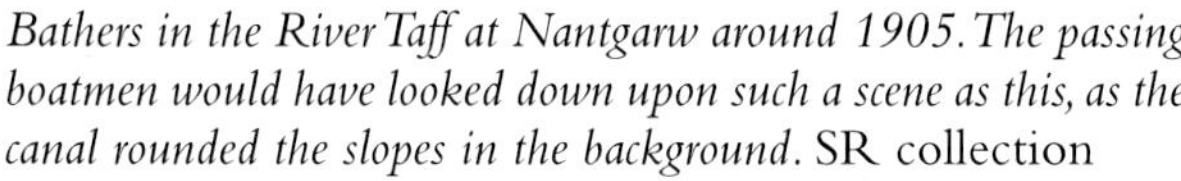

Bathers in the River Taff at Nantgarw around 1905. The passing boatmen would have looked down upon such a scene as this, as the canal rounded the slopes in the background. SR collection

Treble Locks

The view from the top of these locks is dramatic. The Garth Mountain towers to the west and the nearer Craig yr Allt rises on the off side, accommodating the steeply graded Rhymney and Barry Railways on their respective ledges around the mountain to Penrhos Junction. Ahead is the heavily wooded Garth Gap, marking the end of the coalfield and the gateway to Cardiff. To complete this almost aerial prospect, the canal company's Rhiw Ddar reservoir fills the foreground, with the canal bordering it to the west.

The fall is 33 feet but the descent from the top lock looks as though it is twice that figure. Treble Locks form a staircase, one lock running directly into another. Its potential as a bottleneck to traffic in the past can be well imagined.

Taff's Well

Taff's Well is a main road village, avoided by the canal, which takes a rural course to the east through three picturesque locks with whitened cottages. There was once a basin leading to the Garth Ironworks and the canal served a number of limestone quarries. The end of the village comes at Walnut Tree Bridge (18 miles) where the canal passes under the road.

Taff's Well Station (TVR) is 300 yards away and the Junction Hotel is nearby.

The high ridge ahead is remarkable for its beech woods – of outstanding beauty when seen from the boat in autumn.

Across the valley (west) are the remains of the Pentyrch Ironworks and the Little Garth hill is honeycombed with iron ore mines.

Passing through the Garth Gap, the canal leads under the high girders of the great Walnut Tree Viaduct and Tongwynlais comes into view.

Taff's Well (from which the village took its name) and the Pentyrch ironworks weir in 1863, photographed by Francis Bedford. SR collection

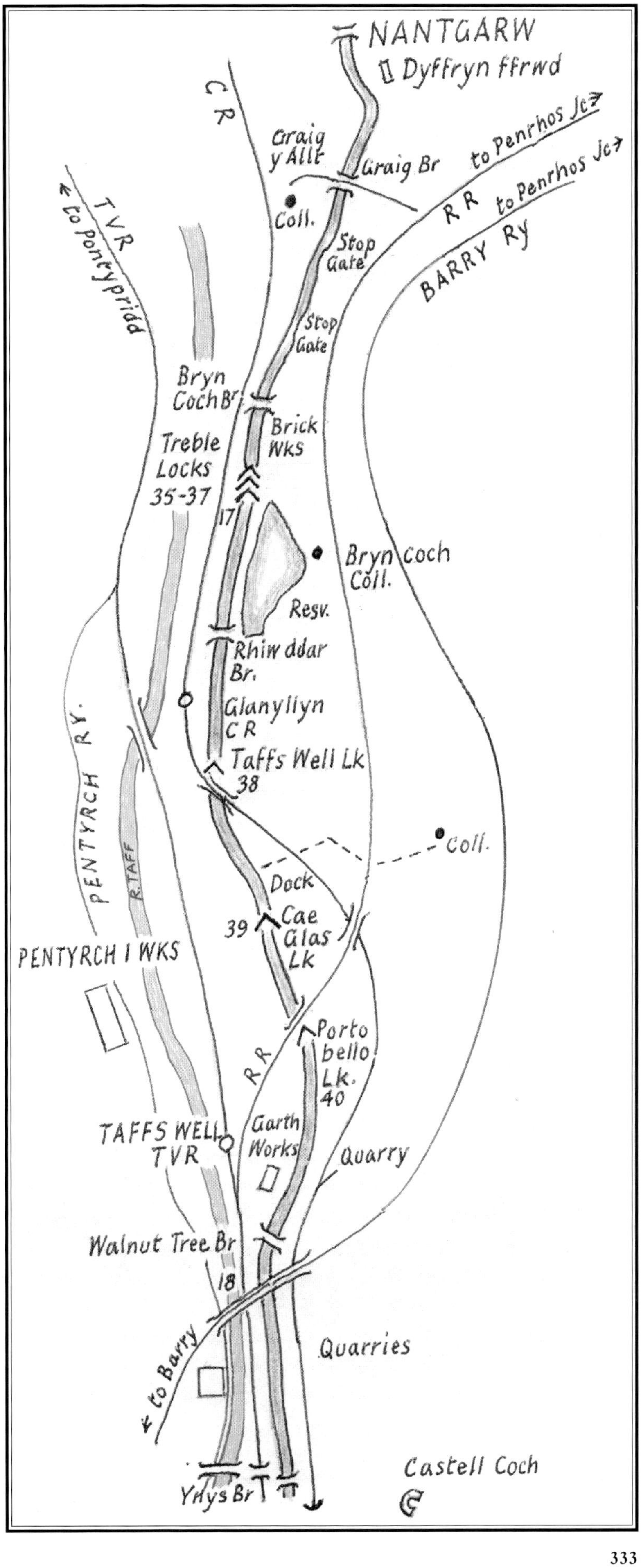

NANTGARW
Dyffryn ffrwd
C R
Craig y Allt
Craig Br
to Penrhos Jc
R R
to Penrhos Jc
BARRY Ry
Coll.
Stop Gate
Stop Gate
TVR
to Pontypridd
Bryn Coch Br
Brick Wks
Treble Locks 35-37
17
Bryn coch Coll.
Resv.
Rhiw ddar Br.
Glanyllyn CR
Taffs Well Lk 38
Coll.
Dock
39
Cae Glas Lk
PENTYRCH RY.
R. TAFF
PENTYRCH I WKS
Porto bello Lk. 40
R R
TAFFS WELL TVR
Garth Works
Quarry
Walnut Tree Br
18
to Barry
Quarries
Castell Coch
Ynys Br

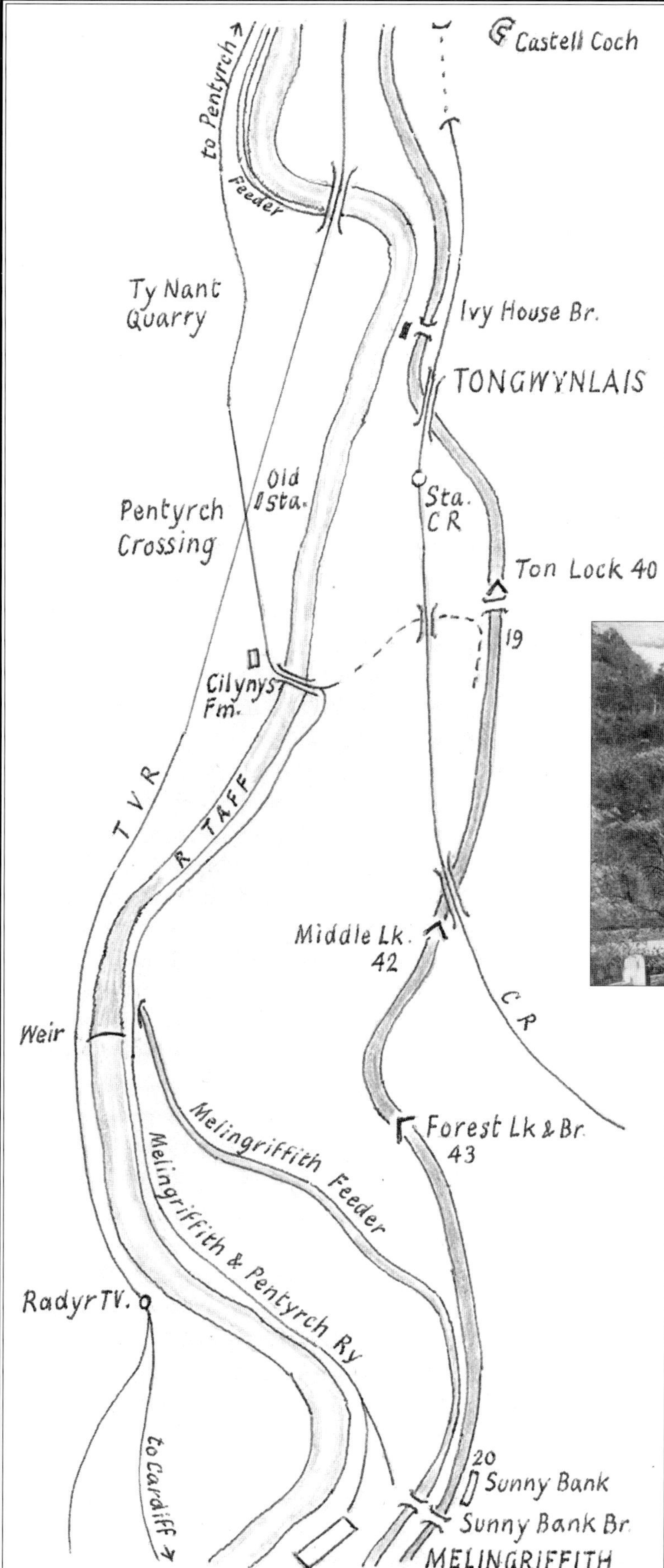

Tongwynlais

The navigation enters the village confined between the River Taff and the Cardiff Railway (1909), where a steep drop into the river has claimed the lives of a number of boat horses. This reach of the canal is known to the boatmen as Price's Pond.

Tongwynlais Station CR is approached from Ivy House Bridge.

The Lewis Arms public house and shops are on the Merthyr road, approached from Ton Lock.

Before leaving this canal village, a boat crew should look north for a last encounter with Castell Coch, set romantically on its hill.

Leaving Ton Lock (No 41), the boat enters a long reach of rural tranquillity, from which it does not emerge until Melingriffith. The canal's off bank is built into a steeply wooded hillside, which continues as the Long Wood for more than a mile. Middle and Forest locks are delightfully placed about midway along this peaceful haven, which is the haunt of herons and kingfishers. The industrial cottages at Sunny Bank mark the approach to Melingriffith and a notorious narrowing in the canal, where boats cannot pass.

A circa 1895 view of Castell Coch, an ancient castle rebuilt by the Marquess of Bute in the 1870s. The canal passes beneath Ynys Bridge in the foreground. SR collection

Melingriffith

The Melingriffith Works feeder, bordered with alder trees, comes within a few feet of the towpath. Water for the tinplate works is taken off the Taff at Radyr weir, across the fields to the west.

Horse boating on the canal is tricky, even dangerous here. Unhitching of the towline is necessary at the iron bridge (1849), where the towpath briefly changes to the east side, confined by a high wall. A horse with a loaded boat can easily be pulled in to the water at the works bridge and basin, where the pinched towpath takes a series of tight right angles. Melingriffith Lock brings relief from the narrows and the canal then returns to its normal width.

At the lock is the Melingriffith pump, with its water driven wheel and massive oak beams. It still delivers water into the canal after use by the tinplate works.

Llandaff Lock

The canal has coal yards and a warehouse here; the settlement, formerly called Llandaff Yard, now prefers the name Llandaff North. At the bridge and lock, the Whitchurch turnpike crosses the navigation.

The Cow & Snuffers is a popular boatmen's pub.

As the boat locks through, the spire of Llandaff Cathedral is seen to the south (1 mile by road over Llandaff Bridge).

Small canal settlements come into view as the boat works through College Lock and then Gabalfa Lock, where John Rhys James has dry docks that carry out boat repair work and also hire canal boats to the Maindy and Blackweir Patent Fuel companies.

The Three Cups is a boatmen's pub on the towpath at Cups Row, on the western side of the canal.

The Cow & Snuffers public house around 1908, looking north east over the canal bridge. The original pub was built around 1812 and is the small white building beyond the grand new construction of 1906 seen here and which by this date had become a small refreshments shop. Note also that the artist has attempted to depict a literal translation of the name on the inn sign; the origins of the Gaelic phrase from which the pub got its name had obviously already been forgotten. SR collection

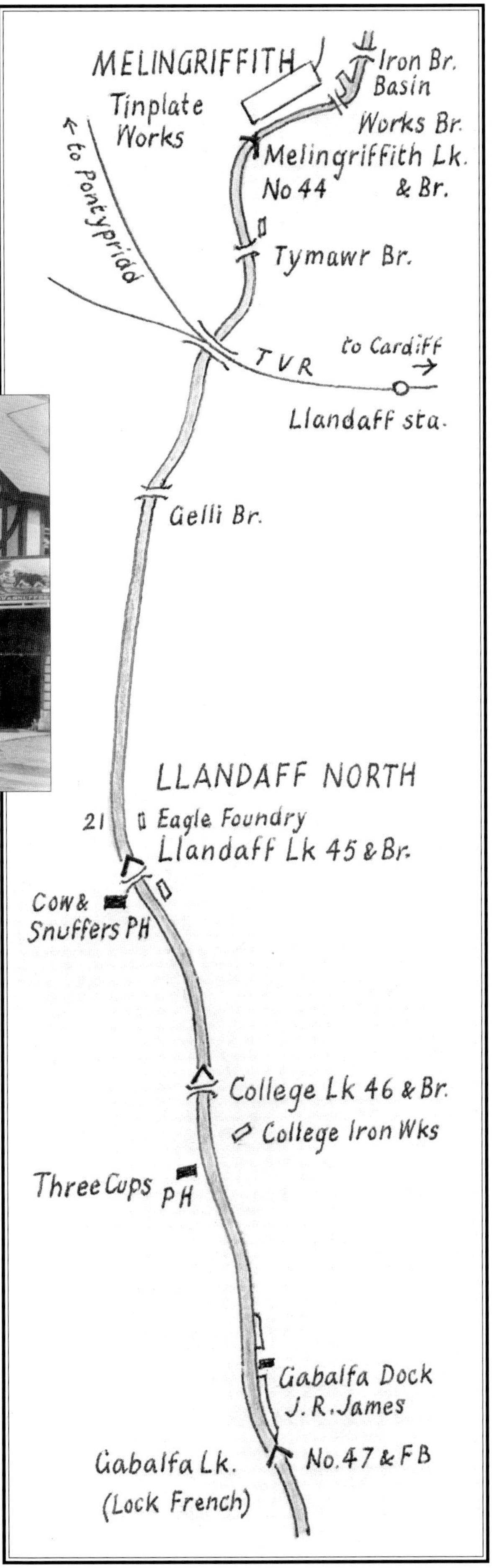

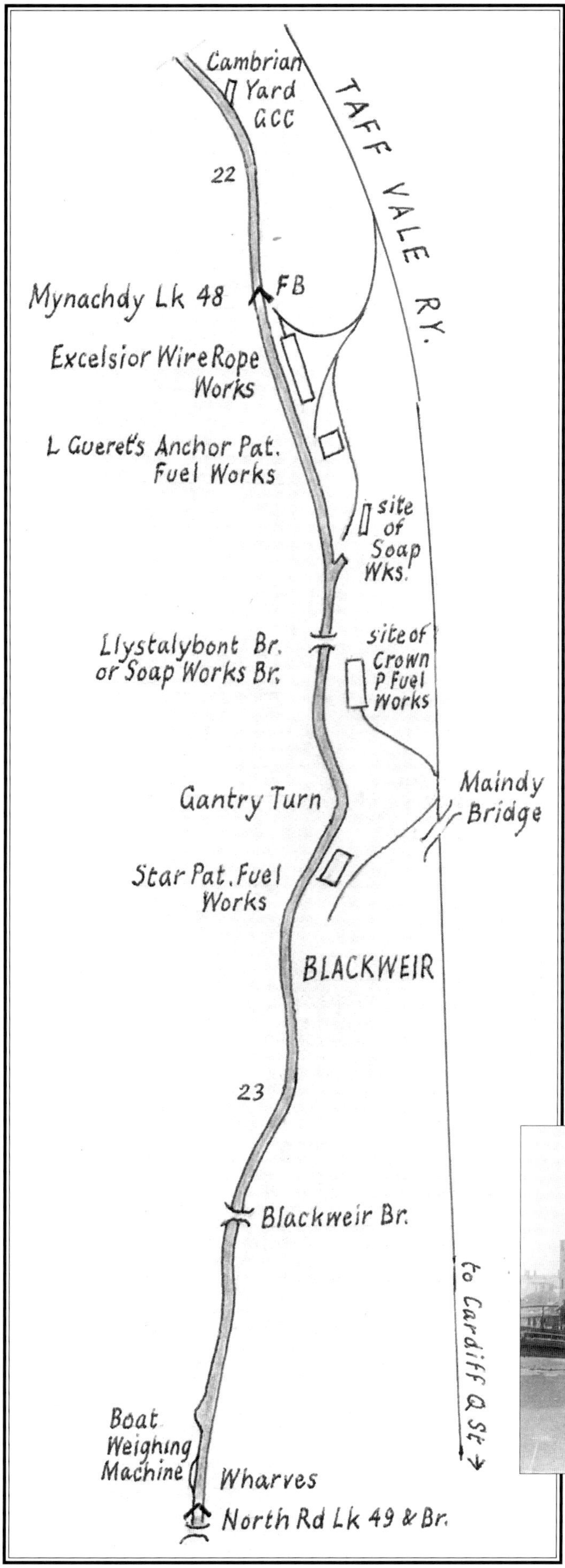

Cambrian Yard GCC
TAFF VALE RY.
22
Mynachdy Lk 48
FB
Excelsior Wire Rope Works
L Gueret's Anchor Pat. Fuel Works
site of Soap Wks.
Llystalybont Br. or Soap Works Br.
site of Crown P Fuel Works
Maindy Bridge
Gantry Turn
Star Pat. Fuel Works
BLACKWEIR
23
Blackweir Br.
to Cardiff Q St
Boat Weighing Machine
Wharves
North Rd Lk 49 & Br.

Mynachdy and Maindy

From Llandaff into Cardiff's city centre, the canal's course is still almost completely rural in character, emphasised by the whitened country style cottages and lock houses belonging to the company. On the off bank, a row of moored company boats indicates the GCC Cambrian maintenance yard and dry dock.

Crews will notice the fall on these locks approaching Cardiff is much less than on the upper ones and so working them is marginally more rapid. Once through Mynachdy Lock, the canal loses its tranquil character. The offside is the domain of the canal-based Patent Fuel industries. Long lines of boats are moored for loading fuel blocks at the works of L. Gueret, who have rails for hauling out boats at Llystalybont (Maindy).

Blackweir

At the next wide bend, called by the boatmen 'the Gantry Turn', the boat passes the works of the Star Patent Fuel Co at Blackweir. Like Gueret's, the Star Company own large numbers of boats and both owners are very active. The crew is kept busy here passing over and under the towlines of approaching boats and horses, returning empty from the Bute Docks.

Industry is left behind at Blackweir Bridge, where the towpath changes sides. Hope Hotel and the Machen Forge public house are in North Road.

The canal runs southwards into the city centre, with North Road and Cathays Park for company to the east and a vista across to the buildings of the University College.

North Road Lock

The boat's permit will be checked by the North Road lockkeeper, who works from a cabin. He will tell you that a record 208 boats, laden and empty, passed through his lock in one day last year – 10 January 1913. All except four were in the Patent Fuel trade.

The scene is picturesque. Cardiff Castle and Lord Bute's thatched gate lodge border the lock. Cardiff's outstanding civic buildings – the City Hall (built 1901-6) and the Law Courts (opened 1906) are across the road in Cathays Park.

Passing through the attractive iron arch of the locktail bridge, the southbound boat is now on the course of Cardiff's mediaeval Town Moat.

North Road Lock looking south, circa 1908, with the distinctive thatched gate lodge alongside. SR collection

Crockherbtown Lock

Crockherbtown Lock, which takes boats under Queen Street, will admit a Down boat (as at North Road) only when an Up boat has emerged from it. At the tail of the lock is a black hole, under the arch below Queen Street ,where two boats can just pass. The Tunnel (115 yards) is too narrow for boats to pass and the towpath runs for only 23 yards. Crews have to pull the boat through by means of a chain along the wall, while the horse is led up a ramp into a lane, to rejoin the boat alongside Hill's Terrace.

Now in welcome daylight again, the boat crew must be alert for approaching boats at Cocks Tower, a sharp corner on the line of the original town walls.

Custom House Bridge around 1920. SR collection

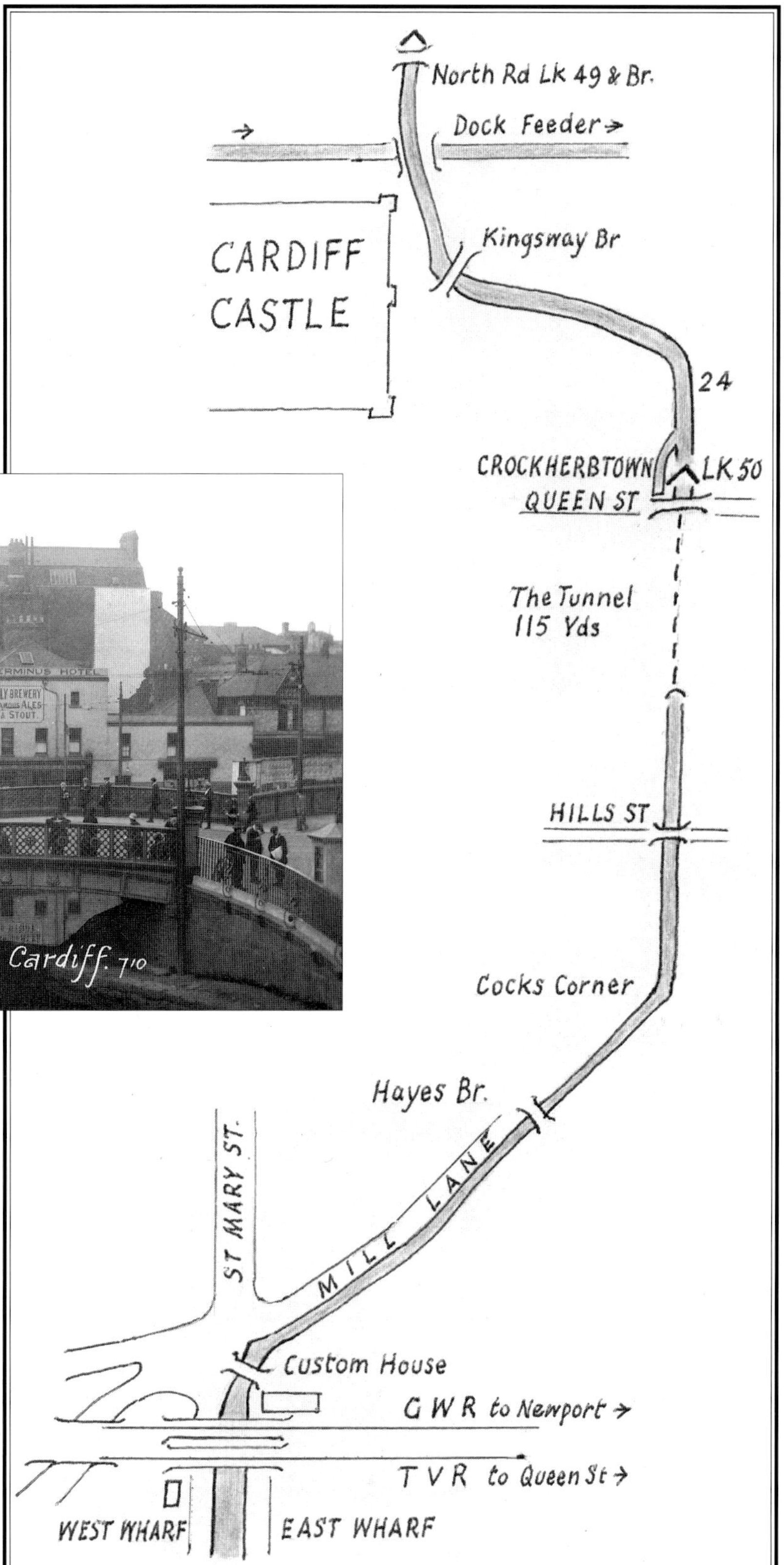

Hayes Bridge

Passing under the Hayes Bridge, the canal runs next to Mill Lane and turns sharply under Custom House Street Bridge at the lower end of St Mary Street.

Cardiff General Station (GWR) is 300 yards away and the Central and Great Western hotels are nearby.

West Canal Wharf

At West Canal Wharf, the voyage from Merthyr ends (24 miles). The GCC's office and wharves are beyond the GWR railway bridges, where boat permits may be handed in.

The Sea Lock pound of the canal continues southwards to the Sea Lock (25$^3/_4$ miles). It is generally busy and unsuitable for horse towage. The canal company does not encourage leisure boating on the Sea Lock pound, which is obstructed by James Street swing bridge and is used by coastal shipping and the sand trade.

Appendix C
GLAMORGANSHIRE CANAL BRIDGES

Ynysangharad to Sea Lock

DIST.	BRIDGE NAME	NOTES
$12^{1}/_{2}$	Pentrebach Quarries Bridge; Farmers Arms Bridge	Access from canal towpath to turnpike road and the quarry behind Farmer's Arms public house. Harrison (1830) does not show it. Shown on 1874 survey of 25in OS map. Most recent crossing was a flat bridge (iron) dated 1879.
	PC&NR (later GWR) Bridge	1881, carrying the railway from Pontypridd to Caerphilly and Newport.
	Quarry Tip Bridge	Shown on Harrison (1830) leading from quarries and turnpike road, across the canal, to a waste tipping point on the river bank. Gone by 1874 OS survey but the site of the tip in the river is discernable, just upstream from the Aberdare Iron Company's tramroad bridge from the canal towpath across the river.
	Duke's Arms Bridge	1816 footbridge giving access from towpath to turnpike road and Duke of Bridgewater's Arms. Shown in Thomas Hornor's painting of 1819 but not on Harrison (1830) or any subsequent map.
$12^{3}/_{4}$	Gwern y Geryn Bridge; Turnpike Bridge; Llanbradach Arms Bridge	1792 stone bridge carrying turnpike road across canal to west side at Treforest and near to the later Llanbradach Arms public house, the turnpike gate and Dr Griffith's Machine Bridge over the River Taff. Widened 1899 to accommodate Pontypridd electric tramway.
$13^{1}/_{4}$	Pwllyhwyad Bridge; Richards' Bridge	1792 stone bridge giving access from the towpath to Pwllyhwyad Farm and taking field path to Coed Glyn Taff and Bryntail. The 1851 census records William Thomas, the farmer of Pwllyhwyad, also being a boatman, with two boatmen sons and employing two further boatmen named Richards. This is possibly the source of the name Richards Bridge.
$13^{1}/_{2}$	Dyffryn Lock Bridge; Lock Lewis Bridge	1792 locktail bridge at Lock 33. Later carried the continuation of Ebenezar Street, Rhydyfelin, to east side of the canal at Springfield.
	Dyffryn Bridge; Kidman's Bridge	1792 stone bridge taking road from the turnpike at Dyffryn Arms, Rhydyfelin, across the canal to Dyffryn Taff Farm and to the hill farm Glyn Taff. In 1851, the 78 year old James Kidman, retired Cardiff salt merchant, was living at Glyn Taff cottage.
	Ty Uchaf Bridge; Treharne Bridge	1792 stone bridge giving access from the towpath across the canal to Tir Treharne and Dynea. Later a field path from the towpath connected with Dyffryn Road and the Druid Houses.
14	Dynea Towpath Bridge	Over entrance to Doctor's Canal 1809. A timber bridge still extant in 1950.
	Maesaraul Bridge; Pont y Glyn	1792 stone bridge carrying lane from the turnpike road at Melin-Gorrwg over the canal to Dynea.
$14^{1}/_{2}$	Foundry Bridge; Morris David's Bridge	1792 stone bridge taking lane from the turnpike road near Melin-Gorrwg foundry across the canal to Gelli-hirion Farm.
$14^{3}/_{4}$	Pentre Bridge; Pont Pentre	1793 stone bridge giving access from Pentre Farm, across the canal, to the towpath and road to the turnpike at Upper Boat. Later (1908) carried footpath from Upper Boat CR station to the Upper Boat halt on the PC&NR.
15	Maesmawr Bridge; Pont Maesmawr; Weaver's Bridge; Caerphilly Road Bridge	1793 stone bridge providing canal crossing for road from the turnpike at Upper Boat to the Caerphilly road to Groeswen, Pen y Groes and the parish church at Eglwysilan on Mynydd Mayo. Site of the coal wharf and tramroad terminus for Maesmawr Colliery.
$15^{1}/_{4}$	Tynywern Bridge	1793 stone bridge carrying footpath across the canal from Tynywern Farm to Groeswen and Pen y Groes collieries.
$15^{3}/_{4}$	Cae Ty Du Bridge	1793 stone bridge for footpath access across the canal between Dyffryn Isaf Farm and the upper road to Eglwysilan, connecting farms around Pen y Groes.
16	Coed Cae Dyrus Bridge	1856 or later, on 1874 OS survey. Probable timber tramway bridge, giving access from the small Coedcaedyrus Colliery (offside N), across the canal and towpath, to waste tips below towpath. Colliery out of use c1900 but bridge still marked as a footbridge on 1921 OS survey.
$16^{1}/_{4}$	Nantgarw Bridge	1793 stone bridge for original Nantgarw-Caerphilly road through Dyffryn Ffrwd, to cross the canal and towpath at site of later Nantgarw Pottery. Approach to the hump-backed bridge was levelled in 1848. Strengthened concrete and girder replacement extant.
$16^{1}/_{2}$	Graig Bridge	1793 stone bridge giving access from Craig yr Allt coal level (below canal towpath) to tipping wharf on opposite side of towpath. This function later replaced by adjacent incline bridge but the stone bridge continued to carry road from Nantgarw village across canal to Tai'r Graig .
	Craig yr Allt Incline Bridge	1859 bridge carrying a tramway incline from Craig yr Allt Colliery to tipping wharf on canal and tipping wharf at sidings on the RR. Shown on 1874 OS survey.
$16^{3}/_{4}$	Bryncoch Bridge	1793 stone bridge giving access from the original route to Cardiff (shown as '*old road to Cardiff*' on Harrison 1830), across the towpath and canal, to the Bryncoch Brickworks.
	Bryncoch Footbridge	Appears on 1880 OS map above the top lock at Treble Locks. It provided access from the towpath to the lower end of the brickworks. Demolished probably after closure of brickworks.
	Treble Locks Dock Bridge	1818 stone towpath bridge across entrance to dock below Treble Locks (Nos 35-7).
17	Rhiw Ddar Bridge	1793 stone bridge carrying original farm road from the turnpike at Glan y Llyn to Rhiw-ddar Farm. The building of Glan y Llyn Station (opened 1911) blocked this route and the bridge was demolished in the same year although the narrows remained. The farm road was diverted to cross railway and canal by new girder bridges c1907 south of Taff's Well Lock (No 38).

DIST.	BRIDGE NAME	NOTES
17¼	Taff's Well Lock Bridge	1793 stone locktail bridge (Lock 38) for farm access across the lock between Ty'r y Wen, Glan y Llyn and fields east of the canal. Extant.
	Rhiw-ddar Iron Bridges	1907 diversion of Rhiw-ddar Farm road over CR and the canal, immediately S of Taff's Well Lock.
	Cardiff Railway Bridge	1907 girder railway bridge crossing the canal between Taff's Well and Caeglas locks.
17½	Caeglas Lock Bridge	1793 stone locktail bridge (Lock 39) carrying footpath from the towpath and lock and lockhouse to Caeglas Dock (of 1856) and across fields to later Taff's Well cemetery.
	Rhymney Railway Bridge	1856 iron railway bridge crossing the canal immediately N of Portobello lock no 40.
17¾	Garth Ironworks Bridge	Iron towpath bridge, dated 1856, over entrance to ironworks basin. Extant.
	Castell Coch Quarry Bridge	c1898-1906 temporary timber railway bridge over canal for contractor's line between the Rhymney Railway (RR) at Walnut Tree Junction and the quarry.
18	Walnut Tree Bridge	1793 stone bridge carrying the Merthyr-Cardiff turnpike road over the canal. The bridge was later enlarged and improved for road traffic but remained a stone arched structure.
	Walnut Tree Viaduct	1901 Barry Railway (BR) Rhymney branch viaduct of steel girders supported on brick piers. It crossed the canal, River Taff and all other roads and railways in the Garth Gap at high level until demolition began in 1969.
18¼	Pentyrch Bridge; Ynys Bridge	1794 stone bridge leading from coal wharf on the turnpike alongside the canal, over the canal and towpath, to the river at Ynys, opposite Pentyrch Foundry. In 1808, a stone bridge was built across the river to extend the road from the canal to Pentyrch Works.
18¾	Ivy House Bridge	1794 stone bridge taking lane over the canal to Ivy House Farm from Tongwynlais.
	Cardiff Railway Bridge	1906 girder bridge over the canal N of Tongwynlais station.
19	Ton Lock Bridge	1794 stone locktail bridge (Lock 41) taking Iron Bridge Road across the canal from the Cardiff turnpike and the river bridge at Cilynys.
	Cardiff Railway Bridge	c1905 girder bridge over the canal and Forest Farm road.
19½	Forest Lock Bridge	1794 stone locktail bridge (Lock 43) giving access from the canal towpath across the lock by field path to the Long Wood.
	Towpath Bridge	An iron bridge taking the towpath over the Parliamentary weir to the Melingriffith feeder. It is a flat bridge and survives with its parapets as part of the Canal Nature Reserve towpath walk. The curved parapet is dated 1851.
20	Sunny Bank Bridge; Velindre Bridge	1794 originally, possibly a stone access bridge for road from Velindre over the canal to Forest Farm. In its final rebuilt form it had a light metal deck and lattice parapets.
20¼	Melingriffith Iron Bridge	1807, replaced earlier swing bridge. 1849 dated iron replacement turnover bridge transferring towpath from W to E side of the canal. Extant but resited near to the Melingiffith pump.
	Melingriffith Works Bridge	1794 bridge replaced in stone 1807. It provided the main road crossing over the canal for entry to the works from the Llandaff to Whitchurch road.
20½	Melingriffith Lock Bridge	1794 stone locktail and turnover bridge (Lock 44) transferring the towpath from the W to E side of the canal.
	Ty Mawr Bridge; Great House Bridge	1794 stone bridge taking farm road from Ty Mawr across the canal to the towpath and fields on the S of the towpath.

Sunny Bank or Velindre Bridge in its rebuilt form, with metal deck and lattice girders, looking north around 1930. The feeder to Melingriffith Tinplate Works is on the left. The canal is passing beneath Long Wood and was quite narrow at this point.
S.C. Fox photo, Neg No 73.146, courtesy WIMM

The concrete bridge built to carry the Western Avenue by-pass road over the canal near Gabalfa. A number of coaches and crowds of people can be seen on top of the embankment and it is thought that this photograph was taken on the occasion of the new road's official opening in 1936. The bridge still survives today. Carol Sharp collection

DIST.	BRIDGE NAME	NOTES
	TVR Main Line Bridge	1840 stone bridge crossing the canal. The iron bridge for the Llandaff Loop line on its S side was constructed in 1900.
20³/₄	Gelli Bridge; Radyr Road Bridge	1794 stone bridge taking road from Gelli Farm to the ford across the River Taff to Radyr church.
21¹/₄	Llandaff Lock Bridge	1794 stone locktail bridge (Lock 45), later widened for road traffic, carrying the road from Whitchurch and Melingriffith to Llandaff Bridge across the River Taff.
21¹/₂	College Lock Bridge	1794 stone locktail bridge (Lock 46) retaining original humpback form to the last. Carried the ancient route from Whitchurch common to the river crossing at Llandaff weir.
21³/₄	Gabalfa Lock Foot Bridge	In its last form, a flat handrailed bridge over locktail (Lock 47) for towpath access to Gabalfa Cottages and Mynachdy. Shown on Harrison 1830.
22	Western Avenue Bridge	c1936 concrete bridge carrying Gabalfa to Ely section of Cardiff's north to west bypass road over the canal. Extant.
22¹/₄	Mynachdy Lock Foot Bridge	Flat handrailed bridge over locktail (Lock 48) for towpath access from Mynachdy Cottages to the Excelsior Rope Works and Mynachdy. Not shown on Harrison 1830.
22¹/₂	Llystalybont Bridge; Soap Works Bridge	Flat cart bridge taking lane from Maindy across canal to the Bute Estate and River Taff. Provided access from towpath across the canal to the soap works and later boat maintenance yard.
23¹/₄	Blackweir Bridge	1794 stone turnover bridge, transferring towpath from W to E side of the canal to avoid Lord Bute's Cardiff Castle estate. The bridge also carried a road from North Road (near Nazareth House) to Lord Bute's private estate.
23³/₄	North Road Lock Bridge; Cathays Lock Bridge; Little Lock Bridge	1794 wooden locktail bridge, replaced 1820 with iron bridge (Lock 49), for access to Cardiff Castle via its West Gate and later picturesque lodge.
	North Gate Bridge; Kingsway Bridge	1794 stone bridge carrying the Cardiff to Merthyr road over the canal at the entrance to Cathays Park. The original canal bridge remarkably survives as a pedestrian underpass, although at least two later road bridges were erected over the top of it to widen the road. The 1885 canal survey regretted that the headroom of the original bridge had not been increased when the road had recently been widened. The 1906 widening resulted in an ornamental iron bridge which lasted until well after the life of the canal. A recent modern bridge has replaced it. Both the replacement bridges are best known in their time as Kingsway bridge.
24	Crockherbtown Arch; Queen Street Bridge	The stone arch carrying Crockherbtown (later Queen Street) in central Cardiff over the canal and towpath immediately below Crockherbtown Lock (Lock 50). The arch was built against the N entrance to the Tunnel and is effectively part of it. Two boats could pass each other under the arch but not in the tunnel proper.
	The Tunnel	115 yards. Towpath for 23 yards only (N end).
	Mr Williams Bridge	(W bank) Assumed moveable bridge across entrance to 'Mr Williams' cut', shown on Harrison 1830.
24¹/₄	Hill's Street Bridge	A post 1920 flat bridge across the canal with no access to the towpath.
	Boat Yard Bridge	(W bank) Assumed moveable bridge across slip from Jenkins' pre-1831 boat yard. Shown on Harrison 1830.

DIST.	BRIDGE NAME	NOTES
	Hayes Bridge; Milkmaid's bridge;	1794 wooden footbridge, ordered to be replaced 1803 and replaced by stone bridge 1821.
	Waterloo Bridge	Stone bridge replaced c1872 to carry Cardiff horse trams over the canal between Mill Lane and Bute Docks.
24½	South Gate Bridge; Custom House Bridge; Wharf Bridge; Cumberland Bridge	1794 Stone turnover bridge taking towpath from E to W bank of canal and the iron wharves at start of the Sea Lock pound. Also acted as a road bridge across the canal. Rebuilt 1860. Final canal bridge replacement c1903 was of iron design, strengthened to carry Cardiff Corporation electric trams.
	South Wales Railway Bridge	c1850 iron girder railway bridge carrying South Wales Railway, later GWR and British Railways. Replaced several times in lifetime.
24¾	East Wharf Iron Bridge	(E bank) c1840 iron bridge over Junction Canal to Bute West Dock. Replaced 1903 by new iron bridge carrying road.
	Timber Pond Bridge	(W bank) 1886 towpath and railway bridge across entrance to the timber pond.
	Hill's Dock Bridge	(W bank) Towpath bridge across entrance to Plymouth Co's loading dock.
25	Jenkins' Dry Dock Bridge; Chaddock's Dock Bridge	(E bank) Moveable bridge across the entrance to the 1817 boat repairing dock. Out of use and filled in before 1942.
	Tredwen's Dry Dock Bridge; Hodge's Dry Dock Bridge	(E bank) Moveable bridge across the entrance to the two boat repairing docks.
	Powell's Basin Bridge	(W bank) Towpath bridge across entrance to Thomas Powell's basin.
	Boat Dock Bridge	(W bank) Towpath bridge across entrance to boat dock.
25¼	Little Dock Bridge; Taff Vale Railway Dock Bridge	(E bank) 1836 flat rolling bridge over entrance to dock.
	Davies' Dock Bridge	(E bank) Towpath bridge over entrance to John Davies's boat dock 1833.
	James Street Swing Bridge	1891 iron swing bridge over canal linking James Street and Clarence Road. Dismantled 1957.
25½	Sea Lock	1864 flat rolling bridge across the lock itself, at towpath level. Designed by Charle de Bergue, it carried a road built by the Taff Vale Railway (TVR Act of 1861) between the Bute Dock area and Ferry Road, where a river bridge took the road to the Ely wharves. Rolling bridge removed by 1902.

Note: 3 June 1818 survey reported 83 bridges on the whole length of the canal.

North Road Lock under a heavy fall of snow circa 1910. The delicate ironwork of the locktail bridge dated from 1820 and gave access to Cardiff Castle via the West Gate. This is not quite the pictureque scene it appears for nothing has moved on the canal since the snowfall; the towpath would have been extremely hazardous for both boatman and boathorse. ILW collection

Appendix D
SAMPLE GCC ACCOUNTS

Above: *Navigation House, seen here circa 1910, was the Canal Company's head offices where the chief clerk and his staff were based, and where the annual accounts were prepared for shareholders.*
Neil Parkhouse collection

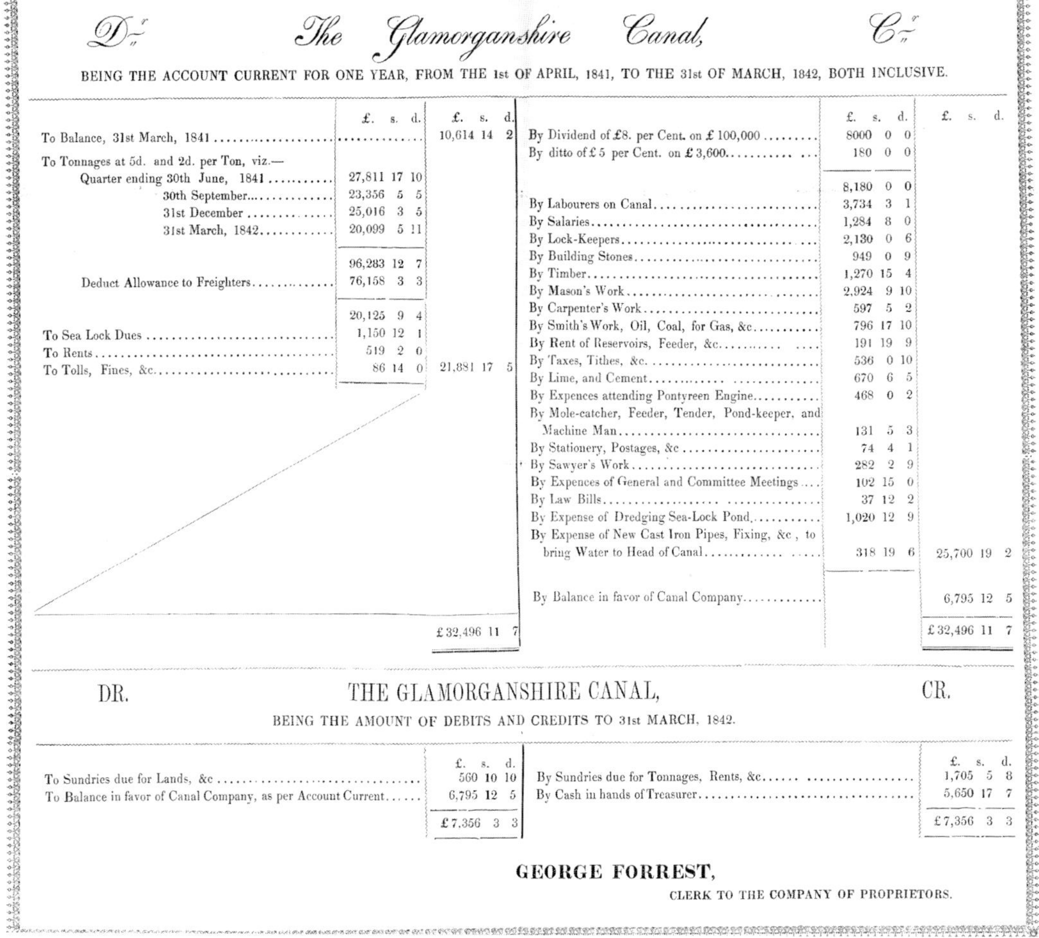

Dr. *The Glamorganshire Canal,* Cr.

BEING THE ACCOUNT CURRENT FOR ONE YEAR, FROM THE 1st OF APRIL, 1841, TO THE 31st OF MARCH, 1842, BOTH INCLUSIVE.

	£. s. d.	£. s. d.
To Balance, 31st March, 1841		10,614 14 2
To Tonnages at 5d. and 2d. per Ton, viz.—		
Quarter ending 30th June, 1841	27,811 17 10	
30th September	23,356 5 5	
31st December	25,016 3 5	
31st March, 1842	20,099 5 11	
	96,283 12 7	
Deduct Allowance to Freighters	76,158 3 3	
	20,125 9 4	
To Sea Lock Dues	1,150 12 1	
To Rents	519 2 0	
To Tolls, Fines, &c.	86 14 0	21,881 17 5
		£32,496 11 7

	£. s. d.	£. s. d.
By Dividend of £8. per Cent. on £100,000	8000 0 0	
By ditto of £5 per Cent. on £3,600	180 0 0	
	8,180 0 0	
By Labourers on Canal	3,734 3 1	
By Salaries	1,284 8 0	
By Lock-Keepers	2,130 0 6	
By Building Stones	949 0 9	
By Timber	1,270 15 4	
By Mason's Work	2,924 9 10	
By Carpenter's Work	597 5 2	
By Smith's Work, Oil, Coal, for Gas, &c	796 17 10	
By Rent of Reservoirs, Feeder, &c.	191 19 9	
By Taxes, Tithes, &c.	536 0 10	
By Lime, and Cement	670 6 5	
By Expences attending Pontyreen Engine	468 0 2	
By Mole-catcher, Feeder, Tender, Pond-keeper, and Machine Man	131 5 3	
By Stationery, Postages, &c	74 4 1	
By Sawyer's Work	282 2 9	
By Expences of General and Committee Meetings	102 15 0	
By Law Bills	37 12 2	
By Expense of Dredging Sea-Lock Pond	1,020 12 9	
By Expense of New Cast Iron Pipes, Fixing, &c, to bring Water to Head of Canal	318 19 6	25,700 19 2
By Balance in favor of Canal Company		6,795 12 5
		£32,496 11 7

DR. THE GLAMORGANSHIRE CANAL, CR.

BEING THE AMOUNT OF DEBITS AND CREDITS TO 31st MARCH, 1842.

	£. s. d.
To Sundries due for Lands, &c	560 10 10
To Balance in favor of Canal Company, as per Account Current	6,795 12 5
	£7,356 3 3

	£. s. d.
By Sundries due for Tonnages, Rents, &c	1,705 5 8
By Cash in hands of Treasurer	5,650 17 7
	£7,356 3 3

GEORGE FORREST,
CLERK TO THE COMPANY OF PROPRIETORS.

Left and page right: *These two sample copies of the accounts illustrate the massive discrepancy between the Parliamentary capped dividend of £8,180 and the income from tonnages, charged at the Parliamentary rates. This resulted in the company returning huge allowances to the freighters as shown. The detailed operating expenses are particularly interesting and merit close study.*
Courtesy GRO

THE GLAMORGANSHIRE CANAL.

Being the Account Current for One Year, from the 1st of April, 1850, to the 31st of March, 1851, both inclusive.

Dr.	£ s. d.	£ s. d.
To Balance 31st March, 1850	....	9,489 8 9
To Tonnages at 5d. and 2d. per Ton, viz. :—		
Quarter ending 30th June, 1850	30,499 2 5	
,, ,, 30th Sept., ,, ...	31,600 3 3	
,, ,, 31st Dec., ,, ...	32,795 12 11	
,, ,, 31st March, 1851	35,254 15 5	
	130,149 14 0	
Deduct Allowance to Freighters	110,779 8 11	
	19,370 5 1	
To Sea Lock Dues	1,286 15 8	
To Rents	400 15 6	
To Tolls, Fines, Interest, &c.	363 11 1	21,421 7 4
		£30,910 16 1

Cr.	£ s. d.	£ s. d.
By Dividend of 8 per Cent. on £103,600... ...	8,000 0 0	
By ,, of 5 per Cent. on £3,600	180 0 0	
	8,180 0 0	
By Labourers on Canal, &c.	1,139 12 9	
By Salaries	1,249 5 0	
By Lock-keepers	2,251 16 6	
By Building Stones	322 9 11	
By Timber	467 18 4	
By Mason's Work	752 16 2	
By Carpenter's Work	621 16 8	
By Smith's Work, Castings, Oil, Coal for Gas, &c.	745 16 10	
By Rent of Reservoirs, Feeder, &c.	191 19 9	
By Taxes, Tithes, &c....	934 4 10	
By Lime and Cement	191 18 5	
By Expenses attending Working and Renewal of Pontyreen Engine	2,961 0 10	
By Policemen, Molecatcher, Feeder-tender, and Pond-keeper	200 7 0	
By Stationery, Postages, &c.	90 9 5	
By Sawyer's Work	123 13 3	
By Expenses of General and Committee Meetings...	84 5 3	
By Dredging Sea Lock Pond	241 17 4	20,751 8 3
By Balance in favour of Canal Company... ...		10,159 7 10
		£30,910 16 1

The Glamorganshire Canal.

BEING THE AMOUNT OF DEBITS AND CREDITS TO THE 31st OF MARCH, 1851.

Dr.	£ s. d.
To Amount due to Sundries	86 0 11
To Balance in favor of Canal Company, as per Account Current..	10,159 7 10
	£10,245 8 9

Cr.	£ s. d.
By Sundries due for Tonnage	1,819 16 1
By Cash in hands of Treasurer	8,425 12 8
	£10,245 8 9

JOHN R. FORREST,
Clerk to the Company of Proprietors.

Appendix E
GUNPOWDER AND SLATE

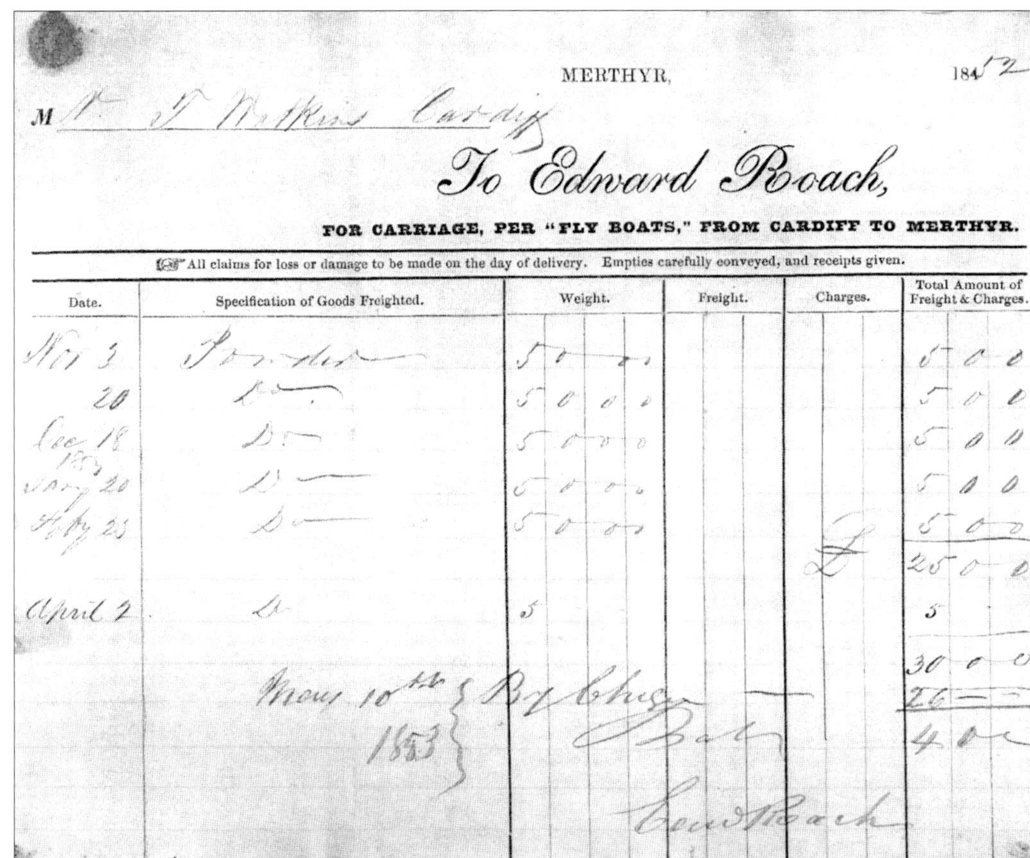

MERTHYR, 1852

M[r] T Watkins Cardiff

To Edward Roach,

FOR CARRIAGE, PER "FLY BOATS," FROM CARDIFF TO MERTHYR.

All claims for loss or damage to be made on the day of delivery. Empties carefully conveyed, and receipts given.

Date.	Specification of Goods Freighted.	Weight.	Freight.	Charges.	Total Amount of Freight & Charges.
Nov 3	Powder	5 0 0			5 0 0
20	Do	5 0 0 0			5 0 0
Dec 18	Do	5 0 0 0			5 0 0
1853 Jany 20	Do	5 0 0 0			5 0 0
Feby 25	Do	5 0 0 0			5 0 0
				£	25 0 0
April 2	Do	5			5
					30 0 0
May 10th 1853	By Cheque				26
	Bal				4 0 0

Edw Roach

For several decades, up until the railways started to take over, the canal fulfilled the role of general carrier. Although the core traffics were in boat loads of Iron, Coal, Stone, Iron Ore, Timber and Market Goods, there were other goods that the canal carried on occasion too. The arbitrary items of ephemera on these two pages give an indication of some of the incidental traffic on offer.

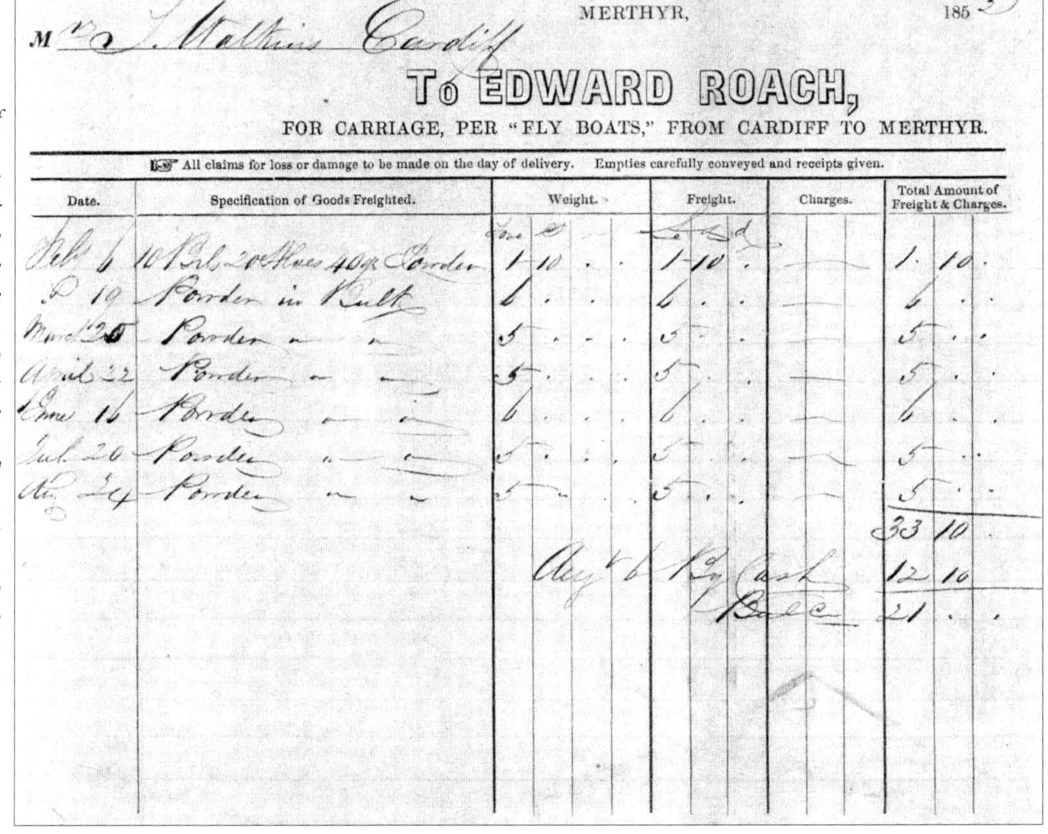

MERTHYR, 1852

M[r] T. Watkins Cardiff

To EDWARD ROACH,

FOR CARRIAGE, PER "FLY BOATS," FROM CARDIFF TO MERTHYR.

All claims for loss or damage to be made on the day of delivery. Empties carefully conveyed and receipts given.

Date.	Specification of Goods Freighted.	Weight.	Freight.	Charges.	Total Amount of Freight & Charges.
Feb 6	10 Brls 20 Hlves 40 qr Powder	1 10	1 10		1 10
Do 19	Powder in Bulk	6	6	—	6
March 25	Powder	5	5	—	5
April 22	Powder	5	5	—	5
June 16	Powder	6	6	—	6
Jul 20	Powder	5	5	—	5
Aug 24	Powder	5	5	—	5
					33 10
	Aug 6 By Cash				12 10
	Bal				21

On this page are examples of invoices from the Merthyr carrier, Edward Roach, to Thomas Watkins, for carrying gunpowder in 1852. The powder probably originated from Ulverston in the Lake District. Watkins kept the powder magazine at Dynea, which appears on the OS map on pages 60-61. Roach was operating a 'Fly Boat' service between Cardiff and Merthyr, with regular departures and carrying any cargoes on offer. Note the invoice shown top is an earlier example of the 1840s, which Roach was apparently using up the last copies of. The lower one is to a different design dated 185-. GRO U/C 106

Port of Cardiff. } An Account of Money Collected by Edward Thomas, as Tolls on Slates brought Coastwise and landed at this Port, in the Year 1829, commencing 1st January, & ending 31st December.

When Received		Ship's Name.	Masters	from whence arrived	Quantity of Slates landed.	Rate	Tolls Received £	s	d	Total.
1829. January	9th	Ann & Mary	J. Jones	Port Madoc	12,900 Dutchess Slates	2d	"	2	2	
February	3rd	Elizabeth	D. Edwards	Beaumaris	48 Tons Queen Slates	4d	"	16	"	
	5th	Ermine	G. Griffiths	Port Madoc	9660 Countess Slates	1d Free	"	"	10	
					12 Tons 13½ Cwt Queen ditto	2d F	"	2	2	
March	15	Ermine	G. Griffiths	ditto	10,372 Saleable Slates	1d F	"	"	11	
April	16th	Lamb	G. Williams	ditto	25,200 ditto	2d	"	4	3	
May	4th	Elizabeth	G. Phillips	Do	3,100 Dutchess Slates	1d F	"	"	3	
					22 Tons 15 Cwt Queen Slates	2d F	"	3	10	
	16	Hopewell	J. Lewis	Conway	10,960 Saleable Slates	2d	"	1	10	
					4 Tons 7 Cwt Queen Do	4d	"	1	6	
June	10	Jenny	J. Evans	Cardigan	8,500 Common Slates	2d	"	1	5	
	30	Elizabeth	G. Phillips	Boscastle	69,980 Common Slates	"	"	8	9	Moiety Free
July	21st	Ermine	G. Griffiths	Port Madoc	3,690 Saleable Slates	1d F	"	"	4	
					22 Tons 4 Cwt 19d Queen Do	2d F	"	3	8	
Septr.	25	Fame	J. Bowen	Cardigan	32,640 Common Slates	2d	"	5	6	
	29th	Vital	J. James	Carnarvon	73 Tons 3 Cwt Queen Slates	"	"	3	4	Moiety Free
					8570 Dutchess Do	"	"	1	1	
Decr.	31	Vigo	J. Jones	Cardigan	48.000 Common Slates	1d F	"	4	"	£ s d
					39.000 Do Do	1d F	"	3	3	3 5 1

Dated 12th Feb: 1830. Edwd. Thomas Receiver.

A whole year's account, for 1929, of roofing slates imported into the canal at Cardiff. The loads have come from several locations in North Wales, including Port Madoc, Conway and Caernarvon, plus one from Beaumaris on Anglesey. Three further cargoes have originated at Cardigan in West Wales and there is one of Cornish slate from the tiny port of Boscastle in North Cornwall. Noteable also are the names applied to the different types of slates: Duchess, Queen, Countess, Common and Saleable. Amongst the vessels noted, both Elizabeth and Ermine brought in three of the cargoes each, Fame was a West Country schooner, built at Fowey in 1816, and Hopewell was a ketch, regularly in the stone and coal trades, sailing out of Lyme Regis. SR collection

Appendix F
GLAMORGANSHIRE CANAL BYE LAWS

GLAMORGANSHIRE
Canal Navigation.

PENALTIES

On Persons who shall be guilty of Offences against the Acts of Parliament and the Bye Laws after-mentioned.

Made for the Preservation and Orderly using of the said Navigation.

Statute 30th, Geo 3rd } THE *master, owner* or *person* having the care of every *Boat, Barge,* or other such *Vessel,* navigating upon the said *Canal,* shall give an exact and true account in *writing,* under his hand, to the collectors of the said *Rates,* at the places where they shall attend for that purpose, of what quantities of *goods* or other *things* shall be in or belonging to such *Boat, Barge* or other *Vessel,* and from *whence* such *goods* or other *things* shall be *brought,* and where the same are intended to be *landed;* and in case any such person shall *neglect* or *refuse* to give such *account,* or to produce his *bill of lading,* to any such *Collector* demanding the *same,* or shall give a *false account,* or shall *deliver* any *part* of the *lading* or *goods* at any *other place* than is or are mentioned in *such account,* with intent to *avoid the payment* of the said *rates,* he shall *forfeit* and *pay* the sum of *Ten Shillings,* a ton for every ton of *goods,* or other *things,* (and so in proportion for any lesser quantity than a ton) which shall be in such *Boat, Barge* or other *Vessel,* of which such *account* shall be so *refused* to be *given,* or of which such *false account* shall be given, or which shall be *delivered out* as aforesaid, (as the respective cases shall be,) and shall also be subject to the payment of the said *rates* herein before granted, and made payable for the same.

THE *masters* or *owners* of all such *Boats, Barges,* or other *Vessels,* shall, and they are hereby required to fix on each side thereof respectively, *correct Indexes* of Copper or Lead, or other metal, of such *graduated dimensions,* and of such convenient *height,* and under such *regulations* as the said Company of Proprietors shall from time to time direct, so that the weight of the *lading* on *board,* may at all times, be thereby ascertained and shewn; and the *names of the owners* of such *Boats, Barges* or other *Vessels* in Copper, Lead or other metal, as aforesaid, or painted in large *capital letters,* shall also by such *masters* or *owners* be affixed on the sides of the said *Boats, Barges* or other *Vessels* in some *conspicuous* manner, and if the *master or owner* of any *Boat, Barge* or other such *Vessel* shall *wilfully navigate* the same upon the said *Canal,* without having such *Index* or *name* thereon, or shall *alter, deface,* or *destroy* the *same* or any *part* thereof, or shall *fix* any *false Index* or *name,* he shall for every such offence, *forfeit* and *pay* a sum not exceeding *Five Pounds,* nor less than *Forty Shillings.*

THE *owner* or *master* of every such *Boat, Barge* or other *Vessel,* shall permit and suffer the same to be *guaged* or *measured,* at the expence of the said Company of Proprietors, whenever it shall be required by the said Company of Proprietors, or such person or persons as shall be appointed by them, for that purpose; provided that no such *Boat, Barge* or other *Vessel* shall be *guaged* or *measured* more than *four times* in any *one Year* and every *owner, master,* or other *person,* having the *rule* or *command* of any such *Boat, Barge* or other *Vessel,* who shall refuse to *permit* and *suffer* the same to be *guaged* or *measured* as aforesaid, shall for every such offence, *forfeit* and pay a sum not exceeding *Five Pounds* nor less than *Forty Shillings.*

THE *owner* or *master* of every such *Ship, Boat* or other *Vessel* as aforesaid, shall be, and is hereby made answerable for any *damage, spoil* or *mischief* that shall be done by such *Ship, Boat* or other *Vessel,* or any of the *Seamen, Boatmen* or *Watermen,* belonging to, or employed in or about the same, respectively, unto any of the *Locks, Bridges, Weirs, Dams, Engines,* or other *Works* in, upon, or near the said *Canal,* or the *Trenches, Aqueducts, Sluices* and *passages* belonging thereto, or by *loading* or *unloading* any such *Ship, Boat* or other *Vessel,* and for any *trespass* or *damage* that shall or may be done to the owners or proprietors of any *buildings, erections, lands* or *tenements* adjoining to the same, or any of them; and such *master* or *owner* shall and may be *sued* and *prosecuted* for the same in any *Court* of *Record,* and if a *Verdict* pass against him, or *Judgment* be given against him, upon demurrer, or by default, the Plaintiff in any such case, shall recover his damages thereby sustained, with *treble* costs of Suit.

IF any *person* shall float any *Timber* on the said *Canal,* or shall suffer the loading of any *Boat* or *Vessel* to lie over the sides of any such *Boat* or *Vessel,* or shall over-load any *Boat* or *Vessel* navigating in, or upon the said *Canal,* so as to obstruct the passage of any other *Boat* or *Vessel,* and shall not immediately, upon notice given to him for that purpose, remove such obstruction, or if any *person* shall throw any *Ballast, Gravel, Stones,* or *Rubbish,* into any part of the said *Canal,* or any Trenches or Water-courses to be made by Virtue of this *Act,* every such person shall, for every offence, forfeit and pay a sum not exceeding *Five Pounds.*

IF any *person* or *persons* shall *wantonly, carelessly* or *negligently open* or cause to *opened* any *Lock, Gate* or any *Paddle, Valve* or *Clough,* belonging to any *Lock* to be erected on the said *Canal,* or suffer any *Boat* or other *Vessel* to strike or run upon any of the *Bridges* or *Locks* thereof, or shall *wilfully flush or draw* off the *Water* from any part of the said *Canal,* or shall leave any of the said Valves or Cloughs *open & running,* after any *Boat* or other *Vessel* shall have have passed any such *lock,* every *person* so offending shall forfeit and pay, for every such offence, any sum not exceeding *Five Pounds,* nor *less* than *Forty Shillings;* and if any person shall *wilfully, maliciously* and to the *prejudice* of the said Navigation, break, throw down, damage, or destroy any Banks or other Works, to be erected and made, by Virtue of this Act, every person so offending, and being thereof lawfully convicted, shall be subject and liable to the like Pains and Penalties as in cases of *FELONY;* and the Court by and before whom such Person shall be tried, shall have power and authority to cause such Person to be punished in like manner as Felons are directed to be punished by the laws and statues of this Realm, or in mitigation of such punishment such Court may, if they think fit, award such Sentence as the law directs in cases of *Petit Larceny.*

Bye Laws.

1 NO Person either to discharge or load any Coal, Iron, Lime or other Merchandise, while the Boat shall continue in the chamber of any Lock, or upon the bank of any Aqueduct, under the penalty of Fifty Shillings for each of the said offences

2 Every Boatman to take a Permit or Bill of particulars of the Lading and Tonnage contained in his Boat, signed by the Wharfinger or Clerk, at the Wharf at which he shall load, in which Bill shall be expressed the particular Wharf or Wharfs such loading shall be discharged at, and the Wharfinger or Clerk receiving the same, shall sign the said Bill of lading as received, and detain the same, for regulating the Tonnage account of his Company, under the penalty of Fifty Shillings.

3. Any Boatman having goods on board not entered in his Permit or Bill of lading, to forfeit a sum not exceeding Forty Shillings.

4 And all Bargemen, &c when they are required by any Lock-keeper, Watchman, &c. are immediately to produce their Permits for examination, under the penalty of Fifty Shillings.

5. That every Boatman is to deliver his Permit at the Canal Office, or to the person or persons appointed to receive the same, as soon as the Boat arrives at the Wharf, and before he begins to unload, under a penalty not exceeding Five Pounds, nor less than Forty Shillings.

6. No Boat to be navigated without having two Boatmen to it, or to be navigated having on board no Permit, signed by one of the Clerks or Lock-keepers, or to be navigated one hour after sun-set, or before day-break, under the penalty of not more than Five Pounds, nor less than Fifty Shillings for each of the last mentioned offences.

7. No Person to land or deposit any Timber, Stones, Iron or other goods whatsoever, on the Towing Path of the Canal, under a Penalty of not exceeding Five Pounds, for every offence, nor less than Forty Shillings.

8. That the Master of every Boat Navigating the Canal, with a Horse, shall at all times provide an able Haulier or Driver to attend such Horse, and that if such Haulier or Driver, shall be absent from such Horse, the Boatmaster shall be liable to a fine or penalty, not exceeding Twenty Shillings, nor less than Five Shillings, for every such occasion, that the Driver or Haulier shall so absent himself.

9. No person to injure any of the Wickets, Hedges, Fences, or Quicksets belonging to the Canal, under the penalty of Forty Shillings.

10. In discharging every Boat, &c. of its loading, the loading to be delivered and placed on the respective Wharfs, in such manner as the Wharfinger of such Wharf shall direct; every empty boat, &c to give way to every loaded Boat, &c until each loaded Boat shall have passed such empty Boat.

11. Every Boat to stop, and the Horse to be taken off, at a post affixed at least seven yards from each end of every Lock, and at all times from each such post, to be gently shafted into each Lock.

12. Every Boat whilst lying either in the Canal or Canal-Bason, to be kept moored at both ends, and no Person wilfully to un-moor, and leave the same un-moored.

13. No Person to ride on any part of the Towing-Path, under any pretence whatever, or to drive any Cattle on any part of the said Towing-Path

14. No Small Boat will be suffered to go through the Crockherbtown Lock for Coal, without leave of the Company's Clerk or Lock-keeper.

15. No Boatman or other Person to be suffered to let the Paddles down without a Windlass.

16. No Person shall load or unload any Coal, Lime, Mine, Ore or Ballast on the Canal, without a platform.

17. Any Person who shall be guilty of any or either of the above-mentioned offences, shall incur and be subject to a penalty not exceeding Five Pounds, nor less than Forty Shillings. The said penalties to be levied and applied, according to the directions of the Acts of Parliament.

June 3rd, 1826.

THOMAS REECE,
Clerk to the Company.

INDEX – GENERAL

INDEX – PEOPLE

The final extent of Cardiff's dock developments, viewed from the air in about 1950. From the bottom, it shows the River Taff, Glamorganshire Canal, West Dock and basin, East Dock and basin, Roath Basin, Roath Dock and Queen Alexandra Dock. WIMM collection